On Essays

Thomas Karshan is Senior Lecturer in Literature at the University of East Anglia. He is the author of *Vladimir Nabokov and the Art of Play* (Oxford University Press, 2011), the co-translator of Nabokov's *The Tragedy of Mister Morn* (Penguin, 2012), and the editor of Nabokov's *Collected Poems* (Penguin, 2013). From 2018 to 2019 he was President of the International Vladimir Nabokov Society. He has published articles on modern British, American, and Russian literature, and essays in the *Times Literary Supplement*, the *London Review of Books*, and elsewhere.

Kathryn Murphy is Fellow in English Literature at Oriel College, and Associate Professor in the Faculty of English, University of Oxford. Her academic work focuses on Renaissance poetry and philosophy, and on the literary essay. She is also a critic and essayist, writing regularly about still-life painting for *Apollo Magazine*, and reviewing Czech literature for the *TLS*. She is currently writing two books: *The Tottering Universal: Metaphysical Prose in the Seventeenth Century*; and *Robert Burton: A Vital Melancholy*, a study of distraction, attention, and *The Anatomy of Melancholy*.

On Essays

Montaigne to the Present

Edited by
THOMAS KARSHAN
and
KATHRYN MURPHY

OXFORD
UNIVERSITY PRESS

OXFORD

UNIVERSITY PRESS

Great Clarendon Street, Oxford, OX2 6DP,
United Kingdom

Oxford University Press is a department of the University of Oxford.
It furthers the University's objective of excellence in research, scholarship,
and education by publishing worldwide. Oxford is a registered trade mark of
Oxford University Press in the UK and in certain other countries

First published in 2020
First published in paperback in 2021

Published in the United States of America by Oxford University Press
198 Madison Avenue, New York, NY 10016, United States of America

British Library Cataloguing in Publication Data
Data available

Library of Congress Cataloging in Publication Data
Data available

ISBN 978–0–19–870786–8 (Hbk.)
ISBN 978–0–19–284861–1 (Pbk.)

Acknowledgements and Note on the Text

Our first debt of thanks is to the brilliant and learned contributors to this volume, who embraced the project, and courteously endured and creatively responded to their editors' queries and revisions. Professor Ned Stuckey-French, author of Chapter 15, 'Creative Nonfiction and the Lyric Essay', sadly died in the summer of 2019, before he could see this book in print, but having revised his essay to its final form. We are proud to have it in the volume and to have worked with him, and are grateful to his wife, Professor Elizabeth Stuckey-French, for corresponding with us about final details at a difficult time.

We are also greatly indebted to Fergus McGhee, who superbly copy edited the entire manuscript, bringing to the job his expertise in the history of the essay, his eye for an unclear or awkward sentence, and his lynx-eyed care for a bibliographically immaculate footnote. Our editors at the Press, especially Aimee Wright and Jacqueline Norton, were graceful in their tolerance of our vacillations, and encouraging and steady in their shepherding of the volume to print. Brian North, our copy-editor assigned by the Press, was likewise extraordinarily attentive and spared us many solecisms. Bhavani Govindasamy, who oversaw the final assembly of the volume, was a pleasure to work with in the final stages. The index is the work of Philippa Jevons; we are very grateful to her for corralling this volume's miscellaneity.

We are also grateful to Robert Boyers and *Salmagundi* magazine for their kind permission to reprint Adam Phillips's 'Up to a Point: The Psychoanalyst and the Essay', which appeared in *Salmagundi* (2013), though without the footnotes added here.

Thanks are also due to the University of East Anglia, the University of Oxford, and Oriel College, Oxford, who supported our work on this volume by offering research leave to the editors and funding various research expenses. Some of Kathryn Murphy's editorial work was undertaken while on a Research Fellowship supported by the Leverhulme Trust. Matthew Bevis and Marcus Waithe were enthusiastic about essays, responsive to queries, and supportive of the editors and the project. Our anonymous readers made many helpful and clarifying suggestions. The editors take full responsibility for remaining errors and waywardness.

We have modernized quotations from texts published before 1800, except in cases where the original spelling was in itself significant.

Contents

List of Figures

Notes on Contributors

Scott Black is Professor of English at the University of Utah. He is author of *Of Essays and Reading in Early Modern Britain* (Palgrave Macmillan, 2006) and *Without the Novel: Romance and the History of Prose Fiction* (University of Virginia Press, 2019) as well as essays on *The Spectator*, Hume's essays, Henry Fielding's novels, eighteenth-century romance, Eliza Haywood, and Heliodorus.

Warren Boutcher is Professor of Renaissance Studies in the School of English and Drama, Queen Mary University of London. He is the author of *The School of Montaigne in Early Modern Europe*, 2 vols (Oxford University Press, 2017), and of numerous chapters and articles on the history of Montaigne's *Essais* and on topics in the European literary and intellectual history of the late Renaissance. He is currently in the early stages of editing *Europe: A Literary History, 1545–1659* (Oxford University Press).

Gregory Dart is Professor of English at University College London. He has published two monographs, *Rousseau, Robespierre and English Romanticism* (Cambridge University Press, 1999) and *Metropolitan Art and Literature 1810–1840: Cockney Adventures* (Cambridge University Press, 2012), and has edited the collection *Restless Cities* (with Matthew Beaumont; Verso, 2010), and two editions of Hazlitt's writings. He is currently General Editor of a new six-volume edition of the *Works of Charles and Mary Lamb* for Oxford University Press, for which he is undertaking to edit three volumes himself, the *Works of 1818*, the *Essays of Elia*, and the *Miscellaneous Prose*.

Markman Ellis is Professor of Eighteenth-Century Studies at Queen Mary University of London. He is the author of *The Politics of Sensibility: Race, Gender and Commerce in the Sentimental Novel* (Cambridge University Press, 1996), *The History of Gothic Fiction* (Edinburgh University Press, 2000), *The Coffee-House: A Cultural History* (Weidenfeld and Nicolson, 2004), co-author of *Empire of Tea* (Reaktion, 2015), and editor of *Eighteenth-Century Coffee-House Culture* (Pickering and Chatto, 2006) and *Tea and the Tea-Table in Eighteenth-Century England* (Pickering and Chatto, 2010). He is currently working on writing and sociability in literary and scientific circles in mid eighteenth-century London.

Stefano Evangelista is Associate Professor of English and Fellow of Trinity College at the University of Oxford, and fellow of the Centre for British Studies of the Humboldt University (Berlin). His main interests include nineteenth-century English and comparative literature, the reception of the classics, and the relationship between literary and visual cultures. He is the author of *British Aestheticism and Ancient Greece: Hellenism, Reception, Gods in Exile* (Palgrave, 2009) and the editor of *The Reception of Oscar Wilde in Europe* (Bloomsbury, 2010), *A. C. Swinburne: Unofficial Laureate* (Manchester University Press, 2013, with Catherine Maxwell), *Pater the Classicist: Classical Scholarship, Reception, and Aestheticism* (Oxford University Press, with Charles Martindale and Elizabeth Prettejohn,

2017), and *Arthur Symons: Poet, Critic, Vagabond* (Legenda, with Elisa Bizzotto, 2018). He is currently working on a monograph on literary cosmopolitanism in the British *fin de siècle*.

Ophelia Field is the author of two historical biographies set in the early 1700s: *The Favourite: Sarah Duchess of Marlborough* (Hodder, 2002 and, revised, by Weidenfeld and Nicolson, 2018), and *The Kit-Cat Club* (Harper Press, 2008), about the club that included the essayists Addison and Steele. She has taught Masters in biography at UCL's Centre for Editing Lives and Letters (CELL) and at the University of Buckingham. She has also taught a course on 'The Art of the Essay' at the Idler Academy and compiled Notting Hill Editions' online 'Essay Library'. Currently, she is working on a new book set in the early seventeenth century and on a collection of personal essays. In parallel, Ophelia is a policy consultant to a wide range of refugee and human rights organizations, including those of the EU, UN, and several major philanthropic foundations.

Denise Gigante, Professor of English at Stanford University, is a specialist in Romantic-period literature. She is the editor of *The Great Age of the English Essay: An Anthology* (Yale University Press, 2009) and *Gusto: Essential Writings in Nineteenth-Century Gastronomy* (Routledge, 2005), two anthologies devoted to the genre of the literary essay, and 'The Essay: An Attempt, a Protean Form', published in *Republics of Letters* (2014). She is currently editing *The Cambridge History of the English Essay* with Jason Childs for Cambridge University Press.

Felicity James is Associate Professor in eighteenth- and nineteenth-century English literature at the University of Leicester. She is currently editing the children's writing of Charles and Mary Lamb for the new Oxford *Collected Works*, and her books include *Charles Lamb, Coleridge and Wordsworth: Reading Friendship in the 1790s* (Palgrave, 2008), and the co-edited (with Ian Inkster) *Religious Dissent and the Aikin-Barbauld Circle, 1740–1860* (Cambridge University Press, 2011) and (with Julian North) *Writing Lives Together: Romantic and Victorian auto/biography*(Routledge, 2017). She co-chairs the Charles Lamb Society, which has held a birthday celebration for Charles Lamb each year since the 1930s; previous guests include Edmund Blunden, and new members are always welcome.

Thomas Karshan is Senior Lecturer in Literature at the University of East Anglia. He is the author of *Vladimir Nabokov and the Art of Play* (Oxford University Press, 2011), the co-translator of Nabokov's *The Tragedy of Mister Morn* (Penguin, 2012), and the editor of Nabokov's *Collected Poems* (Penguin, 2013). From 2018 to 2019 he was President of the International Vladimir Nabokov Society. He has published articles on modern British, American, and Russian literature, and essays in the *Times Literary Supplement*, the *London Review of Books*, and elsewhere.

Kathryn Murphy is Fellow in English Literature at Oriel College, and Associate Professor in the Faculty of English, University of Oxford. Her academic work focuses on Renaissance poetry and philosophy, and on the literary essay. She is the author of several articles on early modern prose, poetry, and poetics, with a particular focus on style and philosophy. She is also a critic and essayist, writing about still-life painting for *Apollo Magazine*, and reviewing Central European literature for the *Times Literary Supplement*. She is currently writing two books: *The Tottering Universal: Metaphysical Prose in the Seventeenth Century*, and *Robert Burton: A Vital Melancholy*.

Fred Parker is a Fellow of Clare College and Senior Lecturer in English at the University of Cambridge. His publications include *Scepticism and Literature: An Essay on Pope, Hume, Sterne, and Johnson* (Oxford University Press, 2003) and, most recently, *On Declaring Love: Eighteenth-Century Literature and Jane Austen* (Routledge, 2018). An article on Addison's *Spectator* essays, 'Addison's Modesty: The Essayist as Spectator', is forthcoming in *Essays on Addison*, edited by Paul Davis for Oxford University Press.

Adam Phillips, is an essayist, psychoanalyst, and a visiting professor in the Department of English and Related Literature at the University of York. He was formerly Principal Child Psychotherapist at Charing Cross Hospital, London. He has edited the essayists Charles Lamb and Walter Pater, writes frequently for the *London Review of Books*, *Raritan*, *Salmagundi*, and other journals, and is the author of numerous volumes of essays, including *Attention Seeking* (2019), *In Writing: New and Selected Essays* (2017), *Unforbidden Pleasures* (2015), and *Missing Out: In Praise of the Unlived Life* (2013), all published by Penguin. He is General Editor of the Penguin Modern Classics Freud translations, and a Fellow of The Royal Society of Literature.

†**Ned Stuckey-French** taught at Florida State University and was book review editor of Fourth Genre. He is the author of *The American Essay in the American Century* (University of Missouri Press, 2011), co-editor (with Carl Klaus) of *Essayists on the Essay: Montaigne to Our Time* (University of Iowa Press, 2012), and co-author (with Janet Burroway and Elizabeth Stuckey-French) of *Writing Fiction: A Guide to Narrative Craft* (Longman, 8th edition). His articles and essays have appeared in journals and magazines such as *In These Times*, *The Missouri Review*, *The Iowa Review*, *Walking Magazine*, *culturefront*, *Pinch*, *Guernica*, *middlebrow*, and *American Literature*, and were listed five times among the notable essays of the year in *Best American Essays*.

Bharat Tandon teaches in the School of Literature, Drama, and Creative Writing at the University of East Anglia. He is the author of *Jane Austen and the Morality of Conversation* (Anthem Press, 2003), and the editor of Austen's *Emma: An Annotated Edition* (Harvard University Press, 2012). He has also published numerous articles on subjects including Austen, Dickens, Cowper, Keats, Hardy, Henry Green, Philip Roth, and twentieth-century periodical culture.

Christy Wampole is an Associate Professor of French at Princeton University. She earned her PhD in French and Italian from Stanford University and has published two scholarly books: *Rootedness: The Ramifications of a Metaphor* (University of Chicago Press, 2016), co-winner of the MLA's 2017 Prize for a First Book, and *Degenerative Realism: Novel and Nation in 21st-Century France* (Columbia University Press, 2020). Her writing has appeared in scholarly journals such as *French Forum*, *MLN*, *Modern Language Review*, *The Yearbook of Comparative Literature*, and *Compar(a)ison*, and she has published essays and opinion pieces in *The New York Times*, *The New Yorker*, and *Aeon Magazine*.

Michael Wood is Professor Emeritus of English and Comparative Literature at Princeton. A longstanding essayist for the *New York Review of Books* and the *London Review of Books*, he is the author, most recently, of *The Habits of Distraction* (Sussex Academic Press, 2018), *On Empson* (Princeton University Press, 2017), and *Alfred Hitchcock: The Man Who Knew Too Much* (New Harvest, 2015). His earlier works include *Literature and the Taste of Knowledge* (Cambridge University Press, 2005) and *The Road to Delphi* (Farrar, Strauss, Giroux, 2003).

Tom F. Wright teaches at the University of Sussex, UK. He is the author of *Lecturing the Atlantic: Speech, Print and an Anglo-American Commons* (Oxford University Press, 2017), and the editor of *Transatlantic Rhetoric: Speeches from the American Revolution to the Suffragettes* (Edinburgh University Press, 2020) and *The Cosmopolitan Lyceum: Lecture Culture and the Globe in Nineteenth Century America* (Massachusetts University Press, 2013). He is writing a book about the history of charisma, and an introductory guide to the concept of 'orality'.

Introduction

On the Difficulty of Introducing a Work of this Kind

Thomas Karshan and *Kathryn Murphy*

1. On Introductions

In 'Of the Resemblance of Children to Fathers', Michel de Montaigne imagined 'a man looking around him at the infinite number of things: plants, animals, metals'. The man is casting about for a cure for his epilepsy, and Montaigne is bemoaning the inadequacy of the art of medicine to the incorrigible plurality of the world, and the idiosyncrasies of its inhabitants. 'I do not know where to have him begin his experiment', Montaigne wrote—or, in French, 'Je ne sçay par où luy faire commencer son essay': I do not know where to make him begin his essay.[1] Montaigne's man nonetheless begins, by taking hold of an elk's horn: a strange and apparently random place to start, but one that makes it possible for him to go on.

A boldness in beginning, despite difficulty in finding a true point of origin, is a frequent characteristic of the essay form. Montaigne's 'Of Books' declares 'I want a man to begin with the conclusion [...] I do not want a man to use his strength making me attentive and to shout at me fifty times "*Or oyez!*" in the manner of our heralds' (365). For Theodor Adorno, in the most compelling modern statement on the essay, the form 'starts not with Adam and Eve but with what it wants to talk about; it says what occurs to it in that context and stops when it feels finished rather than when there is nothing to say.'[2] In other words the essay, the subject of this volume, begins ad hoc and needs no introduction. And yet a collection of essays conventionally demands one: an address to the reader which performs some of the duties of Montaigne's herald, drawing attention to the subject,

---

[1] Michel de Montaigne, *The Complete Works*, trans. Donald Frame (2003), 721; further references given in the text. French from *Les Essais de Michel de Montaigne*, ed. Pierre Villey, 3 vols (1930–1), II, 899. 'Of the Resemblance of Children to their Fathers' is the final essay in the two-book *Essais* which Montaigne published in 1580; a third book was added in the second edition of 1588, and the final posthumous edition of 1595 contained many additions.

[2] Theodor Adorno, 'The Essay as Form', in *Notes to Literature, Volume One*, ed. Rolf Tiedemann, trans. Shierry Weber Nicholsen (1991), 3–23, here 4.

Thomas Karshan and Kathryn Murphy, *Introduction: On the Difficulty of Introducing a Work of this Kind* In: *On Essays: Montaigne to the Present*. Edited by: Thomas Karshan and Kathryn Murphy, Oxford University Press (2020).
© Thomas Karshan and Kathryn Murphy.
DOI: 10.1093/oso/9780198707868.003.0001

defining it, justifying its interest, delimiting its scope, accounting for its origins, and explaining what holds the contributions together.

All of these tasks, however, run against the spirit of the essay, which is miscellaneous and anti-systematic: 'methodically unmethodical', in Adorno's phrase. Defining the essay is notoriously difficult: indeed it is often suggested that 'the one commonly accepted fact about the essay is that indeterminacy is germane to its essence'.[3] At the same time, the essay on essays—what we might call the 'meta-essay'—has been a feature of the form from the start. Montaigne, who originates the term by choosing the title *Essais* for the first edition of his miscellaneous discourses, published in 1580, is self-reflexive and self-baffled by the novelty of this new kind of book. William Cornwallis, with some claim to be Montaigne's first British imitator, included a piece entitled 'Of Essayes, & Bookes' in what is only the second volume of prose works entitled 'essays' printed in English; much later, the genre was sufficiently established for Hilaire Belloc to write 'An Essay upon Essays upon Essays'.[4] The essay is at once resistant to exhaustive definition, and yet—or thus—continually posing and reposing what Denise Gigante has called 'the all-important question: what is the essay?'[5] The seventeen essays collected in this volume likewise participate in the persistent urge to write about essays, despite their characteristic resistance to characterization.

Leigh Hunt had some fun with such paradoxes when in 1819 he called the first essay in a new periodical 'Difficulty of Finding a Name for a Work of this Kind'. He fashioned an introduction out of his perplexity in naming and beginning, like Montaigne describing his epileptic, baffled amid miscellaneous things.[6] Hunt offers an entertaining array of possible titles for his assembly of essays, with each name suggesting something differently characteristic of the form, 'a meaning in their absurdity': 'the Adviser, or Helps for Composing;—the Cheap Reflector, or Every Man His Own Looking-Glass;—the Retailer, or Every Man His Own Other Man's Wit;—Nonsense, To be continued.'[7] The essayist, as the titles of other periodicals tell us, is guardian, spectator, and egotist; a free thinker, the master of his own wit, but also the mere purveyor of commonplaces stolen from others. A genre of paradox, the essay thus comes close to nonsense, a kind of writing to which it bears affinities; and as it begins wherever it chooses, so it is always

---

[3] Claire de Obaldia, *The Essayistic Spirit: Literature, Modern Criticism, and the Essay* (1995), 2.

[4] William Cornwallis, *Essayes* (1600), sigs. Gg8v–Ii8v. For further essays on essays, see the works anthologized in Carl H. Klaus and Ned Stuckey-French (eds), *Essayists on the Essay: Montaigne to Our Time* (2012); Brian Dillon, *Essayism* (2017). Belloc's essay, originally written in 1929, is anthologized in Klaus and Stuckey-French, *Essayists on the Essay*, 51–4. See also Scott Black's essay in this volume.

[5] In the preliminary material for a special issue entitled *The Essay: An Attempt, A Protean Form*, ed. Denise Gigante, *Republics of Letters* 4 (2014), available at http://arcade.stanford.edu/rofl/fora/essay-attempt-protean-form.

[6] For more on Hunt, see this volume, Chapter 1 by Thomas Karshan, 31–2, 37, 48–9; Chapter 7 by Denise Gigante, *passim*, and Chapter 8 by Greg Dart, 169–70, 174–5.

[7] Leigh Hunt, *The Indicator* (1822), 2.

to be continued, never concluded.[8] The essay is 'the Crocodile, or Pleasing Companion; [...] the Pleasing Ancestor; [...] the Ingenious Hat-band': concerned with the quotidian, or the trivial, and the strange, interested at once in tradition and contemporary ephemera. That one proposal is 'Chaos—or the Agreeable Miscellany' suggests both the problem and the pleasures of variety, and names the essayistic trope of miscellaneity that Hunt's own list performs. 'The Hippopotamus Entered at Stationers' Hall', meanwhile, archly indicates the problems of literary form.[9] Since to enter something at Stationers' Hall is to register a work for the purposes of copyright, to introduce the essay there as a hippopotamus is to suggest that it is a paradoxical and monstrous creature which will blunder into and make a mess of established categories of writing and their rule-bound legislation.

The search for a title for assembled essays, and a definition of works 'of this kind', is impossible, Hunt declares: but not therefore either to be given up, or regretted. He nonetheless finds a name—*The Indicator*—and begins. 'There is one good thing [...] which the hunt after a title is sure to realize', he claims: 'a great deal of despairing mirth'.[10] Despite the infinite variety of the stuff of the world, Montaigne likewise suggests in 'Of Experience', 'we fasten together our comparisons by some corner', like the curious elk's horn on which the epileptic lights (998). Taking permission from Montaigne's adhoccery, and Hunt's happily despairing hunt, we here take hold of the elusive essay by several corners, and make our unnecessary introduction out of the long history of problems in defining, naming, and identifying the essay, supplying a background for the book you are reading, and for the persistent urge to write of essays which our contributors also share.

2. On Definitions

From one perspective, it should be easier to define the essay, and supply a story of its origins, than for any other form. Unlike other major kinds of literature—the novel, the epic, the sonnet, tragedy, comedy—the moment of the essay's inception, its Adam and Eve, is clear. When Montaigne published a thick volume of treatises on various topics in 1580, he titled it his *Essais*, and thereby inaugurated a tradition. Before him, the word 'essay' was not used in print for a kind of literary composition; after him, essays proliferated.

But Montaigne's title poses more problems than it resolves. Although the *Essais* are full of characterizations of Montaigne's self and style, and of suggestive uses of

---

[8] Offering a humorous range of rejected titles is itself a trope: see e.g. Aulus Gellius's *Attic Nights*, or *Cabinet* 63 (2017), 17, where the journal lists seventy-one other names it might have had. On Gellius and the miscellaneous tradition, see Chapter 2 by Warren Boutcher.

[9] Hunt, *The Indicator*, 2.   [10] Hunt, *The Indicator*, 1.

'essai' and its verb, 'essayer', Montaigne does not offer a definition. Indeed, the tradition seems founded by accident. Since Montaigne himself nowhere refers to one of his individual discourses as *an* essay, it is usual in scholarship to refer to the individual works as 'chapters'.[11] And though new as a name for literature, the French noun 'essai' pre-existed his application of it to a kind of writing. In the absence of any clear indication of what Montaigne intended, it has become a trope, even a cliché, of essays on the essay to reach for word-history as a route into a characterization of the form: as Claire de Obaldia has remarked, 'etymological evidence [is] always triumphantly brandished at some point or other'.[12] The French 'essai', derived ultimately from the Latin *exāgium*, a weighing, could mean 'trial', 'test', 'attempt', 'sounding', 'sample', 'temptation', 'risk', 'apprentice-ship', 'exercise', or—ironically, given its resistance to introduction—'prelude', 'beginning'.[13] To place it on the title-page of the *Essais* was thus a kind of modesty topos: the discourses printed on these pages, Montaigne suggested, would not be technical or controversial arguments, and should not be taken too seriously as the final, resolved opinions of the author, but instead understood as tentative and experimental discussions, the voice of an amateur or apprentice thinking aloud and liable to correction. Montaigne plays on the full range of its possible mean-ings, to propose essayistic writing as a tentative, risky, and experimental way of rejecting authority and exercising the free-thinking of the author: rather a style and attitude than a form, more frequently a verb than a noun.[14]

When the French term passed into English, however, it was as the name for a genre, however vaguely understood. The earliest citation the *Oxford English Dictionary* finds for the word 'essay' as a noun is in the title of Francis Bacon's *Essayes. Religious Meditations. Places of perswasion and disswasion*, published in 1597.[15] This title carries none of the ambiguity of intention of Montaigne's *Essais*: Bacon's apposition makes clear that 'essayes' names the form of the first set of writings in the book. The same is true of Cornwallis's *Essayes* of 1600, Robert Johnson's *Essaies, or rather Imperfect offers* of 1601, and the title given to John Florio's English translation of Montaigne in 1603: *The Essayes or Morall, Politike and Millitarie Discourses of Lo: Michaell de Montaigne*. Though the verb 'essay' had long been in use, carrying a similar range of meanings to the French, 'assay' was the usual English substantive, and it is only after Bacon that 'essay' begins to

---

[11] See, for instance, Ullrich Langer (ed.), *The Cambridge Companion to Montaigne* (2005), 3. We have not followed this strictly in this volume, however, since many of our contributors discuss Montaigne in his role as model for subsequent essayists.

[12] de Obaldia, *The Essayistic Spirit*, 2; see also Dillon, *Essayism*, 16–17.

[13] See Richard Scholar, *Montaigne and the Art of Free-Thinking* (2010), 67–8.

[14] On the liberating effect of Montaigne's *Essais* on vernacular philosophy and individual thinking, see Warren Boutcher, *The School of Montaigne in Early Modern Europe* (2017).

[15] This is not in fact the first time the word was used in a title: James VI of Scotland, later to accede to the throne of England as James I, published a volume entitled *The Essayes of a Prentise, in the Diuine Art of Poesie*, written in Scots, in 1584. It contained poems, translations, and a short prose treatise on Scots rhyme and prosody.

gain traction as a noun. As late as Thomas Culpeper's 'Of Essayes' of 1671, the foreignness was still remarked: 'The word *Essay*, we have from the French, in which tongue it signifies a trial and probation.'[16] 'Essay' was thus from the first associated in English primarily with a kind of writing.

But what kind of writing? It has proved easier to define the noun 'essay' than the form to which it gave a name. Anthologists and lexicographers are forced to cast a net as wide as possible, offering the barest minimum of characteristics. W. E. Williams's formulation, in the introduction to his 1942 *A Book of English Essays*, was succinct: 'the Essay is a piece of prose, usually on the short side, which is not devoted to narrative'.[17] The *OED* is more expansive: 'A composition of moderate length on any particular subject, or branch of a subject; originally implying want of finish, "an irregular undigested piece" (Johnson), but now said of a composition more or less elaborate in style, though limited in range.'[18] For Williams, the necessary criteria are that it is shortish, in prose, and does not tell a story; for the *OED*'s lexicographer, even the latter two of these stipulations are abandoned: the essay is not too long and is *about* something.

Part of the problem faced in the attempt at definition is that, since Montaigne, the essay has made resistance to definition part of its peculiar work. If, as Montaigne suggests in 'Of Experience', there is 'no quality [. . .] so universal as diversity and variety', then the pursuit of common features is futile. In the famous self-characterization which opens 'Of Repentance', Montaigne claimed:

> I cannot keep my subject still. It goes along befuddled and staggering, with a natural drunkenness. [. . .] I do not portray being: I portray passing. [. . .] This is a record of various and changeable occurrences, and of irresolute and, when it so befalls, contradictory ideas: whether I am different myself, or whether I take hold of my subjects in different circumstances and aspects. [. . .] If my mind could gain a firm footing, I would not make essays, I would make decisions; but it is always in apprenticeship and on trial.   (740)

Montaigne's essay is the opposite of decisions or resolutions: various, changeable, contradictory, befuddled, staggering, drunk. This unruliness—irregularity, or 'the Wildness of those Compositions which go by the Name of *Essays*', as Addison put it in terms which became widespread in the eighteenth century—acts as a warning against attempts at generalization.[19] Indeed, Adorno suggested that the knowledge offered by the essay is not that of definition, but experience, as when someone in a foreign country 'sees the same word thirty times in continually changing contexts'

---

[16] [Thomas Culpeper], *Essayes or Moral Discourses, on several Subjects* (1671), 1.
[17] W. E. Williams (ed.), *A Book of English Essays* [1942], 2nd edn (1963), 11.
[18] See *OED*, *s.v.* 'essay, n., 8'.
[19] Joseph Addison, *Spectator* No. 476 (5 September 1712), in *The Spectator*, ed. Donald F. Bond, 5 vols (1965), IV, 185. For wildness, see Scott Black's contribution to this volume.

and thus 'will have ascertained its meaning better than if he had looked up all the meanings listed'.[20] The actual title which Hunt chose for his periodical—*The Indicator*—suggests a similar attitude: rather than a formula, essays offer a demonstration, pointing at particular things for the reader to recognize. Abstraction is the enemy: William Hazlitt begins 'On Reason and Imagination' by declaring: 'I hate people who have no notion of any thing but generalities, and forms, and creeds, and naked propositions...'[21]

The problem, however, is that pointing at essays, or at things that have been called essays, immediately reveals a baffling and incongruous variety of works. Essays appear at the length of John Locke's *An Essay Concerning Human Understanding* (1690)—belying Williams's insistence on the shortness of essays—or the brevity and lightness of Montaigne's one-page 'Of Thumbs', or the disposable single sheets of the *Spectator*'s daily publications. They can be fervently and committedly political, like the works collected in James Baldwin's *Notes of a Native Son* (1955), or confined to leisure and detachment, as in Montaigne's own works, a paradox explored by Ophelia Field's contribution in this volume. They can be personally confessional, or pseudonymously estranged, via personae like the *Tatler*'s Isaac Bickerstaff or Charles Lamb's Elia; encompass the witness accounts of journalism, as in Hazlitt or George Orwell, or fantasies and dreams, such as Lamb's 'Dream-Children'. Even the suggestion that an essay is a piece of prose finds a challenge in works like James VI and I's *Essayes of a Prentice, in the Diuine Art of Poesie* (1584) or Samuel Daniel's *Poetical Essayes* (1599), the first and third works published in Britain with the word in the title; or in Pope's *Essay on Man* and *Essay on Criticism*.

Some of the works which are essays by common consensus, meanwhile, in fact preferred to call themselves by other names. From the mid-seventeenth century into the eighteenth, the word 'essay' was at once ubiquitous—over 1,500 works were published between 1642 and 1714 with the word in the title—and often interchangeable with 'Discourse' or 'Dissertation', though 'essay' often implies a more tentative approach. Locke, in his dedication and epistle to his *Essay*, shifted back and forth between 'essay' and 'treatise'. Addison and Steele, in the *Tatler* and *Spectator*, preferred 'papers', resisting, like Samuel Johnson after them, too close an association with wayward Montaigne: we go sixty-eight issues of the *Spectator* before we find the first use of the word 'essay', and 101 issues before we come to the first time that the term is applied to the 'little Diurnal Essays' of the periodical itself.[22] Others prefer the modesty of 'studies', 'sketches', 'estimates', 'portraits', 'pieces', or even, in Robert Louis Stevenson, 'gossips'.[23] Brian Blanchfield's recent

---

[20] Adorno, 'The Essay as Form', 15.

[21] William Hazlitt, 'On Reason and Imagination', in *The Selected Writings of William Hazlitt*, ed. Duncan Wu, 9 vols (1998), VIII, 40.

[22] *Spectator* No. 68 (18 May 1711), in Bond, *The Spectator*, I, 289; No. 101 (26 June 1711), in Bond, *The Spectator*, I, 424.

[23] See Hunt, *The Indicator*, essays 2 and 15. For an overview of some of the various names under which essays pass, see Charles Whitmore, 'The Field of the Essay', *PMLA* 36.4 (1921), 551–64, here 561.

volume organizes its twenty-four essays under the title *Proxies*.[24] And the essay has also always lent itself to hybrid forms, from the essayistic novels and novelistic essays of Henry Fielding, George Eliot, Robert Musil, and Milan Kundera (denying the separation of narrative and essay on which definitions insist), the hybrid prose and poetry of Abraham Cowley and Claudia Rankine, to photo-essays, film-essays, and video-essays which are at once unimaginable from the perspective of Montaigne's late sixteenth-century beginnings, and recognizably in a common tradition of experiment, tentative thought, experiential reasoning, and avoidance of definition, resolution, and closure.[25]

The temptation, then, is to make this resistance and capaciousness into the essay's definitive characteristic, the ragbag into which things which resist other names can be corralled. As Hugh Walker wrote in his 1915 *The English Essay and Essayists*—still the most substantial single-author study of the history of the form in English—'just as, in the days before enclosures, stray cattle found their way to the unfenced common, so the strays of literature have tended towards the ill-defined plot of the essay.'[26] Warren Boutcher, in his contribution to this volume, argues against taking the essay as a genre at all, placing it instead in a longer tradition of miscellaneous writing. The essay has been called 'less a genre than quite deliberately an antigenre, designed to flaunt the prescriptiveness in literary matters which had been inherited from a rationalistic rhetorical tradition'; one critic calls it a 'Proteus', saying that 'there is no genre that takes so many shapes and that refuses so systematically to resolve itself, finally, into its own shape'; another, that it is 'a genre legitimated by its existence outside any genre', which 'retains its character only when it constantly intersects with other genres'; a fourth suggests that it is 'a moment of writing before the genre, before genericness—or as the matrix of generic possibilities'.[27] For de Obaldia, there is no such thing as the essay, only essaying, a set of tendencies which can colonize any other literary form. For Rachel Blau du Plessis, 'given that the essay is all margin, marginalia, and interstitial writing, it rearranges, compounds, enfolds, and erodes the notion of

---

Stevenson titles two of his essays 'gossips': 'A Gossip on Romance' and 'A Gossip on a Novel of Dumas's'. For an overview of Stevenson's various titles for his essays, see Robert-Louis Abrahamson, Richard Dury, Lesley Graham, and Alex Thomson, introduction to Robert Louis Stevenson, *Essays I: Virginibus Puerisque, and other papers* (2018), xxxiii–xxxiv.

[24] Brian Blanchfield, *Proxies* (2016).
[25] On Rankine, see Chapter 15, by Ned Stuckey-French, 308–11; on Fielding, Chapter 5, by Fred Parker, 129–31; on Lamb, Chapter 9, by Felicity James; on twentieth-century fiction, Chapter 14, by Michael Wood. On the problem of genre and recognition of form, see de Obaldia, *The Essayistic Spirit*, 1–8, and 23.
[26] Hugh Walker, *The English Essay and Essayists* (1915), 2.
[27] W. Wolfgang Holdheim, *The Hermeneutic Mode: Essays on Time in Literature and Literary Theory* (1984), 20; O. B. Hardison, Jr, 'Binding Proteus: An Essay on the Essay', in *Essays on the Essay*, 11–28, here 12; Mikhail Epstein, 'Essayism: An Essay on the Essay' (1982), in *Russian Postmodernism: New Perspectives on Post-Soviet Literature*, ed. Mikhail Epstein, Alexander Genis, and Slobodanka Vladiv-Glover (2016), 216–22, here 216; Réda Bensmaïa, *The Barthes Effect: The Essay as Reflexive Text* (1987), 91–2.

center in textually fruitful ways.'[28] 'Essay' becomes one of those words, like 'nonsense', 'miscellaneous', or 'etc.', which Susan Stewart describes as making 'a category that is both negative and residual', giving 'us a place to store any mysterious gaps in our systems of order'.[29]

This unlegislated gathering of strays and fugitives, giving a name of form to formlessness, has irked some writers. Samuel Johnson blamed Montaigne for having 'reconciled mankind' to 'licentiousness' 'by the vivacity of his essays': 'he therefore who wants skill to form a plan or diligence to pursue it, needs only entitle his performance an essay, to acquire the right of heaping together the collections of half his life, without order, coherence, or propriety.'[30] In this book we have tried to strike a balance between the licence offered by the title of 'essay', and the worry expressed by Johnson that the word might act as an excuse for not engaging in the proper work of definition. Our book is entitled *On Essays*, not *On Essayism*, and we do not see the essay merely as a 'heap' of ill-assorted writings; or a gesture of amused despair at the inadequacy of categories; or a liberty run to licentiousness. Instead, we take a hint from another passage in Montaigne's 'Of the Resemblance of Children to Fathers', the title of which already hints at a relationship between generation and genre. 'What a prodigy it is', Montaigne exclaims,

> that the drop of seed from which we [humans] are produced bears in itself the impressions not only of the bodily form but of the thoughts and inclinations of our fathers! Where does that drop of fluid lodge this infinite number of forms? And how do they convey these resemblances with so heedless and irregular a course that the great-grandson will correspond to his great-grandfather, the nephew to the uncle?   (701)

It is not difficult to transpose from human genus to literary genre: what Montaigne says here is true of the history of the essay, in which family resemblances skip generations, realize potential in unexpected ways, mutate, recur, lie dormant for decades, then spring to life again. Virginia Woolf, a great historian as well as practitioner of the essay, likewise turned to the metaphor of family resemblance in her 'The Modern Essay' of 1922. 'The form', she concedes, 'admits variety. The essay can be short or long, serious or trifling, about God or Spinoza, or about turtles and Cheapside.' It is nonetheless, as her phrasing suggests, a form; and though 'the family is widely spread', some of whose 'representatives have risen in the world and wear their coronets' while 'others pick up a precarious living in the gutter', it is still a family.[31]

[28] Rachel Blau DuPlessis, 'f-Words: An Essay on the Essay', *American Literature* 68.1 (1996), 15–45, here 20.

[29] Susan Stewart, *Nonsense: Aspects of Intertextuality in Folklore and Literature* (1978; 1979), 5.

[30] Samuel Johnson, *The Rambler*, vols III–V of *The Yale Edition of the Works of Samuel Johnson*, ed. W. J. Bate and Albrecht B. Strauss (1969), V, 77 (No. 158).

[31] Virginia Woolf, *The Essays of Virginia Woolf*, 6 vols, ed. Stuart N. Clarke et al. (1986–2011), IV, 216.

The family suggests a tradition, even if one whose matters of inheritance are chancy and often surprising; and thus this volume, after two more general essays by Karshan and Boutcher, is organized chronologically, from Montaigne to the present. Most contributions focus on one of the typical characteristics of this family, as it finds expression in particular members, but with an eye to the whole tradition, its edges and its blurring with others. Each contribution, like Adorno's traveller in a foreign country, points out the essay or the essayistic in different contexts; each essay, in the spirit of Hunt's indicator, acts as a pointer, towards some of the senses of what the essay can be or has been.

3. On Reading

The previous section might be taken to suggest that the essay sprang fully formed from the head of Montaigne in 1580, and that he is thus the patriarch and single progenitor of that family of essays and essayists which has since scattered across the globe. The etymology, and complicated early uses, however, imply a complicated sequence of tentative beginnings, 'like a circumspect runner trying for a start', in one of Cornwallis's metaphors.[32] Adorno's resistance to a tracing of origins back to Adam and Eve suggests that a single point of origin is the wrong way to think of essayistic beginnings. And Francis Bacon, author of the first published book of English essays, also put novelty and tradition in uneasy relation in the dedication of a manuscript version of his essays, claiming that 'the word is late, but the thing is ancient'; in other words, that while calling a composition an 'essay' was new, the form of writing it designated was not.[33] Like Montaigne's idea of the human person, the essay is at once idiosyncratically novel, and a reworking of inherited features.

Early essayists were confident of who those forebears were. Bacon pointed to Seneca's letters to Lucilius, which, he claimed, were 'but Essays,—That is dispersed Meditations, though conveyed in the form of Epistles'.[34] Montaigne wrote an essay 'In Defence of Seneca and Plutarch', and Joseph Addison similarly nominated Seneca, alongside Montaigne, as his essayistic 'Patterns'.[35] In doing so, they separated themselves from a strain of ornate and orderly oration associated with Cicero, and laid claim to a tradition of miscellaneous, curious, moral writing. Seneca's *Epistulae morales*, or 'moral letters', were a sequence of 124 short Latin texts dating to the first century AD each written on a theme—'On the Terrors of Death', 'On Philosophy and Friendship', 'On the Reasons for Withdrawing from the World', 'On Meeting Death Cheerfully', 'On Grief for Lost Friends', 'On Drunkenness', 'On Gathering Ideas', 'On Discursiveness in Reading', 'On the

---

[32] Cornwallis, *Essayes*, sig. Gg8v.
[33] British Library, MS Add. 4259, fo. 155. Quoted in Francis Bacon, *The Essayes or Counsels, Civill and Morall* [1625], ed. Michael Kiernan (2000), xlvii.
[34] Ibid.   [35] *Spectator* No. 476 (5 September 1712), in Bond, *The Spectator*, IV, 186.

Fickleness of Fortune', 'On Style as a Mirror of Character'. They tend to begin with an anecdote, a memory, a concrete observation, before broadening to generalized and moral statements in a Stoic vein. Plutarch's *Moralia*, written in Greek slightly later in the same century, is a collection of seventy-nine texts on similarly miscellaneous topics, taking in a wider range of subjects than Seneca's *Epistulae*: alongside moral questions of virtue, education, and prudence appear antiquarian discussions, anthropology, natural speculations, and collections of anecdotes and sayings, including 'On Profiting from One's Enemies', 'On Superstition', 'On Isis and Osiris', 'On The E at Delphi', 'On Curiosity', 'Whether Land or Sea Animals are Cleverer', and 'On the Eating of Flesh'.

The inclusion of the word 'moral' in the titles of so many seventeenth-century volumes of essays demonstrates how closely the form was understood as pursuing the same path as the wisdom literature of Seneca and Plutarch, with its witty alternation of general precept and personal speculation: 'their teaching', Montaigne says, 'is the cream of philosophy, and presented in simple and pertinent fashion' (364).[36] Their mosaic of different topics was also enabling: 'the knowledge I seek is there treated in detached pieces that do not demand the obligation of long labor, of which I am incapable. [. . .] I need no great enterprise to get at them, and I leave them whenever I like. For they have no continuity from one to the other' (364).[37] The detachment of their separate considerations, their shortness, and their freedom of form to begin and leave off at will, remarked by everyone from Montaigne to Adorno as key features of the essay, are what appeal. The examples of Seneca and Plutarch served more generally to develop a new style of vernacularized philosophy in the sixteenth and especially seventeenth centuries which privileged matter and particularity over formal or oratorical eloquence, and cultivated a high regard for erudition conducted with a gentlemanly informality, also characteristic of Charles Lamb or Leigh Hunt.

The recognized model of Seneca and Plutarch amplifies the point made by Warren Boutcher in his contribution to this volume, that essays participate in a much longer tradition of various and miscellaneous writing that has always had an evident appeal for writers and readers. Recent anthologists have taken this beyond the scope of the direct genealogies of the European and American essay. Philip Lopate's *The Art of the Personal Essay* includes, in its 'Forerunners' section, passages from Sei Shōnagon's tenth-century *Pillow Book*, from the fourteenth-century Japanese Buddhist monk Kenko, and from the eleventh-century Chinese writer Ou-Yang Hsiu.[38] John d'Agata's *Lost Origins of the Essay* begins at

---

[36] e.g. Florio's Montaigne, *The Essayes or Morall, Politike and Millitarie Discourses* (1603); the final edition of Bacon's essays, *The Essayes or Counsels, Civill and Morall* (1625); or Culpeper's *Essayes or Moral Discourses* (1671).

[37] For the miscellaneous tradition more broadly, see Chapter 2, by Warren Boutcher.

[38] Phillip Lopate (ed.), *The Art of the Personal Essay: An Anthology from the Classical Era to the Present* (1994).

the moment when the use of writing by the Sumerian civilization is first recorded for a purpose other than accounting and administration, in 'The List of Ziusudra'—anticipating the essay's tendency to the mosaic and listing form—and includes texts from Akkadian, from Heraclitus, from Azwinaki Tshipala, who lived in southern Africa c.315 AD, and from Chinese and Japanese traditions, including, again, Sei Shōnagon.[39]

The prominence of the list, and of the essayistic text as a way of corralling different literary and factual material, relates the essay to the modes of reading as gathering that prevailed at the beginning of the seventeenth century. Writing in a five-volume translation of Plutarch's *Morals* published in 1684, the translator Matthew Morgan suggested that Plutarch's 'way was that of Common-Place Book'.[40] The practice of commonplacing assembled quotations, exempla, and aphorisms under thematic headings, and acted as the storehouse of latent ideas from which a schoolboy or writer could draw material to be assembled into more sustained argument, oratory, or literary composition. It digested reading into fodder for writing, and made writing a process of assembly of pre-existing material, rather than the creation of new matter. Montaigne himself acknowledges the potential to view his essays as a kind of anthology of the words of others, a *florilegium*: 'someone might say of me that I have here only made a bunch of other people's flowers, having furnished nothing of my own but the thread to tie them' (984). Bacon's earliest essays barely supplied that thread: his editor Michael Kiernan comments that '[s]ome would view the ten earliest essays [...] as little more than pages from Bacon's commonplace books', raw matter in which sentences were divided by pilcrows, emphasizing that these 'essays' were not pieces of continuous discourse, but the result of a partial process of digestion and compilation, made available to other readers.[41] As Scott Black has argued, early essays are 'primarily "records of reading" rather than of writing'.[42]

Reading and writing were, however, continuous, simultaneous processes, and in essays from the early modern period to the present, quotation and scholarship are tempered and enlivened by experience and individual judgement. Thus Montaigne writes that the 'concoctions of commonplaces, by means of which so many men husband their study, are hardly useful except for commonplace subjects, and they serve to show us off, not to guide us' (984).[43] Or, again, 'We know how to say; "Cicero says thus; such are the morals of Plato; these are the very

---

[39] John D'Agata (ed.), *The Lost Origins of the Essay* (2009).

[40] Matthew Morgan, *Plutarch's Morals translated from the Greek by several hands*, 5 vols (1684), I, sig. a3v.

[41] Michael Kiernan, 'General Introduction', in Bacon, *Essayes or Counsels*, xxxi. For a later example, see John Ufflet's *Wits Fancies: or, Choice Observations and Essayes* (1659), discussed in Scott Black, *Of Essays and Reading in Early Modern Britain* (2006), 3–6 (under the name 'Uffley').

[42] Black, *Of Essays and Reading*, 24.

[43] Ironically, Montaigne is here reworking Seneca's animus against adults relying on quotation and proverb. See Letter XXXVIII.

words of Aristotle." But what do we say ourselves? What do we do? A parrot could well say as much' (121). The essay appropriates quotation, so that what another author said becomes the utterance of the essayist's own voice—or, as Hunt put it, 'Every Man His Own Other Man's Wit'.

Still, the bricolage features of the essay, a fragmentary aesthetics of compilation, persist. Brian Dillon has recently remarked on the essayist's predilection for lists, for the accumulation of disparate material that contains, latently, patterns of relation and extrapolation left to the reader to develop.[44] Morgan's comments on Plutarch register a similar relish, drawing on an image in Erasmus: Plutarch's writing is 'like a piece of Mosaic work, which consists of several Parts, but all extremely Beautiful'.[45] The idea of an essay as a mosaic, an intricate tessellation of material in which the originality and beautiful consists both in the appeal of the individual segments, and the intricacy of their patterning, is still visible in modern compilatory essays, such as Eliot Weinberger's *An Elemental Thing*, a 'serial essay' which concatenates disparate information drawn from the legends and anthropology of many cultures to create an echo-chamber of human variety, or in the generically unassimilable meanders of the books of W. G. Sebald.[46]

The suggestion that each essay is an assembly of disparate materials is elaborated in Scott Black's contribution to this volume. The model suggests that we might read the fragmentary aphorisms of Bacon's early essays rather as a site of potential, than of haphazard unfinishedness. This is what Montaigne suggests in 'A Consideration upon Cicero':

> I am much mistaken [. . .] if any writer has sown his materials more substantially or at least more thickly on his paper. In order to get more in, I pile up only the headings of subjects. [. . .] And how many stories have I spread around which say nothing of themselves, but from which anyone who troubles to pluck them with a little ingenuity will produce numberless essays. [. . .] They often bear, outside of my subject, the seeds of a richer and bolder material, and sound obliquely a subtler note, both for myself, who do not wish to express anything more, and for those who get my drift.   (224)

Montaigne describes the purpose of his 'stories'—the classical *exempla*, the personal and historical anecdotes scattered throughout his work—as a storehouse. Each example contains the possibility for 'numberless essays' to which it might give rise (224). The essay we are reading is a proxy which stands in for innumerable essays that others may have written, that the reader may yet write. They are

[44] Dillon, *Esayism*, 23–8.

[45] See Robert Cummings, 'Versifying Philosophy: Thomas Blundeville's Plutarch', in *Renaissance Cultural Crossroads: Translation, Print, and Culture in Britain, 1473–1640*, eds Sara K. Barker and Brenda M. Hosington (2013), 109.

[46] Weinberger, *An Elemental Thing* (2007); e.g. W. G. Sebald, *The Rings of Saturn* [1995], trans. Michael Hulse (1998).

the 'seeds' from which other essays might grow. In his 'Defence of Seneca and Plutarch', Montaigne describes his own book as 'built up purely from their spoils': in other words, he finds in Seneca and Plutarch not only an enabling example, but also the embedded seeds which germinate in his own writing, which itself supplies germs of possibility for the future reader and writer.

4. On Pedantry

The association of the essay with commonplacing links it to the schoolroom, and to an inculcation of habits of thought and cultural norms: qualities which seemingly run counter to the wildness and licentiousness also attributed to the essay. This paradox leads to a dilemma at the heart of the history of the essay, and scholarship and criticism on it, which casts a considerable irony over a volume of essays on essays written largely by people employed by universities. One of the oddities of the essay is that it begins as a literary genre of tentativeness and resistance to institutionalized knowledge, but is now most commonly written as the standard mode of instruction and assessment and usual genre of school and undergraduate writing, especially in the humanities. Montaigne's long essay 'Of Pedantry' indicts the desiccated paralysis of 'scholars' and contrasts them with his own writing: they 'distinguish and mark off their ideas more specifically and in detail. I, who cannot see beyond what I have learned from experience, without any system, present my ideas in a general way, and tentatively. As in this: I speak my meaning in disjointed parts' (1004). The essay resists scholarship and orderly composition: 'I put forward formless and unresolved notions' (278). He claims to emulate the actual course of thinking, moving wildly from one subject to another in order 'to follow a movement so wandering as that of our mind' (331). His stipulations run directly against what are nowadays the criteria used to assess essays in pedagogical contexts: definition of terms and method, orderly structure and clear argument, lack of digression, impersonality of tone, avoidance of conjecture, provision of evidence, summative conclusions, completeness and coherence. One of the most distinguished essayists of the post-war era, Susan Sontag, was capable of writing in her 'Notes on "Camp"' (1964) that 'the form of jottings, rather than an essay (with its claim to a linear, consecutive argument), seemed more appropriate for getting down something of this particular fugitive sensibility.'[47] Yet a record of fugitive thoughts and sensations is precisely what Montaigne's essays are. It would have come as a surprise to him that the form he inspired has come to be identified with the kinds of spurious coherence he himself denied.

[47] Reprinted in *Against Interpretation and Other Essays* (1966), 276–7.

Sontag shows how the meanings and associations of 'essay' have come to be, in some contexts, completely inverted, placing the editors and writers of this volume in a quandary: as scholars writing on essays, we place ourselves under the immediate suspicion that we will be crushing the freedom which the essay adopts as its right. Yet these ironies are characteristic. Brian Blanchfield justified calling his essays 'proxies' because the word 'expresses a kind of concession to imprecision, a failure', expressing the essay's willingness to pledge itself less to truth and accuracy than to ad hoc and temporary expression, as in Montaigne's insistence that he makes 'essays', not 'decisions'.[48] Yet Montaigne himself, despite his renunciation of abstraction, decisiveness, and rules, is full of aphoristic generalization; Sontag's 'Notes on "Camp"', though issued as numbered 'jottings', likewise have a legislative authority. There is a deep-lying ambivalence between the essay as a strenuous weighing-up, a sober examination, which surfaces in the modern usage in school and university exercises, and the opposed sense of something tentative, preliminary, and provisional—that is, between the essay as try or attempt, and the essay as trial, an ambiguity which John Jeremiah Sullivan has referred to as 'this binary, this yin / yang, this Heisenbergian flickering between two primary meanings'.[49]

Like so much else, this ambivalence is already present in the essay's earliest history. Montaigne himself placed the word 'essai' in pedagogical contexts, yet did so precisely to stress the provisionality of his writing:

> I set forth notions that are human and my own, simply as human notions considered in themselves, not as determined and decreed by heavenly ordinance and permitting neither doubt nor dispute; matter of opinion, not matter of faith; what I reason out according to me, not what I believe according to God; as children set forth their essays [comme les enfans proposent leurs essais] to be instructed, not to instruct[.]   (284)[50]

The schoolboy 'essays' to which Montaigne compares his writings were not the same as the essays that modern pupils and students write in schools and universities, but hesitant attempts to fulfil various set exercises such as those of translation and imitation. That same idea of the essay as a pupil's sketch or draft was expressed by James VI and I—whose tutor, the poet George Buchanan, had also taught Montaigne—when he titled his volume of poems, translations, and poetics *The Essayes of a Prentise, in the Diuine Art of Poesie* (1584). The pedagogical association is still clearer in Florio's address 'To the curteous Reader' in his translation of Montaigne, where he exclaimed '*Why but Essayes are but mens*

---

[48]   Blanchfield, *Proxies*, viii.
[49]   John Jeremiah Sullivan (ed.), *The Best American Essays 2014* (2014), xxiv–xxv.
[50]   See Villey, *Les Essais de Michel de Montaigne*, I, 619.

school-themes pieced together; you might as wel say, several texts'.[51] The 'school-theme' Florio refers to was a proposed subject on which a student had to write a composition, following standard rules of definition and example. Montaigne recalled, in 'Of the Education of Children', tutors 'giv[ing him] a theme in the school fashion': receiving a text on a given subject to recast in elegant Latin (156). By the middle of the seventeenth century, the essay had also become a pedagogical genre, an 'exercise in the grammar school', as the title of Ralph Johnson's *The Scholars Guide* had it:

> An Essay is a short discourse about any virtue, vice, or other common-place. Such be Learning, Ignorance, Justice, Temperance, Fortitude, Prudence, Drunkenness, Usury, Love, Joy, Fear, Hope, Sorrow, Anger, Covetousness, Contentation, Labour, Idleness, Riches, Poverty, Pride, Humility, Virginity, &c.[52]

Johnson supplies rules for 'making' an essay, which, far from the changeable and drunken form inaugurated by Montaigne, work like a recipe for the exhaustive treatment of a topos, beginning by 'express[ing] the nature of it in two or three short Definitions, or Descriptions', establishing its sorts or kinds, its 'causes, adjuncts, and effects', while emphasizing that this should be done 'briefly, without tautology or superfluous good words, in good and choice language'. It is not clear how long the essay's previous history in the schoolroom was, especially since Johnson sends his reader to modern exemplars, referring to the 'larger and complete Essays' of Bacon and Owen Felltham.[53] What is clear is that already by 1665, the fissure in senses of 'essay' had set in.

Johnson differentiates the 'essay' from the 'theme' on the basis of its topic: a 'theme' could approach any subject, rather than just a vice or virtue. The 'theme' predominated over the 'essay' as the standard model of school prose composition for three further centuries. Over the course of the nineteenth century, the distinction between theme and essay in pedagogical contexts began to collapse. According to Ian Michael, the essay ultimately gained supremacy in large part due to its use in the rubrics of competitive public examinations, which were adopted widely from the 1850s, in an attempt to provide a meritocratic way of judging candidates for employment in the expanding professions and civil service, especially the Indian civil service.[54] The emphasis on virtue and vice lingered on in the essay tradition, with candidates for exam papers being asked, for example, to 'assess the characters' of figures from Shakespeare. The purpose of such

---

[51] John Florio, *'To the curteous Reader'*, in Montaigne, *Essayes*, trans. Florio (1603), sig. A5v.

[52] Ralph Johnson, *The Scholars Guide from the Accidence to the University, or, Short, Plain, and Easie Rules for performing all manner of Exercise in the Grammar School* (1665), 13–14.

[53] Ibid., 14.

[54] See Ian Michael, *The Teaching of English: From the Sixteenth Century to 1870* (1987), 309–11, and Peter Womack, 'What are Essays For?', in *English in Education* 27.2 (1993), 42–8.

examinations was to offer candidates an opportunity to demonstrate their own character and merit, independent of any particular area of specialized knowledge or practical aim. The notion that the essay exposed the writer's idiosyncrasy was harnessed to the meritocratic pretensions of a new educational and professional structure, which rewarded students for meeting certain well-recognized if often implicit structural and conceptual models. Peter Womack expresses these mixed messages—write freely, but conform to expectation; be yourself, but adopt the disinterested persona of the essayist—as the product of the ideological fantasy 'that expressing one's individuality and affirming one's membership of the elite [should] become effectively identical'.[55]

The essay's role in the school and university systems thus became, in parallel, at once the codified mode of addressing a topic (along with strictures on structure, with models of four-point and five-point essays recommended by handbooks), and a prompt to a kind of playful composition which, despite or because of its pretence to lightness and spontaneity, did the work of forming an intellectual and social elite.[56] Cyril Connolly wrote in *Enemies of Promise* that as late as 1938, 'countless small boys', suffering under the bad influence of Addison, 'are at this moment busy setting down their views on Travel, the Great Man, Courage, Gardening, Capital Punishment to wind up with a quotation from Bacon'.[57] John Gross, too, remembers with horror being asked in the classroom of the mid 1940s 'to write a light-hearted essay all about nothing' in the tradition of Lamb.[58] One significant institutional survival of the personal essay about character is the American college admission essay, in which applicants are encouraged to draw a moral out of a personal anecdote, often about struggle, and enriched by some element of their reading or studies: 'failure', an expert on the admissions essay tells us, 'is essayistic gold'.[59] However distantly, these essays, too, derive ultimately from the Montaignian sense of *essai* as trial and attempt, a vehicle for writing the experiments of life.

5. On Essays

Given the various ways in which the essay bristles against academic writing—its resistance to introductions, to definitions, to generalization and abstraction, to

---

[55] The argument in this paragraph is drawn from Womack's in 'What are Essays For?'.

[56] For the four-part structure—'introduction, points for, points against, conclusion'—prevailing in British handbooks and the five-part American structure ('introduction, three arguments, conclusion') see Peter Mack, 'Rhetoric and the Essay', *Rhetoric Society Quarterly* 23.2 (1993), 41–9, here 41, 48, and n.13.

[57] Cyril Connolly, *Enemies of Promise* [1938], 2nd edn (1949), 11.

[58] See Gross's 'Introduction' in *The Oxford Book of Essays* (1991), xxi–xxii.

[59] Rachel Toor, 'How to Conquer the Admissions Essay', *The New York Times*, 2 August 2017, at https://nyti.ms/2hnhF6C.

accounts of origins, its freedom from discipline, rules, and criteria—it is no wonder that the field of critical work on the essay is sparse. The essay has been relatively neglected in scholarly and critical accounts, since the characteristics associated with the essayistic—lack of authority, digression, marginality, and so on—are precisely those from which the professional study of literature had to distinguish itself, in order to make a claim to the systematic and methodical qualities that would win it respectability as a university discipline.[60] Remarkably, there is only one substantial history of the essay in English, Hugh Walker's *The English Essay and Essayists* (1915),[61] though there are also several excellent studies of the essay in particular periods,[62] while editors of anthologies have done important work in framing their topics.[63] Though English is the language in which the form of the essay has been most consistently productive, the most compelling theoretical statements have been Central European, from Robert Musil, György Lukács, and Theodor Adorno, an irony reflecting the English and essayistic bias towards practice and empiricism, and away from theory and abstraction.[64]

It is also for this reason that some of the most compelling thinking on the essay appears in the reflections of essayists on their own practice, or on those of other essayists. The implicit reflexivity which so often inhabits Montaigne, as we have seen, is a consistent trait, as Karshan shows in his contribution to this volume, teasing out the ways in which Woolf's great essay 'Street-Haunting' acts as a recapitulation of themes from throughout the essay tradition. Such meta-essays often avoid systematic definitions, preferring to offer their insights indirectly, by performing the features they claim as typical, as in Brian Dillon's recent *Essayism*.[65] The introductions by practising essayists contributed annually since

[60] On the association of the essay with the dilettantish and *belle-lettriste*, see Chapter 7, by Denise Gigante.

[61] See also Walker's earlier 'Miscellaneous Prose', in *The Literature of the Victorian Era* (1910, 1921), 1024–54. Graham Good's *The Observing Self: Rediscovering the Essay* (1988) is more episodic. See also Tracy Chevalier (ed.), *Encyclopedia of the Essay* (1997). The most comparable volume to ours is Alexander J. Butrym (ed.), *Essays on the Essay: Redefining the Genre* (1989).

[62] e.g. Scott Black, *Of Essays and Reading in Early Modern Britain* (2006); Elbert N. S. Thompson, *The Seventeenth-Century English Essay* (1927); George S. Marr, *Periodical Essayists of the Eighteenth Century* (1923); Thomas McFarland, *Romantic Cruxes: The English Essayists and the Spirit of the Age* (1987); David Russell, *Tact: Aesthetic Liberalism and the Essay Form in Nineteenth-Century Britain* (2017). Though not focused solely on essayists, Michael Hurley and Marcus Waithe (eds), *Thinking Through Style: Non-Fiction Prose of the Long Nineteenth Century* (2018), contains several relevant studies. For briefer accounts, see Ted-Larry Pebworth, 'Not Being, but Passing: Defining the Early English Essay', *Studies in the Literary Imagination* 10.2 (1977), 17–27; Robert DeMaria, Jr, 'The Eighteenth-Century Periodical Essay', in John Richetti (ed.), *The Cambridge History of English Literature, 1660–1780* (2005), 527–48.

[63] See Erin Mackie (ed.), *The Commerce of Everyday Life: Selections from* The Tatler *and* The Spectator (1998); Denise Gigante (ed.), *The Great Age of the English Essay* (2008), on the eighteenth-century and Romantic essayists; Gertrude Himmelfarb (ed.), *The Spirit of the Age* (2009) on the Victorian essayists.

[64] See also de Obaldia, *The Essayistic Spirit*; Kuisma Korhonen, *Textual Friendship: The Essay as Impossible Encounter from Plato to Montaigne to Levinas and Derrida* (2006); Blau duPlessis, 'f-Words'; Erin Plunkett, *A Philosophy of the Essay: Scepticism, Experience, and Style* (2018).

[65] See again Klaus and Stuckey-French, *Essayists on the Essay*.

1986 to Robert Atwan's *Best American Essays* anthologies form, taken together, one of the most substantial recent bodies of thought on the essay. Recently, Adam Gopnik has offered an unofficial history of the essay tradition through pieces in the *New Yorker* on Montaigne, Johnson, De Quincey, Wilde, Chesterton, and Beerbohm, while Woolf's essays on essayists, including Montaigne, Addison, Hazlitt, and Lamb, constitute a thorough and insightful, if unofficial, history of the essay.[66]

A glance at the publication dates of many of these studies suggests something particular about the history of academic work on the essay. Though in the earlier part of the twentieth century, the essay played a significant role in the conception of the field of English literature, by the mid century, and certainly for most of the second half, it was a neglected genre: its association with dilettantism and ephemerality, and its resistance to theory and abstraction, making it a less serious or worthy object of research and scholarly attention than the more obviously amenable genres of lyric, novel, or drama. However the twenty-first century has seen a revival of interest in the essay form, and forms of non-fiction prose more generally, at the same time as practice and publication of essays and memoirs has also significantly increased. Non-fiction prose, or creative non-fiction, is now a staple of creative writing and MFA programmes; bookshops host whole sections under titles like 'Literary Essays'; and the publication both of new volumes of essays, and of studies of the essay, participates in the renewed attention to the form. Courses on the essay are increasingly available to undergraduates and graduates; and, in addition to this volume, several new studies have recently been published, or are emerging.[67]

In this volume, we have asked our contributors to accept and even embrace the irony of writing literary criticism and scholarship on the essay. We have ordered the volume, after two general introductory essays, according to the chronology of the essayists who are most central to each chapter, asking our contributors to take a topic general to the history of the essay, to tug on one of the various threads of what is typically essayistic, and to explore and exemplify it with relation to the particular corner they had taken hold of, all the while hoping to illuminate the longer history and more general tradition through particular instances. With the inevitable exception of Montaigne, our focus throughout is on the essay in Britain and America. This is not a *Handbook* of the essay, an apparently comprehensive and general introductory guide to the workings of a form as to the operation of a

---

[66] For Gopnik on Montaigne, see *The New Yorker*, 16 January 2017; on Johnson, see 'Man of Fetters', 8 December 2008; on De Quincey, 'Tory Tabloidism', 16 March 2012; on Wilde, 'The Invention of Oscar Wilde', 18 May 1998; on Chesterton, 'The Troubling Genius of G. K. Chesterton', 7 July 2008; on Beerbohm, 'The Diminutive Genius of Max Beerbohm', 3 August 2015. On Woolf, see Chapter 1, by Thomas Karshan. See also Philip Lopate, *Notes on Sontag* (2009).

[67] See, for example, Gigante (ed.), *The Essay: An Attempt, A Protean Form*; Plunkett, *Philosophy of the Essay*.

machine or contraption; nor is it a *Companion*, suggesting that the essay is a single and singular personage, to an encounter with whom this book might act as chaperone; nor an *Encyclopaedia*, implying that we have delimited and anatomized our subject into its component parts; nor a *History*, suggesting that the essay has a continuous and causally connected past which could be summarized. Instead, we have called the volume *On Essays*, availing ourselves of the essay's own titular habit, which implies at once its tendency to be *about* something, to have in view something which is its subject; while at the same time incorporating an awareness of the writer's intentionality, the taking up of an angle, rather than a claim to definitiveness or completion. We have tried to do justice to the paradoxical, miscellaneous, and amorphous qualities of the form, and the possibilities and potentials they permit, without losing sight of family resemblances, and the various characteristic qualities which, despite their hopscotching across generations, are nonetheless recognizably traits of the essay.

It is precisely this indirect mode of approaching the history of the essay which Thomas Karshan discovers in Chapter 1 of this book, 'What is an Essay?', which shows how Virginia Woolf's 'Street-Haunting' acts as a consummation and recapitulation of the paradoxical, miscellaneous history of the essay as she saw it, looking back to Montaigne and Bacon, and incorporating the eighteenth-century periodical essayists, Hazlitt, Lamb, De Quincey, Hunt, Thoreau, Emerson, Stevenson, Butler, and Belloc. Woolf's weaving of these references covertly into the incidents and accidents of a dusky walk through London in search of a pencil performs the contingent, chancy inheritance of traits across the essay form. Her essay is thus exemplary of something which emerges over and again in the writers discussed in the chapters of *On Essays*: the way in which the history of the essay is always being obliquely reimagined and rewritten when essayists rework tropes from their predecessors. This process continues today: so, for instance, 'Street-Haunting' has been a constant reference and inspiration for Rebecca Solnit, who calls Woolf a 'Virgil guiding me through the uses of wandering, getting lost, anonymity, immersion, uncertainty, and the unknown', and traces her ancestry as an essayist of self-loss back through Woolf to Thoreau.[68]

Chapter 2 in the volume, Warren Boutcher's 'The Montaignian Essay and Authored Miscellanies from Antiquity to the Nineteenth Century', likewise looks to the essay's powers of gathering and anthologizing: though in this case, tracing a long history that sees 'essay' as one name among many for examples of

---

[68] Rebecca Solnit, 'Woolf's Darkness: Embracing the Inexplicable', *The New Yorker*, 24 April 2014 (adapted from an essay in *Men Explain Things to Me* (2014), 85–108). See also Solnit, *A Field Guide to Getting Lost* (2005), 23: 'For Woolf, getting lost was not a matter of geography so much as identity, a passionate desire, or even an urgent need, to become no one and anyone, to shake off the shackles that remind you who you are, who others think you are. [...] Her getting lost was solitary, like Thoreau's.' See also this interview, in which Solnit 'cited Virginia Woolf and Henry David Thoreau as the writers most important to her' (https://www.nytimes.com/2017/08/08/t-magazine/entertainment/rebecca-solnit-writer-resistance.html).

the long tradition of miscellaneous writing, beginning in Aulus Gellius's *Attic Nights*. Boutcher thus accounts for the disparity of the manifestations of the essay, and the difficulty of finding a definition for it, by pointing to Montaigne's coining of the genre as an accident: one which reifies a title meant only to indicate a style and posture.

Nonetheless, as Cornwallis's immediate recourse to reflection on the nature 'of essays' suggests, reflection on the form is as old as the form itself, in English at least. The transformation of essaying into a genre called the essay was largely an English phenomenon in the seventeenth century: more essays were published in English than in any other European language (including French), in part because of the congruence of the essay's informal, anti-systematic, and anti-metaphysical biases with the emergence of English experimentalism and empiricism (a justification for the incongruous title of Locke's *An Essay Concerning Human Understanding*). Kathryn Murphy's contribution to this volume investigates this early English history, and the synonymity of essay, experience, and experiment in the seventeenth century. Chapter 3, 'Of Sticks and Stones', explores how Montaigne's preoccupation with his own idiosyncratic experience turns, in Bacon, to an interest in experience as a cognitive virtue, divested of personality; and thence, across the English seventeenth century, to an association of the essay with the beginnings of experimental science, in Robert Boyle. This trajectory gives some grounding for the essay's paradoxical relationship to science in later periods. On the one hand, for the Spanish philosopher Ortega y Gasset, the essay is 'science, minus the explicit proof', or for Max Bense, a German philosopher of science, 'the essay is an experimental method [...] in the same sense that one speaks of experimental physics'.[69] On the other, for Pater, Woolf, Lukács, and Adorno, the essay is precisely the form that resists science and system. Murphy's chapter shows the common origin of each of these positions in a preoccupation with experience rather than reason or authority as the ground of knowledge.

The following sequence of chapters contains essays which think through tensions between opposites which both seem equally part of the essay's way of being: sociability and solitude, philosophy and popular life, reverie and conversation, individualism and politics. In Chapter 4, 'Time and the Essay', Markman Ellis foregrounds a different sense of experience to that in Murphy's chapter, examining the innovation of Steele and Addison in publishing the essay as a daily paper. As Hazlitt concisely put it, 'the philosopher and wit here commences newsmonger'.[70] The *Tatler* and *Spectator* brought into close combination the witty and philosophical poles of the essay tradition. Although Addison and Steele

---

[69] José Ortega y Gasset, 'To the Reader', reprinted in Klaus and Stuckey-French, *Essayists on the Essay*, 38; Max Bense, 'On the Essay and its Prose', reprinted in Klaus and Stuckey-French, *Essayists on the Essay*, 72.

[70] Hazlitt, 'On the Periodical Essayists', V, 87.

reject the digressiveness of Montaigne, whom they are reluctant even to name, many of their essays share Montaigne's preoccupation with the ephemera of passing fashion and cultural artefacts; others, more moral and philosophical, are reminiscent instead of Bacon, the essayist they prefer to invoke. The periodical essay also marks the shift of the essay's primary locale from the closed gentlemanly spaces of the private study, garden, or experimental closet, as in Montaigne, Bacon, and their seventeenth-century followers, into the coffee-house and city.[71] As Ellis shows, the material history of the periodical essay—both the signs of usage and reading on the single-sheet 'Daily-Papers', and the more substantial gathering of them into bound and collected volumes—demonstrates that the proper place of the *Tatler* and *Spectator* was at once the coffee-shop and the library, and shows their participation simultaneously in the ephemerality of the daily life of commercial London in the early 1700s, and in learned culture and the formation of taste.

This poise between the learned and the popular was part of the periodical's aim: Addison famously wrote in the tenth issue of the *Spectator* that, as 'it was said of Socrates, that he brought Philosophy down from Heaven, to inhabit among Men', so 'I shall be ambitious to have it said of me, that I have brought Philosophy out of Closets and Libraries, Schools and Colleges, to dwell in Clubs and Assemblies, at Tea-Tables and in Coffee-houses.'[72] Fred Parker, in Chapter 5, 'The Sociable Philosopher', traces this purpose of bringing learning and philosophy into the polite world in the later eighteenth century. As Parker points out, Hume extends and complicates Addison's metaphor, claiming that the essayist is an 'Ambassador from the Dominions of Learning to those of Conversation'.[73] The essay thus enriches the conversation of ordinary society with the ideas and discoveries of learning. But it also provides a conduit through which the learned world is supplied with an embodied, situated content of character, situation, and personae. The eighteenth-century vogue for the philosophical dialogue, or the essay in dialogue, something practised by Hume and advocated by Anthony Ashley Cooper, Third Earl of Shaftesbury, shows the period's sense that ideas require a person to whom they are attributed, in order to be evaluated or given credit.[74] At the same time, the essay's digressiveness promotes a philosophical play of thought and free association of ideas which, as Parker says, depends on what Shaftesbury called 'the associating genius of man', in which 'associating' names both the sociability of human beings and their modes of reaching truth, and the essayistic

---

[71] Jürgen Habermas accorded the periodical essay a crucial role in the emergence of the 'public sphere' essential to modern democracy: 'in the *Tatler*, the *Spectator*, and the *Guardian* the public held up a mirror to itself'. See *The Structural Transformation of the Public Sphere*, trans. Thomas Burger (1991), 43.

[72] *Spectator* No. 10 (12 March 1711), in Bond, *The Spectator*, I, 44.

[73] David Hume, *Essays Moral, Political, and Literary*, ed. Eugene F. Miller (1987), 535.

[74] On this, see further Kathryn Murphy, 'The Essay', in Nicholas McDowell and Henry Power (eds), *The Oxford Handbook of English Prose, 1642–1714* (forthcoming).

procedure of apparently unmotivated meandering through adjacent subjects which provides its own revelations of the connectedness of things.

This connection between the eighteenth-century essay and persona, dialogue, and associative digression allies it with the emergence in the same period of the novel. Eighteenth-century novels, like essays, are miscellaneous, and incorporate various discourses into a single intelligible whole, making connections between specialised thought and the ordinary, social world. Henry Fielding opens each of the eighteen books of *Tom Jones* with an essay; Parker shows that, no less than Hume or Samuel Johnson, Fielding's fiction dramatizes the tension between intellect and society, opinions and life. This is the topic, too, of Chapter 6, 'Tristram Shandy, Essayist', in which Scott Black shows how Sterne's *Life and Opinions of Tristram Shandy, Gentleman* makes the eighteenth-century essay's reliance on personae into 'an elaborate joke' about the necessary invention of a fictional life to justify the recording of opinions. If Fielding's essays in *Tom Jones* are issued in the voice of the narrator, Black shows Sterne extending the essayistic persona into novelistic character. Shandy's famous digressiveness performs the association of ideas theorized by Locke in his own *Essay Concerning Human Understanding*. Though dramatically different in heft and philosophical serious-ness, both Sterne and Locke show, again, the association of ideas working out in the form of an essay. Against the backdrop of the habitual characterization of essayistic writing in the eighteenth century as 'wild', Black demonstrates that the perennial difficulty of categorizing *Tristram Shandy* according to the canons of genre, or corralling it within the designation 'novel', can be resolved by consider-ing it as an elaboration of the tendencies of the period's essays.

In Chapter 7, 'On Coffee-Houses, Smoking, and the English Essay Tradition', Denise Gigante shows what happens to these principles of association and soci-ability at the close of the eighteenth century. Through the token of Leigh Hunt's essay 'Mr Gliddon's Cigar Divan', Gigante shows how the eighteenth-century combination of public consumption (of coffee and news) with the sociable discussion of ideas and formation of taste in the coffee-shop shifts to a world of isolated reverie and dream in the smoking houses of early nineteenth-century London. Hunt, nostalgic for the world of Addison and Steele, shapes the essay in resistance to the pressing activity of modern clock-watching, desiring a 'humane openness of intercourse' in which thought and life flow together in easy conver-sation.[75] In keeping with the Romantic return to Montaigne as the presiding spirit of the essay, Hunt follows the smoker into Gliddon's cigar divan, where he finds the Montaignian 'arrière-boutique' or back-room of the mind literalized in an exotic, orientalized space which seems to belong to a world entirely differing from the sociable, commercial one going on around it. What he sees there is something

---

[75] Hunt, 'Coffee Houses and Smoking', in *The New Monthly Magazine and Literary Journal* 16.61 (January 1826), 50–4, here 53.

closer to the cloistered den of De Quincey's Opium-Eater. A volume of Kant's metaphysics replaces Addison's communally-read *Spectator*, and wild hallucinations replace the sociable associations of thought.

In Chapter 8, 'The Romantic Essay and the City', Greg Dart explores how Hunt's contemporaries Charles Lamb and William Hazlitt negotiated between the urban legacy of the *Spectator* and the poetic privileging of scenes of rural life that they found both in their older contemporaries Wordsworth and Coleridge, and in the longer tradition of retirement poetry which had been associated in the seventeenth century with the essay. Like Gigante, Dart finds Lamb and Hazlitt, alongside Hunt, nostalgic for the sociable city of the *Spectator*, but using images such as bells, knocking, and the post as ways to assemble an essayistic 'whirligig of association' which bridges past and present, day and night, reality and imagination. Association, then, in an image which recalls the close of Scott Black's essay, serves as 'a kind of relay between town and country, prose and poetry, the actual and the ideal'. If for Addison and Hume, and in our volume for Black and Parker, the essayist was an ambassador between realms of learning and conversation, in these Romantic essays the role is that of 'a tireless commuter, negotiator, and dialectician'.

Still other forms of sociability and connection are the subject of Felicity James in Chapter 9, 'Charles Lamb, Elia, and Essays in Familiarity'. Lamb's essays long stood in for the continuation of the 'companionable, curious, associative impulse' of the essay, establishing a familiar and almost oral intimacy between writer and reader for which Montaigne and the essay more generally were celebrated—as in Hazlitt's remark that in Montaigne, the reader is 'admitted behind the curtain, and sits down with the writer in his gown and slippers'.[76] In Lamb, as in Montaigne and Seneca, the essay is closely akin to the letter, and the related informality of style suits an era which articulated the ideal, in Wordsworth's preface to the *Lyrical Ballads*, that poetry should be written in 'the real language of men'.[77] James's essay exposes the 'sense of darkness at the other side of the familiar', showing how Lamb's persona Elia is also anagrammatically 'A Lie', a self 'made many', both in that it is 'unreliable or uncanny' and self-inconsistent, and in the way that the supposed intimacy of the persona is established through association or familiarity with an unknowable multitude of various readers. Here, too, we find a paradox vivid since Montaigne: that the essay is an idiosyncratic expression of self and yet at the same time constituted of a patchwork of quotations and mediated voices.

If Black shows how Nietzsche celebrated Sterne for his playfulness and 'antipathy to seriousness', James discusses how Carlyle had attacked Lamb for those

---

[76] Hazlitt, 'On the Periodical Essayists', V, 88.
[77] William Wordsworth, 'Preface to *Lyrical Ballads*', in *The Prose Works of William Wordsworth*, ed. W. J. B. Owen and Jane Worthington Smyser, 3 vols (1974), I, 119.

same qualities, a rejection which continued in the twentieth century with F. R. Leavis and the Scrutineers. In Chapter 10, 'Carlyle, Emerson, and the Voiced Essay', Tom Wright shows how in the mid nineteenth century, on both sides of the Atlantic, the essay continued the effort to voice itself directly and to build a public sphere, not through a virtual coffee-house, or a retreat into a confidential privacy, but by drawing together audiences in lecture halls. Formerly spectator, conversationalist, and correspondent, the essayist now becomes political orator or religious preacher. Yet, as Wright shows, in Carlyle and Emerson the essayist is a listener as well as a speaker, inviting into his essays the imagined voices of their publics, offering 'a space of synthesis amidst the cacophony of society, in which multiple voices speak variously and sometimes in conflict but within a common space'. Emerson likened his essays to a 'panharmonicon', a huge mechanical organ invented at the beginning of the nineteenth century, with the capacity to imitate the sounds of other instruments and thus a whole orchestra. The essayist comes to play a role in imagining the democratic nation into being. The concord suggested by the panharmonicon becomes more difficult to imagine in the later Carlyle, in whose late essays we find the essay not as a familiar friend but as antagonist: reprising the essayist as pugilist and aggressor also discussed in the chapters by Karshan and Murphy. Emerson, meanwhile, as Wright shows, encourages readers to avoid the cacophony by learning to 'trust their own inner voice': a return to that idiosyncrasy of the essayistic persona inaugurated by Montaigne, mistrusted by those modernist successors to Emerson and Carlyle who, like T. S. Eliot, preferred impersonality.[78]

The example of Carlyle, whose later essays were often denied the name of 'essay' on the basis of their vehement political address, raises a further problem of the essay form picked up by Ophelia Field in Chapter 11: the tension between political engagement and designs on the reader, and a tradition of retirement and non-participation in polemic. In 'Retiring or Engaging', Field points out that the retirement and detached spectatorship of Montaigne and Addison are themselves political positions, and that indeed many essayists have valued retirement as the condition of political effectiveness, allowing scope for the liberal conscience, dissent, and self-questioning. Detachment also allows, as in Montaigne's own 'Of Cannibals', a stance of critical anthropology towards one's own society. Field traces from 'Of Cannibals' the strain of the essay which critiques imperialism and slavery, passing through Hazlitt's 'On Reason and Imagination', via Orwell, to James Baldwin and Lewis Nkosi. Hazlitt's argument—that an essay's political value can be found not in its argument, but in its evocative appeal to experience and imagination, thus encouraging readers to, in this case, imagine what it is like

---

[78] Woolf is an exception to this rule. For Eliot's description of Montaigne as 'a fog, a gas, a fluid, insidious element', see 'The Pensées of Pascal', in *Selected Essays* [1932] (1991), 410; for his mockery of the 'Inner Voice', see 'The Function of Criticism', in *Selected Essays*, 29.

to be trapped in the hull of a slave ship—is also visible in the writings of Thoreau, Woolf, Baldwin, Nkosi, and Sontag, whose *Regarding the Pain of Others* combines in its title the essayist's 'aboutness' (writing *on* the pain of others) with the problem of voyeurism and the necessity of taking suffering into account. Such essayists, Field shows, combine the 'advice to princes' tradition of the Baconian essay with the strategic indirection of Montaigne.

The various chapters in the second half of *On Essays* move from this concern with association, sociability, and society, to consider various aspects of a set of debates about the place of the essay as a prose genre somehow poised between 'scientific' or factual writing, on the one hand, and fiction, on the other. Questions about the status of the essay as art or otherwise dominated three great Central European interventions in the theory of the essay in the early and mid twentieth century: György Lukács's 'On the Nature and Form of the Essay' (1910), Robert Musil's reflections on 'essayism' in his novel *The Man without Qualities* (1930–43), and Theodor Adorno's 'The Essay as Form' (1958), a direct response to Lukács. Lukács dismisses the idea that any well-written non-fiction is an 'essay', and accords it instead a unique role in the literary array as giving form to the faintest and most evanescent moments of life; an intermediate form between poetry and philosophy, a kind of 'intellectual poem' which gestures towards the absolute truth of philosophy, science, and system without reaching it. Always a precursor, the essay emphasizes process over verdict or destination.[79] Musil reiterated some of Lukács's judgements, finding the essay's domain 'between religion and knowledge, between example and doctrine', in which 'terms like true and false, wise and unwise, are equally inapplicable'.[80] Musil's hero Ulrich adopts an 'essayism' based on Lukács's account of the essay: a way of living which involves a resistance to system, taking experience hypothetically and assessing and weighing it from various angles, yet inconclusively. The implication in *The Man without Qualities* is that the novel is the right home for such essayism, treating each moment as an overdetermined concretization of various possibilities. Adorno's response to Lukács resisted the assignment of the essay to art and poetry, instead seeing it as the literary form capable of resisting science's abstraction, subjectivity, and universalization, while still articulating a knowledge rooted in culture, history, and the situated moment. For Adorno, the essay 'revolts against the doctrine—deeply rooted since Plato—that the changing and ephemeral is unworthy of philosophy'.[81]

This series of problems about the relation between science, fact, essay, and fiction are at the heart of the chapters in the second half of this volume. In

---

[79] György Lukács, 'On the Nature and Form of the Essay', in *Soul and Form*, trans. Anna Bostock (1971), 7, 11, 18.
[80] Robert Musil, *The Man Without Qualities*, trans. Sophie Wilkins (2011), 271, 273.
[81] Adorno, 'The Essay as Form', 167.

Chapter 12, 'Things Said by the Way', Stefano Evangelista shows that if Lukács had gone back behind Wilde to his progenitor, Walter Pater, he would have found in him an anticipation of many of his own views. Pater took his orientation from some of the same German thinkers as did Lukács. He derives from Friedrich Schlegel's theory of the fragment a view of the essay as an ideally anti-systematic mode, occupying the space between philosophy and poetry and, indeed, between poetry and prose; in Pater we find early examples of that form proximate to the essay, the prose-poem. Like Wilde and Lukács, Pater values the essay as the form which can do justice to the fugitive impressions of art and life that cannot be captured in the less subjective discourse of philosophy and science. In his novel *Gaston de Latour* he paints a portrait of Montaigne which celebrates him for his radical scepticism and principled dedication to doubt. For Pater, the essay is 'the literary form necessary to a mind for which truth itself is but a possibility, realisable not as general conclusion, but rather as the elusive effect of a particular personal experience'.[82] Pater's novel, like Musil's, thus emphasizes less plot and character than free association and lack of closure. For him, as Evangelista argues, 'the essay, not the novel, provided the open-ended and non-hierarchical literary structure that bound together the text and the world outside of language, holding the promise of a utopian coming together of the various branches of human knowledge in ages to come.'

Evangelista notes that Pater evoked this open inter-connected structure by the same image, the web, which George Eliot used to describe her work as a novelist. In Chapter 13, '"Strips of Essayism"', Bharat Tandon takes up the example of Eliot as novelist, essayist, and editor of essays. Tandon finds in Eliot a twofold sense of novelistic essayism: a didactic voice in the mode of Addison or Johnson, making a trial of life, speaking over the narration and offering what James Wood has called 'strips of essayism'; and the miscellany of possible voices which Eliot tries out, channels, convenes, and adjudicates, recalling the polyvocality of Carlyle. So, too, as editor of a periodical, she balances the occasional with the eternal—a parallel combination to the diurnal and the durable which Markman Ellis showed in the *Spectator*.

Michael Wood begins Chapter 14, 'Rational Distortions', with Henry James's turn against this model of essayistic novel writing in authors such as Eliot and Thomas Hardy. Wood identified in Jorge Luis Borges, who wrote short stories disguised as essays, and essays as short stories, a later rebellion against the Jamesian and modernist doctrine of showing rather than telling, continued by a sequence of late twentieth-century novelists in the Borgesian lineage—Angela Carter, Julian Barnes, W. G. Sebald, and Kazuo Ishiguro—who do not just weave essay and fiction together, but 'devise a new role for fiction that thinks,

---

[82] Walter Pater, *Plato and Platonism* (1910), 175.

and [. . .] implicate fiction itself in the act of thinking'. Instead of incorporating facts, or 'passages of speculative rumination', this kind of essayistic fiction instead 'use[s] fiction as a way of trialling, interrogating, or testing ideas'.

The fraught question of the factuality, or facticity, of the essay is the opening preoccupation of Chapter 15, 'Creative Nonfiction and the Lyric Essay', by Ned Stuckey-French, which is devoted to writing which falls under a recent, nearly paradoxical coinage: 'creative non-fiction'. Stuckey-French examines both the rise of this category in creative writing programmes in universities in the United States, and the arguments of the influential theorist and anthologist of the essay John d'Agata, who rejects 'creative non-fiction' in favour of the 'lyric essay'. Stuckey-French then shows how the contemporary essayists Jo Ann Beard, Eula Biss, and Claudia Rankine are all preoccupied by the boundary between fiction and reality, and often transgress it without minimizing its ethical and political significance, in respect of childhood memory, violence, or race.

In Chapter 16, 'Up to a Point', Adam Phillips observes, conversely, how psychoanalysis has resisted expressing itself under the title of 'essay', for fear of being accused of purveying fiction, falling short of the status of a science and a profession—a worry about institutions and professionalism which, as we noted above, also besets academic writing on the essay. Yet the irony is that essayists such as Montaigne, Lamb, and Pater (the latter two of whom Phillips has edited) pioneered the charting of the unconscious and its un-methodical free associations. Here, the dominant theme of 'association' in the first half of the volume finds a further echo. Phillips instead argues for a kinship between the two terms of his title: 'An essay, like a psychoanalysis, is an experiment without a proof.' If some of the most interesting contemporary essays are being written by those who are sympathetic to psychoanalysis but sceptical of its claims to being a science and a profession—Phillips himself, Darian Leader, Jacqueline Rose, Janet Malcolm— that may be not only because they believe that psychoanalysis, like the essay, is an art rather than a science, but nonetheless not fictional; nor even only because it is the essence and tradition of the essay that it allows the wandering pen to match the zig-zags of the irrational mind; but also because the unconscious is recalcitrant to the authority of science and professionalism.

As Christy Wampole says in Chapter 17, 'Dalí's Montaigne' (the last in the book), the essay has always been a form which shows the mind working not in rational discursive argument but via the rich but inchoate images one meets in dreams and objects. As the essay fulfils this quality in itself, it can leave the written word behind, taking advantage of new media and realizing itself in images or in text-image hybrids—whether the mixed photo-essays of Sebald and Rankine discussed by Wood and Stuckey-French, or the various essays in the media of drawing, photography, film, and video that have become a significant part of contemporary essayism. Wampole explores some such essayistic hybrids: Salvador Dalí's illustrations to Montaigne's *Essays* (1947), James Agee's and Walker Evans' photo essay *Let Us Now Praise Famous Men* (1941), Chris Marker's essay-film *Sans soleil* (1982), and John Bresland's video essay *Mangoes* (2010). All of these works, in different ways, bear traces of the influence of Surrealism, a movement with perhaps surprising affinities to the essay. Yet, in Agee and Walker Evans, Marker, and Bresland, such surrealism is closely allied to the everyday, the factual, and the artefactual. In these hybrid forms, technologically unimaginable from Montaigne's perspective, we still find the unfolding patterns of family resemblance which mark the essay: association, experiment, experience.

6. On Potential

The origins of this book are, like those of the essay, distant, cloudy, and shaped by contradiction, emerging from the distinct perspectives of the two editors, who first conceived the project some time in 2009. At that time, the revival of interest in the essay that Ned Stuckey-French's contribution traces back to the mid-1980s was not yet mainstream. Although two new and influential journals of the essay had been founded in the previous decade—*Cabinet Magazine* in 2000, and *n+1* in 2004—and were joined in 2011 by Notting Hill Editions, a London publisher dedicated to essayistic writing, it was still notoriously difficult to sell books of essays. The past decade has, however, seen a substantial growth of interest in the essay among writers, readers, scholars, and publishers, making *On Essays* more timely than we expected; the title of Christy Wampole's 2013 *New York Times* column, 'The Essayification of Everything', gives a sense of the sudden cultural centrality of a genre historically located on the margins.[83] Several exceptionally significant books of essays, or essayistic books, have recently been published, including Leslie Jamison's *The Empathy Exams*, Claudia Rankine's *Citizen*, Ta-Nehisi Coates's *Between the World and Me* (all 2014), Maggie Nelson's *The Argonauts* (2015), Mark Greif's *Against Everything*, and Brian Blanchfield's *Proxies* (both 2016). The success, achievement, and vitality of work by writers on both sides of the Atlantic, such as Olivia Laing, Hilton Als, Adam Phillips, John Jeremiah Sullivan, Eula Biss, Emilie Pine, and Jia Tolentino, suggests the resurgence of the form. Alongside related modes, like memoir and autofiction, some essays now attract as much attention as do novels. Courses and conferences on the essay are becoming ever more common in universities. Though detecting causes of such trends is hazardous, one condition may be the shift in media and its circulation from print to online, serving to soften the boundary between journalism and personal reflection, making opinion both easily accessible and speedily shared, and allowing distinctions between professional, expert, institutional, and

---

[83] Christy Wampole, 'The Essayification of Everything', *New York Times*, 26 May 2013, https://opinionator.blogs.nytimes.com/2013/05/26/the-essayification-of-everything/, accessed 27 October 2019.

private commentators to erode. The increasing dominance of universities over intellectual and even artistic life since the Second World War, and the risk of serious thought being sequestered there, suggests another possible reason for the revival, as a counter-reaction, of a form which allows for both detachment and political force; for serious attention to ephemeral details of life and culture; and for the improvisational hazarding of judgements, arguments, and ideas. Like the novel, with which, as several chapters in this volume show, its history is inter-twined, the essay creates a space in which otherwise disparate genres and conversations can mix; experience and learning enrich one another; and the specialized learning and experimental artistic forms of universities and avant-gardes find or even form a general readership, and grow there. Unlike the novel, the essay realizes these possibilities without claiming the potentially neutralizing licence of fiction.

We are aware that this book will be the first of several studies of the essay emerging in the coming years. As we noted earlier, there is an irony in academic work on a form so resistant to methodical scholarship. Nonetheless, we have ambitions for this volume which go beyond the passive reflection of a revival of interest in the world of literary practice and publishing. Scholarship and criticism have a role to play not only in aiding the teaching and understanding of the history of the essay, but also in informing its future. We hope these chapters indicate the seeds of potential, flourishing variously in different times, places, and circumstances, which the essay contains; and that they can help to keep in sight the full range of what has been possible in the form, as a resource and spring for future reading and writing. As we have already suggested, with Montaigne, the resemblances that essays bear to one another across the history of the genre are 'heedless and irregular', to the extent that the term 'essay' can seem a polite name for a motley scattering of orphans, rejects, remote cousins, adoptions, and forgot-ten or disavowed family resemblances. But such families—such genres—can be the strongest and most creative, depending as they do not on blood ties or lines of descent, but on elective affinities deepened through generations. The essays assembled in this book suggest ways of recognizing shared characteristics, and possibilities for cultivation, across the history of the form.

We thus hope that this volume offers a various array of possible ways to begin, in reading, thinking about, writing about, or just writing, essays, in the knowledge that there will be more to come. But like Montaigne's man grabbing his elk's horn, beginning in one way means leaving the rest of the infinite number of potential starting points still resting on the table. We are aware of the ways in which the choices we have made leave unrealized possibilities. Taking the essayistic privilege of not being obliged to an exhaustive treatment of a subject means acknowledging gaps. No doubt anyone who picks up this book will have favourite essayists to whom we have paid scant attention. Our strategy of commissioning contributors to write about particular essayists in the light of an essayistic theme or trope means that some crucial strands and issues emerge obliquely and repeatedly, rather than as the subject of particular chapters—for example, the essay and visual art; or walking; or poetry; or pedagogy; or race; or gender.[84] These are the lacunae, the essays unessayed, of which we are particularly conscious: no doubt readers will spot other gaps egregious to them, or different ways, other than grabbing the elk's horn we chose, of making a beginning. We hope the gaps will be as fertile as what they separate.

The art of the essay has always involved the arrangement of existing materials into constellations, in which each element has the possibility to participate in different ways of making patterns and determining salience. We have ordered this book chronologically, and we hope that the essays gathered here show a range of what has been possible in this kind, recognizing the ways that the resources of a form can be replenished by engagement with its past. At the same time, the recurrence and chancy reappearance of topics, tropes, characteristics, and themes also show the continuing openness of the essay to experiment, its resistance to generic and generalizing impositions, and its creative reassembly of miscellaneous elements. Our ambition is that this book will help stimulate a growth of scholarly interest in this form, which though it challenges scholarship and literature alike by occupying the no-man's-land between the two, is an essential ambassador between the world of the learned and that of conversation and literature, keeping open channels of communication without which each is impoverished. If, as Chesterton said, the essay is the joke of literature, it can do what good jokes do, and open passages across boundaries: between the various disciplines; between expertise and experience; and between literature and life.[85]

---

[84] On visual art, see chapters by Gigante, Evangelista, and Wampole; on walking, Karshan, Murphy, and Dart; on poetry, Dart, James, and Stuckey-French; on pedagogy, this introduction, Stuckey-French, and Phillips; on race, Field and Stuckey-French. Scarcely any essays were published in the seventeenth century written by women; with the advent of the periodical essay, however, women began both to be conceived as a significant audience for the form, and to write their own counter-periodicals, such as Eliza Haywood's *The Female Spectator* (1744–6). Leslie Jamison includes a rebuke to the trivializing of female memoir and essay-writing in her 'Grand Unified Theory of Female Pain', *The Empathy Exams* (2014), 185–218. See also Cynthia Ozick, 'She: Portrait of the Essay as a Warm Body', in Ozick, *Quarrel & Quandary* (2000).

[85] G. K. Chesterton, 'The Essay' [1932], in Klaus and Stuckey-French, *Essayists on the Essay*, 57, 60.

1

What is An Essay? Thirteen Answers from Virginia Woolf

Thomas Karshan

What we call monsters are not so to God, who sees in the immensity of his work the infinity of forms that he has comprised in it.

Montaigne[1]

The critic is one who glimpses destiny in forms.

György Lukács[2]

1. A Hippopotamus Entered at Stationers' Hall

What is an essay? The essay would rather not answer such an impertinent question—or would answer it only with a shrug offered in retreat. The very word *essay* was from the beginning just such a shrug: an expression of modesty; a defensive mask; a licence, like that of a joke, for saying things without being held accountable for them.[3] Essays have always understood themselves evasively, preferring to define themselves by what they are not. They are not quite knowledge, and they are not quite art.[4] Emerging in opposition to the methods that characterize scientific procedure, they resist being defined theoretically; but deriving from that mass of 'miscellaneous' writing born in the spaces left vacant by the recognized forms of discourse at a given time, they cannot be placed generically. Essays

---

[1] Michel de Montaigne, 'Of a Monstrous Child', in *The Complete Works*, trans. Donald Frame (2003), 654.

[2] György Lukács, 'On the Nature and Form of the Essay: A Letter to Leo Popper', in *Soul and Form*, trans. Anna Bostock, ed. John T. Sanders and Katie Terezakis (2010), 23.

[3] Montaigne's earliest readers indicate that *essai* was first and foremost an expression of modesty, yet urge us to look beyond the title to the substance beneath: E. V. Telle, 'À propos du mot "essai" chez Montaigne', *Bibliothèque d'Humanisme et Renaissance* 30.2 (1968), 225–47 (here, 228–9).

[4] I refer to the debate that often arises in German theories of the essay as to whether the essay is *Kunst* or *Wissenschaft*. *Wissenschaft* is sometimes translated as 'Science', but in the context of this debate has a broader resonance than 'Science' holds in contemporary English, suggesting any discourse or enquiry which aims at systematic knowledge. For this debate, see the Introduction to this volume, 20.

Thomas Karshan, *What is An Essay? Thirteen Answers from Virginia Woolf* In: *On Essays: Montaigne to the Present.*
Edited by: Thomas Karshan and Kathryn Murphy, Oxford University Press (2020). © Thomas Karshan.
DOI: 10.1093/oso/9780198707868.003.0002

are, as Montaigne said, monstrously formless, and, as Samuel Johnson added, dangerously licentious.[5] Claiming the licence to take in anything and everything, essays adopt a potentially unlimited range of forms, and essayists have frequently preferred not to straitjacket themselves in the uniform of a definition. The essay ruins categories and definitions, embracing a wild diversity of possible forms, which is why Leigh Hunt, in his witty list of possible titles for the essay, once called it a 'Hippopotamus entered at Stationers' Hall'.[6] Doubt about its own identity drives the essay; as G. K. Chesterton wrote, 'an essay, by its very name as well as its very nature, really is a try-on and really is an experiment', and for that reason, 'a man does not really write an essay. He does really essay to write an essay', and does so in order 'to find out what it was supposed to be'. The essay, he says, is 'the joke' of literature—the relaxation of its rules, the dissolution of its boundaries.[7] Yet if essayists must risk being told that what they are writing in is not a form at all, to be accounted as nothing when placed amid the recognized methodical discourses and literary genres, that contempt at least offers a sanctuary of neglect, even invisibility, in which many essayists have gladly taken refuge. The essay's apparent nothingness affords it a jester's licence for free speech, its seeming formlessness a shape-shifter's gift for impersonation.

Like so many essayists before her, Virginia Woolf professed impatience with histories and definitions.[8] Yet as she had argued in her essay on Addison of 1919, though the essay may seem to be nothing more than a frame for 'ordinary prose', no form at all, it is through the labours of Addison and the essayists 'that prose is now prosaic—the medium which makes it possible for people of ordinary intelligence to communicate their ideas to the world' (IV, 115). Or, as she put it in 1905, in 'The Decay of Essay-Writing', though the personal essay was the invention of Montaigne, 'the first of the moderns', 'its significance, indeed, lies [...] in the undoubted facility with which we write essays as though this were beyond all others our natural way of speaking'. It is essential to the work of the essay that it should conceal its form. For what appears as free speech is a modern invention made possible by the essay; this apparently 'natural way of speaking' conceals the machinations of a genre; and 'the peculiar form of the essay implies a peculiar

---

[5] See Montaigne, 'Of Friendship', 164. Samuel Johnson, *The Rambler*, vols III–V of *The Yale Edition of the Works of Samuel Johnson*, ed. W. J. Bate and Albrecht B. Strauss, 23 vols (1969), V, 77 (No. 158).

[6] Leigh Hunt, *The Indicator* (1822), 2. This list belongs to a tradition of alternative titles for essays inaugurated by Aulus Gellius in his *Attic Nights* and identified by Warren Boutcher in his chapter in this volume (see 63–5). It continues up to this day in a remarkably similar such list of rejected titles in *Cabinet* magazine: see *Cabinet* 63 (Spring 2017), 17.

[7] G. K. Chesterton, 'The Essay' [1932], in Carl H. Klaus and Ned Stuckey-French (eds), *Essayists on the Essay: Montaigne to Our Time* (2012), 57, 60.

[8] Virginia Woolf, *The Essays of Virginia Woolf*, 6 vols, ed. Stuart N. Clarke et al. (1986–2011), IV, 216. Further references given in the text. See also this volume, Introduction, 3–9.

substance; you can say in this shape what you cannot with equal fitness say in any other' (I, 25).

What, though, is that peculiar substance, and what is its genesis? Though essays defy the recognized categories of theory and genre, they have for that very reason often felt required to offer the apology of a self-description. In Montaigne's rueful words, 'how often and perhaps how stupidly have I extended my book to make it speak of itself!'[9] Those self-descriptions generally take the form not of theoretical pronouncements but of a series of perennial images and metaphors. Many are direct translations of the word *essai* in Montaigne: the essay is apprenticeship, homework, a try, a sally, an experiment, a weighing-up, a valuation, a taste, or a trial. Or they develop Montaigne's own paradoxical descriptions of his writing: the essay is a ramble but also a retreat; an act of friendship and an assault; a sickness and a medicine; a monster, a joke, or a nothing. These metaphors have in turn given rise to the various persistent themes and sub-genres of the essay from Montaigne to the present: the essay on childhood, on failure, on science, on courage, on commerce, on empire, on money, on food, on justice; or on walking, on travel, on retirement, on friendship, on conflict, on prejudice, on illness, on deformity, on humour, and on transience and the ephemeral. And those metaphors have also come to characterize essayists themselves; as Montaigne also said, 'I have no more made my book than my book has made me—a book consubstantial with its author, concerned with my own self, an integral part of my life.'[10]

So, if we are to look for answers to the question of what an essay is, we can find them most abundantly in essays which seem to be about something else: Montaigne's essay 'On Cripples', for instance, which testifies to the form's very deformity, or Hazlitt's 'The Indian Jugglers', which presents the essayist as a juggler with themes. This chapter will explore the question of what an essay is principally through a single such essay by Woolf, her 'Street-Haunting: A London Adventure', which she wrote in the early months of 1927, immediately after finishing *To the Lighthouse*. It is a ramble, the classic Montaignian metaphor—enshrined, for example, in the title of Johnson's *The Rambler*. But is also a haunting, in which Woolf opens herself to being possessed by the spirits of the great essayists and reshaped by the metaphors of the genre, embodied in the various characters she encounters and the rooms she passes through. Into the small space of 'Street-Haunting' Woolf concentrates much of the history of the essay and its predominant themes. By teasing out its allusions, it will be possible to sketch, in turn, many of the major metaphors by which the essay has held up to itself a set of partial mirrors.

---

[9] Montaigne, 'Of Experience', 997.   [10] Montaigne, 'Of Giving the Lie', 612.

2. A Passionate Apprenticeship

The first use of the word 'essay' for a piece of writing in English is the title of James VI of Scotland's 1584 collection of poetry, *The Essayes of a Prentise in the Divine Art of Poesie*. Likewise, William Cornwallis describes himself, as an essayist, as 'newly bound Prentice to the inquisition of knowledge'.[11] Montaigne's essays were early on understood as presenting themselves as apprentice works: in 1584, one of his first readers, La Croix du Maine, wrote that 'this title is [...] is modest indeed, since if you take the word "Essais" as "trials" or "apprenticeship", that is most humble and self-denigrating'.[12] That posture of apprenticeship serves Montaigne's picture of his mind: 'If my mind could gain a firm footing, I would not make essays, I would make decisions; but it is always in apprenticeship and on trial.'[13] As such, the essayist is an apprentice to the wisdom of the past—though not, as Montaigne insists, merely parroting it, or parading it, and not producing what Montaigne called '[t]hese concoctions of commonplaces, by means of which so many men husband their study', but integrating it into his being, and so giving it new life.[14] He rejoiced to take some passage he admired: 'I give it some particular application with my own hand, so that it may be less purely someone else's.'[15] As the various chapters of the present book show, essayists since Montaigne have, by apprenticing themselves to their predecessors, brought recurrent and unexpected life to the traditions of the essay.

Virginia Woolf certainly did so. Among the adolescent journals collected as *A Passionate Apprentice*, the entries from 1899 and 1903 appear, as the editor Mitchell Leaska writes, to consist 'largely of exercises in essay writing'.[16] She may have been inspired by the gift that her brother Thoby astutely made her, on 25 January 1903, her twenty-first birthday, of editions of Montaigne and Bacon; in her letter thanking him, she wrote that she had 'hunted' Cotton's translation of Montaigne for three years, preferring it to the Florio; that 'I always read Montaigne in bed'; that 'the Bacon is one of my choicest works'; and that 'I shall carry it in my fur coat many a mile and many a mile.'[17]

Woolf was the last major essayist to have been a conscious and diligent apprentice in the full tradition which passes from Montaigne and Bacon via Addison and Steele, and on through Hazlitt, Lamb, Hunt, and De Quincey, up

---

[11] Sir William Cornwallis, *Essayes*, ed. Don Cameron Allen (1946), 190.
[12] Quoted in Telle, 'À propos du mot "essai"', 228.   [13] Montaigne, 'Of Repentance', 740.
[14] Montaigne, 'Of Physiognomy', 984.   [15] Montaigne, 'Of Physiognomy', 985.
[16] See Woolf, *A Passionate Apprentice* (1992), vii, and Juliet Dusinberre, *Virginia Woolf's Renaissance* (1997), 10, 16. For other important studies of Woolf and the essay, see Randi Salomon, *Virginia Woolf's Essayism* (2012); Leila Brosnan, *Reading Virginia Woolf's Essays and Journalism* (1997); Beth Carole Rosenberg and Jeanne Dubino (eds), *Virginia Woolf and the Essay* (1997); and Hermione Lee, 'Virginia Woolf's Essays', in *The Cambridge Companion to Virginia Woolf* (2000), 91–109.
[17] Woolf, *The Letters of Virginia Woolf*, vol. I, ed. Nigel Nicolson (1975), 67.

to Stevenson, Belloc, and Chesterton. She was as persistent and acute a historian and theorist of the essay as has ever been, offering two direct theoretical statements: 'The Decay of Essay-Writing', and 'The Modern Essay', her review-essay of the five volumes of *Modern English Essays 1870–1920* edited by Ernest Rhys for *Everyman*. Woolf published hundreds of essays which, collected, fill six volumes. She wrote essays on Montaigne, Addison, Hazlitt, De Quincey, Beerbohm, and many other less remembered essayists, and read diligently for all these pieces. As a young reviewer books of essays were a specialty, and in her reviews we also find preserved fossils of that now forgotten age when, in the late Victorian, Edwardian, and Georgian periods, the essay was a commercial form used to fill out the weekly paper, the products of which are gathered in Rhys's anthology. More substantial essays were published in a number of intellectual journals, perhaps the most significant of which was the *Cornhill Magazine*, edited from 1871 to 1882 by Woolf's father Leslie Stephen, himself a distinguished essayist and historian of the form, to whose *Hours in a Library* Woolf turned frequently throughout her reading life. Stephen's first wife, Minny, was the daughter of Thackeray, who was the *Cornhill*'s first editor and author of the *Roundabout Essays*; while Minny's sister Annie—Aunt Annie, as Woolf called her—was also an essayist, author of the *Blackstick Papers*. Woolf wrote appreciatively on the essays of each of these relations.

3. A Haunting

'Street-Haunting' depicts a woman—Woolf, or a persona—arising one winter dusk from her room to go on a ramble across London on the pretext of buying a pencil at a stationer's shop on the Strand; on the way she surveys other pedestrians, rich and poor, hears snatches of conversation, window-shops, browses in a second-hand bookshop, and visits a boot-shop where she comes across a dwarf woman, one of several such startling encounters. In an essay for the *Yale Review*, published in October of the previous year, 'How Should One Read a Book?' she had said that 'to skip and saunter, to suspend judgement, to lounge and loaf down the alleys and bye-streets of letters is the best way of rejuvenating one's creative power' (IV, 393). In Woolf's next novel, *Orlando* (1928), the title character shape-shifts as they pass down the centuries of English literary history. 'Street-Haunting' does something similar for the essay: it is a summing up of the whole genre, in which Woolf weaves together images and scenes from Montaigne, Addison, Hazlitt, Lamb, Emerson, Belloc, and Chesterton, entering into what she calls 'sudden capricious friendships with the unknown and the vanished' (IV, 487). In one respect, 'Street-Haunting' can be said to perfect the genre, as she said Addison's essays do, which 'exist, perfect, complete, entire in themselves' (IV, 113). Yet it is part of its perfection that 'Street-Haunting' includes much that is grotesque, divided, and imperfect, attaining to the quality of Lamb's essays as Woolf described them in *A Room of One's Own*: 'superior even to Max Beerbohm's, I thought, with all their perfection, because of that wild flash of imagination, that lightning crack of genius in the middle of them which leaves them flawed and imperfect, but starred with poetry'.[18] That crack of genius in 'Street-Haunting' stars with imperfection many of the metaphors in which the essay has been accustomed to see itself reflected, rendering their oddities visible.

A clue to Woolf's purpose is offered by her essay on Montaigne, where she quotes in French a passage from 'Of Cripples': '[. . .] *plus je me hante et connois, plus ma difformité m'estonne, moins je m'entens en moy*' (IV, 78).[19] Like Montaigne, the more she haunts herself and tries to know herself, the more her deformity amazes her and the less she understands herself. As such, 'Street-Haunting' is engaged in something like the project of *To the Lighthouse*, in which, Woolf later wrote, 'I did for myself what psycho-analysts do for their patients.'[20] It holds a particular interest in drawing out the importance of the essay as that form in which the unconscious was charted prior to the invention of psychoanalysis. Not that Woolf was seeking in 'Street-Haunting' to illustrate Freudian theory, though Woolf's brother Adrian had trained as an analyst, and though Woolf was publishing psychoanalytic works at the Hogarth Press: in January 1927, around the time she embarked on writing 'Street-Haunting', the press published Freud's *The Ego and the Id*, and Ferenczi's *Further Contributions to the Theory and Technique of Psychoanalysis*. Only in the late 1930s would Woolf read Freud with respectful interest; in 1927 she was hostile. Rather, we can regard her, like other modernists, as a competitor to Freud, finding ways of exploring the unconscious through experiment with existing literary forms, and discovering in the essay's digressiveness a vehicle for exploring the association of ideas and their conflicts. Her favourite essayist, Charles Lamb, spoke in 'Imperfect Sympathies' of 'the first dawn, the early streaks' of the understanding, its 'surmises, guesses, misgivings, half-intuitions, semi-consciousnesses, partial illuminations, dim instincts, embryo conceptions'.[21] The affinity between the essay and psychoanalysis is remarked by Lamb's editor Adam Phillips, himself a distinguished essayist: 'the literary essay as a form—at least from the early nineteenth century onwards—has not only allowed for the artfulness, the interest of digression, but has also positively encouraged it.'[22]

---

[18] Woolf, *A Room of One's Own and Three Guineas*, ed. Morag Shiach (2008), 8.

[19] In Donald Frame's translation, 'the more I frequent [*hante*] myself and know myself, the more my deformity astonishes me, and the less I understand myself', 958.

[20] Woolf, *Moments of Being*, ed. Jeanne Schulkind (1985), 81.

[21] Charles Lamb, 'Imperfect Sympathies', in *The Works of Charles and Mary Lamb*, ed. E. V. Lucas, 7 vols (1903), I, 546. On Woolf and psychoanalysis, see among others Sanja Bahun, 'Woolf and Psychoanalytic Theory', in *Virginia Woolf in Context*, ed. Bryony Randall and Jane Goldman (2012), 92–110.

[22] Adam Phillips, *Side Effects* (2006), xiii. See also Chapter 16 in this volume, by Phillips.

4. A Room of One's Own

Woolf's lifelong reverence for Montaigne led her to make three pilgrimages to his tower, in 1931, 1937, and 1938.[23] The small study there is described in Leigh Hunt's 'Autumnal Commencement of Fires—Mantel-Pieces—Apartments for Study' as 'sixteen paces in diameter'. Descanting on his 'feeling' 'in favour of smallness', Hunt recommends for the essayist 'a small study, where we are almost in contact with our books', with curiosities upon the mantelpiece, such as an 'old-looking saucer' which, though of little worth, 'overflows [...] with the milk and honey of a thousand pleasant associations'.[24] Celebrations of the little room of the essayist are themselves a sub-genre of the essay, and it is in just such a room that we find Woolf at the beginning of 'Street-Haunting', 'surrounded by objects which perpetually express the oddity of our own temperaments', among them a 'bowl on the mantelpiece', which calls up a scene in 'Mantua on a windy day', in which 'the sinister old woman' who ran the shop pressed the bowl on the author without asking for money (IV, 481).

Montaigne's tower study offers to essayists through the centuries an authority and image for that retirement from which the essayist can observe the world with sceptical, independent eyes. The essayist moves among the quotations that bear the wisdom of the past, but is not enslaved to them, any more than to the commonplaces of the present; rather, the essayist is, quintessentially, a free-thinker, writing on the authority of their own experience. Woolf called the essay 'primarily an expression of personal opinion' (I, 25). ' "I" must always think things for himself, and feel things for himself' (IV, 223). It is a theme on which Hazlitt wrote a whole essay, 'On Living to One's Self': that is, to be 'living in the world, as in it, not of it', 'to be a silent spectator of the mighty scene of things'.[25] Montaigne's little inner room stands for the *arrière boutique* of the mind, a 'back shop all our own, entirely free, in which to establish our real liberty and our principal retreat and solitude', where one can step back from the authority of the powerful.[26] Abraham Cowley wrote against that authority in his essay 'Of Greatness': 'since we cannot attain to Greatness, (says the *Sieur de Montaigne*) let's have our revenge by railing at it'; so Cowley says, 'I love Littleness in almost all things.'[27] Lukács draws out the intellectual power of this littleness, metaphorical as well as real, when he says that the essayist 'ironically adapts himself to this smallness—the eternal smallness of the most profound work of the intellect in face of life—and

---

[23] See Judith Allen, *Virginia Woolf and the Politics of Language* (2010), 1–39.
[24] Hunt, *The Indicator*, I, 6-7.
[25] William Hazlitt, 'On Living to One's Self', in *The Selected Writings of William Hazlitt*, ed. Duncan Wu, 9 vols (1998), VI, 79. Further references are to this edition.
[26] Montaigne, 'Of Solitude', 214.
[27] Abraham Cowley, *Essays, Plays, and Sundry Verses* (1906), 428–9.

even emphasizes it with ironic modesty'.[28] Even the small room of 'Street-Haunting' can accommodate great subjects.

Only two years later, in 1929, Woolf would title her book-length essay on women and literature *A Room of One's Own*, with its famous argument that if a woman is to write fiction, she needs above all £500 a year and a room of her own, that money standing for 'the power to contemplate', the lock on that room for 'the power to think for oneself'.[29] Woolf pays homage to the essay tradition early on, when, finding herself excluded by her gender from Cambridge libraries, she imagines herself into a scene by Charles Lamb, a poor clerk who in 'Oxford in the Vacation' spoke fondly of how he could take imaginative possession of the treasures of learning, and, for a summer's day, 'play the gentleman, enact the student'.[30] Woolf writes, 'Literature is open to everybody. I refuse to allow you, Beadle though you are, to turn me off the grass. Lock up your libraries if you like; but there is no gate, no lock, no bolt, that you can set upon the freedom of my mind.' *A Room of One's Own* reprises the eternal battle of the essay, from Montaigne onwards, against the secluded learning of the universities, their methodical research and linear arguments, their nuggets of fact and 'indisputable proofs', summed up in 'the student who has been trained in research at Oxbridge', and who 'has no doubt some method of shepherding his question past all distractions till it runs into his answer as a sheep runs into its pen', and in 'the professors, the patriarchs', writing on '*The Mental, Moral, and Physical Inferiority of the Female Sex*'.[31] To be sure, the essay had itself long been thought of as a form of patriarchal privilege—as Woolf's father had put it, 'literature written by gentlemen for ladies—that is, for persons disposed to sit at gentlemen's feet'.[32] Yet in *A Room of One's Own*— a work that with its self-interrupting openness and looping digressions is as Montaignian as any in English barring *Tristram Shandy*—Woolf discovers in the essay a form capable of offering resistance to the procedures of patriarchal culture: rather as she says that Jane Austen did when, finding the prose sentence of her own day too male, she devised instead 'a perfectly natural, shapely sentence proper for her own use'.[33]

[28] Lukács, 'On the Nature and Form of the Essay', 9–10.
[29] Woolf, *A Room of One's Own and Three Guineas*, 139.
[30] Lamb, 'Oxford in the Vacation', in Lucas, *The Works of Charles and Mary Lamb*, I, 482.
[31] Woolf, *A Room of One's Own and Three Guineas*, 98; 35–6; 122; 39.
[32] Leslie Stephen, 'The Essayists', in *Men, Books, and Mountains* (1956), 58.
[33] Woolf, *A Room of One's Own and Three Guineas*, 100. For Woolf's adaptation of the essay form to a feminist critique of male culture, see Catherine Sandbach-Dahlströhm, '"Que scais-je?": Virginia Woolf and the Essay as Feminist Critique', in Rosenberg and Dubino (eds), *Virginia Woolf and the Essay*, 275–95.

5. A Piece of Homework

Woolf's adventure begins with the meta-literary pretext of buying a pencil from a stationery shop, a flash of self-consciousness about the conditions of writing that is one of the marks of the genre. Cornwallis opens his first essay, 'Of Resolution', succinctly: 'The world is a book; the words and actions of men commentaries upon that volume.'[34] Woolf quotes from a typical passage in her essay on Montaigne: 'I have taken a road along which I shall go, without stopping and without effort, as long as there is ink and paper in the world.'[35] 'Street-Haunting' belongs to a sub-genre of essays about seeking out or picking up a writing implement. In 'A Piece of Chalk' (1905), G. K. Chesterton finally realises that the writing implement he has been looking for—a piece of chalk—is everywhere beneath his feet on the hills of the South Downs, and—implicitly—that the virtue of experience is also everywhere beneath our feet, requiring only the essayist to take it up and make it visible.[36] And in 'On the Pleasures of Taking up One's Pen' (1908), Chesterton's friend Hilaire Belloc squiggles a cat's cradle of inky digressions in the margin of his own pretended argument, with encomia on a gold pen nib, and mockery of the industrious ideals Belloc was made to write out with his pen as a schoolboy—'Mr Belloc himself masquerading with a fountain pen', as Woolf teasingly pictured him in 'The Modern Essay' (IV, 222).[37]

When Montaigne picked it up, the word *essai* was associated—as it is today—with the schoolroom; the essay has always claimed the schoolchild's concern with stationery, with pen and stains, with waste paper—and with error.[38] Montaigne says he writes 'as children set forth their essays to be instructed, not to instruct'.[39] Cornwallis says of his essays that 'if they prove nothing but words, yet they break not promise with the world, for they say, "But an Essay," like a Scrivener trying his Pen before he ingrosseth his work', or, again, 'I am fallen into an Inkpot, and [...] these papers I use only to make me clean.'[40] The essay expresses error and mess, not clean conclusions. In 'The Decay of Essay-Writing' Woolf had lamented that 'it is to the art of penmanship that we owe our present literature of essays', to the inspiration of 'sheets of paper' to be covered by 'gallons of ink' (I, 26)—beginning, as she says in 'The Modern Essay', 'as close to the top of the sheet as possible, judging precisely how far to go [...] without wasting a hair's breadth of paper' (IV, 222). It is as if in the essay our writing returns to its most minimal origins, in the penmanship we learned at school, when we were apprentices to wisdom, and

---

[34] Cornwallis, *Essayes*, 5.

[35] Montaigne, 'Of Vanity', 876 (cited by Woolf at *The Letters of Virginia Woolf*, IV, 78).

[36] Chesterton, *A Shilling for my Thoughts* (1917), 9–13.

[37] Hilaire Belloc, 'On the Pleasures of Taking up One's Pen', in *On Nothing & Kindred Subjects* (1908), 4–6.

[38] See the Introduction to this volume, 13–16, for the essay and pedagogy.

[39] Montaigne, 'Of Prayers', 284.

[40] Cornwallis in *Essayes*, 'Of Essaies and Books', 190; 'Of Flattery, Dissimulation, and Lying', 225.

not yet fully writing. All the better, then, that Woolf should set out not to buy a pen—which, as she says in her essay on Montaigne, risks turning 'ordinary men into prophets, and changing the natural stumbling trip of human speech into the solemn and stately march of pens' (IV, 72)—but a pencil, that tool of schoolchildren and apprentices; provisional, and open to error and correction. Essays are 'rudimental', as Steele puts it in his imagined letter of a Stationer to the *Spectator*, only the raw material of mature civilization.[41] The essay is a try; its failures are successes, its blotches, scribbles, and erasings themselves revelatory.

6. A Bookshop

It is a paradox that for all their defiant independence from authority, essays are built out of quotations. For all Montaigne's repeated expressions of contempt for the scholarly parade of learning for its own sake, his pages are a maze of citations, and essayists have often been accused of doing little more than rearranging their commonplace books. Ben Jonson was among the first to level this charge: 'such are all the essayists, even their master, Montaigne. These in all they write, confess still what books they have read last—and therein their own folly—so much, that they bring it to the stake raw and undigested.'[42] To call someone an essayist is to describe them as much as a reader as a writer; Scott Black has shown how in seventeenth-century England '"essay" was the name for a tool of reading that enabled a certain competency and skill—a kind of commonplace book where the work of selection and collection that is key to humanist reading is practiced and undertaken', and Graham Good has argued that the essay from its inception is 'commentary which has broken free from its "text"'.[43]

So, before she can reach the stationer's shop to buy her pencil, Woolf must first enter a second-hand bookshop, and pass through one of the essay's sub-genres, the essay on second-hand books and bookshops, where, as Woolf says, 'wild books, homeless books [...] have come together in vast flocks of variegated feather, and have a charm which the domesticated volumes of the library lack' (IV, 487). Orwell's 'Bookshop Memories', of 1936, is a fairly late, disenchanted example of this sub-genre; in Rhys's *Modern Essays* Woolf would have found examples in Belloc's 'On an Unknown Country', about a young man browsing books about travel, escape, and utopia from the outdoor bookshops on Euston

---

[41] *Spectator* No. 304 (18 February 1712) in *The Spectator*, ed. Donald F. Bond, 5 vols (1965), IV, 94.

[42] Ben Jonson, *Explorata, or Discoveries*, ed. Lorna Hutson, in *The Cambridge Edition of the Works of Ben Jonson*, vol. 7, ed. David Bevington et al. (2012), 524–5. On commonplacing and the essay, see the Introduction, 11–13.

[43] Scott Black, *Of Essays and Reading in Early Modern Britain* (2006), 21; Graham Good, *The Observing Self: Rediscovering the Essay* (1988), 3.

Road, and J. C. Squire's 'The Lonely Author', which tells of the ill-assorted books he finds in the smoking-room of a provincial hotel one evening. Behind both is Lamb's 'Detached Thoughts on Books and Reading', with its fond lingering on 'the class of street-readers' who 'filch a little learning at the open stalls', and on the dog-eared pages 'of an old "Circulating Library" Tom Jones, or Vicar of Wakefield', whose 'sullied leaves' 'speak of the thousand thumbs, that have turned over their pages with delight!'[44]

As Woolf says in 'Street-Haunting', 'in this random miscellaneous company we may rub against some complete stranger who will, with luck, turn into the best friend we have in the world'. For her, that friend might be found in 'some grayish-white book from an upper shelf' which she reaches down, 'directed by its air of shabbiness and desertion', and in which she reads of 'an unknown traveller, who stayed at inns, drank his pint, noted pretty girls and serious customs' (IV, 487). Woolf is discreet enough not to fix her new friend with a name, but it is Hazlitt, who in 'On Going a Journey', tells of how he stayed 'at a little inn on the borders of Wales, where there happened to be hanging some of Westall's drawings, which I compared [. . .] with the figure of a girl who ferried me over the Severn'. It is an art of the essayist to find in such apparently chance discoveries and comparisons a hidden fatefulness; what Woolf has happened on, for all its shabby desertion, is the central travel essay in English, the direct inspiration, for instance, of 'Walking Tours' by Robert Louis Stevenson, who says Hazlitt's essay 'is so good' that 'there should be a tax levied on all who have not read it'.[45]

7. A Valuation

In 'Street-Haunting' Woolf is going shopping, and on her way to the stationer's she will pass through the boot-shop as well as the bookshop, and gaze in at the windows of the butcher's, the florist's, the furniture shop, and the antique jeweller's. The beauty of her walk is the gift of commerce. 'Passing, glimpsing, everything seems accidentally but miraculously sprinkled with beauty, as if the tide of trade which deposits its burden so punctually and prosaically upon the shores of Oxford Street had this night cast up nothing but treasure.' She pays tribute to the 'curious trades' pursued by the people who live in 'these narrow old houses between Holborn and the Strand'—the very territory that Addison and Steele

---

[44] Lamb, 'Detached Thoughts on Books and Reading', in Lucas, *The Works of Charles and Mary Lamb*, I, 691, 687.

[45] Hazlitt, 'On Going a Journey', in *Selected Writings*, VI, 166; Robert Louis Stevenson, 'Walking Tours', in *Virginibus Puerisque* [1881], in *The Works of Robert Louis Stevenson*, ed. Edmund Gosse, 20 vols (1906), II, 429. Woolf commented on Stevenson's essay in 'Modern Essays' (*The Letters of Virginia Woolf*, IV, 219).

had made their own. There one finds people who 'are gold beaters, accordion pleaters, cover buttons, or others who support life, with even greater fantasticality, upon a traffic in cups without saucers, china umbrella handles, and highly coloured pictures of martyred saints' (IV, 484–5).

The essayist is an assayer, or a valuer; to essay is, according to Samuel Johnson in the third of his definitions for the verb *to assay*, 'to try the value and purity of metals'. The essayist is frequently concerned with commerce, and its digestion and transformation of raw material into the commodities and toys of civilization. A classic statement is Addison's *Spectator* essay on the Royal Exchange as 'a kind of *Emporium* for the whole earth', through which the fruits of the various parts of the world can be exchanged and combined, so that 'the single Dress of a Woman of Quality is often the Product of a hundred Climates': 'the Scarf is sent from the Torrid Zone, and the Tippet from beneath the Pole. The Brocade Petticoat rises out of the Mines of *Peru*, and the Diamond Necklace out of the Bowels of *Indostan*.'[46] Woolf, who took particular pleasure in Addison's attention to 'little muffs, silver garters, fringed gloves' (IV, 111), would expand upon his pleasure in imperial commerce in a pair of essays she contributed to *Good Housekeeping* in December 1931 and January 1932, 'The Docks of London' and 'Oxford Street Tide'. Woolf traces goods on their passage from the mouth of London, the docks in which 'one sees things in their crudity, their bulk, their enormity', until they have been digested by the great city and deposited in Oxford Street, where 'they have been refined and transformed' (V, 283): the mammoth tusk becoming 'an umbrella or a looking-glass not of the finest quality', while one elephant tusk 'makes a billiard-ball, another serves for a shoe-horn.' And not only does the essayist value; to essay is also to weigh or weigh up, an image Montaigne made his own by the set of scales he chose as his emblem. By venturing down to the docks, Woolf is able to discern behind commodities that weighing and valuing and tasting which naturally concentrates the essayist's interest, watching how 'not only is each package of this vast and varied merchandise picked up and set down accurately, but each is weighed and opened, sampled and recorded' (V, 278). Yet along with this, in *A Room of One's Own*, Woolf presents the essayist as one who can value the world according to other scales than those officially sanctioned. The university—the institution against which she measures her essaying—presides over the discourse which weighs and classifies; the essayist's task is to evaluate what cannot be measured: 'I do not believe that gifts, whether of mind or character, can be weighed like sugar and butter, not even in Cambridge, where they are so adept at putting people into classes and fixing caps on their heads and letters after their names.'[47]

---

[46] *Spectator* No. 69 (19 May 1711), in Bond, *The Spectator*, I, 293, 295.
[47] Woolf, *A Room of One's Own and Three Guineas*, 138.

8. A Taste

As she steps out of her door, Woolf enters a London that is prosperous, proportioned, and civilized: there are 'symmetrical straight avenues of doors and windows'; even the poor 'wear a certain look of unreality, an air of triumph', and eating does not really depend on violence: the butchers' shops are a comely impressionist painting of 'yellow flanks and purple steaks', absorbed into the 'blue and red bunches of flowers' of the adjacent florists', as if meat were decorative. She is, she tells us, 'gliding smoothly on the surface'; although 'we are in danger of digging deeper than the eye approves', she muses, 'let us dally a little longer, be content still with surfaces only' (IV, 482). Bringing to a focus this polite Addisonian scene, she sees through a window 'the privacy of some drawing-room, its easy chairs, its papers, its china, its inlaid table, and the figure of a woman, accurately measuring out the precise number of spoons of tea' (IV, 482). Her taste is measured, exact: or, in the word Woolf notices was Addison's favourite, 'nice' (IV, 109).

The essayist's assay of the world works not only by weighing it up but by tasting it. In Montaigne to essay can be to taste food, and throughout his *Essais* we find operations of mind reduced back to tasting, eating, digesting, and excreting. The essay frequently presents experience as a chewing-over, a taste which is lost if it is swallowed down; the essay is the first taste of things, before they have been digested, and the essay is frequently referred to, as by Johnson in his *Dictionary*, as 'an irregular, undigested piece'. Yet by a paradox typical of the essay, this metaphor is reversible: the task of the essay is also to digest ideas. Of superficial scholars, who regurgitate quotations undigested, Montaigne says that 'it is a sign of rawness and indigestion to disgorge food just as we swallowed it' and that 'the learning that could not reach their mind remains on their tongue'.[48] In 'The Modern Essay', Woolf says that all information and learning should first have been 'assimilated', something Mark Pattison failed to do when, in his essay on Montaigne, he drew on Alphonse Grün's biography, but 'served M. Grün up raw', so that he 'remains a crude berry among the cooked meats, upon which our teeth must grate for ever' (IV, 217).

Woolf's woman at the tea-table incarnates what Addison calls 'the fine Taste', 'the utmost Perfection of an accomplished Man'. Such a person, 'after having tasted ten different Kinds of Tea [...] would distinguish, without seeing the Colour of it, the particular Sort which was offered him'.[49] Addison recommends the *Spectator* 'to all well-regulated Families, that set apart an Hour in every Morning for Tea and Bread and Butter'.[50] (And in fact, Markman Ellis tells us in his chapter in this book,

---

[48] Montaigne, 'Of the Education of Children', 135; 'Of Three Kinds of Association', 757.
[49] *Spectator* No. 409 (19 June 1712), in Bond, *The Spectator*, V, 527.
[50] *Spectator* No. 10 (12 March 1711), in Bond, *The Spectator*, I, 44–5.

surviving copies of the *Spectator* bear three-hundred-year-old stains of coffee, tea, and butter.[51]) The essay confers a civilized authority upon the apparent subjectivity of taste of the 'conversable world' over which Hume said ladies preside, and to which the essayist is ambassador from the world of learning.[52] For Leslie Stephen, it defined the limitations of the *Spectator* that it could not offer any hard meat not easily digested by the ladies.[53] (Montaigne himself had aspired to get his essays past the salon into the ladies' private drawing rooms.[54]) In 'The Decay of Essay Writing', Woolf said that 'the great burden of modern criticism is simply the expression of such individual likes and dislikes—the amiable garrulity of the tea-table—cast into the form of essays' (I, 26), though at the end of her life she would regret her *Times Literary Supplement* essays, pointing the blame for their 'suavity, their politeness, their sidelong approach to my tea-table training'.[55]

That frustration comes to a head in 'Street-Haunting'. The Addisonian view of Woolf's opening paragraphs, which crystallizes in the vision of the woman at the tea-table, is sweet, even enlivening, but ultimately as insubstantial as a cup of tea. The butterfly eye of the spectator cannot discover the 'obscure angles and relationships' that belie proportion and harmony. 'After a prolonged diet of this simple, sugary fare, of beauty pure and uncomposed, we become conscious of satiety' (IV, 482). And it is at this point that Woolf suddenly turns from taste to disgust, beauty to grotesquerie, dream to nightmare, and proportion to deformity, entering a world that belongs less to Addison, Lamb, and Beerbohm, and more to Montaigne, Hazlitt, and De Quincey. After all, just before she had left her room, Woolf had recalled the brown ring on the carpet left by a tea-kettle violently thrown down in a fit by a man angry at Lloyd George's radicalism.

9. A Ramble

For Woolf is more than a spectator: she is casting aside her privileged perspective and opening herself to being seen into. 'As we step out of the house on a fine evening between four and six, we shed the self our friends know us by and become part of that vast republican army of anonymous trampers' (IV, 481). It is a classic essayistic sentiment. As Emerson had said in *Nature* (1836), 'to go into solitude, a man needs to retire as much from his chamber as from society'; entering this true

---

[51] See Chapter 4, 107–8.
[52] David Hume, *Selected Essays*, ed. Stephen Copley and Andrew Edgar (1998), 2. On this conversable world, see Fred Parker, Chapter 5 in this volume, and Kathryn Murphy, 'The Essay', in *The Oxford Handbook of English Prose, 1660–1714*, ed. Nicholas McDowell and Henry Power (forthcoming).
[53] Leslie Stephen, 'The Essayists' [1881], reprinted in *Men, Books, and Mountains* (1956), 58.
[54] Montaigne, 'On Some Verses of Virgil', 781.
[55] Woolf, *Moments of Being*, 150. On essays at the tea-table, see Markman Ellis's essay in this volume.

solitude, 'all mean egotism vanishes' and 'I become a transparent eye-ball; I am nothing.'[56] Woolf draws on this famous image as she steps out the door, leaving behind 'the shell-like covering which our souls have excreted to house themselves, to make for themselves a shape distinct from others, is broken, and there is left of all those wrinkles and roughnesses a central oyster of perceptiveness, an enormous eye' (IV, 481).

In yielding up her social self to join that army of tramps, Woolf joins, too, that tradition of the ambulatory essay in whose bookshop we have already glimpsed her browsing, whose origin is Montaigne's frequent invocation of his own essaying as a ramble, an image with multiple implications. 'I want people', he tells us, 'to see my natural and ordinary pace, however off the track it is.'[57] The essay is as digressive as the mind. As he says in 'On Vanity', 'my style and my mind alike go roaming.'[58]

But Woolf is really engaging in another kind of rambling, the sort we find in Samuel Butler's 'Ramblings in Cheapside', singled out for praise in her review of *Modern Essays*. Butler's 'ramblings' are his chains of associations. He passes, as Woolf says, across ideas as various as 'that a wound in the solicitor is a very serious thing; that Mary Queen of Scots wears surgical boots'; and 'that no one really cares about Aeschylus'. Butler's essay stands as a reproach to what she, quoting Butler, calls 'a fatal "faithfulness to a fixed idea"' (IV, 210). For as Butler says of the turtles he sees in Sweeting's window, 'I was struck not more by the defences with which they were hedged about, than by the fatuousness of trying to hedge that in at all which, if hedged thoroughly, must die of its own defencefulness.' What is true of Turtle, is true of Man; and Butler wisely implies here what Freud would later say: that we die of the defences we make as shells for ourselves, if they prevent us from making connections. It is one of the virtues of essays, by their liberating ramblings, to evade fixed ideas, pierce our defences, and unchain the connections which hold us locked tight.[59] This Woolf pledges herself to doing in 'Street-Haunting', when she closes the door on the 'oddity' of her social self, and on 'the shell-like covering which our souls have excreted to house themselves' (IV, 481). Leaving that shell behind, Woolf goes to join the company of the homeless—the 'derelicts who choose to lie not a stone's throw from theatres' (IV, 485). For 'the good citizen when he opens his door in the evening must be banker, golfer, husband, father; not a nomad wandering the desert, a mystic staring at the sky, a debauchee in the slums of San Francisco, a soldier heading a revolution, a pariah howling with scepticism and solitude' (IV, 486).

---

[56] Ralph Waldo Emerson, 'Nature', in *Nature, Addresses, and Lectures*, vol. I in *The Collected Works of Ralph Waldo Emerson*, ed. Robert E. Spiller and Alfred R. Ferguson (1971), 8, 10.
[57] Montaigne, 'Of Books', 360.   [58] Montaigne, 'On Vanity', 925.
[59] Samuel Butler, 'Ramblings in Cheapside' [1890], in *Modern English Essays 1870–1920*, ed. Ernest Rhys (1923), 5 vols, II, 161–81, here 161.

In her essay on Montaigne, Woolf quotes this from 'Of Exercitation', in Cotton's translation:

> We hear of but two or three of the ancients who have beaten this road [said Montaigne]. No one since has followed the track; 'tis a rugged road, more so than it seems, to follow a pace so rambling and uncertain, as that of the soul; to penetrate the dark profundities of its intricate internal windings; to choose and lay hold of so many little nimble motions.   (IV, 71)[60]

The project of 'Street Haunting' is, tacitly, to find images to body forth these 'dark profundities', 'intricate internal windings', and 'little nimble motions' of the soul: Woolf is entirely Montaignian when she speaks of 'the true self' as 'neither this nor that, neither here not there, but something so varied and wandering that it is only when we give the rein to its wishes and let it take its way unimpeded that we are indeed ourselves' (IV, 486). This is what turns haunting into the adventure alluded to in Woolf's sub-title, 'A London Adventure': 'And what greater delight and wonder can there be than to leave the straight lines of personality and deviate into those footpaths that lead beneath brambles and thick tree trunks into the heart of the forest where live those wild beasts, our fellow men?' (IV, 490–1).

For Woolf, the ramble into darkness is a dream; in 1922, in 'Modern Essays' Woolf had said that the essay aims to 'lay us under a spell with its first word, and we should only wake, refreshed, with its last' (IV, 216). But in 'Street-Haunting', that dream turns darker when, satiated on the 'simple, sugary fare, of beauty pure and uncomposed', Woolf pauses at the door of the boot-shop and asks herself '"What, then, is it like to be a dwarf?"' With the awful immediacy by which wishes are granted in dreams, a dwarf-woman appears at once, 'escorted by two women who, being of normal size, looked like benevolent giants beside her. [...] She wore the peevish yet apologetic expression usual on the faces of the deformed.' In the next essay she wrote after 'Street-Haunting' in the spring of 1927, 'Poetry, Fiction and the Future', Woolf would ask for a form capable of expressing the mind of an age 'full of monstrous, hybrid, unmanageable emotions', 'an attitude which is full of contrast and collision', in which beauty and disgust sit cheek by jowl, and 'emotions which used to enter the mind whole are now broken up at the threshold' (IV, 429–30, 433)—as they are in 'Street-Haunting', at the threshold of the shoe-shop.

In 'Poetry, Fiction and the Future', Woolf found such a form in Elizabethan poetic drama, but six months earlier, she identified another in her *TLS* piece on De Quincey's poetic essays, where she quotes De Quincey on his '"visionary scenes derived from the world of dreams"', and describes the 'horrid transition'

---

[60] Square brackets Woolf's own. 'Of Exercitation' is usually 'Of Practice' in modern translations.

as he suddenly ascends or descends between poetry and prose (IV, 363–4). She refers to the great scene of collision in De Quincey's 'dream-fugue', 'The English Mail-Coach', a hallucinatory variation on Montaigne's 'On Coaches', in which, with the coachman asleep, the coach rides down a pair of young lovers to their violent death. The sleep of reason gives birth to monsters: the 'slumbering coachman' looks like a crocodile, by virtue of 'that gaiety [...] in the dreaming faculty', that reveals within itself a 'latent ferocity' such as lurks beneath the playfulness of tiger or leopard cubs; and the Montaignian digressions of consciousness do not merely coil in and among themselves but smash against one another, allowing an expression of 'this horror' which 'has always been secretly felt by man'.[61]

What Woolf took from De Quincey was a model for the underlying nightmare-logic of 'Street-Haunting'—for the sudden unmediated transmutations of peace into violence, of the Mayfair lady, with her set of pearls like the fantasy from an advertisement, turning into the dwarf women surrounded by her giantesses, trying on shoes, and then in turn metamorphosed into two blind bearded men supporting themselves on the head of a young boy. If this rapid concatenation of image reminds one of dreams as Freud described them, that is not so surprising. What we see in De Quincey is what happens when Montaignian digression is allowed off its leash, approaching that intoxicated or rhapsodic ecstasy, governed only by 'Fortune', in recognition of which Montaigne likened his writing to poetry, 'an art, as Plato says, light, flighty, daemonic'.[62] 'Free association artistically controlled' was Aldous Huxley's phrase for 'the paradoxical secret of Montaigne's best essays'.[63] The association of ideas, on which Freudian theory depends, has been seen as a hallmark of the essay form since the *Spectator* popularized the theory set out by Locke in his *Essay Concerning Human Understanding* (1690).[64] As late as 1923, we still find Hilaire Belloc teasingly expressing Locke's theory, in an essay where he muses on why he finds himself wanting to read Virgil's *Bucolics* in the Bourse at Paris at two o'clock on a summer afternoon: 'as to why this should be so, I cannot tell. Locke would explain it perhaps by his "Association of Ideas": but Locke is dead and gone.'[65]

10. An Assault

A violent conflict within the self is a constant risk in the act of assaying oneself. The essay has often been spoken of as entailing a 'pleasant friendship with the

---

[61] Thomas De Quincey, *Confessions of an English Opium-Eater* [1821], ed. Barry Milligan (2003), 209.
[62] Montaigne, 'On Vanity', 925.   [63] Klaus and Stuckey-French, *Essayists on the Essay*, 90.
[64] See, for example, *Spectator* No. 110 (6 July 1711), in Bond, *The Spectator*, I, 454. On the essay and 'association', see Fred Parker's contribution to this volume, Chapter 5.
[65] Belloc, 'On a Variety of Things', in *On* (1923), 59.

reader', as in A. C. Benson's 'The Art of the Essayist', which Woolf would have read in Rhys's *Modern English Essays*.[66] The essay on friendship, or in praise of a friendship, is a distinct sub-genre, initiated by Montaigne and Bacon's essays 'Of Friendship'. Yet the essayist must be a candid friend, not a flatterer, a distinction Bacon takes over from Plutarch, insisting that 'the Counsel, that a Friend giveth' is necessary because the counsel 'that a Man giveth himself' is bound to fall into either of two opposing traps: it may be flattery, or it may be that 'Calling of a Man's self, to a Strict Account', which is 'a Medicine, sometimes, too Piercing and Corrosive'.[67] But that medicine is just what Montaigne dispenses in his *Essays*, whose opening scenes of military assaying turn inward into a series of assaults and essays against oneself, severe martial tests of one's own virtue such as Montaigne identifies in the ancient philosophers, the Stoics and Epicureans, and in Socrates, who 'tested himself [*s'essayoit*] still more roughly, keeping for his exercise the malignity of his wife, which is a test with the naked blade [*un essay à fer esmoulu*]'.[68]

As Kathryn Murphy shows in her chapter in this volume, the essayist is frequently an aggressive figure, pictured wielding a stick in argument.[69] The essayist may write *for*, or *against*, and is not infrequently, as Hazlitt argues in his classic essay on the subject, 'On the Pleasure of Hating' (1826), a good hater, a counter-enlightenment figure for whom 'Nature seems (the more we look into it) made up of antipathies: without something to hate, we should lose the very spring of thought and action. Life would turn to a stagnant pool, were it not ruffled by the jarring interests, the unruly passions, of men.'[70] His friend Lamb had five years earlier, in 'Imperfect Sympathies', equally repudiated an indifferent egalitarianism, and confessed himself 'a bundle of prejudices—made up of likings and dislikings—the veriest thrall to sympathies, apathies, antipathies', notoriously exercising some antipathies against Scotsmen and Jews.[71] The paradox of the essayist as a figure divided between friendship and hatred, peace and violence, enlightenment and bigotry, is expressed in Leigh Hunt's list of possible titles for essay volumes: 'the Crocodile, or Pleasing Companion;—Chaos, or the Agreeable Miscellany;—the Fugitive Guide;—the Foot Soldier, or Flowers of Wit;—Bigotry, or the Cheerful Instructor;—the Polite Repository of Abuse;—Blood, being a Collection of Light Essays.'[72] Hazlitt had incarnated that blood in his famous essay 'The Fight', where he plays the pugilist and embodies his essayism in the

---

[66] A. C. Benson, 'The Art of the Essayist', in Rhys, *Modern English Essays*, V, 59.
[67] Francis Bacon, 'Of Friendship', in *The Essayes or Counsels, Civill and Morall* [1625], ed. Michael Kiernan (Oxford, 2000), 85.
[68] Montaigne, 'Of Cruelty', 373.   [69] See Chapter 3, 79–80.
[70] Hazlitt, 'On the Pleasure of Hating', in *Selected Writings*, VIII, 118.
[71] Lamb, 'Imperfect Sympathies', in Lucas, *The Works of Charles and Mary Lamb*, I, 544.
[72] Hunt, *The Indicator*, I, 3. See the Introduction to this volume, 2–3.

figure of the boxer, even as in the antipathetic essay, 'The Indian Jugglers', he had embodied the opposing lightness of the essayist juggling with ideas. For Woolf, these potentially violent paradoxes were Hazlitt's essence; he was, she said, 'a two-minded man', and there was something 'divided and discordant even in his finest essays, as if two minds were at work who never succeeded save for a few moments in making a match of it' (V, 495, 498).

In 'Street-Haunting', Woolf briefly raises the figure of hatred, when she assays her own middle-class political complacency and turns a corner on herself. She had been reassuring herself that the poor 'do not grudge us, we are musing, our prosperity; when, suddenly, turning the corner, we come upon a bearded Jew, wild, hunger-bitten, glaring out of his misery; or pass the humped body of an old woman flung abandoned on the step of a public building with a cloak over her like the hasty covering thrown over a dead horse or donkey'. In the dream of 'Street-Haunting', Woolf both sympathetically enters the figure of her hatred, and recoils from it. The spell of 'beauty pure and uncomposed' is broken; antipathy is awoken in her, as in Lamb, by her ambivalent feelings towards Jews, and set jangling against the equal impulse towards sympathy; and 'at such sights the nerves of the spine seem to stand erect; a sudden flare is brandished in our eyes; a question is asked which is never answered' (IV, 484–5). Such hard questions are essential to the moral and political virtue of the essay; as Woolf would write in her 1934 essay, 'Why?', 'the great obstacle to asking questions openly in public is, of course, wealth', and the essay affords the opportunity for 'asking questions of oneself' (VI, 30).

11. A Deformity

It is just such an assay Woolf puts to herself at the pivotal point of 'Street-Haunting', when, in one of those sudden thought-experiments by which Montaigne periodically arrests his complacency, she asks what it is like to be a dwarf. Montaigne before her had called essays 'grotesque and monstrous bodies, pieced together of diverse members, without definite shape, having no order, sequence, or proportion other than accidental'.[73] The deformity of the essay was apt for the expression of 'one's self' as 'the greatest monster and miracle in the world' (IV, 78), as Woolf put it in her essay on Montaigne, and of all the other terrors that collected in her imagination under the name of monster—'this monster, the body' (IV, 318), and the 'monster' that a literary woman will fear herself to seem.[74]

---

[73] Montaigne, 'Of Friendship', 164.   [74] Woolf, A Room of One's Own and Three Guineas, 75.

The dwarf-woman enters the shoe-shop, 'escorted by two women who, being of normal size, looked like benevolent giants beside her'. Yet this phantasm of disproportion and deformity is transformed when she finds the right shoe:

> Look at that! Look at that! she seemed to demand of us all, as she thrust her foot out, for behold it was the shapely, perfectly proportioned foot of a well-grown woman. It was arched; it was aristocratic. Her whole manner changed as she looked at it resting on the stand. She looked soothed and satisfied.   (IV, 483)

As Randi Saloman has acutely perceived, 'the dwarf stands in for the essayist [. . .] patronised and humbled by those who surround her', who 'reveals a completely different side of herself as soon as she has found the appropriate means of expression'.[75] The essay may be a dwarfish, mis-shapen form, flanked by the larger genres, but as Woolf had written in 'The Decay of Essay-Writing', 'you can say in this shape what you cannot with equal fitness say in any other' (I, 24), just as in *A Room of One's Own* she said that Austen devised 'a perfectly natural, shapely sentence proper for her own use'.[76]

Montaigne, too, had embodied the deformity of his essays in the various monstrosities that haunt his pages, from the Siamese twins described in 'Of a Monstrous Child', whose duality evokes the paradoxes of man and nature as surely as Woolf's giantesses do those of the essay itself, through the lame woman prized for her concupiscence who without warning looms up in 'Of Cripples', to the account of Socrates's deformity in 'Of Physiognomy', in which Montaigne comments that 'every well-formed shoe shows the form of the foot within'.[77] The essay on deformity is a well-established sub-genre.[78] Perhaps in response to Montaigne, Bacon wrote 'Of Deformity' in 1612, and four years later Cornwallis responded to it with his essay on 'King Richard the Third', inverting Bacon's view that outer deformity expresses inner crookedness, while in 1754 William Hay, himself a hunchback, would publish *Deformity: An Essay*, claiming Montaigne as his ally against Bacon's aspersions on the deformed.[79] Hay was able to draw on the authority also of Addison, who in the seventeenth number of the *Spectator* had introduced the 'Ugly Club', reflecting that 'it is, methinks, an honest and laudable Fortitude to dare to be Ugly', and that 'it is happy for a Man, that has any of these Oddnesses about him, if he can be as merry upon himself, as others

---

[75] Randi Saloman, *Virginia Woolf's Essayism* (2012), 30.

[76] Woolf, *A Room of One's Own and Three Guineas*, 100.

[77] Montaigne, 'Of a Monstrous Child', 653–4; 'Of Cripples', 963; 'Of Physiognomy', 986.

[78] For two early twentieth-century examples, see Randolph Bourne's 'The Handicapped' [1911] and Jane Addams, 'The Devil Baby at Hull-House' [1916], both of which appeared first in the *Atlantic Monthly* and are anthologized in Joyce Carol Oates (ed.), *The Best American Essays of the Century* (2000).

[79] Cornwallis, 'The Prayse of King Richard the Third', in *Essayes of Certaine Paradoxes* (1616), n.p. William Hay, *Deformity: An Essay* [1754], ed. Kathleen James-Cavan (2004), 24.

are apt to be upon that Occasion.'[80] Woolf's dwarf-woman expresses that Oddness, lurching up from beneath the easy comfort of the Addisonian essay: 'at any moment, the sleeping army may stir itself and wake in us a thousand violins and trumpets in response; the army of human beings may rouse itself and assert all its oddities and sufferings and sordidities' (IV, 482). In the original manuscript, she had also asked, 'In what crevices and crannies did they lodge, this maimed company of cranks and oddities?'[81] In this single sentence Woolf brings into dream-like coalition the apparently paradoxical models of Addison, with his 'oddities', and Montaigne, whom two years earlier she had praised for seeing into the 'crannies and crevices' that 'poetry cannot reach' (IV, 57). By doing so, Woolf can express that paradox, the universal oddity of the individual, which is the quintessential subject of essays, whose 'proper use is to express one's personal peculiarities' (I, 26).[82]

12. A Sport

In the essay we have, then, a form which fits the experience it aims to express by being the perfect match of one deformity to another. But no sooner has the dwarf-woman left the boot-shop than this transformative grace necessarily vanishes. 'As she walked out between her guardians, with the parcel swinging from her finger, the ecstasy faded, knowledge returned, the old peevishness, the old apology came back, and by the time she reached the street again she had become a dwarf.' More than that, 'she had changed the mood; she had called into being an atmosphere which, as we followed her out into the street, seemed actually to create the humped, the twisted, the deformed.' It is as if 'the dwarf had started a hobbling grotesque dance to which everybody in the street now conformed' (IV, 484). The essay no longer offers a form that will perfectly fit and contain experience. It declines the perfection that Woolf saw in Addison's essays. Just as we have seen, through Montaigne, that the essay is as much deformity as form, so we may remember Samuel Johnson's account of it as 'licentious', and call it not a form, nor even a deformity, but a licence—for 'all that is grotesque, absurd, amusing and jocose', as Benson said in 'The Art of the Essayist'.[83]

We might, then, as an alternative to saying that the essay is a monstrosity, say instead that it is a sport, playing on the full scale of that word: a freak of nature, a game, a joke, a whimsy, and a hunt. In 'Street-Haunting' Woolf raises the thought, and not only specifically by calling her essayistic eye 'sportive'; nor merely by

[80] *Spectator* No. 17 (20 March 1711), in Bond, *The Spectator*, I, 75.
[81] The manuscript is in the Beinecke Library at Yale (YCAL MSS 145, Box 13, folder 415).
[82] On this universal oddity in the essay, see this volume, Chapter 3, by Kathryn Murphy, 84–5.
[83] Benson, in Rhys, *Modern English Essays*, V, 56.

basing her great essay upon the slim whimsy of going to buy a lead pencil; but also by comparing her expedition, in the first paragraph, to foxhunting and golfing, isolating the contraries of violence and peace which coalesce in the sport of the essay. Hazlitt had done the same when in 1821–2 he published 'The Fight' and 'The Indian Jugglers', implying the hidden relation between boxing and juggling. Vladimir Nabokov would combine the two metaphors in his Hazlittian 1925 essay *Igra* ('Play', or 'Sport'), in which he opened an account of a boxing fight with an image of god as a 'marvellous juggler' and a vision of all of life as sport.[84] Hazlitt had already pitched the idea of the essayist as a juggler with themes in 1819 in 'On the Periodical Essayists', if only to disclaim it by praising Montaigne for eschewing 'juggling tricks' on the one hand and 'solemn mouthing' on the other.[85] It is the art of 'The Indian Jugglers' to invoke the analogy between essaying and juggling only to disavow it, like a three-cup trickster showing a ball and then hiding it. The view of Montaigne as a jester goes back to Bacon's 'Of Truth', in which he insinuates that Montaigne is a 'jesting Pilate'. Montaigne himself refers to his hero Socrates as a jester and says that man is 'the investigator without knowledge, the magistrate without jurisdiction, and all in all, the fool of the farce.'[86] Indeed, Sainte-Beuve suggested that the best Latin translation for Montaigne's *essai* was *lusus*—jest, sport, or game.[87]

There is a long tradition of seeing the essay as a fundamentally comic mode, with corresponding sub-genres of essays on humour, sport, and games. Adam Gopnik has noted that 'the essay differs from the lyric poem (which does the same kind of thing) by being in prose, but also by being funny and by being clear'.[88] When Addison makes his fundamental distinction between 'the Freedom of an Essay' and 'the Regularity of a Set Discourse', it is in the context of one of his several essays on laughter, a subject for which he clearly considers essaying the appropriate mode of writing.[89] Working in this tradition, Woolf wrote her first familiar essay in 1905 'On the Value of Laughter', there defining true humour as a blend between tragedy and comedy, and describing the humorist by the same image of a perilously balanced acrobat that she would apply thirteen years later to the essayist: the humorist 'not infrequently topples over ignominiously on the other side, and either plunges headlong into buffoonery or else descends to the hard ground of serious commonplace, where, to do him justice, he is entirely at his

[84] The essay was later published in December 1925 under the title of 'Breitenstäter—Paolino', the names of the boxers. See the translation in Vladimir Nabokov, *Think, Write, Speak*, ed. and trans. Brian Boyd and Anastasia Tolstoy (2019), 33–7; here 33.
[85] Hazlitt, 'On the Periodical Essayists', in *Selected Writings*, V, 85.
[86] Montaigne, 'Of Physiognomy', 986; 'Of Vanity', 932.
[87] Cited by Hugo Friedrich in *Montaigne*, ed. Philippe Desan, trans. Dawn Eng (1991), 343.
[88] Adam Gopnik (ed.), *The Best American Essays: 2008* (2008), xviii–xix.
[89] *Spectator* No. 249 (15 December 1711), in Bond, *The Spectator*, II, 465.

ease' (I, 58).[90] In doing so she recapitulated Hazlitt's praise of Montaigne for avoiding the equal pitfalls of juggling tricks and solemn mouthing.

The essay is also comic in form, by virtue of its habitual play with the structures of rhetoric and genre. As such it has a kinship with that other comic form, the mock-epic, with its paradoxes, its inversions, its miniaturism, its saving lightness, and its celebrations of the minimal and base, such as dullness or a lock of hair. It is to this category of the mock-encomium that 'Street-Haunting' belongs, being as it is, amongst much else, a mock praise of a pencil.

13. Everything and Nothing

The whole of the history of the essay, and the deformity of the self, and prosperity and poverty, and violence and play, and so much more, have been made to balance, precariously, on the point of a pencil. 'Street-Haunting' is about nearly nothing at all; it is also about almost everything. Containing everything in nothing, it is, as Woolf nicely said of Addison's essays, 'the shapely silver drop, that held the sky in it and so many bright little visions of human life' (IV, 115). The word 'essay', it has been said, can mean everything, and so risks meaning nothing; but it is also the task of essayists to contain everything in nearly nothing. Encyclopedists, they transgress the fences shutting off one academic or professional specialism from another, drawing together into a single intelligible whole all that falls under the authority of their own odd experience; miniaturists, they focus their thoughts through the smallest or most trivial of objects: Thackeray writes about chasing his hat; Chesterton about the contents of his pockets; Addison the cat-calls of London; Beerbohm some question a forgotten clergyman once tremulously put to Johnson.

To eyes trained by the sciences with their approved methods and theories, by the arts with their recognized genres and appropriate subjects, the essay may seem not merely a monster, or a joke, but a near nullity—as close an approach to nothing as is possible in writing. Hilaire Belloc, who wrote an essay called, 'An Essay upon Essays upon Essays', published volumes of essays *On Everything*, *On Something*, *On Anything*, and *On Nothing*, before publishing one entitled simply *On*. Essays on nothing and on doing nothing are a staple of the genre, from Cornwallis through Fielding and on into Lynd, Belloc, and Priestley; for nothing is whatever is not recognized by the professionals and professors of the day; a praise of nothing inverts established truth and opens up for literature all those elements of existence usually overlooked. As Cornwallis writes in 'The Prayse of Nothing': 'Nothing's *immortal*: Nothing *ever joys*; / Nothing *was ever free from all annoys*.'[91]

---

[90] Compare with a passage on the essayist as acrobat at risk of breaking his neck at II, 212.
[91] Cornwallis, 'The Prayse of Nothing', in *Essayes of Certaine Paradoxes* (1616), n.p.

Or as Belloc puts it in his *On Nothing*, nothing is 'the warp or ground of all that is holiest. It is of such fine gossamer that loveliness was spun'; 'nothing is the tenuous stuff from which the world was made'.[92]

Montaigne said, 'any topic is equally fertile for me. A fly will serve my purpose.'[93] Or even a pencil; or even the death of a moth, the subject of the fragment, unpublished in Woolf's own lifetime, under whose title Leonard Woolf first republished 'Street-Haunting'. Woolf's editors think it likely that Woolf wrote 'The Death of the Moth' a few months after 'Street-Haunting', in September 1927 (VI, 444). In it Woolf, like so many other essayists before and after her, surveys life itself in a form as near as possible to nothingness, fleeting and evanescent, and does her best to prop it up, just long enough to be witnessed, by stretching out the point of her pencil (VI, 443). In the moth, she sees herself— just as she does at the end of 'Street-Haunting', where she reflects on 'the self which has been blown about at so many street corners, which has battered like a moth at the flame of so many inaccessible lanterns' (IV, 491).

---

[92] Belloc, *On Nothing*, xiv, xvi. For other essays on nothing, see Henry Fielding, 'On Nothing' in *Miscellaneous Works: I*, vol. 14 in *The Complete Works of Henry Fielding* (1902), 307–21; Robert Lynd, 'On Doing Nothing', in *If the Germans Conquered England* (1917), 47–53; and J. B. Priestley, 'On Doing Nothing', in *Essays of To-Day and Yesterday* (1926), 35–41.

[93] Montaigne, 'On Some Verses of Virgil', 810.

2

The Montaignian Essay and Authored Miscellanies from Antiquity to the Nineteenth Century

Warren Boutcher

1. Introduction

The essay has a doubly paradoxical identity. It is both a genre and something that is difficult to define as a genre. It is both a schooled form of argument on a given topic, and an unschooled form of rumination on various topics.[1] On the one hand, it is recognized today in the anglophone literary world as one of few genres of non-fiction that count as literature. Its origins are held to lie in the reception of Montaigne in England in the late sixteenth century, which gave rise to the work of early English essay writers such as Cornwallis and Bacon. In the later seventeenth century, the traditional account goes, the genre and its author were exiled by France and welcomed and assimilated with redoubled enthusiasm in England. The genre was re-formed in a distinctively English vein by Addison and Steele, in the early eighteenth century, as the periodical loose paper. This literary-historical narrative builds on nineteenth-century criticism such as the piece by William Hazlitt (1778–1830) entitled 'On the Periodical Essayists', published in *Lectures on the English Comic Writers* (1819).[2]

On the other hand, the qualities we associate with essayistic writing—spontaneity, formlessness, freedom from method—mean that we can find it everywhere: in scientific literature, in novels, in drama, in film, in all sorts of works that carry neither the title 'essay' nor the common features of a genre. So Scott Black shows in the present volume that Tristram Shandy is an essayistic novel, Fred Parker that Hume's works are essayistic philosophy; Michael Wood

---

[1] On the latter, see Peter Mack, 'Rhetoric and the Essay', *Rhetoric Society Quarterly* 23.2 (1993), 41–9.

[2] The lecture was expanded from a *Round Table* essay of 1815, published in *The Examiner* (March 5). See 'On the Periodical Essayists', in *The Selected Writings of William Hazlitt*, ed. Duncan Wu, 9 vols (1998), V, 84–96. References given in the text.

Warren Boutcher, *The Montaignian Essay and Authored Miscellanies from Antiquity to the Nineteenth Century* In: *On Essays: Montaigne to the Present.* Edited by: Thomas Karshan and Kathryn Murphy, Oxford University Press (2020).
© Warren Boutcher.
DOI: 10.1093/oso/9780198707868.003.0003

finds essays in late twentieth-century fiction, and Christy Wampole in works of art, photography, and video.[3]

The present chapter proposes a historical explanation for this paradox. For what has perhaps been lost in contemporary criticism is a sense of how the essay was still embedded in Hazlitt's time in a much broader European tradition of various and miscellaneous writing that long preceded Montaigne, that included him, and that continued long after him.[4] It was defined as a tradition by the fact that it did not contain anything that could be classified according to the generic and professional norms defined by classical poetics, rhetoric, and philosophy, norms that in changing forms persisted through to the mid-nineteenth century. So the tradition comprehended all genres and writings that were not of the order of epic poetry or oratory or philosophy, such as the miscellany, the commentary, the rhapsody, the *silva*, the *farrago*, other types of reference works such as encyclopedias, and writings that were *sui generis*.

This negatively defined tradition accommodated a range of more and less structured types of writing, from learned exercises and treatises of various kinds to lyrical and satirical poetry, familiar letters, Socratic dialogues, antiquarian commentary, and personal notes or records. Before Hazlitt's time, it was more often referred to synecdochically as the miscellany, or miscellaneous literature, than as the essay—though we should always remember that both 'miscellany' and related terms such as 'commentary' retained the capacity to denote quite structured collections or expositions of learning. After Hazlitt's time, 'miscellany' came more usually to mean an anthology of disparate texts, while 'essay' came more regularly to denote a non-fictional literary composition of a deliberately free and mixed kind.

Another way of stating the same thesis is to say that in the tradition of classical learning and letters transmitted via the Renaissance through to the eighteenth century there had developed two complementary orientations for the acquisition, registration, and communication of knowledge: one more regular and scholastic, and one more irregular and amateur. Each orientation could be equally at work in a single text. The first was marked by an order of knowledge and a set of formal arts or disciplines that determined the classification of phenomena and the marshalling of literary resources for the invention and methodical arrangement of persuasive speeches in the persona of an orator (Quintilian); of treatises of positive doctrine in the persona of a philosophical teacher (Aristotle, Galen); or of epic poems or tragedies in the persona of a poet (Virgil, Seneca).

---

[3] See Chapters 6, 5, 14, and 17, respectively.

[4] I use 'various' when describing this literary tradition in a way that includes the senses derived from the Latin *varius*, and that inhere in the term *varia*, which means not only a collection of various types of writing, but writings characterized by *varietas*. See William Fitzgerald, *Variety: The Life of a Roman Concept* (2016).

The second was defined contrarily by the lack of disciplinary order and a more heterogeneous style of discourse: it cultivated, sometimes with purpose, the mixed in kind, colloquial in expression, loose in composition. It also came with less authoritative, less career-oriented, more subjective personae, such as those exhibited in private conversation or in recreational study. It was more suitable for busy, lay readers and audiences than for learned experts and professionals. It could in some contexts be informed by scepticism about conceptions of the value of public rhetoric, or of knowledge as a structured system, or of epic poetry, and of all three as the foundations of learned or literary careers. It might also—as already mentioned—assume an aesthetic purpose based in the deliberate pursuit of effects of spontaneity, heterogeneity, and disorder, effects considered to be more redolent of the everyday flux of conversation and occasion, or of the tumult and variety of Nature or Chaos.

These opposed but complementary orientations corresponded to two broad types of collection of self-contained items of knowledge and wisdom, and of associated observations or notes, in textual compilations that, as a set of genres, both belonged to the various and miscellaneous tradition outlined above: the encyclopedia and the miscellany.[5] Encyclopedic works generally purported to offer a more systematic, comprehensive, and authoritative collection of knowledge across a defined range of fields. Miscellanies in this narrower, generic sense transmitted fragments of learning and learned observation in various fields in a more random, digressive style, in diverse genres such as table-talk and *hypomnemata* (often within the same work), and did not generally espouse structure or claim authority in the same ways. Some of these latter collections were personalized or more definitely 'authored' in one way or another—either through selectivity, or through the disordered interweaving of the personal memoirs or meditations of the compiler or commentator.[6]

Through the eighteenth century, under the influence of Montaigne and his school, moral and natural philosophy came to the fore as the principal fields of miscellaneous literary writing, leaving philology and antiquarianism behind. It was now most likely to be moral wisdom and experience—commonplaces, proverbs, apophthegms, anecdotes, fables, personal notes and memoranda—or items of scientific observation that would be miscellaneously communicated.

Hazlitt makes all this clear in 1819 when he refers to 'that sort of writing' which the periodical essayists have been the most successful at cultivating in England. The periodical essay, in other words, is one, local instance of a much broader kind of writing, a whole 'department of literature'. This writing deals with the 'mixed

---

[5] See Neil Kenny, *The Palace of Secrets: Béroalde de Verville and Renaissance Conceptions of Knowledge* (1991), 35–54 for a particularly nuanced treatment of the relationship between these 'opposed but intimately related' genres in the long sixteenth century.

[6] Amiel Vardi, 'Genre, Conventions, and Cultural Programme in Gellius' *Noctes Atticae*', in *The Worlds of Aulus Gellius*, ed. Leofranc Holford-Strevens and Amiel Vardi (2004), 159–86, 164–84.

mass of human affairs' that do not fall under any 'regular art, science, or profession'. It is, in short, various and miscellaneous. It is not shaped by the requirement to treat of natural science or systems of philosophy in a high-minded way determined by scholarly and textual authorities. It instead 'makes familiar with the world of men and women', which brings it closest to moral philosophy or moral history. It has what might be called an archival or administrative aspect: it 'records [our] actions', 'takes minutes' of 'our dress, air, looks, words, thoughts, and actions'. In terms of style and content it does not deal in 'sweeping clauses' and theories but in 'liberal constructions' and details, facts (84).

If we ask what writers might already have treated this mixed human matter in antiquity, there is only one clue in Hazlitt's piece, in the Latin quotations he selects: the satirical poets Horace and Juvenal. Amongst the moderns it was Montaigne—who (we might add) also quoted both classical poets extensively in Latin—who led the way to this kind of writing. He was a new, literary kind of author of non-fiction. He did not assume the persona or 'character' of a 'philosopher, wit, orator, or moralist' though he became all these just by speaking his mind (85). He did not compare books with rules and systems, or take a standard of excellence from Aristotle. He did not converse like a pedagogue with his pupil. In the wake of his English reception, the periodical essayists applied the 'same unrestrained expression of their thoughts' to temporary and local matters, added a fictitious and humorous disguise (i.e. the character of the *Tatler* or the *Spectator*), and retained the archival function as a matter of daily (in the case of *The Spectator*) or tri-weekly (in the case of *The Tatler*) news (87).

A contemporary of Hazlitt's shall in this chapter provide us with a more detailed window onto the persistence into the nineteenth century of this understanding of the tradition of various and miscellaneous writings to which the essay belonged. In 1796, Isaac D'Israeli (1766–1848), the father of the statesman Benjamin Disraeli, published a short piece entitled 'Of Miscellanies'.[7] It offers a vantage point from which we can recover the history of the essay, and of Montaigne's place therein, as it stood on the cusp of the romantic revolution and the invention of English literature. As D'Israeli wrote, modern and nationalized conceptions of literature and the essay were beginning to take hold. But in his eyes the history of the essay was still part of a much broader history of miscellaneous reading and commentary, conversation and writing, a history stretching back to Aulus Gellius and other classical writers, and across many different genres. As we shall see, D'Israeli captures and aestheticizes this history by invoking the persona of the 'Miscellanist', which he distinguishes from that of the 'Pedant'.

There is one important distinction to emphasize before we proceed. D'Israeli does not employ the term 'miscellany' to denote a medley of texts by different

---

[7] It comprised the first chapter of Isaac D'Israeli, *Miscellanies; or, Literary Recreations* (1796). References given in the text.

authors or from diverse sources, an anthology of the kind often compiled by a publisher. He means, instead, to focus our attention on other dimensions of miscellaneity, from the formal and temporal, to the emotive and discursive. A miscellany in his treatment is a heterogeneous, occasional, spontaneous, irregular form of writing attributable to a single, authorial 'Miscellanist' (though it may include extracts from other authors and sources)—what I am dubbing the 'authored' as opposed to the impersonal, anthological miscellany.[8] The 'miscellaneous'—like the 'essayistic' in modern culture—could refer at one and the same time to the quality of a non-professional authorial persona, a random mode of reading and observation, a varied literary style or mixture of forms, a heterogeneous set of contents, a non-scholarly readership. But, like the 'essay' for most of its history, it is not always or even usually a strictly generic term.

2. The Miscellanist and the Pedant

D'Israeli begins, then, with the antagonism between the characters of the 'Miscellanist' and the 'Pedant'. The Pedant is an arid grammarian, a conjectural critic or philologist who typically abuses Miscellanists. One of them (Joseph Scaliger) had even called 'the venerable father of modern Miscellanies', Montaigne, a 'bold ignorant fellow' (3–5). So although D'Israeli refers to 'literary essays' (3) and the 'essayist' (20) during his piece, he describes Montaigne as the progenitor not of the modern essay, as so many later writers would do, but of 'modern Miscellanies' (5).

In what follows, D'Israeli sketches out the province of the Miscellanist. The sketch is so broad as to seem, at points, to include any literature that does not follow the rules of formal professional scholarship and philosophy—belles-lettres in general, including both learned and fictional writings. For he is delineating not just the character of the Miscellanist, but the species of miscellaneous compositions, and the nature of 'the tasteful, the volatile, and the amiable' readership whose non-pedantic tastes create a demand for non-regular, non-scholarly literature (3)—just as we might now define the 'essay' as a relationship between the persona of the essayist, the form of the essay, and the essayistic reader, all set against more professional and methodical alternatives.

---

[8] On the history of the authored miscellany, see Eric MacPhail, *Dancing Around the Well: The Circulation of Commonplaces in Renaissance Humanism* (2014); Dominique de Courcelles (ed.), *Ouvrages miscellanées et théories de la connaissance à la Renaissance* (2003), especially the chapters by Mandosio and Couzinet; Perrine Galand-Hallyn and Sylvie Laigneau-Fontaine (eds), *La Silve: histoire d'une écriture libérée en Europe de l'antiquité au XVIIIe siècle* (2013), especially the chapter by Frans De Bruyn; Emily Colette Wilkinson, 'The Miscellaneous: A Poetics of the Mode in British Literature, 1668–1759', unpublished doctoral dissertation (Stanford University, 2008).

D'Israeli consolidated this sketch of an alternative, miscellaneous literary culture in a revealing way in the revised version of the chapter that appeared only five years later in 1801. In that version, he opens by identifying the delightful province of the Miscellanists, who form a communication between the learned and the unlearned and introduce elegant philosophy into literature, with what in Germany 'has been termed [...] the ÆSTHETIC, from a Greek term, signifying *feeling* [...] [which] decides on the beautiful by TASTE, and not by *Logic*'.[9] Here, the traditional opposition between more regular and more various presentations of knowledge and wisdom, transmutes into a recognizably modern opposition between hard logic and aestheticized feeling, between formal philosophy and literature.

What kind of persona did a Miscellanist characteristically communicate? Back in the 1796 text, D'Israeli quotes engagingly '*naive* expressions' from Montaigne's preface 'Au lecteur' in French to exemplify 'sincerity', or writing from the heart. Whatever the style of his rhetorical periods, grand and Asiatic or compressed and laconic, it is sentiment and his 'sensations' that matter, drawing us into his works, 'as into my own heart'. The thought is backed up by verses in original French and imitative English by the Montaigne of French poetry, Boileau (7–10). Miscellanists, then, are purveyors of 'pleasing egotism', who reject studied compositions—'sparkling antithesis, and solemn cadences'—to paint themselves in 'domestic negligence' (13–14). They raise no 'artificial emotions' but paint forth their 'little humours', their 'individual feelings', like Plutarch (in Montaigne's estimation), like Addison, Sterne, Richardson, Temple, Dryden (10–12).

Within this agreeably aesthetic, irregular mode of composition, D'Israeli goes on to discriminate a particular 'species of Miscellanies' (14) or shorter, non-systematic non-fiction. This is where D'Israeli begins loosely to define a genre something like the essay. These are short works, often discovered in a 'fugitive state', prompted by the peculiarity of a situation, or the enthusiasm of a prevailing passion (the implicit parallel with lyric poetry should be noted). In their modern, printed incarnations they are associated with certain material formats. The writer of miscellaneous 'loose papers' (18) (including Seneca and Plutarch) or 'little works' (14) is contrasted with 'voluminous writers' (16), by which he means writers who undertake to produce a 'volume' of quarto size or bigger (20). This is probably an allusion to *The Spectator*, No. 124 (23 July 1711), where Addison likewise contrasts the periodical writer, who communicates his thoughts to the world via loose tracts and single pieces, with the pedant or scholar who writes bulky volumes for academic libraries.[10]

---

[9]   D'Israeli, *Literary Miscellanies: including a Dissertation on Anecdotes*, 2nd edn (1801), 67–8.
[10]   See Markman Ellis's contribution to this volume, Chapter 4, 100.

3. The History of the Essay before the Nineteenth Century

What is the significance for the present volume of the late eighteenth-century case of D'Israeli? It suggests we proceed cautiously when, following Hazlitt and later writers, we seek to identify a historical genealogy of the English essay as a distinct, identifiable genre with sub-genres (the personal essay, the character essay, the scientific essay, etc.), a genre with classical precedents but with a clear modern origin in the anglicized Montaigne, and a single line of development through the periodical essayists of the early eighteenth century.[11]

This is not to say we cannot proceed at all. For D'Israeli does indicate a precise provenance for the genre: the *miscellanea* or humanist, erudite 'miscellany' *stricto sensu*; that is, miscellaneous philological studies and fragments of commentary undertaken, originally in Latin and now in English, by grammarians and conjectural critics. The humanist Angelo Poliziano was the first to use this title in his *Miscellanea* of 1489. But many other titles were used in the sixteenth century for these randomly ordered scholarly collections, including *adversaria*, which were collections of scholarly reading notes offered up in the random order of their daily occurrence, rather than methodically under headings.[12]

In the late sixteenth century, Montaigne took the form out of the humanists' hands and gave it to 'the scientific and the moral writer' (4), making himself rather than the text of antiquity the 'idol of his lucubrations' (7)—hence the hostility of the philologist Scaliger. So a form of general commentary on everyday life breaks free from scholarly forms of deliberately varied and disordered exegesis of fragments of classical texts. Montaigne was initiating a battle over the most appropriate style of discourse and persona for the public intellectual who would reach a lay readership with some interest in knowledge and learning, but no time or patience to follow formally elaborated commentaries or theses on particular texts or topics. One way he did this was to appropriate fragments of classical texts for non-philological purposes.

In the more recent English literary tradition Scaliger's hostility equated to that of William Warburton, the professional divine and textual critic, for Joseph Addison (5)—'the first of our essayists' (11). The pedants of the last age, D'Israeli says outright, were the Warburtonians (4). When Bentley and Warburton—the first by conjecturally emending Milton, the second by explaining the Eleusinian mysteries of Virgil, *Aeneid*, book 6—tried to bring the voice and

---

[11] The clarity of this origin is called into question in Richard Squibbs, *Urban Enlightenment and the Eighteenth-Century Periodical Essay: Transatlantic Retrospects* (2014), 43–4.

[12] Jean-Marc Mandosio, 'La miscellanée: histoire d'un genre', in de Courcelles (ed.), *Ouvrages miscellanées* (2003), 7–36; Jean-Marc Chatelain, 'Les recueils d'adversaria aux xvie et xviie siècles', in Henri-Jean Martin and Frédéric Barbier (eds), *Le livre et l'historien: études offertes en l'honneur du Professeur Henri-Jean Martin* (1997), 169–86; Ann Blair, *Too Much to Know: Managing Scholarly Information before the Modern Age* (2010), 126–31.

knowledge of the professional critic to a lay public and to men of taste, they did no more than reveal the singular imbecility concealed under the arrogance of the scholar (6). This left the field open for the true public intellectual—the literary essayist—to triumph, as Montaigne had done in France, in his time. Montaigne still worked up his essays from commentary on textual fragments, but not in a pedantically philological manner.

However, as we have already seen, D'Israeli also associates Montaigne with a whole category of irregular, mixed writings in classical, medieval, and modern European literature—for which the most common designation in early modern catalogues was, again, 'miscellanies', but in a much broader sense that we associated earlier with a negatively defined tradition of various literature. Within that category thrived a kaleidoscope of different kinds of occasional treatises, encyclopedias, and less systematic works in prose and verse compiled by a single author (alongside other miscellanies that were more like impersonal anthologies), and which shared only one characteristic: they were not classifiable either in literary criticism or through the book trade as formal works of epic or dramatic poetry, oratory, history, philosophy, law, medicine, or theology. They were unstably and fluidly labelled with various ad hoc titles—centrally including the 'essay', which itself was developing a broad range of uses alongside and in tandem with 'miscellany'.

The examples D'Israeli gives of the authorial miscellanist's work demonstrate the variety of genres which this orientation or persona could inhabit. They include recent works of the long eighteenth century such as Bolingbroke's Senecan 'Reflections upon Exile', the German Johann Georg Zimmermann's 'Essay on Solitude' (probably the shorter, 1756 version), William Shenstone's essay-poem on economy, William Hay's explicitly Montaignian essay on deformity (1754), and Defoe's first essays of 1697–8 (in the collection *An Essay upon Projects*). But they also range back before Montaigne's time to Italian humanist works including Petrarch's *De vita solitaria* and Pierius Valerianus's collection of literary anecdotes (*De literatorum infelicitate*), and, from late antiquity, Boethius's prose-and-verse *Consolations of Philosophy*. D'Israeli also invokes, as Miscellanists: all the proponents of the French moralist tradition, from Rochefoucault and La Bruyère to the Montesquieu of the letters of Usbek; the classical tradition of commentaries of the kind described in the preface to Aulus Gellius's *Noctes Atticae*; the medieval Occitan tradition of 'Troubadours, Conteurs, and Jongleurs' who composed moralities, histories, and tales in verse and prose.

Before 1800, then, even as we cautiously join critics of the time such as D'Israeli in beginning to trace the properties of an emergent genre in England (the literary essay), we should be aware of the vast field of various and miscellaneous writings in which it remained inextricably embedded. There were two complementary veins in this field, which the same writer might call upon depending on mood, occasion, and purpose—as when Addison points to his vacillations between his more regular and methodical papers and his wilder compositions or essays. In the wilder form of composition, each writer, in a specific cultural and literary context, could negotiate anew, relatively unhampered by norms and rules, the particular shape and title to be taken by his or her piece of disordered, varied, and subjective writing or compilation. To authorize their chosen form or mixture of forms they might draw on the more successful such past negotiations in their own and other literatures, from classical works such as Aulus Gellius's *Noctes Atticae* (prose) and Statius's *Silvae* (verse) to Renaissance works such as Montaigne's *Essais* and Jonson's *The Forrest* or *Under-Wood*. But they were by definition free to invent new titles, new forms for works that were always, to some degree, ad hoc and *sui generis*—because they were mixed in kind, varied in style and content, disordered in composition. Each work in this wilder vein might be unique, because particular to the author's collecting habits, their preoccupations, their circumstances.

4. Aulus Gellius

This is, after all, precisely what is intimated in the first and most frequently cited discussion of the freer form of authored miscellany in classical antiquity: the 'Praefatio' to Gellius's *Noctes Atticae*, which D'Israeli possessed in a contemporary English translation by Rev. W. Beloe.[13] There were other classical works derived from—or which claimed to derive from—irregular personal notes or compilations and which were circulated in relatively disordered forms: Marcus Aurelius's *Meditations*, for example, were a form of *hypomnemata* or notelets, and Aelian's collection of stories about animals was a kind of medley on a specific topic.[14] But from the *quattrocento* Renaissance to D'Israeli's day, Gellius was—sometimes in the company of Macrobius—the principal classical precedent for the miscellaneous author. In his preface, he describes how he came to compose and entitle his work, which consists of various short pieces on literary-critical, philological, and moral questions. When he had in hand any Greek or Latin book, or when he heard anything worth remembering, he collected notes that pleased him, whatever kind they were, without introducing any distinctions or order (I, iii).

The 'Commentaries' (a term which, as we heard earlier, could mean anything from a private journal or collection of notes for private use to exegetical commentary) that result from these 'original annotations' reflect the same irregularity: 'I have used the same accidental arrangement which I had before used in making the collection' (I, iii). He has entitled them 'Attic Nights' (they were composed at night in the countryside of Attica) so as not to attempt to imitate the fine titles invented by other writers who had compiled books of a similar kind. As they had

[13] Aulus Gellius, *The Attic Nights*, trans. Rev. W. Beloe, 3 vols (1795). References given in the text.
[14] Blair, *Too Much to Know*, 20, 82.

got together a 'various, mixed, and as it were immethodical kind of learning' ('variam et miscellam et quasi confusaneam doctrinam'), they 'studied to give their books refined and dainty titles' of various sorts.[15]

Gellius goes on to give thirty of these, which focus the readers' minds either on the variety and richness of the contents, or on the labours of the author, or on particular types of discourse. One of the contemporary essayists whose works were collected by D'Israeli, Vicesimus Knox, wrote an essay on 'the titles of miscellaneous papers' (in imitation of Gellius's 'Praefatio'), in which he vernacularizes and glosses some of the titles. He lists: the 'Muses', for poetical miscellanies; 'Timber, Sylvae, Hylae', authorial collections of 'a store of timber or materials, which themselves, or others, might [...] use in erecting a regular structure'; 'Peplon [...] the [embroidered] Mantle [...] detached pieces on various subjects [...] with every variety of the most vivid coloring and picturesque imagery'; 'the Horn of Almathea' or 'THE CORNUCOPIA', which captures 'the idea of great exuberance and inexhaustible variety'; 'Hive and [...] Honeycomb' which 'conveyed at once the idea of industry and taste in the collector and of sweetness in the collection'; the 'Limon, or the Meadow', which causes the reader to 'expect flowers richly interspersed'; 'Pandecte', chiefly applied to collections of law, but 'extended to miscellaneous books of polite literature', and denoting, in Knox's view, something like the 'monthly magazines'; 'Enchiridion, the Manual', for pocket 'works of small magnitude comprehending things of great moment'.[16]

Gellius goes on to claim that just as he falls short of these writers in care and elegance of style, so he falls short in the dignity of his title, which was just dashed off in rustic fashion (I, v). In fact, the choice he made was probably intended to suggest scholarship and nocturnal toil, and the plurality of self-contained items.[17] The modesty is clearly affected and Gellius's claim is belied by what he goes on to say next. These writers' collections had aimed at quantity, where his is more definitely *authored*. It is selective and purposeful; it aims to provide short-cuts to independent learning across an extraordinary variety of fields (I, vi). It is deliberately disordered and generically diverse—different chapters recall different genres, from *chreiai* and *hypomnemata* to dialogues and symposiums.[18] It has, though, as a form of non-fiction derived from learned study, what would now be described as literary qualities.

---

[15] A more literal rendition would be 'various items of knowledge collected from a mixture of fields in an almost miscellaneous manner'.

[16] Vicesimus Knox, *Winter Evenings; or Lucubrations on Life and Letters*, 3 vols (1788), I, 15–21 (further references given in the text); compare Beloe's translation, I, iv–v. Those Knox does not mention were translated as follows by Beloe: '"My own Readings" [...] "Ancient Readings" [...] "Flowrets" [...] "Inventions" [...] "Lights" [...] "Tapestries" [...] "Helicon," "Problems" [...] "Small Arms" [...] "Memorials," "Practical Hints," "Leisure Amusements," and "Lessons" [...] "Natural History," "Various History," "The Parterre", "The Orchard" [...] "Common Places" [...] "Miscellanies," "Moral Epistles" [...] "Epistolary or Mixed Questions"'.

[17] See Vardi, 'Genre, Conventions', 159–60.   [18] Vardi, 'Genre, Conventions', 179–80.

Behind Gellius's account there is, then, a classical Roman understanding of the broad tradition of various and miscellaneous writings invoked at the start of this chapter. Gellius describes these as *commentarii*; they include works that might now be described as florilegia, handbooks, or encyclopedias, alongside Seneca's moral epistles and Pliny's natural history. In terms of readership, they were meant for a special class of people who were too busy to engage in proper study or extended philosophical reading.[19]

Some of the books within this larger category, however, distinguish themselves literarily by their purposeful selectivity, their variety, their disorderliness. These purport to offer observations on reading and experience in a random order, casually, as they occurred to a particular person, so as to stimulate pleasure and curiosity. Each writer's miscellany—where it has such pretensions to literary distinction—might be mixed, varied, and occasional in its own way, and might therefore be deserving of an ingenious title distinguishing it from others and marking a particular form or occasion specific to the author and his or her circumstances. This was the tradition of titling that Montaigne was following when he entitled his book *Les Essais de Michel de Montaigne* ('The trials or tastings of Michael of Montaigne'): it was an ad hoc title meant to mark both the uniqueness of the book (like 'Attic Nights') and of the persona with which it was consubstantial, rather than to inaugurate a new literary genre.

In the same way, in the volume under discussion, D'Israeli was the first—in his subtitle—to anglicize the French 'récréations littéraires', used by Solignac (1723), Latour (1759), and Cizeron-Rival (1765), as the title for various kinds of literary miscellanies.[20] Although D'Israeli invokes Montaigne and others, what he actually produces under titles such as 'Miscellanies' and 'Curiosities' is a lightly vulgarized version of various kinds of *res litteraria* and *biographia litteraria* that Coleridge was to raise to much greater dignity. His 'literary recreation' is just one, distinctively literary form in which the broader genre of the authored, aesthetically pleasing miscellany was still, at the end of the eighteenth century, manifesting itself in myriad different forms that also included the increasingly prominent 'essay'.

---

[19] Vardi, 'Genre, Conventions', 164–5.

[20] D'Israeli owned a copy of Cizeron-Rival's work. My sources for all statements about D'Israeli's books are *Catalogue of a considerable portion of the valuable library of Isaac D'Israeli [. . .] which will be sold by auction, by Messrs. S. Leigh Sotheby & co. [. . .] on Friday, March 16th, 1849, and three following days* (1849) and the Jisc Library Hub Discover database (formerly Copac), which includes a catalogue of the books in the Disraeli family library at Hughenden Manor, with copy-specific provenance information. Some 294 copies are recorded as 'Ex libris Isaac D'Israeli'. It is uncertain in some cases whether a book was introduced into the library by Isaac or Benjamin.

5. Miscellaneity in D'Israeli's Library

Frans De Bruyn has argued that the eighteenth century might be named the 'Age of Miscellaneity'; the tradition of various and miscellaneous writings had become so ubiquitous in both prose and poetry, 'so diverse in content and purpose as scarcely any longer to be considered a discrete genre, so indispensable to publishers and readers alike as to need no justification'.[21] As the formal and regular genres of rhetoric, poetry, and professional philosophy, and the structured encyclopedia of classical learning, began to lose their grip outside the academy, so the lay readership's demand for varied and pleasing forms of literary learning grew more and more dominant in the field of publishing.

The portions of D'Israeli's library that went on sale after his death and that survived in his son's collection support De Bruyn's contention. We can use its contents as a way of understanding the form in which a whole tradition of writing stretching back to antiquity could be present in the literary culture of the early nineteenth century, and how Montaigne could be considered the father of the modern version of that tradition, and the 'essay' its most durable representative. We are visiting, in particular, four moments in the history of that tradition, through the prism of the Disraeli books: Gellius's moment in Roman antiquity (already discussed); Montaigne's moment at the turn of the sixteenth and seventeenth centuries; the moment of the exile of the essay from France and its welcome in England at the turn of the seventeenth and eighteenth centuries; Isaac D'Israeli's own moment at the turn of the eighteenth and nineteenth centuries.

The catalogue included many different forms of miscellaneous publications, predominantly in English and French, stretching back from the 1830s to the 1530s—though some of these publications contained works dating from the medieval and classical periods. The miscellanies in question ranged from the purely anthological to the single-authored, from more ordered to more random, from scholarly to literary, from poetic to prosaic. D'Israeli possessed a number of modern translations and editions of classical works in the tradition of commentaries and miscellanies. We already know that he possessed the first full translation into English of Aulus Gellius's *Attic Nights* (Beloe, 1795). He also had a few volumes of Cicero's works translated as 'essays on old age and friendship' and 'essay on moral duty', and French editions of Seneca's *Oeuvres* and Plutarch's *Oeuvres morales*.

More significant was his collection of medieval and Renaissance miscellanies, which included Montaigne's *Essais*. He had copies of Tabourot's *Bigarrures* (1614); Alexandri ab Alexandro's *Genialium Dierum libri* (1673), Corrozet's *Thresor des Histoires de France* (1627), the *Holy Commonwealth, or Political*

---

[21] Frans De Bruyn, 'The English afterlife of the *silva* in the seventeenth and eighteenth centuries', in Galand-Hallyn and Laigneau-Fontaine (eds), *La Silve*, 657–88, here 670.

Aphorisms (1659), Bouchet's *Les Serées* (1614), various other treasuries of wit or similes, collections of novels, antiquities. He also had the *Satyre Menippée* (1593), and numerous emblem books.

D'Israeli owned the second edition of John Molle's translation, via Simon Goulart's French, of Camerarius's humanist miscellany: *The living librarie, or meditations and observations historical, natural, moral, political, and poetical* (1625). This edition did not include translations from the third volume, where, in a dedicatory preface, Goulart—the intermediary translator—explained the fluid category of literature to which he was contributing, and the market for which he was catering around the turn of the sixteenth and seventeenth centuries. He says he has added his own observations here and there to Camerarius's text, with the French nation in mind, who desire variety in what they read ('desireuse de diverse lecture'). He then lists the genres of various and miscellaneous writings by ancient and modern authors that meet this desire:

> Medleys of natural history, antiquities, novels, lessons, collections, pandects, treasuries and theatres of examples, anthologies, philological studies, researches, discourses, miscellanies, daily exercises, evening exercises, banquets, table-talks, discourses [*sic*], essays, hoards, observations, and other works.[22]

Here is an early seventeenth-century description of the tradition with which we are concerned throughout this chapter. This list—a descendant of Gellius's— adapts and vernacularizes the neo-Latin genres of various and miscellaneous writing described by Conrad Gessner in the *Pandectæ* as 'varia et miscellanea'. The latter included, for example, Plutarch's *Symposiaca* ('Propos de table' or 'Tabletalk') and collections of *varia historia* and *mirabiles narrationes*. In Goulart's list, the new genre of *essais* takes its place in a broad tradition of miscellaneous literature from reference works to dialogues, from *histoires mêlées* to *leçons* and *trésors et théâtres d'exemples*. This literature was thriving at the end of the sixteenth century and the beginning of the seventeenth century, thanks to a taste for *diverse lecture* in both England and France. It is worth noting that the only survivors—as literary genres—from this list in contemporary literary culture are the novel and the essay.

6. Montaigne

The D'Israeli family library contained copies of the 1657 *Essais*, probably acquired by Benjamin, of the 1669 *Essais*, almost certainly owned by Isaac, and of the

---

[22] Philippus Camerarius, *Les meditations historiques*, ed. Simon Goulart, 3 vols (1610), III, sig. 2¶2r.

fourth, 1711 edition of Charles Cotton's English translation. The latter, still at Hughenden Manor, has Benjamin's bookplate but may have belonged originally to Isaac, who quoted it in his published work (at other times he quoted directly from the French).[23] Isaac's French copy (1669) was of the last edition of the *Essais* to be published in France between 1669 and 1725, as the *Essais* were placed on the Roman Catholic Index in 1674. As paratexts added to later editions reveal, Charles Cotton's translation, first published in 1685, exploited this Catholic and Gallic neglect of one of their own. In the edition owned by the Disraelis (1711), the publisher felt the need to include a 'Vindication' of the work (authorship uncertain). It begins as follows:

> The Essays of *Michel de Montagne* are justly ranked amongst Miscellaneous Books: for they are on various subjects, without order and connexion; and the very body of the discourses has still a greater variety. This sort of confusion does not however hinder people of all qualities to extol these Essays above all the Books that ever they read, and they make them their chief study. They think that other Miscellanies of ancient and modern Books are nothing but an unnecessary heap of quotations, whereas we find in this authorities to the purpose, intermixed with the Authors own thoughts; which being bold and extraordinary, are very effectual to cure men of their Weakness and Vanity, and induce them to seek Virtue and Felicity by lawful means.[24]

At the end of the 'Vindication' Montaigne is declared to be safer and more welcome in England than in despotic France. All the more interesting, then, that the passage quoted above proves to be translated directly from a French work of bibliography that had sought to define a library for a French vernacular readership in the 1660s: Charles Sorel's *La bibliotheque françoise*.[25] The English claimed Montaigne as their own by translating French words.

There is no concern here in 1711 to define a new genre called the 'Essay'. The work is justly ranked amongst an existing category going back to antiquity (the language—'Miscellaneous', 'various subjects', 'confusion'—specifically recalls that of Gellius's 'Praefatio'): miscellaneous books ('livres meslez'). These are books which are various—confused, even—both in their subject and in the very form of their discourse. What sets this one apart from others that merely heap up quotations from classical and modern books is that they are intermixed, in a purposeful way, with the bold and extraordinary thoughts of the author. Furthermore, despite the general confusion and variety, the book can still be

---

[23] See Ingrid A. R. De Smet, 'Isaac D'Israeli, Reader of Montaigne', in Neil Kenny, Richard Scholar, and Wes Williams (eds), *Montaigne in Transit: Essays in Honour of Ian Maclean* (2016), 187–202.

[24] Michel de Montaigne, *Essays*, trans. Charles Cotton, 4th edn, 3 vols (1711), I, sigs. B1r–v.

[25] Charles Sorel, *La bibliotheque françoise*, 2nd edn (1667), sigs. G4v–5r.

seen as a form of conduct manual. There is a general therapeutic purpose: to cure men of weakness and vanity. A miscellany could indeed be seen as an alternative, more recreational way of 'mixing' some instruction more pleasurably into the reader's leisure.[26]

From this point of view, then, Montaigne's text is the most successfully *authored* miscellany of its day, perhaps the most successfully authored since classical works such as Aulus Gellius's *Noctes Atticae*. Many other of Montaigne's contemporaries and early readers either explicitly or implicitly placed his work and assessed its value in relation to miscellaneous writings, whether positively or negatively. They saw it (especially in its fullest version, first published in 1595) as an extravagantly disordered form of miscellany that deceptively promised some order—because although it was divided into chapters with head-ings they turned out neither accurately to describe nor successfully to marshal the digressive and wandering trains of thought they contained. It was marked by a new and intriguing title and an unusually frank and detailed thread of self-commentary—which many of the early readers could have done without. The format of the earliest French editions obstructed the methodical reader, who wished to use the text in more systematic fashion to methodically source and store commonplaces, by offering no marginal citations for the numerous embed-ded quotations and no indexes of the content.

It was Montaigne's intention neither to create a new genre of short literary works called 'essays', nor to be seen to have authored a generic miscellany. He claimed to have authored a completely unique book, *sui generis*, that comprised 'trials', 'tastes', or 'tests' of its author's natural faculties (divided into chapters, not 'essays') conducted by means of the registration and reflective review of a personal written record of his everyday *fantasies*. The term 'essay' denoted a free form of cognitive exercise that internalized and intensified—as a style of thought and writing—the features of informal private conversations between close friends.

When he refers to the book itself, its literary form, rather to than its contents, the word Montaigne most commonly uses is not *essais* but *registre*. The distinction between the two terms is clear when he says, for example, that this 'fricassee' that he is scribbling here is nothing but a 'record of the essays of my life', as Donald Frame translates it, or 'Register of *Essays* of my own life', as it was phrased in D'Israeli's copy of Cotton (III, 411)—that is to say, memoranda of experimental tests and reviews of his mental and physical health or balance.[27] In late classical Latin a *regesta*, and in medieval Latin a *regestum*, was a record of the *res gestae*, the things done—deeds—that were held to be worth recording, whether in the archives of a household estate, a chancery, a legal court or parliament. Some of

---

[26] Mandosio, 'La miscellanée', 9.
[27] Michel de Montaigne, *The Complete Works*, trans. Donald M. Frame (2003), 1007. Further references given in the text.

these archival books were used for more personal memorial writing or 'self-writing' as it has been described in recent scholarship.

By using this word of a printed book that records without rhetorical decorum or logical order the *fantasies* and secular musings of an unexceptional individual, as they occur to him, Montaigne is implicitly claiming that they are as worthy of record as the deeds of a famous nobleman such as Caesar in antiquity or Monluc in his own day, who both wrote history in the form of 'Commentaries' or personalized historical records. This claim and its acceptance by posterity is perhaps Montaigne's most important legacy. His work gave recognized social value or 'nobility' (in the language of the day) to a freer style of reading, thinking, and writing than that taught and advocated by professional intellectuals—even if some of those intellectuals, called humanists, had themselves anticipated in Latin in philological works what he was to do in the vernacular.

On the one hand, Montaigne advertised himself as someone who preferred to acquire the knowledge needed for his thinking and writing without having to read like a professional intellectual toiling through extended, structured works of formal philosophy. He preferred miscellaneous authors like Seneca and Plutarch, who offered their learning and observations in disparate, disconnected pieces, so that one could dip in and out of their works as one pleased. On the other hand, he self-consciously mixed the resulting style of informal and varied learning with a whole medieval tradition of personal archival writing. Even, then, if he does not call his book a miscellany, his text invokes a wide range of different kinds of various and miscellaneous writings, in part to situate itself amongst them, in part to distinguish itself from them—just as Gellius had done in a much more concentrated fashion in his preface. The one time Montaigne uses 'essays' to denote a general form of discourse he is not necessarily thinking of writings. He is referring to the essays of schoolchildren, which may be oral, and which are produced not to instruct others, but to be instructed *by* others, by teachers (284).

Disraeli could have found more negative points of view on Montaigne's brand of miscellaneity, both in the 1711 'Vindication', and elsewhere in his library. Amongst his vast collection of varied and miscellaneous writings, D'Israeli had fifty-one volumes (1735–1808) of the *Gentleman's Magazine*. In the magazine for December 1767, alongside a description of the recent eruption of Vesuvius, anecdotes and observations relating to Oliver Cromwell, and a letter-essay on the doctrine of papal infallibility, readers could find the second, serialized part of the first translation into English of the *Huetiana*, the collected scholarly gossip of Pierre-Daniel Huet. There, they could learn the scholarly bishop's opinion of Montaigne's *Essais*. Properly, they should be called '*Montaniana*, that is, a collection of *Montagne*'s thoughts without order or connection'. This is precisely why they are so agreeable to 'our nation [the French], an enemy to the pains necessary to go through long dissertations', and 'to the present age, an enemy to that application which close and methodical treatises require'. The 'free turn' of his wit, the variety of his style, his metaphorical expressions have made Montaigne 'the Breviary of genteel triflers, and of idle scholars', who seek only 'some tincture of letters, and some knowledge of the world'. He vainly put himself 'above rules'. The persona was little more than the result of boasting about servants and reputation. The self-portrait was no more than 'domestic impertinences'. The only note of admiration for Montaigne's miscellaneity in Huet's translated text comes when he talks about the style of the *Essais*—a 'great variety of Images on all sorts of subjects', a 'numberless train of agreeable metaphors'.[28]

7. Later Seventeenth and Eighteenth Centuries

Where can we find the *Essays* collected amongst miscellaneous books in England at the moment of Cotton's translation, around the turn of the seventeenth and eighteenth centuries? One answer is the so-called 'Term' catalogues that listed a good proportion of the books printed and published in England at quarterly intervals every year between 1683 and 1709. The 1700 edition of Cotton was not listed but the three volumes of the first edition, published in sequence across 1685–6, were. All three appeared in the listings under the category 'Miscellanies'. The main categories used in the Term catalogues were quite crude and do not reflect a careful effort at classification: 'Divinity'; 'Physick' or natural philosophy; 'Histories', which included novels and romances; 'Mathematicks'; 'Poetry and Plays'; 'Law'; 'Musick'; 'Miscellanies'; 'Libri latini', which could include not only Latin- but French-language books; and 'Books reprinted'.[29] Clearly, 'Miscellanies' is from the cataloguers' point of view a catch-all, negatively defined category: all books that cannot be fitted into the other categories. And it does not catch some books that describe themselves as miscellanies and that are naturally sorted under 'Divinity' or 'Poetry'.

But it is nevertheless interesting to consider the company the *Essays* kept, and to discern the outlines at this moment of the whole field of various and miscellaneous literature that, besides shaping the way books were marketed and sold, could be given intellectual and aesthetic significance (whether positively or negatively) by critics such as Huet and the author of the 'Vindication'. Much new natural-philosophical literature of an experimental, therapeutic, or practical ilk was listed under this category alongside the *Essays*: various observations and discourses upon venereal disease; practical observations in surgery, with diverse remarkable cases and cures, approved with testimonials. In other catalogues, many of Robert Boyle's scientific essays were listed as 'Miscellanies'. Books of

---

[28] 'Huetiana', in *Gentleman's Magazine*, vol. 37 (December 1767), 579.
[29] Other categories such as 'Globes and maps', 'Architecture', and so forth, appeared more sporadically.

pedagogical exercises and conduct manuals tended to appear here: the school of manners; counsels, essays, and other miscellanies comprising a lawyer's advice to his son. There were also translated classical works that could not find a place under the more generic categories—Lucian's works, for example. Dialogues were also considered miscellaneous: a dialogue between sobriety and gluttony; modern dialogues in the Lucianic mode. And of course there were various essays, treatises, and tracts of an occasional or polemic nature: a treatise on improving the manufacture of English wool; a censorious essay on the sin of perjury.

Montaigne had a major rival in England at this moment as the figure who made aesthetic and literary sense of this category of books, a rival who, furthermore, made a different kind of sense of it. There is no evidence the Disraelis possessed a copy of Shaftesbury, though it is surely likely that they did. Isaac certainly had a copy of John Brown's 1751 *Essays on the Characteristics*, which attacked Shaftesbury for his slovenly and confused form of composition and for the randomness of his thoughts on revealed religion. Shaftesbury's apologia for his own work is to be found in volume three of the *Characteristics*, where he describes 'the ingenious way of MISCELLANEOUS *Writing*' in a broad and ambivalent fashion that hints at Huet's perspective even as it celebrates the mixed form.[30]

Miscellaneous writing is nothing less than the relaxation of the requirement for '*Regularity* and *Order*', of the 'strict *Laws* and *Rules* of Composition'. Previously, to earn the 'Name of AUTHOR' one had to write a treatise or poem according to the rules. But now, the 'way of MISCELLANY, or *common ESSAY*' was open, in which 'the most confus'd Head' might exert itself (II, 130–1). Although he does not name Montaigne here, Shaftesbury is referring to the Frenchman's achievement of giving the name of author to modern miscellaneous writers. But miscellaneity can inhabit any genre at any moment—it can crop up as a farce at the end of a grave French tragedy, or mix itself throughout an English tragicomedy. Shaftesbury describes himself in the first two volumes of his three-volume work as using more regular and formal kinds of subject and manner and laying them aside as he saw fit—again, using both veins in a single collection (II, 132).

In one of his reflections Shaftesbury reveals the grounds on which he differs from Montaigne, though again he does not mention the name. In his advice to authors he recommends that they distinguish completely between their private exercises and experimental practice and the more artful writings they should publish to the world. It is 'writers of MEMOIRS and ESSAYS' who are chiefly subject to the failure to make this distinction. Who could endure 'to hear *an Empiric* talk of his own Constitution, how he governs and manages it' as, we might

---

[30] Anthony Ashley Cooper, 3rd Earl of Shaftesbury, *Characteristicks of men, manners, opinions, times* [1711], ed. Philip Ayres, 2 vols (1999), II, 129. Further references given in the text.

add, Montaigne does in 'Of Experience'?[31] Shaftesbury thoroughly discourages the publication of all such exercises as come under the notion of this *self-discoursing Practice* (I, 90). His own notebooks, or journals of self-examination, remained, indeed, in manuscript. Shaftesbury thereby banished from the public sphere a whole vein of private memorial writing that had shaped the particular form of frank miscellaneity espoused by Montaigne. Temple similarly progressed from a more Montaigne-like vein in his early essays to the more polite form he espoused later. This suggests that Montaigne's specific brand of essay-miscellany was not as uniformly welcome in England as Hazlitt and others were later to state.

8. Contemporary Essays and Miscellanies in D'Israeli's Library

In D'Israeli's library we can find late eighteenth- and nineteenth-century works across the whole range of varied and miscellaneous literature in which the essay was still embedded. Many were entitled or contained sections entitled 'essays' or 'essais'. Some indicate the consolidation of a genre of short 'papers', derived from Addison and conceived as an illustrious achievement of an English national literature. At the more classical and didactic end of the genre were the *Essays moral and literary* of Vicesimus Knox, a headmaster and preacher, which grew from thirty-eight essays in the first, 1778 edition to 174 essays in the seventeenth edition of 1815. Originating in juvenile college exercises, they combine light treatments of literary topics with disquisitions on forms of moral sensibility.

Knox's oeuvre (not all of which is to be found in D'Israeli's library) identifies him not just as an essayist, but as a miscellanist in a longer European tradition of which he was very aware. Besides anthologies of 'elegant extracts' of prose and poety, and of 'elegant epistles', he also wrote the English vernacular imitation of Aulus Gellius's *Noctes atticae*, entitled *Winter Evenings*, that we encountered above. The chapter quoted earlier becomes, in the later, expanded editions, a Johnsonian critique of the extravagances and pretence into which miscellaneous, periodical literary culture had descended since *The Spectator*, and an argument for the plainer approach he is inclined to use: '[g]ood thoughts delivered in this miscellaneous manner [...] when the reader is not palled with attempts to please him by mere tricks' (I, 72).

Knox goes on to divide the readership for books into the 'professional, philosophical, and miscellaneous'. The first require 'regular and complete treatises'; the second (Bacons, Boyles, Lockes, and Newtons) must penetrate directly to the 'interiora rerum', without diversion. But he is concerned above all with 'miscellaneous readers', who are in the majority. They are socially mixed: 'of all

---

[31] For further discussion of this passage, see Chapter 3 in this volume by Kathryn Murphy, 87.

conditions, of the young and the old, the gentleman and the merchant, the soldier, the mariner, the subordinate practitioner in medicine and law, the philosopher and professor [...] in their leisure hours; and lastly, [...] the ladies'. Shall a merchant with a busy life and a taste for letters 'read folios and dry treatises, in the Aristotelian style and regularity'? Even if he wishes he could, he needs something for amusement, that he can comprehend in a short time, and relinquish without weariness: 'What so well adapted as an elegant miscellany?' (I, 74–6).

It turns out that such a miscellany is not without the sanction of ancient examples. Knox identifies all *Saturæ*, Seneca's *Epistles*, Plutarch's *Opuscula*, Horace's *Sermones*, the *Deipnosophistae* of Athenaeus (learned dinner conversations), Macrobius's *Saturnalia*, and even the *miscellanea* of grammarians as not 'systematical treatises' but 'popular essays' to please and improve the people at large (I, 77). Again, 'essay' is here used not to denote a precisely identifiable genre, but as a broad term for a tradition of varied and miscellaneous writing going back to antiquity.

If Knox gives us a neoclassical and elite perspective on this tradition, then another volume from D'Israeli's library can give us a more populist, vernacular perspective. Two years after the death of the antiquarian Francis Grose, a collection of his 'essays, dialogues, letters, biographical sketches, anecdotes, pieces of poetry, parodies, bon mots, epigrams, epitaphs, &c. chiefly original' was published. The title—whether chosen by the publisher or the author—was of the witty, invented kind first described by Gellius in relation to miscellanies: the 'Olio', meaning a mixed stew.[32] It had been used by Margaret Cavendish as a title to describe a collection of essays, and by Swift and Pope to denigrate the worst aspects of miscellaneous publications.

The Olio is particularly interesting for our purposes for two reasons. Firstly, because the publisher and editor betrays some anxiety that Grose may not have intended his manuscript 'medley' of collected notes to be published as a volume, as an authored miscellany. He is not sure in some cases whether the items are original or copied, and cannot be confident in his classifications of the various kinds of material. Sixteen of the essays, written in the manner of Addison as *The Grumbler*, had appeared serialized in the newspaper *The English Chronicle*, and then had been collected in a volume. But the rest had been found amongst his manuscript papers, the compiler's or writer's intentions unclear.

It is interesting, secondly, because the volume places the 'essay' once again in the broader environment of miscellaneous writings and notes that we have been describing throughout. Besides the items listed on the title-page there were 'observations on different subjects' and 'curious extracts'. The latter includes extracts from a parish register at East Dean, Sussex and 'an odd leaf in the

---

[32] Francis Grose, *The Olio* (1793).

possession of Mr Gostling', alongside another from John Ferne's *The Blazon of Gentrie* (1586). There are transcriptions, accounts, and stories Grose has written down from various sources, including some verses written by 'nearly an Idiot' living at Cirencester, a copy of a hand-bill stuck up in Dublin in 1784, and verses written on the breast of an emblematic figure of Gluttony attached to a public house in Cock Lane. This is a vernacular version of the humanist medley of the Renaissance.

Both Knox's and Grose's works—Knox's with high praise—appeared in another volume of *Essays* collected by D'Israeli: Nathan Drake's five-volume *Essays, biographical, critical, and historical*, illustrative both of the contents of the original *Tatler*, *Spectator*, and *Guardian*, and of the later periodical papers written in imitation of Steele and Addison, up to the year 1809.[33] Drake was central to the process of canonization of the distinctively English periodical essay that began in the 1790s. The short or loose paper was canonized as the transmitter of a tradition of civic and moral wisdom.[34]

Here we can continue to question the traditional account in which, *c.*1660, the French rejected Montaigne and the essay and the English welcomed both, assimilating them as natives. The genealogy Drake traces right up through Addison and Steele to Knox and Grose and co. is different from D'Israeli's in one detail that is particularly interesting for our purposes: his estimation of Montaigne. He goes back to Gellius's preface, and forward to the Italian conduct manuals of Castiglione and Della Casa, through Bacon's *Essays*, La Bruyère's *Characters* (in imitation of Theophrastus), Temple's *Miscellanea*, and Collier's *Essays*. But he is obliged to stop along the way to give us the reason he is not including the most compelling of all collections of essays—Montaigne's: '[h]e is too much of an egotist, and is too frequently unguarded and indecent in his expressions'.[35]

Not surprisingly, this English tradition is held to reach its apogee in Dr Johnson's *The Rambler*. One essay of nearly 400 pages is devoted to his literary life.[36] It was Johnson, of course, who in that very periodical identified Montaigne (without naming him) as the writer who had introduced the licentiousness of lyric poetry into short dissertations.[37] The result, according to Johnson, is that 'he therefore who wants skill to form a plan or diligence to pursue it, needs only entitle his performance an essay, to acquire the right of heaping together the collections of half his life, without order, coherence, or propriety', the three canons

[33] Nathan Drake, *Essays, biographical, critical and historical, illustrative of the Tatler, Spectator, and Guardian*, 3 vols (1805); Nathan Drake, *Essays, biographical, critical, and historical, illustrative of the Rambler, Adventurer, and Idler*, 2 vols (1809–10).

[34] Squibbs, *Urban Enlightenment*, 27–8.

[35] Drake, *Essays, biographical, critical and historical, illustrative of the Tatler, Spectator, and Guardian*, I, 29.

[36] Drake, *Essays, biographical, critical, and historical, illustrative of the Rambler, Adventurer, and Idler*, I, 111–488.

[37] See the discussion in the Introduction to this volume, 8.

of classical literary composition.[38] This is a hostile view of the precedent set by Montaigne's *Essais*: anyone thereafter could take their miscellaneous reading notes and observations of half a lifetime, lump them together, call the whole 'performance' an essay, and publish it as though they were a bona fide literary author.

Squibbs's study suggests that Drake was more typical—and more accurate—than D'Israeli, in downplaying the role of Montaigne, and playing up the role of the 'character' tradition, in the creation of the English periodical essay.[39] So, contrary to the literary-historical stereotype of a Montaigne embraced by the English and rejected by the French, we here find Montaigne written out of the essay tradition in England. Conversely, D'Israeli could have read admiring French accounts of the essayist in his collection, accounts which remind us that if the *Essais* were rejected in France, it was only by leading critics and publishers (he was still read there in older editions), and only for a short period.[40]

9. Conclusion

Montaigne gave a noble authorial persona and a licence to roam to the non-professional and miscellaneous reader-writer, thinker, and observer who did not wish closely to follow formal rhetorical or poetic rules, or to elaborate speculative systems: the Miscellanist, in short. But did he found a literary genre in the strict sense? An 'essay' genre was founded in England at the beginning of the eighteenth century—the loose periodical paper—but it was markedly different in material form, style, and purpose from a book (the *Essays*) of 1,000 pages that contained long and indecent chapters such as 'On Some Verses of Virgil'. The relationship of Montaigne's text to personal archival writing of a candid and self-revelatory kind was largely excluded from the English miscellany and essay tradition as defined by Addison, Shaftesbury, and Johnson. It was then recovered in miscellaneous writings of the English Romantics, including works that were not entitled 'Essays' (e.g. Lamb's 'Confessions of a Drunkard', De Quincey's *Confessions of an English Opium-Eater*, or Hazlitt's *Liber Amoris*).

Montaigne should be seen, then, as a unique, remarkable precedent for European and English miscellanists in general. Where professional humanists had written mixed collections of philological remarks in neo-Latin, he authorized, as a layman writing in the vernacular, a varied form of modern miscellaneous

---

[38]   Samuel Johnson, *The Rambler*, vols III–V of *The Yale Edition of the Works of Samuel Johnson*, ed. W. J. Bate and Albrecht B. Strauss (1969), V, 77 (No. 158).

[39]   Squibbs, *Urban Enlightenment*, 43–4.

[40]   One example is the *Mélanges tirés d'une grande bibliothèque*, of Paulmy d'Argenson and Contant d'Orville (1779–88), which contains an extended praise of the *Essais* as miscellaneous moral philosophy in vol. 15. D'Israeli had fifty-seven volumes of this work.

writing that centred on the qualities of the persona of the author rather than on puzzles arising from the texts of antiquity. He did this in the context of a very broad tradition of varied and miscellaneous writings that had developed in tandem with and in relation to the norms of the classical rhetorical, poetic, and philosophical traditions. When, between the nineteenth and twentieth centuries, the force and social reach of these norms waned, so did the sense of a complementary vein of less regular, more mixed, more varied—even confused—writing that could be found in and across a host of genres, including schoolroom exercises and treatises of various kinds. What was left standing in the twentieth century was a narrower understanding of the 'essay' as a single literary genre, alongside a vague sense that any piece of more informal writing or art could be considered 'essayistic'.

The history of the essay before 1800 should also be understood in relation to broader historical narratives, some of which have only been hinted at here. There is the history of cultural exchange and rivalry across the Channel, especially through the long eighteenth century of alternating war and peace that saw the Anglo-French inventions of the novel and the essay. There is the history of the slow transition from a pan-European world of learning dominated by Latin *litterae*, led by professional scholars, to a nation-based, vernacular world of belles-lettres, periodical culture, and natural-philosophical experiments. The latter world centrally included disseminators or 'public intellectuals' such as D'Israeli, who consciously mediated between expert knowledge and the tastes and experience of lay readers—readers who themselves extracted and compiled, recorded and experienced varied and miscellaneous things outside the contexts of traditional institutions and systems of learning and of public or professional offices. Their patron saint—if not always their precise literary model—was Michel de Montaigne.

3

Of Sticks and Stones

The Essay, Experience, and Experiment

Kathryn Murphy

1. Refuting and Refooting

On Saturday, 6 August 1763, as James Boswell faithfully reported, Samuel Johnson kicked a stone:

> After we came out of the church, we stood talking for some time together of Bishop Berkeley's ingenious sophistry to prove the non-existence of matter, and that every thing in the universe is merely ideal. I observed, that though we are satisfied his doctrine is not true, it is impossible to refute it. I never shall forget the alacrity with which Johnson answered, striking his foot with mighty force against a large stone, till he rebounded from it, 'I refute it *thus*.'[1]

Johnson's famous 'answer' rejects Berkeley both in a performance of obstinate frustration with apparently nonsensical philosophical speculation, and in an insistence on the brute persistence of matter despite such speculation, his throbbing toes manifesting to his satisfaction that the external world is real. Indeed an early spelling of 'refute' was 'refoot':[2] the kick is also a visual pun, and the rebounding foot, rejected by the rock, enacts dialectical refutation.

Like most puns, Johnson's kick is based on an insinuation of logical cogency through accidental similarity. His answer to Boswell and Berkeley is, as is well known, a bad argument, and no refutation at all: an example of the fallacy which logicians call *ignoratio elenchi*, in which a response is irrelevant to the terms of the proposition. It would cost Berkeley nothing to suggest that even Johnson's sensations are merely ideal. But this, of course, would not chasten Johnson, and is indeed his point: his emphatic '*thus*' parodies the logician's *ergo*, and suggests that the experience of frustration with metaphysical speculation, and the pain of a stubbed toe, are a form of persuasion prior to the formal claims of philosophy.

---

[1] James Boswell, *Life of Johnson* [1791], ed. G. Birkbeck Hill and L. F. Powell, 5 vols (1934), I, 471.
[2] See *OED s.v.* 'refute, *v.*'.

Kathryn Murphy, *Of Sticks and Stones: The Essay, Experience, and Experiment* In: *On Essays: Montaigne to the Present.*
Edited by: Thomas Karshan and Kathryn Murphy, Oxford University Press (2020). © Kathryn Murphy.
DOI: 10.1093/oso/9780198707868.003.0004

Though scandalous to the philosopher, Johnson's encounter with the stone belongs to a class of philosophical anecdotes which counter theory with embodied experience. In an ancient example, the philosopher Zeno of Citium is beating a servant for committing theft. The servant claims that he was compelled by fate to steal, and should not be punished for something beyond his control. Zeno responds that, since the same necessity of destiny is forcing him to beat the servant, he cannot desist. If the servant asks Zeno to stop, he contradicts his own argument by implying that Zeno has free-will; if he retains his principles of determinism, he must accept his beating as inevitable, and cease to resist. Or there is another ancient anecdote, retold by Owen Felltham in his essay 'Of Logick': 'When *Diogenes* heard *Zeno*, with subtle *Arguments*, proving that there was no *Motion*: he suddenly *starts up*, and *walks*. *Zeno* asks the *cause*? Saies he again, *I but confute your reasons.*'[3] Diogenes's action coined the phrase *solvitur ambulando*, 'it is proved by walking', or by practical experiment. Like Johnson's kick, these are logical fallacies. Zeno's beating is a complex version of the *argumentum ad baculum*, the argument of the stick, in which violence or a threat, rather than reason, persuades an opponent. But the failure to argue according to the canons of dialectic is the point of the anecdotes. Instead of a 'thus' and QED, they offer gesture. Zeno's application of the stick is both a supplanting of persuasion with violence, and an exposure of how physical experience counters the propositions of philosophy. Diogenes's refusal to speak is his response.

The literary essay shares with such anecdotes recurrent strains of imagery—the stone, the stick, and walking. Johnson himself is a prime example. The title of *The Rambler*, his twice-weekly periodical which housed 208 essays between 1750 and 1752, endorses the essay as an amble, while Leigh Hunt, in his essay 'Of Sticks', records three 'bacular anecdote[s]' concerning Johnson, in each of which a walking stick serves the double purpose of support and of physical threat to accompany verbal argument.[4] The name 'Isaac Bickerstaff', which Richard Steele borrowed from Jonathan Swift as the pseudonymous editor for the period-ical *The Tatler*, which ran from 1709 to 1711, suggests the argument of the stick in the surname, bickering by means of staffs. Recent critics have traced the literary stick in its essayistic habitat.[5] Walking, whether country rambling or city flânerie, is one of the essay's great themes, and often bears epistemological claims.[6] In Thoreau's 'Walking', perambulatory thinking is contrasted with book-learning:

[3] Owen Felltham, 'Of Logick', in *Resolves*, 8th edn (1661), 89. This is a different Zeno: Zeno of Elea.
[4] Emerson, however, doubted Johnson's walking prowess, writing in 'Country Life' that while 'Dr. Johnson said, "Few men know how to take a walk," [...] it is certain that Dr. Johnson was not one of the few'. See *The Later Lectures of Ralph Waldo Emerson, 1843–1871*, ed. Ronald A. Bosco and Joel Myerson, 2 vols (2001), II, 63.
[5] See Denise Gigante, 'Sometimes a Stick is Just a Stick: The Essay as (Organic) Form', *European Romantic Review* 21.5 (2010), 553–65, and Michael Caines, 'Stick and Stickability', *TLS* blog (20 June 2016), at http://timescolumns.typepad.com/stothard/2016/06/stick-and-stickability.html.
[6] On city walking, see Chapter 8 in this volume by Greg Dart.

'you must walk like a camel, which is said to be the only beast which ruminates when walking. When a traveller asked Wordsworth's servant to show him her master's study, she answered, "Here is his library, but his study is out of doors".'[7] The essayist Rebecca Solnit quotes Kierkegaard retailing Diogenes's *solvitur ambulando*, and endorses Husserl's idea that 'walking is the experience by which we understand our body in relationship to the world'.[8] The violence of the argument of the stick, meanwhile, and its association of pain with knowledge, recurs frequently. In Hazlitt, writing is fighting. 'There are two things that an Englishman understands,' he opens one essay: 'hard words and hard blows'.[9] Indeed, in his ideal pugilistic prose, '[e]very word should be a blow: every thought should instantly grapple with its fellow'.[10] The epigraph to his famous essay 'The Fight'—'The *fight*, the *fight's* the thing, / Wherein I'll catch the conscience of the king' (IX, 61)—implies that fisticuffs, like Hamlet's *Mousetrap*, have a heuristic purpose, and are revelatory not as discursive argument but through the experience of event. More recently, Leslie Jamison's *Empathy Exams*, which queries the communicability of suffering and the possibilities and limits of our capacity to experience what others feel, includes an essay which considers the symbolic and personal significance of a punch to the face.[11]

The persistence of these sticks, stones, and walks, the stuff of the assertion of physical sensation over theory, is part of the essay's perennial preoccupation with experience, rather than abstraction or metaphysics, as the ground of knowledge. John Locke's *An Essay Concerning Human Understanding* (1690), the foundational work of British empiricism, was at least by title an essay; David Hume, as Fred Parker discusses in this volume, was likewise an essayist.[12] American pragmatism, turning away from abstraction, rationalism, and idealism towards the practical effects of ideas, takes inspiration from Thoreau and Emerson; their centrality to Stanley Cavell continues the essayistic tradition in American philosophy. Theodor Adorno's 'The Essay as Form' opposes the essay to the 'academic guild' which 'accepts as philosophy only what is clothed in the dignity of the universal and enduring'; the essay, instead, takes 'individual human experience' as its version of 'objectivity'.[13]

This chapter grounds this long association of the essay with experience in the form's emergence in Montaigne and his English successors. Although Adorno

---

[7] Henry David Thoreau, *The Portable Thoreau*, ed. Jeffrey S. Cramer (2012), 560.

[8] Rebecca Solnit, *Wanderlust: A History of Walking* (2002), 27; more generally, 14–29.

[9] William Hazlitt, 'Jack Tars', in *The Fight and Other Writings*, ed. Tom Paulin and David Chandler (2000), 157.

[10] From 'On the Prose Style of Poets', in *The Selected Writings of William Hazlitt*, ed. Duncan Wu, 9 vols (1998), VIII, 8. Further references given in the text.

[11] Leslie Jamison, 'Morphology of the Hit', in *The Empathy Exams* (2014), 69–77.

[12] See Chapter 5.

[13] Theodor Adorno, 'The Essay as Form', in *Notes to Literature, Volume One*, ed. Rolf Tiedemann, trans. Shierry Weber Nicholsen (1991), 3–23, here 4, 8.

paints the essay as the locus of resistance to science and enlightenment, it is no accident that it arises at the same time as philosophical empiricism, nor that Francis Bacon was both the first to publish 'essays' in print in England, and the originator of experimental science. This origin, however, gives rise to paradoxes. Like Johnson, the essay substitutes pain, embodiment, and experience for theory, formality, and logic. But despite the gestures which supplant verbal argument and logical discourse in the anecdotes with which I began, the argument, as Montaigne says in a different context, is of words, and with words it is answered: we do not feel Johnson's pain, or Zeno's servant's, or witness Diogenes walking, but read about it. Thoreau's recommendation of the walk as rumination was doubtless written while sitting. The essayistic substitution of experience for theory relies on the conjuring of the felt experiences of others through words. The subject of this essay is the origin of these paradoxes in the earliest essayists and the epistemological shifts of the seventeenth century.

2. Montaigne's Stones

The word 'experience' had a range of early modern meanings. The most general was similar to modern usage—information gained by the senses, observation, or what one has personally undergone. A still prevalent sense, however, was equivalent to 'essay': '[t]he action of putting to the test; trial'; '[a] tentative procedure; an operation performed in order to ascertain or illustrate some truth'. 'Experiment' and 'experience' were synonymous. In philosophy, meanwhile, an 'experience' was a singular 'piece of experimental knowledge', some fact drawn not from theory or reasoning but from extrapolation of sensory information and repeated action, for example, in an Aristotelian example, that eating chicken is good for a cold.[14] In Aristotle's *Metaphysics* and *Nicomachean Ethics*, such experiences were a weak precursor to knowledge, an undertheorized miscellany of facts appropriate only for ad hoc action, the bricolage of the unlearned. But in the seventeenth century, as Aristotelian university philosophy was increasingly criticized, and observation and experiment played a greater role in natural philosophy, experience was revalued.[15]

For Montaigne to place 'Of Experience' in the capstone position as the final chapter of the final 1588 edition of the *Essais*, then, engaged directly with debates over the valorization of experience. The chapter begins with a generalization about

---

[14] See *OED s.v.* 'experience, *n.* 1a&b, 7b'.

[15] See the special issue *Between Experience and Experiment*, ed. Cécile Alduy and Roland Greene, *Republics of Letters* 2.1 (2010), and my 'Anxiety of Variety: Knowledge and Experience in Montaigne, Burton, and Bacon', in *Fictions of Knowledge: Fact, Evidence, Doubt*, ed. Yota Batsaki, Subha Mukherji, and Jan-Melissa Schramm (2011), 110–30.

the human condition: 'There is no desire more natural, than that of knowledge.'[16] This is a paraphrase of the first sentence of Aristotle's *Metaphysics*, which opens 'All men by nature desire to know'. For Aristotle, the intrinsically curious nature of mankind is demonstrated by the way that information gleaned by the senses is worked upon by reason to generate abstracted knowledge. For Montaigne, however, the same observation evolves into utter scepticism about the human capacity to abstract from the particular to the general. Though experience is 'much more weak and vile' than reason, reason often 'fails us' (599), and experience is the only reliable means of knowledge available to man. The teeming world of nature is so incorrigibly plural that experience is irreducible, and abstractions are thus founded on unacceptable elisions of difference and particularity, since 'No quality is so universal in this surface of things, as variety and diversity [...] Resemblance doth not so much make one, as difference maketh another' (604).[17] As a result, rather than following Aristotle by offering a treatise on the nature of being, the second half of 'Of Experience' is an account of the experience of being Montaigne. He presents his own particular case: observations on his regimen, on what, when, and how he eats, how he sleeps, defecates, has sex, prioritizing his embodied experience over generalization.

The details of regimen are offered to the reader not as instruction, or as fodder for their own abstract extrapolations: this is a register of experience on its own terms. 'I have lived long enough', he claims, 'to yield an account of the usage [*sc.* habits] that hath brought me to this day. If any be disposed to taste of it, as his taster I have given him an assay.' The last phrase reads in Montaigne's French 'j'en ay faict l'essay': literally, 'I have made him this essay'.[18] Though Florio's translation brings out the sense of 'essay' as a taster and metallurgical test of quality, he occludes the direct association of Montaigne's account of himself with the texts gathered together under the title of *Essais*. Florio is more faithful shortly afterwards, in his version of Montaigne's 'toute cette fricassée que je barbouille icy n'est qu'un registre des essais de ma vie': 'all this gallimaufry which I huddle-up here, is but a register of my lifes-Essayes' (608).[19] 'Essais de ma vie' might be translated as 'the experiments of my life'; Florio's 'lifes-Essayes', however, equates the experience of living with the chapters of Montaigne's book. The phrase applies at once to the unsystematic observations of Montaigne's regimen that constitute 'Of Experience', and to the volume as a whole: a gallimaufry, a heterogeneous, recipe-less stew, of the flavours of a lived life.

---

[16]   Michel de Montaigne, *Essayes*, trans. John Florio (1603), 599. Further references given in the text.
[17]   For further discussion, see my 'Montaigne, Robert Burton, and the Problem of Idiosyncrasy', in *Montaigne in Transit: Essays for Ian Maclean*, ed. Neil Kenny, Richard Scholar, and Wes Williams (2016), 223–38.
[18]   Montaigne, *Les Essais de Michel de Montaigne*, ed. Pierre Villey, 3 vols (1930–1), III, 593.
[19]   Montaigne, *Les Essais*, III, 590–1.

Montaigne's move from Aristotle to his own body enacts the period's epistemological shift, in which the humanist preoccupation both with ancient texts of moral philosophy, such as Cicero and Seneca, and with philosophy as subordinate to civic action, led to a mockery and suspicion of the technical logic and metaphysics of scholasticism. The gesture by which Montaigne supplants metaphysics with experience is thus common, but the intimacy of his account is not. This primacy of the individual is explicit: 'I study my self more than any other subject. It is my supernatural Metaphysic, it is my natural Philosophy.'[20] Though the chapter's title might give rise to the expectation of a treatise on the nature of experience, it contains an implicit possessive pronoun: of *my* experience, '*my* lifes-Essayes'. In this lies Montaigne's epistemological argument: there is no experience that is not, at root, *my* experience, and hence no knowing that is not inescapably grounded in the *ad hoc* and *ad hominem*. The essay thus makes the characteristic gesture identified in the anecdotes with which I began, countering metaphysics with bodily experience.

In Johnson's frustration with Berkeley, a stone acted as the mute repudiant of theory. The same recalcitrant object is a recurring preoccupation in the *Essais*, and serves the same purpose. Objecting to the Aristotelian definition taught in the universities, Montaigne uses a stone to complain of that system's infinite regress: 'A stone is a body: but he that should insist and urge; And what is a body? A substance: And what a substance? And so go-on: Should at last bring the respondent to his [...] wits' end.'[21] The more knowledge is abstracted from particulars, the less it is knowledge. A stone was the typical scholastic example of an inanimate corporeal substance, with which animate corporeal substances— men and animals—were contrasted. But Montaigne has an intimate relationship with the stone which makes it ideal for his assertion of experience over theory. He suffered painful manifestations of what he calls his 'gravel' or 'colic paroxysms': kidney stones in the urinary tract. This was the disease which had killed his father—appropriately, if coincidentally, named Pierre—and speculations on whether Montaigne might have inherited it are the starting point of the long essay 'Of the Resemblance of Children to their Fathers'. While 'Of Experience' directs its critique at the abridgements and generalizations of law, 'Of the Resemblance' takes the art of medicine to task, objecting to its claims to prescribe remedies apt to the infinite variety of human circumstance and unpredictable disease. In each, the unsystematized claims of experience are asserted as securer grounds. And in each, accounts of Montaigne's personal struggle with the stone are the crux.

At the beginning of 'Of the Resemblance', Montaigne tells us that the affliction emerged during the 'seven or eight years' (435) in which he had been composing

---

[20] Montaigne, 'Of Experience', in *Essayes*, 604.   [21] Montaigne, 'Of Experience', 636.

the *Essais*. The painful accretion of material within his body parallels the gestation of writing. The stone, like Johnson's stone or Zeno's stick, is a recalcitrant object which asserts a non-verbal argument. The stone is a 'hard, gritty, and massy body' (651) which the larger human body struggles to expel. Though its presence is internal, it is manifest not only to the sufferer, but in visible symptoms:

> Thou art seen to sweat with labour, to grow pale and wan, to wax red, to quake and tremble, to cast and vomit blood, to endure strange contractions, to brook convulsions, to trill down brackish and great tears, to make thick, muddy, black, bloody and fearful urine, or to have it stopped by some sharp or rugged stone, which pricketh and cruelly wringeth the neck of the yard [*sc.* penis][.]   (649–50)

Unlike other diseases, in which diagnosis is troublesome due to 'the uncertainty of their causes, conditions, and progresses', the stone has a 'peculiar commodity': 'it is an infirmity, wherein we have but little to divine. [...] We have no need of doctoral consultations, or collegial interpretations. Our senses tell us where it is, and what it is' (651–2). No need of theory, or the symptom-reading of medical art. The stone is immediately available to the senses, a self-evident token of experience.

Yet the stone has other purposes for Montaigne: not only a confirmation of the primacy of the lived experience of the body, but also an opportunity for verbal elaboration and speculation. In 'Of Experience', the stone is the subject of a long passage in which Montaigne offers 'specious arguments' about its meaning, as an example of the inventiveness of his wit in response to the most unpromising subject. In 'Of the Resemblance', Montaigne notes that he has already 'had trial of five or six long and painful fits of [the stone]' (435). The French verb—'[j]'en ay desjà essayé'—makes clear again the connection between his affliction and his experimental writing.

Prime among the lessons Montaigne derives is an opportunity for the practice of Stoic endurance. He claims that 'it is for my good, that I am troubled with the gravel'. Moreover, '[i]t is an evil that comes and falls into those limbs, by, and with which thou hast most offended' (649): that is to say, the penis. Elsewhere in the *Essais*, the penis is emblematic of a fundamental paradox of embodiment:

> All men know by experience, there be some parts of our bodies, which often without any consent of ours, do stir, stand and lie down again. Now these passions, which but exteriorly touch us, can not properly be termed ours; For, to make them ours, a man must wholly be engaged unto them: And the pains that our feet or hands feel whilst we sleep, are not ours.   (218)

As in 'Of Experience', Montaigne begins with a statement of something true for 'all men' (though not of course for women)—indeed, something known by experience. This supposedly universal truth, however, is related to the most intimate of sensations: the involuntary motions of the penis, demonstrating that bodies are animated by impersonal passions beyond the will. Yet in 'On Some Verses of Vergil', which, despite its title, is largely about sexual intimacy, and especially about penises and their disobedient tendencies, Montaigne writes: 'Each of my pieces [sc. members] are equally mine, one as another: and no other doth more properly make me a man than this. My whole portraiture I universally owe unto the world' (532). Having a penis, moved by desire or excruciated by the stone, is at once the most proper of experiences and the most improper, the most personal and the least. It thus encapsulates a central paradox of the *Essais* as a whole, which are at once absolutely insistent on the idiosyncrasy of their portrait of a single man, and recognized, repeatedly, as a testament to human universality.

This paradox of the common and the idiosyncratic is also raised by the stone in 'Of the Resemblance'. There, the fact that Montaigne, but none of his siblings, inherited the stone from his father is the cause of the title:

> What monster [sc. wonder] is it, that this tear or drop of seed [sc. semen], whereof we are engendered, brings with it [...] the impressions, not only of the corporal form, but even of the very thoughts and inclinations of our fathers? Where doth this drop of water contain or lodge this infinite number of forms? And how bear they these resemblances, of so rash, and unruly a progress, that the child's child shall be answerable to his grandfather, and the nephew to his uncle?   (437)

The questions complicate the idiosyncrasy of experience so significant to the *Essais* as a whole: how can the irreducible facts of bodily experience, and still more bafflingly, apparently individual opinions, desires, thoughts, in fact be a matter of transmission and replication? How can the apparent accidents of the individual turn out to be shared?

Montaigne's struggle with the stone can be extrapolated to two more general paradoxes of the essayistic tradition. The first, the question of transmission of thoughts and inclinations, is also articulable as an issue of literary genre and human genus. Montaigne's experimental writings, characterized by variety and idiosyncrasy, nonetheless spawned imitations and answerable forms, recognizable descendants. The essay's presentation of personal idiosyncrasy is simultaneously concerned with what is common, and readers consistently testify to finding themselves in Montaigne's self-portrait.[22]

---

[22] e.g. Pascal: 'Ce n'est pas dans Montaigne, c'est dans moi que je trouve tout ce que j'y vois'; Emerson: 'I remember the delight and wonder in which I lived with them. It seemed to me as if I had myself written the book, in some former life, so sincerely it spoke to my thought and experience' ('Montaigne; or, The Skeptic', in *Representative Men* [1850], vol. IV in *The Collected Works of Ralph Waldo Emerson*, ed. Wallace E. Williams (1987), 92).

The second paradox relates to the efficacy of arguments of sticks and stones. The emblematic nature of the stone rests, for Montaigne, in the undeniable extremity of pain, which reminds him that he is material and mortal. Yet in being made subject of the witty elaborations and moral sententiae of 'Of the Resemblance' and 'Of Experience', the stone, and Montaigne's writing of it, become subject to the fundamental problem of the communicability of personal experience. Elaine Scarry, in *The Body in Pain*, observes that 'to have great pain is to have certainty; to hear that another person has pain is to have doubt'.[23] Pain is at once the least deniable, and the most incommunicable, of experiences. It reduces the suffering body to inarticulate utterance: to screams, groans, and cries. Montaigne exploits the radical disjunction between the sufferer and the observer, and between the voice of one in pain and a description of it. Immediately after the passage from 'Of Experience' quoted above, in which he describes the blood, sweat, and tears of the stone, Montaigne (speaking of himself in the second person), insists that during this exhibition of symptom, he

> entertain[s . . .] the by-standers with an ordinary and undaunted countenance, by pauses jesting and by intermissions dallying with thy servants: keeping a part in a continued discourse; with words now and then excusing thy grief, and abating thy painful sufferance.   (650)

The spectacle of the suffering Stoic, macerated by pain and simultaneously in a state of calm or jest, was a great emulative idol of Montaigne and the Renaissance more generally, in figures such as Seneca the Younger, Theremenes, or Socrates. Montaigne's behaviour here is a version of such indifference. Yet it also exacerbates the problem identified by Scarry. Verbal 'continued discourse' is a register at odds with blood and groans. For Virginia Woolf, 'the poverty of the language' available for the depiction of pain limits possibilities of expressing the body's experience: the sufferer is 'forced to coin words himself, and, taking his pain in one hand, and a lump of pure sound in the other [. . .], so to crush them together that a brand new word in the end drops out'. We thus need 'a new language [. . .] more primitive, more sensual, more obscene'.[24] For Emerson, Montaigne had already invented that language: he writes of the *Essais* that '[t]he sincerity and marrow of the man reaches to his sentences. [. . .] Cut these words, and they would bleed; they are vascular and alive.'[25] Woolf's 'On Being Ill', strangely, does not mention Montaigne, but in harking after a writing which testifies to the 'daily drama of the body' (101), the personal essay to which he gave rise is surely conceived as its

---

[23] Elaine Scarry, *The Body in Pain* (1985), 7.
[24] Virginia Woolf, 'On Being Ill', in *The Essays of Virginia Woolf*, vol. IV, ed. Andrew McNeillie (1994), 318–9.
[25] Emerson, 'Montaigne', 95.

proper lodging. Prompted by resistance to the metaphysical abstractions of Aristotle, Montaigne gives rise to the tradition of the essay as the testament to the intimate sensations of the body.

3. Bacon's Experimental Discussions

The essay's foregrounding of personal experience, and especially pain, prompts problems which are at once ethical and aesthetic, for writer and reader: the tendency to voyeurism or appropriation in making someone else's pain your entertainment, perfectly captured in the ambivalent senses of the first word in Susan Sontag's title *Regarding the Pain of Others*.[26] It may also trespass on good taste. A disdain for Montaignian self-exposure animated the third Earl of Shaftesbury—himself a writer of informal and conversational prose, and one essay, in the *Characteristicks*. Shaftesbury objected to the 'frothy Distemper' to which 'Writers of Memoirs and Essays', who 'entertain the World so lavishly with what relates to *themselves*', are subject:

> they [...] exhibit on the Stage of the World that *Practice*, which they should have kept to themselves; [...] Who indeed can endure to hear *an Empiric* talk of his own Constitution, how he governs and manages it, what Diet agrees best with it, and what his Practice is with himself? The Proverb, no doubt, is very just, *Physician cure thy-self*. Yet methinks one should have but an ill time, to be present at these bodily Operations. Nor is the Reader in truth any better entertained, when he is obliged to assist at the experimental Discussions of his practising Author, who all the while is in reality doing no better, than taking his Physic in public.[27]

Exposing bodily operations is the whole stuff of 'Of Experience'; for Shaftesbury, this makes Montaigne an 'Empiric', a mountebank or quacksalver who elevates experience over learning. Shaftesbury's phrase 'experimental Discussions' is telling, associating the Montaignian essay with the new practices of scientific experiment, particularly prominent after the foundation of the Royal Society in 1660. Contemporary book titles show that 'essay' could refer to both literary form and epistemological practice. Robert Boyle's *Essays of the strange subtilty, determinate nature, great efficacy of effluviums* (1671), for example, encompasses both the experimental testing of streams of invisible particles, and the textual description of their strange properties.

---

[26] Susan Sontag, *Regarding the Pain of Others* (2003).
[27] Anthony Ashley Cooper, 3rd Earl of Shaftesbury, 'Advice to an Author', in *Characteristicks of men, manners, opinions [...]*, 3 vols (1711), I, 163.

Francis Bacon, figurehead of the emergence of experimental philosophy, was also the first person in England to publish works entitled 'essays'. Bacon's choice of the word for his *Essays or Counsels, Civil and Moral,* given their lack of resemblance to Montaigne's *Essais,* is an apparent puzzle. The differences are immediately manifest. Bacon's style is compressed and lacks digression. His essays are directed at action, not the retirement of the Montaignian library. Idiosyncrasy of voice and confession is avoided. Indeed, in 'Of Wisdom for a Man's Self', self-centredness is explicitly abjured: 'It is a poor centre of a man's actions, *himself.* It is right earth. For that only stands fast upon his own centre; whereas all things that have affinity with the *heavens,* move upon the centre of another, which they benefit.' For Bacon idiosyncrasy is, continuing the astronomical metaphor, 'eccentric': a propulsion of energy away from 'the ends of his master or state'.[28] Instead, Bacon's *Essays* use an impersonal tone and a patrician 'we' which elides idiosyncrasy while assuming a compact of identity between gentlemanly writer and readers.

The differences nonetheless conceal an equal commitment to the essay as a genre of experience. In the dedication to the manuscript presented to Prince Henry in 1611 or 1612, Bacon wrote of his essays that, 'although they handle those things wherein both men's lives and their pens are most conversant, yet [...] I have endeavoured to make them not vulgar; but of a nature whereof a man shall find much in experience, little in books.'[29] This is a book which strives not to be a book: Bacon commits his essays to a performative contradiction, akin to the retailed anecdote of Johnson's stone.

The problem emerges from the contemporary range of meaning of 'experience'. Bacon plays on the distinction between experience as knowledge based on probative experiment or observation, and the technical sense of philosophy, in which 'an experience' is the result of elaboration and generalization of such observations. The topics of his essays, Bacon claims, are familiar matters commonly addressed in writing, yet rarely with the wisdom which emerges from deliberation on such common experience. 'Of Studies' considers the uses and abuses of book learning. Different fields of learning, Bacon writes, 'perfect nature, and are perfected by experience: for natural abilities are like natural plants, that need proyning by study: and studies themselves do give forth directions too much at large, except they be bounded in by experience' (439). What emerges is a complex reciprocity of the meanings of experience. Nature supplies individual and personal experiences, which are various, 'vulgar' (that is, common), and undisciplined. Thus while 'expert [etymologically "experienced"] men can execute, and perhaps judge of

---

[28] Francis Bacon, *Essays or Counsels, Civil and Moral* [1625], in *Francis Bacon: The Major Works,* ed. Brian Vickers (1996, 2008), 386. The image relies on geocentrism: the earth stands still while the heavens rotate around it. Further references given in the text.

[29] Bacon, *The Essayes or Counsels, Civill and Morall* [1625], ed. Michael Kiernan (Oxford, 2000), 317.

particulars, one by one; [...] the general counsels, and the plots, and marshalling of affairs, come best from those that are learned' (439), since learning abstracts from such particulars. But study alone, book-learning, is too general, 'too much at large': it requires the curbing of experience to yoke it to particulars, and allow prudent action. Bacon's essays are thus presented as the result of this oscillating motion: experiential observation, the garnerings of the particular lived life, 'proyned' or pruned by study and thus divested of their idiosyncrasy, but then tempered again by experience to become apt weighing of circumstance, and counsel to action.

The figure of 'a man', who appears in Bacon's description of the essays to Prince Henry, is thus crucial. This 'man' is singular, but not specified and idiosyncratic. Montaigne's chapter 'Of Repenting' opens 'Others fashion [*forment*] man, I repeat [*recite*] him; and represent a particular one' (483). For Bacon, however, the subject of the essay is not particular. The distinction is clear in 'Of Regiment of Health', whose title identifies it with the same concerns of Montaigne's 'Of Experience' and 'Of the Resemblance'. It begins 'There is a wisdom in this, beyond the rules of physic: a man's own observation, what he finds good of, and what he finds hurt of, is the best physic to preserve health' (403–4). In kernel, this articulates Montaigne's argument: one's 'empiric' observation of one's own idiosyncrasy, in the technical sense of unique humoral constitution and circumstances, is better than the general rules and remedies of physicians. But the essay develops not into an account of Bacon's own regimen, but into general precepts of moderation appropriate for any individual. The first person appears three times: twice ventriloquizing the generalized voice of 'a man'—as in '"This agreeth not well with me, therefore I will not continue it"' (404)—and once as a precept: 'I commend rather some diet for certain seasons, than frequent use of physic' (404). Bacon makes the epistemological argument of Shaftesbury's despised 'Empiric', and of Montaigne's *Essais*—that experience and observation are the best ground of practice in physic—while resisting the 'frothy distemper' that would make him take his own medicine in public.

Bacon thus shares with Montaigne the prioritization of experience, but experience schooled and cooled into the impersonal. This is of a piece with his wider epistemological preoccupations. The abandonment of experience was, for Bacon, the cardinal error of contemporary knowledge, since 'men have withdrawn themselves too much from [...] the observations of experience: and have tumbled up and down in their own reason and conceits' (146).[30] The biases attendant on language and reliance on authority are deemed by Bacon 'Idols' of the mind, which his iconoclastic method will demolish.[31] This of course exacerbates the

---

[30] From *The Advancement of Learning*, Book I.
[31] See Bacon, *New Organon* 1.39, in James Spedding, Robert Leslie Ellis, and Douglas Denon Heath (eds), *The Works of Francis Bacon*, 14 vols (1861–79), IV, 53.

performative contradiction: how to write, how to communicate experience, with-out simply reinstantiating the problem? Bacon continually experimented with forms which might render experience without making it dogmatic. He tended to short forms. In the *Advancement of Learning*, he recommended aphorisms for scientific writing because they

> cannot be made but of the pith and heart of sciences: for discourse of illustration is cut off; recitals of examples are cut off; discourse of connexion and order is cut off; descriptions of practice are cut off; so there remaineth nothing to fill the Aphorisms but some good quantity of observation: [. . .] Aphorisms, represent-ing a knowledge broken, do invite men to enquire farther.   (234)

Aphorisms are deliberately unsatisfying, partial, inviting the reader's participa-tion: a provocation to thought. A similar process is at work in Bacon's posthu-mous *Sylva Sylvarum*, an assembly of 1,000 'experiments' (which might thus equally be titled 'experiences', or 'essays'): short texts which discuss not just trials of nature, but notes from reading (from travel books, on coffee; or the ancient belief that 'it is dangerous to pick one's ear whilst he yawneth'); anecdotes about teeth set on edge by the sound of a saw, prophetic dreams, or the peculiar resonance of rooms in Cambridge; curiosities like chameleons or a petrified egg; or banalities, like the evaporation of breath from a window-pane, or sugar glittering when scraped with a knife.[32] All of these are offered to the reader as invitations to seek after the causes of things, and to augment the offered experiment with experience of their own.

The aphorism and experiment, then, deliver experience not as knowledge already established, but instead make the short form itself an experience for the reader. Rather than separating the realms of 'experience' and 'books', Bacon strives to make books experiential. In the 1624 Latin expansion of the *Advancement of Learning*, Bacon distinguished between two ways of delivering knowledge: while the '*Magistral*' method requires the reader's faith in the author's knowledge and authority, the '*Initiative*' 'discloseth and unveils the Mysteries of Knowledges'.[33] The reader of the initiative method enacts the processes by which the author came to know: in reading, he emulates the process of discovery. '*Magistral teacheth, Initiative insinuateth*', Bacon declares, in an echo of a claim in Montaigne's 'Of Repenting': 'I teach not; I report' (484).

It might be objected that, though Bacon's experiments might be initiative, his *Essays* seem magistral. This, however, relies on a passive readerly stance which ignores the implications of the word 'essay', its call for a reader willing to test and weigh. In entitling the final edition *The Essays or Counsels*, Bacon implies a

---

[32] Bacon, *Sylva Sylvarum*, in Spedding et al. (eds), *The Works of Francis Bacon*, II, 553.
[33] Bacon, *Of the advancement and proficience of learning*, trans. Gilbert Wats (1640), 272.

relationship between the terms, which gives special significance to the essay 'Of Counsel'. Counsel hovers between the initiative and magistral modes. On the one hand, it is an assertion of what prudent action would be. On the other, it does not pretend to teach: it is submitted to the judgement of the one counselled. Action will emerge not from blind obedience to its assertions, but from deliberation on them. Matters must be 'tossed upon the arguments of counsel' (379), trialled, tested, and assayed. '[P]rinces', in seeking counsel, 'may extract and select' (380). They use counsel as a touchstone, without necessarily revealing their own purposes, and derive it from multiple sources. Moreover, since 'books will speak plain when counsellors blanch [. . .] it is good to be conversant in them, specially the books of such as themselves have been actors upon the stage' (382): books of counsel are thus literate experience, experience delivered in letters.

Bacon's final version of the essays opened with a newly written essay 'Of Truth', which began with a redolent question: '"What is Truth?" said jesting Pilate; and would not stay for an answer' (341). The context is the questioning of Jesus after his arrest, in other words an interrogation, a trial, an assay. Here, however, it is the 'jesting' interrogator who is weighed and found wanting, in abandoning his question without investigation, in his exasperation at the obliquity of Jesus's replies, in his failure to weigh and wonder in assessing truth. The lesson for the reader is that their own exactions of meaning must be probative, unsatisfied with broken knowledge, willing to experience and experiment.

4. Boyle's Vicarious Experience

Despite his apparent deviation from Montaigne's model, then, Bacon recognized in the essay an apt register for experience and experiment. The alliance of his essays and natural philosophical work, however, raises difficulties for literary histories of the genre. The problem is particularly stark in Adorno's 'The Essay as Form', in which Bacon's twin role as essayist and figurehead of scientific enlightenment is something of an embarrassment. Bacon inaugurates precisely the projects of reason and scientific method that Adorno needs the essay to resist. In the *Dialectic of Enlightenment* Bacon is the father of the 'disaster triumphant' of the 'fully enlightened earth', bequeathing false idols of objectivity and 'the impartiality of scientific language' which disembody the human relationship to objects and other beings.[34] Adorno sees the essay as a locus of resistance more generally to the epistemological canons emergent in the seventeenth century, arguing that the essay 'might be interpreted as a protest against the four rules established by Descartes' *Discourse on Method* at the beginning of modern Western science

[34] Theodor Adorno and Max Horkheimer, *Dialectic of Enlightenment*, trans. John Cumming (German 1944; English 1997; reprinted 2008), 3 and 23.

and its theory', 'challeng[ing] the ideal of *clara et distincta perceptio* and indub-
itable certainty' (14). This is partly a matter of style: the essay, Adorno writes, 'is
related to rhetoric, which the scientific mentality has wanted to get rid of since
Bacon and Descartes' (20). Adorno only acknowledges the paradox in a paren-
thetical aside, in an assertion of the essay's 'critique of system' which keeps Bacon
the target of that critique: 'Since Bacon—himself an essayist—empiricism has been
as much a "method" as rationalism. In the realm of thought it is virtually the essay
alone that has successfully raised doubts about the absolute privilege of method'
(9). Bacon, then, is at once inaugurator of the English essay, and the enemy of its
experiential epistemology.

The paradox is starker in an author whom Adorno does not mention, but who
wrote the seventeenth century's most detailed theoretical account of the essay's
epistemological work: the chemist Robert Boyle. Boyle demonstrated himself an
apt reader of Bacon in his *Christian Virtuoso*, a work which argued for the
compatibility of experimental philosophy with theology. Far from seducing the
experimenter into atheism, he argues, experiments 'dispose a studious Searcher of
Truth [...] for Theology', because they require a searching examination of
experience, rather than a sensualist's pursuit of further stimulating experiences:

> the greater part of the Libertines we have among us, being Men of *Pilate*'s
> humour, (who, when he had scornfully ask'd *what is truth?* would not stay for
> an Answer) do, with great Fastidiousness, decline the Study of all Truths that
> require a Serious and Settled application of Mind.[35]

Boyle approves Bacon's oscillation between experience, study, and the further
tempering of experience, and takes 'Of Truth' as his touchstone: the libertine's
skittish refusal to dwell in difficulty and reflect on experience, 'go[ing] no further
than the Outside of things, without penetrating into the Recesses of them',
engenders a permanently broken knowledge, since truth is discovered 'not only
by Serious Meditation, but by intricate and laborious Experiments' (49).

The opposition of experience and writing in Bacon's dedication to Prince
Henry troubled Boyle more explicitly. If scientific method relies on experience
and witness, on rejecting authority and taking no man's word for it, what role can
writing play? How can someone else's account of an experiment be trusted, if true
experience is unmediated? *Christian Virtuoso* is alert to this problem, not least
because Boyle wants to make claims about the rationality of believing in the Bible,
unverifiable by experience. Boyle's manoeuvre is to acknowledge that 'the word
Experience may admit of diverse Senses'. The more 'restrained acceptation' sees

---

[35] Robert Boyle, *The Christian Virtuoso* (1690), 47–8.

experience as information gained by the senses. More broadly, however, it is understood

> in contra-distinction to *Reason*, so as to comprehend, not only those *Phænomena* that Nature or Art exhibits to our Outward Senses, but those things that we perceive to pass Within our selves; and all those ways of Information, whereby we attain any Knowledge that we do not owe to abstracted *Reason*.

Thus Boyle distinguishes between '*Immediate* and *Vicarious* Experience'. '*Immediate* Experience', also called '*Personal Experience*', 'Man acquires [...] without the Intervention of any external Testimony'. Vicarious experience divides into '*Historical*, and *Supernatural*'. The latter is truth received by revelation. The former is of most relevance here: 'By *Historical Experience*, I mean that, which tho' it were personal in some Other man, is but by his Relation or Testimony, whether immediately or mediately, conveyed to us' (53–6). The introduction of this category allows the experimentally minded man, for whom knowledge must come from observation, to claim others' experience as his own. This has been called 'virtual witnessing', part of the 'literary technology' of the new science.[36] It also has implications for the essay form.

This is confirmed in the 'Proemial Essay [...] with considerations touching Experimental Essays in General' prefacing one of Boyle's earliest natural philoso-phical works. It explained why he 'cast [his experiments] into Essays, rather than into any other form'.[37] His first justification is their resistance to system. The totalizing claims of the old natural philosophy lead to redundancy and the suppression of local observations, particular to circumstance. In that 'form of Writing which (in imitation of the French) we call Essays', however,

> the Reader needs not be clogg'd with tedious Repetitions of what others have said already, so the Writer, having for the most part the Liberty to leave off when he pleases, is not oblig'd to take upon him to teach others what himself does not understand, nor to write of any thing but of what he thinks he can write well.   (9)

It is striking that Boyle's reasons for praising essays are shared by Adorno, 300 years later. For Adorno, the essay 'starts not with Adam and Eve but with what it wants to talk about; it says what occurs to it in that context and stops when it feels finished rather than when there is nothing to say' (4). As in Boyle, the essay is the privileged site of resistance to system:

---

[36] Steven Shapin, 'Pump and Circumstance: Robert Boyle's Literary Technology', *Social Studies of Science* 14.4 (1984), 481–520.

[37] Boyle, 'A Proemial Essay [...]', in *Certain Physiological Essays* (1661), 3. The essay is discussed at length in Scott Black, *Of Essays and Reading in Early Modern Britain* (2006), 67–85.

In the realm of thought it is virtually the essay alone that has successfully raised doubts about the absolute privilege of method. The essay [...] is radical in its non-radicalism, in refraining from any reduction to a principle, in its accentuation of the partial against the total, in its fragmentary character.   (9)

Bacon and Boyle praise and deploy precisely those characteristics of the essay to which Adorno deems them opposed.

Boyle also, like Bacon, sets the essay in opposition to bookishness. He chooses a 'philosophical rather than a rhetorical strain', because 'to affect needless Rhetorical Ornaments in setting down an Experiment [...] were little less improper than it were [...] to paint the Eye-glasses of a Telescope' (11). This suggests that the essay is just a tool, best at presenting its object when it is so perspicuous it cannot be seen. This runs against the non-instrumental notion of the 'literary essay' discussed in the Introduction to this volume, and rinses the essay's lens of the personal colouring which typifies Montaigne. It also seems to confirm Adorno's objection to the supposed anti-rhetoric of science. But there is more here:

> though a Philosopher need not be solicitous that his style should delight his Reader with its Floridness, yet I think he may very well be allow'd to take a Care that it disgust not his Reader by its Flatness [...] though it were foolish to colour or enamel upon the glasses of Telescopes, yet to gild or otherwise embellish the Tubes of them, may render them more acceptable to the Users.   (12)

Boyle's point is minimal: a little honey on the rim of the cup makes medicine more palatable, and a bored reader may welcome a little embellishment to retain and focus their attention. There is, however, a richer possibility. Seventeenth-century telescopes were often bound in leather and tooled in gold leaf, like books. Telescopes were not just for looking through, but for looking at. Boyle's experimental essay can be viewed either as an instrument through which experience can be seen, or as an experience in its own right. Adorno objected to the ways in which dogma is founded on 'the imputation of immediacy to something mediated'; the idea that writing *about* something presents it without also showing its embeddedness in the writer's experience, and in the circumstances of its historical situation (10). For Boyle and Bacon, the fantasy of an unmediated writing, of the cleansed lens of the telescope, is asserted, but simultaneously subverted by the ways in which the essay draws attention to its own manoeuvres of mediation.

This returns us to Shaftesbury's objection to the essayist's frothy distemper. Shaftesbury figured the relationship between reader and essayist as an overly intimate encounter between strangers, in which one performs and the other looks pruriently on. But in Montaigne, Bacon, and Boyle, the relationship is different. If the reader is assumed to be looking *through* the essay, they are being invited not to watch someone having an experience, but to have it themselves. And if they are looking *at* the essay—if, as Montaigne suggests, they are offered the essay as an assay, as something to taste—then the essay is that experience. As Adorno says, the essayist 'does not actually think but rather makes himself into an arena for intellectual experience' (13). The relationship of writer and reader is not, here, contra Shaftesbury, voyeuristic. Instead, the essay is a space for cognitive emulation, for vicarious experience.

5. Conclusion

Adorno's definition of the essay by what it is not—not method, not science, not Bacon—relies then on a misunderstanding of the intimate relationship at the essay's origins with experiment. This was an understanding still available to Hazlitt, writing of 'that sort of writing which has been so successfully cultivated in this country by our periodical Essayists', which he saw to be 'in morals and manners what the experimental is in natural philosophy, as opposed to the dogmatical method' (V, 84).[38] In Bacon and Boyle, the impulse to write essays was congruent with the impulse to perform experiments, and both were, like Montaigne, part of the period's elevation of the epistemological value of experience over the abstractions of metaphysics.

The central preoccupation of the early modern essay with experience and experiment, however, also gave rise to some of the genre's most characteristic conundrums and paradoxes: how to mediate immediate experience, how to render idiosyncrasy common and communicable, how to resist bookishness and dogmatism in a literary genre. The essay shares the paradoxes with which I opened: the pains of the stone (kicked or urinary), the experience of walking, the undeniable fact of a blow all insist on their irrefutable material witness, but are only available to others through reading, through the proxy witness of anecdote and description. What the essay makes available can only be vicarious experience.

Some resolution is suggested in the typical arc of what we might call the essay of experience. As we have seen, Montaigne's epistemological pessimism at the opening 'Of Experience' is salved by a turn to the recounting of himself. Emerson's essay 'Experience' begins by lamenting the maplessness of our encounters with the world and our limited experience of it: 'Where do we find ourselves? In a series, of which we do not know the extremes, and believe that it has none. We wake and find ourselves on a stair: there are stairs below us, which we seem to have ascended; there are stairs above us, many a one, which go upward and out of

---

[38] From 'On the Periodical Essayists'.

sight.'[39] But it ends in a celebration of the possibilities of expansion and a process of perfecting in the succession and fragmentariness of experience. Mark Greif's 'The Concept of Experience' opens with the irreducible particularity of each individual life, the impossibility of having all available experiences, as a tragedy: the 'condition [which] conspire[s] to make life intolerable'. But it then offers a balm in the sharing of vicarious experience, which 'open[s] a door into the inside feeling of somebody else's life', and in the lives of those who 'take a large proportion of their experience from books'. 'Serious reading', he writes, 'often starts from a deep frustration with living',[40] but ultimately leads to a return to living 'deliberately', attending to mundane experience as offering aesthetic opportunity.

Such essays move from an assertion of the inadequacy of experience, its epistemological uncertainties and limitations, to a celebration of variety, changeableness, and partiality as a more authentic kind of knowledge. In this they echo Montaigne. Despite their manifest differences, each of Montaigne, Bacon, Boyle, and their later followers, demonstrate that the essay might be considered not just a substitute for experience and a solace for its inadequacy, but an experience in itself. The essay, from its beginnings to the present, acts at once as a challenge to and a confirmation of one's own experience, an encounter with another and an encounter with one's self. Like Johnson kicking the stone, the essayist and the reader seek a proving confirmation of the reality of the external world. Also like Johnson, however, the encounter proves not that reality, but the vividness of the reader's own experience of reading. The essay leaves us in a constant oscillation between realism and idealism, between the common and the idiosyncratic, between, as Bacon suggested, experience, literary study, and experience.

---

[39] Emerson, 'Experience', in *Essays, Second Series* [1844], vol. III in *The Collected Works of Ralph Waldo Emerson*, ed. Joseph Slater (1984), 27.

[40] Mark Greif, 'The Concept of Experience' [2005], in *Against Everything* (2016), 77–95, here 77, 82, 85.

4

Time and the Essay

The Spectator and Diurnal Form

Markman Ellis

1. Introduction

The Spectator was for nearly two centuries after its publication the most famous example of the essay in the English language.[1] Most unusually for an essay periodical—a form in which an essay, buffered only by a few advertisements, comprised the entirety of a regular publication—it was published daily, Sundays excepted. It ran for 555 numbers between 1 March 1711 and 6 December 1712, with a further eighty numbers in a continuation in 1714. Written mostly by Joseph Addison and Richard Steele, who were responsible for more than 500 of the essays, and assisted by a group of friends, almost every piece was nonetheless ascribed to the fictional editor, Mr Spectator, whose character was described in the first number.[2] The essays were a collaborative writing enterprise, in which Mr Spectator's opinions and prose supposedly floated free of the individual and idiosyncratic thoughts and style of his specific authors.

The Spectator's historical significance is now thought to lie in its contribution to the 'culture of improvement', which championed a new paradigm of politeness and civility in literature and society through the entertaining and accessible format of the essay.[3] In *The Spectator* No. 10, Addison suggested his plan was to make philosophy urbane:

> It was said of Socrates, that he brought Philosophy down from Heaven, to inhabit among Men, and I shall be ambitious to have it said of me, that I have brought

---

[1] Previous versions of this chapter were presented at colloquia at Queen Mary University of London and the University of Queensland, and I am grateful for the advice of those present. Special thanks to Rebecca Beasley, Sophie Butler, Richard Coulton, Mark Currie, Simon During, Thomas Karshan, Kathryn Murphy, Eric Parisot, Joad Raymond, Chris Reid, and Richard Yeo.

[2] Joseph Addison and Richard Steele, *The Spectator*, ed. Donald F. Bond, 5 vols (1965). In his 'Introduction' (I, xlii–lix), Bond gives details of the contributions of different authors. Further references given in the text.

[3] Peter Borsay, 'The Culture of Improvement', in *The Eighteenth Century*, ed. Paul Langford (2002), 189. See also Lawrence E. Klein, *Shaftesbury and the Culture of Politeness: Moral Discourse and Cultural Politics in Early Eighteenth-Century England* (1994), 3–14. See also this volume, Chapter 5 by Fred Parker.

Markman Ellis, *Time and the Essay:* The Spectator *and Diurnal Form* In: *On Essays: Montaigne to the Present.* Edited by: Thomas Karshan and Kathryn Murphy, Oxford University Press (2020). © Markman Ellis.
DOI: 10.1093/oso/9780198707868.003.0005

Philosophy out of Closets and Libraries, Schools and Colleges, to dwell in Clubs
and Assemblies, at Tea-Tables and in Coffee-houses.   (I, 44)

In these four places, Addison and Steele found a model for the new polite
refinement they sought to study, emulate, and inculcate, and evidence for the
spirit of civility and community underpinning a harmonious society balanced
between mutual trust and self-reliance. This chapter explores a different aspect of
The Spectator essay's modernity: its relationship to time. In its diurnal production,
and reception, *The Spectator* approximated the temporality of a newspaper—even
though diurnal publication was a recent innovation, and something only a few
newspapers managed in the early eighteenth century. Most newspapers and
periodicals were published regularly, but only two or three times a week. *The
Daily Courant*, founded in 1702, was the first British daily newspaper. *The
Spectator's* daily publication thus connected it to a journalistic modernity, related
but different to the civic modernity of its promotion of the reform of manners and
politeness.

Before writing this chapter, I conducted an experiment by reading one number
of *The Spectator* each day, approximately matching the date of production (publication) with the date of consumption (reading), albeit with an interval of nearly
three centuries. Beginning in March 2010, more or less 299 years after *The
Spectator* first appeared, I read one paper a day, Sundays excepted, until
December 2011, with essay No. 555, first published on 6 December 1712. Of
course, I had 'read' *The Spectator* before, but in a non-sequential and intermittent
manner. As a student, I read the most important essays as directed by my teachers,
selectively and out of sequence, in an anthology that usefully gave each essay a
summary title. I read the essays on aesthetics for one class, those on social reform
for another, and those on the essay and satire for yet another. I was guided by
thematically organized edited collections.[4] In later research I preferred to use
Donald F. Bond's magisterial five-volume edition for the Clarendon Press, using
its extensive index to find essays on topics in which I was interested (such as taste,
coffee, tea, or wigs). The edition I read each day was the handy complete *Spectator*,
published in four volumes in 1907 by Everyman.[5]

When I told others of my *Spectator*-a-day plan, some reacted with incredulity,
as if it was a form of 'extreme reading'—like that of the journalist who recently
read all the books on an arbitrarily-chosen library shelf.[6] Yet reading *The Spectator*
in order and in daily doses was what Addison and Steele had envisioned.
My purpose was to experience *The Spectator* as it was prepared. This was not

---

[4] Erin Mackie (ed.), *The Commerce of Everyday Life: Selections from the Tatler and the Spectator*
(1998); Angus Ross (ed.), *Selections from the Tatler and the Spectator of Steele and Addison* (1982).
[5] G. Gregory Smith (ed.), *The Spectator*, 4 vols (1950).
[6] Phyllis Rose, *The Shelf: From LEQ to LES: Adventures in Extreme Reading* (2014).

an attempt to recapture the reading experience of the early eighteenth century—which would not be possible for numerous historical reasons. But I hoped at least that I would be able to draw some conclusions about how the diurnal pattern affected *The Spectator*'s production and consumption, and what daily publication—or indeed any chronologically determined repetition—adds to the reader's experience. The chapter pursues this aim by exploring *The Spectator*'s own discourse on the essay form, contextualizing this in relation to its status as a material text, first read in single sheets. As a diurnal periodical, each essay is an adventure in thought located in a particular chronological relationship with the others, but heading off in a new and unanticipated direction. The *Spectator*-a-day experiment reiterated to me that the essay form expects and tolerates this sense of the adventurous sally of thought, but also holds it in tension with material that is intellectually systematic and ambitious.

2. *The Spectator* and the Essay Form

The description of *The Spectator* as an 'essay periodical' identifies several innovations of which it is the type, if not the inventor. As Robert DeMaria has argued:

> In the periodical essay proper several characteristics come together more or less in concert: regular and frequent appearance (daily, ideally); presentation of a particular point of view, often "spoken" by a literary persona or a related group of personae; correspondence with readers (either fictional or real); domination of the periodical by the essay and, ideally, complete identification of the two.

These features, he says, 'combine perfectly' in *The Spectator*—'and perhaps in the six-day a week *Spectator* only'.[7] But although *The Spectator* is the type of the 'essay periodical', the term 'periodical' was not used in this sense until later in the eighteenth century. When Mr Spectator refers to his own production, he calls it a 'Paper' (as in No. 363 (26 April 1712), III, 362), or more disparagingly, a 'Penny Paper' (No. 124 (23 July 1711), I, 506). The term 'paper' had, from the 1690s, been used to identify a journal or newspaper, of which a 'Penny Paper' was a cheap form.[8] As the newspaper evolved in the seventeenth century, it printed discrete and miscellaneous pieces of news information, identified by date and place. As such, it had no enduring association with the prose genre of the essay, although

---

[7] Robert DeMaria, Jr, 'The Eighteenth-Century Periodical Essay', in *The Cambridge History of Literature 1660–1780*, ed. John Richetti (2010), 527–48, here 528.

[8] *The Spectator* cost a penny for the first 445 numbers, until the Stamp Act (10 Anne, cap. 19) levying a half-penny duty on paper was introduced on 1 August 1712, when the price was raised to two pennies.

later periodicals, such as Dunton's *Athenian Mercury* or Defoe's *Review*, included some essayistic prose. The essay in the form practised by Montaigne or Shaftesbury was not associated with newspapers and periodicals, but rather with elite and gentlemanly forms of distribution and dissemination, including both scribal and print publication. In this sense, *The Spectator*'s important innovation of the daily essay periodical presented a contradiction: a penny paper (vulgar, disposable), in which readers found an essay (polite, elite, worth pondering at length).

Embedded in *The Spectator*'s 555 essays is an extended discourse on the essay form. In paper No. 124 (23 July 1711) Addison investigates the intellectual project of *The Spectator*, which, he argues, uses the essay to set knowledge free from the constraints of academic scholarship and pedantry. Mr Spectator contrasts the periodical writer, who 'communicates his Writings to the World in loose Tracts and single Pieces', with the 'Man who publishes his Works in a Volume'. Those 'Bulky Authors', Mr Spectator continues, wrap their thoughts in preambles, verbiage, and windy expressions, and give little attention to style, so that their writing is full of repetitions, tautologies, and enlargements. By contrast, the essay writers, 'who publish their Thoughts in distinct Sheets, and as it were by Piece-meal' must immediately fall into their subject, and adopt a lively manner of expression, if the paper is not to be condemned as dull and thrown away (I, 505–6). Matter must be close together and concise, making a virtue of novelty by being wholly new in itself or its expression. Essays tolerate loose constructions, broken hints, and irregular sketches, but a good essayist, he says, should develop argument, like a treatise in a short compass, and use humour to touch on essential aspects of the topic.

Addison also suggests that while the 'bulky authors' of tracts and volumes are 'bound up in Books and kept in Libraries and Retirements', where they are inaccessible to all but the scholar and pedant, the essayist in penny papers was read by forty or fifty thousand readers. Because of this wide public, Addison suggests that the essay writer's vocation should be philosophical and moral:

> Our common Prints would be of great Use were they thus calculated to diffuse good Sense through the Bulk of a People, to clear up their Understandings, animate their Minds with Virtue, dissipate the Sorrows of a heavy Heart, or unbend the Mind from its more severe Employments with innocent Amusements.

In this way, a periodical like *The Spectator* uses the essay form to 'obtrude', or forcibly offer, knowledge to 'the Public', where it is 'canvassed in every Assembly, and exposed upon every Table' (I, 507).

The Spectator's discourse on the essay continued in No. 249 (15 December 1711), where Addison follows the Montaignian tradition by praising the creative looseness allowed by the essay form: without order or method, the writer has freedom and liberty to pursue his subject in whatever manner is appropriate:

> When I make Choice of a Subject that has not been treated on by others, I throw together my Reflections on it without any Order or Method, so that they may appear rather in the Looseness and Freedom of an Essay, than in the Regularity of a Set Discourse.   (II, 465)

Addison defended this notion several times: in No. 219 (10 November 1711), he described his compositional method as loose and unconsidered, without an attempt to 'Methodise' (II, 351).[9] In No. 476 (5 September 1712), Mr Spectator declares that:

> Among my Daily-Papers which I bestow on the Public, there are some which are written with Regularity and Method, and others that run out into the Wildness of those Compositions which go by the Names of *Essays*.   (IV, 185)

Addison draws a distinction between irregular and methodical essays. Those of a methodical construction have a regularity achieved, he says, when the writer has the whole scheme of discourse in mind before writing. Cicero and Aristotle are the models here. He characterizes their approach using a metaphor from gardening: the methodical essay is like a 'regular Plantation' with ordered paths from which long views of 'Lines and Walks' can be observed from 'Centres', so that the 'Eye commands the whole Prospect, and gives you such an Idea of it, as is not easily worn out of the Memory'. The comparison is with the formal landscape garden. The more irregular papers or essays, however, present several thoughts on a subject, not ranged in order, that seem to grow out of one another. Seneca and Montaigne are the models of the irregular writer, whose essays are likened to a wild 'wood' abounding in 'noble objects' arranged in 'confusion and disorder', allowing one to 'ramble' all day continually discovering new things, but leaving one with a 'confused imperfect notion of the place' (IV, 186). There is little doubt that it is the Montaignian wild landscape which gains Addison's approval.

In No. 435 (19 July 1712), Addison offered a further distinction according to subject, between 'more Serious Essays and Discourses', on philosophical topics 'for ever fixed and immutable' which 'never vary', and 'Speculations': 'Occasional Papers, that take their Rise from the Folly, Extravagance, and Caprice of the present Age', concerning 'Contingent Subjects' that change according to fashion, so that readers in the future will have no notion of what they were about ('Posterity will scarce have a sufficient Idea of them, to relish those Discourses

---

[9] See *OED*, *s.v.* 'methodize, v., 1a': 'To reduce to method or order; to arrange (thoughts, ideas, expression, etc.) in an orderly or systematic manner'.

which were in no little Vogue at the time when they were written'). As a satirist, Mr Spectator observes and ridicules every 'absurd Fashion, ridiculous Custom, or affected form of Speech', even if these topics might appear to some to be beneath his attention (IV, 27). He recalls his attacks on the swelling petticoat, on beauty patches worn to indicate party faction, on coloured hoods, in previous essays (numbers 81, 127 and 265). Here, he goes on to attack one of the new 'Female Extravagancies', which is to ride a horse in a hat, periwig, and riding coat, in imitation of men's apparel, a form of gender confusion that, he suggests, indicates greater moral corruption (IV, 28). Such essays take their lead from contemporary follies, and, as such, are victim to the logic of fashion, destined to rapid irrelevance. These topics, it would seem, can have no perennial value or interest, as the particular folly cannot be expected to last. But rather than becoming simply ephemeral, such papers retain the reader's interest, both for their higher satire on fashion and consumption, and for the detail of quotidian trivia.

In Addison's identification of *The Spectator* as a daily 'Penny Paper', he was aware and prepared to make light of its similarity to low and vulgar literary forms like the newspaper. One avenue for this was speculation about *The Spectator's* place within contemporary print culture. In *The Spectator* No. 367 (1 May 1712), Addison noted the public benefits of his moral argument, as readers' 'Minds are either improved or delighted by these my daily Labours'. But he also noted the 'Material' 'Benefits', that 'arise to the Public from these my Speculations, as they consume a considerable quantity of our Paper Manufacture, employ our Artisans in Printing, and find Business for great Numbers of Indigent Persons' (III, 379). After considering the origin of the paper used in printing (most of it was recycled from rags and used paper, ironically including old newspapers), Mr Spectator reiterated how in this material sense *The Spectator* was much like any newspaper, simply paper imprinted with ink, or as he says 'stained with News or Politicks'. Mr Spectator thus reiterates the continuity between his paper and the wider culture of newspapers, naming *The Post-Man*, *The Post-Boy*, *The Daily-Courant*, *The Review*, *The Medley*, and *The Examiner*. They are all embedded in the same commercial system, and are even distributed by the same newspaper sellers: 'Men, Women, and Children contend who shall be the first Bearers of them, and get their daily Sustenance by spreading them.' Mr Spectator then pauses to consider the numbers employed by *The Spectator* as it progresses from a bundle of rags to a 'Quire of Spectators', supplying employment for many people in the print and newspaper distribution trades ('providing Bread for a Multitude')—though also reminding readers of the collective nature of periodical essay writing (III, 380). A witty tailpiece to the essay imagines what happens to the papers after they are read. Mr Spectator does not imagine that they will be bound up or preserved, but rather, that their fate is to be recycled for quotidian purposes, such as a touch paper to light a pipe, as wrapping for an ounce of spice, or to line the tin of a mutton pie (III, 381). 'Papers' are just paper, and as such, they have value in material culture, in addition to their value as moral philosophy. Addison makes a double point: as a material object, each diurnal essay is ephemeral, and it is most likely that it will be disposed of or recycled; at the same time, though located in a single day, each essay also reaches beyond these limits towards moral and philosophical argument.

3. Reading Daily, Daily Reading

The Spectator's diurnal form afforded it a peculiar tincture, setting it apart from its competitors and predecessors in essay writing, and placing it in continuity, competitive or complementary, with the newspapers. In the first essay, Mr Spectator explains to the reader his intention to 'publish a Sheet full of Thoughts every Morning, for the Benefit of my Contemporaries' (I, 5). Each day's essay was printed on both sides of a folio half sheet, with two columns to each page, and advertisements taking up part of the second page, stretching or shrinking in number in response to the difference in length between the essays. Essay writing was a discipline bounded by space and time.

Mr Spectator also imagines the consumption of his essays as having a chronological and a spatial dimension. In No. 10, Addison imagines *The Spectator* ushering philosophy from the closed scholarly world of closets and libraries, schools and colleges into a new life dwelling in clubs and assemblies, at tea-tables and coffee-houses. These places of sociable reading and debate, the coffee-house and tea-table especially, he imagines within the temporal nexus of the morning:

> I would therefore in a very particular Manner recommend these my Speculations to all well-regulated Families, that set apart an Hour in every Morning for Tea and Bread and Butter; and would earnestly advise them for their Good to order this Paper to be punctually served up, and to be looked upon as a Part of the Tea Equipage.   (I, 44–5)

The Spectator, Addison proposes, should be so common an aspect of everyday routine as to be considered part of the tea-things and a complementary part of the social act of tea consumption. He returns to the scene of the morning tea-table at least twelve more times in *The Spectator*.[10] Readers too situated their reading at tea: John Gay proposed to himself 'the highest Satisfaction, in Reading it [...] over a Dish of Tea, every Morning next Winter'.[11] This zone of domestic and

---

[10] See Nos. 92 (I, 389); 140 (II, 55); 158 (II, 119); 212 (II, 328–30); 216 (II, 342); 246 (II, 454); 276 (II, 575); 300 (III, 73); 323 (III, 182–4); 395 (III, 482); 488 (IV, 231); 536 (IV, 412); 606 (V, 71).

[11] John Gay, *The present state of wit, in a letter to a friend in the country* (1711), 21–2.

feminized politeness is of course important within Mr Spectator's arguments for the gendered transformation of manners. But the essay's regular morning location also reinforces the fact that *The Spectator* is invested in the lived experience of every day. The quotidian is not simply a question of the public sphere of private individuals, to adopt Habermasian phrasing, but also a temporal relationship: reading an essay a day takes about as much time as a cup of tea takes to drink.

The demands of the daily production of the essay fell more heavily on the writers and publishers than the readers. Contemporaries were amazed that Addison and Steele could keep up the pace. One critic, announcing himself in *A Spy upon The Spectator* (1711), referred disparagingly to their '*Daily Burthern of Speculations*'—and wrote that 'I hope Gentlemen who have time upon their Hands will not grudge throwing away a quarter of an hour in a Day reading this Paper'.[12] John Gay, in his survey of periodical publications, *The Present State of Wit* (1711), commented on the daunting obligation set by the writers on themselves. Would they be able to keep up the pace and maintain the quality? Gay said:

> We had at first indeed no manner of Notion, how a Diurnal paper could be continu'd in the Spirit and Stile of our present *Spectators*; but to our no small Surprise, we find them still rising upon us, and can only wonder from whence so Prodigious a Run of Wit and Learning can proceed.[13]

As Gay recognized, the composition of the essays, even if shared between two authors, was a prodigious work of writing.

The diurnal nature of the paper posed production problems, too. The popularity of *The Tatler*, which had been published three times a week, every other day, meant that two printing presses were used to print each issue: a solution that meant setting the type more than once, and by so doing, increasing the cost and complexity of production. With the daily production of the *The Spectator*, as Donald Bond has shown, the difficulties of printing capacity were only increased. The solution was to use two printing houses, each of which was responsible for alternate issues: Samuel Buckley at the sign of the Dolphin in Little Britain, and Jacob Tonson in Chancery Lane.[14] This further divorced *The Spectator* from the news agenda, as each printer was given two days to print sufficient copies from one setting of the type. This solution was only really viable for a paper with no 'news'. This means that *The Spectator*'s avoidance of up-to-date and novel information was structural as much as it was political or philosophical. Some groups of essays were in fact written well in advance, to be used by the printer when needed.

---

[12] *A Spy upon The Spectator: Part I* (1711), iii, 24.   [13] Gay, *The present state of wit*, 19.

[14] Bond, 'Introduction', in *The Spectator*, I, xxi–ii.

The eleven essays on the 'Pleasures of the Imagination' (Nos. 411–21, 21 June–3 July 1712), for example, are thought to have been written years earlier.

Diurnal production at once focused the essay on everyday life, and encouraged it to avoid commentary on matters of state or the political agenda of Westminster, unlike competitors like Daniel Defoe's twice-weekly *The Review* (1703–14). This suited *The Spectator*'s own stated agenda, to reform philosophy and morals, both through didactic intervention and gentle satire. To be focused on the follies of everyday life was of course to have a political aim, but it was not that of the politicians. The technical impediment to newsworthy essays reinforced Mr Spectator's claims to political impartiality, as when he noticed, in the first number, that he was 'resolved to observe an exact Neutrality between the Whigs and Tories' (I, 5).[15] Later, in No. 16, he observed 'as I am very sensible my Paper would lose its whole Effect, should it run into the Outrages of a Party, I shall take Care to keep it clear of everything which looks that Way' (I, 72–3).[16] *The Spectator* found a large and ready audience for its medley of moral and satirical essays that addressed both quotidian folly and moral philosophy. Popular success and daily publication, however, reinforced the technical and material problems of printing enough copies in a single day, and so, somewhat counter-intuitively, almost guaranteed the exclusion from the paper of the diurnal news of politics and affairs of state.

4. Reading *The Spectator* Papers

My experiment of reading one essay of *The Spectator* a day clarified and revealed certain aspects of the diurnal essay. As a reading experience, it reinforced *The Spectator*'s miscellaneity in topic and form. A week in June 1711 had essays on women wearing cosmetic patches on their faces as a sign of party allegiance; on the kind of man who falls into debt; a dream comparison between living artists and the great masters (Raphael, Titian); an essay against duelling; on the odd places that interesting printed text can be found, such as under a pie or in the lining of a hatbox; and finally, on the system and rules of physiognomy and its opposite, the inclination to take against someone for their appearance, identified in the essay as '*Prosopolepsia*' (Nos. 81–6, 2–8 June 1711 (I, 346–69)). As this parade of topics shows, apparent diversity is to some extent subsumed in *The Spectator*'s wider satirical and moral argument about the reform of society. But it would be wrong to overlook how miscellaneous and varied the offering was, and how important that sense of the unexpected is in the diurnal reading of *The Spectator*: there is no way to predict the topic of the next day's essay. This extends to the different prose forms adopted by the essays, as they variously make use of letters, allegories,

---

[15] *The Spectator* No. 1 (1 March 1711).   [16] *The Spectator* No. 16 (19 March 1711).

fables, treatise-like sententiousness, poetry, and fiction. Indeed, one comes to expect, and value, the unexpected change in topic, tone, and form between essays.

As the variety of the essays suggests, they have a distinctive, open-ended quality. An important aspect is that sense of adventure implied by the etymology from the French *essai*, a trial or test. An essay is an excursion in thought, an away-day that ventures forth in unexpected directions. Johnson caught this well in his second definition of an essay as 'A loose sally of the mind; an irregular indigested piece; not a regular and orderly composition'.[17] Brian Lennon has celebrated that aspect in his own essay, 'The Essay, in Theory': 'The essay *is*, in this sense [...] nonchalant, inconsistent, digressive, flexible, personal, subjective, humanistic, tolerant, dynamic, voluptuous', and as such, contrasted with its 'systemic other', the academic article or treatise, which is 'serious, invariant, rigid, impersonal, objective, scientistic, dogmatic, static, ascetic'.[18] The loose sally of the essay as a form is both an internal structure, and, in the case of *The Spectator*, an effect produced by the location of the essay in the context of its neighbours, which together make sallies and digressions across a whole spectrum of thought.

But in reading *The Spectator* diurnally, the reader also begins to discern patterns and eddies in the flow of unconnected papers. The paper has both circadian and infradian rhythms: cycles which last a day or longer than a day. The circadian rhythm of the paper is established by its daily production; beyond this, *The Spectator* also establishes higher-order chrono-bibliographical effects. The papers have a weekly rhythm imposed on them by their Sunday break, a pause that reinforces the rhythmic production of the essays, and acts as a kind of exhalation of collective breath. This is reinforced by Addison's sense that the Saturday papers were themselves more serious, pious, and philosophical, an occasion for moral reflection at the week's end—so that the chronological rhythm also possessed a moral aspect. One Saturday paper (No. 513, 18 October 1712) draws attention to 'the very serious Nature' of the topics addressed on that day, as on others in this hebdomadal location (IV, 320). In addition, there is a subtle alignment of the essays with the seasons, both meteorologically and metaphorically. At one level this is explicit. A paper on the erotic potentialities of May was published in late April ('the Month of May [...] infuses a kindly Warmth into the Earth and all its Inhabitants', III, 371–2).[19] The series of essays depicting Mr Spectator's summer sojourn with Sir Roger de Coverley in the country, celebrating the various delights of a rural summer, were published in July, at the height of summer (Nos. 106–32, 2 July–1 August 1711 (II, 439–512 and III, 1–25)). Other references to meteorology and times of the year, such as to ice and snow—boys skating on the ice in No. 263 (1 January 1712)—reinforce this seasonal synchronism.

[17]   Samuel Johnson, *A Dictionary of the English Language* (1755), n.p.
[18]   Brian Lennon, 'The Essay, in Theory', *diacritics* 38.3 (Fall 2008), 71–92, here 71.
[19]   *The Spectator* No. 365 (29 April 1712).

Further large-scale narrative structures emerge or crystalize as the diurnal progress continues. One of these emerges out of the meetings of Mr Spectator's sociable club, which is imaginatively assembled repeatedly but irregularly. The summer holiday with Sir Roger de Coverley sustains a more concentrated narrative. There are also several series which exhibit a connected argument, such as the sequence of Saturday essays on Milton, a substantial book-by-book analysis of *Paradise Lost*, undertaken over eighteen weeks in 1712; or the eleven consecutive papers on 'The Pleasures of the Imagination' in the same year. More sporadically, many papers note their relation to earlier papers on similar topics, establishing a system of call and response, following up topics and suggestions. In these various ways, then, *The Spectator* created longer chronological structures within the daily sequence of papers.

The publication in folio half sheets caused some material problems. The *Spy upon The Spectator* observed, 'Upon my coming to Town a Friend lent me a huge bundle of Papers, which bore the Title of *Spectators*, and it seems has for some time been publish'd *daily*.'[20] Purchasing the essays by the sheet was not only cumbersome but also expensive, at a penny a paper. Mr Spectator commented: 'My Speculations, when they are sold single, like Cherries upon the Stick, are Delights for the Rich and Wealthy' (IV, 231–2).[21] Nonetheless, *The Spectator* sold in large numbers: in No. 10 (12 March 1711), Mr Spectator estimated that the papers sold 3,000 copies, and modern editors estimate some individual numbers sold in much higher quantities, rising to 20,000 (I, 44).[22] Nonetheless, comparatively few copies have survived. Complete runs of *The Spectator* are rare. There are eleven known extant copies of complete or near complete runs of the first daily edition of *The Spectator*—of which six were consulted in preparation for this chapter (two each in the British Library, in Oxford, and in Los Angeles).[23]

These bound volumes of the single daily papers provide some material evidence about their readers, and the place of the essay in their everyday life. In imagining his reader, Mr Spectator placed the scene of reading according to gender: for men, at the coffee-house table: for women, amidst the family in the morning, reading the paper with their tea and bread and butter. There is a certain amount of evidence in the surviving copies, from the marks left on them, that these places were indeed the location for reading. Some of these marks are what might be

---

[20] Gay, *The present state of wit*, 5.   [21] *The Spectator* No. 488 (19 September 1712).

[22] Bond, 'Introduction', in *The Spectator*, I, xxvi.

[23] The ESTC lists volumes at the following libraries: British Library (two complete runs and one partial); Trinity College, Cambridge; Columbia University; Eton College Library (incomplete Nos. 1–447); Huntington Library; New York Public Library; Bodleian Library (one complete run and one partial); Magdalen College, Oxford (long but incomplete run from Nos. 1–280). In addition, not listed on the ESTC, are copies at the William Andrews Clark Memorial Library at UCLA (a complete run, but not listed on their catalogue) and The Spencer Research Library at the University of Kansas (two copies, one complete 1–635, and one near complete 7–553), from the Collection of Richmond P. and Marjorie N. Bond.

called orthodox marginalia, comprising manuscript commentary or observations, in ink and pencil. Ownership inscriptions comprise some of these marginal annotations, while others seem closer to commentary, speculative comments, and drafts for unassociated compositions. Ink and pencil are also used to leave doodles, smudges, and scribbles. These are commonly not connected with the text of the paper, including flourishes and other exercises of penmanship, scribbles, sums of addition, especially of financial transactions. Marginalia and scribble both suggest that the place of reading is close to the place of writing. But other marks suggest that reading happened in the context of a diverse range of social and bodily practices. Marks made by spills and splashes of fluid (such as, one imagines, of coffee, tea, wine, or beer), as well as miscellaneous oily or buttery smudges, suggest that the place of reading is also close to the place of consumption. In addition, rips, tears, and burn marks remind scholars that these pieces of paper were not highly valued.

An essay in *The Connoisseur* in 1754, an imitation of *The Spectator* written by George Colman and others, imagined a variety of misreading and 'rude treatments' suffered by the material text of the essays after their 'first appearance in a sheet and a half'. When Mr Town, the fictional editor, finds his essays preserved in a file in a coffee-house, he attempts to judge the reception they have met with from the evidence left upon them by their readers.

> I have considered every speck of dirt as a mark of reputation, and have assumed to myself applause from the spilling of coffee or the print of a greasy thumb. In a word, I look upon each paper, when torn and sullied by frequent handling, as an old soldier battered in the service, and covered with honourable scars.

He is concerned to note all the ways his essays have been mistreated. He describes how he found some 'foul proofs' of his essay being used as toilet paper by his printer; some 'supernumerary sheets' being used as a thread-paper by the wife of his publisher; and one paper defaced by a young fellow in the 'blank margin' with a 'filthy list of foul shirts and dirty stockings'. This causes him to draw conclusions about the fate of single sheet publications:

> The repeated abuses of illiterate bakers, pastry-cooks, and chandlers I know I am condemned to suffer in common with other mortal writers. It was ever their privilege to prey indiscriminately on all authors good or bad: and as politicians, wits, freethinkers, and divines, may have their dust mingled in the same piece of ground, so may their works be jumbled together in the lining of the same trunk or band-box.[24]

---

[24] George Colman, *The Connoisseur. By Mr Town, critic and censor-general*, 2 vols (1755–6), 'No. XXIX. Thursday, August 15, 1754', I, 174–9.

In noting these quotidian repurposings, *The Connoisseur* deprecates vulgar misreadings, but also celebrates the diverse range of readers and readings. Colman's essay takes its hint from Mr Spectator's own paper on 'accidental reading', in which he describes the curious enjoyment to be met with from printed texts encountered in unexpected places, such as 'under a *Christmas* Pie', wrapped around a candle, in the lining of a hat box, or pasted onto a kite (I, 361).[25]

The surviving half-folio essays also give some more direct hints about who were their first readers. One paper in the library of Magdalen College, Oxford indicates it was owned by 'Roger Cocke', or 'Cooke', about whom nothing else is known.[26] Another, in the Bodleian Library, has a manuscript ownership inscription of Walsingham Beasley, who was a brewer in St John's Street, Clerkenwell when he died in 1759.[27] Another is inscribed 'For Mr Gougis at ye figure of ye flower de luce / In Corn Hill', perhaps indicating it was subscribed to by a City apothecary.[28] One set of *Spectators*, now in the Spencer Research Library in Kansas, was collected by John Shales, who had been the keeper of John's Coffee House in St Martin's Lane, where he acquired the copies, and subsequently bound them up. Later, in 1747, when Shales had become a messenger or secretary in the Office of Taxes, his bound copy was acquired by Henry Entwisle, who noted this story on a paper pasted into the front end-paper of the volume.[29] These owners and collectors are all men in the middle stations of life, prosperous, enterprising, commercially minded, but not members of the cultural or political elite. The provenance evidence, if such this is, supports the claims made in *The Spectator* about the diversity of men to which it was addressed.

5. Repackaging Daily Papers

After the first few months, many readers did not encounter *The Spectator* in its diurnal half-folio format, but in the octavo and quarto volumes that collected together chronologically determined sets of essays. After first publication in sheets, *The Spectator* was repackaged in various forms, each of which altered

---

[25] *The Spectator* No. 85 (7 June 1711).

[26] 'E Libris Rogeri Cocke', MSS marginalia, *The Spectator* No. 1, 1 March 1711, Magdalen College Library, Oxford, pressmark: Magd.Addison-J. (SPE) 1711 (fol.), No. 1.

[27] Ink autograph signature, twice (once effaced), once in title, 'Walsingham Beasley', *The Spectator* No. 1 (1 March 1711), Bodleian Library Oxford, pressmark: Bodleian Hope fol.88. 'Walsingham Beazley, esq.': death notice, *Gentleman's Magazine*, 3 December 1759.

[28] MSS ink endorsed above title 'For Mr. Gougis at ye figure of ye flower de luce / In Corn Hill this [??]', *The Spectator* No. 126 (25 July 1711), Bodleian Library Oxford, pressmark: Bodleian Hope fol.88.

[29] Henry Entwisle noted in 1747: 'These papers [...] were our messenger's (at the Office for Taxes) John Shales who kept Johns Coffee house in St Martin's Lane and he bound them up[;] the other volume was lent to Blankley & lost.' Note pasted on to front end-paper of the volume in the Spencer Research Library at the University of Kansas: call number: Bond P125. See W. R. Ward, 'The Office for Taxes, 1666–1798', *Bulletin of the Institute for Historical Research*, 25 (1952).

and reformed the reader's experience of the essay. In *The Spectator* No. 47 (24 April 1711), the booksellers offered made-up bound monthly sets of the half-folio papers. The first and most important reformatting was the publication of the essays in octavo and duodecimo editions. Tonson advertised in *The Spectator* No. 227 (20 November 1711) that he was printing by subscription two volumes of the essays in octavo, in a large character, bound and gilt for two guineas, collecting the first 169 essays.[30] This first collected edition referred to itself as 'the Spectators', indicating they were a plural collection. Further volumes continued through to the 555th essay in the seventh volume, followed by an eighth for the 1714 continuation, and a ninth for the spurious 1715 papers.[31] The collected volumes, shorn of their advertisements, and in prestigious format and binding, appealed to a more polite and elite mode of book consumption. A copy of the first seven volumes in the British Library (pressmark C.58.h.3) has a book-plate indicating it was purchased by 'The Right Hon[ble] Henrietta Countess of Pomfret Lady of the Bed Chamber to the Queen'.[32] These multi-volume octavo sets were enormously popular, reaching their sixth edition by 1724, and remaining in print throughout the century.[33] Subsequently, there were five major re-edited editions, including those by Nichols and Barbauld, which kept *The Spectator* in print in the late eighteenth and early nineteenth centuries.

Repackaging the essays in distinct miscellany collections was also successful. In addition to reformatted sets of volumes, specific groups of *The Spectator* papers—the most coherent narrative sequences—were extracted and repackaged as stand-alone publications. *The Spectator* anticipated such collecting: in No. 124 (23 July 1711), referring to the demand for his '*rural Speculations*', Mr Spectator reports that his bookseller has told him of the habit of some customers, 'several having made up separate Sets of them, as they have done before of those relating to Wit, to Operas, to Points of Morality, or Subjects of Humour' (I, 507–8). Some of these reader-created collections are still extant, like a set of the daily papers on Milton bound uniform with an edition of Milton's works in the Bodleian Library.[34] In addition, essays from *The Spectator* were frequently reprinted in anthologies, beauty books, and edited collections through the rest of the century. Continuations and imitations, such as Johnson's weekly *The Rambler* (1750–2), Colman's *The Connoisseur* (1753–4), or Hazlitt's *Table Talk* (1821), also kept alive the reputation of *The Spectator*.

---

[30] An advertisement for the first two volumes of the collected edition appeared in Nos. 227–34, 237, 247, and 248.

[31] Bond, 'Introduction', in *The Spectator*, I, lxxii–lxxiii.

[32] Henrietta Louisa Fermor, Countess of Pomfret (died 1761), Lady of the Bedchamber to Caroline, Princess of Wales, later Queen Caroline, 1714–37.

[33] *The Spectator* No. 555 (6 November 1712), comments that 'an Edition of the former Volumes of Spectators of above Nine thousand each Book is already sold off'.

[34] Bodleian Library, pressmark Vet. A3 c.70 (3). Bound with *The Poetical Works of Mr John Milton* (1695).

These repackagings are relevant to the long and complicated reception history of *The Spectator*, but they also restructure the reader's experience of the essay, especially its relationship to chronology and the passage of time. Collections present the reader with numerous ways to reorganize the miscellaneous structure of the diurnal essays, not least by reading them continuously, without having to wait until tomorrow for the next one. Furthermore, technologies of organization, such as the contents page and index, impose methodical order on the variety, allowing readers to engage with *The Spectator*'s contents by following arguments and topics systematically, rearranging the material to the reader's own thematic ends. The reader can follow a train of thought through any and all of the 555 essays. This kind of 'indexical reading' imparts structure and organization.[35] In the present day, *The Spectator* is habitually read and understood indexically, that is, as a more or less coherent argument. An instance in this essay is afforded by my discussion of the form of the essay, following the topic through essays 124, 249, 219, 476, 435, and 367, in that order, ignoring the hundreds of essays that come between them, and the non-chronological ordering. Indexical reading adds coherence, but occludes the variety and sense of the unexpected of the diurnal essay.

The history of the index to *The Spectator* is notable for the speed with which it was first accomplished, acknowledging the reader's appetite for a thematic approach.[36] The first index covered the first four volumes of the collected edition, and was appended to the fourth volume in late November 1712, before the daily sheets finished.[37] Every volume that appeared thereafter had an index. The entries in *A Compleat Index to the First Four Volumes of the Spectators* (1713) began:

Abigails, (male) in Fashion among the Ladies, *Vol.* 1 *Page* 251.

Absence in Conversation, a remarkable Instance of it in *Will Honeycomb*, *V.* 1 *P.* 439. The occasion of this Absence, *P.* 440, and Means to Conquer it, *P.* 441. The Character of an absent Man out of *Bruyere*, *P.* 443. An Assembly of Absent Men, *V.* 1, *P.* 167.

Absence of Lovers, Death in Love, *V.* 3 *P.* 404. How to be made easy, *P.* 405, 406, 417.

---

[35] The phrase 'indexical reading' is used in various ways by other disciplines: it is used broadly in the sense intended here by Peter Stallybrass, in 'Books and Scrolls: Navigating the Bible', in Jennifer Andersen and Elizabeth Sauer (eds), *Books and Readers in Early Modern England: Material Studies* (2002), 51; and Matthew Brown in *The Pilgrim and the Bee: Reading Rituals and Book Culture in Early New England* (2007), x.

[36] But note the advertised index in *The motto's of the five volumes of Tatlers, and the two volumes of the Spectator, translated into English. To which is added, a complete index to the two volumes of the Spectator* (1712).

[37] Advertised in *The Spectator* No. 533 (11 November 1712): 'This Day is publish'd, *A very neat Pocket Edition of 3d and 4th Volumes of the* Spectator *in 12°. To which is added a compleat Index to the whole 4 volumes. Printed for* S. Buckley *at the Dolphin in* Little Britain *and* J. Tonson *at Shakepear's Head over-against Catherine-street in the* Strand'. Vol. 3 is dated 1712 and Vol. 4 1713 (except in the octavo where these dates are reversed).

Abstinence, the Benefits of it, *V*. 3 *P*. 149.

Academy for Politicks, *V*. 4 *P*. 314. The Regulations of it, *P*. 316 *&c.*

Accompts, their great usefulness, *V*. 3, *P*. 30.[38]

This has a strange distracted poetry of its own, deploying the essays' miscellaneity in new forms of incongruous comedy. Although the author of *The Spectator* index is unknown, it was probably neither Addison nor Steele, but someone from within the bookseller's employ. Although indexes have a long history, they were not typical in English periodicals in this period.[39] The index is composed of alphabetized summary phrases, but not necessarily by what the modern age would identify as a keyword. Furthermore, the index phrases do not summarize the whole essay but point to particular sentiments and arguments identified by volume and page, rather than essay (so that individual essays can have more than one entry). Later editions of the indexes used the essay number, due to the 'Multitude and Variety of the Editions'.[40] Thus the index allows readers to navigate the volumes in search of particular topics, as identified by the indexer. The index further collects summary phrases on the same or similar topics, allowing all the essays on a particular topic to be found and read together. Here, for example, 'absence' can be traced through several *Spectator* essays (Nos. 24, 77, 241, and 244).

The index imposes a new information order on the meandering course of the diurnal essays, methodizing them to a limited extent. In this way, the index is on a continuum with other early modern information management tools, such as commonplace books and later the encyclopedia. Gentlemen and scholars in the humanist tradition had developed a practice whereby they used a specially prepared notebook, a commonplace book, to record sets of 'ideas or themes' 'grouped under one "Head"', so that they might be stored and recalled, using a spatialized order.[41] Indexing in the manner undertaken by *The Spectator* can be seen as a response to these encyclopedic and commonplace-book practices, and as such, as a response both to the plenitude of the essays themselves, and more generally to the perception of the over-abundance of books and periodicals in the period (the so-called early modern information overload).[42]

---

[38] *A Compleat Index to the First Four Volumes of the Spectators*, in *The Spectator*, 4 vols (1713), IV, n.p.

[39] Althea Douglas, 'The Indexes of 18th and early 19th-century magazines', *The Indexer* 14.3 (April 1985), 14–15.

[40] *A general index to the Spectators, Tatlers and Guardians* (1757), vi.

[41] Richard Yeo, 'Ephraim Chambers's *Cyclopædia* (1728) and the Tradition of Commonplaces', *Journal of the History of Ideas* 57.1 (1996), 157–75. See also Alan Walker, 'Indexing Commonplace Books: John Locke's Method', *The Indexer* 22.3 (April 2001), 114–18 and Ann Moss, *Printed Commonplace Books and the Structuring of Renaissance Thought* (1996).

[42] Ann Blair, *Too Much to Know: Managing Scholarly Information before the Modern Age* (2010).

Without an index, the reading experience is closer to the diurnal miscellaneity of everyday life. In his study of the diary and journal, another open-ended literary form closely tied to everyday life, Stuart Sherman outlines how these forms preserve a sense of being in the middle of experience. The diurnal reading process unfolds into the future, not knowing what is going to happen next, at least until tomorrow. But, as this suggests, 'history' in the diurnal papers unfolds backwards through time, so that as each new essay is added to the series, the reader is able to create new connections and narratives between discrete events in the past. This can be witnessed within the text too: in numerous papers, Addison makes a connection back to a previous number, using phrases such as 'those I mentioned in my last Saturday's Paper'—though the reference to Saturday was removed in the collected volumes.[43] Addison imagines an attentive reader who has been following all the papers.

The diurnal *Spectator*, as conceived by Addison and Steele, revelled in the unexpected juxtapositions of essays on different topics and in different modes and styles. In the contest between the diurnal and the indexical, the essay holds within itself the tension between the immediacy and presentism of the journalistic, and something more moral and sententious, more philosophical and presentless. Indexical reading changes *The Spectator*, and in so doing, exposes that ambivalence in the essay form, between on the one hand the everyday sally of thought, the attempt or endeavour, journalistic and disposable, and on the other, the more enduring philosophical thinking of the tract or treatise in miniature. The essay hovers ambiguously between the open-ended potential of the diurnal unexpected and the structured and methodized encounters of indexical reading. It is by sloughing off the quotidian and incomplete status of the diurnal periodical essay that *The Spectator* in particular, and the essay in general, began to aspire to moral seriousness and philosophical sententiousness: what it gives up in that sloughing off is not, however, itself without significance.

---

[43] *The Spectator* No. 363 (26 April 1712).

5

The Sociable Philosopher

David Hume and the Philosophical Essay

Fred Parker

1. Introduction

Shortly after completing his philosophical masterpiece *A Treatise of Human Nature*, David Hume turned to essay writing. His *Essays, Moral and Political* came out in two volumes in 1741–2, and was immediately well received. It was as an essayist, not a philosopher, that Hume made his name, and he continued to write essays for the rest of his life, adding some twenty to subsequent editions, withdrawing others, and reserving the most controversial for posthumous publication. When in 1748 he returned directly to the arguments of the *Treatise* in what we now call *An Enquiry concerning Human Understanding*, this work was in fact published as *Philosophical Essays concerning Human Understanding*, retaining that title over ten years and several editions.

In one sense, this represented a turn away from hard philosophy. The *Treatise* did not sell, and Hume wished to be read; in his later autobiography he made no secret of his desire for literary fame. But to say that in turning to the essay Hume was turning *from* philosophy begs, of course, a large question. At its most general, that question might be put like this: is philosophy best conducted in a way that is *continuous* with our other activities, with our everyday practices of reflection, expression, and social interaction? Or is it best conceived and conducted as a distinct and specialized discourse, a thing *apart*? This question goes back to the origins of Western philosophical thought. For the first emphasis, we might think of the *Symposium* or the historical Socrates, who seems to have philosophized with anyone he came across in the agora, using the most commonplace examples and images to think with. For the second, we need only recall the special training in abstract thinking that Plato requires for his elite philosopher-guardians, or the way that Aristotle, in the *Nicomachean Ethics*, brackets off the life of intellectual inquiry from the other virtues as something optional, both marginal and superior.

Fred Parker, *The Sociable Philosopher: David Hume and the Philosophical Essay* In: *On Essays: Montaigne to the Present.*
Edited by: Thomas Karshan and Kathryn Murphy, Oxford University Press (2020). © Fred Parker.
DOI: 10.1093/oso/9780198707868.003.0006

2. Shaftesbury, Socrates, and 'the liberty of the Club'

From the moment of its birth in the writing of Montaigne, the essay existed in an ambiguous relation to the work of philosophy: philosophical reflection is everywhere in the *Essais*, but given in a mode resistant to systematization, as propositional content is continually refracted and dispersed in the experiential flow of thinking. In the eighteenth-century essay that sense of subjective process largely disappears, but what sometimes remains is an informality that reserves the right to discount coherence and procedural regularity. This informality is expressed in the ideal of an *easy* style: expression which flows naturally, without apparent exercise of will, and announces itself as *sociable*, as reader-conscious and, at least overtly, reader-friendly.

What would it mean to think of such a mode as congenial to the purposes of philosophy? Addison announced *The Spectator* as imitating Socrates in bringing 'Philosophy out of Closets and Libraries, Schools and Colleges, to dwell in Clubs and Assemblies, at Tea-Tables and in Coffee-Houses',[1] but it was Shaftesbury who engaged most thoughtfully with Socrates, and who went furthest in merging the philosophical with the essayistic to the point where the distinction between them vanishes. The writings collected in the *Characteristics* (1711) all signal their distance from systematic discourse, variously adapting or evoking the manner of familiar conversation. The significance of this is made clear in the one piece explicitly called an essay: 'Sensus communis, an essay on the freedom of wit and humour in a letter to a friend'. Shaftesbury begins with a defence of freedom in conversation, 'a liberty in decent language to question everything'. He cites a recent conversation 'upon the subject of morality and religion' which ended in a 'pleasant confusion' as, paradoxically, a case of good intellectual practice.[2] In elucidating this, Shaftesbury travels a long way, sliding from topic to topic with only a tacit implication of coherence. First he dissents from the tendency in contemporary thought to reduce goodness and virtue to reward-oriented utility. What is truly good is good in itself and appeals to a 'social feeling or sense of partnership with humankind' (50). The ethical is thus interwoven with the sociable, and in another large move, our pleasure in this goodness is described as aesthetic, being a pleasure in true proportions, true measures, harmony. The 'pleasant confusion' of the conversation exemplifies, we may infer, this sociable aesthetic.

Shaftesbury's freedom of movement here is almost Montaignian. Connections are loose and associative, rather than logically worked out. But this has its own

---

[1] Joseph Addison and Richard Steele, *The Spectator*, ed. Donald F. Bond, 5 vols (1965), I, 44 (No. 10, 12 March 1711). Further references given in the text. See also Markman Ellis's chapter in this volume, 97–8.

[2] Anthony Ashley Cooper, 3rd Earl of Shaftesbury, *Characteristics of Men, Manners, Opinions, Times*, ed. Lawrence E. Klein (1999), 33, 37. Further references given in the text.

point. 'The most generous spirits are the most combining', Shaftesbury writes, and if the structure of his essay is associative, this is itself a manifestation of 'the associating genius of man', that 'associating inclination' which makes for our sociability, our love of goodness, and our pleasure in beauty (52–3). This in turn bears on the kind of persuasiveness that the essay claims for itself, and the kind of persuasiveness that Shaftesbury recommends in intellectual inquiry generally. There is no question of rational demonstration or systematic argument; *cogency* is set aside, as a coerciveness incompatible with that sociable freedom dear to Shaftesbury's heart. Instead, we are offered truths that an over-subtle or self-centred philosophizing may mislay, but which are intuitively recognized by *sensus communis*—common sense, but also the sense made by a community: sociable intelligence.

Accordingly, an 'easy' and 'familiar' manner is the true style of intelligence. True persuasiveness carries itself lightly, for no argument on, in a broad sense, moral or aesthetic topics can ever compel assent; Shaftesbury declines to be 'drawn from my way of humour to harangue profoundly on these subjects' (68). This intelligent lightness is exemplified by the ancients, particularly Horace, who could treat even 'the very gravest subjects [...] in a free and familiar style' (35), but can be found also in the ideal of free conversation. Shaftesbury's defence of those who freely question everything is compatible with his attack on those who deny the existence of disinterested virtue, only on the basis that the *sensus communis* which underlies good liberal conversation will always keep its participants from anti-social absurdities. Their differences are always, so to speak, provisional, imaginably part of a larger harmony, subordinate to the pleasure of exchange.

This is what Shaftesbury's editor Lawrence Klein calls, in a helpful phrase, his 'philosophical worldliness' (xxvii), a quality which the philosophical essay might seem the perfect form to explore. Yet as every reader notes, Shaftesbury's world is small and sharply defined; it extends only to the well-bred. Politeness requires that freedom of inquiry be limited to 'private society' and 'select companies':

> For you are to remember, my friend, that I am writing to you in defence only of the liberty of the Club and of that sort of freedom which is taken among gentlemen and friends who know each other perfectly well [...] The public is not, on any account, to be laughed at to its face or so reprehended for its follies as to make it think itself contemned. (36)

This emphasis on the 'Club' smooths away the tension which 'philosophical worldliness' might otherwise suggest. Shaftesbury's philosophers are gentlemen, and his gentlemen are inclined to be philosophers; under these conditions of homogeneity the sense of encounter or mediation carried by the philosophical essay is small. But the reader of the *Characteristics*—a published work, but not intended for a wide readership—is in no man's land here: surely not one of the foolish unenlightened public, but also not unequivocally Shaftesbury's 'friend', not confided in as to the content of that anarchic conversation. The Socratic affiliations of the essayistic style, simultaneously fashioning intimacy and intimating irony, are strikingly in play.

3. Hume's Conversational Turn

Hume's 1741–2 *Essays* place the philosopher in a more openly complex relation to the world. The 1742 volume opens with 'Of Essay-Writing', where Hume outlines how 'the Separation of the Learned from the conversible World seems to have been the great Defect of the last Age, and must have had a very bad influence both on Books and Company.'[3] Now, however, these two worlds are coming together, and in writing as an essayist he describes himself as facilitating the exchange between them, an 'Ambassador from the Dominions of Learning to those of Conversation' (535). The emphasis on 'the conversible world' as the proper site of intellectual activity is strong: still, in Hume's image the two realms remain distinct, and there remains a certain irreducible tension between them. An ambassador opens relations, but is also there to negotiate the potential for conflict. Nevertheless—as good manners require—Hume plays down the fact that he is a visitor from another country, emphasizing instead his affiliation to that most conversible of forms, the eighteenth-century periodical essay. The manner of *The Spectator* is, in some of these early essays, clearly evoked. The ambassador image recalls Addison-as-Socrates bringing philosophy into the coffee-house; there is an ostentatious addressing of 'the Fair Sex', the conversible world being one of mixed company, unlike the learned; there are conscious modulations between a more playful and a more serious register, each guaranteeing the other ('To be serious, and to quit the Allusion before it be worn thread-bare [...]', 536); and a few essays are even signed off with a moral allegory, one of the more obviously imitable parts of Mr Spectator's repertoire.

'Philosophy', meanwhile, is portrayed as something uncouth and unsocial, disengaged from the customary world, and disabled or deformed by such disengagement.[4] 'Philosophers are apt to bewilder themselves in the subtilty of their speculations; and we have seen some go so far as to deny the reality of all moral distinctions' (567). In fact, Hume came teasingly close to such a denial in the *Treatise* (he denied that moral distinctions constitute knowledge, though they are

---

[3] David Hume, *Essays Moral, Political, and Literary*, ed. Eugene F. Miller (1987), 534. Further references given in the text.

[4] Where Hume speaks admiringly of 'great Philosophers' in these essays, he is thinking of natural philosophy: Galileo and Newton (550).

realities of experience), but here he allows himself to endorse his readers' com-
monsensical assumption that any such denial must be patently absurd. Thinking
done in isolation from society is likely to go wrong; philosophers really need to get
out more. 'When a philosopher contemplates characters and manners in his
closet, the general abstract view of the objects leaves the mind so cold and
unmoved, that the sentiments of nature have no room to play, and he scarce
feels the difference between vice and virtue' (568).[5] Hence philosophy is declared
less valuable than the study of history, where our feelings are engaged by specific
characters and situations. Elsewhere 'philosophy' is associated with positive
antagonism to natural sentiment: the 'grave philosophic Endeavour after
Perfection [...] strikes at all the most endearing Sentiments of the Heart, and
all the most useful Byasses and Instincts, which can govern a human Creature'
(539). Hume's piquant example of such a 'Philosophic Spirit' is a young
Frenchwoman who, wishing to become a mother, called on an admirer for
assistance but sent him on his way once a child was born. The key thing here is
the woman's self-sufficiency, her striking independence—from others, from the
feelings that might 'govern' her, and from social convention, 'the receiv'd Maxims
of Conduct and Behaviour', which are set firmly aside by 'our Philosophical
Heroine' (542–3). The 'philosopher' is represented in the *Essays* as a figure of
disengagement, self-containment, and self-sufficiency, on whom the conversible
essayist, sociably engaged with his readership and working with the grain of their
interests and beliefs, naturally looks askance.

That Hume, author of the *Treatise*, should distance himself from 'philosophy'
in this way, is only superficially a paradox. In truth, his turn towards the more
sociable orientation of the essay makes good sense in the light of the philosophical
scepticism of the *Treatise*. For Hume's concern was always twofold: with the
rational cogency of his arguments, and with their implications for practical living.
The arguments of the *Treatise* were devastating to the view that we are rational
entities or agents, that we possess any secure rational understanding of how the
world works and why one event follows another, that we have knowledge of our
own essential selves or of the grounds of moral judgement. However, our practical
understanding of the world and our ability to function within it do not therefore
fall apart but hold together, as before, through the force of habit and sentiment.
Reason discovers its own bankruptcy to be so complete that the non-rationality of
our customary beliefs and behaviour cannot count against them, and their status,
although severely damaged from any point of view that seeks for ultimate justi-
fications, is simultaneously enhanced as a result. In the conclusion to the first book

---

[5] The *Treatise* regularly presents Hume as sitting alone in his chamber. See John Sitter, *Literary
Loneliness in Mid-Eighteenth-Century England* (1982), 23–4.

of the *Treatise* Hume memorably staged this turn from philosophical crisis to customary practice:

> The *intense* view of these manifold contradictions and imperfections in human reason has so wrought upon me, and heated my brain, that I am ready to reject all belief and reasoning, and can look upon no opinion even as more probable or likely than another [...]
>
> Most fortunately it happens, that since reason is incapable of dispelling these clouds, nature herself suffices to that purpose, and cures me of this philosophical melancholy and delirium [...] I dine, I play a game of back-gammon, I converse, and am merry with my friends; and when after three or four hour's amusement, I wou'd return to these speculations, they appear so cold, and strain'd, and ridiculous, that I cannot find in my heart to enter into them any farther.
>
> Here then I find myself absolutely and necessarily determin'd to live, and talk, and act like other people in the common affairs of life.[6]

This crucial turn—from the *intense* solitary philosopher to the customary social world—is mirrored by the turn from the *Treatise* to the *Essays*: except that Hume will now explore the possibility of connecting the realms which in the *Treatise* seem utterly separate. It is this which the essay mode makes possible. The Montaignian appeal to the whole sensibility rather than the intellect alone is transposed, in this eighteenth-century mode, into the submission of individual thought to the terms of sociability expected by a communal readership. The principle of sociable connection takes the place of the freedom of subjective association in the earlier model. In the 1741–2 *Essays*, and still more in the *Philosophical Essays* of 1748, Hume continues to think and reflect, but now only under the sign of what is 'conversible'.

4. Johnson: Thinking and Contingency

This need to reconnect the estranged intellectual with the customary social world is felt by other writers at the time. When Samuel Johnson takes up the periodical essay in 1750, with *The Rambler*, he repeatedly returns to this theme. This reflects Johnson's situation as an 'uncourtly Scholar'[7] writing in a crowded marketplace for his daily bread, but it also voices his perception of a more general problem. 'The great fault of men of learning' is their inability to turn their intellect, as

---

[6] David Hume, *A Treatise of Human Nature*, ed. L. A. Selby-Bigge (1978), 269.
[7] Samuel Johnson, *The Letters of Samuel Johnson*, ed. Bruce Redford, 5 vols (1992–4), I, 95.

Socrates extraordinarily did, directly upon the 'relations of life'. (In naming Socrates here, Johnson echoes Montaigne, e.g. in 'Of Physiognomy' or 'Of Experience'.) In consequence,

> they are often despised by those, with whom they imagine themselves above comparison; despised, as useless to common purposes, as unable to conduct the most trivial affairs, and unqualified to perform those offices by which the concatenation of society is preserved, and mutual tenderness excited and maintained.[8]

The solitary intellectual enjoys a freedom of mind that tends dangerously toward the self-sufficiency of reverie:

> There is nothing more fatal [than solitude] to a man whose business is to think [...] The dreamer retires to his apartments, shuts out the cares and interruptions of mankind, and abandons himself to his own fancy [...] He is at last called back to life by nature, or by custom, and enters peevish into society, because he cannot model it to his own will.   (IV, 106; No. 89)

Johnson knows what the cure should be: the acknowledgement of dependency that is involved in social existence. The dreamer-intellectual in the passage just quoted

> must, in opposition to the Stoick precept, teach his desires to fix upon external things; he must adopt the joys and the pains of others, and excite in his mind the want of social pleasures and amicable communication [...] The most eligible amusement of a rational being seems to be that interchange of thoughts which is practised in free and easy conversation.   (IV, 107–8)

This is not unlike Hume's turn from intense philosophy to conversing with his friends, and provides a comparable rationale for cultivating the 'conversible' mode of the essay. But a conversation with Johnson could be a strenuous affair, and Johnson is more reluctant than Hume to give up on self-determination. The intellectual '*must* [...] *teach* his desires' to turn to others; conversation is 'the most *eligible* amusement of a rational being' (my emphases). In the passage from the *Treatise*, by contrast, the turn just 'happens', 'most fortunately', a manifestation of 'Nature' rather than of any agency of Hume, who finds himself 'necessarily determin'd' to live as others do.

---

[8] Johnson, *The Rambler*, vols III–V of *The Yale Edition of the Works of Samuel Johnson*, ed. W. J. Bate and Albrecht B. Strauss (1969), III, 132 (No. 24). Further references given in the text.

Now the essay may be said to be inherently friendly to contingency, and quizzical of design—especially when it is one of a series of essays in the plural, openly occasional and miscellaneous, *rambling* from topic to topic. Johnson confesses this directly in *Rambler* 184: 'the writer of essays', 'unconnected pieces', has an easy task in one way, since he need only expand on some slight reflection or observation, but he pays for this by having continually to find new topics, 'obliged to choose, without any principle to regulate his choice' (V, 201–2). His choice is in the end largely determined by accident, and in this Johnson holds that it resembles our life-choices generally. What this conveys is a complex, or perhaps ambivalent, attitude towards the occasional essay. Its openness to contingency and accident brings it close to the very process of living, but involves it by the same token in the unsatisfactoriness of life lived by chance, without principle or plan. Johnson salutes Montaigne, but cannot approve of him as a model:

> A writer of later times has, by the vivacity of his essays, reconciled mankind to the same licentiousness [as is allowable in lyric] [...] and he therefore who wants skill to form a plan or diligence to pursue it, needs only entitle his performance an essay, to acquire the right of heaping together the collections of half his life, without order, coherence, or propriety.   (V, 77; No. 158)

Since Johnson is himself writing as an essayist, he is hardly repudiating the form altogether. What he seems to be desiderating is a properly philosophical essay, coherent as argument, grounded at once in rational principle and in his readers' experience, and working upon the world to practical effect. What he actually writes are essays which convey the tension inherent in such an ideal. A train of argument leading in one direction is very often counterbalanced by opposite considerations, leading to no strong conclusion. The evident didactic impulse of *The Rambler* is continually obliged to concede how often 'speculation has no influence on conduct' (IV, 160; No. 98). The style of the essays maintains a principled awkwardness in relation to the 'easy' manner of the conversible ideal; the very sentences which recommend 'free and easy conversation', quoted above, are as strenuous in their diction and syntax as in their morality. Johnson's weighty phrasing, in recommending that the intellectual 'excite in his mind the want of social pleasures and amicable communication', is not itself overly sociable or amiable: it evokes, precisely, the *want* of social pleasures, the gap that stubbornly obtains between intellectual reflection and the conversible world. In *Rasselas* he will create a work that expresses this formally, embedding short dissertations on various topics—retirement, poetry, marriage, bereavement, and so on—in a narrative of life flowing on regardless. Imlac's discourse on the dangers of solitary intellectual speculation is full of wisdom, but achieves nothing; the mad astronomer is cured only when the women draw him into social pleasures.

In *The Rambler* the awkwardness of the essays' affiliation to sociability acknow-ledges a comparable, though perhaps more conflicted irony.

Here and there this becomes explicit. In No. 98 Johnson's fictional correspond-ent complains that the Rambler spends too much time in abstruse thought, and should instead descend to

> those little civilities and ceremonious delicacies, which, inconsiderable as they may appear to the man of science [...] yet contribute to the regulation of the world, by facilitating the intercourse between one man and another, and of which the French have sufficiently testified their esteem by terming the knowledge and practice of them *Sçavoir vivre*, 'the art of living'.   (IV, 160–1)

Why not write more like the *Spectator*, whose readers were led to feel they could move between social niceties and philosophical issues without changing gear? Johnson thinks it important to register that criticism, but important also to maintain the dialectical tension between concentrated thinking and social living that gives rise to such complaint. The elusiveness of *savoir vivre*, as well as its desirability, is his subject. In *Rambler* 173 the appearance of pedantry in polite company has something to be said for it, being better at least than 'an affected imitation of fashionable life':

> It ought at least to be the care of learning, when she quits her exaltation, to descend with dignity. Nothing is more despicable than the airiness and jocularity of a man bred to severe science and solitary meditation.   (V, 153)

5. The Art of Diplomacy

Johnson's comment points up the challenge facing Hume as philosophical essay-ist, the danger involved in making the transition between the two worlds *perfectly* easy. Hume himself was alive to this. He withdrew the most Addisonian of the early essays—including 'Of Essay-Writing' and 'Of Moral Prejudices', in which the philosophical Frenchwoman appears—from later editions. He may have felt that as his entry-point into the conversible world, they had served their turn; but he also recognized something mannered in their engagingness that did not sit easily with any more serious intellectual inquiry. For the philosophical Hume is very much present in the *Essays*. By this I mean partly that he has substantial things to say about the political constitution, civil liberty, the relation of culture to com-merce, and so on: but also that the *Essays* retain traces of that philosophical scepticism which challenges (as well as facilitates) the embrace of sociable con-sensus and agreeable conclusions. They promote a sense of the thinker's complex *relation* to 'the conversible World' of his implied reader, rather than his complete identification with it. That relation might be described, thinking back to his image of the essayist as ambassador, as *diplomatic*: the very tact with which Hume embraces the manner and attitudes of the conversible world reveals him as no native of the place.[9]

One way in which this appears is in his handling of oppositions. Hume organizes many of his discussions around formal oppositions: between learning and conversation; in the political essays, between authority and liberty, or court and country; elsewhere, between superstition and enthusiasm, impudence and modesty, simplicity and refinement, the dignity and the meanness of human nature. Such framing seems to recommend a position of moderation or synthesis that smiles at extremism, again in the manner of the *Spectator*. One essay indeed commends 'the middle station of life' as the happiest. But this piece was withdrawn after the first edition, and in other essays the desirable middle point, the position of achievable moderation, remains subtly elusive:

> All questions concerning the proper medium between extremes are difficult to be decided; both because it is not easy to find *words* proper to fix this medium, and because the good and ill, in such cases, run so gradually into each other, as even to render our *sentiments* doubtful and uncertain.   (46)

This sceptical emphasis provides a fine weapon against 'zealots in either party' (608), collapsing most disputes into 'some ambiguity in the expression' (81); but it does so not from the vantage of some secure middle ground, but rather by suggesting how much depends on the light in which a thing is regarded, the manner in which a question is framed.

The positions that emerge will thus depend very much on the conventions that are operative. And although this plays well enough to the conversible world, which is itself the product and the upholder of convention, 'the receiv'd Maxims of Conduct and Behaviour', it also notes that these conventions are conventions, without ultimate sanction. This essayist may agree to smile satirically at a woman so unconventional—so 'philosophical'—as to aim at motherhood while declining marriage, but he himself knows how to think counter-conventionally.[10] 'Of Polygamy and Divorces', for example, sets off with startling boldness. Hume sees no reason in principle why each couple should not draw up its own terms for the marriage contract; duration and exclusivity may vary according to

---

[9] This dynamic tension between the philosopher and the conversible world peaks in Hume's writing of the 1740s. It can be argued that he then moved away from such charged reader-awareness and the kind of commitment to the essay which it involves. The new essays of the 1750s were published not as 'essays' but as *Political Discourses* (1752) and *Four Dissertations* (1757); I have not wanted to draw on them here.

[10] The essay questioning the taboo on suicide was actually printed for a later volume before Hume withdrew it at the last moment as un-conversible, 'at the urging of friends' (577).

circumstances, as has been the case in different cultures, and happens in the animal kingdom. 'All regulations, therefore, on this head are equally lawful, and equally conformable to the principles of nature; though they are not all equally convenient, or equally useful to society' (183). But with that idea of convenience comes the turn: and having dispatched all notion of prescriptive norms, Hume reflects on the practical disadvantages arising from polygamy, and others that arise from the principle of voluntary divorce. This allows him to conclude, with a not quite subliminal archness, on this one-sentence paragraph: 'The exclusion of polygamy and divorces sufficiently recommends our present EUROPEAN practice with regard to marriage' (190). The arc of the essay is thus, as often in Hume's thought, through a potentially subversive freedom of inquiry to an impeccable affirmation of the status quo. This was always predictable from the urbanity with which more radical options were canvassed; the reader never thinks it likely that Hume will leave polygamy on the table. Yet the fact that the familiar affirmation of marriage rests not on God's will or natural law, but entirely on what is most 'convenient', makes a difference. The free thinker aligns himself with his readers at the end, yes, but with an intelligence that recognizes convenience as such: contingent, provisional, unsanctioned. The lightness of the case for lifelong monogamy chimes with the lightness of the essay mode, its hospitality to contingency, where the essayist writes himself free from the weight of authority and the force of system or logic.

'Of the First Principles of Government' exhibits a comparable lightness. Hume takes it as axiomatic that it is 'on opinion only that government is founded' (32), and goes on to distinguish the kinds of opinion that are in play:

> Upon these three opinions, therefore, of public *interest*, of *right to power*, and of *right to property*, are all governments founded, and all authority of the few over the many.   (34)

More traditional would have been to establish the nature of government's right to power, the reality of such a right being the basis of people's opinion that it exists. But Hume makes opinion, not right, fundamental. He offers this as a near-truism about an obvious fact: since the many are stronger than the few, the few can govern only by virtue of a state of opinion which permits them to do so. The words 'founded' and 'authority' refer simply, then, to practicality. But they are words which recall how they might be differently used, as part of an inquiry into the ethical foundation, the true authority, of government—and thereby suggest, through their appropriation for practicality, that they *cannot* be meaningfully used in that way. Opinion is sovereign. And as public opinion is a matter of convention and consensus, the conversible mode of the essay is the appropriate place to establish it.

It is in this context that many of these essays investigate the bounds and contours of *civility*. Hume enquires into questions of social influence and refinement, into the management of conflict in the political realm, into the atmospheric pressure of opinion and of the cultural environment. The *Essays* pay much tribute to modern politeness—which is much greater, Hume notes, than is found among the ancients (128–30)—but are always aware of civility as a construction or artifice:

> Among the arts of conversation, no one pleases more than mutual deference or civility, which leads us to resign our own inclinations to those of our companion, and to curb and conceal that presumption and arrogance, so natural to the human mind.   (126)

> Wherever nature has given the mind a propensity to any vice, or to any passion disagreeable to others, refined breeding has taught men to throw the biass on the opposite side, and to preserve, in all their behaviour, the appearance of sentiments different from those to which they naturally incline.   (132)

This element of artifice, though desirable, has its dangers: 'modern politeness, which is naturally so ornamental, runs often into affectation and foppery, disguise and insincerity' (130–1). Johnson's loud suspicion of politeness is not entirely foreign to the more tactful Hume. Hence alongside the emphasis on 'mutual deference or civility' there is also a quieter running concern with the possibility of detachment and independence, those qualities associated with the 'philosophical' attitude. Independence is discussed in various contexts: the independence of Parliament from the crown, the artist's relation to the polity in which he lives, or, more subtly, the 'delicacy' discussed in the piece which Hume chose to open the *Essays*, 'Of the Delicacy of Taste and Passion'.

'Delicacy' here means sensitivity: the more one has, the more alive one is to both pain and pleasure. Where passion is concerned, this is undesirable, since 'great pleasures are much less frequent than great pains'; delicacy of taste, on the contrary, is to be cultivated, since the pleasures it affords—the books we read, the diversions we engage in, the company we keep—are much more under our own control. The cultivation of a delicate taste can therefore be related to the endeavour of philosophy, understood as usual as a version of stoical self-sufficiency:

> Philosophers have endeavoured to render happiness entirely independent of every thing external. That degree of perfection is impossible to be *attained*: But every wise man will endeavour to place his happiness on such objects chiefly as depend upon himself: and *that* is not to be *attained* so much by any other means as by this delicacy of sentiment.   (5)

Here the essayist, though carefully differentiating himself from the philosopher, still finds house-room for the philosophical ideal of detachment. Indeed, a cultivated taste will actually counteract or 'cure' a passionate engagement with the world, setting us apart. 'Many things, which please or afflict others, will appear to us too frivolous to engage our attention' (6). Only towards the end of the essay does Hume pull this round, and speak more diplomatically:

> But perhaps I have gone too far in saying, that a cultivated taste for the polite arts extinguishes the passions, and renders us indifferent to those objects, which are so fondly pursued by the rest of mankind.   (6)

'On farther reflection', Hume finds that delicacy of taste fosters just those 'tender and agreeable passions' that promote 'love and friendship'—but only, now, 'by confining our choice to few people, and making us indifferent to the company and conversation of the greater part of men'. The man of delicate taste 'feels too sensibly, how much all the rest of mankind fall short of the notions which he has entertained' (7). 'Too sensibly' is a phrase exquisitely poised between the critical and the sympathetic.

How sociable is this? We are returned here to that mix of intimacy and exclusion noted above in relation to Shaftesbury, but here raised into a much higher level of consciousness. Hume's readers are encouraged, of course, to identify themselves with the select few; they have, after all, the good taste to be reading Hume. Still, the gesture of disengagement does not sit well with the *Essays*' overt embrace of the conversible world. Hume's discussion of delicacy implies a dual movement: sociable engagement which coexists with, or is conditioned by, 'philosophical' reserve. This complex implication is conveyed principally as a tone of voice. By placing this discussion at the entrance to the *Essays*, Hume may have wished to set the tone for the essayist's rapport with the reader more generally.

The true essayist is a writer who goes with the flow. The essayist free-associates, subjectively, or freely associates, sociably. They give themselves up. But in the most interesting essayists there is also a countermovement: some intimation of form or purpose, some recognition that flow ends in chaos, some play of irony or insinuation of reserve that corresponds to Montaigne's famous *arrière-boutique* or backshop of the mind. 'Delicacy of sentiment' is one of the terms with which Hume registers this; 'modesty' is another. His essay 'Of Impudence and Modesty' brings the two together. Where individuals are modest,

> their good sense and experience make them diffident of their judgment [...] [and] the delicacy of their sentiments makes them timorous lest they commit faults, and lose in the practice of the world that integrity of virtue, so to speak, of which they are so jealous. To make wisdom agree with confidence, is as difficult as to reconcile vice and modesty.   (554)

'To make wisdom agree with confidence' might be described as the project of the philosophical essay. It is difficult, because of the pressure exerted by modesty, which is here almost a virtue, despite standing outside Hume's normal category of qualities useful or agreeable. Modesty is both social and intellectual: it connects a stance towards the world with the outcome of philosophical thinking: for, to the sceptical Hume, being diffident of one's judgement is no bad thing. 'Modesty and Reserve' appear in the conclusion to *Philosophical Essays concerning Human Understanding* as the hallmark of that '*mitigated* Scepticism' which Hume recommends, and throughout that work 'modest' marks the right kind of intellectual attitude. Locke, for instance, for all the abstractness of his thinking, 'really was a great Philosopher, and a just and modest Reasoner'.[11]

6. Philosophical Essays Concerning Human Understanding

Hume's own 'reserve' in the *Philosophical Essays* can be felt as a poised elusiveness, approximating to Socratic irony, that activates, but declines to determine, the question of an overall intention.[12] The reader is made to wonder to what extent *Philosophical Essays*—not yet *An Enquiry*—is a work with a plot. A volume of *Essays*, in the plural, leads us to expect a set of discrete arguments, among which we may pick and choose: but the first of the *Philosophical Essays* sets the agenda for what sounds like a single project, and several though not all of the following essays have clear links with what comes before or after. In a work which offers a critique of the argument from design, we are continually exercised by the question of Hume's design on his readers. In the third essay, he writes that in all 'Compositions of Genius',

> 'tis requisite that the Writer have some Plan or Object, and tho' he may be hurried from this Plan by the Vehemence of Thought, as in an Ode, or drop it carelessly, as in an Epistle or Essay, there must appear some Aim or Intention in his first setting out, if not in the Composition of the whole Work. (34)

Literary coherence requires the sense of intentionality, though the essayist has licence to 'drop it carelessly'—itself an ambiguous phrase, suggesting both 'deploy it casually' and 'discard it negligently'. In Hume's own first setting out, in his opening essay, he announces his aim as that of uniting the two different species of philosophy, the 'easy and obvious' and the 'accurate and abstruse' (3). The 'easy' philosopher—Cicero and Addison are cited—appeals to his readers' feelings, and may affect their behaviour in the world; an 'abstruse' philosopher, like Locke, is a theorist, who looks to establish fundamental principles and 'hidden truths', and writes not for 'common Readers' but for 'the 'Learned and the Wise' (3). Hume is

---

[11] Hume, *Philosophical Essays concerning Human Understanding* (1748), 249–50. Further references given in the text.

[12] M. A. Box speaks of an 'ironic coyness'. See *The Suasive Art of David Hume* (1990), 206–5.

here recasting his earlier categorization of the learned and the conversible worlds, and as a conversible essayist, he finds that abstruse philosophy has little to recommend it. It 'vanishes' when the philosopher steps out into daylight, under the impact of natural feelings; it induces 'Melancholy' and 'endless Uncertainty'; and it can expect only a 'cold Reception' in the world (7). Nevertheless, some hard thinking may have a practical use in showing us its own limits, so destroying 'that abstruse Philosophy and metaphysical Jargon' which mixes itself with 'popular Superstition' (12). Hume hopes that by

> reasoning in this easy Manner, we can undermine the Foundations of an abstruse Philosophy, which seems to have serv'd hitherto only as a Shelter to Superstition and a Cover to Absurdity and Error!   (19)

Just what this undermining of foundations will involve is not made clear, although Hume's 'easy manner' reassures the reader that the outcome will be perfectly sociable. In the essays that follow, however, the radicalism of Hume's thinking becomes increasingly apparent, as he sets out many of the core sceptical arguments of the *Treatise*—on the non-rationality of arguments from experience, on the primacy of custom and sentiment, on the unintelligibility of causality and the inescapability of necessity. To these he adds the two essays that were to become notorious, destroying the twin arguments for religious belief from miracles and from design, and in the final essay he canvasses the furthest reaches of an extreme scepticism: the irrationality of our belief in the external world, the groundlessness of all our everyday actions, reasonings, and beliefs. At almost every point, however, Hume urbanely reassures his readers: determinism rightly understood leaves morality where it always was, the functions of what we misdescribed as reason are perfectly well performed by custom and instinct, faith rather than reason is Christianity's best support, the querying of the design argument is a mere 'sceptical Paradox' (205) without consequences for practice, and the extremes of scepticism can flourish only 'in the Schools' (246), inside the bubble of abstruse academic thought, and can never take hold on life as it is actually experienced and lived.

Some readers may feel, as many of Hume's contemporaries did, that there is a choice to be made. Is Hume ultimately the sociable essayist, demonstrating through his easy manner how amiably these subversive arguments can be adapted to and reconciled with common life and practice? 'Philosophical Decisions are nothing but the Reflections of common Life, methodiz'd and corrected' (251). Or is Hume really the subversive freethinker in the *Spectator*'s clothing, tapping rather into the essay's older hospitality to free-thinking (evasive of authority, fostering the 'essaying' of radical speculation) that goes right back to Montaigne?[13] Much of the

---

[13] See Richard Scholar, *Montaigne and the Art of Free-Thinking* (2010).

commentary on Hume ever since has been structured around a similar choice: between the constructive naturalist and the radical sceptic. But it is also possible to feel that the *Philosophical Essays* are written so as to hold both possibilities in play, exploiting precisely the tension inherent in the idea of a 'philosophical essay', and thus evading the kind of 'affirmative and dogmatical' response which Hume deplores (249). Consider, for example, the shape of this sentence:

> When he [the Pyrrhonian sceptic] awakes from his Dream, he will be the first to join in the Laugh against himself, and to confess, that all his Objections are mere Amusements, and can have no other Tendency than to show the whimsical Condition of Mankind, who must act and reason and believe; tho' they are not able, by their most diligent Enquiry, to satisfy themselves concerning the Foundation of these Operations, or to remove the Objections that may be rais'd against them.   (248-9)

The sentence invokes a sociable laughter against the absurd excesses of philosophy, but then runs on, tactlessly recalling those philosophical arguments to the point where the ultimate direction of the laughter—against the philosopher or against the whimsical condition of mankind—becomes as uncertain as the syntactic distribution of emphasis. We are conscious of a certain reserve behind the sociable concession that 'all his objections are mere amusements', but this does not, I think, convert to positive irony. Rather, we are struck by how, notwithstanding that reserve, Hume is nevertheless writing in the sociable manner of the essay mode, entering—but as a philosophical sceptic—into the conversible world.

7. Fielding and his Audience

This effect has much to do with Humean philosophy, but it also draws on the potential of the essay at a particular moment in its history, when the writer's intellectual separation from his readership crosses his desire to enter into worldly life. Perhaps, in brief conclusion, I can indicate this through reference to *Tom Jones*, published the year after *Philosophical Essays*. Each of its eighteen books open with what Fielding himself calls essays. Fielding's project in these essay-chapters has something in common with Hume's embassy between the regions of learning and conversation, for Fielding repeatedly insists that the essential qualification for the novelist—the rare, true novelist—is knowledge, *discovery* rather than creativity, a penetrating and discriminating understanding of how things are (316).[14] Hence, he maintains, the ability to write such reflective essays as these is

---

[14] Henry Fielding, *Tom Jones*, ed. Sheridan Baker (1995), 478–80. Further references given in the text.

the hallmark of the true novelist-historian, the reader's guarantee that they are not dealing with a work of mere ignorant romance.

Crucially, however, a large part of this knowledge can be had only through 'Conversation', as the practical knowing that comes from moving in the world (479). Being a man of knowledge in its fullest sense, Fielding must also be a man of the world, and the quality of these 'initial Essays' (137)—familiar in manner, casual in structure, very far from theoretical rigour, often built round an openly entertaining conceit (the novel as tavern food, for example)—announces their willingness to connect with, to exist for, his audience. This operates as a writerly expression of his ethical conviction that true virtue is outward-turning, and consists in 'a certain relative Quality, which is always busying itself without Doors', rather than that prudential wisdom which stays 'at home' (507).

Yet there is a tension here. Once again, the essayist-intellectual's familiar way with his readership carries an equivocal aspect. As his metaphors evoke them, Fielding's readers are set apart from this figure of knowledge. They are the consumers in the novelist's tavern, the subjects in the novelist's new kingdom, the audience in the novelist's theatre. Each of these images establishes the reader's rights and space with one hand, only to constrain or denigrate them with the other. At a public tavern 'all Persons are welcome', with 'a Right to censure, to abuse, and to d—n their Dinner without Controul': nevertheless, Fielding dismisses those who do not know how to value his novel to 'some other Ordinary better accommodated to their Taste' (25). As the audience in his theatre, his readers will judge his characters freely from their various positions in the auditorium, but only 'we, who are admitted behind the Scenes of this great Theatre of Nature' are qualified to discriminate between the action and the person (212). This charged 'we'—poised between a sociable communality, a desire to generalize the personal, and an insinuation of the writer's sovereign authority— may, in this context, mean only the author. Readers without such author-like knowledge are apt to condemn without understanding, damning the book for unreal or minor faults, and failing to see the coherence of its grand design. (As in Hume, the essay's equivocal nature as both casual and purposive gives particular point to questions of design and contingency.) All such incompetent readers, Fielding points out, are likely to be bored or antagonized by these serious essays, whose virtue lies precisely in their dullness. Their dull sobriety makes them 'essentially necessary to this Kind of Writing', for it gives the impression of some serious intent, and offers a foil to the much more entertaining world of the narrative (137–40).

This is playful, of course; Fielding's actual readers are invited to differentiate themselves from those who do not care for serious reflection—the frivolous, the censorious, and the idle. But the effect is complicated—and not only because we *are* keen to get back to Tom and Sophia. Fielding's reader-friendliness coexists with a certain reserve, a potential astringency:

[W]e shall represent Human Nature at first to the keen Appetite of our Reader, in that more plain and simple Manner in which it is found in the Country, and shall hereafter hash and ragoo it with all the high *French* and *Italian* Seasoning of Affectation and Vice which Courts and Cities afford. By these Means, we doubt not but our Reader may be rendered desirous to read on for ever.   (26)

Fielding's consideration for his readers' pleasure glances also at the corrupt nature of their taste. The play of irony is felt as a conceivable antagonism. Thus in the opening to Book 16 Fielding notes that these essays always contain 'somewhat of the sour or acid Kind' (541), so that the irritated reader-critic 'may fall with a more hungry Appetite for Censure on the History itself'. The reader recognizes that Fielding is laughing such censorious readers out of countenance, but also that there really is a good deal of 'sour or acid' in Fielding's thinking for the conventional-minded reader, which may or may not be neutralized by its parodic acknowledgement here.

8. In Conclusion: The Amiable Arsonist

The unforgettable image with which Hume concludes the *Philosophical Essays* has a similarly complex playfulness, a flavour of Socratic irony.

When we run over Libraries, persuaded of these Principles, what Havoc must we make? If we take in our hand any Volume; of Divinity or School Metaphysics, for instance; let us ask, *Does it contain any abstract Reasonings concerning Quantity or Number?* No. *Does it contain any experimental Reasonings concerning Matter of Fact or Existence?* No. Commit it then to the Flames: For it can contain nothing but Sophistry and Illusion.   (256)

The quasi-sociable 'we' slips into an admonitory imperative. The image of Hume's radicalized readers as incendiaries, makers of havoc in gentlemen's libraries, is playful, of course, reassuring of the philosopher's friendly intentions towards the conversible world; but for all that, the sense of something destructive in Hume's thinking is not an illusion. Just as with Fielding, what we have looks like the kind of easy playfulness, or Shaftesburian raillery, which, assuming familiarity, asks merely to be *understood* in order to be loved: but the reader's uncertainty as to whether they do in fact have an understanding with the essayist, or are not rather being seriously challenged by him, connects with that dynamic tension between intellect and the social world which animates a certain kind of 'philosophical essay'.

6

Tristram Shandy, Essayist

Scott Black

1. Tristram among the Essayists

There are few detours in the history of the essay as wondrously strange as
Laurence Sterne's *Tristram Shandy*. Of course to call *Tristram Shandy* an essay
is already to make that history even stranger. But if essays are loose, free, and
unmethodical writings that flit between books and reflections, they likewise seed
other genres, and most notably the one that develops alongside them, the novel.
From Fielding through Eliot and Tolstoy, Musil and Kundera, novelists have
interleaved their plots with inset reflections that suggest a history of the essay
branches into the history of the novel. But even within this lineage of essayistic
fiction, Sterne's book is notably peculiar. Indeed, it seems more an essay than a
novel at all, and in this chapter I will consider it in that light.[1]

Purportedly an autobiography, *The Life and Opinions of Tristram Shandy* never
advances much beyond Tristram's childhood and actually spends most of its time
telling stories of his father and uncle—as well as recording Tristram's comic
frustrations in trying to write his own story. We get far more of Tristram's
'opinions' than his 'life' (and more of the father's and uncle's opinions than
Tristram's). Because of this, the genre of *Tristram Shandy* has been a vexed
question for its readers from the very beginning. An anonymous reviewer of the
first volumes in the *London Magazine* (February 1760) wrote: 'Oh rare Tristam
Shandy!—Thou very sensible—humorous—pathetic—humane—unaccountable!—
what shall we call thee?—Rabelais, Cervantes, What?'[2] Such questions have continued unabated ever since. Modernists and postmodernists claim Sterne's book as
anticipating their self-conscious fictions and anti-novels.[3] More historically minded
critics read the anachronism the other way around, taking *Tristram Shandy* as a

---

[1] I argue that *Tristram Shandy* is not a novel in '*Tristram Shandy*'s Strange Loops of Reading',
Without the Novel: Romance and the History of Prose Fiction (2019), 97–118.
[2] Quoted in Alan B. Howes (ed.), *Sterne: The Critical Heritage* (1974), 52. Thomas Turner wrote in
his diary, 14 September 1762: 'In the even, Mr Tipper read to me a part of a—I know not what to call it
but Tristram Shandy' (quoted in Geoffrey Day, *From Fiction to Novel* (1987), iv).
[3] Modernist: Viktor Shklovsky, 'The Novel as Parody: Sterne's Tristram Shandy', in *Theory of Prose*,
trans. Benjamin Sher (1990), 170. Postmodernist: Raymond Federman, 'Self-Reflexive Fiction or How
to Get Rid of It', *Critifiction: Postmodern Essays* (1993), 19.

Scott Black, *Tristram Shandy, Essayist* In: *On Essays: Montaigne to the Present.* Edited by: Thomas Karshan and Kathryn
Murphy, Oxford University Press (2020). © Scott Black.
DOI: 10.1093/oso/9780198707868.003.0007

belated Renaissance satire.[4] And recently it has been explained as a contextually specific satire on the eighteenth-century novel.[5] Here I suggest another literary context for *Tristram Shandy*: the essay, which despite a lack of recent attention, helps illuminate many of its characteristic features.

The most evident qualities of *Tristram Shandy*—its organization by free association, whim, and distraction, by pleasure, play, and game—are essayistic. Indeed, a century ago Orlo Williams used Sterne as an example of the class of 'essayists who never wrote essays at all', arguing that both *Tristram Shandy* and *Sentimental Journey* 'have all that whimsical discursiveness, that delight in tossing the subject like a shuttlecock, with a resonant battledore of humour, that careless readiness to explore every promising bypath of a theme, which is the essential quality of an essayist'.[6] Taking up Williams's prompt, I suggest that the essay is a missing piece of the formal context of *Tristram Shandy* and that *Tristram Shandy* is a missing piece of the history of the English essay. Sterne adopts many of the traditional habits of the essay to give Tristram's narrative its characteristic style. And in Tristram himself Sterne adapts one of the defining formal innovations of the eighteenth-century English essay, the essayistic persona, to give his book its basic structural device. Tristram Shandy is less a failed or frustrated novelistic narrator than a characteristic (and characteristically peculiar) essayist. In these ways, the essay passes through Sterne with just the kind of playful, digressive swerve that organizes (or perhaps disorganizes) the genre itself in its form and history alike. If *Tristram Shandy* seems a byway in the history of the essay, that is how the essay works. And if the essay seems a distraction from the narrative concerns of *Tristram Shandy*, that is how *Tristram Shandy* works as well.

In turning to *Tristram Shandy*'s relation to the essay, I am returning to an old critical *topos*, but one that has recently fallen off the map. Graham Greene said that Sterne's 'whimsicality was inherited by the essayists, by Lamb in particular'.[7] And critics have noted that Sterne inherited his whimsy *from* the essayists as well, especially Montaigne. Wayne Booth suggested that Sterne borrowed from Montaigne 'elaborate and whimsical commentary as an end in itself, more or less divorced from any other narrative interest', and a 'consistently inconsistent

---

[4] D. W. Jefferson, 'Tristram Shandy and the Tradition of Learned Wit', *Essays in Criticism* 1.3 (1951), 225–48; Melvyn New, *Laurence Sterne as Satirist* (1969); Donald Wehrs, 'Sterne, Cervantes, Montaigne: Fideistic Skepticism and the Rhetoric of Desire', *Comparative Literature Studies* 25 (1988), 127–51; J. T. Parnell, 'Swift, Sterne, and the Skeptical Tradition', *Studies in Eighteenth-Century Culture* 23 (1994), 221–42.

[5] Thomas Keymer, *Sterne, the Moderns, and the Novel* (2002).

[6] Orlo Williams, *The Essay* (1914), 16–17. Arthur Calder-Marshall [1936] considered Tristram Shandy 'half novel, half essay [...] without unity of mood and exhibiting more caprice than plan' (quoted in Lodwick Hartley, *Laurence Sterne in the Twentieth Century: An Essay and a Bibliography of Sterne Studies 1900–1965* (1966), 135). Lionel Stevenson calls it 'a gigantic personal essay, in which the author chats with the reader about everything which interests him, in the manner of Montaigne and Burton' (*The English Novel: A Panorama* (1960), 129).

[7] Quoted in Jefferson, 'Tristram Shandy', 225.

portrait of the author himself, in his character as writer'.[8] Booth uses Montaigne's self-portrait as a way to explain 'the unity of *Tristram Shandy*', but I do not see much unity in either Sterne's portrait or his book.[9] Rather, I think Montaigne's *Essays* offered Sterne an example of a book formed by the kind of open-ended, recursive, and unresolved play that Williams calls a 'delight in tossing the subject like a shuttlecock'.

Montaigne's *Essays* follow accident, change, and chance. Here is a smattering or 'heap' of some of the most salient passages of generic reflection in Montaigne: 'I have no other Officer to put my Writings in Rank and File but only Fortune. As Things come into my Head, I heap them one upon another, which sometimes advance in whole Bodies, sometimes in single Files: I am content that every one should see my natural and ordinary pace, as ill as it is'; 'what are these Things I scribble, other than *Grotesques*, and monstrous Bodies, made of dissenting Parts, without any certain Figure, or other than accidental Order, Coherence, or Proportion?'; 'Could my Soul once take footing, I would not essay, but resolve; but it is always learning and making trial'; 'Those are the bravest Souls that have in them the most Variety, and that are most flexible and pliant [...] Life is an unequal, irregular, and a multiform Motion. [...] The least forced, and most natural Motions of the soul, are the most beautiful; the best Employment, those that are least constrained.'[10] Montaigne thus sees a wandering motion as characteristic of the self, of life, and of writing, and in the *Essays* Sterne finds a model of writing guided by fortune and the oscillations of impulse. Jonathan Lamb calls this a new groundwork of art in which 'rhapsody is being converted into a formal principle, accident into design'.[11]

However, like Booth's earlier insistence on finding a unity in *Tristram Shandy*, Lamb's account of Sterne's use of Montaigne too definitively converts accident into design by finding a formal principle. Rather, recognizing the essayistic aspects of *Tristram Shandy* allows us to account for its evident *lack* of unity, its oddness and wildness, without making that into a principle of oddness and wildness.[12] In locating the tension between accident and contingent design in the figure of Tristram, we can recognize a 'flexible and pliant' narrator defined by, and derived from, the 'unequal, irregular, and multiform' practices of the essay.

Though Montaigne is an evident and noted influence on Sterne, what is less observed is that he was also influenced by Montaigne's British inheritors, who adapted and developed the stylistic and philosophical idiosyncrasies of

---

[8] Wayne Booth, *The Rhetoric of Fiction*, 2nd edn (1983), 224, 226.

[9] Booth, *The Rhetoric of Fiction*, 226–9.

[10] Michel de Montaigne, 'Of Books', *Montaigne's Essays*, trans. Charles Cotton, 6th edn, 3 vols (1743), II, 87; 'Of Friendship', I, 202; 'Of Repentance', III, 20; 'Of Three Commerces', III, 35–8. This is the translation of Montaigne that Sterne read.

[11] Jonathan Lamb, 'Sterne's Use of Montaigne', *Comparative Literature* 32 (1980), 1–41, here 9.

[12] See Melvyn New, 'Sterne and the Narrative of Determinativeness', *Eighteenth-Century Fiction* 4 (1992), 315–30, here 316.

Montaigne's form. *Tristram Shandy* is full of references to essays of all kinds, from Montaigne (in Cotton's translation), to the *Spectator*, to Locke's *Essay*, and even Pope's 'Essay on Man' in the dedication to volume nine. But even this is not the complete picture.

2. The English Essay *circa* 1760

Sterne's use of Montaigne is part of a lively and extensive tradition of British essays during what Paul Korshin calls 'the golden age of essay writing, from 1710 to 1775' and Denise Gigante 'the great age of the English essay'.[13] As he usually does, however, Sterne goes much further than his contemporaries in exploring— and exploding—the possibilities of the forms he adopts; in this case he undoes the relative regularity introduced into the genre by Montaigne's English followers. But while *Tristram Shandy* reclaims the freedom of Montaigne's *Essays* from the controls placed on it by contemporary essayists, it does so by adapting a key innovation of the English genre, the essayistic persona. In order to show how *Tristram Shandy*, and Tristram Shandy himself, are rooted in the tradition of the English essay, this section offers a sketch of the genre *circa* 1760.

Let us start with Ephraim Chambers's *Cyclopaedia*, which Melvyn New calls Sterne's 'primary "reference" work'.[14]

ESSAY, in matters of learning, is a peculiar kind of composition; whose character is to be free, easy, and natural; not tied to strict order, or method, nor worked up and finished, like a formal system.

The matter of an *essay* is supposed to consist principally of sudden, occasional reflections, which are to be wrote much at the rate, and in the manner a man thinks; sometimes leaving the subject, and then returning again, as the thoughts happen to arise in the mind.

At least, this has hitherto been the practice; and Montaign[e], who has got no small reputation by this way of writing, seldom keeps many lines to the subject he proposes: though it is our opinion, that my lord Bacon is a better pattern in the *essay* kind.

Mr Locke, however, and a few other authors use *essay* in a severer sense: the *essay of human understanding*, every Body knows is a regular, artful, laboured Work.[15]

---

[13] Paul Korshin, 'Johnson, the Essay, and The Rambler', in *The Cambridge Companion to Samuel Johnson*, ed. Greg Clingham (1997), 65; Denise Gigante, *The Great Age of the English Essay: An Anthology* (2008).

[14] Melvyn New, 'Introduction', *The Life and Opinions of Tristram Shandy, Gentleman*, vol. 3: *The Notes* (1984), in *The Florida Edition of the Works of Laurence Sterne*, ed. New, Richard A. Davies, and W. G. Day, 8 vols (1978–2000), 25.

[15] s.v. 'essay', in *Ephraim Chambers, Cyclopaedia, or, An Universal Dictionary of Arts and Sciences* (1728).

This is all standard stuff, a good digest of a century's worth of critical commentary.[16] Chambers's account is notable for registering not just the constitutive variety of this 'free, easy, and natural' genre, what Johnson famously calls '[a] loose sally of the mind; an irregular indigested piece', but also for recognizing the variety within the tradition: Bacon's pattern as well as Montaigne's, and the adoption of the genre, or its name, by more systematic, finished works like Locke's *Essay*.[17]

The most popular and influential essayists of the eighteenth century by far were Addison and Steele, whose *Spectator* (1711–12) provided a model for periodical essays throughout the century. Though not as fully improvisatory as Montaigne's *Essays*, the *Spectator* is itself heterogeneous in its modes of writing, and includes unmethodical papers that Addison says partake of 'the Looseness and Freedom of an Essay', and associatively 'run out into the Wildness of those Compositions which go by the Names of Essays'.[18] Addison characterizes his essays' 'Chemical Method' as 'giv[ing] the Virtue of a full Draught in a few Drops', a key component of his 'Socratic' project of bringing 'Philosophy out of Closets and Libraries, Schools and Colleges, to dwell in Clubs and Assemblies, at Tea-Tables, and in Coffee-Houses'.[19] This mediation between scholarship and society, making learning polite and enlightening the public, becomes one of the key tropes of the eighteenth-century discourse of the essay. David Hume repeats it in 'Of Essay-Writing' (1742) when he describes himself as 'as a Kind of Resident or Ambassador from the Dominions of Learning to those of Conversation'.[20] And in his *Essays* (1765), Oliver Goldsmith notes the popularity of 'Essay-writing, which may be considered as the art of bringing learning from the cell into society'—a double-edged sword for Goldsmith, because as learning educates the public it becomes more concerned with popularizing discoveries than making new ones.[21] Towards the end of the century (1779), Vicesimus Knox testifies to Addison's influence in Addison's own terms: 'Addison, like Socrates, to whom he has often been compared, brought down knowledge from those heights which were accessible only to professed scholars, and placed it within the reach of all, who, to natural and common sense, added the advantage of a common

---

[16] For the English essay 1600–1750, see Black, *Of Essays and Reading in Early Modern Britain* (2006). For the English periodical essay through the eighteenth century, see Richard Squibbs, *Urban Enlightenment and the Eighteenth-Century Periodical Essay: Transatlantic Retrospects* (2014).

[17] In his *Dictionary of the English Language* (1755), Johnson defines essay: '1. Attempt; endeavour. 2. A loose sally of the mind; an irregular indigested piece; not a regular and orderly composition. 3. A trial; an experiment. 4. First taste of any thing; first experiment.'

[18] Joseph Addison and Richard Steele, *The Spectator*, ed. Donald F. Bond, 5 vols (1965), II, 465 (No. 249, 15 December 1711); IV, 185–6 (No. 476, 5 September 1712). See Black, ch. 4, and this volume, Chapter 4 by Markman Ellis.

[19] Bond, *The Spectator*, I, 506 (No. 124, 23 July 1711); I, 44 (No. 10, 12 March 1711).

[20] David Hume, *Essays*, ed. Eugene F. Miller (1987), 535. See also Fred Parker's contribution to this volume, Chapter 5, 117.

[21] Oliver Goldsmith, *Collected Works of Oliver Goldsmith*, ed. Arthur Friedman, 5 vols (1966), III, 161–2.

education.'[22] A polite version of Montaigne's 'natural Motions of the soul' and his brave variety are here brought out from the study and offered as the form able to speak to a variety of readers, and to readers in all their own variety:

> The detached nature of these writings, enables the writer to vary his style without impropriety, to be grave or gay, humorous or severe; to lay down positive rules, or to teach by example; to speak in his own person, or introduce an instructive tale. Every volume contains a variety of subjects treated in various manners, and suited to the disposition of different readers, or to the same reader at different times.[23]

The efficacy of the essay as a little, 'chemically' productive, and accreting form was repeated throughout the century. In *The Rambler* (1751) Samuel Johnson wrote that

> The writer of essays escapes many embarrassments to which a large work would have exposed him; he seldom harasses his reason with long trains of consequences, dims his eyes with the perusal of antiquated volumes, or burthens his memory with great accumulations of preparatory knowledge. A careless glance upon a favourite author, or transient survey of the varieties of life, is sufficient to supply the first hint or seminal idea, which, enlarged by the gradual accretion of matter stored in the mind, is by the warmth of fancy easily expanded into flowers, and sometimes ripened into fruit.[24]

Goldsmith adopts this familiar trope in *The Bee. Being Essays on the Most Interesting Subjects* (1765):

> [A]s I intended to pursue no fixed method, so it was impossible to form any regular plan; determined never to be tedious, in order to be logical, wherever pleasure presented, I was resolved to follow. Like the Bee, which I had taken for the title of my paper, I would rove from flower to flower, with seeming inattention, but concealed choice, expatiate over all the beauties of the season, and make my industry my amusement.[25]

This is the classical language of mellification, the work of the bee, a traditional image of reading and learning as digestion that was used to characterize the essay throughout its history; essays do not offer new things, 'only matter well digested',

[22] Vicesimus Knox, 'On Essay Writing', in *Essays, Moral and Literary*, 2nd edn, 2 vols (1779), II, 3.
[23] Knox, *Essays, Moral and Literary*, II, 10.
[24] Johnson, *The Rambler*, vols III–V of *The Yale Edition of the Works of Samuel Johnson*, ed. W. J. Bate and Albrecht B. Strauss, 23 vols (1969), V, 201 (No. 184).
[25] Goldsmith, *Essays* (1765), in *Collected Works*, I, 354.

as one essayist put it in 1655.[26] A 'first hint or seminal idea' from reading or experience is enlarged by the accretion of associations and worked by fancy into flowers; other readers follow in kind, without care and with pleasure, to gather nourishment from those flowers. Essays are the works of digestion in the fields of pleasure, seemingly careless, says Goldsmith, but secretly selective. This can be fruitful but also sticky work.

Montaigne's *Essays* were, of course, the standard model, and they were handled with caution. In *The Adventurer* (1753), Joseph Warton skewers Montaigne's 'many awkward imitators, who under the notion of writing with the fire and freedom of this lively old Gascon, have fallen into confused rhapsodies and uninteresting egotisms', and critiques Montaigne himself for giving 'a catalogue of his private vices, and publish[ing] his most secret infirmaries, with the pretence of exhibiting a faithful picture of himself, and of exactly portraying the minutest features of his mind'.[27] In 'Of Essay-Writing' (1760), Nicolas Charles Joseph Trublet similarly expresses ambivalence about Montaigne and compositions 'in the Essay-Way' that are 'free from the Care of Order and Method':

> Montaigne's Way of Writing was this: When any Thoughts occurred to him on a Subject, he immediately set about writing them. But if these led him into any other that had but the most distant Relation to them, he pursued that new Thought, as long as it furnished him any Matter; returned afterwards to his Subject, which he frequently abandoned again, and sometimes never returned to it more. In short, they were Digressions on Digressions, continual Rambles, but agreeable, and often insensible, to which an incidental Proposition, nay, a single Word often gave Occasion.

In 'Of Conversation', Trublet echoes those who condemn Montaigne for his 'scandalous' openness, but says 'many of these Pieces are the most beautiful in whole Performance. *Montaigne* studied and painted Man by studying and painting himself; which is indeed the best Method of studying him, and the surest Way of painting him to the Life.'[28]

But how much of the man does one want to see? To manage the vanity and impolite exposure associated with the essay, while preserving its lively charms, English essayists introduced a significant innovation that became a defining characteristic of the eighteenth-century genre, the fictional persona. Aaron Hill's

[26] T. C., *Morall Discourses and Essayes* (1655), quoted in Black, *Of Essays*, 23–4. For the classical discourse of digestion and mellification, see Thomas M. Greene, *The Light in Troy: Imitation and Discovery in Renaissance Poetics* (1982), 73.

[27] Joseph Warton, *Adventurer* No. 49 (24 April 1753), 108–9. Montaigne is named as a model in *Spectator* No. 476 (5 September 1712), in Bond, *The Spectator*, IV, 185, and critiqued for his egoism in No. 562 (2 July 1714), in IV, 520.

[28] Trublet, *Essays Moral and Critical* (1760), 5, 9, 28; originally published as *Essais sur divers sujets de littérature et de morale* [1735, 1749, 1754].

preface to the collected *Plain Dealer* (1730) offers a good account of both the problem to be managed and the solution arrived at. After rehearsing the familiar characteristics of the essays—they 'go against all Order and Method whatsoever' and follow Montaigne's pattern in mixing 'a great deal of Wit, much good Observation, and some Learning'—Hill notes the costs and benefits of the genre:

> [Montaigne's] Essays are wild, rambling, and incoherent; some of them don't treat at all of the Subjects proposed, and others might as well have any other Title as those they wear [...] Montaigne [...] first introduced that useful practice of Digression into Treatises upon select Subjects; and by giving us every whimsical Conceit that came into his Head, has led us as it were dancing after his Morality, much more pleasantly than if we walked in Stilts, or were directed by the Leading-Strings, which Seneca had accustomed us to.[29]

Hill wittily refers to the end, and the ends, of Montaigne's *Essays*: ''Tis to much purpose to go upon Stilts, for when upon Stilts, we must yet walk upon our Legs: And when seated upon the most elevated Throne in the World, we are but seated upon our Breech.'[30] The beauties of such natural and naked pleasures are, of course, intimately entangled with their crude exposures. (Are we being teased to look up the stilts to his exposed behind?) So the English essayists adapted the genre to the polite world by inventing a fictional persona who constrains Montaigne's rude vanity:

> The Spectator, and Nestor Ironside, are characters also excellently well adapted to our Pleasures, by our Knowledge of their being Fictitious: For such is our Malignity of Temper, that we can't forgive a real Author acting or thinking oddly or idly, though our Entertainment arises from thence, because we consider him as a reasonable Man, and obliged by a superior Duty to another kind of Behaviour; but we can indulge an imaginary, or assumed Personage in any ludicrous, frolicsome or whimsical Words or Opinions, because we know that he only plays the Fool for our Delight and Amusement, which we grudge him to do for his own. Thus Montaigne's Faults are the Beauties of Bickerstaffe and Ironside [...] Certainly, writing under an assumptive Character is a fine Improvement in this Way; and I believe the Novelty of it, without derogating from the Wit, Humour, and good Sense, or excellent Style of those mentioned papers, made up the greatest Part of their Merit: The little Incidents of human Life, Pieces of Conversation, and familiar Arguments, which may be thrown into Writing under such a Character, give it the Advantage of all other Methods.[31]

---

[29] Aaron Hill, *Plain Dealer* (1730), i–iii.
[30] Montaigne, 'Of Experience', in *Montaigne's Essays*, III, 402.   [31] Hill, *Plain Dealer*, iv–v.

It is striking to find Hill locating the invention of a fictional narrator in the essay, not the novel. (Indeed English novelists by 1730—Delarivier Manley, Jane Barker, Daniel Defoe—had not made the shift from pseudo-factual narrators to 'properly' fictional ones.[32]) It is even more surprising to find Isaac D'Israeli suggesting in 1796 that Sterne's fictional persona is derived from the essay. (Had D'Israeli read no novels?) In *Miscellanies; or Literary Recreations*, D'Israeli echoes Hill's account of the significance of Addison's imaginary or assumed characters, who can safely indulge in the kind of wild, rambling incoherencies and digressive whimsical conceits of Montaigne without being mistaken for a real author:

> Why is Addison still the first of our essayists? He has sometimes been excelled in criticisms more philosophical, in topics more interesting, and in diction more coloured. But there is a pathetic charm in the character he has assumed, in his periodical Miscellanies, which is felt with such a gentle force, that we scarce advert to it. He has painted forth his little humours, his individual feelings, and eternised himself to his readers. Johnson and Hawkesworth we receive with respect, and we dismiss with awe; we come from their writings as from public lectures, and from Addison's as from private conversations.[33]

D'Israeli's account of Addison's continuing popularity at the end of the century demonstrates the long-lasting force of the innovation of 'writing under an assumptive Character'. Both Hill and D'Israeli focus on the conversational intimacy allowed by a playful and fictional persona, whose 'frolicsome or whimsical Words or Opinions' can express '[t]he little Incidents of human Life, Pieces of Conversation, and familiar Arguments', the 'little humours' and 'individual feelings' that give Addison his charm. D'Israeli continues by associating Sterne with this formal innovation: 'Sterne perhaps derives a portion of his celebrity from the same influence; he interests us in his minutest motions, for he tells us all he feels.'[34] It is not clear whether D'Israeli is saying Sterne was directly influenced by Addison and the 'pathetic charm in the character he has assumed' or influenced by that kind of individuated 'private conversation' more generally. But either way, D'Israeli identifies the character Sterne assumes as an essayistic persona.

3. Tristram's Essay

These contemporary discussions of the essay offer a context for the early reception of *Tristram Shandy*, for some of its key features, and for the persona of Tristram

---

[32] See Nicholas D. Paige, *Before Fiction: The Ancien Régime of the Novel* (2011).
[33] Quoted in Howes, *Sterne: The Critical Heritage*, 295. Poor Steele is forgotten.
[34] Quoted in Howes, *Sterne: The Critical Heritage*, 295.

Shandy himself. Sterne's first readers immediately associated him with Montaigne, and they responded to *Tristram Shandy* in terms associated with the genre Montaigne developed. In a famous letter of 1760, Robert Brown wrote that 'I would lay too, that [Sterne] is no stranger to Montaigne'; Sterne responded that Brown was 'absolutely right'.[35] In March 1760 Thomas Newton noted the response to the first volumes of *Tristram Shandy*: 'Many people are pleased with the oddness and wildness of it.'[36] A year later the *Critical Review* characterized the next volumes as 'a work, which seems to have been written without any plan, or any other design than that of shewing the author's wit, humour, and learning, in an unconnected effusion of sentiments and remarks, thrown out indiscriminately as they rose in his imagination.'[37] Such miscellaneous looseness, freedom, and wildness are characteristics Addison associated with the essay, and which became clichés of the English genre. For the *Critical Review* commentator, the novelistic elements are distinctly secondary ('We will venture also to say, that the characters of the father and uncle are interesting and well sustained'), as they were to Walter Scott the following century: '*Tristram Shandy* is no narrative, but a collection of scenes, dialogues, and portraits, humorous or affecting, intermixed with much wit, and with much learning, original or borrowed.'[38] Coleridge's remark that '[t]he digressive spirit [is] not wantonness, but the *very form* of his genius' is just one of many, many comments about Sterne that adopt the discourse of the essay to discuss his work: digression, irregularity, wildness, discursive wandering without system or method.[39]

The attribute of 'wildness', which we've already seen linked with the essay by Addison and with Sterne by Newton, is a frequent observation of critics. Samuel Richardson (1761) wrote that Sterne's 'Unaccountable wildness; whimsical digressions; comical incoherencies; uncommon indecencies; all with an air of novelty, has catched the reader's attention'.[40] Philip Parsons (1779) notes that 'Sterne delighted in that wild wood-note strain of digressive and irregular writing' but complains that 'repeated digressions, and flights under no restraint of method, perplex the mind' because method is necessary to writing.[41] And Jeremiah Newman (1796) waxes lyrical: 'Unembarrassed by those fetters of continuity and coherence, which sound criticism expects from common writers, he considers himself as at liberty, to wander discursively, or rather to leap over barren rocks, or

---

[35] Quoted in Howes, *Sterne: The Critical Heritage*, 102–3.
[36] Quoted in Howes, *Sterne: The Critical Heritage*, 57.
[37] Quoted in Howes, *Sterne: The Critical Heritage*, 127.
[38] Walter Scott, 'Laurence Sterne', *Ballantyne's Novelist's Library*, ed. Walter Scott (1821–4), quoted in Howes, *Sterne: The Critical Heritage*, 373. Nevertheless Scott included *Tristram Shandy* in the Library. Anna Laetitia Barbauld did not include it in her *British Novelists* (1810) and did not consider it a novel (*Selected Poetry and Prose*, ed. William McCarthy and Elizabeth Kraft (2002), 408).
[39] Coleridge, 'Wit and Humour' (1818), quoted in Howes, *Sterne: The Critical Heritage*, 356.
[40] Quoted in Keymer, *Sterne, the Moderns, and the Novel*, 1.
[41] Parsons, *Dialogue of the Dead* (1779), quoted in Howes, *Sterne: The Critical Heritage*, 233–4.

uncultivated precipices, and except, when he occasionally stoops to crop a rose, raise a lily, or drop a sentiment, to gallop without reins, and sometimes without judgment, from Alps to Pyrenees.'[42] Perhaps the best summation comes from the *Port Folio* of Philadelphia (1811), which observes '[t]hose random and wild effusions so utterly repugnant to any thing like system' and continues: 'To prescribe system to Sterne really seems to us like teaching a humming-bird to fly according to mathematics; it is his delightful wildness that enables him to rifle every flower of it sweets, and to give his quivering and delicate rainbows to the sun.'[43] And if critics regularly remark Sterne's wildness—and, like these final comments, often strain to reproduce the effect—Tristram himself notes it too.

'What a wilderness has it been!' exclaims Tristram, looking back over the first five volumes.[44] And while it might go too far to insist, hobby-horsically, that this was necessarily an essayistic wildness, I hope I may ride at a gentle trot and suggest the phrase resonates in the contemporary context of the genre. Many of Tristram's characteristic moves are recognized essayistic habits. Tristram's comment about his 'little books, which I here put into thy hands, [and] might stand instead of many bigger books' (4.22.270) echoes Addison's account of the essay's 'Chemical Method' of giving 'the Virtue of a full Draught in a few Drops'. For Anna Letitia Barbauld, writing in 1810, this was a defining aspect of Sterne's work: 'It is the peculiar characteristic of this writer, that he affects the heart, not by long drawn tales of distress, but by light, electric touches which thrill the nerves of the reader who possesses a corresponding sensibility of frame.'[45] Whether or not Tristram is referring directly to Addison (or Barbauld's sentimental electricity refers to Addisonian moral chemistry), something was clearly in the air, loosely speaking, an ambient generic context in which Tristram's phrase resonates. Tristram does refer to Addison directly elsewhere, as when he proudly makes his own contribution to the labour of learning. In an elaborate and silly passage about the influence of England's irregular climate on the eccentricity of the English—a passage that gathers steam through mock-scholarly references to Dryden and 'one or two' papers of the *Spectator*—Tristram facetiously participates in the *Spectator*'s Socratic project of bringing learning to the public, while comically undermining its earnestness, by noting that the 'irregularity in our characters' also gives the English something to do in bad weather—as demonstrated by this very passage, which Tristram remarks he's writing on 'a very rainy day, *March 26, 1759*' (1.21.57), as if to date his own periodical essay.

---

[42] Jeremiah Newman, *The Lounger's Common-Place Book* (1803), quoted in Howes, *Sterne: The Critical Heritage*, 298.

[43] Quoted in Howes, *Sterne: The Critical Heritage*, 340.

[44] Laurence Sterne, *The Life and Opinions of Tristram Shandy, Gentleman*, ed. Melvyn New and Joan New (2003), vol. 6, ch. 1, 369. Further references given in the text.

[45] Barbauld, *Selected Poetry and Prose*, 408.

It is this kind of joking scholion, of course, that gives the book much of its digressive quality, 'the eternal scampering of the discourse from one thing to another' as Tristram's father has it (speaking of Locke's *Essay*, and thus glossing the associative texture of its nominal genre) (3.18.170). Such digressions, Tristram's inability to drive his mules in a straight line, are said to be the sunshine of reading, its life and soul, and the vital substance of his book (1.14.34–5, 1.22.64). And the mock-scholia are what Tristram half-mockingly offers to correct readers' 'vicious taste' of 'reading straight-forwards, more in quest of adventures, than of the deep erudition and knowledge which a book of this cast, if read over as it should be, would infallibly impart them with' (1.20.52).

What cast of book is this? When Tristram's writing process comes to the fore, and when his digressive 'opinions' interrupt the narratives of his 'life', the book achieves that meta-fictionality so admired, with good reason, by postmodernists searching for their roots. It certainly is startlingly self-reflexive, but it only looks new to critics who neglect the tradition of Renaissance wit. And it only looks old to critics who neglect the tradition of the eighteenth-century essay, which channelled those practices into Sterne's time. Tristram's 'opinions', which punctuate and derail his novelistic 'life', are neither simply innovative nor simply anachronistic, but are derived from the discursive habits of a contemporary genre devoted to adapting and digesting books. But further, might not only the opinions, but the 'life' itself also owe its origin to the English essay?

We earlier saw that, in 1730, when novels still used pseudo-factual narrators, Aaron Hill discussed the invention of a fictional persona in the essays of Addison and Steele. I propose that defining characteristic of the English essay, the introduction of the essayistic persona, is the generative joke of *Tristram Shandy*.[46] At the beginning of the book, Tristram introduces himself by observing that 'there are readers in the world, as well as many other good people in it, who are no readers at all,—who find themselves ill at ease, unless they are let into the whole secret from the first to last, of every thing which concerns you' (1.4.8). The first volumes of Tristram's narrative are testament to how difficult it is really to get to the beginning of things, *ab ovo*, whether in life or art. But he nonetheless tries; and so will I. This passage contains an echo of the opening gesture of the *Spectator*, or the cliché it became in countless subsequent periodical essays: 'I have observed, that a Reader seldom peruses a Book with Pleasure 'till he knows whether the Writer of it be a black or a fair Man, of a mild or choleric Disposition, Married or a Bachelor, with other Particulars of the like nature, that conduce very much to the right Understanding of an Author.'[47] If Sterne takes the persona of Tristram from

---

[46] For the development of the essayistic persona, see Manushag N. Powell, *Performing Authorship in Eighteenth-Century Periodicals* (2012).

[47] *Spectator* No. 1 (1 March 1711), in Bond, *The Spectator*, I, 1. Sterne's passage might also echo the opening of Burton's *Anatomy of Melancholy*, which, as I discuss below, Sterne is fond of using—and abusing.

Addison and Steele, or from the eighteenth-century essay tradition more generally, the entire 'life' that Tristram tells (or never quite tells) looks like an elaborate
joke about the history of the fictional persona invented to record his 'opinions'. Of
course, there is no single point of genesis in this magnificently overdetermined
book—Sterne's miscellany is itself in continual dialogue with his many miscellaneous sources, from Montaigne and Burton to Chambers and Addison. (Tristram's
very origin is a dispersion of spirits compounded by a series of accidents.) My
point is that the 'opinions' overwhelm the 'life' to such an extent that it makes
more sense to read *Tristram Shandy* in relation to a genre of opinions than one of
lives. Indeed, we know just enough about Tristram's life to understand the etiology
of his opinions. The irregular, digressive, and fragmentary account of the life fully
accounts for the irregular, digressive, and fragmentary habits of the writing
persona, though it accounts for little else.

4. Gathering, Twisting, Floating

What does reading Tristram Shandy as an essayist get you? 'To read *Tristram* as
Sterne's novel', says Eric Rothstein, 'is to read a controlled book.'[48] Likewise, to
read *Tristram Shandy* as a satire is to read Tristram, the butt of Sterne's critique,
against a pious horizon at the edge of the text.[49] In both cases, Tristram's persona
is part of a coordinated, controlled project pointing towards a larger order—
outside of the text itself, of course—that makes sense of the failures, the play, and
the oddness of the work. As either an ancient project of Renaissance wit and
Scriblerian satire or a modern project of mock-novelistic life-writing, *Tristram
Shandy* achieves unity and coherence, whether moral or aesthetic. But in recognizing a genre of 'opinions' alongside the modern 'life', we have a way to account
for the book's oddness that does not need, generically, to resolve such wildness
into a larger unity. To read *Tristram Shandy* as Tristram's essay is to read a less
controlled book, one organized (or disorganized) by pleasure. Situating *Tristram
Shandy* in the context of the essay allows us to focus on this foundational and
often overlooked aspect of both the book and the genre: their origins in pleasure,
and indeed the communication of pleasure.

Goldsmith was no fan of Sterne, but he was as popular and typical an essayist as
any in the decade of *Tristram Shandy*. Returning to his self-portrait will help draw
out some of these implications: 'wherever pleasure presented, I was resolved to
follow. Like the Bee, which I had taken for the title of my paper, I would rove from

---

[48] Eric Rothstein, *Systems of Order and Inquiry in Later Eighteenth-Century Fiction* (1975), 77.
[49] Wehrs, 'Sterne, Cervantes, Montaigne', 130; Parnell, 'Swift, Sterne, and the Skeptical
Tradition', 237.

flower to flower, with seeming inattention, but concealed choice.'[50] This is usefully boilerplate, a partial echo of Montaigne: 'I do nothing without Gaiety; Continuation, and a too obstinate Endeavour, darkens, stupefies and tires my Judgment.'[51] But while Goldsmith suggests his essays only seemingly chase pleasure and rove inattentively, while actually concealing a purpose, Sterne's book follows Montaigne more closely. As Booth says, Montaigne is 'playful', and reading *Tristram Shandy* within the history of the essay does suggest that 'the satire is for the sake of the comic enjoyment, and not the other way around'.[52] From this perspective, Tristram looks more like a post-Scriblerian essayist than a Scriblerian satiric butt, closer in tone to Fielding's delight than Swift's bitterness.[53] If Walter Shandy is a satirized modern spider, spinning his ineffectual systems from the confusions of his own mind, Tristram is a bee, gaily roving in the garden.[54]

In identifying the eighteenth-century English essay as a defining genre of *Tristram Shandy*, and Tristram himself as an essayist, I am endorsing readings of Sterne as playful. This is not to deny Sterne's piety, but to suggest that those kinds of issues, and what Richard Lanham calls the critical 'pressure toward seriousness', lie outside the game space of the book, which is a separate sphere of play and pleasure that need not be read against a serious horizon.[55] Lanham himself sees Tristram playing a classical rhetorical game: 'Tristram, like Rabelais, *plays* with the older models. The forms of classical historical narrative constitute his game.'[56] We can certainly add to Lanham's list of classical forms (history, biography, rhetorical manuals, mirrors of princes, travel books), the modern form of the essay. Indeed if the forms Tristram plays with are classical, his play with them is essayistic in its following pleasure without achieving a final form. Essays, by definition, do not finish their work—if they do they are no longer *essais*—but rather relay their work, and share their play, with others. This participatory aspect of game-playing remains undeveloped in Lanham's account but it is worth explicating. Our readerly relationship with Tristram is game-like in a couple of

---

[50] Goldsmith attacks Sterne's 'Bawdy and Pertness' in Letter 53 of *Citizen of the World* (*Collected Works*, II, 221–5).

[51] Montaigne, 'Of Books', in *Montaigne's Essays*, II, 88.

[52] Booth, *The Rhetoric of Fiction*, 230, 222.

[53] See Ashley Marshall, 'Henry Fielding and the "Scriblerians"', *Modern Language Quarterly* 72 (2011): 19–48, here 45.

[54] Walter is 'systematical' (1.19.49) and spidery, spinning every thread of his hypotheses out of his own brain (5.16.336) while knocking down all others (5.35.357). And Walter's story is set in the context of the Scriblerians while Tristram carefully dates his own observations to the present (1.18.42, 1.21.57, 5.17.339, 9.1.546).

[55] Richard Lanham, *Tristram Shandy: The Games of Pleasure* (1973), 164, 2, 41–2. Lanham writes: 'Surely our role (as audience) points rather to admiring Tristram's performance than to weeping for a world where such desperate enactments need take place. We should admire him not for his success in reenacting the blooming and buzzing confusion of an absurd world but for his success, as a precocious child in the garden of Western culture, in pleasing himself' (126).

[56] Lanham, *Tristram Shandy*, 23.

senses: it takes place within a 'sheltered space' that has no other end than pleasure and it is played with others.[57] Tristram offers a reflexive model of our own activities of reading him—an invitation to adopt his attitude, play with his book, and indeed continue the play that constitutes his book with that book itself. Like Montaigne's, Tristram's book offers an open-ended and never fully redeemed invitation to participate in the activities—variously ridiculous, ludic, moral, and, occasionally, wise—that are written in (and as) the text, without any other end than play. 'If anyone shall tell me, that it is to undervalue the *Muses*, to make use of them only for sport, and to pass away the Time: I shall tell him, that he does not know the value of Sport and Pastime so well as I do; I can hardly forebear to add further, that all other end is ridiculous.'[58]

Recognizing in the essay an eighteenth-century context of this kind of play helps update and more locally historicize the practices of belated Renaissance wit—miscellaneous mixture, digestion, digression, arcane learning, bookish quotation—that distinguish Tristram's writing. It also reminds us that the literary context of Sterne's Britain extends beyond the novel. Once we identify the essay as a contemporary context, Tristram himself, one of *Tristram Shandy*'s supposedly novelistic features, no longer seems derived from the novel at all. Nor does much else. Thomas Keymer argues that Fielding's novels mediate Sterne's use of Montaigne: 'Fielding gets in first, too, when adopting from "the celebrated Montaigne, who promises you one thing and gives you another"' (*Joseph Andrews*, 2.1), the quintessentially Shandean idea—or so one might have thought it—of a chapter that fails to get around to its advertised content.'[59] But there is no need to posit the influence of Fielding when Sterne could have taken this directly from Montaigne, or from the preface to Cotton's translation, which highlights this quintessentially Montaignian feature, or from the tradition of the English essay that intervened between Montaigne and Sterne, which includes Fielding's adaptation of the essay in his novels.[60] Or from all of these. As Lanham says, *Tristram Shandy* 'is no one thing'.[61] Indeed, it can look like a miscellaneous mixture of genres of mixture and miscellany: satire, encyclopedia, novel, as well as essay.[62] But the essay's approach to variety is distinctive: pleasure and play without internal order and without an external organizing horizon. Other genres do

---

[57] For the 'sheltered space' of games, and for a summary of recent scholarship on play, see Robert N. Bellah, *Religion in Human Evolution: From the Paleolithic to the Axial Age* (2011), esp. 2–3, 8, 111–12.

[58] Montaigne, 'Of Three Commerces', in *Montaigne's Essays*, III, 49.

[59] Keymer, *Sterne, the Moderns, and the Novel*, 33.

[60] Montaigne, *Montaigne's Essays*, I, 4. For Fielding's use of the essay, see Black, *Of Essays*, ch. 5, and Fred Parker in this volume, 129–31.

[61] Lanham, *Tristram Shandy*, 20–1.

[62] For encyclopedias, see Jack Lynch 'The Relicks of Learning: Sterne among the Renaissance Encyclopedists', *Eighteenth Century Studies* 13.1 (2000), 1–17.

other things, but the essay works like a game, and not least in its open-ended invitation to play along.

I will end with an essayistic gesture, one I make self-reflexively to conclude my chapter as well as to make a couple of last remarks on the genre and Sterne's own reflexive use of it. That kind of recursion is my point. In discussing Sterne's sarcastic comments on scholarship, I make myself, like Tristram, the butt of a joke, but also do with him what he does with his texts, which do the same with theirs, and so on all the way down. Tristram's exclamation as he throws the key to his study into the well at the beginning of volume five is often quoted, with a sigh, by those of us writing about *Tristram Shandy*:

> Tell me, ye learned, shall we for ever be adding so much to the *bulk*—so little to the *stock*?
>
> Shall we for ever make new books, as apothecaries make new mixtures, by pouring only out of one vessel into another?
>
> Are we forever to be twisting, and untwisting the same rope? for ever in the same track—for ever at the same pace?
>
> Shall we be destined to the days of eternity, on holy-days, as well as working-days, to be shewing the *relics of learning*, as monks do the relics of their saints—without working one—one single miracle with them?   (5.1.309–10)

The apothecaries' mixtures and the twisted rope, as John Ferriar noted when he accused Sterne of plagiarism in 1798, are taken from Robert Burton's *Anatomy of Melancholy*.[63] Sterne is making a characteristically essayistic gesture here with Burton, subtly and slyly quoting one of those 'vertiginous sources' that itself quotes other texts to discuss the uses and abuses of quotation.[64] I call this essayistic because towards the end of the previous volume (4.25.284), Sterne makes a similar move when he has Yorick complain about Homenas's sermon by referring to Montaigne's complaint that quotations can make their host text seem even more dull, insipid, and void of wit.[65] Montaigne says this as part of his defence of his 'making Use of nothing but my own proper and natural Force and Ammunition', 'the natural Parts I have, of which this is the Essay'.[66] That typically Montaignian 'use' is what Sterne performs *with* Burton, not just by using his book but by doing himself what Burton does with his books too:

> For my part I am one of this number, *nos numerus sumus*: I do not deny, I have only this of Macrobius to say for myself, *Omne meum, nihil meum*, 'tis all mine,

---

[63] Robert Burton, *The Anatomy of Melancholy*, ed. Holbrook Jackson (2001), 23–4.

[64] Lanham notes 'Sterne's fondness for vertiginous sources' in *Tristram Shandy*, 102.

[65] Montaigne, 'Of the Education of Children', *Montaigne's Essays*, I, 156.

[66] Montaigne, 'Of the Education of Children', *Montaigne's Essays*, I, 155.

and none mine. As a good housewife out of divers fleeces weaves one piece of cloth, a bee gathers wax and honey out of many flowers, and makes a new bundle of all, *Floriferis ut apes in saltibus omnia libant* [as bees in flowery glades sip from each cup], I have laboriously collected this cento out of divers writers.[67]

Sterne's particular use of Burton's honey, his own contribution to the stock, is the line about relics and miracles. This is a tonally tricky passage in light of *Tristram Shandy*'s satire on Dr Slop's Catholicism, but I think Tristram really means it. After all, we want something miraculous from the textual relics we work with, something that repays our faith and makes all this preservation, commentary, and transmission worth it, right?

The miracle Tristram wants is perhaps the real, ordinary activity that is satirically named by his extravagant rhetoric. The final irony of Tristram's ironic question is that he *does* want what the metaphoric inflation undercuts: the 'miracle' is a satiric joke that hides an earnest wish to make something of his reading. The essay is a nominalization of the verb, to essay, and the genre never strays far from the activities of trying, testing, weighing. Its tentative, exploratory patterns register the pressure of the writer's activity, personality, and even (as detractors are quick to note) vanity. But the modesty of the form—a first draft, a rough sketch—mitigates this charge, in part, because no essay claims to be finished; when it is, it is something else. An essay, then, awaits its reader in order to be not completed, but continued in turn and in kind. Sterne's 'miracle' makes such use of Burton, which I take to be the ordinary experience of finding yourself in another's book and seeing what you, in turn, can make of it.

As an essayist, Tristram is a reader turned writer, and he models the pleasures of play across books. Nietzsche remarks this quality of Sterne's writing:

> His antipathy to seriousness is united with a tendency to be unable to regard anything merely superficially. Thus he produces in the right reader a feeling of uncertainty as to whether one is walking, standing: a feeling that is closely related to floating. He, the supplest of authors, communicates something of this suppleness to his reader. Indeed, Sterne unintentionally reverses these roles, and is sometimes as much reader as author.[68]

The lightness that distinguishes Tristram's voice, and gives us a sense of floating, is an effect of the recursive nature of the genre he adopts. Tristram plays with his texts and invites us to play with his own in turn, offering a response that awaits a further response. If the essay is the contemporary eighteenth-century genre that names Tristram's playful roving through his readings, it remains 'contemporary'

---

[67] Burton, *The Anatomy of Melancholy*, 24–5.
[68] Nietzsche, *Human, All Too Human*, trans. R. J. Hollingdale (1996), 239.

in the broadest sense: naming that kind of response for Sterne's anachronistic sources (Montaigne, Burton), for Sterne's contemporaries (Johnson, Goldsmith), and for Sterne's readers (Nietzsche, me, you) alike. Like their readers—indeed as the proffered registers of their responses—essays themselves float. Tossed like shuttlecocks between readers, essays communicate, perform, and invite a suppleness of reading that is at once careless and carefree, anachronistically layered, and always contemporary, whether in 1580, 1760, or right now.

7

On Coffee-Houses, Smoking, and the English Essay Tradition

Denise Gigante

The art of smoking is a contemplative art; and being naturally allied to other arts meditative, hath an attachment to a book and a newspaper.
Leigh Hunt, 'Mr Gliddon's Cigar Divan'[1]

1. Introduction

For the literary periodical essayist of the eighteenth century, living was, or ought to be, an art. The *ars* tradition on which this art of living was based began with Horace's *Ars poetica*, and continued through French neoclassicism (e.g. Nicolas Boileau's *L'art poétique*) to the English Enlightenment, when it opened up from the more limited realm of fine art to include a range of arts associated with living. The Latin *ars* was a way of doing, being, or knowing, and sociable, everyday arts, such as dining, coffee-drinking, smoking, and conversation, defined the neoclassical culture of taste. Taste differed from classical aesthetics, which had for its goal the transcendence of lived reality through the contemplation of beauty—and which was, in this sense, more an art of dying (*ars moriendi*) than of living. Taste, by contrast, was a lived aesthetic; it fostered sociability in the coffee-houses where people smoked and conversed. The art of conversation in turn informed the conversational style of the literary periodical essays which flourished at this time. The periodical essay differed from earlier forms of the literary essay in a single feature: the serial persona, which gave the periodical its name and personality. Hence, *The Tatler*, *The Spectator*, *The Rambler*, *The Idler*, *The Adventurer*, *The Connoisseur*, *The Lounger*, *The Trifler*, *The Hypochondriack*, and so on down the line of the literary periodical essay tradition in English. The early periodical personae combined the figure of the newspaper journalist with the fictional idea of character. When the literary periodical essayist ventured out, with his pipe and his snuff, to read the papers at St James's—or White's, or Button's—he interacted

---

[1] [Leigh Hunt], 'Mr Gliddon's Cigar Divan', in William Hone (ed.), *The Table Book*, vol. 2 (1828), 680. Further references given in the text.

Denise Gigante, *On Coffee-Houses, Smoking, and the English Essay Tradition* In: *On Essays: Montaigne to the Present.* Edited by: Thomas Karshan and Kathryn Murphy, Oxford University Press (2020). © Denise Gigante.
DOI: 10.1093/oso/9780198707868.003.0008

with real persons in the coffee-houses of Enlightenment London. In doing so, he punctured the ontological bubble to which he had been confined as an essayistic fiction.

But did the belletristic mode of the periodical essay, in which journalism aspired to literary art, depend on a culture (however imaginary) that had passed away by the end of the century of taste? In January 1826, the Spectator's literary-periodical heir, James Henry Leigh Hunt, published an essay titled 'Coffee Houses and Smoking' in which he lamented the fact that the coffee-house culture surrounding the early essayists had dissolved. Hunt's essay is elegiac in tone, as its belated persona, Harry Honeycomb, strolls through the Covent Garden district of London, where many of the Enlightenment coffee-houses had been clustered. His persona is a spin on the character of Will Honeycomb, an ageing gallant of the Spectator's Club. 'As I never pass Covent Garden (and I pass it very often) without thinking of all the old coffee-houses and the wits', Harry Honeycomb complains, 'so I can never reflect, without impatience, that there are no such meetings now-a-days, and no coffee-room that looks as if it would suit them. They do not allow smoking in the best coffee-houses, and where they do, so many other things are allowed, that no gentleman would remain.'[2] Harry has been left behind in a world without the clubs or communal spaces that had defined the earlier essay tradition. For by the Romantic period, the lively arts associated with the culture of taste had given way to a loftier ideal of art detached from everyday life.

Ultimately what we find, in Hunt's sequel to 'Coffee Houses and Smoking', is a new form of the coffee-house as the last stand of the English periodical essayist. His essay 'Mr Gliddon's Cigar Divan' takes up where Harry Honeycomb left off after having stumbled, through the back wall of Arthur Gliddon's tobacco shop in King Street, Covent Garden, into an Orientalized cigar divan (Figure 7.1). To Harry, the new form of the smoking room appears as a vision in a dream. Hunt describes it as 'in good oriental keeping, and a proper *sesame*, when on touching a door in the wall, you find yourself in a room like an eastern tent, the drapery festooned up around you, and views exhibited on all sides of mosques, and minarets, and palaces rising out of the water' (II, 675). The door leading through the back wall of Gliddon's tobacco shop serves as a pivot, one that spins the literary periodical persona out of the tradition that had defined him and into the mode of imaginary reverie that distinguishes the literary periodical essayist of the romantic period. But what, after all, did the so-called art of smoking have to do with the essay, or belles-lettres more broadly speaking? That is the question, and now that we have asked it, let us go and make our visit: let us follow Harry Honeycomb through streets that lead less tediously than an argument to the fate of the English periodical essayist in the cultural palimpsest of Covent Garden.

---

[2] Hunt, 'Coffee Houses and Smoking', in *The New Monthly Magazine and Literary Journal* 16.61 (January 1826), 50–4, here 51. Further references given in the text.

Mr. Gliddon's Cigar Divan.

KING STREET, COVENT GARDEN.

Figure 7.1 'Mr Gliddon's Cigar Divan', in William Hone (ed.), *The Table Book*, vol. 2 (1828), 673–4.

Source: Image courtesy of the British Library.

2. Smoking as an Ornamental Art

Harry Honeycomb = delights 'to think of the times when smoking was an ornament of literature' (50). As he wanders the streets of Covent Garden in 'Coffee Houses and Smoking' haunted by the ghosts of the early periodical personae and their clubs, he calls to mind an illustration of the Spectator's Club from a pocket-book edition of *The Spectator*, of the kind Hunt himself was in the habit of carrying on his ramblings. The image features the members of the club gathered around a table in a coffee-house, smoking their pipes. 'Captain Sentry is going to light his pipe at the candle; Sir Roger is sitting with his knees apart [. . .] in the act of preparing his,—perhaps thinking what a pretty tobacco-stopper the widow's finger would have made', recounts Harry, confessing that he 'longs to be among them' (51). He is alluding to the engraving designed by Thomas Stothard for John Sharpe's 1804 edition of *The Spectator* in the series of *British Classics* produced by John Bell. Although the actual illustration includes no text to identify the individual members of the Spectator's Club, Harry knows them as well as if he were among them. One Spectatorial smoker whom he does not name, however, is his own literary progenitor and namesake, William Honeycomb. The Spectator abbreviates the name as 'Will', and Hunt alters that name to Harry, the familiar form of Henry. Will is the ageing lady's man of the Spectator's Club, and Hunt, at the age of 41, is slyly identifying with him through a pseudonym—fleshed out as a persona—associated with his own name, James Henry Leigh Hunt.

Hunt uses the pseudonym 'Harry' elsewhere. His poem addressed to Arthur Gliddon's wife Anastasia, 'La Bella Tabaccanista; or, the Fair Tobacconist of Covent-Garden', published in *The Examiner* in 1819, bore the signature 'Harry Brown' (a cognomen suited perhaps to the colour of tobacco).[3] Although periodical personae had gone up in smoke, like the notes the Spectator once burned in his pipe, pseudonyms were very much part of literary culture in Hunt's day.[4] Hunt himself had rejected the convention in 'The Round Table', an essay series published in *The Examiner* in the spirit of 'our good old periodical works'. The authors of 'The Round Table', says Hunt in the opening number, 'profess to be no other than what we are:—in other words, we assume no fictitious characters, or what an acquaintance of ours, in his becoming disdain of the original French, would call *names of war*.'[5] William Hazlitt was the principal author of the Round Table, and his essays in general dispensed with the essayistic convention of persona. Charles Lamb, by contrast. who was present at the Round Table though he contributed no essays to the series, cultivated an antiquated prose style and clung stubbornly to the practice of the early essayists in their use of personae. Hunt was caught in the middle, recognizing the degree to which the device of the serial persona had become superfluous and yet longing nostalgically for the age of serial personae.

Smoking may have been an ornament of literature in the age of the Spectator, but by the Romantic period ornaments were no longer in fashion. In what amounts to an aesthetic manifesto for Romanticism, William Wordsworth's 'Preface to *Lyrical Ballads*' condemns literary ornamentation in high-sounding words: 'It is not, then, to be supposed that any one, who holds that sublime notion of Poetry which I have attempted to convey, will break in upon the sanctity and

---

[3] Hunt, 'La Bella Tabaccanista; or, the Fair Tobacconist of Covent-Garden', *The Examiner* 603 (18 July 1819), 459.

[4] See Joseph Addison, *The Spectator* No. 46 (23 April 1711), in *The Spectator*, ed. Donald F. Bond, 5 vols (1965), I, 198.

[5] Hunt, 'The Round Table' No. 1, in *The Examiner* 366 (1 January 1815), 11.

truth of his pictures by transitory and accidental ornaments, and endeavour to excite admiration of himself by arts, the necessity of which must manifestly depend upon the assumed meanness of his subject.'[6] Ornaments, associated with 'arts' in the plural, are tied to the neoclassical *ars* tradition. For Wordsworth, they are the tools of the belletrist, not the poet. They are historical rather than philosophical, transitory rather than eternal, and accidental rather than essential. For a philosophical poet like Wordsworth, they are gauds, seducing the reader from the sublime power of poetry to the charms of artful speech.

Wordsworth was echoing the Kantian idea that ornamentation is supplemental—accessory and contingent, rather than essential and necessary—to beauty, and at worst a detraction from it. Kant writes in his 1790 *Critique of Judgment* that 'if the ornament itself does not itself consist in beautiful form, but is merely attached, as a gold frame is to a painting, then it impairs genuine beauty.'[7] Beauty was no longer to be assessed through an *art* of judgement that involved distinguishing beauties from defects.[8] It involved a purposiveness that obviated particularity, and aesthetic judgement accordingly involved the apperception of ideal form. An ornament such as a frame, if it seemed a natural extension of the beautiful object, could contribute to a judgement of the beautiful, but only to the degree that it submitted to formal purposiveness, thereby diminishing its own status as an ornament. By the time Hunt was writing, therefore, ornaments had become a clog on the purity of art. From beauties or marks of distinction, they had devolved into blemishes.

Harry Honeycomb's nostalgia for the times when smoking was an ornament of literature—like the nostalgia inscribed in his own name—connects Hunt's peri-odical persona not just to the smoking congeniality of the Spectator's Club, but to a pluralistic conception of literature as belles-lettres, or an assemblage of beauties. The 'honeycomb' image itself, as a storehouse of specifically literary sweets, traces back to the Roman essayist Seneca. Seneca's eighty-fourth epistle is a *locus classicus* for reflecting on the work of the literary essayist:

> We should follow, men say, the example of the bees, who flit about and cull the flowers that are suitable for producing honey, and then arrange and assort in their cells all that they have brought in; these bees, as our Vergil says, 'pack close the flowing honey, and swell their cells with nectar sweet' [...] We also, I say, ought to copy these bees, and sift whatever we have gathered from a varied course of reading, for such things are better preserved if they are kept separate; then, by

---

[6] William Wordsworth, 'Preface to *Lyrical Ballads*', in *The Prose Works of William Wordsworth*, ed. W. J. B. Owen and Jane Worthington Smyser, 3 vols (1974), I, 141–2.

[7] Immanuel Kant, *The Critique of Judgment*, trans. Werner S. Pluhar (1987), 71.

[8] Addison modelled this practice in *The Spectator*, devoting twelve papers to the beauties of each of the books of *Paradise Lost* (Nos. 303, 309, 315, 321, 327, 333, 339, 345, 351, 357, 363, and 369) and one paper to its blemishes (No. 297).

applying the supervising care with which our nature has endowed us,—in other words, our natural gifts,—we should so blend those several flavours into one delicious compound that, even though it betrays its origin, yet it nevertheless is clearly a different thing from that whence it came.[9]

The belletrist (howbeit an anachronism with respect to Seneca) sips the beauties of literary tradition and stores them away in little cells. Whether the *topoi* of the commonplace book or the more ancient repositories of mind, the honeycombed beehive is the product of individual taste, and the surname of Harry Honeycomb suggests an explicitly literary man of taste.

Oliver Goldsmith also draws on the analogy between the bee and the belletrist in his literary periodical series *The Bee* (1759). Goldsmith's serial persona is a creature inclined to pursue its own taste, as he explains in the opening essay of the series: 'Like the Bee, which I had taken for the title of my paper, I would rove from flower to flower, with seeming inattention, but concealed choice, expatiate over all the beauties of the season, and make my industry my amusement.'[10] Goldsmith's motto for the paper underscores the analogy between discrete literary beauties and the kind of sweets found in a honeycomb: '*Floriferis ut Apes in saltibus omnia libant, / Omnia Nos itidem*' ('As bees dancing among flowering plants sip up all the nectar, so we your words').[11] The role of the literary periodical essayist as a belletristic critic is to point out the beauties of English literature, his own taste guiding the selection.

In the opening number of *The Indicator* (1819–21), Hunt explains that he has taken the name of his periodical persona from the *cuculus indicator*, a bee-cuckoo or honey bird, which hovers above trees where honey can be found.[12] The same idea lies behind Hunt's signature of a pointing hand, which he used to sign his literary contributions to *The Examiner*, and tellingly also his essay 'Mr Gliddon's Cigar Divan', the sequel to 'Coffee Houses and Smoking'. This typographical sign, the manicule, is the mark of the belletrist, indicating where the sweets in the honeycomb of literary tradition are to be found. Beauties were extractable as ornamental features of belletristic texts, and reviews of belles-lettres took the form of a string of quoted beauties punctuated with commentary. Literary anthologies were called *Beauties*. The man of taste collected beauties—on shelves, in commonplace books, and in the storage cells of a cultivated mind. The honeycomb as an assemblage of beauties was a symbol of the belletristic aesthetic.

---

[9] Lucius Annaeus Seneca, *Epistulae morales/Moral Epistles*, trans. Richard M. Gummere (2014), 277–9.

[10] Oliver Goldsmith, *The Bee; Being Essays on the Most Interesting Subjects* (1759), 3.

[11] My translation of Goldsmith's quotation from Lucretius (*De rerum natura*, 3: 11–12) on the title page of *The Bee*.

[12] Hunt, *The Indicator* No. 1 (13 October 1819), reprinted in Hunt, *The Indicator* (1822), 1.

Harry Honeycomb's elegy for the ornamental art of smoking in 'Coffee-Houses and Smoking' is thus also, and primarily, an elegy for the *ornamentality* underwriting the form of the literary periodical essay as a key genre of English belles-lettres. In the essay form, an aggregation of ornamental features—anecdotes and epigraphs, epistles and eponymous personae, accidental associations and encounters—contributes to the form's generic plasticity, at the same time detracting from the teleology of sustained narrative and the structure of systematic argumentation. It should be noted that Addison himself, in a series of *Spectator* essays on the difference between true and false wit (Nos. 58–63), rejected literary ornamentation: antiquated or ornate poetic diction, quibbles, conceits, typographical shapes (picture poems), anagrams, acrostics, and other rhetorical flourishes. But at the same time, the singularity and contingency of ornamentality defined the essayistic aesthetic. Washed up on the other side of the century of taste, Harry Honeycomb is *himself* an ornamental relic, and of the very tradition that defined English belles-lettres.

3. Smoking and Suburbanity

The smokers of Harry Honeycomb's day, cordoned off from each other in the private libraries and fireside armchairs of the suburbs, reflected the failure as well as the success of the early periodical essayists in their effort to cultivate a taste by which they could be appreciated. As Harry Honeycomb casts a wistful eye at the old haunts of Sir Roger and his friends in Covent Garden, he muses that 'we must consider what Steele and Addison would have liked had they lived now, and witnessed the effect of the Spectators of other men. It is they that have helped to ruin their own pipes and wine, and given us a greater taste for literature and domesticity' (53). After a century's proliferation of the Spectator project throughout the literary periodicals of the eighteenth century, there could be no going back to the more free-flowing (and exclusively male) world of the Enlightenment coffee-house. 'People confine themselves too much to their pews and boxes', Harry complains. 'In former times there was a more humane openness of intercourse' (51). The segregating booths ('pews and boxes') of the coffee-house, like the private box pews of churches, suggest a virtuous morality connected to tasteful society. But polite reserve and hushed conversation can also add up to an atomized community.

Eight years after 'Coffee Houses and Smoking', Hunt was still brooding over the contrast between the coffee-houses of his own day and those of the early periodical essayists. 'The company did not sit in boxes, as at present', he explains in his *London Journal*, 'but at various tables which were dispersed through the room. Smoking was permitted in the public room: it was then so much in vogue that it does not seem to have been considered a nuisance.'[13] However idealized Hunt's vision of an Enlightenment coffee-house might be, it registers the loss of a certain vitality in coffee-houses whose patrons had become separated into their own little private spheres. 'I need not tell my Reader', Addison's Spectator had declared, 'that lighting a Man's Pipe at the same Candle, is looked upon among Brothersmokers as an Overture to Conversation and Friendship'.[14] Harry longs for this more fluid, convivial space associated with the coffee-houses of Queen Anne's day. While it is easy to dismiss such longing as an idealization involving a fiction of a reality that did not exist, we might also call it a *fictional reality* that one might actually inhabit. Hunt was, after all, familiar with the various pseudo-realities and fictionalities made possible through the literary periodical essay tradition, and he is at his best as a writer in a form whose 'humane openness' never closed off into any of the self-contained fictional worlds represented by the novel, the genre of belletristic reading most closely allied to domesticity and the private, suburban fireside.

Literary periodical essays, first in their newspaper format as broadsides, later in newspaper columns or in magazines, were meant to circulate, and circulate they did in the coffee-houses of their day like the serial personae for whom they were named.[15] But by the 1820s, the periodical papers had become absorbed into thicker monthly and quarterly journals that resembled books. As such, they were better suited to individual private spheres of belletristic reading than to the more communal space of the coffee-house. In an essay 'On Periodical Essays' published in *The Examiner* in 1808, Hunt compares the periodical essayist favourably to authors of books, saying that the essayist does not approach his audience 'in all the majesty of a quarto or all the gaiety of a beau duodecimo, smooth and well dressed'; rather, he 'claims a peculiar intimacy with the public', and 'If you do not like him at first you may give up his conversation; but the author of a book is fixed upon you for ever, and if he cannot entertain you beyond the moment, you must even give him sleeping room in your library.'[16] This essay 'On Periodical Essays', published nearly twenty years before 'Coffee Houses and Smoking', was prophetic, for by 1826, just as urban coffee-house culture had shrunken into more suburban units demarcated by booths, the republic of letters had scattered into the private patterns of suburban bookishness.

The ornamental art of smoking transformed as well. The last of the old-style smokers whom Harry Honeycomb can recall was a clergyman who had also been a man of the world:

---

[13] Quoted from James Peller Malcolm's *Anecdotes of Manners and Customs of London*, in Hunt, *Leigh Hunt's London Journal*, Supplement to Part I (1834), lxiii.
[14] *The Spectator* No. 568 (16 July 1714), in Bond, *The Spectator*, IV, 539.
[15] See this volume, Chapter 4 by Markman Ellis.
[16] Hunt, 'On Periodical Essays', in *The Examiner* 2 (10 January 1808), 26.

He had seen the best society, and was a man of the most polished behaviour. This did not hinder him from taking his pipe every evening before he went to bed. He sat in his arm-chair, his back gently bending, his knees a little apart, his eyes placidly inclined towards the fire; and delighted, in the intervals of puff, to recount anecdotes of the Marquis of Rockingham, and 'my Lord North'. The end of his recreation was announced to those who had gone to bed, by the tapping of the bowl of his pipe upon the hob, for the purpose of emptying it of its ashes. Ashes to ashes; head to bed. [...] I think I could drop off with a decent compromise between thought and forgetfulness, sitting with my pipe by a fireside, in an old elbow-chair.   (50)

This smoker of Honeycomb's acquaintance drops the names of two former prime ministers, Charles Watson Wentworth, second Marquess of Rockingham, and Frederick North, Lord North, former leaders of the Whig and Tory parties, respectively. Party politics had no place in a republic of letters, and like the early periodical essayists who, despite their Whiggish sympathies, made an effort to steer clear of political affiliation, this smoker 'of the old school' shows his political disinterestedness by conversing with representatives of both parties (50). Like the members of the Tatler's and Spectator's Clubs, he is anecdotal—and to that degree, compatible with the ornamentality of the essay tradition in which such clubs figured prominently. But there is this difference: Honeycomb's acquaintance smokes alone at his hearth, rather than with a club in a coffee-house.

Of all the members of the Spectator's Club, this old-school smoker reminds Harry most of Sir Roger de Coverley, the affable country squire, though the lack of tasteful urbanity that distinguished Sir Roger from the Spectator has here become a tasteful *suburbanity*. Hunt uses this term in his essay 'Men and Books' to describe the pipe-smoking Thomas Warton, a belletrist whom he distinguishes from the typical Oxford scholar. There was 'more magnanimity and heroism' in Thomas Warton's edition of Milton, Hunt asserts, 'aye, and in the pipe he smoked of an evening, under certain circumstances of *suburbanity*, than in all the daring and large-minded comments upon *Phi* and *Tau* made by the interchangers of that felicitous designation'. Although Warton was an institutional academic, a Fellow of Trinity College, Oxford, and Professor of Poetry from 1757 to 1766, he was also a belletrist: an amateur, or 'hearty *lover*' of poetry and other forms of fine writing.[17] Warton's edition of Milton's *Poems Upon Several Occasions* addressed the same general audience as Addison's *Spectator* papers on *Paradise Lost*, and his pipe-smoking suburbanity, as a latter-day ornamental art, shows the Addisonian 'Pleasures of the Imagination' in praxis: a phrase Addison coined in *The Spectator*

---

[17] Hunt, 'Men and Books', in *The New Monthly Magazine and Literary Review* (January 1833): 31–7, here 32.

to describe aesthetic experience, and more particularly (as he would demonstrate with respect to Milton) the tasteful pleasures of belles-lettres.[18]

A respite from study as much as from sloth, belletristic reading was neither hard work nor mental vacancy. According to Addison, the pleasures to be gained from it, 'do not require such a Bent of Thought as is necessary to our more serious Employments, nor, at the same time, suffer the Mind to sink into that Negligence and Remissness, which are apt to accompany our more sensual Delights, but, like a gentle Exercise to the Faculties, awaken them from Sloth and Idleness, without putting them upon any Labour or Difficulty'.[19] Not coincidentally, this is how Harry Honeycomb describes the pleasures of smoking. 'In smoking, you may think or not think, as you please', he says. 'If the mind is actively employed, the pipe keeps it in a state of satisfaction, supplies it with a side luxury, a soft ground to work upon' (50). Fertile, soft, and earthy as ploughed dirt, tobacco gives the smoker 'ground to work upon', which may yield verse—as in the georgic metaphor of ploughed lines—or other forms of tasteful expression. The contemplations of the smoker take place somewhere 'between thinking and no-thinking' (51). They are equally remote from the socially inaccessible regions of vegetable existence on the one hand, and scholarly thought and disquisition on the other. Addison uses the words 'Sloth', 'Idleness', 'Negligence', and 'Remissness' interchangeably to refer to the former condition of mentally inert animality, while the opposite extreme involves mental labour, difficulty, and a 'bent of thought' ponderous enough to bow the human animal beneath its weight. The pleasures of the imagination, by contrast, involving both sensation and sense (moderate mental activity), qualify (like the contemplations of the smoker) as tasteful experience.

The Spectator, in Addison's words, had sought to bring philosophy 'out of Closets and Libraries, Schools and Colleges, to dwell in Clubs and Assemblies, at Tea-Tables, and in Coffee-Houses'.[20] These were the sociable environments in which the pleasures of the imagination transpired, and in which the contemplative smoker enjoyed what Harry calls 'a decent compromise between thought and forgetfulness' in his portrait of the old-style smoker above. The puff of smoke takes the hard, abstemious edge from the scholar, rendering him conversable in the pauses he takes to reflect. 'If you wish to be idle, the successive puffs take the place of thinking', Harry says: 'There is a negative activity in it, that fills up the place of the real' (50). This 'negative activity' is a version of Wordsworth's 'wise passiveness' as an antidote to the 'savage torpor' of everyday existence.[21] One can

---

[18]   *The Spectator* No. 411 (21 June 1712), in Bond, *The Spectator*, III, 536.
[19]   *The Spectator* No. 411 (21 June 1712), in Bond, *The Spectator*, III, 539.
[20]   *The Spectator* No. 10 (12 March 1711), in Bond, *The Spectator*, I, 44.
[21]   Wordsworth, 'Preface to *Lyrical Ballads*', in *Prose Works*, I, 129. On 'wise passiveness', see Wordsworth's poem 'Expostulation and Reply' from *Lyrical Ballads*, in *Lyrical Ballads, and other Poems, 1797–1800*, ed. James Butler and Karen Green (1992), 108.

read the smoke floating upward in wispy phantoms from the contemplative head as a visible sign of resistance to the same forces of modernity that Wordsworth identifies in his 'Preface to *Lyrical Ballads*' as marshalled against the pleasures of the imagination. Yet while Hunt's old-school smoker might seem to fit right in with the members of the Spectator's Club, he is as alienated from their world as Harry. He is content to smoke in his own home and go to bed. Perchance to dream. For dreaming was the form the pleasures of the imagination took in the literary periodical essays of the romantic period.

4. The Cigar Divan

When Harry Honeycomb at last reaches his 'friend Gliddon's snuff and tobacco-shop in King Street' his thoughts are still running on the old-school smokers. 'Ay; here, said I, is wherewithal to fill the boxes of the Steeles and Congreves, and the pipes of the Aldriches and Sir Roger de Coverleys. But where is the room in which we can fancy them? Where is the coffee-house to match? Where the union of a certain domestic comfort with publicity—journals of literature as well as news,—a fire visible to all,—cups without inebriety,—smoking without vulgarity?' (52). Given the complicated fictionality of the tradition in which he is participant, it is fitting that Harry Honeycomb should imagine a convivial Oxford scholar like Henry Aldrich filling his pipe in company with the fictional squire from *The Spectator*. Although Hunt does not name his friend Arthur Gliddon, who opened London's first cigar divan in the rooms behind his tobacco shop in Covent Garden, Harry conscripts him into his own pseudo-reality by calling him Gliddon.

In historical actuality, there were many Gliddons. Two years before Arthur Gliddon's cigar divan opened, Hunt wrote to his friend from Italy, chastising him for his epistolary silence: 'If you can't write a whole letter, Mrs Gliddon must help you. What of Mr John Gliddon? [. . .] What of Mr Thomas Gliddon, and Alicia Gliddon, and Mrs Gliddon, senior, and all the Gliddons, you Gliddon?'[22] Arthur's brother-in-law, George Gliddon, who had lived in the East, was the person Harry Honeycomb had to thank for bringing the idea of the cigar divan to London from Constantinople.[23] Arthur Gliddon's cigar divan, the first of many that would spring up in the metropolis in the nineteenth century, returned the coffee-house to its origins in the symbolic world of Orientalism.

Here we would do well to recall that while the institution of the coffee-house had become identified with the European Enlightenment, the original coffee-houses of London prepared coffee in the Turkish fashion, served tea in China

---

[22] Hunt to Arthur Gliddon, 24 July 1823, quoted in Anne Gliddon, *The Gliddons in London 1760–1850*, ed. Wendy Norman (2000), 35.
[23] Gliddon, *The Gliddons in London*, 22.

bowls (called dishes), and were often depicted in illustration with turbaned servers. Coffee followed the trade routes to England from the East, from Yemen originally (as most accounts have it) to Constantinople, where, in the mid sixteenth century, the first coffee-houses opened. Pasqua Rosee, the employee of an English trader in Turkish goods, opened London's first coffee-house in St Michael's Alley in 1652. Like others that began to appear throughout Europe in the seventeenth century, from Le Procope in Paris to the Blue Bottle in Vienna, Rosee's coffee-house was Turkish in flavour.[24] These early English coffee-houses did not disguise their Orientalism, though it soon wore off in an era of Tatlers and Spectators who made coffee-drinking and conversation signs of British culture.

Coffee came from the East only to be associated with the West, while tobacco came from the West only to be associated with the East. In both 'Coffee Houses and Smoking' and its sequel, 'Mr Gliddon's Cigar Divan', Hunt credits Sir Walter Ralegh, sponsor of colonial ventures in Virginia, with having imported the fashion of pipe-smoking to England (52, 679). The word 'cigar' itself derives from the Spanish *cigarro*, and in turn from the Mayan *sik'ar*, a New-World term for smoking.[25] In the latter essay, Hunt puts himself in dialogue with other wits and essayists, including Charles Lamb ('L'), over a cup of coffee at Gliddon's. 'Talking of the refreshments of different ages, it is curious to see how we identify smoking with the Eastern nations', observes 'L', 'whereas it is a very modern thing among them, and was taught them from the west. One wonders what the Turks and Persians did before they took to smoking; just as the ladies and gentlemen of these nervous times wonder how their ancestors existed without tea for breakfast' (678). Such nervous times were a reflection of nervous, caffeinated citizens. The physician George Cheyne associated nervous conditions with the English in *The English Malady; or, a Treatise of Nervous Diseases of all Kinds, as Spleen, Vapours, Lowness of Spirits, Hypochondriacal, and Hysterical Distempers, &c.* (1733). But nervous stimulants entered the nation from outside, from both the East and the West, and Lamb, who spent his days at that imperial centre of East–West relations, the offices of the British East India Company in London, knew the futility of plumbing a commodity, like a cigar or cup of coffee, to its symbolic depths in a global economy.

By the 1820s, coffee and tea, cigars and tobacco, were all part of what David Cannadine calls a 'remarkable transoceanic construct of substance and sentiment', whose best description, he suggests, is '*imperialism as ornamentalism*'.[26] Cannadine

---

[24] On the coffee-house phenomenon, see Bryant Lillywhite, *London Coffee Houses: A Reference Book of Coffee Houses of the Seventeenth, Eighteenth and Nineteenth Centuries* (1963); Brian William Cowan, *The Social Life of Coffee: The Emergence of the British Coffee House* (2005); and Markman Ellis, *The Coffee House: A Cultural History* (2004).
[25] The etymology of 'cigar' is from *Encyclopedia Britannica Online*; the *OED* outlines some philological conflict and proposes that the cigar-shaped cicada may lie behind the Spanish *cigarro* (*s.v.* 'cigar, n.').
[26] David Cannadine, *Ornamentalism: How the British Saw Their Empire* (2001), 122.

posits 'Ornamentalism' as a corrective to Edward Said's Orientalism, which understands imperialism in terms of race, rather than the class hierarchies that are Cannadine's concern.[27] When we think about the Orient, he argues, we think 'about chiefs and emirs, sultans and nawabs, viceroys and proconsuls; about thrones and crowns, dominion and hierarchy, ostentation and ornamentalism'.[28] As opposed to the Western ideals of neoclassicism, the ornament emerges in the political and social vision of Ornamentalism as triumphant: a symbolic construct in which East and West are inextricable, as centre and periphery, metropolis and colony, turn each other inside out.

To the degree that the cigar represents the latest fashion in smoking, moreover, it is somewhat at odds with the contemplative life symbolized by the old-style, ornamental smoker. In an attempt to explain the shift from the pipe to the cigar in the ornamental art of smoking, Hunt quotes from the prospectus to Gliddon's cigar divan, which he seems to have written for his friend:

> The recreation of smoking, which was introduced into this country in an age of great men, by one of the greatest and most accomplished men of that or any other age, was for a long time considered an elegance, and a mark of good-breeding. Its very success gradually got it an ill name by rendering it too common and popular; and something became necessary to give it a new turn in its favour,—to alter the association of ideas connected with it and awaken its natural friends to a due sense of its merits. Two circumstances combined to effect this desirable change. One was the discovery of a new mode of smoking by means of rolling up the fragrant leaf itself, and making it perform the office of its own pipe; the other was the long military experience in our late wars, which have rendered us so renowned; and which, by throwing the most gallant of our gentry upon the hasty and humble recreations eagerly snatched at by all campaigners, opened their eyes to the difference between real and imaginary good-breeding, and made them see that what comforted the heart of man under such grave circumstances, must have qualities in it that deserved to be rescued from an ill name.   (680)[29]

The cigar is here a commodified pipe. It is quick and easy; and once used, it is used up. It is interchangeable with any other cigar in the box. It requires none of the ornamental adjuncts of pipe-smoking, from snuff box to tobacco stopper. In short, it has been rolled up and packaged for convenience, like the very Englishmen Harry would like to see out of their boxes.

---

[27] See Edward Said, *Orientalism* (1978).   [28] Cannadine, *Ornamentalism*, 126.

[29] On Hunt's authorship: the style of the prospectus for Gliddon's cigar divan matches (and borrows phrases from) both 'Coffee Houses and Smoking' and 'Mr Gliddon's Cigar Divan'. It includes the same genealogy of smoking as the former, and the only record of it is in the latter.

In conversation with Harry Honeycomb, Gliddon points to a sign at the back of his shop, and his 'open sesame' reveals the fate of the literary periodical essayist: a belletrist in a cigar divan, a culturally ornamental space at the centre of a global nexus of trade. 'It was rather two rooms thrown into one', Harry says, 'and with a fire in each; a divan of ample dimensions runs round it; lamps of ground glass diffuse a soft, yet sufficing light; the floor is carpeted; two cheerful fires offer double facility of approach, a twofold provocation to poke and be self-possessed; around are small mahogany tables, with chairs, in addition to the divan; and in the midst of all, stands a large one, profusely covered with the periodical works of the day, newspapers, magazines and publications that come out in numbers' (52). To stir the fire with an air of self-possession had been the prerogative of Sir Jeoffrey Notch of the Tatler's Club, whose ancestry put him one social 'notch' above the other members of the Club and gave him first dibs on the fire poker.[30] But had Sir Jeoffrey woken up after more than a century's sleep in Gliddon's version of the coffee-house, he might not have been able to approach either of the fires with the same air of possession. The old oak seats had stretched out luxuriously into Oriental divans. Oriental carpets covered the floors. Pink drapery festooned the walls, fluting up into a Turkish Crescent. And the painted walls blinked open onto views of mosques, minarets, and Turkish palaces.[31] Through a seemingly magical hole in the wall of a respectable business, one passed into a world of Orientalized fantasy.

What Hunt depicts in his essay on 'Coffee Houses and Smoking' is the symbolic prehistory as well as future of the eighteenth-century periodical essay tradition. Michel de Montaigne, in his essay 'Of Solitude', speaks of an *arrière-boutique*, a back shop of imaginative freedom into which the essayist may retreat from his more public façade. 'We must reserve a back shop all our own, entirely free, in which to establish our real liberty and our principal retreat and solitude', writes the essayist.[32] This same *arrière-boutique* as a place of retreat from the busy world, a private storehouse of subjectivity behind one's public front, is materialized in the back rooms of Gliddon's tobacco shop. Indeed, for all Hunt's effort to revive the tradition of 'our good old periodical works', the literary essays that stand out from the Romantic period tend to reject the sociability associated with earlier coffee-house culture by retreating into dreams and visions.[33] In this respect, one might place Thomas De Quincey's 'Confessions of an English Opium-Eater' in a category with Hazlitt's reverie-like essays (e.g., 'On a Sun-Dial', 'On Going a Journey') and Lamb's dreamy periodical essays that appeared under the signature Elia ('Dream Children: A Reverie', 'Old China', and 'The Child Angel', among

---

[30] Richard Steele, *The Tatler* No. 132 (11 February 1710) in *The Tatler*, ed. Donald F. Bond, 3 vols. (1987), II, 266.
[31] Gliddon, *The Gliddons in London*, 22.
[32] Michel de Montaigne, *The Complete Works*, trans. Donald M. Frame (2003), 214.
[33] Hunt, 'Round Table', 11.

them). Dreamlike reverie also characterizes much poetry of the period, from Coleridge's 'Kubla Khan; or, A Vision in a Dream' to John Keats's 'The Fall of Hyperion: A Dream'. Coleridge, like De Quincey, was addicted to opium, and Keats produced his late work under the influence of laudanum. Both poets—Keats in verse, Coleridge in a preface—attribute their hallucinatory visions to an 'elixir', which we can identify as an opiate.[34] Percy Shelley calls this mode of visionary reverie a 'waking dream' in *The Triumph of Life*.[35]

Hunt could hardly have recognized the spectre he was raising of an Orientalized subculture that was soon to emerge in other smoky back rooms and opium dens when he speculated, 'what a number of elegant and cheerful places lurk behind shops, and in places where nobody would expect them. Mr Gliddon's shop is a very respectable one; but nobody would look for the saloon beyond it' (675). The familiar snuff and tobacco shop, in other words, is a commercial facade for a more covert entity whose respectability is not as immediately apparent. Secrecy, luxury, and even suspicion seem bound up in the affair. Hunt observes that 'a person's surprise would hardly be greater, certainly his comfort not so great, in passing from the squalidness of a Turkish street into the gorgeous but suspicious wealth of the apartment of a pasha, as in slipping out of the mud, and dirt, and mist, and cold, and shudder, and blinking misery of an out-of-door November evening in London, into the oriental and carpeted warmth of Mr Gliddon's Divan' (675). The Ornamentalism of the East was taking root in the symbolic heart of the West, in Covent (or perhaps Covert) Garden. 'I begin to think I am a Turk under the influence of opium, who take my turban for a hat, and fancy I'm speaking English', Hunt writes (676). Harry, too, might be excused for doubting whether he is hallucinating in the manner of his contemporary, the English Opium-Eater.

In 'Suspiria de Profundis', a sequel to his 'Confessions of an English Opium-Eater', De Quincey claims that his purpose in those earlier essays had been to show the influence of opium on dreaming, and more importantly, *to demonstrate the faculty of dreaming*. Dreaming was a counteractivity, opposed to the 'fierce condition of eternal hurry' that characterized modernity.[36] De Quincey warned that 'unless this colossal pace of advance can be retarded (a thing not to be expected) or, which is happily more probable, can be met by counter-forces of corresponding magnitude, forces in the direction of religion or profound philosophy, that shall radiate centrifugally against this storm of life so perilously

[34] John Keats, *The Fall of Hyperion*, l. 47, in *The Poems of John Keats*, ed. Jack Stillinger (1978), 479; Samuel Taylor Coleridge, preface to 'Kubla Khan' in *Christabel; Kubla Khan, a vision; The Pains of Sleep* (1816).

[35] Percy Bysshe Shelley, *The Triumph of Life*, l. 42, in *The Complete Poetical Works of Percy Bysshe Shelley*, ed. Thomas Hutchinson (1905, 1965), 508.

[36] Thomas De Quincey, in *Confessions of an English Opium-Eater and Other Writings*, ed. Robert Morrison (2013), 82.

centripetal towards the vortex of the merely human', the result must be 'a regency of fleshly torpor'.[37] De Quincey's 'fleshly torpor' is a variant of Wordsworth's 'savage torpor', both conditions the inevitable result of a headlong rush into modernity. 'At length I rouse myself from my reverie', Hazlitt writes, 'and home to dinner, proud of killing time with thought, nay even without thinking.'[38] Such are the pleasures of the imagination in a world ruled by the clock—defiantly idle, somewhere between thought and no-thought. But the pleasures of the imagination in these late periodical essays aimed less at a disinterested, Spectatorial view of the world than at the altered realities that might be glimpsed through the ground-glass lamps of Gliddon's cigar divan—lamps that spread 'a soft yet sufficing light' in a room beyond daylight.[39]

In De Quincey's self-portrait of the essayist, moreover, the Opium-Eater smokes alone. Whereas the Spectator sought to bring philosophy out of the closet and into the world of sociability, we find De Quincey's Opium-Eater sequestered in 'the interior of a scholar's library, in a cottage among the mountains, on a stormy winter evening'.[40] Rather than the daily periodicals, a book of German metaphysics sits on his table. A metaphysician verging on Faustian magician, he would be out of place in the coffee-houses of the early periodical essays. Instead of the Spanish tobacco the Tatler takes to share at the Graecian, he chooses a stimulant derived from the Oriental poppy to indulge in solitude. Phenomenal and phantasmatic, isolated and yet imbricated in that global nexus of East and West which we may call Ornamentalism, he has shut up shop, and retreated into his own sombre and dysfunctional *arrière-boutique*, a victim of the very medium used to transport him there.

In 'Suspiria de Profundis', De Quincey suggests that just as chemistry can bring to light hidden layers of a manuscript, opium-smoking can bring to consciousness memories buried deep within the brain.[41] This metaphor of the palimpsest, anticipating Freudian psychology and cultural analysis, may be instructively applied to the literary topography of Covent Garden as a landscape comprising the layered textuality of the English literary periodical essay tradition.[42] From his position in Gliddon's cigar divan, Harry Honeycomb looks one way and imagines that he sees Sir Richard Steele in 'the man with the short face'; looking the other

---

[37] De Quincey, *Confessions of an English Opium-Eater*, 82.
[38] William Hazlitt, 'On a Sun-Dial', in *The Selected Writings of William Hazlitt*, ed. Duncan Wu, 9 vols (1998), IX, 159.
[39] On the paradigm shift from the mimetic mirror to the lamp of inner vision, see M. H. Abrams, *The Mirror and the Lamp: Romantic Theory and the Critical Tradition* (1953).
[40] De Quincey, *Confessions of an English Opium-Eater*, 61.
[41] De Quincey, *Confessions of an English Opium-Eater*, 136–7.
[42] On Freud's analysis of Rome as a palimpsest, see Sigmund Freud, *Civilization and its Discontents*, trans. James Strachey (2005), 44.

way, he discovers Joseph Addison 'in black, looking something like a master in chancery' (53). Hunt himself, in the voice of his manicule persona in 'Mr Gliddon's Cigar Divan', sees the spectre of John Dryden emerging from Rose Alley on his way to spend the evening with his club at Will's (675). Ultimately, these late periodical essays suggest, the palimpsest of the modern world was legible only through the visionary imagination of the dreamer.

8

The Romantic Essay and the City

Gregory Dart

What I mean by living to one's-self is living in the world, as in it, not
of it: it is as if no one knew there was such a person, and you wished
no one to know it: it is to be a silent spectator of the mighty scene of
things, not an object of attention or curiosity in it; to take a thoughtful, anxious interest in what is passing in the world, but not to feel the
slightest inclination to make or meddle with it.

Hazlitt, 'On Living to One's-Self'[1]

1. Two Traditions: The Urban Periodical Essay and the Poetry of Rural Retirement

There are two traditions behind the Romantic familiar essay. The most obvious
line of inheritance leads back through the eighteenth-century urban periodical to
the *Tatler* and *Spectator*. In Hazlitt's 'On Living to One's-Self' (1821) it is difficult
to pass over that resonant line about being 'a silent spectator of the mighty scene
of things' without recalling Mr Spectator's resolution to 'retire into Town, if I may
make use of that Phrase, and get into the Crowd again as fast as I can, in order to
be alone', or the assertion at the beginning of his twenty-four hours in London,
that 'it is an inexpressible Pleasure to know a little of the World, and be of no
Character or Significancy in it.'[2] Hazlitt's essay recalls this mode of metropolitan
spectatorship but cannot long sustain it, for no sooner is it invoked than the lens
retracts and another, more distant perspective slides into view:

It is such a life as a pure spirit might be supposed to lead, and such an interest as
it might take in the affairs of men, calm, contemplative, passive, distant, touched
with pity for their sorrows, smiling at their follies without bitterness, sharing
their affections, but not troubled by their passions, not seeking their notice, nor

---

[1] William Hazlitt, 'On Living to One's-Self', first published in *Table-Talk* [1821], *The Selected
Writings of William Hazlitt*, ed. Duncan Wu, 9 vols (1998), VI, 79. Further references given in
the text.

[2] Joseph Addison, *Spectator* No. 131 (31 July 1711) in *The Spectator*, ed. Donald F. Bond, 5 vols
(1965), II, 20–1; Richard Steele, *Spectator* No. 454 (11 August 1712) in Bond, II, 98.

Gregory Dart, *The Romantic Essay and the City* In: *On Essays: Montaigne to the Present.* Edited by: Thomas Karshan and
Kathryn Murphy, Oxford University Press (2020). © Gregory Dart.
DOI: 10.1093/oso/9780198707868.003.0009

once dreamt of by them. He who lives wisely to himself and to his own heart, looks at the busy world through the loop-holes of retreat, and does not want to mingle in the fray. 'He hears the tumult, and is still.'   (VIII, 91)

The final quotation is from Book IV of William Cowper's *Task* (1785), that great mock-epic of rural domesticity, and so too is that striking phrase about looking at the world 'through the loop-holes of retreat'.[3] Generically speaking, this is the literary equivalent of changing trains: one minute we had seemed to be travelling towards the metropolitan marketplace in the spirit of the eighteenth-century periodical; the next the wheels of civic engagement have been put into reverse and we are circling round and back towards the countryside in the wounded spirit of early modern 'retirement' poetry. It is a subtle shift, an associative side-step, no doubt encouraged by Cowper's 'loop-hole'. But such locomotive interchange between adjoining tracks of feeling is highly characteristic, I would argue, not only of 'On Living to One's-Self', but also of the Romantic familiar essay more generally, whose unstable intellectual position on the challenge of modernity is also an unstable geographical position, and whose anxious self-questionings often manifest themselves as unexpected modulations of register and genre.

2. The Alienated Spectator

The template that Addison and Steele bequeathed to the familiar essay form was one in which all roads led to the City. At the heart of the *Spectator* was the fictional club of Mr Spectator, Roger de Coverley, Andrew Freeport, and their friends, whose dialogue was designed to balance the competing claims of Whig and Tory, town and country. But over and above this atmosphere of tolerant politeness there shone the steady appeal of modern commerce. Addison's paean to the Royal Exchange (in No. 69) is the most famous example of this; but even more significant, in a way, is the celebration of the 'Change as a kind of cathedral of modern urbanity at the climax of Steele's twenty-four hours in London (No. 454). Out in Covent Garden in the late morning, Mr Spectator makes use of the anonymity of the city to window-shop on a window-shopper, following a female 'Silk-Worm' as she flits from store to store. The silk-worms serve a purpose, Steele tells us, because 'they are ever talking of new Silks, Laces and Ribands, and serve the Owners in getting them Customers', though they never buy anything them-selves. And then later that afternoon, having moved east to the City, Steele's narrator theatrically declares himself 'the richest Man that walked the *Exchange*

---

[3] 'I behold / The tumult, and am still', in *The Task* [1785], IV, ll. 99–100, and ''Tis pleasant, through the loop-holes of retreat / To peep at such a world', IV, ll. 88–9, in William Cowper, *Poetical Works*, ed. H. S. Milford, (1905), 184.

that day; for my Benevolence made me share the Gains of every Bargain that was made'.[4] In sum what this essay presents us with is a prelapsarian version of Poe's 'Man of the Crowd', in which there is no alienation between viewer and viewed, or between visual and actual consumption, because the identification of the narrator with commercial modernity is so complete. Never has the periodical prose-writer been so happy in his role as glorified silk-worm—advertising, far more than criticizing, what the market has on offer.

No such whole-hearted identification was possible for the Romantics. The closest thing to an official inauguration of the Romantic familiar essay took place on 1 January 1815, when Leigh Hunt launched 'The Round Table' in his liberal newspaper *The Examiner*. Born during a brief window of public tranquillity, politics was the wicked fairy overlooked at its christening, with the stated aim of the new series being to revive the inclusive 'club' spirit of those 'good old periodical works' the *Tatler* and *Spectator*.[5] Largely the work of Hunt and Hazlitt, 'The Round Table' was short-lived but influential, ushering in a new golden age for the essay, most notably in the pages of *Blackwood's* (1817–), John Scott's *London* (1820–), Hunt's own *Indicator* (1819–21), and Henry Colbourn's *New Monthly* (1821–). Like the *Spectator* 'The Round Table' intermingled philosophical, social, and literary criticism, offering essays 'On Philosophical Necessity', 'On Methodism', and 'On Milton's Versification'. It also found room for several proto-Dickensian urban sketches, including Hunt's notorious 'On Washerwomen'. But in spite of this rich variety, there lingered a nagging suspicion that, as Hazlitt himself acknowledged in the Preface to the collected edition, 'The Round Table' had fallen 'somewhat short of its title and original intention' (IX, 19).

The problem was that by mid 1816 post-war distress and popular agitation had swollen to such a degree that, for both Hazlitt and Hunt, the political essay had begun to displace the familiar one as the order of the day. On 5 January 1817 the forty-eighth and last of the 'Round Table' series—Hazlitt's 'On Actors and Acting'—made its appearance in *The Examiner*. A week later the same writer was writing in the same paper 'On the Connection between Toad-Eaters and Tyrants'. Where two years previously, at a time of post-war optimism, the emphasis had been upon literature as a collaborative pursuit, now Hazlitt was representing it as self-seeking and divisive. 'There is no class of persons so little calculated to act in *corps* as literary men', he wrote; 'they are governed not by the spirit of unanimity, but of contradiction.' So far from being consensus-seekers in the field of politics, writers were the most extreme and eccentric actors in it. 'They [...] are ready to prove the best things in the world the worst, and the

---

[4] *Spectator* No. 454 (11 August 1712), in Bond, *The Spectator*, IV, 101, 102.
[5] Leigh Hunt, 'The Round Table', from *The Examiner* (1 January 1815), in *Selected Writings of Leigh Hunt*, ed. Robert Morrison and Michael Eberle-Sinatra, 6 vols (2003), II, 6.

worst the best', Hazlitt continued, 'from the pure impulse of splenetic over-weening self-opinion.'[6]

Even when it made a comeback at the end of the decade, the familiar essay retained an impulse to retirement. Often the city, with its relentless getting and spending, and its increasingly vociferous class politics, was precisely what it wanted to escape. As Hunt himself put it in the first issue of his *Indicator* in October 1819: 'the Editor has enough to agitate his spirits during the present eventful times, in another periodical work [i.e. *The Examiner*]', hence in this new one he would 'attend to no subject whatsoever of immediate or temporary interest. His business is with the honey in the old woods.'[7] In this last phrase Hunt was making a very deliberate fusion of the symbolic and the literal, bringing together the 'old woods' of early English literature—Chaucer, Spenser, Milton, and the Elizabethans, an enthusiasm for which he was hoping to revive, and the 'old woods' around Hampstead, where the author was then living. Essays about the teeming streets were not beyond him—his 'On the Sight of Shops' and 'On the Graces and Anxieties of Pig-Driving' are very Steele-like in tone and subject matter—but in general he preferred to keep a distance from the *forum*. Professing himself 'accustomed to use his pen, as habitually as a bird his pinion, and to betake himself with it into the nests of bowers of more lasting speculations, when he has done with public ones', Hunt declared himself 'determined to keep those haunts of his recreations free from all noise and wrangling, both for his own pleasure, and for those who may choose to accompany him'.[8] This was retreat of a distinctively modern and suburban kind: the setting up of a close relationship between the spaces or 'haunts' of recreation, little private nests and bowers on the edge of the city, and the space of belles-lettres itself, as embodied by *The Indicator*. And what this promoted, as we can see from an essay such as 'Walks Home at Night', was a notion of life as a regular commute between city and suburb, *Examiner* and *Indicator*, the realm of business and an (increasingly privatized) realm of culture.

In the early modern period, the 'retirement' tradition had still had an overwhelmingly classical air, and offered itself as a virtuous retreat from city and court corruption. But with the commercial development of the eighteenth century it began to take on a more 'thoughtful, anxious' character. Early in Book III of Cowper's *Task* (1785) the poet rails against London as a haven of prostitution and fraud where 'vice has such allowance, that her shifts / And specious semblances have lost their use', before suddenly modulating into a new and more personal key:

---

[6] Hazlitt, 'Literary Notices No. 22: The Times Newspaper: On the Connexion between Toad-Eaters and Tyrants', *The Examiner* (12 January 1817), 26.
[7] Hunt, *The Indicator* No. 1 (13 October 1819), 1.   [8] Hunt, *The Indicator* No. 1, 1.

I was a stricken deer, that left the herd
Long since; with many an arrow deep infixed
My panting side was charg'd when I withdrew
To seek a tranquil death in distant shades.[9]

Here a familiar trope of retreat—that of the 'stricken deer'—is transformed into an expressive statement of alienation, not least because it stands in such an unexplained and enigmatic relation to what has gone before. In moments such as this the moral damage of the city is depicted as something sublime, beyond description, representable only as a strange non-sequitur. Strong in Cowper, this current is even more powerful in Wordsworth, who was to render the 'dissolute' city's corruption of Luke, the son of old Michael the shepherd, in equally mysterious terms: 'ignominy and shame / Fell on him', the poet announces abruptly at the climax of his tragic pastoral of 1800, 'so that he was driven at last / To seek a hiding place beyond the seas'.[10]

Coming to maturity at a time of revolutionary upheaval and ever-increasing urbanization, the Lake Poets gave extra intensity to Cowper's rhetoric of retreat. This was a feature of many of Wordsworth's *Lyrical Ballads*—of 'Michael' and 'Tintern Abbey'—and it also found its way into his celebrated Preface to the second edition, which complained of the 'savage torpor' generated by the 'increasing accumulation of men in cities'.[11] In Coleridge, too, the effect of metropolis upon mental life was regularly invoked and deplored. In his 1797 conversation poem 'This Lime Tree Bower my Prison' he reflected sympathetically on how his London friend Charles Lamb had 'pined / And hunger'd after Nature, many a year, / In the great City pent, winning thy way / With sad yet patient soul, through evil and pain / And strange calamity!'[12]

3. Healthy Associations: Lamb, Hazlitt, Hunt, and the Essay of Urban Nostalgia

Lamb had grown up in Cowper and Coleridge's poetic shadow, and in his early verse he did nothing to contradict their anti-urban bias.[13] But with the publication

[9] Cowper, *The Task*, III, ll. 108–11, in *Poetical Works*, 162.
[10] William Wordsworth, 'Michael', ll. 454–6, in *Lyrical Ballads, and other Poems, 1797–1800*, ed. James Butler and Karen Green (1992), 267.
[11] Wordsworth, 'Preface to *Lyrical Ballads*', in *The Prose Works of William Wordsworth*, ed. W. J. B. Owen and Jane Worthington Smyser, 3 vols (1974), I, 129.
[12] Samuel Taylor Coleridge, 'This Lime-Tree Bower, My Prison', ll. 28–32, in *Poetical Works I: Poems (Reading Text)*, ed. J. C. C. Mays (2001), in *Collected Works of Samuel Taylor Coleridge*, ed. Kathleen Coburn, 23 vols (1983–), XVI, 352.
[13] See, for example, 'Composed at Midnight', first published in *Blank Verse* [1798], *Works of Charles and Mary Lamb*, ed. E. V. Lucas, 7 vols (1903), V, 24–5. Further references given in the text.

of Wordsworth's Preface his dissipated spirits were called home. One of Wordsworth's key assertions, in both his literary theory and his poetic practice, was that rural landscape, ever-changing with the seasons and yet also reassuringly permanent, provided the best foundation for the human personality. It was the securest ground for the growth of general concepts out of particular sense impressions, extracting virtue out of natural objects through the association of ideas. Locality bred morality, and Nature kept one sane. When it came to the city, by contrast, Wordsworth's presumption was that, because everything in it was so remote and impermanent, the values that it inculcated would be the same. Man in the city would have no moral landmarks to lay a course by; he would be adrift in a sea of signs. But Lamb, born and bred in the Temple, was instinctively resistant to this charge, feeling bound to insist that he too had his time-honoured associations and his virtuous chains of feeling: 'My attachments are all local, purely local—' he told the poet in January 1801, 'old chairs, old tables, streets, squares, where I have sunned myself, my old school,—these are my mistresses—have I not enough, without your mountains?—I do not envy you. I should pity you, did I not know that the Mind will make friends of any thing.'[14] And in 'The Londoner', a short essay published a year later in the *Morning Post*, he worked this sentiment up to a considerable pitch of lyric feeling:

> Where has spleen her food but in London? Humour, Interest, Curiosity, suck at her measureless breasts without a possibility of being satiated. Nursed amid her noise, her crowds, her beloved smoke, what have I been doing all my life, if I have not lent out my heart with usury to such scenes! (I, 47)

Reworking Steele's old model of commercial spectatorship into a perverse usury of the streets, in which profit is extracted from sympathizing with the pleasures and pains of others, 'The Londoner' provided a blueprint for the metropolitan essay of the future. But it was only twenty years later, with the growth of the literary magazines, that the conditions were ripe for it to be put into practice.

Lamb's opening sally in this vein, 'The South-Sea House', which first appeared in the *London Magazine* in August 1820, was written in the persona of a scholarly clerk 'Elia', and began by reworking the old metropolitan club motif beloved of Steele and Addison. What it presented was a group portrait of some of the clerks that Lamb had known during his brief stint at the House nearly thirty years before. With wistful humour, the essayist reminisced about Evans the ageing Macaroni, Thomas Tame, who had 'the air and stoop of a nobleman', John Tipp and Plumer, amateur musicians, and Henry Man, the amateur author (II, 4). The eccentricities

---

[14] Charles Lamb, *Letters of Charles and Mary Lamb*, ed. Edwin Marrs, 3 vols (1975), I, 267–8.

and hobby-horses of these men were recalled and celebrated, as befitted the sub-genre. But where Lamb's portrait was unusual was in its over-determined insistence that, even in 1792, these men had already seemed like living relics, poverty-blanched bachelors, amiable but outmoded. The South Sea Company had been founded in 1711, the same year as the *Spectator*, but had been in gradual, irreversible decline more or less ever since (especially after the notorious 'Bubble' of 1720). Lamb's former colleagues were perfect representatives of their parent company in this respect. And when viewed in this light, Lamb's group portrait may be seen as containing not only a series of general thoughts about the effects of time and change in the City, but also a more specific lament about the slow decline of the Addisonian ideal.

The implicit contrast with Mr Spectator, on his visit to the Royal Exchange, is a strong one; for where the former had freely admitted weeping for joy at the spectacle of busy commerce uniting the world, Elia is forced to discover a new and perverse pleasure in his old institution's cloistral quiet, transcending the continuing terrors of his day job in contemplation of the administrative ruins of the past: 'Living accounts and accountants puzzle me', he says. 'I have no skill in figuring. But thy great dead tomes, which scarce three degenerate clerks of the present day could lift from their enshrining shelves [...] are very agreeable and edifying spectacles. I can look upon these defunct dragons with complacency' (II, 2). Discovering a pocket of picturesque retirement on the corner of Threadneedle Street, Lamb's essay somehow manages to occupy a realm at once inside and outside the City. It works as a sepia imitation of a *Spectator* sketch. But it also functions as a metropolitan lyrical ballad, wherein the South Sea House, like poor Margaret's ruined cottage, is transformed from the poignant image of a 'poor neighbour out of business' into an 'agreeable and edifying' spectacle (II, 2).

There is a similar nostalgia for bygone forms of urban sociability in many of Hazlitt's familiar essays, notwithstanding their greater openness to contemporary politics. But tellingly, when he wanted to criticize the coffee-house politicians of his day, it was not Steele and Addison that he resorted to by way of a contrast, but Francis Beaumont and Ben Jonson at the Mermaid Tavern another hundred years before. 'Then where there hath been thrown / Wit able enough to justify the Town', as he says, quoting Beaumont's 'Letter to Jonson' in his June 1822 essay 'On Coffee-House Politicians'. 'I cannot say the same of the Southampton,' he continued, speaking of his own local, just off Chancery Lane, 'though it stands on classic ground, and is connected by vocal tradition with the great names of the Elizabethan age':

What a falling off is here! Our ancestors of that period seem not only to be older by two hundred years, and proportionably wiser and wittier than we, but hardly a trace of them is left, not even the memory of what has been.   (VIII, 192)

Ignoring the *Tatler* and *Spectator*, Hazlitt reaches back to the early seventeenth century, a time when he imagines city and country, prose and poetry to have stood in a more open relation to one another. This attitude was shared by many in the *Examiner* group. Only a few months prior to this Lamb's Elia had made a similar link between the Temple, where he and his sister had been brought up, and the Arcadian landscapes of Spenser and Marvell. 'What a transition for a countryman visiting London for the first time', he exclaimed, 'the passing from the crowded Strand or Fleet-street, by unexpected avenues, into its magnificent ample squares, its classic green recesses!' (II, 82–4).[15]

The earliest and most self-conscious deployment of this kind of historical fantasy was in Leigh Hunt's 'Pleasant Memories Connected with Various Parts of the Metropolis', which was first published in *The Indicator* in October 1819, only a month after the Peterloo Massacre. In it Hunt indulged London's literary associations to the full, while at the same time making us aware of the various other kinds of association—social and political—that such daydreaming was keeping at bay.

> Health will give us a vague sense of delight, in the midst of objects that would tease and oppress us during sickness. But healthy association peoples this vague sense with agreeable images. It will comfort us, even when a painful sympathy with the distresses of others becomes a part of the very health of our minds. We can never go through St Giles's, but the sense of the extravagant inequalities in human condition presses more forcibly upon us; and yet some pleasant images are at hand even there to refresh it. They do not displace the others, so as to injure the sense of public duty which they excite; they only serve to keep our spirits fresh for their task, and hinder them from running into desperation or hopelessness. In St Giles's church lie Chapman, the earliest and best translator of Homer; and Andrew Marvell, the wit and patriot, whose poverty Charles the Second could not bribe. We are as sure to think of these two men, and of all the good and pleasure they have done to the world, as of the less happy objects about us.[16]

Here pleasant images from literary history provide a momentary distraction from urban misery, but only in order to give liberal optimism a much-needed shot in the arm. This was how Leigh Hunt wanted his familiar essays to work in theory, as morale-boosting diversions. In practice, however, their tendency was always to want to segregate and protect 'healthy association' from the contaminating influence of the *polis*. This was not an attempt to depoliticize it per se but rather to suburbanize and privatize it, to whisk it away from any connection with Cato Street or Spa Fields. The impulse was most clearly evident in the *Indicators* that

---

[15] First published in the *London Magazine* in September 1821 and reprinted in *Elia* (1823).
[16] Hunt, *The Indicator* No. 3 (27 October 1819), reprinted in *The Indicator* (1822), 20.

Hunt wrote in the first weeks and months after Peterloo, essays such as 'Country Houses near Town', 'Autumnal Commencement of Fires', and 'To Any One Whom Bad Weather Depresses', where one can see a trim garden being marked out solely for the private imagination to play in.[17] Even in the St Giles essay quoted above we can sense a deep desire to treat literature as a means of escape underlying all those anxiously repeated insistences to the contrary. For no sooner are the 'pleasant images' of Chapman and Marvell brought in to refresh the liberal spirit than they begin to derail and distract it, instantly accruing fetish status like charms or secular icons.

4. The Enfranchised Quill: Lamb's Lucubrations

For Leigh Hunt political journalism was the day job, familiar essay-writing the recreation. For Lamb the day job was, simply and straightforwardly, that of being a clerk in the City of London. Literature was what happened at night and at the weekends. But when seeking to give definition to his own reading and writing space, Lamb was not content simply to distinguish it from public affairs, or his daily labour at the office. He also wanted to differentiate it from what he called 'reviewing', 'the accursed critical habit, the being called upon to judge and pronounce', which had grown to such prominence with the rise of the magazines (I, 129).[18] If poetry, especially the poetry of the Lake School, can be thought of as being 'in retreat' in this period, then the aggressive new reviewing culture, exemplified most notably by the *Edinburgh Review*, the *Quarterly* and *Blackwood's*, was one of the things it was retreating from, a culture so anonymous and cut-throat that it was sometimes likened to street crime.[19] Coleridge deplored the treatment Wordsworth had received from Jeffrey and Hazlitt, setting up a loose distinction between his favoured mode of amateur 'genial criticism', which sympathized with poetry and the poetic impulse, and professional 'reviewing', which was often coldly adversarial in comparison. Lamb shared Coleridge's and Wordsworth's deep aversion to periodical criticism (not least after the *Quarterly's* insensitive rewriting of his 1814 review of *The Excursion*), and when giving definition to his own brand of familiar essay in the 1820s, he openly offered it up to his readership as that most paradoxical of things—a form of metropolitan retreat.

In Steele's *Tatler* 'Isaac Bickerstaff' had addressed some of his essays 'from my own apartment', representing portions of his periodical as having been written in

---

[17] These essays appeared in *The Indicator* No. 1 (13 October 1819), 6–8; No. 2 (20 October 1819), 9–11; and No. 5 (10 November 1819), 33–5, respectively.
[18] From 'The Tragedies of Shakspeare'.
[19] See Gregory Dart, *Metropolitan Art and Literature 1810–1840: Cockney Adventures* (2012), 70.

private at the end of the day (and not, as was more usual, in a City coffee-house).[20] This topos was further extended when the periodical was published in book form, being presented to the public as *The Lucubrations of Isaac Bickerstaff.*[21] 'Lucubration', the act of reading or writing at night, had connotations of excessive scholarliness and obscurity. It was a comic trope, and in this case referred back to Swift's original conception of Bickerstaff as an eccentric astrologer.[22] But notwithstanding its prominent appearance on the title page of the collected *Tatler*, neither the notion of lucubration nor its associations had any real relevance to Steele's handling of the essay form. Only in Lamb's Elian essays of the 1820s were its imaginative possibilities explored. Presenting 'Elia' as a man who (like himself) works all day at a counting house, Lamb celebrated the night as the only time for him to think or study:

> The enfranchised quill, that has plodded all morning among the cart-rucks of figures and cyphers, frisks and curvets so at its ease over the flowery carpet-ground of a midnight dissertation.—It feels its promotion.[23]

Night is Elia's only resort, but it is also a rich one, because it sponsors a new kind of freedom and ambition for prose-writing. This notion is everywhere in Lamb, but is perhaps most enjoyably expressed in a 'Popular Fallacy' from 1826, which quibbles with the notion 'That We Should Lie Down with the Lamb'. At the most literal level this essay is a simple celebration of candlelight as a civilizing force. 'Wanting it', Elia speculates, 'what savage and unsocial nights must our ancestors have spent, wintering in caves, and unillumined fastnesses! They must have lain about and grumbled at one another in the dark' (II, 271). Gradually this builds into a picture of the night as the true home of conversation, speculation, and, in particular, poetic activity: 'It is a mockery, all that is reported of the influential Phoebus', the essayist continues. 'No true poem ever owed its birth to the sun's light' (II, 272). Celebrating the night as the bringer of inspiration, Lamb invokes two sons of London—Milton and Jeremy Taylor, one a poet, the other a writer of religious essays and sermons, as night-workers of the first order. 'Milton's Morning Hymn on Paradise, we would hold a good wager, was penned at midnight; and Taylor's richer description of a sun-rise [in *Holy Dying*] smells decidedly of the taper.' Buoyed by such examples, Elia then goes on to confess a growing confidence in himself:

---

[20] See, for example, *The Tatler* No. 1 (12 April 1709), in *The Tatler*, ed. Donald F. Bond, 3 vols (1987), I, 1.

[21] *The Lucubrations of Isaac Bickerstaff, Revised and Collected by the Author*, 4 vols (1712).

[22] See, for example, George Mayhew, 'Swift's Bickerstaff Hoax as an April Fool's Joke', *Modern Philology* 61.4 (May 1964), 270–80.

[23] From 'Oxford in the Vacation'.

Even ourself, in these our humbler lucubrations, tune our best measured cadences (Prose has her cadences) not unfrequently to the charm of the drowsier watchman "blessing the doors"; or the wild sweep of winds at midnight. Even now a loftier speculation than we have yet attempted courts our endeavours. We would indite something about the Solar System.—*Betty, bring the candles.*

(II, 272)

Several years before Lamb's 'Popular Fallacy', Coleridge had devoted key chapters of the *Biographia Literaria* (1817) to re-establishing the formal difference, radically undermined by the Preface to *Lyrical Ballads*, between poetry and prose. Metre, for Coleridge, was the sign, if not the symptom, of a crucial distinction, a distinction which had to do with poetry's higher organization and purpose: 'I write in metre', he insisted, 'because I am about to use a language different from that of prose.'[24] For him, the esemplastic power at work in imaginative poetry was an important metaphor for, and indeed a leading example of, the divine creativity at the heart of nature. Poetry had a religious quality that prose did not. Seen in this context, Lamb's 'prose has her cadences', backed up by the references to Milton and Jeremy Taylor, is a clear attempt to remind Coleridge of the spirit of the seventeenth century, a lucubratory moment which had sponsored visionary flights in prose as well as verse.

Lamb's reference to the watchman recalls an early poem of Coleridge's, where young bards had been pictured scribbling away in their 'city garrets', struggling in vain to address that 'Sister of love-lorn poets, Philomel!':

> While at their window they with downward eye
> Mark the faint lamp-beam on the kennell'd mud,
> And listen to the drowsy cry of Watchmen,
>   (Those hoarse, unfeather'd nightingales of Time!)[25]

But the deeper allusion, and allegiance, is to Milton's 'Il Penseroso', in which the sound of the 'Belman's drowsy charm' blessing the doors 'from nightly harm' had introduced an image of the poet himself, letting 'his lamp at midnight hour / Be seen at some high lonely Tower', as his mind roved between heaven and earth, 'the spirit of Plato to unfold'.[26] Drawing this company around him, Lamb insists that prose also 'has her cadences', and that, under special conditions (as, for example, at night), it too might be able to take on some of the expansiveness of lyric poetry, and 'indite something about the Solar System'. But in the final sentence this

---

[24] Coleridge, *Biographia Literaria*, ed. James Engell and W. Jackson Bate, 2 vols (1983), in *Collected Works*, VII: II, 69.

[25] Coleridge, 'To the Nightingale' (1795), ll. 1–6, in *Poetical Works I (Reading Text)*, in *Collected Works*, XVI, 227.

[26] John Milton, *Il Penseroso*, ll. 83–96, in *Complete Poems*, ed. Gordon Campbell (1980), 35.

impulse is ironized, for in the very act of making a first preparatory step towards the fulfilment of this sublime ambition, the essay returns fetishistically to its earlier, more modest theme. And that is where it ends, or breaks off—in a neat joke which is also an admission of failure: '—*Betty, bring the candles*'.

Writing some fifteen years after Lamb's death, Thomas De Quincey lamented the short-windedness of his prose style. Making reference to his clerkship and domestic care of his sister, De Quincey argued that 'all his life [. . .] he must have read in the spirit of one liable to sudden interruption' and that his writing had suffered in consequence. 'The instances are many in his own beautiful essays', wrote the Opium-Eater, 'where he literally collapses, literally sinks away from openings suddenly offering themselves to flights of pathos or solemnity in direct prosecution of his own theme.'[27] He then went on to contrast Lamb's style with his own, criticizing the former's lack of 'rhythmus, or pomp of cadence'.[28] John Wilson had made a similar point in a slightly different way in his (otherwise very sympathetic) review of Lamb's *Works*, arguing that 'there is a sort of timidity about him that chains his wings. He seems to want ambition.'[29] The suggestion was that Lamb's tendency towards brief flights and self-interruption was, quite literally, a shortcoming. But that is not the only way of interpreting the imperfections of Elia. Indeed from another perspective it might be seen as exhibiting a deep understanding of his chosen genre. To Lukács, writing nearly a century later, the essay was at bottom a Socratic form, because it was one in which the longing for 'the essential', for 'form and value', was forever being interrupted and forestalled. This was not a weakness, however, but a 'profound life-symbol', a crucial portion of the wisdom it had to impart:

> Plato knew exactly why he burned the tragedy he wrote in his youth. For a tragic life is crowned only by its end; only the end gives meaning, sense and form to the whole, and it is precisely the end which is always arbitrary and ironic here, in every dialogue and in Socrates' whole life.[30]

Like Milton's Penseroso, Elia uses the midnight hour 'the spirit of Plato to unfold', but it is not Plato the essentialist that he ends up emulating, but Plato the essayist. He looks for truth but finds life.[31] In *The Spirit of the Age*, which was published in the same year as the 'Popular Fallacies', Hazlitt noted this tendency of Lamb's to hover on the borderline between the everyday and the ideal, like the piece of soot

---

[27] Thomas De Quincey, 'Final Memorials of Charles Lamb', *North British Review* (November 1848), 194.

[28] De Quincey, 'Final Memorials', 195.

[29] John Wilson, 'Works of Charles Lamb', *Blackwood's* (August 1818), 599.

[30] György Lukács, 'On the Nature and Form of the Essay: A Letter to Leo Popper', in *Soul and Form*, trans. Anna Bostock, ed. John T. Sanders and Katie Terezakis (2010), 30.

[31] Lukács, 'On the Nature and Form of the Essay', 27.

flapping on the bar of the grate in Coleridge's 'Frost at Midnight'. 'Ideas savour most of reality in his mind', he wrote, 'or rather his imagination loiters on the edge of each, and a page of his writings recalls to our fancy the *stranger* on the grate, fluttering in its dusky tenuity, with its idle superstition and hospitable welcome!' (XI, 180).[32] Here Hazlitt openly celebrates the indecisive, intermittent quality of Lamb's writing, its phantom familiarity, its self-mocking erudition.

5. Hazlitt, Coleridge, and the Whirligig of Association

Foregrounding the play of association between present and past, town and country, and poetry and prose, was very much a feature of Hazlitt's familiar essays of the 1820s. So too the appeal—and impossibility—of retirement. Witness his 'On Living to One's-Self' which, like the above-mentioned 'Frost at Midnight', begins by a country fireside on a winter evening (the essay is advertised as having been written at Winterslow Hut, Wiltshire on 18–19 January 1821):

> I never was in a better humour than I am at present for writing on this subject. I have a partridge getting ready for my supper, my fire is blazing on the hearth, the air is mild for the season of the year, I have had but a slight fit of indigestion to-day (the only thing that makes me abhor myself), I have three hours good before me, and therefore I will attempt it. It is as well to do it at once as to have it to do for the week to come.   (VIII, 90)

There is an irony here, and one that Hazlitt makes much of, which is that the topic he has chosen is all about intellectual and moral independence, and yet the conditions under which he is contemplating it, which are that of a freelance essayist writing to a deadline, effectively exclude him from this state. Sure enough, the more Hazlitt meditates on the sublime detachment that might define 'living to one's-self', the more he finds himself railing against his literary enemies back in the metropolis. The whirligig of association is forever linking poles and opposites. Re-engaging with metropolitan culture is presented as something that the essayist can scarcely prevent himself from doing, being temperamentally incapable of equanimity, but it is also presented as something that he has no real choice about, given his status as a professional writer. Splendid isolation, or sublime self-exile, is posited as an alluring ideal, but one open only to poets and peers. Quoting the final stanzas of the third Canto of Byron's *Childe Harold* beginning 'I have not loved the world, nor the world me', Hazlitt chips in with a pointed comment: 'sweet verse embalms the spirit of sour misanthropy: but woe betide the

---

[32] From 'Elia and Geoffrey Crayon'.

ignoble prose-writer who would thus dare to compare notes with the world, or tax it roundly with imposture' (VIII, 97). In 'Frost at Midnight' the poet's inability to inhabit fully the rural idyll that lay before him had been blamed on his childhood in the city. But in 'On Living to One's-Self' it has its basis in pure economic necessity. In Hazlitt's hands as in Lamb's, the Romantic familiar essay has become that most interesting of creatures—a lyrical medium, but one that is continually being interrupted by the most prosaic, and pragmatic, of concerns.

Given new prominence by its republication in *Sibylline Leaves* in 1817, 'Frost at Midnight' was a poem that functioned as both an inspiration and a provocation to the London essayists. It was a provocation because it was determined to read every sign of the country in the city as a reminder of urban alienation. It was an inspiration because, even more than 'Tintern Abbey', it was deeply invested in exploring the associative links between them. The poet, sitting alone one night in his rural cottage with his young baby boy sleeping by his side, suddenly sees a 'fluttering stranger' in the fire. According to popular superstition this sooty film was thought to portend the visit of some townsman or family member, and in 'Frost at Midnight' it reminds the poet of how he used to pore over the fire when he was at boarding-school in the city, hoping for sightings of similar 'stranger[s]'. 'Pent 'mid cloisters dim', and seeing 'naught lovely but the sky and stars', the young boy had longed all the while to be back at his 'sweet birth-place' in the country, where 'the old church-tower / Whose bells, the poor man's only music, rang from morn to evening, all the hot Fair-day / [...] Most like articulate sounds of things to come!'[33] What the stranger and the bells provide, in this scenario, are reminders of a former promise, the promise of an education in and through Nature, which the poet hopes his young son will benefit from, even if it is now too late for him. 'Therefore all seasons shall be sweet to thee', he concludes, addressing the little baby in the crib beside him, 'Whether the summer clothe the general earth / With greenness [...] / Or if the secret ministry of frost / Shall hang them up in silent icicles, / Quietly shining to the quiet Moon' (ll. 65–7, 72–4, in I, 456). This final mention of 'the secret ministry of frost' takes us back to the first line of the poem, but in a very different spirit from the opening, for what was once, as it were, a mere visual metaphor, a description of the way frost creeps slowly across a landscape, is now shot through with religious significance—a symbol of nature's 'eternal language'.

Hazlitt's closest engagement with 'Frost at Midnight' is in the last essay he wrote, 'The Letter Bell' of 1830. Life, the essay begins by asserting, is too vast and various to contemplate from a distance; but take a tuning fork to some part of it, and the reverberations will travel in all directions:

---

[33] Coleridge, 'Frost at Midnight' (1798), ll. 52–3, 28–9, 33, in *Poetical Works I (Reading Text)*, 455. Further references given in the text.

Ask the sum-total of the value of human life, and we are puzzled with the length of the account and the multiplicity of items in it; take any one of them apart, and it is wonderful what matter for reflection will be found in it! As I write this, the *Letter-Bell* passes: it has a lively, pleasant sound with it, and not only fills the street with its importunate clamour, but rings clear through the length of many half-forgotten years.   (XVII, 377)

These two sentences might pass for a miniature blueprint for the familiar essay, beginning with the particular and moving indirectly and by a process of association towards something more abstract and general. From the point of view of the treatise (such as Hazlitt's own early *Essay on the Principles of Human Action*), it looks unsystematic and amateurish, but its great advantage comes from the way it is able to follow the workings of the mind. More than any other literary form (with the possible exception of the blank verse conversation poem) what it aspires to is not so much thought's distillate but its process of fermentation—the manner in which ideas resonate and communicate with one another.

The letter-bell was a bell rung in the streets by early nineteenth-century postmen as a prompt for people to come out and present their letters for posting. When Hazlitt hears it the reverberations are as many and as complex as they are for Lamb when he hears 'the bell which rings out the Old Year' at the beginning of his 1821 essay 'New Year's Eve'. First, it reminds Hazlitt of the moment, some thirty years previously, when he had first come up to London, and owed a letter to his people back home. 'It made me feel that I had links still connecting me with the universe', he writes, 'and gave me hope and patience to persevere':

At that loud-tinkling interrupted sound (now and then) the long line of blue hills near the place where I was brought up waves in the horizon, a golden sunset hovers over them, the dwarf-oaks rustle their red leaves in the evening breeze, and the road from [Wem] to [Shrewsbury], by which I first set out on my journey through life stares me in the face as plain, but from time and change not less visionary and mysterious, than the pictures in the *Pilgrim's Progress*.

(XVII, 377)

Like an amalgam of Coleridge's 'fluttering stranger' and his old church bell, the letter-bell is both a reminder of family ties and a herald of things to come. Not only does Hazlitt's essay follow the same procedure as 'Frost at Midnight' in the way that it talks about landscape and memory, the early productions of the Lake School are part of what it wants to remember:

I should notice, that at this time the French Revolution circled my head like a glory, though dabbled with drops of crimson gore: I walked comfortable and cheerful by its side—

And by the vision splendid
Was on my way attended.
It rose in the east: it has again risen in the west.   (XVII, 377)

The letter-bell takes the essayist back to the 1790s, and reminds him of his youthful idealism; it is an idealism, moreover, that he has never relinquished, and that he may yet live to see fulfilled (the mention of the re-emergence of the 'vision splendid' in this, the sunset of his life, is a reference to the recent outbreak of the 1830 revolution in Paris). As so often in such cases, Hazlitt quotes Wordsworth to make a link between the *Lyrical Ballads* and the radical enthusiasm of the 1790s (for the two always went together in his mind). Key to the pleasure and pride that Hazlitt feels on hearing the letter-bell is that it reminds him of the essential consistency of his feelings, especially his political feelings: 'This is the reason I can write an article on the *Letter-Bell*, and other such subjects; I have never given the lie to my own soul. If I have felt any impression once, I feel it more strongly a second time; and I have no wish to revile or discard my best thoughts' (XVII, 378). This, as Hazlitt then goes on to make clear, is in stark contrast to Coleridge, Wordsworth, and Southey, who for all their professed interest in continuities have not remained faithful to liberty's cause.

So what is the larger meaning of Hazlitt's letter-bell in this context? Coleridge's 'stranger' was an associative image that ranged both backward and forward in time, binding the different portions of the poet's life together. But emotionally it only ever looked one way: back to the countryside. In the case of the letter-bell, however, there is a return ticket. On its initial appearance it reminded the essayist of his friends back home, and of the need to write to them; but in more recent instances it is also capable of drawing him deeper into the metropolis. 'Or if the Letter-Bell does not lead me a dance in the country', he writes, 'it fixes me in the thick of my town recollections':

It was a kind of alarm to break off from my work when there happened to be company to dinner or when I was going to the play.   (XVII, 378)

The letter-bell is an injunction to write, but it is also a reminder of the larger context in which writing takes place; it is a bridge between the individual and the communal. Sometimes, Hazlitt says, when he was looking over an old engraving on a wintry evening, it was 'the only sound that drew my thoughts to the world without, and reminded me that I had a task to perform in it' (XVII, 379). The letter-bell, in short, is a perfect symbol for the Hazlittian familiar essay, acting as a kind of relay between town and country, prose and poetry, the actual and the ideal. In Keats's 'Ode to a Nightingale' the bell-like resonance of the word 'forlorn' calls time on the poet's great excursion into faery land, 'tolling [him] back to his sole self'.[34] But in Hazlitt the letter-bell is always a welcome interruption, a constructive spoke in the wheel.

Historically, the letter-bell was part of a concrete network of communications and connections that made up the early nineteenth-century mail system. But it was also, to Hazlitt, 'a conductor of the imagination' that could ferry things back and forth, across space and time, and link the different corners of life together. In the city it reminded you of the country; in the country it reminded you of the city. It was a tireless commuter, negotiator, and dialectician. This emphasis on association as a dynamic and wide-ranging network of response is characteristically Hazlittian. Whereas in Hunt's recreational writings, as we have seen, association often seeks to restrict itself to what is healthful and pleasant, in Hazlitt it is always insistently, even dogmatically open. Wherever one might happen to be in a Hazlitt essay—whether in the countryside or in a coffee-house, at the House of Commons or in an art gallery—it is only ever one short step to anywhere and everywhere else.

Not every sight or sound is equally associative, 'The Letter-Bell' concedes, and as if to reinforce the point devotes some of its later paragraphs to thinking about dustman's bells, postman's knocks, and the sight of Mail-Coaches pouring out of London of an evening. Significantly, the essay ends with a reference to Book IV of Cowper's *Task*, whose 'loop-holes of retreat' had been so attractive to 'On Living to One's-Self', but which is cited here in order to show the deep interpenetration of town and country. The passage chosen is from the beginning of the book, which depicts the Post-Boy, 'the herald of a noisy world', trudging through the winter night to deliver his 'close-packed load':

> He whistles as he goes, light-hearted wretch!
> Cold and yet cheerful; messenger of grief
> Perhaps to thousands, and of joy to some;
> To him indifferent whether grief or joy.[35]

This is characteristically Cowperian in its imagining of the meeting between city and country as one of cold, modern indifference intruding upon a sensitive, picturesque communality, a feeling that is expressively played out in the blank verse itself, the final line deliberately flattening the jaunty rhythm of its predecessors. Prompted by such thoughts, Hazlitt ends the 'Letter-Bell' by referring once again to the July Revolution, and to the manner in which its news has been spread abroad:

> The picturesque and dramatic do not keep pace with the useful and mechanical. The telegraphs that lately communicated the intelligence of the new revolution to

---

[34] John Keats, 'Ode to a Nightingale', ll. 71–2, in *The Poems of John Keats*, ed. Jack Stillinger (1978), 371.

[35] *The Task*, IV, 12–15, in *Poetical Works*, 183.

all France, within a few hours, are a wonderful contrivance, but they are less striking and appalling than the beacon-fires (mentioned by Aeschylus), which lighted from hill-top to hill-top, announced the taking of Troy and the return of Agamemnon.   (XVII, 382)

Coleridge's ambition for the 'fluttering stranger' in 'Frost at Midnight' was that it should become a 'toy of thought'. Nor is it unusual to see poetry cultivating such aspirations. What is rarer, but what one encounters again and again in the Romantic period, is a similar ambition lurking at the heart of the familiar essay. Most essays are capable of floating theories or telling stories; relatively few are capable of speaking in and through their images, their pattern of resonances, their form.

It is this harmonic quality that distinguishes the best work of Lamb, Hunt, Hazlitt, and De Quincey, and which they often strove to foreground in their work. Explaining the relationship between the 'Vision of Sudden Death' in his 'The English Mail-Coach' and the concluding 'Dream-Fugue' that followed it, De Quincey used a musical metaphor, showing how all the elements of his anecdote of the near collision of two night-coaches had been encouraged to blend 'under the law of association, with the previous and permanent features investing the mail itself' to produce a deliberately polyphonic climax.[36] In the case of 'The Letter-Bell', whose final lines are quoted above, what we have is an essay that can be read either tragically or triumphally depending on the meaning with which one chooses to load the letter-bell itself. One can see it as a tocsin of liberty whose prophecy is (by the end of the essay) fulfilled, or one can read it as an emblem of the endangered poetry of life ('the picturesque and dramatic do not keep pace with the useful and mechanical'). Both readings are equally prominent, equally viable, but it is perhaps the great achievement of this essay, and of others like it, that it is less interested in choosing between these alternatives, than in dramatizing its own rich ambivalence, its ability to move in two directions at once.

---

[36] De Quincey, 'Explanatory Notices', from *The English Mail-Coach and other Writings*, in *The Works of Thomas De Quincey*, 16 vols (1878), IV, xiii.

9

Charles Lamb, Elia, and Essays in Familiarity

Felicity James

1. Introduction: Re-Familiarizing Lamb

Let us start our journey into the familiar essay with two moments, years apart, of unfamiliarity, of strangeness and loss. The first is an evening in January 1798, in London's Inner Temple. Charles Lamb, still recovering from the death of his mother at the hands of his sister, Mary, the previous year, had rushed away from a gathering of friends with his feelings 'wrought too high not to require vent', as he tells his correspondent.[1] Walking alone in the Temple, his birthplace, he composed one of his most successful poems, 'The Old Familiar Faces'. 'Where are they gone, the old familiar faces?' the poem begins, and each verse enumerates his losses—his murdered mother, his ill sister, his absent friends—until we get to its great cry of loneliness:

> Ghost-like, I paced round the haunts of my childhood.
> Earth seem'd a desert I was bound to traverse,
> Seeking to find the old familiar faces.[2]

The poet has become a ghost to his own haunts, estranged from all he once held familiar, the halting pace of the verse echoing his uncertainty as he goes out into his solitary future.

In the second moment, the 'Ghost-like' poet of 1798 transforms himself into the 'queer spirit' Elia. That description comes from a mock obituary, 'Character of the late Elia', published in the *London Magazine* for January 1823. The piece would later become the 'Preface' for the *Last Essays of Elia*: it comes in the midst of Lamb's successful run as one of the chief attractions of the *London Magazine*. Just when he is enjoying his first taste of widespread popularity, Lamb toys with killing off his creation—if, indeed, Elia ever really existed in the first place. A 'two years'

---

[1] Charles Lamb to Marmaduke Thompson, January 1798, in Edwin W. Marrs, Jr (ed.), *The Letters of Charles and Mary Anne Lamb*, 3 vols (1975–8), I, 124–5.
[2] Lamb to Marmaduke Thompson, 124–5.

Felicity James, *Charles Lamb, Elia, and Essays in Familiarity* In: *On Essays: Montaigne to the Present*.
Edited by: Thomas Karshan and Kathryn Murphy, Oxford University Press (2020). © Felicity James.
DOI: 10.1093/oso/9780198707868.003.0010

and a half existence has been a tolerable duration for a phantom', writes the obituarist, one Phil-Elia. He goes on to discuss the oddness and crudeness of this phantom's essays. 'I am now at liberty to confess', Phil-Elia tells us, 'that much which I have heard objected to my late friend's writings was well-founded. Crude they are, I grant you—a sort of unlicked, incondite things—villainously pranked in an affected array of antique modes and phrases.'[3] If his style is lacking, so is his content. Elia 'gave himself too little concern what he uttered', says Phil-Elia, and 'would interrupt the gravest discussion with some light jest'.[4] Both the lack of seriousness and the affectedness are compressed into the word 'prank', which nicely, pointedly, brings together the idea of a hoax or trick with an obsolete late sixteenth-century term meaning ostentatiously dressed, or decorated with folds.[5] And such layers of borrowed finery, such deliberate prankings and teasings, reinforce Phil-Elia's central question—who is the essayist? His words are his, and yet not his, filched from the works of others. His essays are 'unlicked, incondite things', like the 'unlick'd bear-whelps' of Shakespeare's *3 Henry VI*. Even the name Elia is stolen, purloined from a former colleague, and in any case, it is an anagram of its own untrustworthiness: 'a lie'. And the lies keep coming: even before we have got to the piece in the January issue of the *London Magazine*, we have encountered a piece by 'Elia's Ghost', and the editorial has reassured us that Elia's '*ghostship* has promised us very *material* assistance in our future Numbers', unsettling our notions of the author and authorial sincerity.[6]

Lamb and Elia, 'the man and his familiar', in the words of A. C. Ward, were a constant presence in the essays of the nineteenth and into the twentieth century.[7] His work exerted a powerful influence on the development of the familiar essay genre, and part of the purpose of this chapter is to bring 'Elia's Ghost' into full view in contemporary conversations about the essay—and to remember the complexity and strangeness of his writing. The second, intertwined, purpose is to use Lamb to deepen our understanding of the many nuances of the familiar essay, and what we mean by the familiar in all its different senses. Etymologically, the term is derived in English partly from the French *famylier* and partly from the Latin *familiāris*, both of which have as their primary meaning 'belonging to the family' or 'relating to the household': 'private, personal, of or belonging to a family, closely associated, intimately connected, well-known, habitual'. This sense of something well-known, intimate, and accustomed then leads into the larger sense of familiar as related to the essay. The familiar essay is written in a

---

[3] 'A Character of the Late Elia', *London Magazine* 7.37 (January 1823), 19.

[4] 'A Character of the Late Elia', 20.

[5] As in Spenser's line, 'Some prank their ruffs, and others trimly dight / Their gay attire', from the *Faerie Queene* (1.4.14), a work Lamb knew well. See Edmund Spenser, *The Faerie Queene*, ed. A. C. Hamilton (2001, 2007), 65.

[6] *London Magazine* 7.37 (January 1823), 3.

[7] Lamb, *Everybody's Lamb, Being a Selection from the Essays of Elia, The Letters, and the Miscellaneous Prose*, ed. A. C. Ward (1933), xvii.

conversational style: it uses familiar language, in the sense of words which are 'homely, plain; easily understood', and frequently returns to topics which are themselves familiar, 'habitual, ordinary, usual'.[8] It borrows from those older connotations of close relationship to create a form of language which is 'free, casual, informal', one which would be used between friends or relations, and as such, as we will see, it has links with the familiar letter.

It also carries stranger meanings, which Lamb, in particular, brings to the fore. For all its associations with the ordinary and homely, the 'thing call'd Familiar' carries along with it an alternative meaning of a witch's companion: 'Familiars in the shape of mice, / Rats, ferrets, weasels, and I wot not what', in the words of a Lamb favourite, *The Witch of Edmonton* (1621).[9] As Phil-Elia reminds us, when he describes Elia as a 'queer spirit', the familiar is closely related to the uncanny. Indeed, Phil-Elia's characterization of Elia's style shows several different meanings of 'familiar' at play: Phil-Elia, despite his sharp critique of his 'late friend's' style, is clearly related to Elia, 'belonging to [his] family, closely associated'; he knows his style intimately. And yet despite this familiarity in one sense, in another sense it turns the familiar inside out. For Elia's style is far from 'homely' or 'ordinary': it is encrusted with ornament and archaism, deliberately odd. This reminds us that the familiar essay may be haunted in many ways. Although essayists from Montaigne to Hazlitt emphasize the importance of conversational, plain, straightforward language, this exists in a certain tension with the essayist's creation of a persona, whose words may not quite be the author's own. They may, indeed, be borrowed from someone else entirely, given the essayistic tendency towards quotation and allusion. Elia's essays revel in the use of 'antique modes and phrases', turning the familiar, at moments, into something baroque. They also love to hoax, and with their deliberate lies and evasions, they direct 'the reader's attention to the persona', in the words of David Shields, 'the unreliable mask of the "I"'.[10] Phil-Elia captures something of the strangeness of what Lamb does with the familiar: at once intimate and alien, ostensibly friendly but in fact disconcerting, continually unsettling expectation.

For twentieth-century readers, all this 'pranking' proved difficult. Lamb's style dwindled into an 'assumed and easily assimilable bag of tricks, little literary touches which give the illiterate something predigested for toothless gums to mumble, and cheat him into believing that he is in contact with great thoughts'.[11] This is Denys Thompson, in 'Our Debt to Lamb', published in Lamb's centenary year, 1934, in the *Scrutiny* anthology edited by F. R. Leavis, *Determinations*. Thompson's wilful—yet not imperceptive—reading proved highly influential in

[8] See *OED*, *s.v.* 'familiar, *n., adj.*, and *adv.*'
[9] Lamb, *Specimens of English Dramatic Poets, who Lived about the Time of Shakspeare* (1808), 176.
[10] David Shields, *Reality Hunger* (2011), 159.
[11] Denys Thompson, 'Our Debt to Lamb', in F. R. Leavis (ed.), *Determinations* (1934), 207.

shaping Lamb's twentieth-century reputation, and tells us a good deal about the ways in which the familiar mode itself fell from favour. For Thompson, familiarity breeds contempt. The familiar essay is a fawning thing, getting too close for comfort. Complacent, self-satisfied with its own small world, it encourages lazy reading and irrationality. Thompson's scorn shows us a moment of shift in the history of the essay, away from the personal, subjective, elusive Elian style which had been so dominant through the later nineteenth and early twentieth centuries. The result has been that we have, in some ways, forgotten how to read such style— the dismissal of the *Scrutineers* has had a long reach.

One hundred years ago, pre-Thompson, we would have had little difficulty in understanding what was meant by the familiar mode. We would have grown up reading Lamb, Hazlitt, and Hunt, particularly Lamb; as schoolchildren we would have cut our literary teeth on 'Dissertation upon Roast Pig'. For everybody knew Lamb, as the title of Ward's 1933 anthology, *Everybody's Lamb*, suggests. And following Lamb, Hazlitt, and Hunt were a host of familiar essayists who birrelled merrily into the early twentieth century: Augustine Birrell himself, whose *In the Name of the Bodleian, and Other Essays* (1905) opens with a reference to Elia, and wanders, Lambishly, through second-hand bookshops, libraries, theatres, and gardens; E. V. Lucas, editor of Lamb's works, who produced a staggering number of light essays on all manner of *Adventures and Enthusiasms* (to borrow the title of a 1920 volume): London policemen, ponies, circuses, conjuror's rabbits, punctuality, door-stops. Through these variegated essays, there seemed to be an agreement that, in the words of A. C. Benson, 'the charm of the familiar essayist depends upon his power of giving the sense of a good-humoured, gracious and reasonable personality and establishing a sort of pleasant friendship with his reader'.[12] Not information or facts, but a companionable, curious, associative impulse is at the heart of this kind of essay.

It was an easy step from such good humour to the toothless maundering decried by Thompson. Such an approach ran counter to the rational strain of critical thinking he wished to encourage: the sort of essay produced by, say, Addison, who, in Thompson's view, 'presumed a reader with a mature mind, with serious interests and a scale of values approximating his own'. Those serious interests were key to the *Scrutiny* project itself: Leavis had completed his own PhD on 'The Relationship of Journalism to Literature', with specific reference to the early periodical press and Addison.[13] *Determinations*, as Leavis suggested in the introduction, was similarly intended to encourage a 'serious interest in literature', which might have a wider import: 'Not only must the seriousness involve, it is likely to derive from, a perception of—which must be a preoccupation with—the

---

[12] A. C. Benson, 'The Art of the Essayist', in Carl H. Klaus and Ned Stuckey-French (eds), *Essayists on the Essay: Montaigne to Our Time* (2012), 40.
[13] Michael Bell, *F. R. Leavis* (1988), 4.

problems of social equity and order and of cultural health.'[14] Thompson, a headmaster eager to put his literary criticism to practical use, employed this idea of seriousness as a touchstone, and found the Romantic familiar essayists wanting. If Addison, and by implication the Leavisites, promote 'useful amusements', Lamb flatters the 'unthinking man in the street', sharing his interests such as 'drink, gastronomy and smoking' and encouraging his indolence and ignorance.[15]

For Thompson, Lamb's familiarity is 'offensive' in two main senses. Firstly, he sees the essays as simply pandering to old familiar prejudices, and therefore unchallenging. They never require the 'reader to re-orientate himself', offering up 'experiences acceptable because they are already in stock'. Secondly, Lamb's tone as Elia is *over*familiar, 'often so exacerbating that one wants to shout "don't breathe in my ear"'.[16] This easy, insincere intimacy, so at odds with the 'lay-pulpit' essay of spiritual improvement practised by the eighteenth-century greats, had, Thompson felt, fostered a particularly revolting strain of commercial writing and '"low-brow" propaganda'.[17] It is the Elian style, 'fake personality' layered with allusion, archaism, and quotation, which poses the greatest problem for Thompson: he deems it an 'embarrassing, confectionary manner', an 'offensive affectedness'.

These last quotes are from the 1934 edition of Thompson's practical education handbook *Reading and Discrimination*. In one exercise he set extracts of Addison alongside a passage from Lamb, and then a contemporary advert for a barber's shop, or 'Sartorial Temple'. 'In the eighteenth century', he instructs his readers, 'the essay was a medium for serious writers […] Lamb reduced it to a vehicle for charming whimsies', and he draws his students' attention to the pernicious influence of Lamb's 'pseudo-literary style unvitalized by living speech', which he thinks has had a lasting influence on the 'modern essay and advertisement'.[18] Such objections were a key part of a larger change in Lamb's critical fortunes, and in the decline of the familiar essay itself. Sated by centenary celebrations of 'Saint Charles', critics would in increasing numbers turn against Lamb, or rather, the Victorian version of Lamb the sentimental essayist. The Victorians had seized on Lamb as the embodiment of familial duty, whose nostalgic style was easily conflated with his own tragic history, especially once his biography—and the details of his sister's matricide—had become public knowledge in the latter part of the nineteenth century. There had been some dissenting voices—Carlyle's disgust at him as a stuttering, gin-soaked 'emblem of imbecility'—but for the most part Lamb enjoyed an unprecedented popularity and identification with the

---

[14] Leavis, 'Introduction', in *Determinations*, 2.   [15] Thompson, 'Our Debt to Lamb', 206.
[16] Thompson, 'Our Debt to Lamb', 203.   [17] Thompson, 'Our Debt to Lamb', 217.
[18] Thompson, *Reading and Discrimination* (1934), 39–40; 104–5. By the time of the 1979 edition of the same text, his scorn had had the desired effect: Lamb had vanished from the curriculum, and no extracts from his work appear in the text.

familiar essay itself through the Victorian and Edwardian periods.[19] This popularity worked against him as the twentieth century wore on. For Mario Praz he became the 'quintessence of the spirit of bourgeois intimacy', whose essays display 'their jewel-like decoration of learned allusion' in Biedermeier fashion; for Cyril Connolly, more crudely, he was one of the 'delicious middlers', revelling in trivialities.[20] And as Lamb declined, so too did the fortunes of the familiar essay. The Thompsonian accusation of 'a fundamental lack of seriousness or purpose' lingered through the twentieth century, shaping classroom teaching, academic research, and more general attitudes. By 1955, Clifton Fadiman could write 'A Gentle Dirge to the Familiar Essay', suggesting that it was on the way to extinction, consigned to the musty shelves of second-hand bookstores and the footnotes of literary history.[21]

Yet just when it seemed forgotten, at the tail-end of the twentieth century, it has had an unusual resurgence. In the words of Anne Fadiman, the 'survival of the familiar essay is worth fighting for', and she describes her 2007 volume *At Large and At Small* as her 'contribution to the war effort', both continuing and refuting her father Clifton's work on the familiar essay some fifty years before.[22] Essayists like Fadiman, David Shields, or Nicholson Baker are finding in the form the space to digress, to tackle issues at once personal and universal, large and small. The spirit of Elia is once again being invoked to guide them. 'Let me confess at the outset,' says Fadiman, 'that I have a monumental crush on Charles Lamb', whom she imagines as a friendly 'shade' guiding her own 'converse' with the reader.[23] A 'shade', reminiscent of Elia as ghost or 'queer spirit'—Fadiman isn't afraid to acknowledge the 'weird and dark' aspects of Lamb, and the strange aspects of the familiar. His baroque wildness is acknowledged in a different way by Phillip Lopate, who sees Lamb as having had a wide, albeit unacknowledged, influence on the development of postmodern writing, suggesting that his legacy shapes the fragmentary, auto/biographical, shape-shifting creations of the late twentieth and early twenty-first centuries, novel, essay, and memoir:

> If you would seek a template for the giddy, runaway, self-referential verbal production in today's post-modern stars such as Thomas Pynchon, John Barth, Dave Eggers, Rick Moody, David Foster Wallace, and Nicholson Baker, look to Sterne and Lamb.[24]

---

[19] Joseph E. Riehl, *That Dangerous Figure: Charles Lamb and the Critics* (1998), 54–5.

[20] Mario Praz, *The Hero in Eclipse in Victorian Fiction* (1956), 68; Cyril Connolly, *Enemies of Promise* (2008), 13. See Riehl, *That Dangerous Figure*, 89–111, for excellent discussion of 'Lamb's Ill-Starred Centenary'.

[21] Clifton Fadiman, *A Party of One* (1955), 349–53. For a full discussion of changing attitudes, see G. Douglas Atkins, especially *On the Familiar Essay: Challenging Academic Orthodoxies* (2009).

[22] Anne Fadiman, *At Large and At Small: Confessions of a Literary Hedonist* (2007), xi.

[23] Fadiman, *At Large and At Small*, 26.   [24] Lamb, *Essays of Elia*, ed. Phillip Lopate (2003), xv.

Lamb's writing, as we'll see, is haunting on its own terms; it also haunts our own age. Returning to Lamb helps us to understand the many modes of the familiar—from the homely to the baroque, from intimacy to strangeness—and to construct an alternative history for the allusive and subjective strain of essayistic writing which was never fully extinguished by Thompson and New Critical scorn.

2. Traditions of the Familiar

As we've seen, 'familiar' can be an unexpectedly loaded term. For Thompson, the negative association was to the fore. An essay which is familiar, in his reading, is one which goes no further than the known, which deals in prejudice and stale ideas; it also carries a double meaning of inappropriate intimacy, of getting too close and too vulgar. Those derogatory senses of the word have hung around the genre for many decades. But we would do well to remember the larger tradition of familiar discourse, conveying both the sense of homely and easily understood language, and also the idea of close association: the author speaking to the reader as freely and casually as he would to a friend or relation. Such a tradition stretches back to Cicero's letters *Ad Atticum* and *Ad Familiares*. Petrarch's discovery and imitations of Cicero established an epistolary style of intimate plain speaking as an important model from the fourteenth century onwards, exerting both a rhetorical and political influence, and slowly making its way into the English vernacular.[25]

Petrarch describes his own edited letters, *Rerum Familiarum Libri* [*Books of Familiar Matters*], written between 1325 and 1366, as being themselves an exercise in familiarity: a text where '*multa familiariter deque rebus familiaribus scripta errant*'. This has been translated as having 'little anxious regard to style, but where homely matters are treated in a homely manner', or 'written on a variety of personal matters in a rather simple and unstudied manner'.[26] In addition to ethical advice on topics such as facing mortality, on virtue and moderation, Petrarch's letters offer a form of life-writing, 'an image, in some sort, of my mind and character, hewn out with great labour', in which reflections on his life become a way of opening up larger questions.[27] His ascent of Mount Ventoux, for example, is at once an autobiographical account of his own changing emotions, an allegorical reflection on surmounting difficulties, and a statement of authorial identity and influence, as he reads Augustine's *Confessions* on the mountainside. The close attention paid to setting is an important strand: Petrarch creates a

---

[25] See Gary Schneider, *The Culture of Epistolarity: Vernacular Letters and Letter Writing in Early Modern England, 1500–1700* (2005), 42.

[26] From Petrarch's prefatory letter, 'To his Socrates', I: i. Translated, respectively, by James Harvey Robinson, *Petrarch, the First Modern Scholar and Man of Letters* (1909), 145, and by Aldo S. Bernardo, *Rerum Familiarium Libri I–VIII* (1975), 11.

[27] Robinson, *Petrarch*, 145.

portrait of his surroundings, 'about fifteen miles from Avignon, a delightful valley, narrow and secluded, called Vaucluse [...] I transferred thither myself and my books'.[28] The reference to his books, too, is characteristic. His familiar discourse includes not only friends and contemporaries but literary predecessors: quotations and readings of earlier authors are woven into his reflections, and he includes letters to authors including Horace and Livy. Thus we have a sense of these letters stretching backwards into literary tradition and forwards to embrace the reader. A specific person—the addressee of a letter, or the dedicatee of a work—is often invoked directly to create a context of familiarity, so that the general reader, too, is co-opted into this intimate address.

This rhetoric of intimacy has been explored by Kathy Eden, who shows how Petrarch's rediscovery of Cicero's letters formed an important staging post, with Erasmus and Montaigne, in the development of Renaissance familiar style, closely linked to epistolarity.[29] We can see the same emphasis on familiar language echoing through the three authors, as when Montaigne tells us of the importance of conversational style: 'The speech I love is a simple, natural speech, the same on paper as in the mouth', he tells us in his essay on educating children, 'a speech succulent and sinewy, brief and compressed'.[30] His subject matter is familiar, in that he uses his life, his lived ordinary experience, as a subject of enquiry, and, like Petrarch telling us about the Vaucluse, he informs the reader about his surroundings and invites us into his library with its view of 'my garden, my farmyard, my courtyard, and into most of the parts of my house', curving to offer the essayist 'at a glance all my books, arranged in five rows of shelves on all sides'.[31] Like Petrarch and Erasmus, quotation and allusion shape his style; his address to the reader is mediated through his '[a]ssociation with books'.[32] Here we have the hallmarks of later familiar writing: the careful crafting of a persona who adopts a conversational style, either as letter-writer or as intimate friend. That intimacy with the reader is then developed through physical description of settings—and settings, crucially, in which reading takes place, whether that is Petrarch's mountainside or Montaigne's library. Trust me, says the familiar writer, for I too am a reader.

We will return to the importance of this 'converse with books', but let's follow, for a moment, the development of familiar language. The eighteenth century saw an upsurge of 'familiar' writings, which often sit—as Petrarch's own pieces do—between essay and letter. Samuel Parker's 1701 *Familiar Letters upon Occasional Subjects*, for example, addresses doctrinal controversies and questions of government as well as helping the reader steer a course through the difficult waters of style and polite conversation—avoid 'Rustic, Vulgar, or Childish Topics', advises Parker, although now and then a 'Casual *Dash* of 'em, like *Mint* in a *Salad*, can

---

[28] Robinson, *Petrarch*, 69.   [29] Kathy Eden, *The Renaissance Rediscovery of Intimacy* (2012).
[30] Michel de Montaigne, *The Complete Works*, trans. Donald M. Frame (2003), 154.
[31] Montaigne, *The Complete Works*, 762, 763.   [32] Montaigne, *The Complete Works*, 761.

give Relish to better Things'.[33] By the time Parker's book made it into a second edition, the idea of the letter had receded, and it was retitled *Essays on Divers Weighty and Curious Subjects*: a nice illustration of the ways in which essays and letters might fulfil similar functions—offering advice, opinions, social guidance and moral reflections—as well as the semi-public aspect the familiar letter could take on.[34] Manuals of the letter became popular—Samuel Richardson's *Familiar Letters on the most Important Occasions*, for example—as newly 'letter-literate' readers sought to master familiarity in style and content.[35] Both the periodical essay and the letter-writing manual offered lessons in how to approach familiar topics, and how to adopt an easy, familiar style in a changing world of social relations. Gauging the level of familiarity was crucial, so as not to become 'one of those familiar Coxcombs', or fall in with a 'Set of familiar Romps' complained of in the pages of the *Spectator*.[36] Instead, the familiarity aimed at was that of Addison himself, as described by Johnson, 'an English style, familiar but not coarse, and elegant but not ostentatious'.[37] In behaviour, familiarity should consist of properly regulated 'social pleasures and amiable communication', as Johnson writes in the *Rambler* essay No. 89: 'A wise and good man is never so amiable as in his unbended and familiar intervals.'[38]

But in the hands of the Romantics, the familiar took on different, more radical, implications. The term is central to *Lyrical Ballads*, for example, and in the 'Advertisement' of 1798 it forms an important part of Wordsworth's defensiveness. A reader unsympathetic to the volume's conversational 'experiments', imagines the poet, may find that 'many of his expressions are too familiar, and not of sufficient dignity'.[39] This is hardly an apology, of course, but a challenge, since such 'familiar' expressions form the basis for radical experiments with language and form in *Lyrical Ballads*. In the wake of Revolutionary disappointment, these first-generation Romantics strive to address social relations and how familiar relationships might be reconfigured, describing homely situations—the position of the old, the poor, the outcast—in the 'real language of men'.[40] This finds its way into the Romantic familiar essay through the engaged responses of Lamb and Hazlitt. In their treatment of the mundane, and their dwelling on lived

---

[33] Samuel Parker, *Sylva. Familiar letters upon occasional subjects* (1701), 74.

[34] Parker, *Essays on divers weighty and curious subjects [. . .] Occasionally written in familiar letters to several persons* (1702).

[35] Samuel Richardson, *Letters written to and for particular friends: on the most important occasions* (1741). For further discussion, see Clare Brant, *Eighteenth-Century Letters and British Culture* (2006).

[36] *The Spectator* No. 508 (13 October 1712); No. 492 (24 September 1712), in *The Spectator*, ed. Donald F. Bond, 5 vols (1965), IV, 305, 246.

[37] James Boswell, *Life of Johnson*, ed. R. W. Chapman (1998), 161.

[38] Samuel Johnson, *The Rambler*, vols III–V of *The Yale Edition of the Works of Samuel Johnson*, ed. W. J. Bate and Albrecht B. Strauss (1969), IV, 107, 108.

[39] William Wordsworth, 'Advertisement to *Lyrical Ballads*', in *The Prose Works of William Wordsworth*, ed. W. J. B. Owen and Jane Worthington Smyser, 3 vols (1974), I, 116.

[40] Wordsworth, 'Preface to *Lyrical Ballads*', in *Prose Works*, I, 119.

experience—eating, drinking, walking, setting off to see a fight or staying in bed on a cold morning, crowding into the theatre or rambling in Hertfordshire fields— their essays exhibit a similar interest in reinventing the ordinary. Certainly, in a Hazlitt essay such as 'On Familiar Style', we can directly trace the ways in which his conversational language echoes the intentions of *Lyrical Ballads*. 'It is not easy', Hazlitt's essay begins, 'to write a familiar style': it demands 'precision' and 'purity of expression', finding words which are 'common' and fitting them to an exact purpose.[41] Like Wordsworth's defence of his 'too familiar' language two decades previously, Hazlitt pleads 'guilty to the determined use of acknowledged idioms and common elliptical expression' in order to create a particular style free from cliché and pomposity, drawn from 'common conversation'.

And yet. And yet we come up against the oddness of Lamb. For all his engagement with other Romantics he is his own man, and the Elian voice, 'villainously pranked in an affected array of antique modes and phrases', seems at odds with Hazlitt's recommendation of language suited to 'common conversa- tion', and with the longer tradition of familiar style as homely or plain. This apparent contradiction is key to understanding Lamb's contribution to the devel- opment of the familiar essay. Elia takes the essay in some strange new directions— yet also, as we will see, keeps one eye on earlier traditions and reinvents them for his own purposes. In so doing, he darkens the familiar essay, and makes it, above all, a strange and teasing expression of personality.

3. Haunting the Familiar

We saw with our opening poem 'The Old Familiar Faces' that the familiar had an especially potent meaning for Lamb as a writer. Its claustrophobic pacing—that 'Ghost-like, I pac'd' enacted in the halting rhythm of the verse—reinforces the slow loss of each relationship, from mother to friend to lover to (implicitly) sister: 'some they have died, and some they have left me, / And some are taken from me'. But this isn't just about the poet's own awkwardness and grief. The unusual form is lifted from Lamb's reading of the Jacobean dramatist Philip Massinger, and his use of feminine rhymes, with their unstressed final syllables, as in these lines from 'A Very Woman':

> In the best language my true tongue could tell me,
> And all the broken sighs my sick heart lend me,
> I sued and serv'd. Long did I love this lady.[42]

---

[41] William Hazlitt, 'On Familiar Style', in *The Selected Writings of William Hazlitt*, ed. Duncan Wu, 9 vols (1998), VI, 217. Further references given in the text.
[42] Lamb, *Specimens of English Dramatic Poets*, 431.

This odd echo is what makes 'The Old Familiar Faces' Lamb's most successful poem: the unacknowledged assumption of an older form gives it an inexpressible dimension, as if somehow we are able to sense the layers of haunting behind and between the lines.

It's worth dwelling on this moment of ventriloquization because this is an important staging post in the development of Elia's allusive voice. In this early example, we see how Lamb was learning how to draw from older, lesser-known writers, making them an integral part of his language, writing them into his own rhetoric of familiarity. In the case of the lines above, two years before the poem was written, we find Lamb singling them out in a letter to Coleridge to commend 'the fine effect of his double endings'. 'Are you acquainted with Massinger?' he asks Coleridge, quoting liberally both from him and from 'a little extract book I keep, which is full of quotations from B[eaumont] and F[letcher] in particular'.[43] The same Massinger lines are quoted as an epigraph at the start of Lamb's contribution to Coleridge's *Poems on Various Subjects* (1797) alongside a dedication to his sister Mary. They must have carried a special meaning for Lamb, veteran himself of a six-week stay in Hoxton madhouse, since Massinger's play, *A Very Woman*, influenced by Burton's *Anatomy of Melancholy*, contains a portrait of severe depression: 'Melancholy [...] near of kin to madness'. But simply sharing Massinger's words with Coleridge seems to have afforded some consolation in the midst of Lamb's melancholy, commemorated in the structure of 'The Old Familiar Faces'. Where are the old familiar faces? The answer is within the poem itself, which carries in its structure and sound a consolatory echo of shared reading: friends may be absent, but poetry runs between them.

Such shared allusions are often Lamb's way of enacting or evoking intimacy— his letters are thick with references to Elizabethan literature into which he strives to initiate others: Massinger, Beaumont and Fletcher, Quarles, Jeremy Taylor, Richard Baxter and Robert Burton. We find him in the late 1790s hunting down rare editions of seventeenth-century texts for Southey and Lloyd as a mark of friendship, and allegorizing his family situation in a blank verse Elizabethan tragedy of betrayal, guilt, and violence, *John Woodvil*. In 1800, on the suggestion of Coleridge, he wrote 'the forgery of a supposed Manuscript of Burton the Anatomist of Melancholy'.[44] In the *Anatomy of Melancholy* Lamb found another model for familiarity, since Burton searched for ways in which to render his discussions of 'frenzy, lethargy, Melancholy, madness [...] more familiar and easy for every man's capacity'.[45] Lamb takes on Burton's own 'familiar' language, and makes it part of his own rhetoric of friendship, deepened because his friends,

---

[43] Marrs, *Letters*, I, 31.   [44] Marrs, *Letters*, I, 189–90.
[45] Robert Burton, *The Anatomy of Melancholy what it is. With all the kindes, causes, symptomes, prognostickes, and severall cures of it* (1621), 11.

such as Coleridge, recognized the 'Melancholy, madness' at work in Lamb's own life. Burton's eerie, depressive essayistic style, and the wildness and violence of Elizabethan playwrights such as Massinger, underscore Lamb's familiar mode: they are at once a reminder that there is often something sinister and uncertain in Lamb's writing, and, simultaneously, a counterweight to that darkness—since they function as a reminder of the enduring power of shared, familiar reading.

These, then, are the origins of the 'pseudo-literary style' noticed by Thompson: an early apprenticeship in Elizabethan and seventeenth-century texts, from plays to sermons, which becomes part of a language of shared reading: emotional, expressive, affectionate, but also carrying within it a reminder of the darkness and depression these friends had experienced together. In Elia this finds its ultimate expression, in the digressive, playful, hoaxing essays of the *London Magazine*, which turn the familiar mode in a new direction. Here allusions, archaisms, touches of autobiography and baroque seventeenth-century style become a badge of familiarity: what might at first read as estranging and riddling in fact looks back to, and helps to cement, a bond of friendship, with other writers and future readers.

The first essay of Elia nicely brings together all those different aspects of familiarity, with its portrait of the gloomy South Sea House, so well-known a London landmark, opening into an Ossianic 'desolation something like Balclutha's'.[46] At the heart of the city, we find a forgotten ruin: a version of the 'desert' we encountered in 'The Old Familiar Faces'. Yet as the essay goes on, we find that this desolation is, in fact, alive with association, peopled with memories, which Elia teasingly invites the reader to recover and share. For Lamb had actually worked at the South Sea House in 1791–2—rather than, as the essay claims, 'forty years back' (3). He had known the clerks he mentions, some of whom were still alive. 'Elia' was a name shamelessly borrowed—or as Lamb would later put it, 'usurped'—from a contemporary at the South Sea House, Felix Ellia. Ellia was a hapless author, just about the same age as Lamb, who had published his first, ill-received novel, *Theopha*, in 1798, when *Rosamund Gray* had first appeared. Lamb's assumption of the name began as a literary hoax, before Ellia died in September 1820, but, in spite of Lamb's statement that he was a 'fellow clerk of mine at the South-Sea House', Felix Ellia the real languished forgotten until relatively recently.[47] Moreover, as Gregory Dart explores in Chapter 8 in this volume, the South Sea House is also a 'metropolitan lyrical ballad' which shows how deeply Lamb had been shaped as a writer by his friendship with Wordsworth and Coleridge, and his attentive reading of their work, in the 1790s. Part homage,

---

[46] Lamb, 'The South-Sea House', in *The Works of Charles and Mary Lamb*, ed. E. V. Lucas, 7 vols (1903), 1. Further references given in the text.
[47] See David Chandler, '"Elia, the Real": The Original of Lamb's *Nom De Plume*', *Review of English Studies* 58 (2007): 669–83.

part joke, it shows the many languages Elia is able to move between, a metropolitan periodical author, but also a clerk, a reader of old books such as Ossian, a Romantic poet.

It's no surprise that Elia should have chosen the site of a famous hoax as his first subject, since 'The South-Sea House' is itself an exercise in deception, as the allusion to Ossian hints—it is the creation of 'ELIA', or, unscrambled, 'A LIE'. Contemporaries familiar with Lamb himself, or those who were able to pick up the scattered clues through the *London Magazine*, may have recognized elements of Lamb's own life within the essay, hidden among the descriptions of those South Sea clerks, or his allusions to 'STC' and 'Cousin Bridget'. It is these 'living autobiographical touches' which, as Gerald Monsman has observed, mark the difference between Elia and earlier essay personae such as Steele's 'Isaac Bickerstaff'. This shows us another important aspect of Elia's familiarity: a way of creating a temporary community in the essays. Felix Ellia lives again, ventriloquized through the pages of *Essays in Elia*, like the clerks of the South Sea House. As we learn in the Phil-Elia obituary, Elia loves to 'imply and twine with his own identity the griefs and affections of another—making himself many, or reducing many unto himself'. Through his Elian persona, his hoaxes, his assumed identities, Lamb the familiar essayist strives towards 'making himself many'.[48] There are two ways to read this, both drawing on the familiar: in one sense, it might convey something unreliable or uncanny, continually shapeshifting. Yet, even though Elia can't be relied upon, there might be something consoling in this mutability. For as the reader struggles to work out the truth, he or she becomes involved in the personal essay, a version of the rhetoric of intimacy invoked by Kathy Eden in her discussion of Renaissance familiar style. As Elia 'mak[es] himself many', he creates a larger family of writers and readers—a way of compensating for the grief and disappointment of the 1790s and of peopling the 'desert' in which he had found himself.

This is built into his literary style, both through scenes of shared reading and through allusion. Like Montaigne inviting us into his library, Lamb, as Elia, frequently presents us with scenes of reading, book-collecting, triumphant hunts on city bookstalls. 'The South-Sea House', for instance, among its bygone clerks, celebrates 'Henry Man, the wit, the polished man of letters, the author, of the South-Sea House', whose works, including poems on a walking stick, a china plate, and 'a familiar epistle' to the treasury bench at Bignell's coffee house, apostrophize the everyday. Elia rescues his two forgotten volumes 'from a stall in Barbican, not three days ago' and finds him 'terse, fresh, epigrammatic, as alive' (6). Here the man is identified with the book; in 'Detached Thoughts on Books and Reading', the process is reversed and Elia's books become men, 'kind-hearted' or 'shivering',

---

[48] 'A Character of the Late Elia', 20.

'ragged veterans' in their bad bindings (173). And Elia's familiarity with books occasionally has an erotic charge, as in his love of Shakespeare copies which have been 'oftenest tumbled about and handled' (174), or his 'having been once detected—by a familiar damsel—reclined at my ease upon the grass, on Primrose Hill (her Cythera), reading—*Pamela*' (176). Those breathless pauses suggest what might be going on beneath the surface of this ostensibly respectable scene of shared reading, followed by a blush. The tinge of the erotic reappears in Elia's description of the 'sullied leaves', the 'very odour' of old circulating library copies of *Tom Jones* and *The Vicar of Wakefield*:

> How they speak of the thousand thumbs, that have turned over their pages with delight!—of the lone sempstress, whom they may have cheered (milliner, or harder-working mantua-maker) after her long day's needle-toil.   (173)

Of course, there's also another element of familiarity going on in this description, because the unsung, hard-pressed mantua-maker is a covert tribute to Mary Lamb. The allusion is continued by the ending of 'Detached Thoughts on Books and Reading', which closes with a long quotation from her poem 'Two Boys', from *Poetry for Children*, with its portrait of a boy reading from a street book stall. Books, and the image of the reader, create familiarity on a number of levels. Such allusions, bringing together essayist, friend, and reader in a moment of 'converse with books', are a characteristic Elian feature: another comes in 'The Two Races of Men', where Elia remembers 'Comberbatch, matchless in his depredations!' Here Coleridge, under the hoax name he adopted during his short-lived reinvention as a dragoon, is summoned up through the absences he has left in Elia's library—'that foul gap in the bottom shelf facing you, like a great eyetooth knocked out—(you are now with me in my little back study in Bloomsbury, reader!)' (25). The reader, enfolded in the library, becomes thus included in the relationship between the friends: a snatch of familiar language, 'you are now with me', which allows the reader to participate in a larger familiar relationship. Elia goes on to describe Comberbatch's annotations, 'legible in my Daniel; in old Burton; in Sir Thomas Browne', which serve to write their friendship into literature in a different way. He ends with an exhortation to the reader: 'I counsel thee, shut not thy heart, nor thy library, against S. T. C.' (27). It's in moments like these we see an Elian take on the close relationship between essay and letter we glimpsed elsewhere in the eighteenth century—Lamb frequently reused phrases from his letters to friends in his essays, and here the essay itself becomes an open letter both to Coleridge himself and to the reader of the *London Magazine*.[49]

---

[49] For an account of the ways in which Elia continues epistolary conversations, see Felicity James, 'Charles Lamb, Samuel Taylor Coleridge, and the Forging of the Romantic Literary Coterie', in *Re-evaluating the Literary Coterie, 1580–1830*, ed. William Bowers and Hannah Leah Crummé

Such familiar allusions allow continuity, too, with a whole community of earlier authors. Sometimes, as in 'The Old Familiar Faces' or his forgeries of Burton, Lamb adopts past literary forms; sometimes, as in *The Essays of Elia*, his allusions come through echoes and quotations, so that his writing style itself comes to embody 'converse with books'. It might, indeed, go beyond 'converse': Elia tells us in 'Detached Thoughts on Books and Reading' that 'Books think for me' (172). As Hazlitt comments in 'On Familiar Style', Lamb's sympathy with older authors takes his writing beyond imitation, beyond pastiche. He is, says Hazlitt, 'thoroughly imbued' with their spirit, and 'there is an inward unction, a marrowy vein, both in the thought and feeling, an intuition, deep and lively, of his subject' (VI, 219). Years of friendship meant Hazlitt was deeply, intimately, attuned to Lamb's prose, able to echo the strange blend of the quasi-religious and the erotic in his language, and also able to capture the slippery, self-alienated aspect of his work, the oddness of his familiarity. For that idea of unction seems itself a seventeenth-century notion, drawn from Burton or Baxter: 'marrowy', too, is a very seventeenth-century word, carrying with it echoes of the Marrow Controversy, but also, in Hazlitt's phrase— 'marrowy vein'—something physical, experienced in both 'thought and feeling'. Hazlitt is thus able to express the way the intellectual and the sensual collide in Lamb's work, as in 'New Year's Eve', when Elia exclaims:

> And you, my midnight darlings, my Folios; must I part with the intense delight of having you (huge armfuls) in my embraces? Must knowledge come to me, if it come at all, by some awkward experiment of intuition, and no longer by this familiar process of reading?   (30)

Familiar, here, means not only accustomed, but also intimate: this intuition is not experimental, but, as Hazlitt would have it, deep and lively, something which is physically experienced through the embrace of the book. For Lamb, 'familiar' expression is drawn not from 'common' conversation, as Wordsworth and Hazlitt suggest, but from readings (literally) held in common.

One other aspect of the Elian familiar is also worth touching on in this context: the way in which he often reworks ideas familiar, even to the point of cliché, from previous essayists. 'New Year's Eve', for instance, rewrites Montaigne's meditations on mortality in the essay 'That to study Philosophy, is to learn to die'.[50] But whereas Montaigne counsels the reader to acquaint himself with the notion of death, Elia keenly refutes it. Montaigne tells us that he has made himself

---

(2016), 137–57, and for the ways in which Lamb and Hazlitt converse in their *London Magazine* essays, see Heather B. Stone, 'William Hazlitt, Charles Lamb and the *London Magazine*, 1821', *Wordsworth Circle* 44.1 (2013), 41–4.

[50] For the purposes of comparison in this section I have used the translation by Charles Cotton which Lamb most probably used, since he quotes Cotton at the end of the essay.

'so familiar' with the thought of death that it is 'no trouble at all': 'never Man was so distrustful of his Life, never Man so indifferent for its Duration'.[51] 'I have heard some profess an indifference to life', writes Elia, but he himself has, he tells us, an 'intolerable disinclination to dying' which deliberately flies in the face of Montaigne's counsel (30). He resists that easy familiarity with death: we're back with the poet in 'The Old Familiar Faces', haunted by the knowledge of how unnaturally death has erupted into his family, obsessively dwelling upon but also trying to repress the knowledge that his sister has killed his mother. This horrifying, intimate contact with death makes Elia pettishly reject the Addisonian insights of essays such as No. 289 of *The Spectator*, for 31 January 1712. Here, Mr Spectator is 'guided by the Spirit of a Philosopher' to reflect, like Montaigne before him, on the 'several various ways through which we pass from Life to Eternity', and ends his reflections with a passage from Antiphanes, advising the reader not to grieve for deceased friends, '*We our selves must go to that great Place of Reception in which they are all of them assembled, and in this general Rendezvous of Mankind, live together in another State of Being.*'[52] 'A new state of being', retorts Elia, 'staggers me', and he goes on passionately to defend his current state, complete with sensual and intellectual pleasures:

> Sun, and sky, and breeze, and solitary walks, and summer holydays, and the greenness of fields, and the delicious juices of meats and fishes, and society, and the cheerful glass, and candle-light, and fireside conversations, and innocent vanities, and jests, and *irony itself*—do these things go out with life?
>
> Can a ghost laugh; or shake his gaunt sides, when you are pleasant with him?
>
> (29–30)

Yet Lamb can also write under the pseudonym of 'Elia's Ghost'; at the close of 'New Year's Eve' he retreats 'under the phantom cloud of Elia' (29). The essayist is half a ghost already, flirting with the afterlife. The afterlife he seeks, however, is in the reader's mind, who will be able to recognize these familiar sensory pleasures. To underline this point we close with a quotation not from Montaigne himself but from his translator Cotton's verses on 'The New Year'. 'How say you, reader,' asks Elia, 'do not these verses smack of the rough magnanimity of the old English vein? Do they not fortify like a cordial?' (32) Reading, sensuous engagement with words which 'smack' and 'fortify', is a way of cheating mortality: it is Elia's version of Montaigne's 'converse with books' which allows the writer to live on through the reading of others.

---

[51] Montaigne, *Essays of Michael, seigneur de Montaigne in three books*, trans. Charles Cotton (1700), I, 104.
[52] No. 289 (31 January 1712), in Bond, *The Spectator*, III, 27, 30.

4. Rewriting the Familiar

For Elia does live on, sometimes in surprising ways. His influence on Modernist writers remains to be uncovered, in the work of Edmund Blunden and Virginia Woolf, for instance. Woolf, who read the *Essays of Elia* at 15 and repeatedly, ambivalently returned to Lamb throughout her life, and describes him as an 'exquisite' writer, a 'technically perfect' essayist: 'the essays of Montaigne, or Lamb or Bacon haunt the mind'.[53] And Elia haunts her descriptions of walks by night, of reading, of the common reader browsing in libraries, and of illness. 'On Being Ill', particularly, seems to evoke her reading of the Romantics as she muses on the strange new perspective opened to the invalid, how, viewed from the sickbed, 'the world has changed its shape'.[54] This reminds us strongly of Hunt's *Indicator* essay 'Getting up on Cold Mornings', with its bed-bound perspective, lapped all round in the 'warm and circling amplitude' of the blankets, and again of Lamb's 'The Convalescent', another great Romantic bed essay.[55] Here the pain and grief of illness changes the dimensions of the bed, the self, the world: the very sheets become a 'wavy, many-furrowed, oceanic surface', the invalid a monarch over the 'whole state of sickness' (186). 'How sickness enlarges the dimensions of a man's self to himself!' says Elia (184), contemplating the selfishness and inwardness of illness, and for Woolf, too, each familiar object is altered, friends 'changed, some putting on a strange beauty, others deformed to the squatness of toads, while the whole landscape of life lies remote and fair, like the shore seen from a ship far out at sea'.[56] This mixture of deformity and beauty, the familiar and the strange, the 'oceanic' disorientation of vision, is distinctly shaped by Lamb. What drew Woolf to his writing was also her awareness of the family struggles with mental illness, the true subject of 'On Being Ill'. But perhaps this was also a factor in her doubts about Lamb. No one who has read Carlyle's description of him as weak and imbecilic 'ever rids his mind completely of the impression', she writes, worrying that he is not, in the end, to be taken seriously.[57] Her ambivalence means that his Modernist legacy has yet to be fully traced; it also points to the 'new corrosive critical attitude' which was growing through the twentieth century.[58]

---

[53] '[H]is essays, which are of course, technically perfect', comes in a letter to to Janet Case (18 September 1925), in *The Letters of Virginia Woolf*, vol. III, ed. Nigel Nicolson (1977), 211; the reference to Montaigne and Lamb comes from *The Essays of Virginia Woolf*, vol. V, ed. Stuart N. Clarke (2009), 171.

[54] Virginia Woolf, 'On Being Ill', in *The Essays of Virginia Woolf*, vol. IV, ed. Andrew McNeillie (1994), 319.

[55] Leigh Hunt, 'Getting up on Cold Mornings', *The Indicator* XV (1820), 118; Lamb, 'The Convalescent', *London Magazine and Review* 7 (1825), 376–9.

[56] Woolf, 'On Being Ill', 319.

[57] Woolf, 'A Friend of Johnson', in *The Essays of Virginia Woolf*, vol. I, ed. Andrew McNeillie (1986), 272.

[58] Riehl, *That Dangerous Figure*, 87–9.

In closing, though, I want to look forward to Lamb's relevance in an age when the essay is being rediscovered, and reinvented. Modern essayists—David Shields, Nicholson Baker, Phillip Lopate, Anne Fadiman—seem deliberately to have channelled the Elian spirit, producing different versions and interpretations of the familiar essay which, curiously, amplify precisely the aspects to which Thompson so objected. Shields, for example, singles out Lamb's 'theatrical reticence, the archaism, the nostalgia, the celebration of oddity for its own sake' which 'helped change the English (and American) idea of what an essay should be', and which have clearly shaped his own writing.

At first glance Shields' 'manifesto' *Reality Hunger* seems far removed from Elia's belletrist, nostalgic mode, with its chapters on 'trials by google' and 'reality tv', its meditations on dub reggae, King Tubby, Baz Luhrmann, and The Bachelor. Shields, as didactic in his way as Thompson before him, is sick and tired of the novel. Narrative, and plot, keep readers fettered to an outmoded form (incidentally, Elia also complains that 'Narrative teases me. I have little concern in the progress of events' (75)). 'The novel is dead', writes Shields, 'long live the anti-novel, built from scraps'.[59] And building from scraps is just what Shields does: each chapter is divided into smaller numbered sections—short paragraphs, sentences, sometimes only fragments, often quotations from others. There's a baroque extravagance to his borrowing which echoes Lamb's, with snippets of verse and letters and essays layered upon one another. Shields describes his technique as 'sampling'—using familiar words in new contexts, so that the 'mix breaks free of the old associations'—less an author than a 'scissors-and-paste man', connecting pieces in a 'bricolage', 'collage', or 'mosaic'. And to bring home his point, his description of sampling is lifted from 'Paul D. Miller, aka DJ Spooky', 'scissors-and-paste' is borrowed from Joyce, 'bricolage' from Sebald. The book contains 'hundreds of quotations that go unacknowledged in the body of the text', which Shields tells us is his means of 'trying to regain a freedom that writers from Montaigne to Burroughs took for granted', of questioning terms such as appropriation and plagiarism, hoax and con. Possibly truthfully, possibly not, he tells us that his publishers required a list of citations which he has provided at the back of the book, but that if 'you would like to restore this book to the form in which I intended it to be read, simply grab a sharp pair of scissors or a razor blade or box cutter and remove pages 207–219 by cutting along the dotted line'.[60] That instruction is a performance of intimacy with the reader, asking him or her to participate physically to become a cutter (if not a paster)—restoring the book to its rightful, writerly form. It's not too far from Lamb's asking us to come into his library, that sense of writer and reader achieving familiarity through the handling of volumes.

---

[59] Shields, *Reality Hunger*, 115.   [60] Shields, *Reality Hunger*, 209.

This is a common strain in modern familiar writing. Anne Fadiman opens her first volume of essays, *Ex Libris*, with a paean to the books 'whose textures and colours and smells have become as familiar to us as our children's skin'; she closes it with her love of second-hand books, complete with 'smears, smudges, under-linings and ossified toast'.[61] It's no surprise to encounter Lamb in this essay, rejoicing in finding a 'copy of Quarles for ninepence!!!': Elia's love of 'sullied leaves' and soiled circulating library copies is a touchstone for Fadiman.[62] There's also a hint of the erotic, as with those 'huge armfuls' of book enjoyed by Elia, and his love of old volumes, 'tumbled about and handled'. Fadiman's first essay describes amalgamating her books with those of her husband, some five years after their marriage. 'We physically handled—fondled, really—every book we owned', she tells us.[63] These range from books familiar through personal relation-ship—'Books by Friends and Relatives' occupy a special category of shelves next to the bed—to those familiar through long reading: 'my genital-pink paperback of *Couples*, read so often in my late teens [...] that it had sundered into a triptych held together with a rubber band'.[64] There is a recurrent image of the essayist climbing into bed with a book, 'a bed that was lumpy with books' already; discussing the Fadiman family reading habits she says that they believed in 'carnal love', leaving their books splayed, sucked dry, marked 'promiscuously'.[65]

The fetishistic power of the physical book is similarly evoked by Nicholson Baker in both his essays and his essayistic, digressive, conversational novels. Sometimes these discussions of 'pre-enjoyed book' are overtly sexual: the narrator of *Vox*, for instance, browses a used bookstore in a state of high excitement, since the novels 'looked *handled. All* of their pages were turned. And turned by whom? Turned by women [...] The intimacy of it!'[66] Elsewhere, the urge is more rarefied; transcribing quotations into his commonplace books, Baker the essayist is 'momentarily reanimating' authors, 'slowly unwinding their sentential shrouds'.[67] He feasts on all forms of the written word, from the 'thick, butter-coloured paper' of outmoded card catalogues to the 'champagney hue' of old newspapers.[68] He haunts library discard rooms and mourns the violence inflicted on public book collections, weeding, pulping, selling off; Baker himself saved huge runs of early US newspapers jettisoned by the British Library, and sees in their 'time-tanned pages', like the card catalogues 'dirt-banded' by readerly fingers, a way to read the past.

The book gives the familiar essayist something to hold on to, sometimes literally, in the face of loneliness, grief, desolation, just as Elia embraces his 'midnight darlings, my Folios'. Handling a copy of a favourite book, seeking out

[61] Anne Fadiman, *Ex Libris: Confessions of a Common Reader* (1998), x, 121.
[62] Fadiman, *Ex Libris*, 123, 35.   [63] Fadiman, *Ex Libris*, 6.   [64] Fadiman, *Ex Libris*, 7.
[65] Fadiman, *Ex Libris*, ix, 32–3.   [66] Nicholson Baker, *Vox* (1992), 69.
[67] Baker, *The Way the World Works* (2012), 47.
[68] Baker, *The Size of Thoughts* (1996), 157; *The Way the World Works*, 141.

forgotten volumes on bookstalls or in the library discard skip, and ensuring their survival through quotation or allusion or the use of their unfamiliar language, the essayist asserts continuity with the past and into the future. Death is, temporarily, banished, although, as we saw in 'New Year's Eve', it always lurks at the edges of the best familiar essays. It's no coincidence that the familiar essayist so often likes to work at night, frisking over 'the flowery carpet-ground of a midnight dissertation', embracing 'midnight folios' and surrendering to their 'owl self'.[69] With their 'cheerful glass, and candle-light', their 'cosily delimited interior', they are carving out a little space for themselves in the darkness.[70]

And it is this sense of darkness at the other side of the familiar, kept just at bay by reading, writing, and the carefully constructed persona, which may be Lamb's lasting contribution to the essay. We can glimpse it not only in the more obviously Elian essayists of our time—Fadiman, Baker—but also in the in the 'giddy, runaway, self-referential verbal productions', to borrow Lopate's words, of post-modern writers such as David Foster Wallace. In the very early work 'The Planet Trillaphon as It Stands in Relation to the Bad Thing', a missive from the world of antidepressants, we see Foster Wallace negotiating a mixture of conversational familiarity and desolation. 'I've been on antidepressants for, what, about a year now', begins the narrator, in characteristically laconic mode; he goes on to document the paralysing, lonely, helplessness of his situation, akin to the 'desert' in which the poet finds himself in 'The Old Familiar Faces'.[71] Like Lamb, Foster Wallace finds a way out, if a fragile one, through word-play, humour, shared allusion, and the creation of an authorial persona, by turns hapless and knowing. In 'Getting Away from Already Pretty Much Being Away from It All', for instance, a visit to the Illinois State Fair becomes a queasily grotesque assault on the senses, the 'green reek of fried tomatoes', the 'grisly sound-carpet' of deep fat fryers, the 'pubic-hair-shaped' Curl Fries, fluorescent 'Jetsonian' DIPPIN DOTS.[72] The narrator is borne along by it all, half-disgusted, half-compelled. He quivers with nerves at the sight of The Zipper ride; the Dessert Competitions inflict severe intestinal distress. Eagerly anticipating a corn dog, he stops to admire the prize pigs, and comments that his sense of irony 'has been honed East-Coast keen, and I feel like a bit of a schmuck in the Swine Barn'.[73] As Foster Wallace writes, the essay is partly 'an attempt to explain, for the mainly cosmopolitan readers of *Harper's*, some of the effects rurality, physical distance, lack of stimulation, etc. have on people'.[74] This is reminiscent of the way Dart describes the Romantic essay as negotiating between pastoral and metropolitan, past and present; it is also

---

[69] Fadiman, *At Large and At Small*, 73.   [70] Fadiman, *At Large and At Small*, 67.
[71] David Foster Wallace, 'The Planet Trillaphon as It Stands in Relation to the Bad Thing', in *The David Foster Wallace Reader* (2014), 5.
[72] Foster Wallace, 'The Planet Trillaphon', 727–9.
[73] Foster Wallace, 'The Planet Trillaphon', 721.
[74] Foster Wallace, 'The Planet Trillaphon', 761.

a reflection on the essayist's own childhood, a trip back into the 'middle-of-the-ocean lonely' of the Midwest, now that he has fashioned a new, word-loving, ironically 'East-Coast keen' persona for himself. But we close the essay with the narrator fearfully observing the 'Near-Death Experiences' of the fairground, culminating in a bungee-jump undertaken by, symbolically, an 'East-Coaster'. As he waits to watch him fall, the essayist is overtaken by a sense of doom, of remembered childhood nightmare: 'and the sun and sky and plummeting Yuppie go out like a light'.[75] The persona can no longer be kept up: the essay itself has reached a full stop. But is it wishful thinking to see in those closing lines an echo of Elia's fight against mortality in 'New Year's Eve': 'Sun, and sky [...] do these things go out with life?' It's half a rejection of Elia, just as Lamb himself had rejected Montaigne and Addison, but it's also a homage. Engrained in Foster Wallace's work, even at its darkest, is a love of quotation, allusion, citation, which asserts his continuity with earlier writers and future readers, and which shows the long reach of Elian experimentation with the familiar.

We opened with a question—'Where are they gone, the old familiar faces?' The answer comes in the pages of the essay. Lamb's creation of Elia allowed him converse with friends, with books, and with future readers, in a way which may have alleviated the lonely alienation apparent in that early poem. And while it may have seemed through much of the twentieth century that the familiar essay was in terminal decline, we close with a sense of its resurgence in different forms, in the writings of Shields, Fadiman, Baker, and Foster Wallace. 'Elia', as the *London Magazine* had it in March 1823, 'is *not* dead'.[76]

---

[75] Foster Wallace, 'The Planet Trillaphon', 758.
[76] 'The Lion's Head', *London Magazine*, vol. 7 (March 1823), 243.

10

Carlyle, Emerson, and the Voiced Essay

Tom F. Wright

1. Introduction

Hanover Square Rooms, Mayfair, London, a spring afternoon in 1839. A large paying audience eagerly awaits the arrival of the essayist Thomas Carlyle, who will deliver his new writings on 'Heroes' in person. A record of the event by Leigh Hunt for the *Examiner* described the Scottish author's manner as follows:

> When he enters the room and proceeds to the sort of rostrum whence he delivers his lectures, he is, according to the usual practice in such cases, generally received with applause; but he very rarely takes any more notice of the mark of approbation [...] Having ascended his desk, he gives a hearty rub to his hands, and plunges at once into his subject. [...] He is not prodigal of gesture with his arms or body; but there is something in his eye and countenance which indicates great earnestness of purpose, and the most intense interest in his subject. You can almost fancy, in some of his most enthusiastic and energetic moments, that you see his inmost soul in his face.[1]

A few years later, on a cold January evening, the more modest Tompkins Lyceum on Staten Island, New York is filled with a congregation assembled to hear America's finest essayist, Ralph Waldo Emerson. As with Carlyle, observers thought something in his performance helped to explain his ideas, and one newspaper noted how:

> Commencing on a key, he would continue on the same up to the last word or two, and then drop into a deep musical tone which was very impressive. Occasionally at the end of a sentence he would suddenly stop, for what seemed like a long time, and, with his eyes uplifted upon his audience, looking like one

[1] Leigh Hunt, excerpted in Thomas Ballantyne, *Passages Selected from the Writings of Thomas Carlyle* (1855), 21.

Tom F. Wright, *Carlyle, Emerson, and the Voiced Essay* In: *On Essays: Montaigne to the Present.* Edited by: Thomas Karshan and Kathryn Murphy, Oxford University Press (2020). © Tom F. Wright.
DOI: 10.1093/oso/9780198707868.003.0011

inspired. Everyone in the audience seemed to stop breathing, as if afraid to mar the solemn impression produced.[2]

The literary essay can be one of the most intimate of forms, offering a curiously confidential connection to an author's unfolding thoughts. But as these scenes testify, it can also be a social art. Both of these texts present the essayist as a charismatic force, whose intent can be understood fully only by witnessing their words come to life energized by the dynamics of a live assembly. As one of Emerson's earliest biographers wrote of these occasions, 'the essayist needs to be interpreted by the lecturer; for his voice and manner become a fine commentary on his written thought, giving to it new and unexpected meanings.'[3] These two passages invite us to interpret Carlyle's tense physicality and Emerson's improvisatory cadences as indivisible from their message. Moreover, they encourage us to perceive the presence of an audience—applauding and rebuked in the first, astonished and reverent in the second—as central to the meaning of events. They offer up an image of the essayist not as solitary explorer but as leader, whose didacticism, 'earnestness of purpose', and moments of 'inspired' insight help to guide the community. Together, they present a vision of the emergent public function of the literary essay in the nineteenth-century public sphere on both sides of the Atlantic.

This new role was in part a novelty of the period's media landscape. Beginning in the 1820s, the spread of lecture halls known as 'lyceums' throughout the American republic, and the simultaneous flowering of Mechanics' Institutes in the cities of Britain, gave a new impetus to spoken non-fiction and allowed men of letters, thinkers, and scientists to reach wider publics and forge new careers.[4] Many essays from earlier periods of the English tradition had also been designed as spoken texts, but this Victorian phenomenon was unprecedented in scale. The essayist and orator drew closer than ever before; theatres, temples, and town halls joined the coffee-house as the spiritual home of the essay. The influence of this phenomenon, and of the kinds of scenes captured above, helped shape the aesthetic of Victorian essays, their subject matter, range of reference, and the ways in which essayists imagined and addressed their publics.

---

[2] 'A series of letters published in The Gazette of Stapleton, N.Y.', quoted in *Ralph Waldo Emerson: His Life, Writings and Philosophy*, ed. George Willis Cooke (1881), 258.

[3] Cooke, *Ralph Waldo Emerson*, 260.

[4] See Martin Hewitt, 'Aspects of Platform Culture in Nineteenth Century Britain', *Nineteenth-Century Prose* 29.1 (Spring 2002), 1–32. The most comprehensive recent studies include Angela Ray, *The Lyceum and Public Culture in the Nineteenth-Century United States* (2005) and Donald Scott, 'The Popular Lecture and the Creation of a Public in Mid-Nineteenth-Century America', *Journal of American History* 66.4 (1980), 791–5. See also Tom F. Wright (ed.), *The Cosmopolitan Lyceum: Lecture Culture and the Globe* (2013) and Tom F. Wright, *Lecturing the Atlantic: Speech, Print and an Anglo-American Commons 1830–1870* (2017).

However, as I argue in this chapter, the status of these essays as 'social' was also a property of the newly public ambitions and political imagination of the texts themselves. One tradition of the literary essay tends to presume intimate communion; a conversation by a fireside, perhaps, or an intimate confession. As William Hazlitt put it, the experience of Montaigne's essays is one in which the reader is 'admitted behind the curtain, and sits down with the writer in his gown and slippers'.[5] In the mid nineteenth century, another tradition came to the fore: one more explicitly oratorical than conversational. In this distinctively Victorian lineage, essayists such as John Ruskin, Matthew Arnold, or Henry David Thoreau often borrowed heavily from the rhythms of public speaking and preaching, placing as much emphasis upon rhetoric and persuasion as upon self-reflection. Perhaps more importantly, essayists in this tradition strove to emphasize the collective, with a focus on communal predicaments and shared solutions, with the essayist simulating not one-to-one intimacy but a triangular relationship between speaker, reader, and a wider audience often imagined as a crowd of listeners.

One critical tradition has been to see such essays as examples of 'Sage' writing, or didactic non-fiction that chastises and instructs readers from a position of assumed wisdom and charismatic authority.[6] Yet we might also usefully see this as a tradition of the 'voiced essay': a form explained not only by its didacticism or suggestively sermonic qualities but by its engagement with orality on the level of style and idea. This chapter explores the essays of Carlyle and Emerson as the most prominent examples of this tradition. As I show, both authors drew strength from 'oratorical' styles, reimagining their readerships as circles of listeners, and using tropes of ventriloquism and vocal orchestration in the service of quite distinct political visions. Thinking about their writings as multi-levelled charismatic vocal and social performances provides a new way of thinking about the essay and its audience at a historical moment of productive tension between competing forms of social authority.

2. Forging Oratorical Styles

The kinship of the Scottish social critic and his younger New England Transcendentalist ally was one of the foundational bonds of nineteenth-century transatlantic literary culture. Their shared stylistic traits mean that they occupy a prominent place in the development of the literary essay. Though celebrated in his

---

[5] William Hazlitt, 'On the Periodical Essayists', in *The Selected Writings of William Hazlitt*, ed. Duncan Wu, 9 vols (1998), V, 88.

[6] See John Holloway, *The Victorian Sage: Studies in Argument* (1953) and George P. Landow, *Elegant Jeremiahs: The Sage from Carlyle to Mailer* (1986).

time more for his longer historical works, Carlyle's *Critical and Miscellaneous Essays* (1838), the seminal piece 'Chartism' (1840), the series of lecture-essays *On Heroes and Hero Worship* (1841), the pieces that make up *Past and Present* (1843) and his notorious *Latter-Day Pamphlets* (1850) remain his more enduring and widely read writings.[7] They sit alongside Emerson's *Nature* (1836), 'The American Scholar' (1837), *Essays: First Series* (1841), and *Representative Men* (1850) as some of the most influential essayistic writings of their age.

From the outset, readers have found it useful to think about the experience of these works in terms of a voice speaking directly to the reader. For the young Walt Whitman in 1840s Brooklyn, the words of the Scottish philosopher fell on his ears like 'one of those far-off Hebraic utterers' whose words 'bubble forth with abysmic inspiration [...] rude, rasping, taunting, contradictory tones'.[8] During the same years, as an undergraduate in England, Matthew Arnold fancied that he heard a 'voice oracular' addressing his 'bodily ear' from Concord, Massachusetts: '[t]o us at Oxford, Emerson was but a voice speaking from three thousand miles away'.[9] Emerson and Carlyle also regarded these vocal qualities as essential features of the other's work. 'He does not write in the written dialect of the day', the American was fond of remarking of his Scottish mentor, 'but he draws strength and motherwit out of the spoken vocabulary'.[10] Upon receiving his copy of 'The American Scholar' essay, Carlyle returned this vocal compliment, writing to his friend that 'I could have *wept* to read that speech; the clear high melody of it went tingling through my heart.'[11]

These associations with oral delivery seem natural given their links with the phenomenon of Victorian popular lecturing. Both Carlyle and Emerson became essayists at this moment of intellectual flux when the blurring of sacred, secular, and political discourse opened up new modes of public address. However, their attitudes to the phenomenon were quite distinct. In the case of Emerson, the oral delivery of essays to a listening public became the defining feature of his career. He turned to the lecture form after abandoning a promising Boston preaching career, and by the 1840s had become one of the transatlantic circuit's most celebrated speakers, delivering over 1,500 lectures in total.[12] Carlyle was a far more reluctant

---

[7] He complained in an 1829 letter to Goethe that he was 'still but an Essayist, and longing more than ever to be a Writer in a far better sense' (Thomas Carlyle to Goethe (3 November 1829), in *The Collected Letters of Thomas and Jane Welsh Carlyle*, ed. Charles Richard Sanders et al. (1970–), 44 vols, V, 29).

[8] Walt Whitman, *Specimen Days: & Collect* (1882), 178.

[9] Matthew Arnold, 'Written in Emerson's Essays' [1849], l. 3, in *The Poems of Matthew Arnold*, ed. Kenneth Allott, 4 vols (1965), I, 52; Arnold, 'Emerson', from *Discourses in America* [1885], in *The Complete Prose Works of Matthew Arnold*, vol. X, ed. R. H. Super (1974), 167.

[10] See, for example, Ralph Waldo Emerson, 'New England', in Ronald A. Bosco and Joel Myerson (eds), *The Later Lectures of Ralph Waldo Emerson, 1843–1871*, 2 vols (2010), I, 64.

[11] Carlyle to Emerson (8 December 1837), in Joseph Slater (ed.), *The Correspondence of Emerson and Carlyle* (1964), 44.

[12] Recent discussions include Mary Kupiec Cayton, *Emerson's Emergence: Self and Society in the Transformation of New England 1800–1845* (1992); Thomas Augst, *The Clerk's Tale: Young Men and*

performer, and claimed to Emerson that he was only 'driven' into the 'lecture-room [...] with bayonets of Necessity clapt to my back'. He endured only four short but highly lucrative London seasons between 1837 and 1840, during which his live performances of his essays were one of the highlights of the capital's literary year.[13]

The vocal analogy, however, went beyond lecture culture. Such comparisons were also made possible because of the extent to which both gave to their prose the stylistic qualities of oratorical performance. Whereas the essays of Francis Bacon or William Hazlitt might have aspired to simulate one-on-one conversation, Emerson and Carlyle's style aimed for a register that frequently seems transplanted from the era's dominant sites for public speech: the political stump, public meeting, pulpit, or lectern.[14] Like numerous innovators of the English-speaking essay tradition, they integrated into their style what Walter Ong has called 'oral residue'.[15]

Emerson's early style in particular seems shaped as much for the ear as the eye. He was an admirer of the speechmaking of Whig politicians such as Daniel Webster and Unitarian preachers such as Edward Taylor, and strove to emulate aspects of their dynamic style in his writings.[16] As many readers have noted, his early essays rely heavily on sonic patterning, with a musical quality that turns the rippling euphony and anaphoric repetitions of moments such as this one from 'The American Scholar' into a form of incantation, appealing to audience memory:

> Every day, the sun; and after sunset, night and her stars. Ever the winds blow; ever the grass grows. Every day, men and women, conversing, beholding and beholden.

Often, the rhapsodic intensity of these earlier essays aspires to the metrical flow of verse. Take the exuberant pantheistic opening to the 'Divinity School Address' (1838):

Moral Life in Nineteenth-Century America (2003), 114–57; Bonnie Carr O'Neill, '"The Best of Me Is There": Emerson as Lecturer and Celebrity', *American Literature* 80.4 (2008), 739–67; Tom F. Wright, 'Listening to Emerson's "England" at Clinton Hall, 22 January 1850', *Journal of American Studies* 46 (2012).

[13] Carlyle to Emerson (16 March 1838), in Slater (ed.), *Correspondence of Emerson and Carlyle*, 41. Carlyle's four lecture series were: 1837, 'German Literature', Hanover Rooms; 1838, 'History of Literature', Willis Rooms; 1839, 'Revolutions of Modern Europe', Marylebone Institution; 1840, 'On Heroes and Hero-Worship', Marylebone Institution. See Owen Dudley Edwards, 'The Tone of the Preacher: Carlyle as Public Lecturer in *On Heroes*' in Carlyle, *On Heroes, Hero-Worship and the Heroic in History*, ed. David Sorensen and Brent E. Kinser (2013).

[14] See Angus Hawkins, *Victorian Political Culture: Habits of Heart and Mind* (2015), 113.

[15] Walter J. Ong, *Orality and Literacy: The Technologizing of the Word* (1982), 11.

[16] See Lawrence Buell, *New England Literary Culture from Revolution Through Renaissance* (1989), 1.

In this refulgent summer, it has been a luxury to draw the breath of life. The grass grows, the buds burst, the meadow is spotted with fire and gold in the tint of flowers. The air is full of birds, and sweet with the breath of the pine, the balm-of-Gilead, and the new hay.[17]

As Lawrence Buell has pointed out, moments like this 'yield the most when they are not just scanned by the eye but also heard by the mind's ear'.[18] Their effect relies on the tension between seductively alliterative rhythms and unexpected diction, and such moments are not simply musical but also thematic. With its insistence on the idea of 'breath', its phonemic swell and vowel patterning, Emerson's language becomes an impassioned speech-song whose sensual qualities not only mimic that of the glories of nature, but sound a clarion call against what Emerson saw as modern Christianity's deafness to the natural sublime.

Carlyle's style also alternates between melody and dissonance, and famous passages such as the lyrical stretches of 'Midas', the opening essay of *Past and Present* (1843), seduce readers with its iambic cadences: 'With unabated bounty the land of England blooms and grows; waving with yellow harvests; thick-studded with workshops.'[19] However, the Scot's prose is far more famous for its harsh vocal tones. While his early literary essays were a model of Johnsonian formal balance, as his authorial persona and style developed his prose drifted gradually towards a more obviously oratorical vehemence reminiscent of an impassioned public speaker. Elsewhere in *Past and Present* the melodramatic onslaught of erotemic rhetorical questions, exclamations, personification, and collective pronouns generate rhythms redolent more of stump or dispatch box, almost conjuring the speaker's tense theatricality:

[...] but who are they that cause these wrongs, who that will honestly make effort to redress them? Our enemies are we know not who or what; our friends are we know not where! How shall we attack any one, shoot or be shot by any one? Oh, if the accursed invisible Nightmare, that is crushing out the life of us and ours, would take a shape; approach us like the Hyrcanian tiger, the Behemoth of Chaos, the Archfiend himself; in any shape that we could see, and fasten on![20]

This oratorical flamboyance has divided opinion. Geoffrey Hartman has defended Carlyle's sometimes grotesque mixture of neologisms, jolts, and admonishment

---

[17] Emerson, 'Divinity School Address', in *Nature, Addresses, and Lectures*, vol. I in *The Collected Works of Ralph Waldo Emerson*, ed. Robert E. Spiller and Alfred R. Ferguson (1971), 76.

[18] Buell, *New England Literary Culture*, 101.

[19] Carlyle, 'Midas', in H. D. Traill (ed.), *Past and Present*, vol. X in *The Works of Thomas Carlyle* (1896, 2010), 1.

[20] Carlyle, 'Manchester Insurrection', in *Past and Present*, 15.

as a deliberately 'richer, rougher English'.[21] Attendees at his London lectures seemed to agree, with one commenting on 'his hard, expressive, compound phrases, dragged out with vast energy, from the chamber of his capacious mind, by, as it were, a cable of harsh-sounding broadest-of-broad Scotch'.[22] For many readers, however, this style has been a hindrance. Matthew Arnold urged students to 'flee Carlylese as you would the devil', whilst Friedrich Nietzsche saw it as key to the problem of 'the absurd muddle-head Carlyle'.[23] While clearly indebted to classical rhetorical tropes and techniques, Carlyle's onslaught of erotema, exclamation, and exhortation violates Ciceronian or Quintilian precepts. Yet the style of his essays might be seen less as an attempt to bring English closer to German, as is often claimed, than an attempt to bring written language closer to the condition of fervent stump oratory.

One motivation for this embrace of an oratorical style was the two writers' repeatedly stated desire to simulate something more natural and robust than written essayistic argument. Emerson praised the essays of Montaigne precisely in these terms, proclaiming that 'I know not anywhere the book that seems less written.'[24] In his essay 'The American Scholar' he argued that whilst books are presented as backward artefacts that 'pin' the reader 'down' audiences 'drink' the orator's words because 'he fulfils for them their own nature'.[25] Carlyle often advanced a similar view, arguing in 'Characteristics' that the distinction between orality and literacy was akin to the 'superiority of what is called the Natural over the Artificial [...] The Orator persuades and carries all with him, he knows not how [...] in a state of healthy unconsciousness'.[26] This Romantic yearning for pre-literate expression not only suffused the poetry of the age, of course, but also influenced the essay form. Ivan Kreilkampf has recently described this tendency of the writing of the period to emulate public speech as an 'ongoing romance with voice as cure for print culture's ills' with the live speaker idealized as 'a vanishing source of charismatic power, one freed from all the binds and compromises of bureaucratic knowledge'.[27] In this way, readers of Emerson's and Carlyle's essays respond not to poised rational argument nor the disinterested informality of the

---

[21] Geoffrey Hartman, 'The Sacred Jungle', in *The Geoffrey Hartman Reader* (2004), 249.

[22] Jonathan Dix, *Lions: Living and Dead* (1854), 147. See also Harriet Martineau, quoted in Rosemary Ashton, *Thomas and Jane Carlyle: Portrait of a Marriage* (2002), 212; Charles Sumner to George S. Hillard (14 June 1838), in Edward L. Pierce, *Memoir and Letters of Charles Sumner*, 4 vols (1839), I, 317–18.

[23] Friedrich Nietzsche, quoted in Rolf-Peter Horstmann, *Beyond Good and Evil: Prelude to a Philosophy of the Future* (2001), 142; Arnold, quoted in Frederic Harrison, *Studies in Early Victorian Literature* (1895), 32. For the argument that Carlylese is German, see Hartman, 'The Sacred Jungle', 247–9.

[24] Emerson, 'Montaigne; or, The Skeptic', in *Representative Men*, vol. IV in *The Collected Works of Ralph Waldo Emerson*, ed. Wallace E. Williams (1987), 95.

[25] Emerson, 'Divinity School Address', 86.

[26] Carlyle, 'Characteristics', in H. D. Traill (ed.), *Critical and Miscellaneous Essays III*, vol. XXVIII in *The Works of Thomas Carlyle* (1899, 2010), 7.

[27] Ivan Kreilkamp, *Voice and the Victorian Storyteller* (2005), 70.

familiar essay, but to their cultivation of a persona whose rhetoric simulates the energies of oral encounter. And more subtly, this was also a persona that relied upon allowing readers to feel that they were being spoken to en masse.

3. Constructing an Audience of Listeners

'Listening' was a key term for both essayists, who used it to capture the kind of social attentiveness they sought in their audience. As Carlyle's career developed, metaphors of attention evolved from visual to aural. In 'Characteristics' he railed against a society that merely 'painfully listens to itself'; by the essays of *Past and Present*, the critique of the 'unlistening multitudes' is sharpened, and the essayist urged his audience to 'cease to be a hollow sounding-shell of hearsays, egoisms, purblind dilettantisms' and become a 'faithful discerning soul'.[28] In Emerson's greatest essays such as 'Self-Reliance' (1841), tropes of listening are also widespread, and his argument continually returns to the idea of what 'the soul hears'.[29] In an influential modern reading of Victorian fiction, Garrett Stewart has argued that direct address found in novels ('Dear Reader...') helped forge 'the encoded presence of a reading consciousness to a narrative text'.[30] Carlyle's and Emerson's essays adopted a related but crucially different strategy by reversing the logic of print and encoding the complex presence of readers as listeners.

Carlyle's essays often invoked the presence of a live listener. In 'The Diamond Necklace' (1837) he invited his readers to 'listen to a plain varnished tale, such as your dramatist can fashion' and conceived of his own readership as 'my own listening circle', and as he brought various voices to life, he encouraged readers to 'let us listen'.[31] In similar fashion, the essays of Emerson also solicit the presence of those listening, such as in his invocation of not readers but 'audience' in 'Self-Reliance', when predicting that, 'I might not carry with me the feeling of my audience in stating my belief.'[32] The Transcendentalist's pieces also went further in staging moments of two-way oral contact with imagined listeners. Perhaps the most memorable example occurs in the culminating moments of 'Circles' (1841), where he confronts his 'hearers' directly:

O circular philosopher, I hear some reader exclaim, you have arrived at a fine Pyrrhonism, at an equivalence and indifference of all actions [...] [But] let me

---

[28] Carlyle, 'Characteristics', 22; 'Chartism', in *Critical and Miscellaneous Essays IV*, vol. XXIX in *The Works of Thomas Carlyle* (1899, 2010), 151; 'Morrison's Pill', in *Past and Present*, 26.

[29] Emerson, 'Nature', in *Nature, Addresses, and Lectures*, 9.

[30] Garrett Stewart, *Dear Reader: The Conscripted Audience in Nineteenth-Century British Fiction* (1996), 12.

[31] Carlyle, 'The Diamond Necklace', in H. D. Traill (ed.), *Critical and Miscellaneous Essays III*, 361, 326.

[32] Emerson, 'The American Scholar', in *Nature, Addresses, and Lectures*, 65.

remind the reader that I am only an experimenter. Do not set the least value on what I do, or the least discredit on what I do not, as if I pretended to settle anything as true or false. I unsettle all things.[33]

Speaker, reader, and hearer become here partners in a process of communicative action, with sequences such as this casting the 'reader' as one who not only 'hears' but whose inner voice is in turn heard by the composing speaker. In this way, the Emersonian essay regenerates its message from utterances that move towards what Mikhail Bakhtin called 'answerability', not only inviting response but also folding imagined responses into the drama of the text.[34] In this way, the literary essayist addresses both an implied audience of like-minded readers and a live audience that is rhetorically oppositional.

Reading these essays, we can imagine ourselves in a range of possible scenes of listening. At points, we might imagine their writings as Parliamentary testimony or Senate floor orations. Particularly in the case of Carlyle, they might equally be interpreted as transcriptions of one of his notorious monologues; an experience recorded by Margaret Fuller, who having visited Chelsea complained that the Scot 'does not converse, only harangues [...] it is the nature of a mind accustomed to follow out its impulse as the hawk its prey'.[35] For Emerson's part, the sheer abstraction of his ideas might find us agreeing with Carlyle's particularly striking critique in a letter to his friend that 'we find you a Speaker, indeed, but as it were a *Soliloquizer* on the eternal mountain-tops only, in vast solitudes where men and their affairs lie all hushed in a very dim remoteness.'[36]

Yet sometimes these imagined scenes might be more intentionally specific. The authors' choice of sometimes prefacing pieces with explanations of their initial spoken context (for instance, 'Delivered before the Senior Class in Divinity College [...] July 15, 1838') re-connected readers to a scene of original oral delivery, and to read them was to conceive oneself as part of a community of imagined fellow listeners.[37] One encounters a more organic effect of presence in numerous comparable essays of the period, such as John Ruskin's 1857 'The Political Economy of Art', whose opening retains phrases ('I see that some of my hearers look surprised at the expression. I assure them, I use it in sincerity') that allow readers to imagine their presence in crowds such as Ruskin's original

---

[33] Emerson, 'Circles', in *Essays, First Series*, vol. II of *The Collected Works of Ralph Waldo Emerson*, ed. Joseph Slater (1979), 188.

[34] Mikhail Bakhtin, 'Speech Genres' in Michael Holquist, Vern McGee, and Caryl Emerson (eds), *Speech Genres and Other Late Essays* (1986), 139.

[35] Margaret Fuller, 'Things and Thoughts in Europe, No. IX', *New York Daily Tribune* (19 February 1847), in *These Sad but Glorious Days: Dispatches from Europe, 1846–1850*, ed. Larry J. Reynolds and Susan Belasco Smith (1991), 101.

[36] Carlyle to Emerson (3 November 1844), in Slater (ed.), *Correspondence of Emerson and Carlyle*, 134.

[37] Emerson, 'Divinity School Address', 76.

audience at the Manchester Athenaeum.[38] Similarly, references in Carlyle's 'Hero as Man of Letters' (1841) to 'our present meeting here!' place us back into an audience with the author.[39] Thanks to moments like this, certain essays always remain contextually bound.

Readers of these essays might just as easily imagine themselves before a pulpit. As much as in the widely published sermons of their contemporaries John Keble, John Henry Newman, or Henry Ward Beecher, religious form and training resonated in Carlyle's and Emerson's essays. As John Morrow has noted of the former, 'the moral and rhetorical impulses that might have been deployed in the pulpit were now called up in the service of literature [...] chastisement, rebuke, and a certain roughness or even violence of expression'.[40] They had abandoned the Church of Scotland and New England Unitarianism respectively in favour of a broader secular form of cultural engagement, yet both saw the remains of their former vocation in the other. In the critique of his friend's writing quoted above, Carlyle used the comparison in a loaded fashion, complaining that 'it is a *sermon* to me, as all your other deliberate utterances are.'[41] This sense of translated religiosity was also understood by their audiences. The crowd for Carlyle's first 1840 lecture 'sat silent, [...] as if it had been gospel'; and one contemporary observed of Emerson that 'his aim has always been that of the preacher, differing only in manner of treatment and in range of matter.'[42]

If most conversational essays rely for their charm and power on the sense of being addressed by a like-minded peer, the Victorian voiced essay by contrast involved imagining oneself conjured into a passive embodied assembly. To read essays as the writers seemed to intend was to give way to the charisma of a motivational speaker: just as the true orator, according to Emerson, must be 'inwardly drunk with a certain belief', reading these essayists we become moment-arily party to this intoxication.[43] In another sense, however, there was a partici-patory element, since printed texts of lectures and sermons were among many forms frequently read aloud in group settings in the nineteenth century. Prolific orators such as Emerson were acutely aware of these multiple scenes of potential reading, and that the orator's initial rendition was merely one of many potential re-imaginings of the composition. In one sense, therefore, collections of their essays became akin to anthologies of performance scores.

[38] John Ruskin, 'The Political Economy of Art', in Lloyd J. Hubenka (ed.), *Unto This Last: Four Essays on the First Principles of Political Economy* (1967), 1.

[39] Carlyle, 'The Hero as Man of Letters', in Sorensen and Kinser (eds), *On Heroes*, 102.

[40] John Morrow, *Thomas Carlyle* (2006), 29.

[41] Carlyle to Emerson (3 November 1844), in Slater (ed.), *Correspondence of Emerson and Carlyle*, 134.

[42] Carlyle to Jean Carlyle Aitken (6 May 1840), in *Collected Letters*, XII, 134; George Willis Cooke, *Ralph Waldo Emerson: His Life, Writings and Philosophy* (1881), 263.

[43] Emerson, 'Eloquence', in *Society and Solitude*, vol. VII in *The Collected Works of Ralph Waldo Emerson*, ed. Robert E. Spiller, Alfred R. Ferguson, Joseph Slater, and Jean F. Carr (1971), 47.

Both Carlyle and Emerson saw their essays as attempts to create a figurative 'circle of listeners' that transcended the social and racial exclusions of their actual performances. By embedding in print this triangular relationship between speaker, listener, and fellow attendants, Emerson and Carlyle helped strengthen what Benedict Anderson has called the 'deep horizontal comradeship' of an abstract imaginary congregation: a sense of simultaneity that aimed to bring into being and solidify a circle of listeners that was at times both national—of the British people or citizens of the American republic—and wider than the nation, aspiring to the broader 'we' of Euro-American modernity.[44] But while both seemed to aim for the same form of secular listening public, they did so for quite different political and creative ends. One of the most interesting points of divergence lay in their attitude towards the communities of listener that they created.

4. Orchestrating Voices

These two authors differed from many of the essayists discussed in this book in that theirs was for the most part a strikingly impersonal style. Only very rarely do we find flashes of first-person reflection, reminiscence, or straightforward testimony in their pages. Instead they create a 'circle of listeners' in order to in effect stand back from their own essays, preferring to adopt the pose of detached orchestrators of ideas. Their essays play host to a congregation of different voices, so that the authorial voice becomes not only an inspired speaker but also a devout listener: a fascinating means of articulating positions and thoughts with which the author is not identified. The voiced essay becomes a space of synthesis amidst the cacophony of society, in which multiple voices speak variously and sometimes in conflict but within a common space.

This is particularly true of Carlyle, who peoples his essays with a varied cast of voices who sound off against each other. In his essays on historical subjects, this approach took the form of voicing personae from past eras. Just as his most famous long work *The French Revolution* (1837) wove its narrative from a succession of speakers representing abstract social forces such as the 'Voice of France', essays such as 'Mirabeau' and those in *Past and Present* explored a playwright's instinct for interweaving historical voices into *tableaux vivants*, inviting readers to 'listen to the following utterances' from a cast of long-dead characters.[45] By contrast, in the seminal essays on what he famously called the 'Condition of England' question, Carlyle chose to impersonate the contending voices of the present-day nation. In 'Characteristics', he declares that, 'from this

---

[44] Benedict Anderson, *Imagined Communities: Reflections on the Origin and Spread of Nationalism* (1991), 35.
[45] Carlyle, 'Mirabeau', 423.

stunning hubbub, a true Babel-like confusion of tongues, we have here selected two Voices'.[46] There is a theatrical element to this antiphonal approach which invites comparison with the influential contemporary method of early nineteenth-century British actor Charles Mathews, whose ubiquitous one-man show 'mono-polylogues' involved him embodying a dozen or more characters in one perform-ance. For Carlyle, such ventriloquism was frequently a vehicle of satire, impersonating voices for the purpose of mockery, in a manner that generated Carlylese at its most grotesquely (and sometimes unintentionally) comic, as here in the 'Happy' essay of *Past and Present*: 'there began, in a horrid, semi-articulate, unearthly voice, this song: "Once I was hap-hap-happy, but now I'm *mee*serable! Clack-clack-clack, gnarr-r-r, whuz-z".'[47]

But this ventriloquism was not just satiric method but part of a vision of the political essay as vehicle for humanitarian sympathy. Carlyle began 'Chartism' by calling on 'friends of the people' to 'interpret and articulate the dumb deep want [...] for that great dumb toiling class which cannot speak'.[48] His essays sought to meet this need for clarity by making audible those 'thoughts unpublished [...] going on in every reflective head', dramatizing viewpoints that others had ignored and bringing to life the 'inarticulate uproar' of the dispossessed.[49] It was a gesture he developed in 'Midas', where he moved from the description of rural poverty to inhabit the voice of the social mechanism that kept the poor subordinated:

fifteen millions of workers [...] And behold, some baleful fiat as of Enchantment has gone forth, saying, 'Touch it not, ye workers, ye master-workers, ye master-idlers; none of you can touch it, no man of you shall be the better for it; this is enchanted fruit!'[50]

At moments such as this, the literary essay took on what Carlyle saw as the proper role that Parliament had abdicated: offering a full account of the people's needs and the solutions that 'dwell in all thinking heads' but remained unspoken, 'hovering [...] on the tongues of not a few'.[51] Ventriloquism here offers clarity as an antidote to cultural confusion, and suggests a form of quasi-novelistic omniscience whose panoramic scope was part of Carlyle's impact on contempor-aries such as Charles Dickens and Charles Kingsley.

Emerson's essay aesthetic also relied upon the dextrous juggling of a wide range of voices. He celebrated the discursive freedom of his new medium of the lecture-essay in terms of its vocal diversity, praising it as a form in which 'everything is admissible, philosophy, ethics, divinity, criticism, poetry, humor, fun, mimicry, anecdotes, jokes, ventriloquism. All the breadth & versatility of the most liberal

---

[46] Carlyle, 'Characteristics', 33.   [47] Carlyle, 'Happy', in *Past and Present*, 155.
[48] Carlyle, 'Chartism', 121.   [49] Carlyle, 'Midas', 1; 'Chartism', 122.
[50] Carlyle, 'Midas', 1.   [51] Carlyle, 'Chartism', 192.

conversation [...] all may be combined in one speech; it is a panharmonicon.'[52] Like this panharmonicon, a nineteenth-century technological novelty which imitated the sounds of multiple instruments simultaneously, Emerson's essays hum with resonances of a series of synthesized voices. Most famously, they gave voice to the mute glories of nature, allowing it, in the words of one astute recent reading of his essays, to 'testify' for itself.[53] Blending pantheism and Swedenborgian mysticism, he promoted the literary essay as the channel through which nature could speak: the means by which to break what he called in 'The Divinity School Address', 'the never-broken silence with which the old bounty goes forward [that] has not yielded yet one word of explanation'.[54]

Yet Emerson too, like Carlyle, tended to orchestrate imagined speakers, with 'Self-Reliance' shifting into the voice of the 'Caliph Ali', and *Nature* concluding in the persona of an 'Orphic Bard'. His most arresting method was the staging of dialogues in which the authorial voice confronts opposing views directly as heard speech. The totemic line 'A foolish consistency is the hobgoblin of little minds', in 'Self-Reliance', for example, is countered swiftly as follows:

Ah, then, exclaim the aged ladies, you shall be sure to be misunderstood! Misunderstood! It is a right fool's word. Is it so bad then to be misunderstood?[55]

More elaborately, the essay's other well-known injunction—'Whoso would be a man must be a nonconformist'—generates the following imagined dialogue:

I remember an answer which when quite young I was prompted to make to a valued adviser, who was wont to importune me with the dear old doctrines of the church. On my saying, What have I to do with the sacredness of traditions, if I live wholly from within? my friend suggested,—"But these impulses may be from below, not from above." I replied, "They do not seem to me to be such; but if I am the Devil's child, I will live then from the Devil." No law can be sacred to me but that of my nature.[56]

In this rare moment of personal intrusion, the essay articulates and closes off the alternate 'impulse' with a stark statement of principle, leaving us with discordant voices raised in uneasy competition. This antiphonal chorus leads critics such as Sharon Cameron to read Emerson's essays as an erasure of personality, since at their heart is 'anonymous voice, which is not a recognizable voice because not

---

[52] 'New England: Genius, Manners and Customs' in *The Later Lectures of Ralph Waldo Emerson, 1843–1871*, I, 48.

[53] See Shari Goldberg, 'Emerson: Testimony without Representation', in *Quiet Testimony: A Theory of Witnessing from Nineteenth-Century American Literature* (2013), 23–4.

[54] Emerson, 'Divinity School Address', 76.

[55] Emerson, 'Self-Reliance', in *Essays, First Series*, 26.   [56] Emerson, 'Self-Reliance', 30.

legible as a single person's voice'.[57] Reading these essays presents a paradox to each reader. As we navigate these competing voices, do they weave together as part of a dialectical journey towards truth, or do they remain a chorus of unresolved cries?

In these ways, acts of citation and vocalization displaced confession, resulting in a series of subtle tensions. Both essayists wanted to promote themselves as chief listeners, to efface themselves as speakers and narrative agents, and to either rebuke or give solace to voices they harboured. As Vanden Bossche has written of Carlyle's *French Revolution*, 'the narrator' aimed to seem 'not the manipulator of the voices but the product of them'.[58] Yet both demanded submission, as if to oracles with profound knowledge of all worldly subject, sentiments, and sensibilities. If their essays employed ventriloquism then, as Steven Connor's work on the thrown voices of the nineteenth century has shown, 'ventriloquists also faced and enacted a version of the same aesthetic problem' that confronted 'post-Romantic writers: namely, how to balance the imperious claims of the individual, appetitive poetic self and the severalness of the many lives into which he longed to enter and vanish.'[59] Their respective solutions to this over the course of their essayistic careers are highly revealing.

The classic Carlyle persona of the 1830s and 1840s was the essayist as seer, demanding trust in his powers of interpretation, vocalization, and orchestration. Readers valued essays such as 'Chartism' for their inspired diagnosis of social problems, and for the access they provided to certain ideas found almost nowhere else. And yet, perhaps inevitably, as his career as an essayist developed, this exceptional power and remarkable cultural centrality was lost, and the evolution of Carlyle's handling of voices offers a means of tracing his popular and conceptual decline. By the time of the *Latter-Day Pamphlets* (1850), Carlyle is no longer in sympathetic concord with his readers, but is rather pleading with them in a hectoring frenzy. In notorious essays such as 'Discourse on the Nigger Question' or 'The Stump-Orator', his stylistic melodrama—dashes, semicolons, erratic italicization, and an overabundance of exclamation marks—seem now to capture the cries, gestures, and emotional contortions of an agitated companion lately abandoned. Some of the former vocal tropes remain, such as when the premise of the essay 'Downing Street' is framed in terms of a heard voice: 'from all corners of the wide British Dominion there rises one complaint [...]'.[60] However, as Bossche rightly notes, in these late essays the style 'cuts off' a previous range of speakers 'and allows only Carlyle's own persona to speak', reducing the brilliance

---

[57] Sharon Cameron, *Impersonality: Seven Essays* (2007), 93.

[58] Chris Vanden Bossche, *Carlyle and the Search for Authority* (1991), 68.

[59] Steven Connor, *Dumbstruck! A Cultural History of Ventriloquism* (2000), 297.

[60] Carlyle, 'Downing Street', in H. D. Traill (ed.), *Latter-Day Pamphlets*, vol. XX in *The Works of Thomas Carlyle* (1899, 2010), 87.

of his former dialogue between narrator and the warring factions of English society to a dispiriting monologue.[61]

Carlyle had always maintained a challenging relationship to his audience. It was there both in print and in the approach he took to his public lectures: consider the disdain for applause captured in the opening quote of this chapter, or the observation recorded by one young female audience member in her diary that 'when the audience cheered, he would impatiently, almost contemptuously, wave his hand, as if that were not the sort of homage which Truth demanded.'[62] It is strange, then, that in the late essays the degree of almost confrontational intimacy with his audience is sharpened. By turns urgent and laconic, he beseeches his readers as 'my sublime benevolent friends', 'O my surprising friends!' and 'O my astonishing benevolent friends!', and fills almost entire paragraphs with a succession of vehement rhetorical questions even more zealous and pleading than those of his earlier style.[63] The voice is no longer pedagogue, or choreographer, but aggravated malcontent, calling over the heads of disillusioned contemporaries to the emerging generation and to posterity. And yet who is really still listening to this late Carlyle? It is fitting perhaps that these late essays turn to such direct addresses at the very moment that Carlyle's increasingly rigid authoritarian ideology had cost him most of his audience. In their feverish attempts at intimacy, these late essays reveal an author mourning a lost constituency, aware of a generation of listeners who have abandoned the counsel of his increasingly authoritarian voice.

By contrast, Emerson's solution to the paradox of positioning himself at once as both speaker and listener was to turn the challenge back on his audience. A central metaphor of his writings was the claim that readers should trust their own inner voice. Drawn in part from Quaker imagery, this is the keynote of 'Self-Reliance', where he urges readers to 'listen to the inward voice and bravely obey'; it is also the theme of 'Spiritual Laws' (1841), where he argues that 'there is guidance for each of us' in listening to speech from within.[64] This urge to listen to intuition also takes on a cultural nationalist aspect in 'The American Scholar' where, having 'listened too long to the courtly muses of Europe', the process of personal renovation necessary for American democratic individuality is figured in terms of giving voice to an 'ill-suppressed murmur' of the national sublime.[65] Emerson's classic essays therefore urged readers to listen to themselves rather than his own voice. While both he and Carlyle tend to retire behind a web of citation and impersonation, it was the American's emphasis on his reader's voice that ultimately made

---

[61] Bossche, *Carlyle and the Search for Authority*, 135.

[62] Caroline Fox, journal (20 May 1847), quoted in Rosemary Ashton, *Thomas and Jane Carlyle: Portrait of a Marriage* (2002), 212.

[63] Carlyle, 'Model Prisons', in *Latter-Day Pamphlets*, 60–1.

[64] Emerson, 'Self-Reliance', 30; Emerson, 'Spiritual Laws', in *Essays, First Series*, 110.

[65] Emerson, 'The American Scholar', 63.

his strain of impersonality more endearing. It was a paradoxical form of essayistic authority, and one which his most famous poetic disciple Whitman saw as Emerson's key strength, in that this urging onwards of the essays 'breeds the giant that destroys itself', as part of essays that foresaw their own obsolescence.[66]

5. Charismatic Texts

To grasp the distinction between the ends towards which Carlyle and Emerson's voiced essays were geared, we might return to the energies of the scenes with which this chapter began. In the London lecture hall, Carlyle is presented, seemingly against his will, as the 'Hero as Man of Letters', one of the titles of his performed pieces. In the following century Max Weber would secularize the Greek term *khárisma* and re-imagine it as a divinely imparted gift of leadership.[67] Here we witness both Carlyle and his observers reaching towards a similar idea in their account of the social effects of his apparently heroic social engagement, empathy, and ventriloquism. As he declared in 'The Hero as Poet' lecture in the series, 'truly, it is a great thing for a Nation that it get an articulate voice; that it produce a man who will speak forth melodiously what the heart of it means!'[68] The Carlylean voiced essay sought to fulfil such messianic expectations, to synthesize vast social currents into one strong central voice. The unresolvable tensions between the act of speaking and listening mean that some subjectivities will never be heard, and the act of corralling voices offers merely an illusion of democratic inclusivity.[69]

Never convinced by Carlyle's model of greatness, Emerson saw great men as those that allowed will to flow through them. At the lectern on Staten Island we see an essayist figured more as motivational speaker than hero, merely claiming to model a habit of perception, casting a powerful gaze back upon the crowd, 'eyes uplifted on the audience', and asking of listeners and readers alike that they trust not him but their own powers of comprehension.[70] His essays disperse the gift of meaning through a series of woven voices just as, in the terms he used in 'Self-Reliance', 'It must be that when God speaketh he should communicate, not one thing, but all things; should fill the world with his voice; should scatter forth light, nature, time, souls, from the centre of the present thought.'[71]

[66] Walt Whitman, 'Emerson's Books, the Shadow of Them' (1882) in Richard M. Bucke, Thomas B. Harned, Horace Traubel, and Oscar L. Triggs (eds), *The Complete Writings of Walt Whitman* (1902).
[67] Max Weber, *The Theory of Social and Economic Organization*, trans. A. M. Henderson and Talcott Parsons (1924, 1947), 328, 358ff.
[68] Carlyle, 'The Hero as Poet', in Sorensen and Kinser (eds), *On Heroes*, 135.
[69] For elaborations on this critique, see Nancy Fraser, *Rethinking the Public Sphere: A Contribution to the Critique of Actually Existing Democracy* (1990), 6.
[70] 'A series of letters published in The Gazette of Stapleton, N.Y.', 258.
[71] Emerson, 'Self-Reliance', 30.

Different though their ends might have been, both authors tried to push the often materially focused genre of the essay form towards larger, spiritual concerns through an engagement with voice as idea and practice. By marrying secular, sacred, and oratorical rhythms, these essays attempt to teach us how to listen, presenting citizenship and social sentience as a matter of auditory perception. Looking back at the history of the essay through ideas of performance and speech reminds us that the form has never been solely introspective or intimate. And in a nineteenth-century moment of slippage between media forms and cultural registers, the literary essay took on a new social urgency as a form of public moralism, displaced secular sermon, and civic performance.

11

Retiring or Engaging

Politics in the English Essay

Ophelia Field

1. Introduction to a Paradox

Susan Sontag, opening her 1972 essay 'On Paul Goodman', described herself as a literary hermit working for over a year in 'a tiny room in Paris, sitting on a wicker chair at a typing table in front of a window which looks onto a garden'. The serenity of Sontag's cloister was disturbed, however, as 'each morning someone brings me the Paris *Herald Tribune* with its monstrous collage of "news" from America, encapsulated, distorted, stranger than ever from this distance: the B-52s raining eco-death on Vietnam [. . .]'.[1] The essay form is often a gesture towards the author's desire for pause or retirement, in the classical sense of standing back and claiming a more profound wisdom or wider perspective, but for Sontag this detachment also brought a kind of incredulous alienation.[2] She was torn between the essay's desire to 'draw its curtain', as Virginia Woolf put it in 1925, and the need to self-consciously record the chaos of world events that the curtain may hide.[3]

One image of the essayist is that epitomized by Graham Good as a 'middle-aged man in a worn tweed jacket in an armchair smoking a pipe by a fire in his private library in a country house somewhere in southern England, in about 1910, maundering on about the delights of idleness, country walks, tobacco, old wine, and old books [. . .]',[4] or by Robert Louis Stevenson's 'idler' who 'will not be heard among the dogmatists. He will have a great and cool allowance for all sorts of people and opinions. If he finds no out-of-the-way truths, he will identify himself with no very burning falsehood.'[5] Such Edwardian essayists saw the French

---

[1] Susan Sontag, 'On Paul Goodman', *Under the Sign of Saturn* (1972, 2002), 3.
[2] This position derives from the favourable sense of *otium* in Cicero and Seneca, in turn drawn from an earlier Athenian assumption that independent judgement depends upon the ability to retire and disengage whenever one wishes (which, in practice, depends upon social rank and wealth).
[3] Virginia Woolf, 'The Modern Essay', from *The Common Reader, First Series* [1925], in *The Essays of Virginia Woolf*, vol. IV, ed. Andrew McNeillie (1994), 216.
[4] Graham Good, 'Preface' to *The Observing Self: Rediscovering the Essay* (1988), vii.
[5] Robert Louis Stevenson, 'An Apology for Idlers' [1877], in *The Works of Robert Louis Stevenson*, ed. Edmund Gosse, 20 vols (1906), II, 358.

Ophelia Field, *Retiring or Engaging: Politics in the English Essay* In: *On Essays: Montaigne to the Present.*
Edited by: Thomas Karshan and Kathryn Murphy, Oxford University Press (2020). © Ophelia Field.
DOI: 10.1093/oso/9780198707868.003.0012

grand-père of the Anglo-Saxon essay, Montaigne, as an ancestor in their own image: a privileged nobleman, reclusively retired in his book-lined tower and dedicating himself to '*libertati suae tranquillitatique et otio*' ('freedom, tranquility, and leisure'). They aligned such retirement with the kind of conservatism that considers itself apolitical and seldom availed themselves of the capacity for wide-angle-lens political insight or commentary created by Montaignian retirement. This has remained a popular image of 'essayism' until very recently, even though some of the most canonical and brilliant essayists in English (Bacon, Swift, Hazlitt, Orwell) have also been considered among the language's most political writers.[6] The English 'political essay' tradition therefore presents, as Sontag's self-description dramatized, an apparent paradox.

This chapter traces, via the landmarks of Addison, Hazlitt, Woolf, Orwell, Baldwin, and Hitchens, how these and other major essayists in the English language tradition have grappled with the nature of political writing. The contrary pulls of retirement versus public engagement are most evident in the essayists' self-justifying accounts of their own positions—the continual battle between the duty they felt to 'be political' and their ultimately stronger ambition to produce literary art of universal and lasting value. Whenever firmly engaged, they tried to prick the consciences of retiring readers, or at least found themselves directed towards this effort, rather than some more confrontational polemic, by the essay's conventions of politeness and familiarity. In addition, this survey explores issues such as how political engagement is frequently linked to gaining the first-hand experience so important to any essayist's moral authority, how the Montaignian personal lens inflects the essay's treatment of public issues, and how, for several authors, the essay form itself symbolizes resistance against more absolutist forms of thought.

The English essay generally steers its politics away from the narrowly partisan, towards moral philosophy. Milton's *Areopagitica* (1644) remains perhaps the most famous universalization of a localized political complaint, in its framing of protest against the Licensing Order of 1643 as a general principle of intellectual freedom. Though Milton himself did not describe it as an essay, its reception as such established an association between the essay and the cause of individual liberty that remains implicit today. The prominence of anti-imperialism among

---

[6] Both the self-questioning angst of liberals since 2016, and the social movements now giving voice to those who have suffered racism and sexism, have generated a rich revival of personal-political essay writing, less beholden to the image of the essayist as detached, peaceable, and impartial and hence less entangled in the paradox that this article explores. In the Preface to *Feel Free* (2018), Zadie Smith acknowledges the changed tone of public discourse that makes several of her collected essays sound slightly dated: 'It is of course hardly possible to retain any feelings of ambivalence—on either side of the Atlantic—in the face of what we now confront' (xii). A new fearlessness and urgency can be heard in collections such as *The Fire This Time*, ed. Jesmyn Ward (2018) or *Can We All Be Feminists?*, ed. June Eric-Udorie (2018), and in book-length essays such as *Why I'm No Longer Talking to White People About Race* (2017) by Reni Eddo-Lodge.

the English essay's recurring themes is one clear symptom of this liberal orientation. The essay also remains the form to which fiction writers most often tend to resort when their professional and personal liberties, or those of their colleagues, are under serious threat from censorship, as was the case during the Cold War or under apartheid in South Africa.[7] The literary status of the essay itself becomes politically appealing, with the form's freedom from established critical definition and classical poetics, as well as from the constraints of formal logic and academic apparatus, attracting a disproportionate number of authors who hold individual liberty as the ultimate political value.

2. Eighteenth-Century Consciences

In 'Of Husbanding your Will', Montaigne discusses how his recipe for mixing private and public duties differs from his late father's: while happy to praise those, like his father, selflessly devoted to the public good, Montaigne explains that he himself seeks a clearer 'excuse' before being 'driv[en] into the market place'.[8] Montaigne's own path was complex: though he wrote his essays in retirement, he was also an important mediator in the religious wars between Rome and Navarre, a two-term Mayor of Bordeaux, and a radically independent thinker who dared express surprisingly progressive views on colonialism in the New World. In 'Of Cannibals', for example, Montaigne uses an encounter with three Amerindians in Rouen as a basis for questioning not only the presumptions of the Christian missions recently launched in Brazil, but also, through alien eyes, the gross inequalities of sixteenth-century France. This anthropological self-reflection, highlighting the slaves, enslavers, and savages within Western European societies, was bequeathed as an important theme to the English literary-political essay.

Montaigne's assertion, in his 1580 Preface, that he wrote with 'no goal but a domestic and private one' (2) was both a conventional Renaissance pose, belied by his essays' influential commentary on political matters,[9] and also the assertion of a genuinely original dimension in his work—the personal, self-confessional tone that sets it so far apart from the work of other early modern essayists. Francis Bacon's *Essays* (1597–1625) were similarly Janus-faced, divided between the private and the public, though reversing Montaigne's tendency: couched in impersonal prose, but intimate in their provision of advice to the reader. Bacon described his

---

[7] See, respectively: Arthur Miller's essay 'The Sin of Power', *Index on Censorship* 7 (May 1978), 3–6; or Nadine Gordimer's essay 'A Writer's Freedom' (1976), in *Telling Times: Writing and Living 1954–2008* (2010).

[8] Michel de Montaigne, *The Complete Works*, trans. Donald M. Frame (2003), 935. Further references given in the text.

[9] Henri IV, for example, is known to have admired Montaigne's essay 'Of the Disadvantage of Greatness'. See Gore Vidal, 'Montaigne', *Times Literary Supplement* 4656 (26 June 1992), 3.

primary model, Seneca's *Moral Epistles to Lucilius*, as addressed simultaneously inward and outward: 'dispersed meditations, though conveyed in the form of Epistles'.[10] On the one hand, Bacon's *Essays* belong in the Renaissance tradition of advice to princes and courtiers, and indeed Bacon intended to present a manuscript version to Prince Henry. On the other, the successive print publications of the volume brought it to a wider readership, for whom Bacon's advice on governing, empire, and the conduct of courtly life was aspirational rather than practical.

The essay's intended audience further broadened by the time that the early eighteenth-century English periodicalists, Joseph Addison and Richard Steele, innovatively addressed 'the Bulk of the People', including many Bacon would have dismissed as mere 'vulgar capacities'.[11] Addison and Steele wrote as though they believed their readers were as clubbable, educated, and urbane as themselves, though this was in fact a flattering conceit calculated to instil these very qualities in an audience known to include brewers, washerwomen, and other semi-literate listeners at provincial public readings. We might call this nationally unifying purpose of *The Spectator*, refashioning its audience in the authors' own collective self-image, a kind of integrative propaganda employed for long-term political ends.[12]

The *Spectator* and *Tatler* contained commentary on current affairs geared to this early mass readership, alongside classical allusions and fanciful allegories more suited to an aristocratic reader who might have considered bald partisanship and mercantile economics beneath him. The masked editors debated with correspondents, both real and fictional, the level of topicality that forthcoming issues should contain: as the *Tatler*'s fictional editor, Isaac Bickerstaff Esq., declared: 'Some of my Readers thank me for filling my paper with the flowers of Antiquity; others desire News from Flanders.'[13]

This ambivalence was not restricted to readers; Addison aspired to be a literary essayist like John Dryden, standing impartially above the factional fray and concealing his party loyalties; he expressed amazement 'that the Press should be only made use of [. . .] by News-Writers, and the Zealots of Parties; as if it were not more advantageous to Mankind to be instructed in Wisdom and Virtue than in Politics.'[14] Like Bacon and Dryden, Addison aimed to write according to the

---

[10]   Francis Bacon, 'Preface' to *Essays* [1612], in *The Works of Francis Bacon*, ed. James Spedding et al., 15 vols (1860–4), XI, 340.

[11]   Joseph Addison and Richard Steele, *The Spectator* No. 124 (23 July 1711), in *The Spectator*, ed. Donald F. Bond, 5 vols (1965), I, 507. Bacon, *The Advancement of Learning* [1605], Book I, in *Francis Bacon: The Major Works*, ed. Brian Vickers (1996, 2008), 139.

[12]   See Jacques Ellul, 'The Characteristics of Propaganda' [1962], in *Propaganda: The Formation of Men's Attitudes*, trans. Konrad Kellen and Jean Lerner (1969), 74–9.

[13]   Richard Steele, *The Tatler* No. 164 (27 April 1710), in *The Tatler*, ed. Donald F. Bond, 3 vols (1987), II, 411.

[14]   *The Spectator* No. 124 (23 July 1711), in Bond, *The Spectator*, I, 507.

Tacitean ideal '*sine ira et studio*' (without anger and partiality), a pose particularly attractive after the civil strife of the seventeenth century.[15] Addison therefore defined essayistic politics as starting precisely where party politics ended. Mr Spectator's manifesto was to 'observe an exact Neutrality between the Whigs and the Tories, unless I shall be forced to declare myself by the Hostilities of either side'.[16]

This, however, was somewhat disingenuous. Addison and Steele were 'Junto Whigs', with Addison employed as an Under-Secretary of State prior to his most productive period as an essayist, and as a Secretary of State in the decade following. Published two days behind events, the *Tatler* and *Spectator* eschewed the cut and thrust of daily politics, but this did not make their authors any less engaged. Addison sought to avoid direct confrontation with the Tories in government after 1710, and spoke of 'bridling' Steele's Whig radicalism, but their stridently active Whig friend Arthur Maynwaring was fanning the flames of Steele's political zeal in equal measure. The periodical essays that emerged from this tug of war, with Steele's conscience stuck in the middle, were compromises between persuasion and meditation, activism and detachment. While ostensibly non-partisan, most of the essays obliquely furthered the Junto Whig cause, reforming English culture along the lines of a distinctively Whig aesthetic, or endorsing a Whig model of political economy. They champion the 'middling sort' over other classes, defend freethinkers, praise the mercantile city, or promote Whiggish stylistic principles in every art from music to cookery. What makes the pieces essayistic is that they promote the Junto's ideology only implicitly, under a veneer of genteel and ironically humorous detachment.

A good example of a political pamphlet, addressed to the wider electorate, but smuggled in under the classical robes of the periodical essay form, is Addison's *Spectator* on the theme of national credit finance, published in March 1711.[17] A motto from Lucretius signals that this will be a fictionalized essay, and references to Ovid and Homer likewise indicate its literary credentials. Mr Spectator describes 'rambling' through the city until he comes upon the Bank of England, a Whig-dominated institution. Looking inside the Bank's hall, Mr Spectator thinks about various 'Discourses' on the decay of public credit (like Defoe's recent 'Essay upon Publick Credit'), and considers all such previous pamphleteering to have been 'defective' for being too partisan. An allegorical dream sequence follows, describing Public Credit as a beautiful virgin on a golden throne.

---

[15] See Kathryn Murphy and Anita Traninger, 'Introduction', in *The Emergence of Impartiality* (2014), 24–5.

[16] *The Spectator* No. 1 (1 March 1711), in Bond, *The Spectator*, I, 5.

[17] *The Spectator* No. 3 (3 March 1711), in Bond, *The Spectator*, I, 14–17.

She is subject to vapours—fragile, capricious, and impressionable—and pairs of phantoms, caricatures of Jacobitism and Republicanism, rush in to threaten her. The even-handedness of these threats supposedly shows the author's neutrality and scepticism about party politics. Lastly, however, kindly ghosts come and refill the virgin's bags with gold; these ghosts represent religious moderation, civil liberty, and the Hanoverian heir. There is nothing politically neutral about this outcome. Though many Tories had backed the 1701 Act of Settlement that promised to bring in the Hanoverians, the salvation of the sickly virgin (Queen Anne) from Jacobite invasion is a specifically Whig narrative, as is the implication that the Pretender's arrival would empty the nation's coffers. The immediate context was, as Trevelyan first highlighted, the threat of a Tory takeover of the Bank's Governors at the April 1711 election—a takeover Addison's closest associates were involved in narrowly averting.[18] No contemporary reading this essay could imagine Mr Spectator as anything but a Junto Whig, for all his insistence that he is merely spectating.

The gentility of the essay form was supposed to sugar the pill of political argument for the tea table. Yet that gentility and ambiguity also made the papers unfit for purpose when urgent rallying-cries were needed. Steele therefore abandoned the periodical essay in favour of the pamphlet in the winter of 1713–14 when, with the health of Queen Anne declining rapidly, he believed Britain was reaching a true crisis point. Steele's *Crisis* sold an unprecedented 40,000 copies or more by subscription alone. Addison's *Freeholder* similarly dropped the guise of a detached narrator during the Pretender's attempted invasion of Scotland in the winter of 1715–16, though Steele complained it still did not sound the alarm loudly enough ('[T]he Ministry made use of a lute, when they should have called a trumpet').[19] Such writing defines English 'essayistic politics' by what it is not: short-termist, unashamedly partisan, and rhetorically coercive.

Their contemporary, Jonathan Swift, similarly had two distinct modes of political writing: the pamphlet essays written in the heat of controversy and the pay of Tory Ministers during 1710–14, such as the philippic 'Conduct of the Allies' (1711) intended to destroy the Duke of Marlborough, and Swift's far more artful, satirical essays that are still read as literature today, such as 'A Modest Proposal [. . .]' (1729). In the latter, the politics becomes 'essayistic' to the extent that its arguments against poverty, violence, and colonialism are raised above the transient circumstances that inspired them. Such literary essays were only written after Swift entered his long years of Irish retirement and could view Westminster politics with the jaundiced eye of an exile and historian.

[18]   George Macaulay Trevelyan, *England Under Queen Anne*, 3 vols (1930–4), III, 105.
[19]   Steele quoted in Samuel Johnson, 'Addison', in *The Lives of the Poets* [1781], vols XXI–XXIII of *The Yale Edition of the Works of Samuel Johnson*, ed. W. J. Bate and Albrecht B. Strauss (2010), XXII, 630.

3. Romantic Consciences

Before they became political adversaries, Swift had once suggested to Addison, or perhaps Steele, the idea for a satirical essay, inspired by Montaigne's 'Of Cannibals' and prefiguring *Gulliver's Travels*, in which British party politics would be described by several Iroquois who had recently visited London.[20] Addison realized this idea in *Spectator* No. 50 (27 April 1711). Alongside Montesquieu's *Lettres persanes* (1721), this number of the *Spectator* inspired an entire strand of later eighteenth-century essays that evidenced political clear-sightedness through the 'alien eyes' trick: notably Horace Walpole's 'Letter from Xo-Ho, a Chinese Philosopher at London' and Oliver Goldsmith's 'Chinese Letters' in the *Public Ledger*, published in 1762 as *The Citizen of the World*.[21] Such literary devices—de-familiarizing for the amusement of familiar readers, and emphasizing the alienation and detachment of the essayist's narrative persona—made political commentary witty, but not pressing. They directed essayistic politics towards the pseudo-anthropological, and away from any radical incitement to protest or action.

William Hazlitt and several other essayists of the early nineteenth century reacted against precisely such eighteenth-century artificiality, and, fired by Montaignian candour, tried to return a more heartfelt passion against injustice to the English political essay. Whereas Addison had read Montaigne similarly to twentieth-century post-Marxist critics, disdaining him as an incorrigible 'egotist', Hazlitt celebrated Montaigne as 'the first author who [...] wrote not to make converts of others to established creeds and prejudices, but to satisfy his own mind of the truth of things'.[22] Hazlitt identified *The Spectator*'s major flaw as being the absence of a personal—that is, Montaignian—component. In Hazlitt's preface to his *Political Essays* (1819), he therefore strives to combine an Addisonian tone with the insistent subjectivity and confessionalism of his own Romanticism, as well as the more pugnacious political engagement of a Steele or a Swift:

> I am no politician, and still less can I be said to be a party-man: but I have a hatred of tyranny, and a contempt for its tools; and this feeling I have expressed as often and as strongly as I could.   (IV, 5)

---

[20] Jonathan Swift, *Journal to Stella*, ed. George A. Aitken (1901), 203 (entry for 28 April 1711).

[21] Leigh Hunt's sixth *Political Examiner* on what a 'simple Chinese' would make of pensions given to babies, while learned men starve in garrets, is another example of this literary trope ('The Political Examiner', in *The Examiner* 6 (7 February 1808), 82).

[22] *The Spectator* No. 562 (2 July 1714), in Bond, IV, 520. On post-Marxist critics, see Biancamaria Fontana, *Montaigne's Politics* (2008), 22. William Hazlitt, 'On the Periodical Essayists' [1819], in *Selected Writings of William Hazlitt*, ed. Duncan Wu, 9 vols (1998), V, 85. Further references given in the text. Kingsley Amis similarly defined pure 'essayism' as requiring a 'complacent indifference' to one's readers: see Kingsley Amis, *New Maps of Hell* (1961), 88.

Both Hazlitt and Leigh Hunt defended freedom of expression in the face of their direct persecution by Lord Liverpool's ministry, with several essays such as Hunt's 'On the Censorial Duties of the Press with Regard to the Vices of the Court' (*Examiner*, January 1813) prompting, and in turn replying to, seditious libel charges. Hazlitt, too, was threatened with prosecution after March 1817. Hunt's and Hazlitt's use of the periodical therefore drew upon an alliance between the essay form and the cause of civil liberty dating back to *Areopagitica*'s championing of free speech.

Yet, at the same time, Hazlitt and Hunt shared an ambition for their periodical essays to be elevated above the scrap of Radical journalism, typified by William Cobbett's *Weekly Political Register* (1802–35). Hunt declared a primary aim of his *Examiner* (1808–36) to be the addition to British political writing of 'philosophical spirit', by which he meant Ciceronian morality and Enlightenment scepticism.[23] Hunt's essayistic persona as 'an angry young bourgeois' was commercially successful partly because Hunt was not, in fact, consistently angry: he reflected at times a contempt for party politics by washing his hands of Whitehall and reviewing lyric poetry instead.[24]

Hazlitt, as we have seen, valued the essay for its Montaignian freedom, which correlated to his political liberalism. But he also valued it as a space in which to explore his conflicted personal feelings about retirement. In one piece, Hazlitt allies the pleasures of the familiar essay to the retired serenity of the private library, where 'the reader is admitted behind the curtain, and sits down with the writer in his gown and slippers' (V, 88).[25] Elsewhere, however, it is the essay's extrovert spirit of journalistic inquiry that he values, mocking Jeremy Bentham for lecturing on human wants and needs from precisely such slippered comfort:

> What should Mr Bentham, sitting at ease in his arm-chair, composing his mind before he begins to write by a prelude on the organ, and looking out at a beautiful prospect when he is at a loss for an idea, know of the principles of action of rogues, outlaws and vagabonds?   (VII, 82)[26]

Hazlitt, though likewise writing from the armchair of literature, had previously worked as a reporter on the *Morning Chronicle*, and so could claim first-hand experience as the source of his own essayistic authority.

Having more political designs upon his readers than Montaigne, Hazlitt saw the essay form as uniquely congenial to advocating difficult truths, thanks to its ability to appeal, through figurative language, to the visual, sensual, personal, and

---

[23] Jerome J. McGann, *The Romantic Ideology: A Critical Investigation* (1983), 31.
[24] Lawrence Huston Houtchens and Carolyn Washburn Houtchens (eds), *Leigh Hunt's Political and Occasional Essays* (1962), 36.
[25] From 'On the Periodical Essayists'.
[26] From 'Jeremy Bentham', in *The Spirit of the Age* [1825].

domestic. In 'On Reason and Imagination' (from *The Plain Speaker* (1826)), Hazlitt asks: 'Would you tame down the glowing language of justifiable passion into that of cold indifference, of self-complacent, sceptical reasoning, and thus take out the sting of indignation from the mind of the spectator?' (VIII, 43). (This warm 'sting' of the personal and passionate was what Hazlitt missed in Mr Spectator.) Hazlitt saw experience of the world, combined with fresh language, as twin requirements for bringing home political truths to apathetic readers and making them feel implicated in the oppressions perpetrated in their names.

Hazlitt occasionally used a rhetorical identification between himself and the reader to unite them as downtrodden everymen—speaking, for example, of those whose 'power is at the expense of our weakness; their riches of our poverty; their pride of our degradation' (I, 127).[27] Such authorial identifications with the oppressed masses were less frequent, however, than appeals to the solitary and privileged reader's individualism as a grounds either for self-interest or empathy. Hazlitt thus tended to propose arguments in favour of social change that started close to home—he approved, for example, a remark from Paley's *Moral Philosophy* (1785) that he who refused to give charity is hurt by the refusal just as much as the denied recipient. Hazlitt added that the same moral self-harm applies 'with respect to the atrocities committed in the Slave-Trade' (VIII, 45).[28]

Immediately prior to this analogy, Hazlitt had asked the genteel reader to imagine being in the hull of a slave ship, or to envisage 'the practice of suspending contumacious negroes in cages to have their eyes pecked out, and to be devoured alive by birds of prey' (VIII, 43). What should be emphasized, however, is that these vivid examples supported a larger aesthetic argument about the use of figurative language, rather than building a pro-abolitionist argument located amid contemporary political debate. The subject of the essay in question is reason and imagination, not the slave trade. Throughout his work, Hazlitt's references to other topical political controversies, such as Catholic Emancipation or Castlereagh's foreign policy, similarly exemplify a wider literary-philosophical point in passing, rather than featuring as ends in themselves. The political imperative of the *Political Essays* was, in this way, always subservient to a larger aesthetic purpose.

As Tom Paulin brilliantly demonstrated in *The Day-Star of Liberty* (1988), Hazlitt's prose has a concealed poetics that is committed to 'gusto' and to the 'heat of the moment'.[29] But there remains an important difference between this aesthetic, inherited from his father's Unitarian polemics, and subject matter that is focused, above all, on a topical objective. Hazlitt's writing is passionate and purposeful, and his essays are full of assertions about the value of specificity, yet

---

[27] From 'Coriolanus', in *Characters of Shakespear's Plays* [1817].
[28] From 'On Reason and Imagination'.
[29] Tom Paulin, *The Day-Star of Liberty: William Hazlitt's Radical Style* (1988).

what makes him an essayist and not a journalist was a continual, overriding sense of larger philosophical and personal purpose. In his 1830 essay 'Personal Politics', for example, his ringing attacks on Charles IX and X are only illustrations of a wider moral paradox: that a king can be 'an exceedingly well-meaning, moral man' and yet 'embroil his subjects and the world in disastrous wars and controversies', and that we are the unknowing victims of each era's 'prejudices [...] which have nothing to do with the looks, temper or private character of those who hold them'.[30] This emphasis on the philosophical was most clearly revealed in Hazlitt's stated ambition, in 'A Letter to William Gifford, Esq.' (1819), to be remembered as, above all, a 'thinker' (V, 383). Hazlitt admired his political adversary Edmund Burke not so much for the facility or the political impact of his oratory as for applying metaphysics to politics and thereby gaining the status of 'an acute and accomplished man of letters—an ingenious political essayist' (IV, 211).[31] Even *The Spirit of the Age* (1825), which 'aims to communicate a momentous and insistent topicality', simultaneously indicates by its title—comparing Hazlitt's *Zeitgeist* with that of other eras—how firmly Hazlitt's eye was fixed on posterity.[32]

4. American and Modernist Consciences

Echoing Hazlitt's claim that the best public service the 'true' author can offer is if he 'conceals himself and writes' (VIII, 260), Virginia Woolf recommended to her fellow writers in the early 1930s that 'if one wishes to better the world, one must, paradoxically enough, withdraw and spend more and more time fashioning one's sentences to perfection in solitude.'[33] However, in the case of Hazlitt (whom Woolf portrayed as forced to write 'articles upon politics' only because he grew so poor that there was no longer a symbolic 'curtain to the window'), Woolf saw that the determinedly and eccentrically subjective element, Hazlitt's ego, interfered with his reformist intentions, if not with the indisputable brilliance of his prose.[34] She had already found a more agreeable precedent for her own position in the reclusive persona of Henry David Thoreau.

---

[30] Hazlitt, 'Personal Politics' [1830], in *Literary Remains of the Late William Hazlitt*, ed. William Hazlitt [1836], reprinted 1983, 36–7.

[31] From 'Character of Mr Burke, 1817', in *Political Essays* [1819], and previously published as part of the article 'Coleridge's Literary Life' in *The Edinburgh Review* 28 (August 1817), 488–515.

[32] Tom Paulin, *The Day Star of Liberty: William Hazlitt's Radical Style* (1988), 229.

[33] From 'On the Difference between Writing and Speaking', in *The Plain Speaker* [1826]; Woolf, 'George Gissing', in *The Common Reader, Second Series* [1932], in *The Essays of Virginia Woolf*, vol. V, ed. Stuart N. Clarke (2009), 537.

[34] Woolf, 'William Hazlitt', *The Common Reader, Second Series* [1932], in *The Essays of Virginia Woolf*, vol. V, 497.

Thoreau's essays were in fact written as call-to-arms prose, intended primarily for the lectern and in opposition to the kind of library-window detachment that permeated the Victorian British book review essay—a legacy of the Augustan and Romantic containment of politics within the vessel of cultural and philosophical criticism described above.[35] Thoreau was interested, as a critic of American materialism and imperialism, in awakening the reader's conscience and inciting political resistance, yet he was also the originator of the Horatian–Buddhist–hermit strain in American essaying—the epitome of the retiring writer. In 'Civil Disobedience' (1849), for instance, Thoreau, following his refusal to pay poll tax as a protest against the Mexican War, explained his decision to take political action as a question of personal ethics placed in order of logical priority: 'If I devote myself to other pursuits and contemplations, I must first see, at least, that I do not pursue them sitting upon another man's shoulders. I must get off him first, that he may pursue his contemplations too.'[36]

Woolf's 1917 critical essay on Thoreau, however, ignored this lucid explanation of how the American approached his ethics in strict sequence (engagement before retirement) and chose to instead perceive a mysterious paradox, a contradiction of simultaneity, in Thoreau's attitude towards political life. Woolf quotes Thoreau on finding contemporary American politics 'insignificant', and yet

> this egoist was the man who sheltered runaway slaves in his hut; this hermit was the first man to speak out in public in defence of John Brown; this self-centred solitary could neither sleep nor think when Brown lay in prison. The truth is that anyone who reflects as much and as deeply as Thoreau reflected about life and conduct is possessed of an abnormal sense of responsibility to his kind, whether he chooses to live in a wood or to become President of the Republic.[37]

Woolf echoed Hazlitt on Montaigne when she concluded that Thoreau's books were 'not written to prove something in the end'. Thoreau's essays, she observed, were instead 'written as the Indians turn down twigs to mark their path through the forest'.[38] This telling image suggests retreat and indirection as strategies by which the essayist may seek both to lay and yet disguise his or her intellectual path, and to resist the domination of the slave-masters, in whatever form. The image argues, figuratively, for the possibility of engagement by means of retirement. The political impact of such a strategy may be less immediate and measurable than if one were to lay down the pen for the sword (or the sword-like pen) but the methods were more pure in their literary pacifism.

---

[35] On the Victorian lecture-essay, see further Chapter 10 in this volume by Tom Wright.
[36] Henry David Thoreau, 'Civil Disobedience' [1849], in *Collected Essays and Poems*, ed. Elizabeth Hall Witherell (2001), 209.
[37] Woolf, 'Thoreau', in *The Essays of Virginia Woolf*, vol. II, ed. Andrew McNeillie (1987), 137.
[38] Woolf, 'Thoreau', 136.

This, at least, was Woolf's view on the matter in the 1920s, when she focused on retirement to a room of her own. By June 1938, when *Three Guineas* was published in book form, Woolf had grown more conflicted. Again, she uses the extended essay to dramatize a question of personal conscience: the conflict between her wish to advocate for pacifism on the eve of war, and her equally strong wish to avoid a corrupted and corrupting public sphere designed by men. To many early readers, the personal drama of the piece seemed self-centred: writing about patriarchy as the root cause of global conflict was too essayistic a theme in the immediate run up to the Munich Agreement, and angered those who felt it was the time only for well-aimed arrows at narrow targets, or at least for a united front.[39] In her diary, Woolf worried that *Three Guineas* would be 'a moth dancing over a bonfire'.[40]

Three Guineas remains a deeply misunderstood book due to its daring intermingling of the personal and political. Its epistolary form allows the interspersing of a passionate private voice (that of a semi-fictional narrator, the archetypal daughter of an educated father) with a more didactic tone. In the first of its letters, the prince to whom she plays adviser is an unnamed representative of a peace society (one who happened to have a lot in common with Woolf's friend Viscount Cecil of Chelwood, President of the League of Nations Union). At the same time, Woolf's veneration of Montaigne, which she expressed in several earlier essays, meant that she allows her thoughts to flow freely, playing anarchically with elements of factuality, photo-journalism, and footnotes. Her passionate anger bursts out in lurid, poetic scenes, such as the imagined burning of the women's college that will 'scare the nightingales and incarnadine the willows' while daughters 'heap armful upon armful of dead leaves upon the flames' and their mothers cry 'we have done with this "education"!' from the upper windows.[41] With the conflagrations of the Second World War not hard to imagine at this date, was this essayistic freedom, which connected public and private resentments, narcissistically offensive or politically provocative?

5. Orwell, Baldwin, and other Guerrilla Fighters

While Woolf condemned patriotism for generating war, George Orwell's essays during the Second World War sought to reunite the English intellectual class with a sense of English patriotism. With fascism breaking into the private sphere,

---

[39] See, for example, Q. D. Leavis's scathing review of Woolf's book: 'Caterpillars of the Commonwealth Unite!', *Scrutiny* 7.2 (September 1938), 203–14. Even Woolf's brother-in-law, Clive Bell, called *Three Guineas* her 'least admirable production': cited in B. K. Scott, *Refiguring Modernism*, vol. 1: *The Women of 1928* (1995), 173.

[40] Woolf, *The Diary of Virginia Woolf*, ed. Anne Olivier Bell, 5 vols (1977–84), V, 142.

[41] Woolf, *A Room of One's Own and Three Guineas*, ed. Morag Shiach (2008), 202–3.

exterminating the option of authorial retirement, Orwell saw the essay form not as a covert path of escape, but rather as a preciously illuminated clearing in which 'the liberal tradition can be kept alive' amid impending darkness.[42] What he sought to protect was the liberty to criticize, question, and self-question: Milton's dialectic principle of 'trial by what is contrary'.[43] The essay form's dialectical roots give it a tendency towards self-criticism, making essayistic politics predominantly deconstructive, not programmatic. For essayists from Montaigne to Orwell, each surrounded by over-zealous contemporaries, self-questioning, and the right to contradict oneself, was a part of the personal freedom they defended.

Orwell valued the fundamental provisionality of most English essayists' political convictions and conclusions, based as they are upon the subjectivity of personal experience. In 'Antisemitism in Britain' (April 1945), for example, Orwell confesses: 'In this essay I have relied almost entirely on my own limited experience, and perhaps every one of my conclusions would be negatived by other observers.' Orwell emphasized his faith in the truth-as-I-know-it of radical philosophical doubt, which separates the essay from other forms such as the treatise, sermon, or article, with their positivistic claims; as his contemporary, E. M. Forster, put it: 'I probably differ from most people, who believe in Belief, and are only sorry they cannot swallow even more than they do. My law-givers are Erasmus and Montaigne, not Moses and St Paul.'[44]

Orwell's denunciations of cant, cliché, and Groupthink—most famously in 'Politics and the English Language' (1946)—were, like Hazlitt's call for 'the glowing language of justifiable passion', motivated by a democratizing impulse to widen the audience for political debate and by conviction that eliminating hollow language was a political duty in its own right. Language and form will determine content, Orwell argued, but they can also be the manifestation of our individual and intellectual liberty. The essay form's default mode of gentlemanly familiarity, with its minority appeal to an educated readership, however, continued to constrain its political arguments, even in Orwell. Orwell's early essays, 'Shooting an Elephant' (1936) and 'A Hanging' (1933), thus echo Hazlitt's moral point about the slave trade, arguing that the British Empire's colonial system deformed its rulers as much as its victims. Similarly, Orwell's later essays defending freedom of expression exemplify the tendency to attack the well-meaning complacency of fellow liberals, his likely readers, rather than the more obvious target of their post-war totalitarian enemies. 'The Prevention of Literature' (1946) takes as its unlikely first target, for example, the well-meaning attendants at a PEN

---

[42] George Orwell, 'Looking Back on the Spanish War' (written 1942, published 1943), reprinted in *The Collected Essays, Journalism and Letters of George Orwell*, ed. Sonia Orwell and Ian Angus, 4 vols (1970), II, 249.

[43] John Milton, *Areopagitica* [1644], in *John Milton: The Major Works*, ed. Stephen Orgel and Jonathan Goldberg (1991), 248.

[44] E. M. Forster, 'What I Believe' [1939], reprinted in *Two Cheers for Democracy* (1951, 1970), 75.

tercentenary celebration of Milton's *Areopagitica*, who debate freedom of expression with so many caveats and with such delicate avoidance of party politics that they end up sounding, to Orwell, indistinguishable from the Soviet censors.[45]

For Orwell in the interwar years and 1940s, as for Addison at the end of Anne's reign or Hazlitt in the 1820s, the issue was how to work within a period of history where party politics and war dominated every aspect of social and cultural life. Orwell reflects, in 'Why I Write' (1946), with the self-deprecating modesty of the Montaignian essayist, on the prosaic compulsion of his circumstances: 'In a peaceful age I might have written ornate or merely descriptive books, and might have remained almost unaware of my political loyalties. As it is I have been forced into becoming a sort of pamphleteer.'[46] According to Orwell, 'the essence of pamphleteering is to have something you want to say NOW, to as many people as possible', whereas the essay thrives on a retrospective tone of cool detachment, and thereby—to quote Cynthia Ozick—'defies its date of birth'.[47] By Orwell's own definition, therefore, his longer and more ambitious essays are never pamphlets, despite the form in which half a dozen were first published.

Most of Orwell's well-known political essays furthermore contain a dominant element of retrospective memoir. The title of 'Looking Back on the Spanish War' (1943) very obviously signals this removal in style and time from what Orwell calls the emotive 'newspaper and radio hypnosis' of the 1930s. It is politics recollected in tranquillity. Even Orwell's earliest essays are artful memoirs of anti-colonialism, written over a decade after he was posted as an Indian Imperial Policeman in Burma. The estrangement of historical perspective and memoir create a useful aura of wisdom and impartiality around Orwell's essayistic voice, as he criticizes the moral confusion of his younger self.

James Baldwin's best-known political essays, too, are predominantly memoir. Aware, like Orwell, that his readers will largely be 'uptight, middle-class white people', Baldwin's essays played with the relative 'levels' of all three parties to the essayistic pact—the educated author, the familiar reader, and the exotic subject (namely, himself). Holding this trump card—moral authority based on autobiographical experience—Baldwin expressed disdain for those in the American Beat Generation who (not unlike Orwell, eager to 'to get right down among the oppressed') were busy 'imitating poverty, trying to *get down*, to *get with it*'.[48]

[45] Orwell, 'The Prevention of Literature' [*Polemic* 2 (January 1946)], reprinted in *Collected Essays*, IV, 59.

[46] Orwell, 'Why I Write' [1946]. Elsewhere he was more aphoristic: 'When you are on a sinking ship, your thoughts will be about sinking ships' ('Writers and Leviathan' [1948–9]). Both reprinted in *Collected Essays*, I, 4, and IV, 407.

[47] Orwell, 'Pamphlet Literature' [*New Statesman and Nation* (9 January 1943)], reprinted in *Collected Essays*, II, 283–5; Cynthia Ozick, 'She: Portrait of the Essay as a Warm Body', *Quarrel & Quandary* (2000), 178.

[48] Orwell, *The Road to Wigan Pier* (1958), 148. James Baldwin, 'If Black English Isn't a Language, Then Tell Me, What Is?', *New York Times* (29 July 1979), section 4, 19.

Again, Baldwin limited his political arguments to those that could be usefully addressed to his familiar (liberal, white) readers. His refrain is that racism and segregation mutilate the soul of the white American as much as the black, and it is the complacency and inaction of his anti-racist allies that comes under most sustained fire. Thoreau had observed in 'Civil Disobedience' that

> There are thousands who are *in opinion* opposed to slavery and to the war, who yet in effect do nothing to put an end to them; who, esteeming themselves children of Washington and Franklin, sit down with their hands in their pockets, and say that they know not what to do, and do nothing [...].[49]

Martin Luther King similarly addressed not Southern racists but, in 'Letter from Birmingham Jail' (1963), the eight Alabama clergymen who considered themselves his moderate allies, yet who sat 'idly by'.[50] Inspired by King, Alice Walker's first published essay, 'The Civil Rights Movement: What Good Was It?' (1966–7), condemned the white civil rights activists who had turned into introverted hippies. In these examples, the question of retirement versus engagement is projected outward, from the author's conscience onto that of the complacent reader.

Whereas Orwell took pleasure in toughening up a cozy and complacent form, exploiting its informality and flouting its staider characteristics, Baldwin used the tradition of classical English essayism (by way of New York literary journalism) in order to join a club that otherwise might have refused him entry. He is perhaps the clearest instance of a writer consciously choosing the English literary essay for political writing because of its associations with Enlightenment reason and politeness. A wry knowledge that, in speaking to white readers, Baldwin is providing Baconian counsel to his princes combines, in work such as 'Down at the Cross' (1963), with a searing anger that is contained and controlled by the refinement of his form and diction.

Interweaving personal memoir and political analysis, Baldwin inspired a later generation of essayists who championed what came to be called 'identity politics'.[51] He also inspired contemporary essayists such as the South African Lewis Nkosi, who admired Baldwin's writing for being 'highly provisional, endlessly deferred, designed to obstruct any easy or uncomplicated play of identities: a syntax so fluid and mutable that it all but drove black radicals crazy'.[52] There was,

---

[49] Thoreau, 'Civil Disobedience', 207–8.
[50] See, similarly: Bertrand Russell, 'Civil Disobedience', *The New Statesman* (17 February 1961), in which he urged the average, complacent reader in the second person ('If you join it [...]') to participate in his mass protest against Polaris and Britain's nuclear policy.
[51] For example, Adrienne Rich in 'Split at the Root: An Essay on Jewish Identity' (1982) and more recently Claudia Rankine's lyric essays in *Citizen* (2014).
[52] Lewis Nkosi, 'The Mountain', *Transition* 79 (1999), 104.

Nkosi knew, something oil-and-water in the mix of essayism and radical politics that Baldwin was stirring. The nature of Baldwin's self-aware approach, bearing witness rather than merely spectating, became even more starkly evident in Nkosi's own *Home and Exile* (1965), a book of essays in which the author, as Nadine Gordimer put it, performed an 'acrobatic position' by writing in a genteel, white form, while keeping 'a foot in the black proletariat of the township'.[53] Publishing in exile, Nkosi apologized if his 'intimacy' with the subject matter made it 'impossible sufficiently to sustain a tone of irony and detachment that would be a supreme asset'.[54]

Echoing a comment from Orwell on the need for a writer to be 'an unwelcome guerrilla on the flank of a regular army', Baldwin spoke in 1966, at the midpoint of the Vietnam War and the US race riots, of the American writer 'fighting an astute and agile guerrilla warfare with that American complacency which so inadequately masks the American panic'.[55] Guerrillas are not merely militant, but also covert: they infiltrate complacency and surprise it from within. This is sardonically clear in 'Alas, Poor Richard', where Baldwin meets another black intellectual at a party in Paris and they share an unspoken mutual recognition of a necessary personal charade performed within the much larger 'hoax' that is 'the great cocktail party of the white man's world', meaning the whole Protestant Western culture.[56] His use of the English essay tradition, conventionally characterized by personal meditation, tolerant good humour, and apolitical common sense, was Baldwin's way of 'doing white-face' as guerilla camouflage.

6. Polemical Exceptions

In the latter twentieth century, the English essay form's long-established antiimperialism lent itself well to a line of essayists with a normative and activist position against expansive US foreign policy, most notably Norman Mailer, Gore Vidal, Noam Chomsky, Edward Said, and Christopher Hitchens (until the Bosnian War changed his outlook).[57] They all continued the tradition of the literary essay's self-identification, morally and imaginatively, with the victims of

---

[53] Nkosi's writing was aimed, Gordimer continued, 'at white readers, to rouse white consciousness to black frustration' rather than at his fellow black Africans. See Nadine Gordimer, 'English-Language Literature and Politics in South Africa' [1976], in *Telling Times: Writing and Living 1950–2008* (2010), 249.

[54] Nkosi, *Home and Exile* (1965), i.

[55] Orwell, 'Writers and Leviathan' [1948–49], in *Collected Essays*, IV, 413. James Baldwin quoted in Fern Marja Eckman, *The Furious Passage of James Baldwin* (1966), 213.

[56] Baldwin, 'Alas, Poor Richard', in *Nobody Knows My Name* (1961), 168.

[57] Said, in the 1980s, described his choice of the essay—'a comparatively short, investigative, radically skeptical form'—as a rebellion against the professional humanist critic's general policy of 'noninterference' in the world beyond the ivory tower (Edward W. Said, 'Introduction: Secular Criticism', in *World, The Text and The Critic* (1983), 26, 2).

empire: Montaigne's Brazilians, Addison's and Swift's Iroquois, Hazlitt's slave-ship, Thoreau's invaded Mexicans, Orwell's executed Burmese, Baldwin's guerilla fighter, and Sontag's napalmed Vietnamese villagers.

Christopher Hitchens in particular took pride in drawing his essayistic ancestry back to Orwell and Hazlitt, but also to the even more politically engaged archetype of Thomas Paine, about whom Hitchens wrote an admiring biography. Like Paine's revolutionary pamphlet *Common Sense* (1776), Hitchens's gregarious, flare-gun writing differs from the anti-polemical style of most English political essayists. Yet, on his book jackets, Hitchens had his publishers list his 'pamphlets' (concerning the Iraq War and Mother Teresa, for example) as distinct from his essays. The distinction drawn is not solely one of length; it is also a distinction of purpose, defined by breadth of audience and transience of topicality.

In the Preface to his final essay collection, *Arguably* (2011), Hitchens explains the book's dedication to three martyrs in the cause of Arab pluralism, invoking the memorial to the Oxford Martyrs that stood beneath his college window—the ultimate symbol of political commitment juxtaposed with the ultimate symbol of academic detachment. Hitchens, lest we mistakenly classify him as a mere spectator, mentions his role in organizing a 1969 rally at the memorial in support of a martyr to Czech democracy.[58] His famous hatchet job on Isaiah Berlin in 1998 was similarly based on the rejection of liberal essayism as a cover for cowardice and conservatism, summarizing Berlin's 'general view that the main enemy was activism'.[59] Hitchens had no patience with marking twigs in the Thoreauvian forest, where political opinion can be camouflaged—or easily lost—within the lyrical, familiar, and personal essay modes.

Hitchens, however, also expressed his tiredness, looking back, with the 'ongoing polemic [. . .] between the anti-imperialist Left and the anti-totalitarian Left', in which he had been involved all his life.[60] By 9/11, Hitchens had sided with those who accused essayists like Chomsky of indulging in self-flagellation, taking too far the habit of the English political essay of addressing only those failings close to home and most under the reader's democratic, domestic control. Hitchens therefore resigned from writing for *The Nation* in 2002 on the basis that its editors regarded 'John Ashcroft as a bigger threat than Bin Laden'.[61] Hitchens's sympathies had decisively fallen more on the anti-totalitarian than the anti-imperialist (anti-interventionist) side, and, in the Preface to *Arguably*, he remarks, with a modesty learnt from Orwell: 'This may not seem much of a claim, but some things need to be found out by experience and not merely derived from principle.'[62]

---

[58] Christopher Hitchens, 'Preface' to *Arguably* (2011), xv.
[59] Hitchens, 'Moderation or Death', *London Review of Books* 20.23 (26 November 1993), 3–11.
[60] Hitchens, 'Preface', xvii.
[61] Hitchens, 'Taking Sides', *The Nation*, (26 September 2002), at https://www.thenation.com/article/taking-sides.
[62] Hitchens, 'Preface', xvii.

Towards the end of the same Preface, Hitchens recalled a line from Nadine Gordimer suggesting that the serious essayist should always try to write posthumously. This not only echoes Cynthia Ozick on the essay's defiant timelessness, and Hazlitt's ulterior interest in his posthumous literary reputation, but also suggests an aspiration towards total liberty from 'fashion, commerce, self-censorship, public and perhaps especially intellectual opinion'.[63] Knowing he had only months left to live, Hitchens observed, with bitter irony, that he was currently refining this particular art.

Hitchens's response to Gordimer's remark can be seen as a particularly intense expression of the paradox underlying the English political essay: the simultaneity of engagement and disengagement, involvement and impartiality, free-thinking and familiarity. Hitchens's hero, Orwell, had castigated 1920s novelists for having 'a too Olympian attitude' to the immediate social issues surrounding them, yet even Orwell, as we have seen, sought the lofty vantage point of the memoirist, biographer, or historian in his political essays.[64] For many intellectuals, the essay form, brief and yet philosophical in its nature, has answered the need felt by Sontag in her Paris quarters, 'to strip down, to close off for a while, to make a new start with as little as possible to fall back on'; embarking on such a solo expedition, it is difficult to wear a placard or carry a banner.[65]

---

[63] Hitchens, 'Preface', xix.
[64] Orwell, 'Inside the Whale' [1940], reprinted in *Collected Essays*, I, 493.
[65] Sontag, 'On Paul Goodman', 3.

12

Things Said by the Way

Walter Pater and the Essay

Stefano Evangelista

[...] although road and end do not make a unity and do not stand side by side as equals, they nevertheless coexist: the end is unthinkable and unrealisable without the road being travelled again and again; the end is not standing still but arriving there, not resting but conquering a summit.

György Lukács, 'On the Nature and Form
of the Essay: A Letter to Leo Popper'

1. Introduction

In a period that saw a sharp increase in the production and circulation of periodical essays and, as a result, a constant evolution of the relationship between journalism and literature, Walter Pater stands out as one of the practitioners of the essay as an autonomous and complete art form, in the sense that György Lukács gives to this concept in his letter to Leo Popper.[1] Pater understood the essay as a space for linguistic and formal experiment, dissolving the distinction between criticism and creation, prose and poetry. In his hands even the boundary between the essay and the novel became porous, inasmuch as both genres provided him with opportunities to combine historical and philosophical knowledge with a highly individual literary subjectivity. Pater illustrates how, in the late Victorian period, the essay became a means to reconfigure the relationship between analytical thought and the literary imagination in a way that, as we shall see, would attract the scorn of later writers such as T. S. Eliot. Even more than Eliot, though, Pater was deeply aware that he was writing within a canon that went beyond the boundaries of English and, despite the misgivings of Eliot and other British modernists, his work is central to a nineteenth-century European tradition

---

[1] György Lukács, 'On the Nature and Form of the Essay: A Letter to Leo Popper', in *Soul and Form*, trans. Anna Bostock, ed. John T. Sanders and Katie Terezakis (2010), 16–34, here 34.

Stefano Evangelista, *Things Said by the Way: Walter Pater and the Essay* In: *On Essays: Montaigne to the Present*. Edited by: Thomas Karshan and Kathryn Murphy, Oxford University Press (2020). © Stefano Evangelista. DOI: 10.1093/oso/9780198707868.003.0013

which stems from the German Romantics' ground-breaking theorization of criticism as an art form, and then reaches Britain by way of mid century France and the critical and essayistic writings of Théophile Gautier and Charles Baudelaire.

It is therefore surprising, though not uncharacteristic for such an elusive writer, that Pater's only extant definition of the essay lies half-buried in one of his lesser-known later writings, the chapter on 'The Doctrine of Plato' in his last published book, *Plato and Platonism* (1893). Here Pater describes the essay as

> that characteristic literary type of our own time, a time so rich and various in special apprehensions of truth, so tentative and dubious in its sense of their *ensemble*, and issues. Strictly appropriate form of our modern philosophic literature, the essay came into use at what was really the invention of the relative, or 'modern' spirit, in the Renaissance of the sixteenth century.[2]

The essay is for Pater the most modern literary form: it embodies scepticism and relativism by its refusal to impose rigidity and an artificial sense of resolution where there should be variety and provisional formations. It represents a way of thinking that systematically privileges part over whole (*ensemble*) and means over ends (issues). In dating the birth of the modern essay to the sixteenth century, Pater is of course thinking of Montaigne; but in a footnote to this passage, he stresses the linguistic migration from French to English, referring readers both to Dr Johnson's definition of the essay as a 'loose sally of the mind', and to a lesser-known earlier definition from Nathan Bailey's 1721 etymological dictionary, which lists a 'suggestive use' of the word among miners, lapsed from our own *OED*, as a 'little trench or hole, which they dig to search for ore' (175). This unusual definition brings out the ideas of tentativeness and unexpected richness that Pater found so apt, while the Saxon word 'ore', with its accidental homophony with the French 'or' (gold), embodies the dialogue of French and English and the compound of the precious and the commonplace that Pater found characteristic of the genre.

In 'The Doctrine of Plato', Pater theorizes the essay as an independent literary genre, with a set of conventions and a history of its own. He argues that the essay in its modern form is the latest of three literary methods that have been employed in the course of history to write down philosophical thought. The first and most ancient is poetic, and is preserved in the rare surviving texts of ancient philosophers such as Parmenides, in which ideas are conveyed by means of intuition, imagination, and obscurity. In the course of history, philosophical poetry was substituted by a second form that was its opposite: the treatise, employed by philosophers like Aristotle, Aquinas, and Spinoza, in which, according to Pater,

---

[2] Walter Pater, *Plato and Platonism* (1910), 174–5. Further references given in the text.

'native intuition had shrunk into dogmatic system, the dry bones of which rattle in one's ears' (174). The essay arises as the dialectical synthesis of the previous forms, mediating between the intuitive and associative energy of the former and the rigid systematization of the latter. Its intellectual flexibility results from the fact that it is essentially a hybrid genre, fusing poetry and philosophy.

Pater argues—as Lukács would also do a few years later—that the Platonic dialogue is the progenitor of the essay in its modern form: its dialectical method of arriving at truth by trial and accident anticipates the freedom and elasticity of the essay as developed by Montaigne.[3] For Pater, Montaigne is at once the quintessential essayist and the quintessential representative of the modern mind, because truth for him is always a function of doubt. The essay provided the French writer 'with precisely the literary form necessary to a mind for which truth itself is but a possibility, realizable not as general conclusion, but rather as the elusive effect of a particular personal experience; to a mind which, noting faithfully those random lights that meet it by the way, must needs content itself with suspension of judgement, at the end of the intellectual journey, to the very last asking: *Que scais-je?* Who knows?—in the very spirit of that old Socratic contention, that all true philosophy is but a refined sense of one's ignorance' (175-6).

The image of the essay as journey introduced here creates an evocative spatial metaphor for the essay as a process of exploration, hesitation, loitering, meandering, and revisiting which is of course particularly apt to describe Pater's own prose style, with its paratactic structure and deferrals of meaning. Just as Plato would sometimes show Socrates discussing philosophy during walks in and around Athens in order to give a dramatic backdrop to the lack of premeditation of his teachings, Pater uses the journey to suggest the essential aimlessness of essayistic writing. Here the most significant insights take place 'by the way', that is, accidentally, but also en route, in the middle rather than at the end point of the speculative thrust. Pater's location of important meaning 'by the way' is a recurring *topos* in his speculations on the essayistic method. In the 'Preface' to *The Renaissance* (1873) he declares his scepticism towards critical works that have attempted to find a 'universal formula' of beauty in art and poetry, claiming instead that their value 'has most often been in the suggestive and penetrating things said by the way'.[4] The failure to systematize is the success of the essay as Pater conceives it. In the later book on Plato, the metaphor of the essay as journey allows Pater to highlight what he calls the 'large and adventurous possibilities' (175) of an often side-lined literary genre that, in comparison to the epic (another genre in which journeys play an important role) or the novel, might appear deceptively modest.

---

[3] Cf. Lukács, for whom Plato is the 'greatest master of the [essay] form' (29).
[4] Pater, *The Renaissance: Studies in Art and Poetry*, ed. Donald L. Hill (1980), xix. Further references given in the text.

2. Aesthetic Criticism and the Essay

The dialectic of philosophy and poetry that Pater discusses in *Plato and Platonism* is already present in *The Renaissance* in the form of a whole series of related pairings that help Pater to conceptualize his mission as critic and, most importantly in this context, as essay writer: objectivity and subjectivity, science and literature, specialization and dilettantism. Pater's deliberate emphasis on poetry, rather than literature more broadly—a peculiarity underlined in the altered subtitle of later editions of *The Renaissance*, *Studies in Art and Poetry*—reveals a likely source in the writings of Friedrich Schlegel. In one of his best-known philosophical fragments, Schlegel puts forward a utopian vision of a 'progressive' and 'universal' poetry (which he calls 'romantic poetry'), capable of taking over, in the modern period, the traditional role of the epic, by providing 'a mirror of the whole circumambient world, an image of the age'. He explains: 'Its aim isn't merely to reunite all the separate species of poetry and put poetry in touch with philosophy and rhetoric. It tries to and should mix and fuse poetry and prose, inspiration and criticism, the poetry of art and the poetry of nature.' Schlegel's definition of poetry is unbound by the formal conventions we usually associate with the genre. In fact, *mutatis mutandis*, his ideal of philosophical poetry gives rise to a poetic philosophy, embodied in the prose fragment as ideal fusion of poetry and criticism. Schlegel's philosophical fragments are condensed essays that deliberately reveal the limits of rational discourse by emphasizing incompleteness and provisionality in their very form: undisciplined by the constraints of the philosophical treatise, they have their 'real essence' in 'the state of becoming', as Schlegel writes about his 'universal' poetry.[5] Pater did not employ the fragment form in his writings and his prose is hardly ever aphoristic, but he understands the essay as a poetic form in the sense theorized by Schlegel.

The legacy of Schlegel's philosophical poetry comes to the fore in Pater's idea of 'aesthetic criticism', which he coined by openly evoking the German tradition of the philosophy of art (or *philosophische Ästhetik*) that comprises Schlegel's *Fragments* as well as works by Baumgarten, Kant, Hegel, and others. Aesthetic criticism forms the backbone of Pater's theory and practice of the literary essay as synthesis of imaginative and critical faculties. In the 'Preface' to *The Renaissance*, Pater famously defines his critical method by setting out a series of fundamental questions that the 'aesthetic' critic should ask himself:

What is this song or picture, this engaging personality presented in life or in a book, to *me*? What effect does it really produce on me? Does it give me pleasure? and if so, what sort or degree of pleasure? How is my nature modified by its

---

[5] Friedrich Schlegel, *Friedrich Schlegel's* Lucinde *and the Fragments*, trans. and ed. Peter Firchow (1971), 175.

presence, and under its influence? The answers to these questions are the original facts with which the aesthetic critic has to do; and, as in the study of light, of morals, of number, one must realise such primary data for one's self, or not at all.

(xix–xx)

The emphasis falls away from the material or textual object of inquiry and onto the critic's self. The aesthetic critic—the best possible critic as Pater conceives him—is not a knower of hard facts but a soft being, characterized by intellectual malleability and a heightened capacity for feeling. It follows that in Pater's view the essay—no matter how analytical and scientific—will inevitably contain an autobiographical trace, as it provides the textual record of a 'temperament', defined as the 'power of being deeply moved by the presence of beautiful objects' (xxi). The aesthetic critic will not try to eradicate this trace of the self by means of an impossible performance of objectivity and by removing individual or subjective elements from the language and style of his works, because the very nature of the essay according to Pater is to stage a *relationship* between the object and the critic—a relationship characterized by preference, emotional intensity, proximity, and pleasure.

Matthew Arnold had famously set out the purpose of criticism as to 'see the object as in itself it really is', advocating a rigid separation between 'the creative effort of the human spirit [and] its critical effort'.[6] Pater revises Arnold by arguing that 'the first step towards seeing one's object as it really is, is to know one's own impression as it really is, to discriminate it, to realise it intensely' (xix). Pater's impression, with its emphasis on subjectivity, contingency, and fleetingness, counters Arnold's notion of the objective critic. Nodding again to Schlegel's defence of the philosophical value of poetry, Pater points out the crucial function of sensual perception and the emotions in bringing abstract knowledge into focus and giving it shape as a literary text. As he would argue in the essay on Plato, however, the question of shape is complicated because, while the essay provides a structure to articulate speculative thought, it must also convey that that structure is provisional and meaning unfixed. In other words, in order to be true to the philosophical logic of the impression, the essay must struggle against the fixity of its material medium, the unalterable impression of type on the page. The essay is the record of the critic's personal journey through his subject matter—a journey that, even if repeated, would never be the same again.

In the 'Conclusion' (the other extended methodological reflection in *The Renaissance*), Pater elaborates on this point by using as his epigram the famous paradox of the Greek philosopher Heraclitus, according to which no one can step into the same river twice. In the realm of criticism as much as in speculative

---

[6] Matthew Arnold, 'The Function of Criticism at the Present Time', in *The Complete Prose Works of Matthew Arnold*, vol. III, ed. R. H. Super (1962), 258.

thought, Pater implies, no two experiences are the same, because both critic and object are embedded in time and every encounter between them produces different results. A successful essayistic style, for Pater, will preserve this freshness of the encounter with the object, recreating its conditions. In the light of Heraclitean philosophy, Pater redeploys the discourse of pleasure he sets up in the 'Preface' in order to offer controversial advice to his readers, who are here urged 'to be for ever curiously testing new opinions and courting new impressions', and are told that to 'see and touch' is preferable to 'mak[ing] theories about the things we see and touch' (189). The essayistic mentality in other words (the idea of 'testing' here deliberately recalls the etymological meaning of the word 'essay') becomes an epistemology and even a way of life.

If the 'Preface', by eroding the distance between subject and object, reduces the authority of the critic as impartial observer, the 'Conclusion' celebrates loss of critical distance as a potentially ecstatic experience. This is what is meant by Pater's famous call to 'burn always with this hard, gem-like flame' (189). Schlegel had pointed out a tendency in philosophical poetry to 'lose itself in what it describes' and to 'hover at the midpoint between the portrayed and the portrayer'.[7] Likewise, Pater is very ready to concede that aesthetic criticism is vulnerable to the seductions of the intellectual and material world and, according to him, the literary essay should make, by its form and style, this potential weakness visible rather than hiding it behind a protective shield of rationality. It follows that the critical essay welcomes elements of 'passion' (a word on which he places a lot of emphasis in the 'Conclusion'); and, as far this is possible, it seeks a form of productive contamination with its object, absorbing its ideas and formal properties.

This openness to be challenged and transformed in unpremeditated ways, together with a constant refusal to fix and conclude, is an essential component of the philosophical scepticism that Pater would later associate with Montaigne. The 'Conclusion' suggests that philosophical and religious scepticism have a heightened historical urgency in the nineteenth century, when modern science has offered positive proof for the theory of relativism embraced by the old philosophical tradition that goes from Heraclitus to Montaigne. In the essay on Winckelmann, also in *The Renaissance*, Pater reiterates the connection between philosophical relativism and modern science, visualizing it this time through the memorable image of 'a magic web woven through and through us, like that magnetic system of which modern science speaks, penetrating us with a network, subtler than our subtlest nerves, yet bearing in it the central forces of the world' (185). The magic web is Pater's symbol of the interconnectedness of modern culture. Linking the individual body to the external principles of physical and

---

[7] Schlegel, *Friedrich Schlegel's* Lucinde *and the Fragments*, 175.

moral laws, the image of the web is a heartening vision of the boundlessness of human knowledge. The concept of magic alerts us once again to the crucial role that poetry, in Schlegel's enlarged definition, plays in this ideal: for the intricacy of the network system does not require to be unravelled (following the method of science and philosophy) but rather transfigured into new cognitive patterns that endlessly recombine into new formations.

The ambition to transfigure, rather than simply describe or explain, the object by means of critical prose is what motivates Pater's extensive use of devices traditionally associated with poetic genres, such as metaphor, synaesthesia, and symbolism, as well as his attention to the rhythmic patterns of language. Pater's essays translate the principles of aesthetic criticism into a hybrid medium that critics today call 'aesthetic prose' and that, like Schlegel's philosophical poetry, fuses 'poetry and prose, inspiration and criticism'. Nowhere are these character-istics of aesthetic prose more evident than in the ekphrastic renditions that are scattered throughout the essays in *The Renaissance*. The best-known of these, Pater's celebrated description of Leonardo's Mona Lisa as 'older than the rocks among which she sits' and a 'vampire [who] has been dead many times' (99), was reprinted by W. B. Yeats in the opening of his 1936 *Oxford Book of Modern Poetry*, a gesture that pays homage to its ambiguous generic status as prose poem, although the hybridity of the original was lessened by Yeats's choice to break up Pater's prose into blank verse. The same stylistic traits are in evidence in Pater's ekphrastic descriptions of Botticelli, one of which it is worth reproducing in full:

Perhaps you have sometimes wondered why those peevish-looking Madonnas, conformed to no acknowledged or obvious type of beauty, attract you more and more, and often come back to you when the Sistine Madonna and the Virgins of Fra Angelico are forgotten. At first, contrasting them with those, you may have thought that there was something in them mean or abject even, for the abstract lines of the face have little nobleness, and the colour is wan. For with Botticelli she too, though she holds in her hands the "Desire of all nations," is one of those who are neither for Jehovah nor for His enemies; and her choice is on her face. The white light on it is cast up hard and cheerless from below, as when snow lies upon the ground, and the children look up with surprise at the strange whiteness of the ceiling. Her trouble is in the very caress of the mysterious child, whose gaze is always far from her, and who has already that sweet look of devotion which men have never been able altogether to love, and which still makes the born saint an object almost of suspicion to his earthly brethren. Once, indeed, he guides her hand to transcribe in a book the words of her exaltation, the *Ave*, and the *Magnificat*, and the *Gaude Maria*, and the young angels, glad to rouse her for a moment from her dejection, are eager to hold the inkhorn and to support the book. But the pen almost drops from her hand, and the high cold words have no meaning for her, and her true children are those others, among whom, in her rude home, the intolerable honour came to her, with that look of wistful inquiry on their irregular faces which you see in startled animals—gypsy children, such as those who, in Apennine villages, still hold out their long brown arms to beg of you, but on Sundays become *enfants du choeur*, with their thick black hair nicely combed, and fair white linen on their sunburnt throats.   (44–5)

In such elaborately crafted passages the objects of criticism, here Botticelli's painting *Madonna del Magnificat*, provide the starting point for literary experiments in impressionistic writing that, as Yeats realized, become self-sufficient fragments within the essay and can be detached from its fabric and enjoyed for their formal qualities. As is typical of Pater, the structure tends towards parataxis, emphasizing delay and creating a series of short digressions and a sense of meandering within the spatial field of the art work which are conducive to many small flashes of insight that give the impression of being tangential or unplanned. Description and interpretation blend into a potentially confusing whole, as the voice of the essayist merges with the craft of the artist, playing literary variations on the effects of colour, touch, and sound suggested by the painting and adding details which are not on the canvas, such as the snowfall that Pater evokes in order to elucidate Botticelli's lighting technique without making recourse to technical or analytic language; without, in other words, disrupting the imaginative fabric of his prose.

Like his description of Leonardo's Mona Lisa as a 'vampire', his characterization of Botticelli's virgin as a religious sceptic ('one of those who are neither for Jehovah nor for His enemies') who almost withdraws from the touch of the cold, divine child takes liberties with its material, remoulding it into poetic language and thus updating its novelty and aesthetic and moral challenges for the modern age. The result is that Pater's aesthetic prose presents itself to the reader as no less an object of interpretation than Botticelli's canvas. Transferring these insights from the microcosm of the ekphrasis to Pater's handling of essayistic writing more broadly, we could say that Pater's essays deliberately deepen the enigma of the object rather than convey a devious sense of clarity and perfect mastery. His lyrical style thus tends to obscure the fundamental quality of referentiality that characterizes the literary essay—its dependence on a pre-existing object—bringing it to relinquish its responsibility to elucidate something outside it.

Oscar Wilde cherished this irresponsible side of Pater and, in his Pater-inspired critical dialogue 'The Critic as Artist' (1891), jokes about Pater's Mona Lisa having supplanted the real thing, as visitors to the Louvre can no longer stand in front of Leonardo's masterpiece without being spell-bound by the famous cadences of Pater's prose. This is a symptom of excellence for Wilde:

Who [...] cares whether Mr. Pater has put into the portrait of Monna Lisa something that Leonardo never dreamed of? [...] the picture becomes more wonderful to us than it really is, and reveals to us a secret of which, in truth, it knows nothing, and the music of the mystical prose is as sweet in our ears as was that flute-player's music that lent to the lips of La Gioconda those subtle and poisonous curves.[8]

Wilde's humorous plea for the creative power of criticism captures a key feature of the critical essay as revealed by Pater: that its relation to the object is essentially intertextual rather than explanatory, derivative, or ancillary, straddling the divide between what we now call primary and secondary texts.

In this sense, Pater is a perfect embodiment of what Adorno praises as the 'decadent intelligence' of the essayist, which, according to Adorno again, hostile critics perceive as a tendency to over-interpret and, by so doing, to create meaning where there is none.[9] Pater's essays are decadent in this sense because of their highly self-reflexive and self-conscious nature, which causes meaning to drift away from the object of enquiry and to gravitate instead towards the text itself— a characteristic which was praised by Wilde as an effective way of advocating the aesthetic autonomy of the essay genre just as it was also frowned upon by several contemporary critics who attacked Pater's analyses as fanciful and potentially misleading.[10] But these same features also make the genre of the art essay, especially as practised by Pater, Decadent in the historicized sense of the term that applies to some strands of late nineteenth-century literature: that is to say, Pater demonstrates how the essay was attractive to a Decadent sensibility that preferred to look for inspiration in pre-existing texts and arte-facts rather than in the actual world and believed that art and literature should not be limited by the obligation to provide a truthful representation of what is outside them.

Pater's achievement as essayist came under attack in the early twentieth century, most famously perhaps by T. S. Eliot, at a time in which literary

[8] Oscar Wilde, 'The Critic as Artist', in *Criticism: Historical Criticism, Intentions, The Soul of Man*, ed. Josephine M. Guy (2007), *The Complete Works of Oscar Wilde* (2000–), IV, 156–7.

[9] Theodor Adorno, 'The Essay as Form' ['Der Essay als Form'], trans. Bob Hullot-Kentor and Frederic Will, *New German Critique* 32 (1984), 151–71, here 152. The evocative expression 'decadent intelligence' is in fact a free translation and it is cited here in the spirit that, like essays, translations sometimes create productive meanings which were only *in nuce* in the original. Adorno's German reads: 'Dem, der deutet, anstatt hinzunehmen und einzuordnen, wird der gelbe Fleck dessen angeheftet, der kraftlos, mit fehlgeleiteter Intelligenz spintisiere und hineinlege, wo es nichts auszulegen gibt.' Adorno's open allusion to Nazi anti-Semitism shows his intellectual and political contempt for those critics that would limit the remit of the essay according to traditional criteria of utility and rationality. Rationalism is, for him, the political enemy of the essayistic mentality; just as the essayistic mentality is allied, politically as well as aesthetically, with those forms of art that the Nazis denounced as degenerate.

[10] See for instance, J. A. Symonds, [signed review], *The Academy* (15 March 1873); and, more tartly, Margaret Oliphant, [unsigned review], *Blackwood's Magazine* (September 1873); both of whom took particular exception to Pater's reading of Botticelli's Madonnas. Reprinted in *Walter Pater: The Critical Heritage*, ed. R. M. Seiler (1980), respectively 57–61, here 59; and 85–91, here 88–9.

Decadence had gone out of fashion.[11] Eliot's definition of bad criticism as 'nothing but an expression of emotion' is explicitly formulated in reaction to the late nineteenth-century essays of Pater, Algernon Charles Swinburne, and Arthur Symons.[12] Eliot objected to these critics' hybrid of prose genre and poetic technique which, to his mind, blurred analytic thought and promoted amateurism. He scorned aesthetic criticism—the cornerstone of Pater's essayistic style—as a psychological aberration, 'the satisfaction of a suppressed creative wish'.[13] Eliot's commitment to criticism as a profession (in the same essay he praises Coleridge as 'a professional with his eye on the technique'[14]) brings him to uphold a series of oppositions—intellect vs. emotion, clarity vs. disorder, finish vs. sketchiness, criticism vs. creativity—that the previous generation of English critics had allegedly confused.

But the confusion of genres and registers to which Eliot objects was, as we have seen, a deliberate characteristic of the art essay; nor was it confined to England alone. As well as German aesthetic philosophy, Pater's aesthetic criticism looked to mid nineteenth-century France, a period that Eliot otherwise holds in high esteem as marking the onset of a productive literary modernity identified with the writings of Baudelaire.[15] Baudelaire, however, together with his older contemporary Gautier, had been a crucial source of inspiration for Swinburne and Pater, who littered their early essays with implicit and explicit references to their French models. Gautier in particular, in his art historical essays, had elaborated a vivid impressionistic style full of lyrical turns that was imitated by Swinburne, first, and then by Pater, whose essay on Leonardo, for instance, is in dialogue with Gautier's 'Leonardo da Vinci' (1858) and 'The Amateur's Guide to the Museum of the Louvre' (1867).[16]

This experiment with an impressionistic, highly elaborate essayistic style that travelled from France to England was linked to a broader redefinition of 'the literary' that took place in the second half of the nineteenth century in the metropolitan culture of both nations, prompted by the sharp rise of journalism and of the periodical industry. The practitioners of the aesthetic or impressionistic essay occupied an ambiguous position in relation to magazines and newspapers. Writers like Gautier, Swinburne, and Wilde thundered about the levelling of culture imposed on them by the periodical press and journalists' commercialization

---

[11] On Pater's complicated reception among modernist writers, see F. C. McGrath, *The Sensible Spirit: Walter Pater and the Modernist Paradigm* (1986); and Perry Meisel, *The Absent Father: Virginia Woolf and Walter Pater* (1980).

[12] T. S. Eliot, 'The Perfect Critic', in *The Sacred Wood: Essays on Poetry and Criticism* (1921), 1–14, here 14.

[13] Eliot, *The Sacred Wood*, 7.   [14] Eliot, *The Sacred Wood*, 17.

[15] While Eliot argued for the importance of Baudelaire, he was also keen to disassociate the French author from what he thought was a distorting English reception by Swinburne and Pater. Eliot, 'Baudelaire', *Selected Essays* (1963), 419–30.

[16] Catherine Maxwell traces the genealogy of aesthetic prose from Gautier to Swinburne and Pater in *Swinburne* (2006), 81–105.

of the written word. At the same time, however, they took on paid work for periodicals and newspapers; and the middlebrow critics and journalists whose ignorance and bigotry they bemoaned would often publish in the pages of the same journals. Wilde's complaint in 'The Critic as Artist' that 'journalism is unreadable, and literature is not read' is typical.[17] Wilde draws a sharp separation between lowbrow journalism and 'literature' by self-consciously emphasizing the literariness of his essays—in this case by employing a dialogue form which nods back to the Platonic tradition that Pater also singles out as pre-eminent in the history of the essay. However, at the same time, the fact that his essay was originally published in a periodical, the *Nineteenth Century*, complicates the assumption that there can be a clean distinction between the two.[18]

Pater also worked as a paid journalist and, as Laurel Brake has demonstrated, his literary works were shaped by his lifelong relationship with the periodical press.[19] Unlike Swinburne and Wilde, though, Pater was not a polemicist. But given the supreme importance that Pater places on subjectivity in the 'Preface' to *The Renaissance*, it is unsurprising that he should feel uneasy about the intellectual promiscuity of the periodical medium, where his essays were read side by side with other topics and other authors and, as was common practice at the time, often published anonymously. After their first journal publication in the *Westminster*, the *Fortnightly*, and the *Contemporary Review*, most of Pater's essays reappeared in collections that were either overseen by Pater himself or by his literary executor, C. L. Shadwell, after his death. In adopting this practice of collecting periodical essays into book form, Pater followed what was already a fairly well-established tradition: Matthew Arnold's *Essays in Criticism*, for instance, had appeared in 1865.[20] But he also contributed to the growth in popularity of the collected-essays form among writers with aesthetic and Decadent leanings, such as Swinburne, John Addington Symonds, Vernon Lee, Wilde, Ouida, and Symons, all of whom brought out volumes of collected essays in the last three decades of the nineteenth century. Reissuing his periodical essays in book form enabled Pater to reclaim his own signature from the overwhelming plurality of journal publishing, implicitly reasserting at the same time the aesthetic credentials of the essay as a literary genre

---

[17] Wilde, 'The Critic as Artist', 135. The essay was originally published as 'The True Function and Value of Criticism' in the *Nineteenth Century*, in 1890.

[18] On the dialectic between journalism and literature in Wilde's career, see the editors' introduction to *Journalism* (2013), vols VI–VII of *The Complete Works of Oscar Wilde*, ed. John Stokes and Mark W. Turner (2000–). Laurel Brake examines the case of Swinburne in ' "A Juggler's Trick"? Swinburne's Journalism 1857–75', in *Algernon Charles Swinburne: Unofficial Laureate*, ed. Catherine Maxwell and Stefano Evangelista (2013), 69–92.

[19] Brake, *Print in Transition, 1850–1910: Studies in Media and Book History* (2001), especially 183–96.

[20] Laurel Brake dates the beginning of this tradition to Francis Jeffrey's experiment of bringing out his anonymous essays from the *Edinburgh Review* in book form, in 1844 (Brake, *Print in Transition*, 225).

by lifting it from the ephemerality of the periodical medium, which in this period exercised a shaping influence on the novel no less than the literary essay.

3. The Novel and the Essay

Not all modernists disliked Pater. In an essay entitled 'The Modern Essay' (1922), Virginia Woolf praised Pater for successfully conveying 'a vision, such as we get in a good novel where everything contributes to bring the writer's conception as a whole before us'.[21] Woolf draws attention to Pater's mastery of the form or style of essay-writing which, she argues, requires a literary skill that is less easy to see but in fact more difficult to achieve than other literary genres. She even echoes Pater's words in the 'Preface' when she claims that the chief aim of the essay 'is simply that it should give pleasure'.[22] Woolf's comparison between the essay and the novel has been systematically pursued in recent years by Claire De Obaldia, who has pointed out that the two genres emerge roughly at the same period and share the same ability to combine different literary modes. Both forms moreover place 'ordinary life and common man as everybody knows them at the centre of [their] investigations', aiming to popularize philosophical and scientific ideas for the benefit of a generalist readership which is not interested in the drier and more difficult forms of the treatise or specialized article.[23]

While in her view the novel has an intrinsically essayistic quality because of its tendency to incorporate other genres and forms of writing, De Obaldia also identifies a type of 'essayistic novel', which is characterized by a foregrounding of generic mixture: 'since the integration of the essay-fragment into its fictional frame is not done by way of a dissolution, the demarcation of the essayistic material results in a confrontation between the cognitive and the aesthetic, theory and practice, potentiality and actualization, fragment and whole [...], which brings about the disruption of narrative sequence.'[24] De Obaldia argues that, as a critical category, the essayistic novel is much more prevalent in German literary criticism, where it is applied to works by writers including Schlegel, Goethe, Thomas Mann, Robert Musil, and Hermann Hesse. Pater's own experiments with the novel form warrant the extension of this critical category to the English late nineteenth century.

In the late 1870s and 1880s, after the *succès de scandale* of *The Renaissance*, Pater turned to fiction. The first product of this new career was *Marius the*

---

[21] Virginia Woolf, 'The Modern Essay', in *The Essays of Virginia Woolf*, vol. IV, ed. Andrew McNeillie (1994), 216–27, 218.

[22] Woolf, 'The Modern Essay', 216.

[23] Claire De Obaldia, *The Essayistic Spirit: Literature, Modern Criticism, and the Essay* (1995), 14–15.

[24] De Obaldia, *The Essayistic Spirit*, 21; see also 194–206.

Epicurean (1885), a historical novel set in ancient Rome. *Marius* is often described as a philosophical novel; but the designation 'essayistic novel' is more appropriate, as the narrative is interspersed with long digressions on religion, literature, art, history, and philosophy. Chapters titles like 'Euphuism', 'New Cyrenaicism', and 'Stoicism at Court' make it clear that the novel is structured around a series of topics that the narrative lays out like an intellectual map of the Latin second century, which the reader navigates alongside the fictional protagonist.

Victorian reviewers were predictably baffled by *Marius* which, in the words of an anonymous critic of the *Pall Mall Gazette*, could 'hardly be called a story at all'.[25] This was, however, precisely the point. Pater had stretched the boundaries of the novel in order to fit those qualities that he valued so much in the essay, such as free association and lack of closure. The result is a corrosion of plot and narrative structure which disrupts the expectations of those who 'read for the story', as the reviewer of the *Pall Mall Gazette* put it, or approach *Marius* as one of the many conversion romances set in ancient Rome that were popular at the time.[26] Pater himself later stressed the thematic contiguity of the novel to his previous work as critic, inviting readers to approach *Marius* as an extended elaboration of the controversial theory of art for art's sake put forward in the 'Conclusion' to *The Renaissance*.[27]

The novel's full title—*Marius the Epicurean: His Sensations and Ideas*—is indeed another permutation of that dialectic of poetry and philosophy that, after Montaigne and Schlegel, Pater had seen as the motor of the essay genre. So, while the story is focalized through the character of Marius, a soft Paterian subject like the 'I' of the 'Preface' to *The Renaissance*, whose authority rests in a heightened susceptibility to sensual impressions, it is narrated in the third person by a nineteenth-century narrator who is aware of his and the readers' historical distance from the action and frequently situates the fictional events within a longer historical perspective. The sense of generic hybridity comes to the fore in a series of episodes in which Marius encounters either actual works of literature such as Apuleius's *Golden Ass*, of which Pater provides a partial translation, or real historical characters such as the emperor Marcus Aurelius and the philosopher Lucian, in which case Pater weaves into the narrative direct quotations or paraphrases of their works (respectively, the *Meditations* and the philosophical

---

[25] Unsigned review, *Pall Mall Gazette* (18 March 1885), 4–5; reprinted in Seiler, *Walter Pater*, 117–19, here 117.

[26] Seiler, *Walter Pater*, 118. *The Times* called *Marius* 'fine writing and hard reading'; reprinted in Seiler, 125. Simon Goldhill provides a study of Victorian historical fiction set in ancient Rome in *Victorian Culture and Classical Antiquity: Art, Opera, Fiction, and the Proclamation of Modernity* (2011), 193–244. Goldhill's emphasis is, however, on assimilating Pater to the mainstream Victorian tradition of historical fiction. See also Norman Vance, *The Victorians and Ancient Rome* (1997), 197–221.

[27] This injunction appeared in a footnote appended to the third edition of *The Renaissance* in 1888 (Pater, *The Renaissance*, 186).

dialogue *Hermotimus*). The novel thus becomes a digressive intertextual hybrid that incorporates translation and criticism into a classic *Bildungsroman* plot, troubling the distinction between narration and interpretation.

The desire to fuse fictional and essayistic techniques is also the inspiration behind a series of short fictions that Pater published between 1878 and 1892, which he called 'imaginary portraits' and which are best understood, as Lene Østermark-Johansen points out, as exercises in biographical form that use fictional elements to thwart the 'referentiality expected from both portraiture and biography'.[28] But the hybridization of fiction and essay is even more extreme in Pater's second and last novel, the unfinished *Gaston de Latour*. Like *Marius*, *Gaston* is a historical *Bildungsroman* that focuses on the intellectual development of a young male protagonist against the backdrop of a period of momentous historical transition: this time the action takes place in sixteenth-century France, in the aftermath of the Reformation. If the character of Marius represents the troubled decline of classical civilization at the onset of the Christian era, Gaston embodies the birth of the modern man—the Renaissance ideal to which Pater had been strongly attracted from the beginnings of his career. The essayistic style is essentially the same as in the previous novel: the narration incorporates learned disquisitions on the arts and literature of sixteenth-century France, often compared to later French culture and the 'modernity' of the late nineteenth century. As Gerald Monsman has pointed out, the constant filtering of the events through memory, ideas, and multiple perspectives dissolves the dramatic action so radically 'that the fictional protagonist seems almost to be reading about the age in which he lived'.[29]

Pater published *Marius* directly in book form but he decided to serialize *Gaston* in *Macmillan's Magazine*—a project that he abandoned half way through, in October 1888, for unclear reasons: he was either dissatisfied with what he had written or, as a slow writer and compulsive reviser, he could not keep up with the pressure of monthly publication.[30] In any case it is telling that, when one further chapter appeared in the *Fortnightly Review* little less than one year later, it was as a

---

[28] Pater, *Imaginary Portraits*, ed. Lene Østermark-Johansen (2014), 4. A full examination of the imaginary portrait, while relevant to the study of how Pater blends the literary essay and fiction, is beyond the scope of this chapter. Besides Østermark-Johansen's detailed introduction, see Elisa Bizzotto, 'The Imaginary Portrait: Pater's Contribution to a Literary Genre', in *Walter Pater: Transparencies of Desire*, ed. Laurel Brake, Lesley Higgins, and Carolyn Williams (2002), 213–23; and Max Saunders, *Self Impression: Life-Writing, Autobiografiction, and the Forms of Modern Literature* (2010), 29–70.

[29] Pater, *Gaston de Latour: The Revised Text*, ed. Gerald Monsman (1995), xl. Further references given in the text.

[30] The first book version of Gaston was issued as 'an unfinished romance' in 1896 by Pater's executor C. L. Shadwell, who after Pater's death added surviving manuscript material to the published chapters. A new critical edition of the novel, edited by Gerald Monsman, has recently been published as part of OUP's ongoing *Collected Works of Walter Pater* (2018-), too late for consultation. References in this essay are to Monsman's previous edition of 1995, which adds further manuscript material to Shadwell's.

free-standing essay rather than as a book instalment or short story: 'Giordano Bruno. Paris: 1586' is a characteristic piece of biographically inspired criticism that fed into a contemporary interest in the Italian philosopher, fuelled by the recent appearance of complete scholarly editions of his Latin and Italian writings.[31] When Pater later revised the essay on Bruno into 'The Lower Pantheism', the title of the chapter as it appears in the novel version, he only had to add a couple of introductory pages to achieve the generic transformation from essay into narrative fiction.

Bruno is one of several historical figures whom Gaston encounters in the course of the narrative. Chief among these is undoubtedly Montaigne, who in the novel personifies the spirit of the sixteenth-century Renaissance. Gaston meets Montaigne just as the latter had embarked on the *Essais*, having given up his legal career. There is something autobiographical in Pater's depiction of the 'homely epicureanism' (44) that characterizes Montaigne's way of life and of the philosopher's 'continual journey in thought, "a continual observation of new and unknown things", his bodily self remaining, for the most part, with seeming indolence at home' (43). Pater's narrative is thick with quotations from Montaigne (here from the essay 'Of Vanity'), which he uses to lend authenticity to his fictional character and, at the same time, to direct readers *away* from the novel, to non-fictional elements that emphasize its hybrid status between fiction and criticism, characterization and interpretation.

Pater dwells in particular on Montaigne's 'disinterestedness' and his radical scepticism, encapsulated by his motto, 'doubt everywhere' (53), which gains a special poignancy in the religious climate of the late Victorian years and reminds readers of the 'Conclusion' to *The Renaissance*. He notes Montaigne's sociability and his endless delight in conversation, drawing attention, as he would do in his work on Plato, to the oral and dialogic origins of the essay genre. Again as in his analysis of the 'genius' of Plato, Pater pushes this genealogy further backwards from speech to inner speech, borrowing in both instances Matthew Arnold's famous image of 'the dialogue of the mind with itself' to describe, as he puts it in *Gaston*, the 'endless *inward* converse of which the Essays were a kind of abstract' (44).[32] What for Arnold was a specific characteristic (and, in an important sense, a specific disadvantage) of modernity, is for Pater a universal characteristic of the great essayistic tradition that goes from Plato to Montaigne. Pater therefore suggests that we should view the *Essais* as an essentially autobiographical work of self-discovery in which subjectivity and impression transfigure the ostensible objects of enquiry, to reveal a portrait of the critical temperament as Pater had theorized it in the 'Preface' to *The Renaissance*.

---

[31] See Monsman's notes to Pater, *Gaston de Latour*, 178.

[32] Cf. Pater, *Plato and Platonism*, 177 and 183. Arnold's quotation comes from the author's preface to the 1853 edition of *Poems*.

The descriptions of Montaigne's creative process, as witnessed first-hand by Gaston, highlight the epiphanic nature of essay-writing, its meaning, like its inspiration, concretizing by the way, here and there, in a way that eludes rationality and full authorial control, kindled by moments of intensity:

> Movement, some kind of rapid movement, a ride, a hasty survey of a shelf of books, best of all a conversation like this morning's with a visitor for the first time,—amid the felicitous chances of that, at some random turn by the way, he would become aware of shaping purpose. The beam of light or heat would strike down, to illuminate, to fuse and organise the coldly accumulated matter of reason, of experience. Surely some providence over thought and speech led one finely through those haphazard journeys!   (44)

The extended fictional characterization of Montaigne brings into focus the elements of Pater's theory of the literary essay that are scattered here and there in his other writings: the metaphor of the journey, the philosophical value of inconsistency, the intimate relation between chaos and enlightenment, the importance of things found 'at some random turn by the way'.

Pater believed that the essay and the novel share a similar set of narrative strategies and fundamental epistemological questions. It is not coincidental, therefore, that the portrait of Montaigne in *Gaston* should contain a semi-hidden cameo of the image of the magic web conceived many years earlier to allude to the transfiguring power of the essay form: with its conjunct references to magic and weaving, a tapestry depicting 'Circe and her sorceries' owned by Montaigne takes readers back to the familiar image from *The Renaissance*, miniaturized and made more mythical in this later text. In a further self-reflexive turn, Pater depicts Montaigne himself as a thinly disguised version of the Homeric Circe, interrupting Gaston's intellectual journey with a bewitching hospitality that holds the protagonist spellbound, as in a 'long day-sleep' (46), for nine months.

In the second half of the nineteenth century Pater was not the only writer who conjured the image of the web to instruct his readers on how to navigate the disparate and sometimes competing forms of knowledge generated by modern culture. In *Middlemarch* (1872), a work roughly contemporaneous with *The Renaissance*, George Eliot also used the web to represent the intricacy of the social relations described in the novel and the decentred nature of its plot. The web for Eliot was also a metaphor for the art of the novelist who, 'in unravelling certain human lots, and seeing how they were woven and interwoven', makes a microcosmic intervention into the problem of human knowledge, as faced at large by her contemporaries.[33] Pater's use of the web is equally self-reflexive. But for him

---

[33] George Eliot, *Middlemarch*, ed. David Carroll (1986), 139.

the essay, not the novel, provided the open-ended and non-hierarchical literary structure that bound together the text and the world outside of language, holding the promise of a utopian coming together of the various branches of human knowledge in ages to come. It is in this inconspicuous and often side-lined literary genre that he saw the power to reconcile objectivity and subjective perception, and to provide a cognitive map of human knowledge as relative, provisional, and taking shape in unexpected places along the interminable and labyrinthine road to truth.

13

'Strips of Essayism'

Eliot, Hardy, and the Victorian Periodical Essay

Bharat Tandon

1. Writing in Tongues

In an essay on V. S. Pritchett (himself an accomplished novelist-essayist), one of the most notable literary essayists of recent times, James Wood, commented on a distinctive characteristic of the mainstream English novel, one that he perceived as contrasting with Pritchett's own, more 'Chekhovian' aesthetic:

> The English novelists, after all, are remarkably intrusive, always breaking in to speak over their characters and tell us what to think, mummifying them some-what in strips of essayism: this is true of Fielding, Eliot, Forster, and on to Angus Wilson and A. S. Byatt. In Chekhov, however, the prose has the texture of its content: it doesn't seek to illuminate its perfection but lightens a path for its own developing cognition.[1]

One can see what Wood is getting at here; looking at the authors he mentions (and many others would serve as well), one might feel there to be an insecurity, an anxiety of genre afflicting this strand of the novel—almost as if, in English literary fiction, representation needed a stern underpinning of opinion in order to be taken seriously. In this light, Wood's broader suspicion of the 'informational' in modern world fiction is understandable: compare his assessments of contemporary 'Hysterical Realism' ('Information has become the new character') and Tom Wolfe ('the prosaic factuality of his information').[2] After all, one can discern, in much fiction of the last twenty years, a tendency, largely derived from Sterne, in which an imaginative concern with obsessive knowledge sets off trains of factual association, which go on to stand in for more traditional forms of plot-business.

However, this tells only part of the story; after all, since its beginnings (if such points could ever be fixed objectively) the novel in English has been defined by the

---

[1] James Wood, 'V. S. Pritchett and English Comedy', in *The Irresponsible Self: On Laughter and the Novel* (2004), 284.

[2] Wood, 'V. S. Pritchett and English Comedy', 174, 204.

Bharat Tandon, *'Strips of Essayism': Eliot, Hardy, and the Victorian Periodical Essay* In: *On Essays: Montaigne to the Present.*
Edited by: Thomas Karshan and Kathryn Murphy, Oxford University Press (2020). © Bharat Tandon.
DOI: 10.1093/oso/9780198707868.003.0014

shifting relations that it has set up between the narrative and the informative. One only has to look back to the generic muddle of prose narrative in the late seventeenth and early eighteenth centuries, out of which the English 'novel' emerged, to see that 'strips of essayism' have bolstered fiction's effects as well as simply 'mummifying' them. In Victorian fiction, as I shall be exploring here, the idea of the 'essayistic', and its associated styles, offers novelists such as Eliot and Hardy a distinctive means of engaging with those broader aesthetic and cultural debates about knowledge and proof, belief and unbelief, which their novels both reflect and enact. But, while Eliot can often play narrative and essayism off each other in a sophisticated, mutually supporting double-act, Hardy, that inveterate, sceptical revisionist, inhabits similar stylistic shapes, only to turn those very shapes into questions about the eclectic and perhaps irreconcilable multiples that he saw as fundamental to modern consciousness.

In what follows, I shall be exploring how Victorian essayism, moving between periodicals, books, and novels, sought to register such contrarieties. The eclecticism of experience was for Victorian readers not simply an abstract idea, but frequently an inescapable part of the experience of reading itself. If, as Geoffrey Hill has contended, '[a]nything less like a "single world" than the nineteenth century it would be hard to discover [...] the epoch was marked by a drastic breaking of tempo and by an equally severe disturbance of the supposedly normative patterns of speech', then those divisions are often literalized in the form, look, and imagined voices of texts.[3] 'Periodicals', Margaret Beetham suggests,

> are heterogeneous in that they are made up of different kinds of material. Many mix text and pictures. Indeed the relation of blocks of text to visual material is a crucial part of their meaning. Even where it does not use visual and literary material together, the periodical is still characteristically a mixed form.[4]

One practical result of this was that single, occasional pieces might constellate themselves over time into larger, interrelated wholes that writers could not anticipate at the time—as witnessed by the career of Arnold, a critic whose permanence, like that of many contemporaries, crystallized out of the provisional. As Walter E. Houghton has noted,

> Arnold was not a writer of books; he was a writer of periodical literature [...] The periodical creation of books was sometimes accidental. As many authors

---

[3] Geoffrey Hill, 'Redeeming the Time', in *Collected Critical Writings*, ed. Kenneth Haynes (2008), 88.
[4] Margaret Beetham, 'Towards a Theory of the Periodical as a Publishing Genre', in Laurel Brake, Aled Jones, and Lionel Madden (eds), *Investigating Victorian Journalism* (1990), 24.

knew, they tried out an idea in an essay only to discover that fresh angles of the subject sprang up demanding another essay, and so on until the collection, perhaps with fresh links, became a book.[5]

So much for the material make-up of texts, and the formal interactions between essays and volumes; however, both Hill and Wood make particular mention of the role of voice in articulating Victorian cultural authority, whether a 'disturbance of the supposedly normative patterns of speech' or the presence of writers 'breaking in to speak over their characters'. In this chapter, I wish to pay particular attention to the phenomenon of 'voice' as both literal referent and figurative quality in the essays and novels of Eliot, Hardy, and in periodical contributors, in order to suggest that the action of the narrating and discoursing voices in these works serves to create channels of communication between the disparate subjects and scales with which they engage.[6] Theoretical writing about the nature of the essay has often had recourse to the idea of individual personality as a model for describing the features of the form. Carl H. Klaus, for example, connects the ideas of Montaigne and Adorno on the essay, noting that 'the form of the essay will appear to reflect the process of a mind in action, but a mind that is always in control of itself no matter how wayward it may seem to be', and going on to describe 'a highly complex and problematic kind of writing—an enactment of thought and a projection of personality that uses language dramatically, as in a monologue or a soliloquy'.[7] It is notable that Klaus's terms look back to Coleridge, whether consciously or not, and particularly to Coleridgean ideas such as 'the mind's self-experience in the act of thinking' and 'the drama of reason'.[8] And if personality in essays is going to be figured in terms of drama, then the voices that give that drama life and body are going to be particularly worthy of attention— even if these voices can only guarantee and underwrite so much in themselves, not possessing the power to validate themselves entirely on their own terms. As Wittgenstein pithily reminds us, '[c]ertainty is *as it were* a tone of voice in which one declares how things are, but one does not infer from the tone of voice that one is justified'.[9]

[5] Walter E. Houghton, 'Periodical Literature and the Articulate Classes', in Joanne Shattock and Michael Wolff (eds), *The Victorian Periodical Press: Samplings and Soundings* (1982), 21–2.

[6] For more on 'voice' in the nineteenth century, in the writings of Carlyle and Emerson, see this volume, Chapter 10 by Tom Wright.

[7] Carl H. Klaus, 'Toward a Collective Poetics of the Essay', in Carl H. Klaus and Ned Stuckey-French (eds), *Essayists on the Essay: Montaigne to Our Time* (2012), xxii–xxiii, xxvi.

[8] Samuel Taylor Coleridge, *Biographia Literaria*, ed. James Engell and W. Jackson Bate, 2 vols (1983), in *Collected Works of Samuel Taylor Coleridge*, ed. Kathleen Coburn, 23 vols (1983–), VII: II, 124; Coleridge, letter to Thomas Poole (28 January 1810), in *Collected Letters of Samuel Taylor Coleridge*, 6 vols, ed. Earl Leslie Griggs (1956–71), III, 282.

[9] Ludwig Wittgenstein, *On Certainty*, trans. D. Paul and G. E. M. Anscombe (1969), 6.

2. Essayism and Essays

When evaluating what writers like Eliot might have gained from both occasional and more (supposedly) solid forms, then the word 'essayistic' and its cognates, and the problematic transit of these terms in the latter part of the nineteenth century, merit close scrutiny. For example, two periodical articles from 1887 highlight both the desire to describe the quintessence of essayism and the difficulty of doing so with authority. In 'The Essay as a Literary Form and Quality' (whose very title strains to hold two distinct states of being in a meaningful relation to each other), Francis N. Zabriskie attempts a working definition of essayism, even as that definition seems to recede before him. 'History, criticism, philosophy, description, or any kind of information or research, may enter into its subject-matter', he argues of the essay. 'But these do not in themselves constitute a genuine essay, any more than swallows can make a summer, or piety and music are sufficient for a hymn.' In a similar vein, he dismisses much nineteenth-century periodical writing from his canon, claiming that '[t]hese masterful and often leonine vivisections of authors, these eloquent creations on paper, these able state papers, these splendid historical tapestries or biographical portraitures, have no more relation to the true essay than a Roman toga or a coat of mail has to a dressing-gown or a pea-jacket'.[10] Yet a reader navigating Zabriskie's florid prose might complain of the lack of any positive definition to counterbalance this. The *Saturday Review*'s unimpressed response to the piece rightly points out that '[t]o define a thing by what it is not appears to be an irresistible temptation to Mr. ZABRISKIE'.[11]

Of course, Zabriskie might have countered that his whole point about essayism was that it isn't a 'what' at all, but a 'how': '*the style is the essay*', he insists, citing the familiar roll-call of Plutarch, Bacon, Montaigne, and Emerson, and the closest he does come to a definition is in terms of an attitude rather than a quantity, which 'treats its subject by a series of suggestions rather than by a chain of reasoning, or even of logical connection'.[12] That said, as witnessed by the equivocal wording of his essay's title, the fact that this is not the only way in which the idea can be understood says much about the status of periodical essayism in the period. All the *Saturday Review* can do in the end is turn Zabriskie's emphases on their heads ('"*The essay is the style*", not "The style is the essay"'), pointing a reader towards a seemingly infinite regress of mutually uncomprehending definitions: 'this essay on essayists is undiluted essayism'.[13] The friction witnessed simply in two essays may appear daunting, but it is nevertheless a condition which any Victorian writer of

---

[10] Francis N. Zabriskie, 'The Essay as a Literary Form and Quality', *The New Princeton Review* IV (July–November 1887), 227, 241.
[11] 'Essays, Essayists, and Essayism', *The Saturday Review of Politics, Literature, Science, and Art* 64.1665 (24 September 1887), 412.
[12] Zabriskie, 'The Essay as a Literary Form and Quality', 229, 231.
[13] 'Essays, Essayists, and Essayism', 413.

the 'essayistic' needed to face—and this apparent contradiction will be my focus in what follows. Zabriskie's attempted definition harks back to the Renaissance senses of the *essai*, and much Victorian writing did gain signally from those qualities of the provisional and associationist identified with the older definitions of 'essayistic'—not least because of the opportunities offered by the material conditions of writing and publication which I sketched earlier.

The Zabriskie debate illustrates some of the dominant senses of 'essayistic' in the nineteenth century; however, looking back to Wood's worry about English fiction's 'strips of essayism', what irks him about this discursive tradition is not its suggestiveness but, rather, its tendency to be too sure of itself, and (especially important for my argument here) to vocalize that modal assurance by 'talking over' its characters in a voice of authority. The bet-hedging qualifications of Zabriskie's title, with its apparent contradictions ('The Essay as Literary Form and Quality'), may in fact point to a contradictory impulse at the heart of nineteenth-century essayism itself.

Indeed, it may even be that, at this particular point in the nineteenth century, the word comes close to incarnating two antithetical ideas at once—on the one hand, we have the essay as an occasional, suggestive, and glancing voice, elusive of certainty, and on the other hand we have the voice of the essay as one that often appears to be policing, closing down, and 'talking over' just those essayistic features beloved of Zabriskie. It is in the shifting interplays between these apparently opposite forms of the essay that Eliot and Hardy discover the qualities that animate their peculiarly textured novels, in which different scales of representation and understanding contend for dominance. And, as I shall go on to investigate, these contentions are given substantial form in a mode of address that balances a sense for the traditional 'essayistic' virtues of the occasional against those impulses towards the determinate and the taxonomic which are equally constitutive of Victorian cultural desires. Time and again in this writing, observation is found aspiring towards precept, in a voice trying rhetorically to will *is* into *ought*.

3. What We Know

George Eliot was not only a novelist and essayist but also the distinguished editor of essays at the *Westminster Review*. Her 'Prospectus' for John Chapman's relaunch of the *Westminster Review* in January 1852 tries, among other things, to balance general precept against particular example, as the periodical lays out its plans for intellectual and social reform:

> The fundamental principle of the work will be the recognition of the Law of
> Progress. In conformity with this principle, and with the consequent conviction

that attempts at reform—though modified by the experience of the past and the conditions of the present—should be directed and animated by an advancing ideal, the Editors will maintain a steady comparison of the actual with the possible, as the most powerful stimulus to improvement. Nevertheless, in the deliberate advocacy of organic changes, it will not be forgotten, that the institutions of man, no less than the products of nature, are strong and durable in proportion as they are the results of a gradual development, and that the most salutary and permanent reforms are those, which, while embodying the wisdom of the time, yet sustain such a relation to the moral and intellectual condition of the people, as to ensure their support.[14]

As the prospectus unfolds, phrases directly or indirectly implying fixed or singular ideas ('the Law of Progress', 'an advancing ideal', 'the institutions of man') are tasked to exist in a context which still acknowledges the presence of flux and multiplicity—epitomizing those dilemmas which, as I have argued, Victorian essayism needed to take on board. And nowhere in the prospectus are those pressures more apparent than in the phrase 'the wisdom of the time': which, like so many other variant terms for *Zeitgeist* ('Spirit of the Age', and so on), covertly acknowledges all the diverse cultural pressures that its simplifying form is perilously holding at bay. The two singulars, 'the wisdom' and 'the time', may be grammatically identical, but while the former could just about be argued to have one referent, the latter could only ever be a cordon set up around plurality to render it manageable. Nor is this the only problematic singular term at work in the Prospectus: 'the wisdom of the time' is, in the vision of the *Westminster*'s future practice, almost immediately tempered by an implicitly more pragmatic and circumspect appeal to 'the moral and intellectual condition of the people'. Therefore, if the review's political and intellectual policy is to be one of modulating a large, abstract commitment with reference to specific instances (which is the passage's clear implication), then 'the people' must also be a multitude hidden beneath an ostensibly singular term. These diverse cultural pressures mentioned above, were, then, just some of the responsibilities that Marian Evans had to take on during her editorial stewardship of the *Westminster Review* from 1852 to 1854, and which she recast in new, creative forms in her new role as George Eliot from the end of that decade. In this light, it is notable that the one *Westminster* essay which is most often discussed as the intellectual fulcrum between the careers of Evans and Eliot, 'The Natural History of German Life' from 1856, grapples in comparable ways with the contending demands of abstract principle and specific instance. Evans's approving review of W. H. Riehl's sociological observations takes particular pains to praise his focus on the actual and the particular as opposed to

---

[14] 'Prospectus', *Westminster Review* 57.111 (January 1852), iii.

the typological, becoming in the process not only an implicit aesthetic and ethical manifesto, but also a stylistic template, for the works of a novelist who was not to exist in the public domain until several months later. 'If we need a true conception of the popular character to guide our sympathies rightly', she argues,

> we need it equally to check our theories, and direct us in their application. The tendency created by the splendid conquests of modern generalization, to believe that all social questions are merged in economical science, and that the relations of men to their neighbours may be settled by algebraic equations,—the dream that the uncultured classes are prepared for a condition which appeals principally to their moral sensibilities,—the aristocratic dilettantism which attempts to restore the "good old times" by a sort of idyllic masquerading, and to grow feudal fidelity and veneration as we grow prize turnips, by an artificial system of culture,—none of these diverging mistakes can co-exist with a real knowledge of the People, with a thorough study of their habits, their ideas, their motives.[15]

Anticipating some of the arguments that Ruskin was to make against Political Economy in *Unto This Last* four years later, Evans very specifically paints 'the splendid conquests of modern generalization' as insufficient, until sharpened by contact with the empirical 'real knowledge of the People'. However, as in the Prospectus, the 'People' does not carry the force of the contrast all by itself, as witnessed by the need that Evans has to specify the word's multiple referents by supplementing it with the clearly plural 'habits', 'ideas', and 'motives'. On one level, the difficulties manifest in both pieces testify to the awkward fact that the word 'people' in English, without the benefit of inflection, has to do duty for both the generalizing, singular idea (the Latin *populus*) and the plural aggregate of diverse individuals (the Latin *homines*). That said, the historical accident of a largely uninflected language's having to stand in for its ancestors is not the only reason why Victorian periodical writing can often find itself caught in overt and covert *glissades* between the singular and plural.

Another reason can be traced back to the specific nature of the nineteenth-century periodical market. The fact that so many of the major publications were strongly identified with party interests (the Tory *Blackwood's*, the Whig *Edinburgh Review*) or editorial personae (*Household Words* as the public projection of Dickens's aesthetics and politics) placed a double burden on contributors: that of doing justice to the specifics of their immediate subjects, even while their writing had to harmonize tonally with a less personalized (or, in the case of Dickens, *over*-personalized) collective and corporate identity. As Fionnuala Dillane has noted, 'Evans has a clear sense not only of the compromises that are

---

[15] 'The Natural History of German Life', in *Westminster Review* 66.129 (July 1856), 55.

an intrinsic feature of periodical publication but also of the impossibility of each individual mind reaching its ideal readers unmediated.'[16] One only need look at the way *Blackwood's* quickly metamorphosed in the popular imagination into 'Maga' (making it sound not unlike some exotic pagan deity), to recognize the force of 'brand identity' in the periodical market; but such pressures could also be felt at a local level, as with all those *Household Words* contributors who were obliged to give their work a tincture of the 'Dickensian', imitating the 'Inimitable', in order to fit in with the magazine's larger public presence. As Percy Fitzgerald, himself once identified as one of 'Dickens's Young Men', later recalled, '[o]ne result of his extraordinary influence was—he seemed, indeed, a sort of literary Gladstone [...] It is difficult now to understand the tricks that were played with this strained and exaggerated sham "Dickensese".'[17]

Thus, writers would often find themselves caught between readerly expectations on the one side, and implicit or explicit editorial coercion on the other. 'House Style' could work in Victorian periodicals as both a specific stylistic demand and a more nebulous aesthetic philosophy or political ideology, and it was often the essayistic voice itself that was charged with navigating between the particulars of what an article or essay was describing and the larger values of the publication for which the individual contributions should be seen to speak, combining empirical scrutiny with a larger cultural diagnosis. Not, in other words, unlike the signal techniques of George Eliot's fiction; although, as I shall go on to illustrate, there is, eventually, a clear winner in the contest between the two techniques.

'My table is covered with books,' Marian Evans wrote to Cara Bray from 142 Strand in October 1851, '—all to be digested by the editorial maw—I foresee terribly hard work for the next 6 weeks.'[18] Her grimly comic metaphor catches the fact that the *Westminster Review* under her editorship was going to need to fulfil diverse expectations, working as a 'digest' of contemporary ideas and texts (as witnessed by the regular 'Contemporary Literature' round-ups), but also potentially 'digesting' the raw materials in front of it. Even taking this widespread element of active, public participation into account, the *Westminster Review*'s position in the intellectual sphere of 1850s London is an unusual one. To look at Marian Evans's correspondence from this period is to witness, even by mid nineteenth-century standards, an extraordinarily varied engagement with cultural commentators. At the same time, once the new *Westminster* has made its way into the unpredictable world of readerly reception, she has to register the sheer range of responses that it has prompted ('It is amusing enough to compare the diverse and

---

[16] Fionnuala Dillane, *Before George Eliot: Marian Evans and the Periodical Press* (2013), 36.
[17] Percy Fitzgerald, *Memoirs of an Author*, 2 vols (1894), II, 156.
[18] George Eliot, to Mrs Charles Bray, October 1851, in *The George Eliot Letters*, ed. Gordon S. Haight, 9 vols (1954–78), I, 371.

contradictory opinions given by people and journals on every single article in the Review. Mr Johnson agrees with you in having an antipathy to James Martineau— therefore won't read the article. Herbert Spencer has tried and can't').[19]

As with the contests between the singular and the plural that I earlier noted at work in the *Westminster*'s prospectus, part of Evans's task as editor was clearly to maintain the review as a channel for open public debate, whilst also paying due attention to Chapman's ideal, as ventriloquized in the Prospectus, of serving the broader 'Law of Progress'. However, as her letter admits, this might be a difficult balance to strike, not least because of any periodical's inability to legislate for how different readers would read and respond to it. For one thing, as Beetham points out, '[i]t is an unusual reader of any periodical who reads every word "from cover to cover" let alone in the order in which they are printed. Most readers will construct their own order [...] The periodical, therefore, is a form which openly offers readers the chance to construct their own texts.'[20] That said, a periodical such as the *Westminster* was not completely at the mercy of readerly freedom. For one thing, the material structure of the periodical might at least 'frame' a reader's movement through the text—even if it could neither dictate nor police it. Aside from the divisions and sub-divisions between sections (which impose, however loosely, a grammar and syntax of reading), the text of the *Westminster* sometimes offers another kind of subliminal framing or marginal commentary, through the presence of the advertisements on the inside covers of individual numbers. For example, a reader of the bound version of Volume VII in 1855 would have been able to read not only a spiky review of Coventry Patmore's *The Angel in the House* ('We seem, as we read, to see our old playfellow, the ever-youthful, well-formed Grecian Eros, metamorphosed into a High Church parson, with spectacles, stand-up coat-collar, and a white cravat'), but also, inside the front cover of the April number, Chapman's advertisement for Evans's translation of *The Essence of Christianity*, which has the effect of supplementing the review's doctrinal suspicions of Patmore's alleged High-Churchiness with a suggested, more radical alternative.[21]

But, as I have been arguing throughout this chapter, the 'conversations' set up within the structural and material being of the text are not the only elements at work: the essayistic voice itself, in its addresses to its implied readers, also has an important role in navigating between the local details of the *Westminster*'s individual contributors and viewpoints, and the underlying notion of a linguistic or ideological 'House Style' (and, given how much of the *Westminster* was both conceived and written under Chapman's roof in his years at 142 Strand, 'house style' carries an extra resonance here). One of Victorian journalism's most overt

---

[19]   Eliot, to Sara Sophia Hennell (21 January 1852), in Haight, II, 4.
[20]   Beetham, 'Towards a Theory of the Periodical as a Publishing Genre', 26.
[21]   *Westminster Review*, vol. VII (1855), 283.

debts to earlier traditions of English essayism (especially the Romantic essay) is its recourse to the first-person plural, in order to mark the transit from observation to inference. If 'we' often works, as it does in the Patmore review, simply as an accepted substitute for 'I', appropriating to cultural commentary the force of the majestic plural or 'Royal We', there are also many instances where it works as the fulcrum between the two seemingly contradictory senses of the 'essayistic' that I have been describing—notably, in Evans's own pieces. Leslie Stephen offered a sharp analysis of the phenomenon of the first-person plural, observing in 1895:

> What is meant by the editorial "We"? The inexperienced person is inclined to explain it as a mere grammatical phrase which covers in turn a whole series of contributors. But any writer in a paper, however free a course may be conceded to him, finds as a fact that the "we" means something very real and potent. As soon as he puts on the mantle, he finds that an indefinable change has come over his whole method of thinking and expressing himself. He is no longer an individual but the mouthpiece of an oracle. He catches some infection of style, and feels that although he may believe what he says, it is not the independent outcome of his own private idiosyncrasy.[22]

That 'indefinable change' Stephen mentions can repeatedly be seen at work in Evans's essays and reviews—a mode of magical thinking which transforms raw observations almost unannounced into ethical examples. 'Every one who was so happy as to go mushrooming in his early days', she writes at the opening of her 1855 review of Kingsley's *Westward Ho!*,

> remembers his delight when, after picking up and throwing away heaps of dubious fungi, dear to naturalists but abhorred of cooks, he pounces on an unmistakable mushroom, with its delicate fragrance and pink lining tempting him to devour it there and then, to the prejudice of the promised dish for breakfast. We speak in parables, after the fashion of the wise, amongst whom Reviewers are always to be reckoned.[23]

At this stage in the piece, her use of 'we' is a fairly simple journalistic convention, like Stephen's 'mere grammatical convention', tipping a large ironic wink to a reader; however, when she moves on to analyse the artistic politics of Kingsley's historical novel, the pronoun does more purposeful rhetorical work:

> His view of history seems not essentially to differ from that we have all held in our childish days, when it seemed perfectly easy for us to divide mankind into the

---

[22] Sir Leslie Stephen, *The Life of Sir James Fitzjames Stephen* (1895), 216.
[23] 'Belles Lettres', in *Westminster Review*, 64.125 (July 1855), 288.

sheep and the goats, when we devoutly believed that our favourite heroes, Wallace and Bruce, and all who fought on their side, were "good", while Edward and his soldiers were all "wicked".[24]

Now, Evans is deliberately hardening the pronoun into an anthropological generalization, even while she argues *against* the dangers of unqualified generalization, looking back to the Prospectus, with its contrast between the 'wisdom of the time' and the 'condition of the people', and forward to the concerns of 'The Natural History of German Life'. There is also much in Evans's Kingsley review that anticipates the early fiction of her alter ego, such as the description of Humboldt ('he could have imagined that a certain group of Indians were the remnants of a race which had sunk from a state of well-being to one of almost hopeless barbarism'), which looks forward to the famous opening sentence of *Silas Marner* six years later ('certain pallid undersized men, who, by the side of the brawny country-folk, looked like the remnants of a disinherited race').[25] But it is particularly in the relationship between voice and authority that Eliot's fiction is most indebted to Evans's essayism: while 'we' in the latter stages of the review never loses its larding of ironic humour, 'when we devoutly believed' gestures towards an unironic sincerity, the voice of the analyst or cultural sage, that will be one of the main voices of the mature novels.

That imaginative and ethical concern with the value and limitations of generalized wisdom, and its debts to the quiddity of experience, which I have traced at work in pieces like 'The Natural History of German Life', is cast afresh when the scale of attention shifts to those valuable details which are proverbially the great quarry of the realist novel. And rarely in Eliot's novels is the back-and-forth movement between idea and example, between the voice of personal testimony and the majestic plural, more pronounced and more morally charged than at the end of *Middlemarch*. A disembodied voice, never named in the novel, is coming to the end of its story, one which not only tells of many named characters, but, as a reader comes to realize over the course of 900 pages, has been doubling as a work of intellectual genealogy, the pre-history of a narrating voice in search of its origins, of a narrator in search of her literary parents:

A new Theresa will hardly have the opportunity of reforming a conventual life, any more than a new Antigone will spend her heroic piety in daring all for the sake of a brother's burial: the medium in which their ardent deeds took its shape is for ever gone. But we insignificant people with our daily words and acts are

---

[24] 'Belles Lettres', 292.
[25] 'Belles Lettres', 293; Eliot, *Silas Marner* [1861], ed. David Carroll (1996), 5.

preparing the lives of many Dorotheas, some of which may present a far sadder sacrifice than that of the Dorothea whose story we know.[26]

The 'Finale' of *Middlemarch* blends some of the analytical techniques of the *Westminster Review* essays with a rhetorical appeal to older and more traditional imaginings of community ('we insignificant people with our daily words and acts'), becoming in the process a kind of agnostic sermon; it typifies what Eliot's novels learn from the applications of the essayistic voice that one can see and hear at work in journalistic pieces such as the *Westward Ho!* review. One of the most characteristic trajectories in the novels' narrative modes is the one illustrated in the Finale: that familiar move from observation ('the medium [...] is for ever gone') to inference and sociological conclusion ('But we insignificant people [...]'). In *Adam Bede*, for example, the facts of Seth's initial attachment to Dinah Morris ('He was but three-and-twenty, and had only just learned what it is to love') quickly modulate into one of the finest passages of extrapolation in early Eliot:

> Love of this sort is hardly distinguishable from religious feeling. What deep and worthy love is so? whether of woman or child, or art or music. Our caresses, our tender words, our still rapture under the influence of autumn sunsets, or pillared vistas, or calm majestic statues, or Beethoven symphonies, all bring with them the consciousness that they are mere waves and ripples in an unfathomable ocean of love and beauty: our emotion in its keenest moment passes from expression into silence; our love at its highest flood passes beyond its object, and loses itself in the sense of divine mystery.[27]

Eliot often figures the connections between individual experiences and the 'unfathomable' totality of existence, and between cause and effect, in terms of 'waves and ripples', much as contemporary scientists like John Tyndall did in order to illustrate their own theories of the world's workings ('every wave and every ripple asserted its right of place, and retained its individual existence, amid the crowd of other motions which agitated the water').[28] In *Silas Marner*, Dunstan Cass makes a very specific and determinate exit in Part I, Chapter 3 ('With that, Dunstan slammed the door behind him'). A reader may not be able to hear the acoustic echoes of that slamming, but the causal consequences of his disappearance ripple outwards across Eliot's narrative into a broader narrative inference: 'The lives of those rural forefathers, whom we are apt to think very prosaic

---

[26] Eliot, *Middlemarch* [1871–2], ed. David Carroll (1986), 825.

[27] Eliot, *Adam Bede* [1859], ed. Valentine Cunningham (1996), 37.

[28] John Tyndall, *Sound: A Course of Eight Lectures Delivered at the Royal Institution of Great Britain* (1867), 255.

figures—men whose only work was to ride round their land, getting heavier and heavier in their saddles, and who passed the rest of their days in the half-listless gratification of senses dulled by monotony—had a certain pathos in them nevertheless.'[29] At first, it seems that the particular instance of Dunstan's action is only there to act as a prompt for the larger sociological generalization about the squires (who are themselves 'naturally selected' for social extinction between the two halves of the novel). However, as in 'The Natural History of German Life', it is also true that the generalization is designed, paradoxically, to persuade a reader to see through archetypes and fictional clichés to the flawed, three-dimensional beings beneath them: one sense of 'essayistic' is coming to the aid of its supposed antithesis.

On one level, one could argue that these instances are evidence of Eliot's fiction fulfilling its aesthetic and ethical remit, as the novels' polyphony shares out voices and allegiances in order to register the intractably plural material on which a reader's sympathetic imagination is being invited to work. If, as she writes of *Westward Ho!*, 'human beings, human parties, and human deeds are made up of the most subtly intermixed good and evil', then narrative too might need to move between scales of existence as well as individual identities, in order to do justice to such intermixture. Indeed, some of Eliot's best modern critics have emphasized multiplicity as being central to her style. David Carroll remarks that Eliot 'saw her fictions as "experiments in life" and, as such, each experiment proceeds by the testing, juxtaposing, comparing, and contrasting of different ways of making sense of the world until coherence reaches its limit and breaks down into incoherence'. (As Kathryn Murphy notes in Chapter 3 in this volume, the Renaissance essay can also be thought of as an 'experiment in life'; suggesting another link between the different genres.)

Then again, returning to Wood's particular suspicion of 'essayism' in fiction, could one also argue that Eliot's narrative voices are open to the charge of 'breaking in to speak over their characters'? I discussed earlier how in Victorian periodical writing, the voice of essayistic authority could serve to link an article's particulars back to a publication's official or de facto house style. While nothing in Eliot's fiction ever approaches the 'improved' version of *Pride and Prejudice* that Jane Austen jokingly imagined for her sister Cassandra ('it wants to be stretched out here & there with a long Chapter—of sense if it could be had, if not of solemn specious nonsense—about something unconnected with the story; an Essay on Writing, a critique on Walter Scott, or the history of Buonaparte'), the texture of the novel's prose is one in which numerous voices and registers are often focalized and guaranteed by the voice of cultural interpretation.[30] Polyphony, then, may be

---

[29] Eliot, *Silas Marner*, 30.
[30] Jane Austen to Cassandra Austen (4 February 1813), in *Jane Austen's Letters*, ed. Deirdre Le Faye (1995), 203.

an essential part of the ethical being of Eliot's work, but some voices are, nevertheless, more equal than others; or, to cast it in the terms of Isaiah Berlin's analogy, Eliot's fiction is full of narrative foxes that want to be philosophical hedgehogs.[31]

There are even times at which it seems as if accepting the dominance of the generalizing voice is the price of the novels' magnanimity—a circumstance which takes on greater importance when one considers how many of them are historical—or, perhaps better, *historiographical* novels. *Middlemarch* may be, as I mentioned above, her most sustained and explicit attempt at an intellectual genealogy of her own late nineteenth-century moment, but all her novels share something of this impulse—notably *Silas Marner*. 'In the days when the spinning-wheels hummed busily in the farmhouses', runs the novel's opening phrase, locating Eliot's story both generically (glancing at the 'once upon a time' formulae of folk-tales whilst marking its distance from them) and historically.[32] Time and again in *Silas Marner*, the movement from particular to general is matched by a movement from past to present. In the summary of Silas's Lantern Yard life, the narrator observes of the community's religious detective-work: 'But the members were bound to take other measures for finding out the truth, and they resolved on praying and drawing lots. This resolution can be a ground of surprise only to those who are unacquainted with that obscure religious life which has gone on in the shelter of our towns.'[33] Even more inventively, Silas's emergence into a world of social sympathy is traced with the eye of a novelist who also moonlights as a comparative anthropologist, although the sequence of roles is reversed:

> Hitherto he had been treated very much as if he had been a useful gnome or brownie—a queer and unaccountable creature, who must necessarily be looked at with wondering curiosity and repulsion, and with whom one would be glad to make all greetings and bargains as brief as possible, but who must be dealt with in a propitiatory way, and occasionally have a present of pork or garden stuff to carry home with him, seeing that without him there was no getting the yarn woven.[34]

Even by Eliot's high standards, this is an extraordinary sentence: with consummate subtlety (and cheek), the focus and tone move repeatedly between ventriloquizing a modern, analytical outsider ('unaccountable creature', 'in a propitiatory way'), and the *style indirect* voice of a Raveloe insider ('a useful gnome or brownie', 'a present of pork or garden stuff'), so as to keep all the novel's different ways of seeing in play, to keep 'modern generalization' in dialogue with the views of individual 'People'. However, *Silas Marner* as a whole does not consistently

---

[31] See Isaiah Berlin, *The Hedgehog and the Fox: An Essay on Tolstoy's View of History* (1953).
[32] Eliot, *Silas Marner*, 5.   [33] Eliot, *Silas Marner*, 13.   [34] Eliot, *Silas Marner*, 129–30.

maintain such an equitable balance between its centres of consciousness: rather, like so many of the novels, it sets up an ontological hierarchy of narrative voices, in which, more often than not, a modern, encyclopedic perspective incorporates and trumps the older and other ones that it is describing.

In the light of Marian Evans's historical beliefs, this slant is understandable: for instance, Comte's version of development was both indisputably progressive and irreversible, as seen in Harriet Martineau's rendering of the theory:

> In the final, the positive state, the mind has given over the vain search after Absolute notions, the origin and destiny of the universe, and the causes of phenomena, and applies itself to the study of their laws,—that is, their invariable relations of succession and resemblance. Reasoning and observation, duly combined, are the means of this knowledge.[35]

And 'the final, the positive state' is the point from which *Silas Marner*'s narration originates, even if it is a perspective which sympathetically encompasses and acknowledges its ancestors. The novel may lay contending styles of interpretation alongside each other (Silas's Nonconformist-haunted atheism, that Christianity of spirit over letter embodied by Dolly Winthrop, and so on), but these are all overlaid by a voice that knows better, even if, by its own logic, it can never know everything, since it too will be outpaced in turn by what Eliot's narrator elsewhere calls 'the growing good of the world', *Middlemarch*'s answer to the *Westminster*'s 'Law of Progress'.[36] In his insightful *Spectator* review of the book version of *Middlemarch*, R. H. Hutton got right to the heart of the question:

> Without counting George Eliot's bitterer sarcasms,—which are only too numerous, though hardly so numerous, we think, as in former books, and sometimes not altogether pleasant,—the wealth of genuine humour in *Middlemarch* is astonishing. And it is, so far as this, of the Shakespearian kind,—that it proceeds out of a fullness of insight into the commonest modes of thought and feeling which brings them before us to the very life; only it does not usually proceed from any considerable measure of *sympathy* with that mode of thought and feeling, as it does in Shakespeare [...] On the contrary, George Eliot laughs *at* the common modes of thought and feeling much more than with them, and it is only astonishing that, this being so, it seldom or never leads her to exaggerate common people's sayings into pure farce, or to starve them into pure inanity.[37]

---

[35] *The Positive Philosophy of Auguste Comte, Freely Translated and Condensed by Harriet Martineau*, 3rd edn, 2 vols (1893), 2.

[36] Eliot, *Middlemarch*, 825.

[37] R. H. Hutton, 'The Humour of *Middlemarch*', *The Spectator* (14 December 1872); reprinted in *A Victorian Spectator: Uncollected Writings of R. H. Hutton*, ed. Robert Tener and Malcolm Woodfield (1989), 201–2.

Whether or not one concurs with the severity of Hutton's judgement, he is responding to something fundamental in Eliot's aesthetics: whether navigating between the moment and 'the Law of Progress' in the *Westminster Review*, or adjudicating between the many narrative scales of the novels, the voice of inference and diagnosis offers her at least a semblance of authority, the chance to be heard above the clamour of debating voices, even at the cost of 'speaking over' them. It is an authority which, as I shall now explore, Hardy's fiction often creatively declines.

4. Parallel Lines

Among the many grimly comic *aperçus* preserved by Hardy in his transferred autobiography (almost all written by him, but attributed to his wife Florence), one of the most resonant comes from May 1886:

> Reading in the British Museum. Have been thinking over the dictum of Hegel— that the real is the rational and the rational the real—that real pain is compatible with a formal pleasure—that the idea is all, etc., but it doesn't help much. These venerable philosophers seem to start wrong; they cannot get away from a prepossession that the world must somehow have been made to be a comfortable place for man.[38]

Over the course of his life, Hardy came to lose that consoling 'prepossession', and accordingly, in fiction, non-fiction, and poetry, his language is frequently not a comfortable place, either for man or for the variety of ways in which humans have tried to make the world safely understandable. Indeed, this grouchily profound journal entry encompasses much that is most characteristic of Hardy's mature writing: moving from the abstractions of Hegelian thought ('that the real is the rational'), to his colloquial dismissal of what those thoughts might achieve ('the idea is all, etc., but it doesn't help much'), playing out in its bathos the tragicomedy of human ideas discovering that the world is so much more and other than themselves. And central to this imaginative endeavour is Hardy's resistance to precisely that hierarchy of narrative voices on which Eliot relies. Both of the contrasting yet complementary senses of the 'essayistic' which I described above in relation to Eliot have an end, or at least the ghostly presence of an end, in sight: the experimental Renaissance essay finds its end in the act of exploring, while the more prescriptive version will try and shepherd the data it discovers towards a desired conclusion and inference. Eliot's fiction is always fundamentally

---

[38] Thomas Hardy, 'Florence Hardy', in *The Early Life of Thomas Hardy, 1840–1891* (1928), 234.

committed to a secular teleology, to the idea of a point of convergence and synthesis; even if, by the logic of history she inherits from Comte and Darwin, that end may be unknowably far in the future, beyond the make-believe of any ending that a human individual might imagine. However, having lost his belief in any conventional form of religious higher power, Hardy in turn abjures such teleological faith, and refuses to grant any styles of language a higher status than others; thus, stripped of the very authority on which Eliot's writing relies, the different voices in his texts have to contend on equal terms. In this Darwinian 'Struggle for Life', then, there are no 'Favoured Races'.

Many of Hardy's contemporaries were quick to point out parallels, whether stylistic or thematic, between his fiction and Eliot's; for instance, in his fulsome praise of Hardy in the *British Quarterly Review* from 1881, Charles Kegan Paul noted that 'George Eliot has for the most part taken a society which changes little—homely people with homely lives. It has been remarked that a boundless sympathy was her characteristic, but on a somewhat low level. Mr Hardy, in the same way, but to an even greater extent, takes life where it changes least, and considers it in its most simply human aspects.'[39] Given Marian Evans's recent death and its impact on metropolitan literary culture, it is understandable that Kegan Paul should bring together Hardy's achievement with Eliot's legacy, but even during Eliot's lifetime, the writers were being bracketed together: the *Spectator* famously suspected the serial version of *Far from the Madding Crowd* of being Eliot's work, and even Henry James's typically waspish review of the book version remarked that Hardy had 'caught very happily her trick of seeming to humour benignantly her queer people and look down at them from the heights of analytic omniscience'.[40] However, such comparisons may lead a reader to underplay the crucial differences between the two novelists, the way in which Hardy, like a curmudgeonly literary hermit-crab, moves into the structures bequeathed to him by Eliot's example, yet turns them into a different beast altogether.

It was not only Hardy's choice of social focus that led critics to yoke him with Eliot; like Eliot before him, the textures of his narratives respond to the plural nature of nineteenth-century existence, playing that variety out in the mixture of their registers. The debt is palpable in passages such as this, in *Far from the Madding Crowd*:

> The only superiority in women that is tolerable to the rival sex is, as a rule, that of the unconscious kind: but a superiority which recognizes itself may sometimes please by suggesting possibilities of capture to the subordinated man.

[39] Charles Kegan Paul in *British Quarterly Review* 73 (1881); reprinted in R. G. Cox (ed.), *Thomas Hardy: The Critical Heritage* (1970), 81.

[40] Henry James, review in *The Nation*, 495 (24 December 1874); reprinted in Cox, *Thomas Hardy*, 28.

This well-favoured and comely girl soon made appreciable inroads on the emotional constitution of young Farmer Oak.[41]

and in the much-discussed final chapter of *Tess of the d'Urbervilles*:

Upon the cornice of the tower a tall staff was fixed. Their eyes were riveted on it. A few minutes after the hour had struck something moved slowly up the staff, and extended itself upon the breeze. It was a black flag.

'Justice' was done, and the President of the Immortals, in Aeschylean phrase, had ended his sport with Tess. And the d'Urberville knights and dames slept on in their tombs unknowing.[42]

Both these passages have elements that bear stylistic comparison with Eliot's fiction: the commingling of analytical generalization with narrative contingency, the dramatizing of eclectic experience through multiple registers (although Eliot would never have allowed herself the grisly figurative humour of juxtaposing 'fixed' and 'riveted'). But there is one important difference: nowhere in Hardy's fiction can a reader feel secure of the existence of that hierarchy of registers, with the result that the 'essayistic' voice, while at least as present as it in Eliot, does not have anything like the dominance, or the unifying force, that it has in the earlier novelist's work. John Bayley captures this quality well when he remarks of the fertile 'instability' of the novels' prose: 'There is a sharp contrast in it between the physical perceptions, which are always his own, and the opinions and ideas which seldom are: it is indeed a part of his honesty to advertise their coming from somewhere else.'[43] At the end of *Tess*, the blatancy of 'in Aeschylean phrase' combines with the Jamesian scare-quotes around '"Justice"', to tag both the allusion and the sentiment as coming clearly from 'somewhere else'; but this is just as true of the generalizing, aphoristic voice that opens the fourth chapter of *Far from the Madding Crowd*. In Hardy, then, *everything* potentially comes from somewhere else, so that 'strips of essayism' remain just that. As in Eliot, multiple registers answer to and embody the multiple hermeneutic modes in which the late nineteenth century was compelled to live at once; however, there is no longer any reassurance that one way of speaking or understanding trumps another, nor any promise of synthesis, a promise that the novels' different sight-lines will converge, or be made to appear to do so.

In 'Memories of Church Restoration' (1906), Hardy wrote that 'the opposing tendencies excited in the architect by the distracting situation can find no

---

[41] Hardy, *Far from the Madding Crowd* [1873–4], ed. Ronald Blythe (1978), 73.
[42] Hardy, *Tess of the d'Urbervilles* [1891], ed. David Skilton (1978), 489.
[43] John Bayley, *An Essay on Hardy* (1978), 17.

satisfactory reconciliation'.[44] And so it is in Hardy's fiction: the essayistic and the novelistic, with their distinctive blends of cherished particulars and broad diagnoses, speak alongside, not over each other, in an art that makes a virtue of its own irreconcilabilities, and marks Hardy himself out as one of the first great cartographers of that modern landscape described by William James, a landscape beyond convergence and conclusion, where everything remains 'essay':

> There were times when Leibnizes with their heads buried in monstrous wigs could compose Theodicies, and when stall-fed officials of an established church could prove by the valves in the heart and the round ligament of the hip-joint the existence of a "Moral and Intelligent Contriver of the World". But those times are past; and we of the nineteenth century, with our evolutionary theories and our mechanical philosophies, already know nature too impartially and too well to worship unreservedly any God of whose character she can be an adequate expression. Truly, all we know of good and duty proceeds from nature; but none the less so all we know of evil. Visible nature is all plasticity and indifference—a moral multiverse, as one might call it, and not a moral universe.[45]

---

[44] Hardy, *Thomas Hardy's Personal Writings*, ed. Harold Orel (1967), 217.

[45] William James, 'Is Life Worth Living?' [1895] in *Writings 1878–1899*, ed. Gerald Myers (1992), 489.

14

Rational Distortions

Essayism in the British Novel after Borges

Michael Wood

1. Catching Fire

The essay-novel, or the novel that did much of the work often associated with the essay, flourished in the United Kingdom after 1945, and especially in the 1980s and 1990s. To understand the particular qualities of this flourishing, we need to go back a little in time.

English novelists of the eighteenth century didn't think essays and novels were the same, but they didn't think they were all that different either, and they were sure they could inhabit the same pages. Fielding prefaced each of the eighteen books of *Tom Jones* with a discursive essay; Sterne's *Tristram Shandy* could be thought of as a garrulous essay masquerading as a novel.[1] There are essays small and large dotted throughout the novels of Balzac and Stendhal, as well as those of Tolstoy and Eliot. And in the case of Virginia Woolf, as Hermione Lee says, '[t]he overlap between essays and fiction is pervasive'.[2]

Something had happened, however, in the meantime. Tolstoy and Eliot didn't know they were creating what Henry James called 'loose, baggy monsters', baggy in part because they were so fond of essays.[3] The modern streamlining of the novel found its rationale in James's prefaces to the New York edition of his work, and even more perhaps in Percy Lubbock's *The Craft of Fiction* (1921), an enormously influential schematization of James's aesthetic for the novel. Readers were to trust the tale and not the artist, as D. H. Lawrence suggested only a little later, and even Proust, who had not read James or Lubbock but had picked up parallel prescriptions from a related intellectual climate, had the narrator of his novel remark that 'a work in which there are theories is like an object with its price-tag still

---

[1] See this volume, Chapter 5, by Fred Parker, for discussion of Fielding, 129–31, and Chapter 6, by Scott Black, for discussion of Sterne, and the essay and eighteenth-century novel more generally.

[2] Hermione Lee, 'Virginia Woolf's Essays', in *The Cambridge Companion to Virginia Woolf*, ed. Sue Roe and Susan Sellers (2010), 98.

[3] See Henry James, *The Art of the Novel: Critical Prefaces*, ed. R. P. Blackmur (2011), 84.

Michael Wood, *Rational Distortions: Essayism in the British Novel after Borges* In: *On Essays: Montaigne to the Present*. Edited by: Thomas Karshan and Kathryn Murphy, Oxford University Press (2020). © Michael Wood.
DOI: 10.1093/oso/9780198707868.003.0015

attached'.[4] Proust, that great theorizer? Well, yes. Both his work and that of James himself are full of wonderful essays. But a good purist theory rides easily over contradictions.

The effect of the theory, once it was diffused into a casual-seeming but well-policed orthodoxy, was so strong that the novels of Mann and Musil, in their devotion to essayism, looked rather like defiances of an orthodoxy, and William Empson could write that 'much of Proust reads like the work of a superb appreciative critic upon a novel which has unfortunately not survived'.[5] Insofar as the New Criticism interested itself in the novel, which was not very far, this was its theory too: no heresy like the heresy of paraphrase, and digression still worse. Woolf, as we have seen, was following a quietly deviant path of her own, but Joyce was magnificently in line, enough to give the line a boost beyond anyone's imagining.

The twentieth century saw some practical dissent from the orthodoxy, and there are magnificent discursive passages in the novels of Iris Murdoch, William Golding, and J. G. Ballard. There are fine instances in the realm of science fiction too, as well as in certain forms of non-scientific fantasy. But the orthodoxy held, and to some extent still holds, at least in creative writing programmes and the minds of conservative critics: showing is primary, telling confined to its proper, minor place, and reflection outlawed.

In this chapter I want to explore works that not only dissent from the orthodoxy but discreetly invert it. They don't return to the old easy crossing of boundaries between novel and essay, or they don't merely return; they devise a new role for fiction that thinks, and they implicate fiction itself in the act of thinking. The essayistic qualities of fiction here are less the extent to which a novel incorporates discursive passages on topics not immediately pertinent to its developing narrative; or passages of speculative rumination, as we find in Fielding or Eliot, for example; or the way in which a novel incorporates facts. Rather, this chapter is interested in novels which use fiction as a way of trialling, interrogating, or testing ideas, indulging in the etymological sense of essaying, and the ways in which this unsettles the senses of both 'fiction' and 'essay'. When Julian Barnes won the 1986 Prix Médicis for the essay, the book in question was his novel *Flaubert's Parrot*. Were the judges behind the time or ahead of it; making a category mistake or sensing a new direction?

A rather mysterious distinction made by T. W. Adorno may help us to pursue the question. He argues that the essay, as distinct from the article or the monograph, 'stops where it feels itself complete—not where nothing is left to say'.[6] This is almost

---

[4] D. H. Lawrence, *Studies in Classic American Literature* (2003), 14; Marcel Proust, *In Search of Lost Time*, trans. Ian Patterson, 6 vols (2002), VI, 190.

[5] William Empson, *Seven Types of Ambiguity* (1966), 249.

[6] Theodor Adorno, 'The Essay as Form', trans. Bob Hullot-Kentor and Frederic Will, *New German Critique* 32 (Spring–Summer 1984), 152.

true of the works I want to consider. They do stop, and they never suggest that nothing is left to say. But because of their allegiance to the sceptical lineage of the essay they also create a feeling of something less than completeness. The story ends but the analytic questions it proposes are still trying to find their focus.

The shadowy but omnipresent figure in this development is Jorge Luis Borges, although to speak of his influence (or perhaps of any one writer's) is to speak too loud. The tracing is easier if we think of American authors. John Barth and Thomas Pynchon openly acknowledge Borges in their work, and Tony Tanner, in his masterly critical work *City of Words*, saw Borges, along with Nabokov, as a presiding spirit over what he called the 'lexical playfields' of American fiction since the 1950s. There are plenty of open references to Borges in Europe too, in the work of Georges Perec and Italo Calvino, for example. Calvino suggested that Borges had an important effect on 'literature in Italian, on literary taste and even on the idea of literature itself'.[7] It's true that Salman Rushdie said Borges was one of his 'passports' to literature; that Julian Barnes remembers in detail a lecture Borges gave in Oxford; that Graham Swift generously if rather vaguely acknowledges the impact of magical realism.[8] But it is quite a way from magical realism to Borges, a memory may be just a memory, and Rushdie made more visible use of the passports called Gabriel García Márquez and Günter Grass.

This is not to say Borges is less present in Britain than in the United States, only that we need to look for him in literary works, without counting on too much help from open declarations. This Borges is well represented in the sly joke that governs the prologue to *Ficciones* (1944). He asserts that writing big books is just too much work, 'a laborious and impoverishing extravagance'. 'A better course of procedure', he says, 'is to pretend that these books already exist, and then to offer a résumé, a commentary.' Carlyle and Samuel Butler have done this, Borges says, but their discussions of books have the defect of being books themselves, and he himself, 'more reasonable, more inept, more indolent', has kept the idea of imaginary works but chosen simply 'to write notes' on them.[9] The creative mischief of the joke lies in its apparently casual dismissal of the orthodoxy I have been describing. Borges is implying not only that commentary is permissible within a text of any kind, but that we might prefer to concentrate on the commentary. And in his story 'The Approach to Al-Mu'tasim', he does exactly what he proposes in his prologue: describes a non-existent novel and writes an essay about it.

Borges is unlikely to have read Adorno's reflections on the essay form, but he manifestly implements one of the philosopher's significant claims and redirects

---

[7] Italo Calvino, *Why Read the Classics*, trans. Martin McLaughlin (1999), 237.

[8] Salman Rushdie, 'Introduction' to Günter Grass, *On Writing and Politics, 1967–1983*, trans. Ralph Manheim (1985), x; Julian Barnes, 'La Vida, una maldita cosa detras de la otra', *Clarín*, suplemento cultural (13 June 1996); Patrick McGrath, 'Graham Swift', *BOMB Magazine* 15 (1 April 1986).

[9] Jorge Luis Borges, *Ficciones*, trans. Anthony Kerrigan (1962), 15.

another. Adorno writes of the material of the essay as 'individual experience, unified in hope and disillusion' (156). This is the mood of much of Borges's writing. His essays and his fiction announce their failure with such grace and irony that it looks like success, creating an Argentinian reflection of what Thomas Harrison describes as a general modern fate: the need 'to formulate [...] truth in its absence'.[10] Of course in important ways this failure *is* a success: an absent truth is not a dead truth, or a lie.

And then, taking his cue from Lukács, who wrote that 'the essay is always concerned with something already formed, or at best, with something that has been', Adorno says 'the effort of the essay reflects a childlike freedom that catches fire, without scruple, on what others have already done' (152). The image of catching fire is splendid, and this is what often happens. But Borges widens the range. He implies that essays can also tackle what no one has done yet except the essayist. This is a way of saying fiction can reflect on fiction but it also points to a deeper, more elusive and productive worry. In the works of Angela Carter, Julian Barnes, W. G. Sebald, and Kazuo Ishiguro the very notion of the 'already formed', of what 'has been', comes into question, and reality, along with fantasy, looks like a slightly premature classification.

2. Everything Excessive

Angela Carter was no doubt exaggerating when she said that Borges's work, as English readers and writers came to know it in the wake of his sharing the first Formentor Prize with Samuel Beckett in 1961, 'rocked the entire mainstream to its foundations', or turned him into 'a kind of household god' for the very people who didn't know how dangerous he was, but she was right about his long-term effect.[11] In a piece written three years earlier, in 1979, Carter not only offers a more nuanced view of Borges (his 'finest stories [...] radiate an icy, serene disquiet, sometimes a mysterious and desolating anguish'), she actually describes what was already her own practice. She says of 'Tlön, Uqbar, Orbis Tertius', the first story in *Ficciones*, that it is 'full of real dread', and concerns 'the imposition of a fictive culture that displaces reality'.[12] This is precisely the subject of her novel *The Infernal Desire Machines of Dr Hoffmann* (1972), but it is also significant that the dread and the fictive culture, in her novel as in Borges's story, are evoked in a combination of detailed fantasy and speculative argument.

The novel is structured around two related insights: that reality can be willed or even just described into being, as with racism or false accusations that take effect; that the reality we know, the solid ground of old realist novels, has become shaky

---

[10] Thomas Harrison, *Essayism* (1992), 220.   [11] Angela Carter, *Shaking a Leg* (1997), 35–6.
[12] Carter, *Shaking a Leg*, 460.

and vulnerable, and so is no longer our stubborn opponent but our unreliable, threatened ally. It is very hard to see how these insights could be pursued without the dimension of overt, analytic reflection that the essay can lend to a novel, but also hard to see how the process could come alive if there were not some serious mutual leakage between the modes, such that the mixed form enacts the invasion.

Carter's novel is narrated by a man called Desiderio, who is not quite able to live up to the allegorical transparency of his name. He does lots of desiring but he also has a lingering affection for reason, and for the world as it is before fantasy starts changing everything. Magical things happen to an unnamed city when 'the Reality War' begins (24). It suffers a 'phantasmagoric redefinition' (12), and becomes a place of endless mirages: 'Nothing in the city was what it seemed' (3). The cathedral vanishes, for example, 'in a blaze of melodious fireworks' (26). Desiderio tells us that only dreams appear real to the city's inhabitants now—because they are known to be dreams—'while the stuff of our waking hours, so buffeted by phantoms, had grown thin and insubstantial enough to seem itself no more than seeming' (14).

He works for the Minister of Determination, 'who wanted to freeze the entire freak show the city had become back into attitudes of perfect propriety' (4), which sounds pretty unappealing, but one of the points of the book is to frighten us into a respect for such loyalty to the world as it is. The plot of the novel involves various erratic travels—a few months with an indigenous people that lives in boats, a long sojourn with a close relative of Count Dracula, a session in a Sadean brothel among animals and appliances borrowed from Surrealism, a spell among centaurs in Africa—that are a bit too violent and lengthy for their own narrative good, but just what Carter needs for the essayistic aspect of her work. Desiderio encounters many instances of the malleability of reality, and also a spectacular instance of its opposite: sheer nature, what happens without the intervention of anyone's fear or desire. He makes this discovery through the sudden destruction of a provincial town:

> The landslide could only be a simple assertion of the dominance of nature herself who, in the service only of the meaningless, reintegrated the city with chaos and then, her business done, casually abandoned it. It was an event of too massive arbitrariness for me to comprehend [...]   (139)

The book celebrates what it attacks, it doubts both desire and reason, and it recruits all kinds of pieces of culture for its purposes: Debussy, Satie, Lautréamont, film theory, Gothic novels, pornography high and low, and much more. It has dozens of ideas, and it turns plot and character into weird vestiges, memories of what other writers use. The story-line—young man falls in love with the titular doctor's daughter but in the end has to kill parent and child—is what the novel announces and then largely ignores; and the characters are either incarnations of arguments or clusters of allusions to types and myths. Desiderio's description of the sinister, imperious Count is subtle and revealing:

> I think what made him so attractive to me was his irony, which withered every word before he spoke it. Everything about him was excessive, yet he tempered his vulgarity—for he was excessively vulgar in every respect—with a black, tragic humour of which he was only occasionally conscious himself.   (143)

It comes as a salutary shock to realize that this is a manifesto, or rather a mock-manifesto hiding a real one. Irony, vulgarity, a humour that 'only occasionally' knows itself: these are features of the novel itself, of course, but not in fact of the essay woven into it. That essay is certainly ironic but not withering; vulgar only insofar as it resists the idea of good taste; and fully aware of what it is up to. In spite of the nod to Proust in the name of Desiderio's love Albertina, Carter thinks the great modern writers would even greater if they laughed at themselves more. It's important to know that desire can make or destroy the world, and that reason and reality are all too often keen to collaborate in their own demise. Carter's essay-question is how we are to live under such conditions, what a liberated, enlarged idea of sanity might mean for us. Perhaps we can't be saved except by vulgar ex-truths that will survive mockery.

3. In-Between Times

Carter's novels look like novels, whatever their debt or allusive connection to Borges may be. There are also, however, novels that don't look like novels. *Flaubert's Parrot* (1984) is a case in point, as its Prix Médicis category suggests, but it doesn't look like an essay either. It looks like a loosely assembled memoir, or a series of long journal entries. The sections are thematically arranged, and although the themes are whimsically chosen they all circle around the life and work of Gustave Flaubert. There is a 'case against' Flaubert, an ironic reconstruction of his mistress's view of him, a chronology, a 'Flaubert bestiary', a mock examination paper, and a parody of a *Dictionary of Received Ideas*.

The narrator, Geoffrey Braithwaite, is very funny, in spite of his dogged dejection, and his first essay-question is which of the stuffed parrots still available for inspection served as the model for the transcendental parrot at the end of Flaubert's story 'A Simple Heart', which turns into the Holy Ghost. There are candidates at Flaubert's house at Croisset, and at the museum in Rouen. And then, at the end of the book, Braithwaite discovers three more possibilities in another local museum. It's known that Flaubert borrowed a parrot to help him write his story, but does anyone know which one it was, or whether it was any of these five? Does it matter?

It doesn't matter concretely, even to Braithwaite. But certainty in such an instance would be an encouraging, if comic model for certainty in other cases regarding objects or events in the past. Braithwaite is asking if there is a way back from fiction to reality, and he needs to know because, as we guess before we are very far into the book, he is himself a version of Flaubert's famous sad sack Charles Bovary, Emma's husband, since he too is a doctor and his wife was unfaithful and has committed suicide. He knows that Flaubert was not joking when he said that everything one invents is true.

There are plenty of differences to separate Braithwaite from Charles Bovary— his Englishness for one thing, the fact that he has read the novel for another—and his wife is no mere echo of Emma Bovary: 'She wasn't corrupted; her spirit didn't coarsen; she never ran up bills' (164). And again: 'I'm not saying that Ellen's secret life led her into despair. For God's sake, her life is not a moral tale. No one's is' (166). Still, Braithwaite is unremittingly aware of the connection. We may think he is telling us all this stuff about Flaubert, showing off his knowledge, pretending he may write a scholarly article or a book, solely in order to avoid talking about his wife. And we shan't be wrong, not least because he says we're not—or perhaps not. 'Ellen's is a true story; perhaps it is even the reason I am telling you Flaubert's story instead' (86).

But there is one thing Braithwaite wants more than displacement of his grief, more than certainty about the past or an escape from fiction. He wants desperately *not* to believe, as almost everything he learns tells him he should, that there are no answers, that history just happens and then vanishes. He is grimly sarcastic about what he calls 'our own wry and unfoolable age', 'our pragmatic and knowing century' (69, 88). The implication is that we can't be fooled because we don't care enough about the truth to miss it.

'How do we seize the past?' he asks. 'Can we ever do so?' The question recurs with variations. 'How do we seize the foreign past?' 'So how do we seize the past? As it recedes, does it come into focus?' (14, 90, 100). Braithwaite's pain, his book-length attempt to shift his failure to understand (or to forget) his wife into a disquisition on the notionally understandable Flaubert, are what make this work a novel, and not an eccentric critical study borrowing a novel's framework. But Braithwaite's explorations open up to us not only the psychology of a suffering man, but a series of essayistic questions about knowledge of others and the past, quite different in their fields of action from the questions Carter poses but very similar in structure and content. Braithwaite continues to use the word fiction as if he knew the facts. In one instance it means local legends; in another he associates it with dream and imposture. But he has learned the Borgesian lesson so important to Barnes and his contemporaries: 'I have to invent my way to the truth' (165). Another, more delicate way of putting this in Braithwaite's case might be to say one can give up being unfoolable without becoming a fool, and there is a wonderful image of this possibility in his thought about changing seasons and cross-channel ferries:

> I like these out-of season crossings. When you're young you prefer the vulgar months, the fullness of the seasons. As you grow older you learn to like the in-between times, the months that can't make up their minds. Perhaps it's a way of admitting that things can't ever bear the same certainty. Or perhaps it's just a way of admitting a preference for empty ferries.   (83)

Giving up the old certainty is not the same as giving up on certainty entirely, just as not making up your mind is quite different from deciding not to decide.

Barnes's next book, *Staring at the Sun* (1986), looks like a novel, albeit a novel full of questions, but the work after that, *A History of the World in 10½ Chapters* (1989), is something else again. It is in the end as much a novel as *Flaubert's Parrot* is, but it looks like a series of essays, and the appearance is an essential part of the effect. At its emotional centre is an unnumbered chapter called 'Parenthesis', in which a man writes about a sleeping woman and worries about love and its chances of resisting history. The other chapters are numbered 1 to 10, so this must be the half named in the title. It's a fragile proportion, especially since the chapter ends by identifying the history of the world as the enemy. 'And when love fails, we should blame the history of the world [...] Our love has gone, and it is the fault of the history of the world.'[13] But this is not the narrator's final thought. The odds are not at all good, but 'in the night the world can be defied' (244). This is the implication of a marvellous reading, a few pages earlier, of Auden's famous line 'We must love one another or die.' Auden himself came to believe the sentence was simply a lie, and didn't reprint the poem. Barnes's narrator says Auden's later view is 'narrow or forgetful', and suggests these interpretations: 'we must love one another because if we don't we are liable to end up killing each other'; 'we must love one another because if we don't [...] then we might as well be dead' (231).

But why is our man so attuned to the chances of unhappiness, so talkative about the history that threatens him? Perhaps he is thinking of the opening of another Auden poem: 'Lay your sleeping head, my love, / Human on my faithless arm'. He might want to switch the adjectives of the second line and worry about the woman's head lying faithless on his human arm. Whatever he feels, this is the heart of the novel, and his worry is the source of all the other chapters, which take the form of a series of essays and short narratives. The parenthesis itself is littered with metaphors and emblems that evoke the other chapters of the book: waves, currents, captains, ships, swimming, Columbus, the Titanic. The first chapter is

---

[13] Barnes, *A History of the World in 10½ Chapters* (1990), 244. Further references given in the text.

narrated by a woodworm that managed to stow away on Noah's ark, and a later chapter reconstructs the trial of a tribe of woodworms by an ecclesiastical court in fifteenth-century France. Deathwatch beetles show up in these and other stories. The general theme is species survival, as figured in the ark, and the ark in turn provokes a series of maritime fables and allusions. The other eight chapters narrate the invasion of a cruise ship by terrorists (the passengers are said to board 'two by two' (33)); the adventure of a woman who escapes to a desert island, perhaps in her mind, perhaps in the actual world; the story behind and of Géricault's painting 'The Raft of the Medusa'; a nineteenth-century journey to Mount Ararat; two ship disasters framing a speculation on the myth of Jonah; drownings during a film shoot in South America; the construction of a North Carolina model of Noah's vessel; and the narrator's arrival and afterlife in an unexpectedly cosy and horribly eternal heaven, the ultimate ark.

There is manifestly no single solution suggested by these tales and reflections but taken together they do represent a funny, frightened, and very particular history of a threatened world. It might be consoling, if you are worrying about whether love can survive the world's onslaughts, to think that history itself is a form of fiction—'fabulation' is the word Barnes's narrator prefers (109, 110, 112, 240). Wouldn't this help, if you were 'scared by history', 'bullied by dates' (239)? Alas no, because here as in *Flaubert's Parrot* and in Angela Carter's world, the loss of history may be worse than the loss of love.

There is a remedy in Barnes's writing, and a surprising one, that is even clearer in *A History of the World* than in earlier work. It's surprising because it is not a feature we associate with the apparently so fastidious Barnes: a vulgarity different in reach and content from Carter's, but vulgarity all the same. Its chief mode is the terrible pun, the tasteless connection or slippage of idiom. The animals are not going to 'rock the boat' when they are on the ark, but they may have 'the stuffing knocked out of them', and 'put back into them—before they are braised or boiled' (4, 27). What is the chance of the survivors of the Medusa being rescued? 'A drop in the ocean' (134). The myth of Jonah and the whale is 'a fishy story, as you might expect' (175). The man enjoying the afterlife says 'I knew I was in seventh heaven' (288). There is nothing to be said for these jokes as jokes; everything to be said for them as anarchic invasions of seriousness, chronic wreckages of tone. In a much later work, *Levels of Life* (2013), an open combination this time of essay, fiction, and moving memoir, there are also blatant and lumpy clashes of literary and figurative uses ('Opera cuts to the chase', 'If I cannot hack it without her, I will hack at myself', 'thinking [. . .] can cut both ways') but they are even more closely linked to the idea of pattern and repetition, reappearance, even resurrection.[14] Barnes shows us impeccably how much we need shape and design and taste, how

---

[14] Barnes, *Levels of Life* (2013), 92,113, 80.

we can't live without them. Like love, they are part of our resistance to the unfortunate, one-way history of the world. But we also need to laugh at them, however lightly, let them play the clown, drop their dignity. This way they afford the characteristic double consolation of the essay: the mind makes meaning and also understands how meaning flickers and fades and looks like a too solemn fable.

4. Darker Histories

When W. G. Sebald asserts that '[m]y medium is prose, not the novel', the remark cries out with everything it does not say.[15] It does not say he writes essays or memoirs, and it does not say he avoids fiction. He has a reason, as we shall see in a moment, for distinguishing between fiction and the novel—a distinction we have not really needed to make so far in this chapter.

Fiction is not a new English word as far the dictionary goes, but it finds a new application in the 1960s. If we don't look to Borges (or his translators) for a source or a clarification, we could look to the poetry of Wallace Stevens or the echoes of Stevens's thought in the critical work of Frank Kermode. In each case the word means something like 'imaginative contribution to our understanding of the real, hypothetical behaviour or proposition that illuminates what is not hypothetical'. Stevens, for example, writes of 'the fiction of an absolute', and 'the more than rational distortion, / The fiction that results from feeling'.[16] Kermode says a fiction is 'consciously false' yet 'helps us to make sense of and move in the world'.[17] It can't be tested like a theory, it can only work for us or fall into neglect. It can also, we might add, be ignored or ridiculed, and it can, as Kermode says, keep some very bad company—it is not always easy to separate it from pernicious myth. Borges would add that 'consciously false' is a little too confident about our knowledge. When the invented alien world takes over in 'Tlön, Uqbar', we are told that 'in all memories, a fictitious past occupies the place of any other. We know nothing about it with any certainty, not even that it is false.'[18] That's how it is with fictions. They formally declare their independence of the truth, make no literal claim to it. However, they can't be guaranteed not to tell the truth they are supposedly liberated from. 'Who can ever boast', Borges says in one of his finest lines, 'of being a mere imposter'?[19] We may, alas, intend to lie and then tell the truth in spite of ourselves. This instability of fiction is part of the enormous usefulness of the concept, and one of the reasons why the writing of fiction may need to conscript the essay.

---

[15] Quoted in W. G. Sebald, *Campo Santo*, trans. Anthea Bell (2006), xi.
[16] Wallace Stevens, *Selected Poems* (2011), 217, 219.
[17] Frank Kermode, *The Sense of an Ending* (2000), 64, 37.   [18] Borges, *Ficciones*, 34.
[19] Borges, *Ficciones*, 71.

Sebald was a German writer whose first major essayistic work was *Vertigo* (1990), translated into English only when other books had made him famous. We need to remember this context when we read him, as we need to read his English texts as the (however excellent) translations that they are. He is important in this chapter not only because of the standing he rapidly earned among English-speaking writers and readers but also because he represents a different essay terrain—as far as stance and subject matter go—from the one we have been looking at, one that is almost antithetical to it. Sebald doesn't ask how we are to seize the past or how we are to cope with a reality that is caving in to dream. He asks how we are to live with a past that will not let us go. 'They are ever returning to us, the dead', he writes in *The Emigrants* (1996).[20] The same book describes an artist whose studio is full of scrupulously undisturbed dust, which this man has come to understand, 'he loved more than anything else in the world. He felt closer to dust, he said, than to light, air or water' (161). The protagonist of *Austerlitz* (2001) is constantly subject to the pull of what he calls 'the vortex of past time', and asks 'Might it not be that we also have appointments to keep in the past[?]'.[21] He's not really asking. His life is a series of such appointments, often kept, often missed, and sometimes kept and missed at the same moment. They take place in old Belgian fortifications and English train stations, in Prague and in Theresienstadt/Terezín. Austerlitz and the unnamed narrator meet up occasionally over several decades, have long talks each time, which the narrator reports in apparently faithful detail. Austerlitz came to England from Czechoslovakia as a child on a *Kindertransport*; his parents died in different camps. We learn this only gradually, though, as Austerlitz himself did. The novel here (which is not a novel, he would say) is the story of his appointments with the past. The essay, which is threaded into every page, is a meditation, in which the narrator also plays a discreet part, on a history that will not go away.

Over the course of the narrative, Austerlitz completes his studies in architecture, becomes an academic in London, and retires. He decides, in what is perhaps the most haunting moment in this magnificent book, that his 'true place of work should have been there in the little fortress of Terezín' (283), the place once built for the Empress Maria Theresa, later used so notoriously by the Nazis. He is thinking of the fortress and not the camp, and specifically of the records room in the fortress, and he is doing his thinking in the new *Bibliothèque nationale* in Paris, not at all far from the railway station that shares his name. He doesn't like the vast spaces of the new 'Babylonian library' (288), which a member of the staff regards as seeking by its architecture 'to exclude the reader as a potential enemy' (286).

---

[20] Sebald, *The Emigrants*, trans. Michael Hulse (1996), 23. ['So also kehren sie wieder, die Toten', *Die Ausgewanderten* (1992), 36.]

[21] Sebald, *Austerlitz*, trans. Anthea Bell (2001), 129, 258. Further references given in the text.

Sebald gives us a full page photograph of the library from the outside, taken by a photographer who seems keen to exclude himself. By contrast the room at Terezín seems bare but welcoming, and this time Sebald provides a visual two-page spread. This is the picture Austerlitz says he has seen, and indeed since he did not enter the fortress, his phrase 'at the sight of the records room' must mean at the sight of this photograph: 'a large-format photograph showing the room filled with open shelves up to the ceiling where the files on the prisoners [...] are kept today' (283). There's a small desk, a table with chairs, an open door, and a clock on the wall. The shelves are divided into square or rectangular boxes, like pigeon-holes for mail; none of them is full, the files tilt sideways. We are looking at (I take it) a reproduction of an actual photograph of an actual room, a record of a place of records. We are sharing the view with a fictional character—two fictional characters, Jacques Austerlitz and the narrator—and a real author, as well as with thousands of real readers. We don't have to get too dizzy at the complication of this vision, but it's worth noting that Austerlitz's idea of this room as 'true place of work' both shapes our seeing, and is in turn filtered through all the lenses on offer. Do we think we could also work here? The place is austere but old-fashioned; it's empty, it's waiting for us. How could we work here? There are no books, only prisoners' files, orderly, abandoned arrangements of paper in memory of people who are (most of them surely) now dead; the clock will always say six o'clock. The answer to these questions matters less than our realization of how deeply they take us into the emotional world of an imaginary character caught up in a far from imaginary history. Babylon, Austria, Paris, Terezín: what do we get if we put them together?

What Austerlitz gets from this conjunction, as from quite a few others, is a theory of design, and what the narrator calls 'a kind of historical metaphysic' (13). 'The marks of pain', he says, 'trace countless fine lines through history' (14). Railway architecture, he says, carries stories of 'leave-taking and the fear of foreign places, although such ideas were not part of architectural history proper' (14). But then Austerlitz is not a proper architectural historian. He is interested in 'the family likeness' between one building and another, and the way further resemblances unfold: among 'law courts and penal institutions [...] stock exchanges, opera houses and lunatic asylums, and the dwellings built to regular grid patterns for the labour force' (33). A state archives building in Prague reminds him of 'a prison [...] a monastery, a riding school, an opera house, and a lunatic asylum' (144–5). We note the recurring locales, sites of confinement and artifice. Of music too. Austerlitz is thinking of the *Bibliothèque nationale* when he comes to his quietly lurid conclusion about humankind and its buildings, but other times and places have clearly invaded the library, and our objection to his claim is not going to be its range, only its assertion of an inevitable doom:

> I came to the conclusion that in any project we design and develop, the size and
> degree of complexity of the information and control systems inscribed in it are

the crucial factors, so that the all-embracing and absolute perfection of the concept can in practice coincide, indeed absolutely must coincide, with its chronic dysfunction and constitutional instability   (281).

The argument from size and complexity to perfection to dysfunction has some serious gaps in it, but Sebald is not trying to lecture to us, and he wants us to see Austerlitz's claim as both historically interesting and oddly tilted, the proposition of a man with a semi-magical theory of architecture. And we do see a sort of fable lurking in the claim. An ambitious concentration camp project, let's say, will fail because of its 'absolute perfection'. This is comforting, but how many people will have to suffer and die before the project fulfills its promise of failure? An opera house or a railway station or a library will fail for the same over-reaching reason, because, as Austerlitz says earlier, 'outsize buildings cast the shadow of their own destruction before them' (19). But there is more than size at work here. Is this a fable about ambition, about the folly of grandeur? No, it's a story about the past blindly writing the script of the future, and may imply, in the mind of this solitary, meditative person, an almost theological conviction that concept and practice cannot meet except in disaster. This is what it means for events to be 'forever just recurring' (197) ['immer gerade jetzt sich ereignende'].[22] Time passes, for Austerlitz as for anyone else. It just doesn't stay passed.

There are moment in Sebald's writing where his narrator at least has a more conventional view of time and memory: 'I think how little we can hold in mind, how everything is constantly lapsing into oblivion' (*Austerlitz* 24). He also worries about 'the entire questionable business of writing' (*Emigrants* 230). But these moments are rare. Oblivion itself keeps casting up material memories, like a sea leaving objects on a shore. Wherever he goes, the narrator of all of these works is 'confronted with the traces of destruction, reaching far back into the past'; he is in no serious danger of forgetting that 'our history [...] is but a long account of calamities'.[23] As for the writing, he makes mistakes, but only when he thinks the task is easy, when he commits a 'wrongful trespass' (*Emigrants* 29) in imagining he knows more than he does about another person. And in a suggestive irony, it is through an account of Borges's 'Tlön, Uqbar, Orbis Tertius' that Sebald shows how far he is from the fear of fiction that marks the essayistic work of Carter and Barnes.

He doesn't seem far at first. The narrator of *The Rings of Saturn* returns to the Borges story—he has already alluded to it once—as an analogue for his own 'uncertainty' about whether he saw or imagined a couple sprawled on the beach in front of him. But then he conjures up the whole story—which 'deals with our

---

[22] Sebald, *Austerlitz* (2001), 281.
[23] Sebald, *The Rings of Saturn*, trans. Michael Hulse (1999), 3, 295. Further references given in the text.

attempts to invent secondary or tertiary worlds' (69)—in a mixture of translation and paraphrase of alarming ease. And when he comes to the moment when 'the labyrinthine construction of Tlön [...] is on the point of blotting out the known world' (74), he reads Borges's tone as inviting admiration for a vastly successful intellectual hoax: 'already the history of Tlön has superseded all that we formerly knew or thought we knew; in historiography, the indisputable advantages of a fictitious past have become apparent' (74).

Let me recall the more literal version:

> its history [...] has obliterated the history which dominated my childhood. Now in all memories, a fictitious past occupies the place of any other. We know nothing about it with any certainty, not even that it is false. (*Ficciones* 34)

Sebald makes no mention of Borges's connecting the hoax to recent ideologies:

> Ten years ago [Borges is writing, or pretending to write, in 1947], any symmetrical system whatsoever which gave the appearance of order—dialectical materialism, anti-Semitism, Nazism—was enough to fascinate men. Why not fall under the spell of Tlön and submit to the minute and vast evidence of an ordered planet? (*Ficciones* 34)

This sounds more than a little like Austerlitz's theory of ambitious architecture. Of course Sebald has not missed the connection, and we have to read his 'indisputable advantages' ironically. He thinks the whole hoax is a masterpiece of mischief. But his tone tells us something else. His own constant but careful use of fiction is so securely related to (regrettably) unalterable fact that he can't think of fiction as a danger outside of fiction. The novel, for him, blurs the boundaries, and that is why he says it is not his medium. He has cheered himself up, recovered his sense of certainty, by retelling the tale of a tale. His history is infinitely darker than that of Barnes and Carter; his epistemological confidence recalls that of Dr Johnson, who thought he could refute the philosopher Berkeley by kicking a stone.[24]

5. Other Places

Salman Rushdie and Graham Swift inscribe essay-themes into their novels—that is, they often return to the older, relaxed tradition of the novel—but neither of them plays with the form of the essay in the manner of Carter, Barnes, and Sebald. Kazuo Ishiguro, however, does continue this latter tradition, not so much through

---

[24] See Chapter 3 in this volume, by Kathryn Murphy, 78–9 for this anecdote.

openly essayistic prose as through narrative arrangements that can only be conceived as ongoing questions. It's not an idle connection to think here for a moment that Ishiguro was Carter's student at the University of East Anglia. 'We'd have these big arguments', he recently told a journalist. 'She'd always say I didn't fill in enough.'[25] He's still filling in only selectively. In his latest work, *The Buried Giant* (2015), we learn more than we can possibly want to know about the self-torture of a group of monks—we know the degree of their consciousness of guilt by the horror of their punishments—but the world we are moving in is more than a little vague. The time and place are post-Arthurian England, when the kingly peace is ending, and Saxons and Britons are about to be at each other's throats. Part of the story concerns an elderly Briton couple seeking to join their son. They are hampered by the plague of memory loss that has descended on their community, and their quest is also an allegorical journey into death. This is all rather slow, and certainly tame compared with the episode of the monks. But the couple gets involved with a Saxon warrior who has a task: to slay the dragon whose breath is causing all the forgetting. The three of them meet one of Arthur's knights, rather ancient now, who seems to have been entrusted with the same job. Not quite, though. It comes as a deep and troubling shock to learn that his job is exactly the opposite: to save the dragon the other knight wants to kill. In other words, he is to preserve the epidemic of forgetting as a social balm, and not allow harsh memories of massacre to stir up further bloodshed. The Saxon in this context represents not only the new order, the violent Nordic England that will make Britons obsolete, but a will to truth of the kind Thomas Harrison associates with the essay as a form.[26] Ishiguro is asking us to rethink the very idea of such a will, and we shall come to different conclusions according to our temperaments and politics, and indeed according to where we find relevance for our thought. Do we always want the truth? If we do, are we right? Is forgetting a gift or just a mode of censorship?

As we ask the questions, we understand the strategy behind Ishiguro's choice of setting: a half-imaginary ancient England and not, as he mentions in the interview, a historical France, South Africa, Yugoslavia, or Japan. It's not that he doesn't want us to ponder the relation of his questions to these places. That is what he wants. But he wants us to think of other places too, of any place at all where the dragon might be needed, or might need to be killed. There is no truth and reconciliation on offer here, no amnesty and moving on; only truth and murder on the one hand, a reign of angry vengeance if the forgetting ends, and ignorance and oblivion on the other, a safer but stupider world.

---

[25] Gaby Wood, 'Do you feel these emotions too?', in *The Daily Telegraph* (28 February 2015), 4–5.
[26] He suggests that essayism occurs at the 'juncture where reason has abolished truth but not the will to truth' (*Essayism*, 219–20).

These questions are too precise and too difficult for a novel that would want to exclude the essay; too unsettled and unsettling for an essay that would want to conclude, to assert a point of view. Where they are, though, in *The Buried Giant*, in the 'more than rational distortion' of an all too imaginable world, they remind us that the novel and the essay desperately need each other's doubts, and they confirm the strength and the promise of the tradition we have been exploring.

15

Creative Nonfiction and the Lyric Essay

The American Essay in the Twenty-First Century

†Ned Stuckey-French

1. Introduction: The Renaissance of the American Essay

For much of the twentieth century critics claimed the American essay was dying or dead. Then in the mid 1980s the body stirred, and Phillip Lopate announced that the patient had been alive all along, living in disguise as op-eds, columns, or 'pieces'.[1] The problem of how to diagnose or define the essay is not new. It might even be endemic, for in a sense the essay was split at the root between Montaigne's personal, digressive openness and Bacon's careful, instructive aphorisms. But if the essay has always seemed divided or even amorphous, it has also been protean, and as Edward Hoagland pointed out in 1976, 'the extraordinary flexibility of essays is what has enabled them to ride out rough weather and hybridize into forms that suit the times.'[2]

Hoagland's remark proved prescient. What was dying in 1976 was a conception of the essay that tied it to three very different but equally uninspiring associations: a belles-lettres past; composition classrooms; and verifiable truth. Within a decade the essay in the United States would enter a renaissance. In the last forty years there has been an explosion in the number of writing programmes, which have come more recently to embrace creative nonfiction; a steady increase in outlets for publication for that form; and fertile discussion about the 'lyric essay' and the nature of 'truth' in nonfiction. Inspired by these debates and taking advantage of this institutional support, young writers have created essays that are formally adventurous and politically engaged. No figure has been more controversial or influential during this period than John D'Agata. As writer, theorist, and director of the University of Iowa's top-ranking programme in nonfiction writing, D'Agata has instigated and framed many of the current debates about the essay. A fierce opponent of the term 'creative nonfiction', D'Agata has championed the phrase

---

[1] See Phillip Lopate, 'The Essay Lives—in Disguise', *The New York Times Book Review* (18 November 1984), 1, 48–9.
[2] Edward Hoagland, 'What I Think, What I Am', *The New York Times Book Review* (27 June 1976), 190.

†Ned Stuckey-French, *Creative Nonfiction and the Lyric Essay: The American Essay in the Twenty-First Century* In: *On Essays: Montaigne to the Present.* Edited by: Thomas Karshan and Kathryn Murphy, Oxford University Press (2020).
© †Ned Stuckey-French.
DOI: 10.1093/oso/9780198707868.003.0016

'lyric essay' as the banner for a radical art-for-art's sake position which insists that the essay should aim at a higher truth, akin to poetry, which for him means it must disdain the constraints of mere fact and eschew the overtly political. D'Agata's efforts have helped to create a climate in which writers directly or indirectly influenced by him have been inspired to engage in radical formal experiments. Ironically and, I will argue, fortunately, some of the best of these writers have bent D'Agata's theory of the lyrical towards their own ends. They have initiated formal experiments while never forgetting that the essay can and must engage with the hard facts of the world, including violence and racism. In the work of the three contemporary essayists on whom this chapter will focus—Jo Ann Beard, Eula Biss, and Claudia Rankine—we shall see that just as political insight requires honesty and a respect for the facts so does the art of the essay require a deep understanding of the relationship between memory and imagination.

2. Creative Nonfiction and the American University

Even as he celebrated the essay's flexibility, Hoagland bemoaned the fact that while there were two anthologies that collected the year's best short stories, there was nothing comparable for the essay. Soon that would change. In 1986 Robert Atwan convinced Houghton Mifflin to launch the *Best American Essays* series and soon the essay was in vogue. That same year the Association of Writers and Writing Programs (AWP) noted that 'the fastest growing creative writing programs are in nonfiction'.[3] Progress, however, has been uneven. Of the 418 graduate programmes in creative writing that AWP lists at the time of writing, only 212 offer degrees in creative nonfiction.[4] The essay has also been saddled with the unfortunate title of 'nonfiction', which, as Scott Russell Sanders points out, is 'an exceedingly vague term, taking in everything from telephone books to *Walden*, and it's negative, implying that fiction is the norm against which everything else must be measured. It's as though, instead of calling an apple a fruit, we called it a non-meat.'[5]

During the post-war period, students encountered essays mainly in first-year writing anthologies. The essay was seen as a service genre, used to model rhetorical modes for beginning writers or to discuss other more 'literary' genres.[6] In the early 1990s, however, several new and important historical anthologies began

---

[3] Mary Rose, Associated Writing Programs, telephone conversation (2 November 2000), quoted by Douglas Hesse, 'The Place of Creative Nonfiction', in *Creative Nonfiction*, a special issue of *College English* 65.3 (January 2003), 238.

[4] *The AWP Official Guide to Writing Programs* and the *AWP 2012–13 Annual Report on the Academic Job Market*, at http://guide.awpwriter.org.

[5] Sanders, 'Interview with Scott Russell Sanders', interview conducted by Robert K. Root, *Fourth Genre* 1.1 (Spring 1999), 123.

[6] See Lynn Z. Bloom, 'The Essay Canon', *College English* 61.4 (March 1999), 401.

to appear.[7] Journals devoted to the essay were also launched (though they held onto the *nonfiction* tag like a comfort blanket): *Creative Nonfiction* (1993), *Fourth Genre: Explorations in Nonfiction* (1999), *River Teeth: A Journal of Nonfiction Narrative* (1999), and *Assay: A Journal of Nonfiction Studies* (2014). Creative nonfiction, as Wendy Bishop put it in a 2003 issue of *College English*, was 'suddenly sexy'.[8]

The history of the University of Iowa's Nonfiction Writing Program is representative of both the essay's late arrival and its improved status within the academy. In 1922, Iowa became the first university in the United States to accept creative work as the thesis for an advanced degree. In 1936, it set up the Iowa Writers' Workshop, the nation's first degree-granting creative writing programme.[9] Finally, forty years later, six professors in the Iowa English Department founded the Nonfiction Writing Program as an all-purpose expository writing strand. Under the direction of Carl Klaus and then Robin Hemley it soon established its position of leadership within the growing field of nonfiction.

3. The Emergence of the Lyric Essay

John D'Agata came to Iowa in 1998 as a poetry student in the Writers' Workshop and stayed to earn a second MFA degree in nonfiction. As an undergraduate at Hobart College, he had worked in both genres. In 1997, with his mentor at Hobart, Deborah Tall, D'Agata helped edit a special issue of *Seneca Review* devoted to what they called the lyric essay. The issue opened with a two-page manifesto heralding this 'fascinating sub-genre that straddles the essay and the lyric poem'. Their definition of the lyric essay emphasized form over content. 'These "poetic essays" or "essayistic poems"', they wrote, 'give primacy to artfulness over the conveying of information. They forsake narrative line, discursive logic, and the art of persuasion in favor of idiosyncratic meditation.' Lyric essays 'partake' of what D'Agata and Tall saw as the traditional essay's 'overt desire to engage with facts' and 'its allegiance to the actual', but also utilize poetry's 'density' and its 'distillation of ideas and musicality of language'. They proceed 'by association' and 'juxtaposition'. A lyric essay, they argued, takes 'shape mosaically—its import visible

---

[7] These include Gerald Early (ed.), *Speech and Power: The African-American Essay and Its Cultural Content from Polemics to Pulpit, Vols. I and II* (1992, 1993); Lopate (ed.), *The Art of the Personal Essay: An Anthology from the Classical Era to the Present* (1994); Joyce Carol Oates and Robert Atwan (eds), *The Best American Essays of the Century* (2000); John D'Agata (ed.), *The Next American Essay* (2003); D'Agata (ed.), *The Lost Origins of the Essay* (2009); Carl Klaus and Ned Stuckey-French (eds), *Essayists on the Essay: From Montaigne to Our Time* (2012); and D'Agata, *The Making of the American Essay* (2016).

[8] Wendy Bishop, 'Suddenly Sexy: Creative Nonfiction Rear-Ends Composition', in *Creative Nonfiction*, a special issue of *College English* 65.3 (January 2003), 257–75.

[9] Iowa Writers Workshop website, at https://writersworkshop.uiowa.edu.

only when one stands back and sees it whole'. Tall and D'Agata believed this new form was transformative: 'We turn to the lyric essay—with its malleability, ingenuity, immediacy, complexity, and use of poetic language—to give us a fresh way to make music of the world. [...] If the reader is willing to walk those margins, there are new worlds to be found.'[10]

Their campaign for the lyric essay won immediate attention, and D'Agata's stock began to rise. He published his first book, *Halls of Fame*, in 2001 and soon after launched an influential trilogy of anthologies—*The Next American Essay* (2003), *The Lost Origins of the Essay* (2009), and *The Making of the American Essay* (2016). In 2013 he succeeded Hemley as director of the Iowa Nonfiction Writing Program, which, at the time of writing, he continues to lead.

D'Agata has played an important role in the essay's revitalization. If the essay lies somewhere along a spectrum between journalism and poetry, D'Agata has nudged it towards the latter pole, challenged its formal conventions, won it new literary credence, and helped draw younger writers to it. Blurring genres, or queering the essay (as some critics have termed it), has opened essayists up to new ways of writing.[11] Essayists now work more impressionistically. They use the page differently, employing typography, white space, section breaks, and images in fascinating ways. They have also embraced the digital revolution and begun to compose in multi-modal ways, using hyperlinks, video, software applications, and social media.[12]

Critics have argued, however, that D'Agata's theory of the lyric essay has led to a needless, even dangerous, blurring of fact and fiction.[13] He has, they said, moved beyond giving 'primacy to artfulness over the conveying of information' to actually fudging facts. D'Agata counters that the essay's connection to research, facts, commerce, and political engagement is suspect, even retrograde. In the introduction to *The Lost Origins of the Essay* he declared, 'I am here in search of art. I am here to track the origins of an alternative to commerce.'[14]

Concerns that the dirty money of commercialism and the blandness of journalism might contaminate the literary essay and drag it down the hierarchy of genres are not new. Nor is the hope that an infusion of poetry might save the patient. Articles might inform, polemics persuade, and sermons save, but essays

---

[10] John D'Agata and Deborah Tall, 'New Terrain: The Lyric Essay', *Seneca Review* 72.1 (Fall 1997), 7. Also available at http://www.hws.edu/academics/senecareview/lyricessay.aspx.

[11] David Lazar, 'Queering the Essay', and Kazim Ali, 'Genre-Queer: Notes Against Generic Binaries', both in *Bending Genre: Essays on Creative Nonfiction*, ed. Margot Singer and Nicole Walker (2013), 15–20 and 27–38.

[12] See this volume, Chapter 17, by Christy Wampole.

[13] See, for instance, Dinty W. Moore, 'D'Agata's Trickery and Manipulations: Dinty W. Moore Speaks Out', *Brevity's Nonfiction Blog* (27 February 2012), at https://brevity.wordpress.com/2012/02/27/dagatas-trickery; Hannah Goldfield, 'The Art of Fact-Checking', *The New Yorker* blog (9 February 2012), at http://www.newyorker.com/books/page-turner/the-art-of-fact-checking; and William Deresiewicz, 'In Defense of Facts', *The Atlantic Monthy* 319.1 (January/February 2017), 90–9.

[14] John D'Agata, 'Introduction' to *The Lost Origins of the Essay*, ed. D'Agata (2009), 3.

should reveal, digress, and even sing. As early as 1863, for instance, Alexander Smith claimed that '[t]he essay, as a literary form, resembles the lyric, in so far as it is moulded by some central mood—whimsical, serious, or satirical. Give the mood, and the essay, from the first sentence to the last, grows around it as the cocoon grows around the silkworm.' The essayist, claimed Smith, is 'a chartered libertine' and has no 'duty to inform' or 'cancel abuses'. He is a 'poet in prose', a 'flower', and a 'skylark' who is 'born to make music' and only 'incidentally stay the pangs of vulgar hunger'. Ideally, wrote Smith, 'The essay should be pure literature as the poem is pure literature.'[15] Smith's goal may have been to acquire some of the prestige and purity of poetry for the essay, but in doing so he diminished the essayist. The essay merely expresses a mood. Freed from worldly duty, the essayist flies like a bird, but is only as conscious as a silkworm, as literate as a flower.

D'Agata's rejection of worldly concerns might seem to have much in common with modernism—Baudelaire's *l'art pour l'art*, or Valéry's dream of *la poésie pure*—but even so high a modernist as Virginia Woolf believed that essayists could negotiate the pressures of mass culture *and* produce art. In 'The Modern Essay' (1925), she identified the problem succinctly: 'To write weekly, to write daily, to write shortly, to write for busy people catching trains in the morning or for tired people coming home in the evening, is a heart-breaking task for men who know good writing from bad.' The task was hard but a writer such as Max Beerbohm, she argued, succeeded because he 'had no gospel to preach and no learning to impart', but gave us 'himself' instead so that 'the spirit of personality permeates every word that he writes'.[16]

About the same time Woolf turned to Thomas De Quincey as a model for how an essayist might write lyrically while honouring the truth of memory. Critics, Woolf complained, believe 'nothing is more reprehensible than for a prose writer to write like a poet' and argue that 'poetry has one mission and prose another'. De Quincey, Woolf believed, knew better. He accepted that our minds are both rational and imaginative, and saw that dreams and memories have much in common. Both are made of images that slide away from us unless captured by words. In memory, Woolf wrote, 'scenes have something of the soundlessness and the lustre of dreams. They swim up to the surface, they sink down again into the depths.' De Quincey invented '"modes of impassioned prose"' that enabled him to describe his memories with precision. Such prose did not make him a poet, or even a 'lyric writer', according to Woolf. De Quincey was 'a descriptive writer, a reflective writer', but he did not describe actual events. He described his memory of those events, and memory has its own truth. We live in the present, the rest of

---

[15] Alexander Smith, 'On the Writing of Essays', in *Dreamthorp: A Book of Essays Written in the Country* (1863, 1913), 26–7. See also William Dean Howells, 'The Editor's Easy Chair' ['The Old-Fashioned Essay'], *Harper's Magazine* (October 1902), 802.

[16] Virginia Woolf, 'The Modern Essay', from *The Common Reader, First Series* [1925], in *The Essays of Virginia Woolf*, vol. IV, ed. Andrew McNeillie (1994), 223, 220.

life available only through memory, and 'it is only by gathering up and putting together these echoes and fragments that we arrive at the true nature of our experience'.[17]

4. The Essay between Art and Science: Lukács and Adorno

In Central Europe, at roughly the same time Woolf's piece appeared, the discussion of the essay's relationship to poetry took a more philosophical and political turn. In a 1910 letter to Leo Popper, György Lukács referred to essays as 'intellectual poems' (*intellektuelle Gedichte*), in the sense that they are at once art *and* criticism. Art and criticism seek different kinds of truth, but the essay, argued Lukács, is a middle or hybrid genre:

> People say that the critic must always speak the truth, whereas the poet is not obliged to tell the truth about his subject-matter. It is not our intention here to ask Pilate's question nor to enquire whether the poet, too, is not impelled towards an inner truthfulness and whether the truth of any criticism can be stronger or greater than this. I do not propose to ask these questions because I really do see a difference here, but once again a difference which is altogether pure, sharp, and without transitions only at its abstract poles.[18]

More than forty years later in 'The Essay as Form', Theodor Adorno rejoined this issue of the essay's mixed nature. He began by quoting Lukács: 'The essay form has not yet, today, travelled the road to independence which its sister, poetry, covered long ago; the road of development from a primitive, undifferentiated unity with science, ethics, and art.'[19] 'In Germany', Adorno added, 'the essay is decried as a hybrid', and neither 'discontent with the mentality that reacts to the situation by fencing up art as a preserve for the irrational' nor discontent with 'identifying knowledge with organized science [...] has changed anything in the customary national prejudice'.[20] Adorno fled Germany in 1934 and lived abroad until 1949. His references to fencing the irrational, organized science, and Germany's national

[17] Virginia Woolf, 'Impassioned Prose' [1926], in *Essays*, vol. IV, ed. McNeillie, 361, 366, 363, 367.
[18] György Lukács, 'On the Nature and Form of the Essay: A Letter to Leo Popper', in *Soul and Form*, trans. Anna Bostock, ed. John T. Sanders and Katie Terezakis (2010), 26. 'Pilate's question' refers to John 18:38, and to the famous opening to Francis Bacon's 'Of Truth': ' "What is Truth?" said jesting Pilate, and would not stay for an answer' (in *Francis Bacon: The Major Works*, ed. Brian Vickers (1996, 2008), 341).
[19] Lukács, 'On the Nature and Form of the Essay', 29, quoted by Theodor Adorno in 'The Essay as Form', trans. Bob Hullot-Kentor and Frederic Will, *New German Critique* 32 (Spring/Summer 1984), 151. 'Der Essay als Form' appeared originally in *Noten zur Literatur I* (1958) and was first collected in Adorno, *Gesammelte Schriften*, 11 (1974).
[20] Adorno, 'The Essay as Form', 151.

prejudice had a new and ominous ring after Auschwitz.[21] Lukács, meanwhile, served during the 1956 Hungarian uprising as Minister of Culture in Imre Nagy's short-lived anti-Soviet government. After the Soviet Union crushed the revolt, Lukács recanted publicly and avoided the fate of Nagy, who was executed in 1958, the year Adorno published 'The Essay as Form'.

For Lukács the essay is trying to define itself in relation to poetry and criticism; for Adorno the abstract poles that define the essay's range are art and science; but the concerns of the two men are similar. Perhaps taking as his cue Lukács's allusion to Pilate's question—the first line in the first essay in what is considered the first collection of English essays—Adorno reminds us that Bacon was both the developer of the scientific method and an essayist: 'Since the time of Bacon, who was himself an essayist, empiricism—no less than rationalism—has been "method".'[22] Method for Adorno is suspect, for it can tend towards certainty, dogma, and eventually, totalitarianism. Fortunately, the essay, in both its Montaignian and Baconian iterations, has offered a check: 'Doubt about the unconditional priority of method was raised, in the actual process of thought, almost exclusively by the essay.'[23]

From the safety of West Germany Adorno criticized Lukács politically, saying he should not have stayed in the Communist Party or engaged in public self-criticism, but he agreed with Lukács about the essay's hybridity. The uniqueness of the essay derived for him from the fact that it was 'radically un-radical' and 'methodically unmethodical'. For Adorno, the essay is a kind of anti-genre, neither poetry nor criticism, neither science nor art, but a third thing that borrows from both. For him the essay carries its scepticism with it at all times, and as a consequence 'the law of the innermost form of the essay is heresy'. The essay, he claimed, 'shies away from the violence of dogma'.[24]

5. Art not Fact: John d'Agata and the Lyric Essay

Lukács and Adorno lived and wrote under the shadow of totalitarianism. They looked to the essay as a form that sought truth without the dictates of method, and respected independent thought. D'Agata and Tall were writing in 1997 when post-modern distrust of objective truth was in vogue. In the *Seneca Review* they admitted: 'Perhaps we're drawn to the lyric now because it seems less possible (and rewarding) to approach the world through the front door, through the myth

---

[21] See Adorno's now famous remark, 'To write poetry after Auschwitz is barbaric' ('Cultural Criticism and Society (1949)', in *Prisms*, trans. Samuel Weber and Shierry Weber (1981), 34).

[22] 'Of Truth' was in fact only written for the final version of Bacon's *Essayes*, published in 1625, twenty-eight years after his first collection. On Adorno and Bacon, see Chapter 3, by Kathryn Murphy, 91–3.

[23] Adorno, 'The Essay as Form', 157.   [24] Adorno, 'The Essay as Form', 157, 161, 171, 158.

of objectivity. The life span of a fact is shrinking; similitude often seems more revealing than verisimilitude.'[25] Since then D'Agata has become increasingly preoccupied with this theme. In a note to the reader on the first page of *The Next American Essay*, he announced, 'I want you preoccupied with art in this book, not with facts for the sake of facts.'[26] Since *Halls of Fame* (2001), he has written two books. The first of these, *About a Mountain* (2010), focuses on the Yucca Mountain nuclear waste dump and the 2002 suicide in Las Vegas of a young boy named Levi Presley. The second, *The Lifespan of a Fact* (2012), was written with Jim Fingal and tells the story of how the article that led to *About a Mountain* was fact-checked. *Harper's* turned the article down when its editors decided D'Agata had fudged too many of its facts. D'Agata then sent it to *The Believer*, and Fingal, who was an intern at that magazine, was charged with fact-checking the piece. At first D'Agata and Fingal argued about relatively small violations of the truth—the name of Presley's school, the colour of a fleet of dog-grooming vans (they were pink but D'Agata wanted purple because 'I needed the two beats in "purple"')—but D'Agata's demands soon escalated. He wanted to have another suicide-by-jumping on the same day Presley killed himself changed to a suicide-by-hanging 'because I wanted Levi's death to be the only one from falling that day. I wanted his death to be more unique.'[27] The co-authors of *The Lifespan of a Fact* compounded their problem when they admitted—after the book came out—that they had taken 'the relatively dry fact-checking document', dramatized it 'a bit', and 'knowingly amped up the hostility of [their] comments'.[28]

D'Agata's distrust of 'facts for the sake of facts' has also led him towards an art-for-art's sake position that would have horrified Lukács and Adorno. He is avowedly apolitical. In an interview for *Guernica*, Ariel Lewiton asked why he shied away from the political in his selections for *The Making of the American Essay*. To which he replied,

> It partly has to do with my own taste and it partly has to do with a sense of timeliness, of wanting to avoid having to explain the political contexts of essays. But most importantly it has to do with wanting to divorce the essay from being read exclusively as a form that's tied to its subject matter, or that is propelled by its subject matter.[29]

---

[25] D'Agata and Tall, 'New Terrain', 8.   [26] D'Agata, *The Next American Essay*, 1.
[27] D'Agata, *The Lifespan of a Fact* (2012), 18.
[28] For the (non)use of 'dickhead', see Josh Dzieza, 'John D'Agata's Fact-Checking Problem', *The Daily Beast* (21 February 2012), at http://www.thedailybeast.com/articles/2012/02/21/john-d-agata-s-fact-checking-battle.html. For altering facts, see Weston Cutter, 'Doubling Down: An Interview with John D'Agata and Jim Fingal', in *Kenyon Review* (23 February 2012), at http://www.kenyonreview.org/2012/02/doubling-down-an-interview-with-john-dagata-and-jim-fingal.
[29] Ariel Lewiton, 'John D'Agata: What We Owe History [An Interview]', *Guernica* (15 February 2016), at https://www.guernicamag.com/what-we-owe-history/. *The Lifespan of a Fact* became a national phenomenon and was reviewed on National Public Radio, and in the *Los Angeles Times*, *The New York Times* (twice), *The New Republic*, and *The New Yorker*. *Harper's* excerpted it. More

Many of D'Agata's contemporaries have found his conception of the lyrical essay liberating, but his attitude towards facts simplistic and his avoidance of politics impossible.

6. Truth if not Fact: Jo Ann Beard

Jo Ann Beard might seem at first glance to agree with D'Agata about the question of truth. Asked about the boundary between fiction and nonfiction in a 2014 interview, she allowed, 'In some of my work that boundary has been permeable.' She quickly added, however, that she does 'care quite a lot about the truth-factor in my own work, if not the fact-factor', before going on to wonder '[i]f there is such a thing as factual truth (there isn't) (or maybe there is)'.[30] Her second-guessing in that pair of parentheses points towards the difficulty.

We get a clearer understanding of Beard's take on the relationship between truth and fact in the preface to her essay collection, *The Boys of My Youth* (1998), where she recounts one of her first 'pre-verbal memories'. She tells in the present tense the story of a night when she was a baby. Her parents have put her in her crib for the night. She is too young to talk, 'like a baby monkey in a cage'. Detail is piled upon detail: 'the satin edge of my blue blanket, the chewable plastic ring that hangs down almost to the mouth level on a piece of green cord, and a boy doll named Hal with blue eyes and lickable hands and feet made of vinyl'. Her mother puts Hal next to her head but he is too close, 'exactly where I don't want him'. So she smacks Hal, and we get our first bit of dialogue: '"You don't want to hurt *Hal*," my mother says sadly. "I thought Hal was your *friend*".' This is not just dialogue, but dialogue with inflection that is recalled verbatim by a 'pre-verbal' child.[31]

Then, in case we did not get the impossibility of what she is proposing, Beard leaves the present of the story and addresses us directly: 'I tried to check out that particular memory with my mother when I grew up. I asked her if she remembered a night when I cried and cried, and couldn't be consoled, and they kept coming in and going back out and nothing they did could help me.' To which her mother answers, 'I don't remember any that *weren't* like that.' We realize that this preface comments on the problem of memory by enacting that problem. It reminds us that the narrative essays that will follow will be composed of research, recollection, and imagination. Her mother's stories are confused with her own memories until she doesn't know which is which. Multiple nights are conflated

recently, a dramatic adaptation of the book opened on Broadway in October 2018 starring Daniel Radcliffe as Fingal and Bobby Cannavale as D'Agata.

[30] Heidi Sistare, 'An Interview with Jo Ann Beard', *Slice* (4 November 2014), at https://slicemagazine.org/jo-ann-beard.

[31] Jo Ann Beard, 'Preface', *The Boys of My Youth* (1998), xi–xii. Further references given in the text.

into one. On the book's publishing page Little, Brown and Company placed this disclaimer: 'The events described in these stories are real. Some characters are composites [...]'. Both disclaimer and preface set up a contract with the reader in which it is agreed that the stories are true even if not every detail is verifiable or strictly accurate. Unlike D'Agata, Beard respects her reader by signalling in advance that imagination will supplement memory. She reminds us how easy it is to fool one's self and how hard, yet important, it is to try not to fool one's self. Tall and D'Agata merely nodded towards the essay's 'allegiance to the actual', but for Beard that allegiance is at the heart of her project. Memory is patchy, history is sly, and some facts contradict others, but she owes it to her readers, her self, and the people she writes about to try to follow the truth, wherever it takes her.

A publisher or author plays a role in establishing the contract with the reader, but so too can a bookseller, anthologist, or editor. A confusion of genres took place when Beard's breakthrough piece, 'The Fourth State of Matter', appeared in *The New Yorker*'s 1996 summer fiction issue with a note identifying it as 'personal history'. Again, Beard explained the implications:

> I think right around then too *The New Yorker* became interested in the idea of creative nonfiction vs. fiction, and how there was a kind of gray area between the two. So my piece was published in the fiction issue, but they stated it was something in between fiction and nonfiction, a "true" story, as we say. That changed things for me professionally.   (5)

For many readers any fogginess about genre burned away quickly because the essay's narrative was about an event that had been in the news—a shooting that began in the Physics Department at the University of Iowa where Beard worked as an assistant on a journal, and which ended elsewhere on campus with six people dead (including the shooter) and a seventh paralysed. Beard also braided at least two other narrative threads into the story of the shooting: her dog is dying and her marriage is ending. All three strands are about loss. One of the victims, Christoph Goertz, a world-renowned space physicist, is her close friend. The first half of the essay focuses on her friendship with Chris, who clearly respects and cares for her. They share coffee and the newspaper, and are allies in the department's squabbles, squabbles that will escalate into violence. Early on Beard drops a hint about what is to come. Her colleagues, she says, are 'space physicists, guys who spend days on end with their heads poked through the fabric of the sky, listening to the sounds of the universe. Guys whose own lives are ticking like alarm clocks getting ready to go off, although none of us are aware of it yet' (75). Like Jo Ann and Chris we are preoccupied with the dying collie, the 'vanished husband', the squirrels in her attic, and, in Chris's case at least, the meaning of the universe, and so we read past this bit of foreshadowing.

In her essay Beard might seem to some to be breaking her contract with the reader by inserting an extended scene that she herself did not witness, but she does not because of how she sets up the scene to make it clear what she knows for a fact and what she is speculating on. She lets us know that she left the office early that day and passed Gang Lu on her way out of the building. Gang Lu, the as-yet unidentified shooter, is sullen, awkward, dissociated. He 'stands stiffly', 'answers questions in monotone', and has 'expressionless eyes'. Then, in a single rushing paragraph that includes passages from his letters home, Beard speculates about what he is thinking; indeed she moves into a very close third-person point of view. She is able to do this because, having worked with him, she knows him well and because she has done almost forensic research into what happened. She knows for instance that he does not think she respects him, that he thinks she is lazy or at least nonchalant, and that he feels no need to respect her. She also lets us know that he has in the pockets of his coat a .38 calibre handgun and a .22 calibre revolver, a fact she could only have learned later. This is rendered within the present tense of the scene, but is simultaneously informed by the haunted retrospection of Beard herself, who by sheer dumb luck survives the carnage he will soon wreak:

> He's sick of physics and sick of the buffoons who practice it. The tall glacial German, Chris, who tells him what to do; the crass idiot Bob, who talks to him as if he is a dog; the student Shan, whose ideas about plasma physics are treated with reverence and praised at every meeting. The woman who puts her feet on the desk and dismisses him with her eyes.   (86)

After this last reference to Beard, seen through Gang Lu's eyes, there is a section break and then we are plunged into the shooting:

> Friday-afternoon seminar, everyone is glazed over, listening as someone at the head of the long table explains something unexplainable. Gang Lu stands up and leaves the room abruptly; goes down one floor to see if the department chairman, Dwight, is sitting in his office. He is. The door is open. Gang Lu turns, walks back up the stairs, and enters the seminar room again. Chris Goertz is sitting near the door and takes the first bullet in the back of the head.   (89)

Beard never tells us how she knows what happened at the murder scene. She doesn't have to. She knows the attitudes and feelings of everyone present because she knows these people personally *and* because she did her research, including examining the police files. She has already told us that she left work early so we know she is creating this scene retrospectively and through other sources. The level of detail could come only from after-the-fact forensic analysis, which she indicates as her source by mimicking its style, rendering the scene as notes, fragments, and short sentences.

The political issues are not submerged in Beard's essay but neither are they explicit. She is primarily a narrative essayist. An explosion of guns, mental illness, and cultural conflict has torn her life apart, but Beard leaves readers to draw their own conclusions concerning these problems. As Beard pointed out in an interview, *The New Yorker*'s publication of 'The Fourth State of Matter' was made possible not only because of the magazine's interest at that time in the 'gray area' between fiction and nonfiction, but also by the fact that 'people were really interested in this issue of workplace shootings, and I think my story gave them a certain kind [of] glimpse into what that experience felt like from the inside of one of those incidents. I had very unfortunate subject matter that was also timely.'[32] D'Agata emphasized form over subject matter when theorizing the essay; Beard acknowledges that the appeal of an essay can depend on both.

7. Race as Fact and Race as Fiction: Eula Biss

Beard graduated from the Iowa Nonfiction Writing Program in 1994 and left for New York before D'Agata arrived in Iowa City. Eula Biss, on the other hand, studied with D'Agata at Iowa, receiving her MFA in 2006. D'Agata published some of her first pieces in *The Seneca Review* and she thanked him in the acknowledgements of her 2011 essay collection, *Notes from No Man's Land: American Essays*. Like D'Agata, Biss saw herself as a poet first: 'I began writing nonfiction by writing poetry, which is nonfiction in the sense that it's not fiction.'[33] Her distinction echoes Sanders's 'non-meat' criticism of the term 'creative nonfiction' while not necessarily pitting lyricism and the verifiable against each other. Nevertheless, working with D'Agata opened her eyes to the possibilities of the essay: 'Naming something is a way of giving it permission to exist. And this is why the term *lyric essay* was so important to me when I first learned it.'[34] Her essays are lyrical but also erudite and political, in the manner of what Lukács called 'intellectual poems'. Unlike D'Agata she stakes a claim within an explicitly political tradition. Just as James Baldwin evoked the titles of Richard Wright's 1940 novel, *Native Son*, and Henry James's 1914 autobiography, *Notes of a Son and Brother*, in the title of his first essay collection, so does Biss's title evoke Baldwin's *Notes of a Native Son*, while also slyly reminding us of her gender.

---

[32] Amy Yelin, 'Jo Ann Beard Interview', *Yelinwords*, 5, at https://yelinwords.files.wordpress.com/2014/05/joannbeardfinal.pdf.

[33] E. B. Bartels, 'Non-Fiction by Non-Men: Eula Biss', interview in *Fiction Advocate* (16 January 2017), at http://fictionadvocate.com/2017/01/16/non-fiction-by-non-men-eula-biss.

[34] Eula Biss, 'It Is What It Is', in *Bending Genre: Essays on Creative Nonfiction*, ed. Margot Singer and Nicole Walker (2013), 196.

Several of the pieces in *Notes from No Man's Land* explore race and gender. Like Baldwin, she does this through the lens of her family, which she describes as 'mixed'. After her parents divorced, her mother, who is white, married a black man and that man's daughter became Biss's stepsister; her 'mother's sister married a black man from Jamaica and had two children', one of whom came to live with her family when Biss was in junior high; she later lived with the other cousin in Brooklyn; and her mother's other sister adopted a Cherokee daughter (79).[35]

Biss differs from Beard in that she does not braid together personal stories so much as oscillate between modes of discourse. She does tell family stories, but unlike Beard she discusses political issues and regularly cites the work of other writers. In 'Relations', for instance, she alludes to the time following her parents' divorce when her mother converted to a West Indian religion and began dating a black man, and then moves quickly to larger questions about what her mother's choices might say about class, gender, and race before finally invoking the race theorist and Harvard Law professor Randall Kennedy:

> Someone once accused my mother of adopting the identity of whichever man she was with. It does seem that my mother has been trying to escape her own white, middle-class, Protestant background ever since she dropped out of high school and got on a Greyhound bus, but shouldn't she be allowed out if she wants out? Especially since she has sacrificed, in various ways, just about all the privilege to which she could ever have laid claim. A multiracial society, Randall Kennedy recently wrote, "ought to allow its members free entry into and exits from racial categories."[36]

It is not uncontroversial, and not unconnected to privilege, to claim that racial categories are or ought to be volitional. Most of Biss's essay, however, focuses on mixed-race relationships that are involuntary rather than intentional—cousins, half-siblings, and adopted children. Living with her mixed-race cousin in her twenties pushed Biss to think about race, identity, and privilege. As a child her cousin had worried her mother loved her brother more because his skin was lighter, though she is also light enough to pass sometimes as white. '"It's hard for me," my cousin mused once as we waited for a train, "I have a lot of white family." At the time, I couldn't fully appreciate what she was saying because I was hurt by the implication that I was a burden to her' (32). Her cousin's honesty prompts Biss to think harder about racial difference: 'I was mistaken for a white boy twice, and once I was mistaken for Asian. But I was never taken for black' (29). Biss takes these small asides and the realizations they force upon her and expands them by

---

[35] Biss, 'Black News', in *No Man's Land: American Essays* (2009), 79. Subsequent essays are from this collection, with references given in the text.
[36] Biss, 'Relations', in *No Man's Land*, 27–8.

situating them in a larger context. Race itself does not become a 'fact' until racism makes it operate as one. Her cousin's comments about family and passing are juxtaposed against memories of the dolls (one black, one white) Biss and her sister had as children. Their dolls are contrasted with those discussed in the 'doll tests' of psychologists Kenneth and Mamie Clark, which exposed the effects of race on African American children and helped decide the Brown v. Topeka Board of Education school integration case. Finally, the whole essay is framed by Biss's discussion of the custody battle that resulted when a white woman who, after a bungled uterine implant, gave birth to twins—one black, one white, one her biological baby, the other the child of a black couple who were clients of the same fertility clinic. Beard showed the quotidian being blown open by violence. Biss takes stray particulars (a child's doll, an offhand comment by her cousin), turns them over in her mind with an almost Montaignian persistence, and finds their significance by nesting them like Russian dolls inside more public discussions of race and identity.

Though Biss studied with D'Agata she does not fudge or dismiss facts; instead, she seeks them out and follows where they lead, and they lead consistently to politics. D'Agata told Lewiton he wanted to avoid having to explain the political contexts of essays and did not want essays to be tied exclusively to their subject matter. Biss, on the other hand, consciously situates her essays within their political contexts and because her subject matter is often race she does not manipulate facts but tries instead to investigate how facts are manipulated, how 'fictions' (such as race) are turned into 'facts'. This empirical approach is on display in her essay 'Time and Distance Overcome'. In this piece Biss deploys short, impressionistic sections that function more like stanzas than paragraphs. These passages proceed disjunctively and their logic is not fully apparent on first reading, or as Tall and D'Agata put it, the shape of such essays' mosaic becomes 'visible only when one stands back and sees it whole'. The essay is divided into three sections, each composed of short segments, some just one sentence long. The opening section tells the story of Alexander Graham Bell's improbable invention—the telephone—and the initial resistance to it. Here is the first of these historical data points:

> "Of what use is such an invention?" the New York World asked after Alexander Graham Bell first demonstrated his telephone in 1876. The world was not waiting for the telephone.   (3)

People were sceptical that every house and business could or should be connected by a system of poles and wires. The telephone was seen as a rich man's toy, an unneeded extravagance. Towns and property owners saw the poles and wires as unsightly affronts. People resisted and chopped down the poles. The narrative tension in Biss's essay comes not from who will win the 'War on Telephone

Poles'—we know how it will turn out—but from the surprising vehemence of people's initial response.

After a section break, Biss ambushes the reader with a new bit of unexpected history: 'In 1898, in Lake Cormorant, Mississippi, a black man was hanged from a telephone pole. And in Weir City, Kansas. And in Brookhaven, Mississippi. And in Tulsa, Oklahoma, where the hanged man was riddled with bullets' (6–7). Beard had planted bits of foreshadowing (though readers might not have recognized them, at least consciously); Biss offers no hints of what is to come, and what comes is a horror that is national in scale. As the litany of lynching continues Biss interrupts it with apparently banal comments that have a haunting and horrifying ring in their new context. This, for instance:

> The children's game of telephone depends on [the] fact that a message passed quietly from one ear to another will get distorted at some point down the line.   (7)

Or this:

> Early telephone calls were full of noise. "Such a jangle of meaningless noises had never been heard by human ears," Herbert Casson wrote in his 1910 *History of the Telephone*. "There were sputtering and bubbling, jerking and rasping, whist-ling and screaming."   (8)

She also quotes W. E. B. Du Bois and Claude McKay on resistance, lending the piece additional political gravity just as her quotations from Kennedy and others did in 'Relations'. Her narrative takes a grimly ironic turn, for the resistance is now to the lynchings not the poles. There were riots, she tells us, 'in Cincinnati, New Orleans, Memphis, New York, Atlanta, Philadelphia, Houston...' This second section ends with the nation torn apart by race but tied together by '14,000 miles of copper wire and 130,000 telephone poles' (10).

The final section of just four segments takes a sharp turn toward the personal when Biss reveals that her grandfather was a lineman whose back was broken when a telephone pole fell on him. Then she divulges that she told her sister the writing the essay changed her formerly romantic view of telephone lines: 'Nothing is innocent, my sister reminds me. But nothing, I would like to think, remains unrepentant' (11). She continues her meta-commentary in a bibliographical note, revealing that she too was blindsided by the facts: 'I began my research for this essay by searching for every instance of the phrase "telephone pole" in the *New York Times* between 1880 and 1920, which resulted in 370 articles.' Then, having stumbled across three articles about lynchings, she launched a new search for the word 'lynched' during the same time period. It turned up 2,354 articles (202).

Biss's book is about trying to see and hear more clearly, which means recog-nizing the fog and static of America's racism within each of us. In what can be read as a correction to D'Agata's rigid separation of fact and fiction, Biss reminds us that race is both a 'social fiction' and a 'social fact'. She understands that she is white and her cousin is not, but all Americans, she argues, are defined by race and caught in a 'heavily trafficked' and 'uncomfortable no-man's land'. To describe the paradox of this shared no-man's land she quotes the critic and novelist Albert Murray: 'For all their traditional antagonism and obvious differences the so-called black and so-called white people of the United States resemble nobody else in the world so much as they resemble each other' (17).[37]

8. Making Race Visible: Clauda Rankine's *Citizen*

Claudia Rankine approaches the issue of race in America from a history that is closer to that of Biss's cousin than Biss's, but she too is out to help her readers see how race functions. She was born in Kingston, Jamaica, and came to the Bronx when she was 7 years old. Her mother and father worked at a hospital—she as a nurses' aide, he as an orderly. In an interview Rankine talks about her upbringing in a way that echoes and amends Biss's quotation from Murray:

> I'm now in my fifties, so it's hard for me to think of myself as not the American citizen that I am. But I do know, growing up in my household with two Jamaican parents, that American blackness was referred to as American blackness and American whiteness was referred to as American whiteness.[38]

Rankine's latest book, *Citizen: An American Lyric*, makes use of short dramatized scenes, bits of prose poetry, photographs, screenshots, and reproductions of paintings, collages, and sculpture. The book takes the mosaic approach to essay form that Tall and D'Agata called for into new territory, but for Rankine form follows function. *Citizen*'s formal innovations ask the reader to rethink not just lyricism and the essay but also race and citizenship, and in so doing reject D'Agata's assumption that an essayist interested in form must resist the political demands of her subject matter, indeed of her experience.

Rankine's expectations of her reader begin with the book's cover, which bears an illustration of a black-and-white photograph of David Hammons's art installation *In the Hood*. Hammons's work consists of a hood cut from a sweatshirt and hanged from a wall. A wire has been inserted with the drawstring, holding the hood open so as to evoke the absent head. The title of the piece also gestures to the

---

[37] The quotation is from Murray's essay collection *The Omni-Americans: Black Experience and American Culture* (1970, 1990), 22.

[38] Aaron Coleman, 'The History behind the Feeling: A Conversation with Claudia Rankine', *The Spectacle* (23 September 2015), at http://thespectacle.wustl.edu/?p=105.

absent (presumably black) body inside the sweatshirt as well as to the neighbour-hood where that person lived. Hammons created his work in 1993, but the image of it on Rankine's 2014 book cover evokes the hooded torture victims of Abu Ghraib (2004), and 17-year-old Trayvon Martin, who was shot and killed in his hoodie in 2012. Rankine's epigraph, which comes from the opening of Chris Marker's 1983 film essay *Sans Soleil*, also emphasizes the visual: 'If they don't see happiness in the picture, at least they'll see the black.' The words and the cover signal that this text, like Du Bois's exploration of the veil or Ellison's of invisibility, will be concerned with making race visible.[39]

The book, designed by Rankine's husband, the photographer John Lucas, is interspersed with images that help us see what Rankine's words say. One image is a well-known photograph of the August 1930 lynching of two African American teenagers, Tom Shipp and Abe Smith, in Marion, Indiana. Lucas (with permission) has removed Shipp and Smith from the photograph. We see only the white crowd standing below the absent bodies—men in shirts and ties, women in print dresses, some laughing, some looking into the camera, one man pointing towards the now absent bodies. Maria Windell has summarized the effect: 'By removing the lynched bodies, *Citizen* reframes the politics of (the) exposure by refusing to allow violence or the gaze to define the black body—literally rendering it invisible—and focusing on the perpetrators.'[40]

The book's visual experiments are several and various. They are taken from high culture and low, and include screenshots from the news and reproductions of art installations. The first image in the book is a snapshot of a sign for 'Jim Crow Road' in a contemporary suburban neighborhood. The book's last two images are prints of Joseph Mallard William Turner's *The Slave Ship* (1840). The street sign reminds us of racism's continuing and quotidian horror. The two reproductions of Turner's painting take us to racism's past. The first is a print of the entire painting. Because the ship is in the distance and the sunset behind it is rendered in such a whirl of colour, it is hard to recognize the painting's details or even its subject. In the credits the second print is titled a 'detail of fish attacking slave'. By zooming in Lucas exposes the manacled leg of a drowning slave, forces the painting's full horror upon us, and reclaims Turner's original title: *Slavers Throwing Overboard the Dead and Dying, Typhoon Coming On.*

The majority of the book's images are screenshots from Lucas and Rankine's video essay *Zidane*, one of several on which they (like Biss and her husband John

[39] For more on Marker's 'dislocated subject' and how he revolutionized the film-essay, see this volume, Chapter 17, by Christy Wampole, 338–41.

[40] Maria W. Windell, 'Citzenship in *Citizen*', from 'On Claudia Rankine's *Citizen: An American Lyric*, A Symposium, Part I,' *Los Angeles Review of Books* (6 January 2016), at https://lareviewofbooks. org/article/reconsidering-claudia-rankines-citizen-an-american-lyric-a-symposium-part-i.

Bresland) have collaborated.[41] The screenshots mimic the video's use of super slow-motion to replay a single instant in the 2006 World Cup final when the great French soccer player Zinedine Zidane, after a raft of racist taunts by one of the Italian players, head-butted his opponent. Zidane was given a red card and sent off, in his last game before retiring. Italy won on penalty kicks when the match finished 1–1 after extra time. *Citizen* excerpts the video's script, which Rankine offers in a voiceover and which is composed of the words of Zidane, his Italian opponent, and quotations from Richard Wright, James Baldwin, Frederick Douglass, and others. Again, words and images work together to help us see beyond the moment by hearing the history beneath it.

Just as Lucas uses documentary and fine art images and techniques such as elision, close-ups, and slow-motion, so does Rankine in her text move between large, public moments when race is on display and smaller, everyday moments when even those receiving a racist slight doubt their eyes and ears. A white man cuts in line at a pharmacy saying he 'didn't see' the black person ahead of him. A white child on a plane lets her mother know she does not want to sit next to the black person in the window seat.[42] In response to these micro-aggressions the narrator says, 'Did I hear what I think I heard? Did that just come out of my mouth, his mouth, your mouth?' (9). The march of first-, second-, and third-person pronouns implicates us all in these racial interactions. Most notable among Rankine's use of pronouns is an intentionally ambiguous second person. The narrator addresses herself, the reader, and others at once. Paula Cocozza has described the effect of this technique on the reader:

> *Citizen*'s "you" refuses to denote a single addressee, let alone one gender or one racial identity. Its referent changes from line to line. It telescopes in and out, singularises, pluralises, reverses, and its shifts keep the reader mobile, continually asking: Which one am I? Where do I fit in? It is impossible to read without questioning your own part in the racist social structures it recounts.[43]

Rankine's use of second person enables her to expand and disguise the narrator, but unlike D'Agata, she is out to challenge, not fool, the reader. The ambiguous second person lets Rankine create a narrator who is and is not her, who is not necessarily black or female, and whose experience is multiple and communal.

---

[41] In 2010 Bresland included *Zidane* in a suite of video essays he curated for the online magazine *Blackbird*. See John Bresland, 'On the Origin of the Video Essay', *Blackbird* 9.1 (Spring 2010), at http://www.blackbird.vcu.edu/v9n1/gallery/ve-intro/intro_page.shtml. Christy Wampole's essay in this volume also discusses at length Bresland's video essay 'Mangoes' (in which Biss appears) (see Chapter 17, 341–5).

[42] Claudia Rankine, *Citizen: An American Lyric* (2014), 16. Further references given in the text.

[43] Paula Cocozza, 'Poet Claudia Rankine: "The Invisibility of Black Women is Amazing"', *The Guardian* (29 June 2015), at https://www.theguardian.com/lifeandstyle/2015/jun/29/poet-claudia-rankine-invisibility-black-women-everyday-racism-citizen.

Rankine then sets these small moments against larger, widely known instances of racist aggression, such as the Trayvon Martin shooting or the response to Hurricane Katrina. Her 'book tracks the small to the large', she says, because 'if people in their daily lives begin by believing and saying these small things, they will add up to major, major aggressions against people just because of the color of their skin.'[44]

These larger public moments are also shared and documented, which presents Rankine with special problems and opportunities. At the centre of *Citizen* is a piece about African American tennis star Serena Williams and how she is treated by white fans, judges, players, and sportscasters. Rankine, unlike D'Agata, welcomes fact-checking. Her Serena Williams essay makes an argument about race and she wants honest debate about facts:

> That essay was dependent on the fact that a reader could go to YouTube and look up the moments I referred to in her life. I didn't want anyone who disagreed with my take on events or remembered them differently not to have a chance to access the moments for themselves.[45]

But Williams is also a celebrity and Rankine's task is also to humanize her and make her real. Because *Citizen* is a book of nonfiction she had to do it from the outside, which required a new kind of lyricism:

> How do you show the effect of all this injustice on a human body? On an actual somebody? And how is that somebody read by the public? I didn't want it to be a traditional lyric because I wasn't trying to create an internalized consciousness for Serena Williams. I was talking about an invisible accumulation of stress in the body, so I had to show how it worked over time. I needed a form that would allow me to do that, and so I ended up with the essay.
>
> That said, it's a lyric essay, not an essay essay, because it was written to fit into *Citizen*.[46]

This last sentence addresses a problem that Rankine had to solve in order to write her book, but it also speaks to the way in which the essay is, in its present moment, caught between retreat and departure. The term *lyrical essay* was equally important to Biss. It gave her essays permission to exist. No one has done more to advocate for the lyric essay than D'Agata. Like Beard and Biss, he studied the form and history of the essay in Iowa during a time of ferment and growth, his

---

[44] Gwen Ifil, 'Using Poetry to Uncover the Moments that Lead to Racism', interview on PBS *NewsHour* (4 December 2014).

[45] David Ulin, 'The Art of Poetry No. 102—Claudia Rankine', *Paris Review* 219 (Winter 2016), 143.

[46] Ulin, 'The Art of Poetry', 144–5.

argument for the lyrical essay generating much of that ferment. All of these writers have contributed immensely to the recent renaissance of the essay, but that renaissance rests on a rich tradition. Essayists have long been preoccupied with the relationship between the factual and the poetic. That history of the lyric essay extends back through Lukács and Woolf to Howells, Smith, and De Quincey, and even to Montaigne and Bacon. A tradition, however, can only move forwards and find what is next if it is gifted with skilled and imaginative practitioners, writers like Beard, Biss, and Rankine who write essays that are lyrical and true, beautiful and engaged.

16

Up to a Point

The Psychoanalyst and the Essay

Adam Phillips

> Professions create traditions that exceed their own histories.
>
> Louis Menand, *The Marketplace of Ideas*[1]

Psychoanalysts don't usually write essays; they tend to write lectures or papers or chapters, or what are called, perhaps optimistically, contributions; Melanie Klein, according to her editors, wrote works, and Lacan, from a quite different tradition, wrote *Écrits*.[2] And when their writings are selected or collected, though the word may be used by way of introduction essays are not what these writings are entitled. Nor indeed what they are often entitled to be called. When Ernest Jones, for example, the founder of the British Psychoanalytical Society, published a collection of his writings in 1948, it was called *Papers on Psychoanalysis*; when the International Psychoanalytical Library published a selection of what the editors called John Rickman's 'papers' in 1957 the book was entitled *Selected Contributions to Psychoanalysis*; it being assumed, I think, that there was something to contribute to called, say, the progress of psychoanalysis. As late as 1999, when Julia Borossa edited a selection of Ferenczi's writing for Penguin, it was entitled *Selected Writings*. There is no collected or selected essays of Klein, or of Anna Freud, Winnicott, Milner, Laing, or Khan.

So it is striking, for example, when the psychoanalyst Charles Rycroft refers to his 1991 book *Viewpoints* being his 'third volume of essays' (and indeed quotes John Maynard Keynes's *Essays in Biography* in his introduction).[3] And having announced in the first sentence of that introduction that it is essays he has written, he goes on immediately to tell the reader of his withdrawal from the British Psychoanalytical Society—'because of its resistance to any unorthodox views'—and of his beginning to write for *The Observer*, *New Society*, *New Statesman*, *TLS*,

---

[1] Louis Menand, *The Marketplace of Ideas: Reform and Resistance in the American University* (2010), 116.

[2] This essay first appeared, without footnotes, in *Salmagundi* 178/9 (Spring 2013).

[3] Charles Rycroft, *Viewpoints* (1991), 1, 3.

Adam Phillips, *Up to a Point: The Psychoanalyst and the Essay* In: *On Essays: Montaigne to the Present.*
Edited by: Thomas Karshan and Kathryn Murphy, Oxford University Press (2020). © Adam Phillips.
DOI: 10.1093/oso/9780198707868.003.0017

and the *New York Review of Books* on what he calls 'matters psychoanalytical'.[4] For Rycroft, as a psychoanalyst in the British Society, calling his book a volume of essays—and by implication his previous books—is like a declaration of independence. He has withdrawn from the ruling institution and he has written for a wider audience. Writing essays, and the literary essay as a form—at least in this psychoanalytic context—is a resistance, a protest, a refusal to meet certain criteria. It is a disengagement from something in order to be able to engage with something else.

The avoidance of the essay as a term of art in psychoanalysis—Rycroft being the exception that proves what is a kind of rule—is not simply or solely the consequence of psychoanalysis's forlorn attempt to keep itself fairly and squarely within the realm, and the cultural prestige, of science. It is, as it were, a considered refusal. Because everything in psychoanalysis endorses Marianne Moore's famous epigraph to what she pointedly called her *Complete Poems*, 'Omissions are not accidents'; there being a link, as she intimates, between completion and omission.[5] Psychoanalysis, that has been so illuminating about omission and about fantasies of completeness—about the paradoxical idea that something becomes complete through omission—has, for reasons that may be of interest, discarded the essay as a useful term and a useable form. It is a strange omission, and not an accidental one.

Because of the uncertainty of its status—as an art or a science, as psychology or metaphysics, as religion or therapy, and so on—psychoanalysis has often had to define itself by saying what it is not. And one of the ways psychoanalysts have done this is by determinedly not writing essays. So psychoanalytic writing may have something to tell us about the essay—what it represents, what distinguishes it, what it forecloses—through its refusal of the genre; through its preference for writing writings and papers and lectures and contributions, and works. What is there about the essay, or about the writers of essays, that one might want to disassociate oneself from? What are psychoanalysts writing that makes the essay form unsuitable? What does an essay involve you in, that you might not want to be associated with? What, in short, are essays or indeed essayists assumed to be like if psychoanalysts want to disidentify from them? Geoffrey Hartman perhaps offers us a clue when he writes in the Preface to his book *The Third Pillar*, 'My contributions are, on the whole, neither erudite nor highly specialised, but rather essays'; psychoanalysis has always feared not being a specialism, and has wanted to sound erudite while never quite knowing what it should be erudite about.[6] There are, of course, lots of forms that psychoanalysts don't use, or claim to use in their writing, and yet the essay, given Hartman's definition of the genre, might seem to

---

[4] Rycroft, *Viewpoints*, 1.
[5] Marianne Moore, *The Complete Poems of Marianne Moore* (1968), vii.
[6] Geoffrey Hartman, *The Third Pillar: Essays in Judaic Studies* (2011), 1.

be rather more germane to the so-called discipline of psychoanalysis than most. Not much harm would be done, seemingly, if a psychoanalyst said he was writing an essay; or included the word in his professional vocabulary. It is sometimes more interesting when the least unacceptable thing is omitted. What, we might wonder, could the psychoanalyst fear from both within and outside his profession, if he claimed, as Rycroft did, to be writing essays? It seems like rather a ludicrous question, and it also is one.

When Judith Butler said in an interview that 'crafting a sexual position [...] always involves becoming haunted by what's excluded. And the more rigid the position, the greater the ghost, and the more threatening it is in some way' she could also be taken to be saying, in a rather psychoanalytic way, that any genre is haunted and defined by the genres it excludes.[7] And indeed that how you exclude something informs both its return and the form its haunting takes. It would be melodramatic to say that psychoanalytic writing is haunted by the essay form; or to intimate that the choosing and using of a literary genre is necessarily akin to the crafting of a sexual position. And yet, from a psychoanalytic point of view, the exclusion could be taken to be, in both senses, over-determined. Freud was famously struck in his *Studies in Hysteria* when, as he put it, his case-histories 'read like short stories'; he had wanted them to have what he calls 'the serious stamp of science', they were 'intended to be judged' like 'psychiatric' case-histories.[8] If they read like short stories they smacked of the literary. And for psychoanalysts, by the same token, to write essays, or to write psychoanalytic essays, might also smack of the literary (Rycroft's introduction quotes George Eliot, T. S. Eliot, and Iris Murdoch as well as Keynes on Goldsworthy Lowes Dickinson). The question, obviously, is what does the literary smack of such that the literary would be something that the psychoanalyst fights shy of in her writing? As though there is something that needs to be excluded from psychoanalytic writing, something which haunts it which is called the literary, or in this case the literary essay; and despite the obvious fact that great works of literature are routinely quoted and praised to the skies by psychoanalysts; though often, of course, as evidence of the truth of psychoanalysis (and the essay, unlike poetry, the novel, and drama, is the genre least often referred to, I suspect, in psychoanalytic writing; certainly in the British tradition of psychoanalysis there are few if any references to Addison or Steele, or Johnson, or Lamb or Hazlitt, or Pater, or Chesterton, or Eliot or Woolf, to mention the most obvious candidates; and Freud, perhaps surprisingly, never quotes Montaigne). It makes a certain kind of sense that psychoanalysts wouldn't want to think of themselves as writing fiction or

---

[7] 'Gender as Performance: An Interview with Judith Butler', by Peter Osborne and Lynne Segal, *Radical Philosophy* 67 (Summer 1994), 32–4.

[8] Sigmund Freud, *The Standard Edition of the Complete Psychological Works of Sigmund Freud*, ed. James Strachey and Anna Freud, 24 vols (2001), II, 160–1.

indeed poetry or drama; but the essay seems somehow more inviting, less of a threat, to use Judith Butler's word, to the psychoanalytic project.

It would be silly to make a drama out of something that is hardly a crisis; but in a psychoanalytic context even Virginia Woolf's vague, struggling definition of the essay in her review article 'Modern Essays' of 1922 (later revised for inclusion in *The Common Reader* (1925)) almost begins to make sense. 'A novel has a story', she writes,

> a poem rhyme; but what art can the essayist use in these short lengths of prose to sting us wide awake and fix us in a trance which is not sleep but rather an intensification of life—a basking, with every faculty alert, in the sun of pleasure?[9]

And her answer is that the essayist 'must know—that is the first essential—how to write'.[10] We know what she might mean, in a collusive sort of way, even though novelists and poets must also know how to write, whatever that might mean. But perhaps psychoanalysts, when they write their papers, lectures, and contributions, don't think of themselves writing, or don't want to think of themselves doing that; or writing in the traditions of the literary essay. In its by now traditional form the psychoanalytic paper begins with what is appropriately called an abstract; then it begins again with a proposal or a suggestion, sometimes called a hypothesis, based on observations made in the clinical situation; this is preceded or followed by a review of the so-called literature and some clinical vignettes that are supposed to validate the hypothesis. There is then a conclusion in which there is often a modest disclaimer about how Freud, Klein, Bion, Winnicott, or Lacan have already said this or something similar; and sometimes we are left with a challenging question, or set of possible implications. It is clear, in short, what and who the psychoanalytic writer is aligning him- or herself with, what the interpretative community is that is being addressed. It is certainly not a version of the albeit rather romanticized eighteenth-century coffee-house culture, nor the avid Victorian reading public. Because psychoanalysts now tend to write for each other, and for a scientific community whose recognition (and cultural legitimacy) they crave. Whether or not the essay as a genre circulates in a way the often rather elitist and embattled profession of psychoanalysis might fear or be wary of; or whether it smacks of amateurism—despite the patent absurdity of being professional about the unconscious and sexuality—the essay has not been the chosen genre of the psychoanalysts. It would be portentous, as I have said, to suggest that in the psychoanalytic literature, as it is in fact called, the essay is repressed. It is, though, certainly not included.

---

[9] Virginia Woolf, 'The Modern Essay', in *The Essays of Virginia Woolf*, vol. IV, ed. Andrew McNeillie (1994), 216.

[10] Woolf, 'The Modern Essay', 216.

In what is called *The Complete Psychological Works of Sigmund Freud*—which is neither complete nor self-evidently psychological though it goes under the unfortunate name of *The Standard Edition*—there are, it is worth noting, only two of Freud's works which are entitled, at least in their English translation, essays, *The Three Essays on the Theory of Sexuality* (1905) and *Moses and Monotheism: Three Essays* of 1939 (the word 'essay' incidentally is not in the index of the *Standard Edition*). Both controversial, and both, in their different ways, about origins, neither of these remarkable books of three essays—three being the privileged number in psychoanalysis—are more obviously essays, or essayistic, than a lot of Freud's other writings (Freud refers to what he calls, or what his translators call, the 'essays' in *Totem and Taboo* and *The Future of an Illusion*, but the books are not called books of essays; and he refers to his 'essay' of 1901 'On Dreams', but he titles it 'On Dreams').[11] It would be pointless to attempt a generic definition of the essay let alone speculate about how Freud might define the genre; and even though there are family resemblances between these two works they are not particularly salient. But there is one thing, I think, worth considering; and this is that the *Three Essays on the Theory of Sexuality* were, in the words of James Strachey, Freud's translator and editor, 'submitted by their author, in the course of a succession of editions over a period of twenty years, to more modifications and editions than any other of his writings, with the exception of, perhaps, *The Interpretation of Dreams* itself'.[12] *Moses and Monotheism*, being among the very last things Freud wrote, was not subject to revision or emendation. *The Three Essays on the Theory of Sexuality* kept announcing as it were its incompleteness.

There is, of course, no way of knowing whether Freud would have added or omitted anything from *Moses and Monotheism*; but the *Three Essays* kept on being, in Freud's view—that is, retrospectively—full of omissions and in need of elaboration and qualification. No one, of course, has had, as yet, the last word on anything; but there was something not about sexuality, but about the theory of sexuality, that for Freud went on being unfinished. The so-called essays on the theory of sexuality were then exactly essays as defined by the *OED*: 'The action or process of trying or testing [...] Cf. assay [...] An attempt, endeavour [...] A first tentative effort in learning or practice [...] a first draft [...] A composition of moderate length on any particular subject [...] originally implying want of finish, "an irregular, undigested piece" (Johnson), but now said of a composition more or less elaborate in style, though limited in range'.[13] An 'essayist' the *OED* defines as 'one who makes trials or experiments'.[14] For Freud, not incidentally, sexuality—not to mention its theorizing—was a trying and a testing, a trial and an

---

[11] See Freud, *Totem and Taboo*, in *The Standard Edition*, XIII, xiii; Freud, *The Future of an Illusion*, in *Mass Psychology and Other Writings*, trans. J. A. Underwood (2004).
[12] See Freud, *The Standard Edition*, VII, 126.   [13] *OED*, s.v. 'essay, *n*. 1a, 2, 5a, 7a&b, 8'.
[14] *OED*, s.v. 'essayist, *n*. 1'.

experiment; as was psychoanalysis itself. Each psychoanalytic session itself being, in the words of the *OED*, a 'composition of moderate length' that is also something of a trial and an experiment; and can, of course, be trying and testing for both participants.

Gillian Beer has written very interestingly about how, as she puts it, 'the techniques of production in nineteenth-century fiction, particularly serialization, also help to shape Freud's account of his working method, and perhaps the method itself with its series of encounters.'[15] If the serialized nineteenth-century novel is akin to the serialized sessions of a psychoanalysis—and from which the fiction called a case-history can be written—then so too could the nineteenth- (and eighteenth-) century essay be usefully linked to the once new form of treatment called psychoanalysis; in which something is tried out in words with no aspiration to the complete or the definitive; in which enlarging one's experience can take priority over winning an argument, proving a point, or coming to conclusions (Johnson's *Dictionary* definition of the essay as 'A loose sally of the mind [...] not a regular and orderly composition', is a useful definition of a psychoanalytic session).[16] And in which the sessions, like the essays of any given writer, develop an idiom, and a disparate continuity; which is partly the continuity of incompletion. The concluding words of Freud's *Three Essays* tell us, after over a hundred pages of fascinating speculation, that no theory of sexuality is, as yet, either possible or plausible. 'The unsatisfactory conclusion, however, that emerges from these investigations of the disturbances of sexual life', Freud writes, 'is that we know far too little of the biological processes constituting the essence of sexuality to be able to construct from our fragmentary information a theory adequate to the understanding alike of normal and of pathological conditions.'[17] The essay as a genre thrives on the conclusion that conclusions are unsatisfactory. That it's all in the trying, and the trying it out. An essay, like a psychoanalysis, is an experiment without a proof. It is experimental writing—again, rather like psychoanalytic writing—but without its avant garde associations. The essay, it should be noted, though an experiment, a trying of something, is a stable form, not subject to much innovation.

'In the realm of thought', Adorno wrote grandly in 'The Essay as Form', 'it is virtually the essay alone that has successfully raised doubts about the absolute privilege of method.'[18] Certainly when it came to sexuality and its theories, Freud found—as his *Three Essays* and their prolific footnotes extended themselves through six editions of the text—that privileging the method of psychoanalysis raised doubts about method, about psychoanalysis, about sexuality, about

---

[15] Gillian Beer, 'Introduction' to *The Wolfman and Other Cases* (2002), viii.

[16] Samuel Johnson, *A Dictionary of the English Language* (1755), n.p.

[17] Freud, *The Standard Edition*, VII, 243.

[18] Theodor Adorno, 'The Essay as Form', in *Notes to Literature, Volume One*, ed. Rolf Tiedemann, trans. Shierry Weber Nicholsen (1991), 9.

theorizing, and about the absolute privileging of anything (or anyone). It is difficult to know quite what to make of Adorno's assertion about the essay form—and the phrase 'virtually the essay alone' suggests that he had his doubts—but it does draw attention to the essay as a sceptical form; and it can make us wonder in relation to Freud's *Three Essays* whether psychoanalysis is a method—whether it ever was a method, and whether and why it became one— and what method might have to do with the unconscious, or with sexuality, and the theorizing about it. And, of course, why Freud called his formative book on sexuality a book of essays. When Harold Bloom writes, 'Freud's theory of the mind or soul, after a century or so, is alive and valuable while his scientism is quite dead. I urge us to regard him as the Montaigne or Emerson of the twentieth century', he is urging us to regard Freud as he did not, mostly, regard himself; that is, as an essayist, with all that that entails, which in Bloom's terms means being a theorist without being a scientist.[19] The essayist is the writer who extricates theory from science.

And Freud's *Three Essays* were not, it should be noted, on sexuality but on the 'Theory' of sexuality (in Shaun Whiteside's new Penguin Freud translation it is called *Three Essays on Sexual Theory*; the *Standard Edition* equivocates, calling it on the cover of Volume VII *Three Essays on Sexuality*, while calling it by its real title on the contents page). Essays are often 'on' something or other but there is clearly a difference between an essay on sexuality and an essay on a theory of sexuality; or this, at least, Freud's essays might make one wonder about. Is there sexuality or only theories of sexuality might be a good question to try out in an essay. As would the question, what is a theory of sexuality a theory of?

Freud warns us—and this is where what Freud calls in his Preface his 'field of scientific work' joins up with the essay's aesthetic of the unfinished (and the unfinishable)—that his *Three Essays* could never 'be extended into a "complete theory of sexuality"'.[20] And we only need these essays, he writes in the Preface to the fourth edition, because we can't see what is in front of us. 'If mankind had been able to learn from a direct observation of children, these three essays could have remained unwritten.'[21] Freud had to write these essays because our perception is distorted by our wishes; because we wanted to see children as innocent we couldn't see them as they are; and because we couldn't see children as they are we couldn't see our sexuality for what it is. It is interesting, and unusual, for the essayist to tell us what would have had to happen to make the writing of his essays unnecessary (and it may be an interesting question—the sort of thing that can be thrown off in passing in an essay—to ask of any piece of writing, what could have happened that would have made the author not need to write it?). For Freud his *Three Essays* are a corrective for the failures, the avoidances of empirical enquiry;

---

[19] Harold Bloom, *The Anatomy of Influence* (2011), 14.
[20] Freud, *The Standard Edition*, VII, 131, 130.   [21] Freud, *The Standard Edition*, VII, 133.

what direct observation shied away from the *Essays* had to investigate. What science had turned a blind eye to the essayist could be curious about; the essay itself—like sexuality—being perhaps the form that keeps making links between curiosity and sociability. The implication being that one of the preconditions for sociability is shared curiosity.

His essays, Freud intimates, seek to reveal something that has been concealed. 'The progressive concealment of the body which goes along with civilization keeps sexual curiosity awake', he writes in the *Three Essays*. 'The curiosity seeks to complete the sexual object by revealing its hidden parts.'[22] Our curiosity can go to sleep—we want to sleep off our desire—so we need concealment to keep it awake; and our curiosity is the way we try and complete something—call it the object of desire—that cannot be completed (we can never have total knowledge, total access, total possession). Essays, which are nothing if not curious, seek to go on trying to complete something that cannot be completed. 'It is out of the question', Freud writes, that his *Three Essays* 'could ever be extended into a complete "theory of sexuality"'.[23] It is, we can surmise, the impossibility of completion that frees the essayist to write, that frees our sexual curiosity to be somehow endless. So a Freudian question here might be, how are we imagining the object of desire when we believe that the essay might be the best way to approach it? Not simply, what is the essayist wanting, but what is the essay a good way of wanting? And what is it about the essay form that makes it this good way of wanting? These are among the questions prompted by Freud calling his great book about sexuality a book of essays.

Freud's *Three Essays*, that is to say, draw our attention to the way the essay as a genre investigates our sense of an ending, our sense of what completion might be; both what we might be wanting by wanting it, and what we imagine it might do for us. We can ask of any piece of writing, what makes this the end? And in what sense, if at all, has it turned out to be the promised end? But in an essay—like a lyric poem or a short story, unlike a novel or a play, or indeed an epic poem—we know the end is always near; essays tending to be, like lyric poems as A. R. Ammons intimates in a phrase from his poem *Essay on Poetics*, 'slight completions'.[24] Freud ends his *Three Essays* by saying that he has reached an 'unsatisfactory conclusion', and that he has barely begun to have an 'adequate' theory of sexuality. Freud offers us the (ironic) satisfaction of being unsatisfied. The essays, like the sexual satisfactions Freud describes in these essays, are nowhere near complete. The desire for completion is all there is to desire, at least in Freud's account. The desire for completion is the nearest we are ever going to get to completion.

---

[22] Freud, *The Standard Edition*, VII, 156.   [23] Freud, *The Standard Edition*, VII, 130.
[24] A. R. Ammons, 'Essay in Poetics', l. 90, in *The Complete Poems of A. R. Ammons*, ed. Robert M. West, 2 vols (2017), I, 543.

If we go back to Freud's words, to Freud's misgivings in the *Studies in Hysteria*, there was what he called 'the serious stamp of science', and then there was the short story, possibly less serious than science, but certainly less scientific. And not quite what Freud wanted his writing to sound like. But somewhere in between the serious stamp of science—the psychiatric case-history, the scientific treatise or paper—and the fictional short story there is, we might say, the essay. The essay which can incorporate both—the empiricism of the scientist and the fabulation of the writer of fiction, 'direct observation' and fantasy—without excluding either. Or can take from both without having to declare an exclusive allegiance. The essay tends to allow for, if not to actually encourage, digression—like psychoanalytic treatment there is no rule about keeping to the point; but it has points to make. And even though, of course, essays can be written by and for so-called specialists or experts, it doesn't tend to be a recondite or esoteric form, at least in the British and American traditions of the literary essay. The essay has been good at genial scepticism, hospitable curiosity, the sociability of knowledge; and, of course, at inspired dogmatism. So—at least in its enlightenment versions—the essay can be, to put it psychoanalytically, the genre in which we are free of the tyrannical parents. And so it lets us imagine what it would be like to live (and write) as if there were no tyrannical parents. This, paradoxically, is not something the ethos of psychoanalysis has always encouraged.

What Freud's *Three Essays*, and the subsequent disavowal of the essay in psychoanalysis after Freud reveals, I think, is that the writing of psychoanalysis—if not its clinical practice—has been tyrannized by the wish to get something right at the cost of saying something interesting and useful. Another way of saying this would be to say that it has not allowed itself to be Emersonian. Comparing his essays on Byron with his editing of Byron, the critic and scholar Jerome McGann had this to say:

> Under the horizon of a literary practice that has idealised the standard critical edition, however, critical commentary itself reflects that aspiration to—that apparition of—finishedness [...] Even writing in the essay form we have wanted to get things right, to say something definitive (the supreme quality, we used to imagine, of the critical edition). And while we can achieve this under certain limitations and conditions, we can never know that we have done it. (Alas, we often imagine that we do know such things).[25]

'Even writing in the essay form we have wanted to get things right, to say something definitive'; as if, even in the essay, we haven't been let off the hook, that the essay could or should be the form in which we can get things other than

---

[25] Jerome McGann, *Byron and Romanticism* (2002), 6.

right, say something that need not be definitive. As if there is no refuge from this distraction of what McGann calls finishedness, and I have been calling completeness. But then there is McGann's wonderfully definitive point: 'while we can achieve this under certain limitations and conditions'—this rightness, this definitiveness—'we can never know that we have done it'. There is hope but not for us. What the literary essay offers the psychoanalyst, and that the psychoanalyst has refused, is the opportunity to be neither definitive nor right, but in a psychoanalytic way. The psychoanalyst, in other words, could do in his writing what he should be doing in his clinical work. But to do this he might need to start writing essays, to let the essay form inform what he does. And then we will be able to see what, if anything, the psychoanalyst can contribute to the essay.

17

Dalí's Montaigne

Essay Hybrids and Surrealist Practice

Christy Wampole

1. Introduction

A hand attached to a sinewy arm writes delicately with a feather quill in an open book. The arm, its bicep muscles exposed, is buttoned to a skull that rides atop a tortoise through a desertscape. This ink-rendered frontispiece of Salvador Dalí's 1947 illustrated edition of Michel de Montaigne's *Essais* shows the compatibility of Surrealism and essayism as expressive, image-reliant forms (Figure 17.1).[1] Through the visible bones and muscles, Dalí conveys in a very literal sense Montaigne's desire to appear *tout nu*, completely exposed to his reader. In the image, the essayist's brain moves slowly through the world, collecting impressions along the way and transferring them directly from the head to the page. It is the essayist's vocation, Dalí suggests, to wander, to dream, and to collect images.

The introduction of a visual element to essayistic practices in the twentieth century—in the form of photograph, film, and video—allowed the essay hybrid to remain suspended in an interstitial space between the documentary and the dream world. This chapter analyses the conjunction of image and text in essayistic hybrids such as the photo essay, essay-film, and video essay and explores the possibilities of estrangement—the transformation of the everyday into the alien—that emerge from the encounter between visual and verbal expression. The familiar etymology of 'essay' suggests that the essayist is committed to some kind of trying or attempting. Texts assay in one way, images in another; their mutual influence allows for the essay to benefit from the kind of productive strangeness lauded by the Surrealists.

Such new hybrid forms as the photo essay, essay-film, and video essay are obviously more visual than the literary essay. Nonetheless, image-centred tableaux were always a key feature of the latter. Readers of Montaigne are likely to have a picture in their minds of the author falling off a horse or exposing himself, completely naked, like those who 'dwell under the sweet liberty of nature's

---

[1] Michel de Montaigne, *Essays of Michel de Montaigne*, trans. Charles Cotton, illus. Salvador Dalí (1947).

Christy Wampole, *Dalí's Montaigne: Essay Hybrids and Surrealist Practice* In: *On Essays: Montaigne to the Present.* Edited by: Thomas Karshan and Kathryn Murphy, Oxford University Press (2020). © Christy Wampole. DOI: 10.1093/oso/9780198707868.003.0018

Figure 17.1 Salvador Dalí, untitled illustration, originally published in *Essays of Michel de Montaigne*, trans. Charles Cotton (1947), n.p.

Art: © 2019 Salvador Dalí, Fundació Gala-Salvador Dalí, Artists Rights Society.

primitive laws'.[2] In fact, Montaigne clues his readers in on his painterly imagination already in the introductory 'Au lecteur': 'car c'est moy que je peins': it is myself I paint.[3] Yet this picture will differ from reader to reader; it has not been fixed by the essayist himself. All essayists rely on images and imagery, but the introduction of the camera and the artist's pen to essay-making changes the form's nature and expands the expressive capacity of the essayist while potentially diminishing the imaginative freedom of the spectator-reader.

A striking example of the transition from word to image in the life of the essay genre occurred in 1947 with Dalí's illustrated edition of Montaigne's *Essays*, commissioned by Doubleday Press. While other artists such as Gustave Doré had produced naturalistic engravings to accompany the *Essays*, Dalí was the first to allow the fantastical imagination to guide his drawings.[4] Using rich colours and his customary dream-like imagery, the Spanish Surrealist translates the essayist's thoughts into allegories. Abstract concepts are morphed into human figures and suspended in an hallucinatory world where the laws of physics and logic do not apply. In his illustration of Montaigne's 'Of Drunkenness', this state of mind is depicted as a woman with a thorny body and a rose sprouting from her chest. Dalí's visual renderings reveal a latent oneiric tendency in Montaigne's prose, showing the extent to which everyday life is naturally infused with arbitrariness and uncanny beauty. The digressive, open-ended thought of Montaigne finds a correlative in Dalí's visual free association.

This postdated collaboration makes obvious many shared affinities between Surrealism and essayism. By essayism, I mean the open-ended 'trying out' of a theme by a reflective subject, particularly in the form of prose (the essay or essayistic novel) or in a visual form (the photo essay, essay-film, or video essay). A mode in favour of the dissolution of boundaries between art and science, intention and chance, and introspection and engagement with the world, essayism shares with Surrealism several features: both operate using a logic of digression and free association; both take interest in the subjective inner life of the individual and in the process of self-discovery; both disregard formal strictures, celebrating instead what Adorno called in the essay a 'childlike freedom'; both rely on sensory perception, memory, intuition, and imagination; and, importantly, both tend to rely heavily on images.[5] In the hybrid visual forms of the photo essay, essay-film, and video essay, essayism gravitates naturally beyond the confines of literature.

---

[2] Montaigne, 'To the Reader', n.p.

[3] Montaigne, 'Au Lecteur', in *Les Essais de Michel de Montaigne*, ed. Pierre Villey, 3 vols (1930–1), I, 4.

[4] Doré completed these drawings in the late 1850s. One illustration, meant to accompany tome one, book 2 of the *Essays*, is viewable through the Bibliothèque nationale's digital library Gallica, at http://gallicalabs.bnf.fr/ark:/12148/btv1b10322204b.

[5] Theodor Adorno, 'The Essay as Form', trans. Bob Hullot-Kentor and Frederic Will, *New German Critique* 32 (Spring–Summer 1984), 151–71, here 152.

The images that result are no less essayistic than text; they simply give a new form to the act of attempting. What results is a juxtaposition of images, tried out on the spectator as a visual digression, the image-work of a meditative subject.

While Surrealism was a specific, historically and geographically located movement with great influence beyond its time and place, essayism is more diffuse and less localizable; it is not a movement and has no clearly defined method, no manifesto, and no political intentions. Nonetheless, it is possible to highlight specific and remarkable similarities between the use of images by Surrealists and essay hybridists. Surrealism might be described as an enlistment of images in the service of self-discovery. These images allow a meditative subject to work through her memories, dreams, misunderstandings, errors, and anxieties, much in the vein of Freudian *Durcharbeitung* (working through). Though it would be a stretch to call Montaigne a proto-Surrealist, it is accurate to say that his loosened style and its heritage in subsequent essayistic writing opened the door for the kind of digressive image sampling integral to Surrealism.[6] The influence also works in reverse: I claim that the newer hybrid essayistic practices (photo essay, essay-film, and video essay) take up the Surrealists' project of disclosing the subconscious aspects of the psyche via pictures, and in doing so, bring to the fore features latent in the tradition of the literary essay.

These hybrid, imagistic forms are more economical than the literary essay in conveying the kinds of impressions that would require an abundance of words. The brevity and suggestiveness of many literary essays already tend away from the long-windedness of discursive prose; the addition of the image to its expressive repertoire in the new hybrids allows the essay to increase meaning while maintaining its usual textual frugality. These hybrids allow for a multiplication and expansion of the singular reflective voice, moving beyond the constraints of thematic cohesion which the literary essay already stretches, and using images as emancipatory stimuli for conflating the conscious and the subconscious, in a way which furthers the inclination of the literary essay to think associatively and to render the dynamism of thought processes. In each case, latent tendencies in the essay tradition as a whole are realized in ways not available through text alone.

The special properties of the image, moving or still, allow the dream to enter waking life: its economy, colour, movement, visual rhythm, appeal to the fantastical component of the human imagination, repeatability or reorderability, exaggerative power, and its capacity to be manipulated, edited, or synthesized. In both surrealism and essayism, the image is a useful tool for contingent thinking, that is,

---

[6] In an unpublished conference talk, Réginald Dalle argued that Dalí's Surrealism shares many features with Montaigne's humanism. In his abstract, he writes, 'Le but de cette communication est de montrer grâce à diverses illustrations choisies comment Salvador Dalí a su saisir par son génie créateur et artistique le génie de Montaigne et voir que le surréalisme dalinien est proche de l'humanisme de Montaigne'. See Réginald Dalle, 'Montaigne vu par Salvador Dalí', *Montaigne et les Essais, 1580–1980, Actes du Congrès de Bordeaux* (Juin 1980), ed. Pierre Michel et al. (1983).

reflection that does not have a pre-established itinerary but lets itself be guided by the new configuration of each passing moment, and resembles the logic of dreams. I argue that the images attempt to show through a first-person perspective—as seen through the eye of the camera—the complicated subjectivity of observant, thinking individuals who summon up pictures following the digressive logic of the essay and the dream. In this, the hybrid essayists turn to the Surrealists as strong antecedents and models. My claims will be supported by a close analysis of four essay hybrids: Dalí's illustrated edition of Montaigne's *Essays* (1947), James Agee and Walker Evans's photo essay *Let Us Now Praise Famous Men* (1941), Chris Marker's essay-film *Sans soleil* (1982), and John Bresland's video essay *Mangoes* (2010).

2. Dalí and Surrealist Essayism

The Surrealists privileged images over words, particularly words in their literary iteration. In one of their many declarations, the Surrealists wrote that '[w]e have nothing to do with literature; but we are quite capable of making use of it when necessary like anyone else'.[7] Salvador Dalí certainly made use of it in his commissioned illustrations of Montaigne's *Essays*, which consisted of both black ink drawings and brilliantly coloured watercolour and ink illustrations. In this case, the literary text is at once the artist's font of inspiration and what constrains his work; because he was asked to illustrate the essays, they provided structure to an otherwise unbound flux of images. While there are plenty of episodes in the essays that lend themselves to illustration, Dalí was not content to produce mimetic depictions of exempla or anecdotes. Instead, he opted for allegorical renderings of passages that are not so neatly imagined in pictures. The reader who comes across the images dispersed throughout the book is put in a special position; she or he is invited to determine the relationship between Dalí's image and Montaigne's text but not to conjure her or his own image.

The black ink illustration for the essay 'Of Thumbs' is signature Dalí (Figure 17.2); in the dark shadows and near architectural bearing of the thumbs, one recognizes Giorgio Di Chirico's influence—a digitized Di Chirico. A little grass, the hint of a ground, and the strong light source suggest that the figures are somewhere outside; nearly all of Dalí's dreamscapes are set in an otherworldly outdoors. He is an externalizer of the internal, as he tries to render al fresco the unventilated complexities of human interiority. The thumb in the foreground resembles an erected condom with its rolled up edges at the bottom; the phallic implications of the image stand out like a sore thumb. These six statuesque

---

[7] José Pierre (ed.), *Tracts surréalistes et déclarations collectives* [1922–39], 2 vols (1980), I, 34.

XII

OF THUMBS

Tacitus reports, that among certain barbarian kings their manner was, when they would make a firm obligation, to join their right hands close to one another, and intertwist their thumbs; and when, by force of straining, the blood it appeared in the ends, they lightly pricked them with some sharp instrument, and mutually sucked them.

[161]

Figure 17.2 Salvador Dalí, untitled illustration, originally published in *Essays of Michel de Montaigne*, trans. Charles Cotton (1947), n.p.

Art: © 2019 Salvador Dalí, Fundació Gala-Salvador Dalí, Artists Rights Society.

phalluses are surrounded by six people—a finger for each—who take up various positions, but who all display their own thumbs. What could be more surreal? One wonders whether Georges Bataille's 'The Big Toe' could be read as a surrealist refashioning of Montaigne's 'Of Thumbs'.[8]

If Dalí overstates Montaigne's theme, inflating the thumbs to gargantuan proportions and reiterating them insistently, he at the same time performs a compelling exercise in thematics. After all, what is a theme? It is the isolation or amplification of a particular concern, the privileged inscription of a space dedicated to one topic, to the exclusion of others. When essayists announce the theme of an essay, usually through the title, they delineate the dimensions of their content, surveying its field. Digression within this field is welcome as long as the theme remains a potentially reliable centre to which the essayist can return. Yet essayists occasionally toy with the expectations set up by their titles, using them as mere jumping-off points to which they never return or as enticing hooks used to flirt with the reader, an irony shared by the Surrealists who rely on their wit and the frustration of readerly expectations to stage playful surprises. Surrealist digressive practice, even less restricted than the essayist's, works like a pinball machine; a thought or some external stimulus ricochets the mind from surface to surface. It has no theme per se, no centre around which to circle, only a starting point. This leads to a claim: essayism has centric tendencies, while Surrealism tends to be eccentric. Dalí's illustrations are of interest in part because the commission constrains him to illustrate *something specific*; he is not granted the usual licence to let his fantasies fly completely free, as is customary in Surrealist automatism. Because 'Of Thumbs' presents an obvious and easily illustrated theme, the illustrator's constraint is clear and his images remain centred.

But what about more abstract themes that don't lend themselves easily to illustration? How would one render 'Of the Force of the Imagination' visually, for example? It would seem that such a title invites total freedom on the part of the artist. Dalí's treatment confirms this (Figure 17.3). His outdoor dreamscape shows the undoing of gravity as architectural forms come apart and mountains, rocks, and trees hover in midair. A yellow-green cube floats in the foreground with a bowl and pomegranate suspended above it. Three human figures levitate and reach upward. The image caption reads '*Fortis imaginatio generat casum*' ('A strong imagination begets the event itself'), the dictum Montaigne cites to begin his essay. The anti-gravitational aspect of Dalí's illustration, which tries to resist the downward pull of the *casus* or fall, suggests a pinpointing of the imagination and the images it generates as located somewhere upward and beyond. The word 'Surrealism' already suggests this spatialization; even though the movement deals heavily with the subconscious, it could never have been called

---

[8] See Georges Bataille, 'The Big Toe' [1929], ed. and trans. Allan Stoekl, in *Visions of Excess: Selected Writings, 1927–1939* (1985).

Figure 17.3 Salvador Dalí, untitled illustration, originally published in *Essays of Michel de Montaigne*, trans. Charles Cotton (New York: Doubleday & Company, inc., 1947), n.p.

Art: © 2019 Salvador Dalí, Fundació Gala-Salvador Dalí, Artists Rights Society.

'Subrealism'. The 'sur-' prefix reinforces the above-and-beyondness of the free associative, image-based practice, depicted as the surpassing of reality.[9] The essay is already an open form in that it is bound to very few conventions and its style and content resist the gravitas of ideology, but the incorporation of Dalí's images allows Montaigne's essay to aim for the yonder. The image, in the form of wall-hung paintings, frescos, the altar, dreams, or the spectacle of a cloudscape or a starry sky, is above our line of sight. Here the essay hybrid borrows this uplifting effect, targeting what is beyond.

Most of Dalí's colour illustrations are allegorical in that they suggest that a second, secret meaning accompanies the 'literal' one. Two images—one in colour, the other in black ink—accompany the essay 'Of Drunkenness'. The latter, as one might anticipate for an allegorical depiction of inebriation, shows a recumbent Dionysian figure out in nature raising his glass towards the spectator. The colour image, on the other hand, conjugates Thanatos and Eros as the heads of two cadaver figures are absorbed into the rose-like body of a woman (Figure 17.4). A rose sprouts from the middle of her chest, thorns protrude from her sides, and petals fall from her arm. The rotting figures, seated across from one another on tree stumps, have perhaps gotten drunk together and are sharing the same intoxicated vision. Alcohol decomposes their consciousness. The rose-woman is drunkenness in a human form, delighting the senses but pricking the drunkards as well. She arouses but cuts. However, this is only one of many possible readings; inevitably, the allegory veils its meaning. Moving away from the literal and towards the figurative, imagery becomes subjectivized. The mind's eye is liberated from objects as the subject takes over. Dalí is not under the thumb of mimetic representation; the phenomenon of drunkenness has no fixed image, which gives him permission to craft his own.

When Arthur Benson defined the essay as 'a thing which someone does himself', he emphasized the self-reliance of the essayist as free subject, as a creator of customized connections.[10] The freedom that binds essayist and Surrealist is one of the key features of their poetics. Assaying, through words or pictures, requires a certain autonomy from the constraints of form, mimetic representation, and even logic. Essayism and Surrealism are permanent invitations to digress, to dream, and to discover or test an idea without committing to it. In Montaigne's case, he proffers a brief Western history of the thumb, leaving the reader to reflect on the cultural power a single digit contains. He politicizes the thumb. Furthermore, he shows implicitly that he just as easily could have dedicated an essay to the index finger or the pinky. Every part of our bodies and every banal object that surrounds

[9] Appropriating the term coined by Apollinaire in 1917, André Breton defines Surrealism in his 1924 manifesto thus: 'Surrealism is based on the belief in the superior reality of certain forms of associations neglected until now, in the omnipotence of dream, and in the disinterested play of thought' (André Breton, *Manifestoes of Surrealism*, trans. Richard Seaver and Helen R. Lane (1972), 26).

[10] Arthur Benson, 'The Art of the Essayist', in *Modern English Essays*, ed. Ernest Rhys (1923), 50.

Figure 17.4 Salvador Dalí, untitled illustration, originally published in *Essays of Michel de Montaigne*, trans. Charles Cotton (New York: Doubleday & Company, inc., 1947), n.p.

Art: © 2019 Salvador Dalí, Fundació Gala-Salvador Dalí, Artists Rights Society.

us is a potential catalyst for essayistic thinking. Dalí's treatment of the thumb is as fragmented as that of Montaigne. These two aesthetic practices shun the conventions set forth by earlier generations of writers and artists and rely instead on the improvisational genius of the daydreamer.

Salvador Dalí's illustrations of the *Essays* are significant because they demonstrate the natural sympathies between essayism and Surrealism. The twentieth century saw both the essay's hybridization and its surrealization, as the inclusion of images coaxed the genre towards the kind of unexpected juxtapositions, blending of the conscious and subconscious, and imagistic economy specific to Surrealist practices.

3. Evans and Agee Keep It (Sur)real

In the late 1930s, the American photographer Walker Evans and the American writer James Agee took on an unorthodox essayistic project that would allow them to forge a double subjectivity through which the suffering farmers of the Dust Bowl would be observed and studied. Originally commissioned but then rejected by a New York magazine as a journalistic piece on US cotton tenantry, Evans and Agee's *Let Us Now Praise Famous Men* was finally published in 1941. On first leafing through the book, one might assume it to be a straightforward piece of documentary journalism, until this sentence in the preface appears: 'The immediate instruments are two: the motionless camera, and the printed word. The governing instrument—which is also one of the centers of the subject—is individual, anti-authoritative human consciousness.'[11] This is the first of many signals of the experimental nature of their project and its reliance on Surrealist principles, particularly apparent in Agee's essays that accompany Evans's photographs, written while he was reading Freud.[12] Indeed, Hugh Davis has called the project 'a work of surrealist ethnography'.[13] Agee uses his own memories, flaws, dreams, and the tangled threads of impressions he collected in the field to work through his anxieties about the project, never sure that he will have done justice to the reality of his subjects. He prizes 'works of the imagination', which 'advance and assist the human race, and make an opening in the darkness as nothing can', and

---

[11] James Agee and Walker Evans, *Let Us Now Praise Famous Men* (2001), x.

[12] William Schultz has argued that the text to *Let Us Now Praise Famous Men* is Agee's 'covert autobiography' and that traces of the 'primal scene schema' can be found in the book. See Schultz, 'Off-Stage Voices in James Agee's *Let Us Now Praise Famous Men*: Reportage as Covert Autobiography', *American Imago* 56.1 (1999), 75–104.

[13] Hugh Davis, 'The Making of James Agee', unpublished doctoral dissertation, University of Tennessee (2005), 53. Elsewhere Davis argues that Surrealism greatly influenced both Evans and Agee: see '"Drinking at Wells Sunk beneath Privies": Agee and Surrealism', in *Agee Agonistes: Essays on the Life, Legend, and Works of James Agee*, ed. Michael A. Lofaro (2007), 85–104, especially 86.

sees in the unmediated and incommunicable experiences of his travels in the South a kind of surreality.[14] He pre-emptively admits the failure of the project because no images or words could communicate the surreal experience of direct contact with the people and places he and Evans encountered (Figure 17.5). The text abounds with free associations, oneiric lists, dream imagery, and, in some sections, what resembles unrestrained, Surrealist-inspired automatic writing: one passage, a single sentence that lasts a page and a half, ends '[...] beneath the table the dog and the puppy and the sliding cats, and above it, a grizzling literal darkness of flies, and spread on all quarters, the simmering dream held in this horizon yet overflowing it, and of the natural world, and eighty miles back east and north, the hard flat incurable sore of Birmingham'.[15]

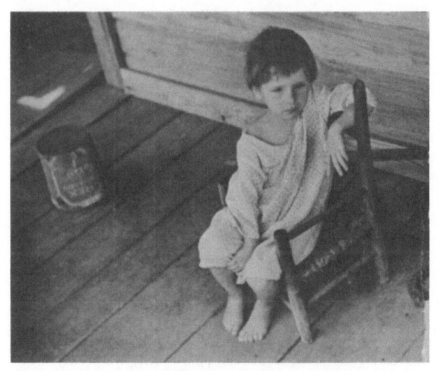

Figure 17.5 Walker Evans, untitled photograph, originally published in James Agee and Walker Evans, *Let Us Now Praise Famous Men* (1939), n.p.

[14]   Agee and Evans, *Let Us Now Praise Famous Men*, 205.
[15]   Agee and Evans, *Let Us Now Praise Famous Men*, 193.

The role of the camera is fundamental in Agee and Evans's project and is held superior to the writer's pen in its ability to document a specific scene.[16] Agee explains that one reason he cares 'so deeply for the camera' is that it is 'incapable of recording anything but absolute, dry truth'.[17] He argues that 'the camera seems to me, next to unassisted and weaponless consciousness, the central instrument of our time.'[18] The nature of the photographic image as trace allows for a phenomenon to leave a lasting mark, albeit dislodged from its original context. This dislodging is the photographic equivalent of the characteristic digression of the literary essay. Surrealism takes particular interest in decontextualized images, pictures that leave their residue on the psyche as on a photographic plate. Rosalind Krauss claims that 'surrealist photography exploits the very special connection to reality with which all photography is endowed. [...] On the family tree of images [the photograph] is closer to palm prints, death masks, cast shadows, the Shroud of Turin, or the tracks of gulls on beaches.'[19] Agee expresses the desire for an even more fundamental kind of trace-making when he laments the fact that the project had to appear as a book.[20] For him, the ideal format would have been radically different:

If I could do it, I'd do no writing at all here. It would be photographs; the rest would be fragments of cloth, bits of cotton, lumps of earth, records of speech, pieces of wood and iron, phials of odors, plates of food and of excrement. [...] A piece of the body torn out by the roots might be more to the point.[21]

Agee wanted pure trace—or, even better, the trace-leaving phenomena themselves. In Evans's photographs, one sees the hard faces of the sharecroppers and their families, their brows as furrowed as their fields. He also captures the objects and places that surround them: a pair of worn boots abandoned in the sterile sand, an empty bed, the dilapidated interiors emptied of people. The necessity of a direct and personal encounter with the *trouvaille* or found object, a component of Surrealist practice, has an afterlife in the photographs of *Let Us Now*

---

[16] Agee argues that words 'are the most inevitably inaccurate of all mediums of record and communication' (Agee and Evans, *Let Us Now Praise Famous Men*, 209). For lack of a better medium, his goal as essayist is to try to let the phenomena he approaches express themselves 'in [their] own terms' (Agee and Evans, *Let Us Now Praise Famous Men*, 208).

[17] Agee and Evans, *Let Us Now Praise Famous Men*, 206.

[18] Agee and Evans, *Let Us Now Praise Famous Men*, 9.

[19] Rosalind Krauss, 'Photography in the Service of Surrealism', *L'Amour fou: Photography and Surrealism*, ed. Rosalind Krauss and Jane Livingston (1985), 15–42, here 31.

[20] 'The photographs are not illustrative. They, and the text, are coequal, mutually independent, and fully collaborative. [...] This is a *book* only by necessity' (Agee and Evans, *Let Us Now Praise Famous Men*, xi).

[21] Agee and Evans, *Let Us Now Praise Famous Men*, 10.

Praise Famous Men, albeit as surrogates for unmediated contact.[22] Because the encountered objects, people, and places cannot be delivered into the hands of the reader, the photograph is the closest proxy. In this collaboration, Evans is a hunter of images while Agee is a collector of impressions. The project is composed of two kinds of traces, those left on film and those left on the psyche.

Let Us Now Praise Famous Men required two people to come to fruition. The essay is not typically a collaborative endeavour. One voice expresses a single subjectivity. This is true even in the case of Dalí's illustrated edition of Montaigne because the images were added after the fact; the two men, separated by centuries, were independent agents. However, the collaboration of Agee and Evans, and essay-films like Chris Marker's *Sans soleil*, which as we will see required a hired narrator, a production crew, and film clips from other directors, suggest that the essay is not necessarily a solitary undertaking.

In fact, comparing Evans's pictures and Agee's text, the two seem at times to be having two different conversations. If we take the photographs alone, there are few visible traces of Surrealist influence, no hint of Man Ray or Hans Bellmer. Most of the images are black and white portraits or shots of interiors, landscapes, or objects, like the pair of shoes left in the dirt (Figure 17.6). There is nothing conspicuously experimental in their composition and their mode seems purely documentary. Yet in conjunction with Agee's essays, they change character, and accrue dream-like, meditative qualities. Through the pictures, meanwhile, Agee's ruminations are given context; grounded in an unequivocally real place and time. Since Montaigne, the essay has been conceived as dialogic; he imagined the pieces as his side of a conversation he'd never be able to have with his deceased best friend Étienne de la Boétie, who was commemorated in the essay 'On Friendship'. Essayists often write with an intimacy toward their interlocutors who will never answer them. The essay hybrids of the twentieth and twenty-first centuries at times attempt to incorporate the absent interlocutor and realize a dialogue only implicit for the companionless essayist. Even between friends, conversations are sometimes difficult. These tensions can be felt in *Let Us Now Praise Famous Men*: the photographer tended towards the real, the writer towards the surreal.

Agee and Evans's collaborative photo essay illustrates the power of the photographer to go where the essayist cannot and vice versa. The essay has thus added another dimension to its already rich expressive repertory, with the photograph providing residual evidence of experiences actually lived. Furthermore, the images placed before the reader provide an occasion for reverie and aesthetic contemplation

---

[22] On the Surrealist *trouvaille*, see 'La Trouvaille (the lucky find); le hasard objectif (objective chance); le trouble (the surrealist uncanny)', in Margaret Cohen, *Profane Illumination: Walter Benjamin and the Paris of Surrealist Revolution* (1993), 140–5.

Figure 17.6 Walker Evans, untitled photograph, originally published in James Agee and Walker Evans, *Let Us Now Praise Famous Men* (1939), n.p.

Source: Copyright © 1941 by James Agee and Walker Evans, and renewed 1969 by Mia Fristch Agee and Walker Evans. Reprinted by permission of Houghton Mifflin Harcourt Publishing Company. All rights reserved.

and set the essay reader on a different course than a pictureless essay. The image is an interrupting force, a surface from which thoughts will be deflected in a new direction. One image shows, for example, a rustic hearth with a sign above it that reads 'PLEASE BE QUITE [*sic*] Every body is welcome', written in a childlike hand, a picture with the power to summon thoughts about literacy, poverty, community, and perhaps even democracy, despite its minimalism. It is an invitation to the reader to digress in a new way. Since we dream and think through images, it is enriching to include them as a resource for the meditative subject alongside the written word. This acceptance of the image as a viable form of essayistic expression accommodates Agee's claim that 'Humans may be more and more aware of being awake, but they are still incapable of not dreaming.'[23] The photograph has the power to ground the prose in the actual world through its authority as trace and provides at the same time a kind of dream image to supplement the written word. The photo essay is a form of lucid dreaming.

[23] Agee and Evans, *Let Us Now Praise Famous Men*, 209.

4. Marker's Dislocated Subject

In the late 1940s, Alexandre Astruc proposed the metaphor of the 'camera-as-pen', insisting that cinema would be futureless unless it adopted the language of the essay and embraced the possibilities of the non-mimetic and the abstract.[24] Conversely, the essay adopted the camera as a different kind of pen, one capable of recording impressions in a new medium.

The consensus today is that the essay-film 'rests somewhere between fiction and nonfiction cinema', fictional in its tendency to give the imagination an open, laboratorial space, and nonfictional in its use of footage of events that actually happened and places that really exist.[25] If one considers the essayistic novel as a 'novel that thinks', one could by analogy define the essay-film as a film that thinks.[26] There is certainly plenty of thinking in Chris Marker's *Sans soleil* (1982), which, as Michael Richardson has noted, 'shows a clear link with a surrealist perspective'.[27] The assaying subject is decentralized. It is not Marker who speaks; instead, the film's thoughts are delivered through several mediators. Narrated by an anonymous woman, the textual portions of the film are observations and reflections delivered to her by a fictional correspondent named Sandor Krasna who travels in Japan, Iceland, the Cape Verde Islands, Guinea-Bissau, and other locations. Along with these words, he delivers filmed images to his interlocutor; this combination of text and living picture creates enigmatic, dream-like digression with a philosophical underpinning.

Many of the clips used by Marker are archival excerpts from other directors. Like the essayist who feels compelled to cite the wisdom of others constantly, Marker and many other makers of essay-films cite filmmakers past by folding their images into the new essayistic project. Reinforcing Roland Barthes's depiction of Japan as an empire of signs, Marker explores death, life, sex, sleep, consumption, memory, and countless other themes through representative images and semiotic codes that differ greatly from those of his native France. He does not show the similarities between the East and the West, only the most jarring

---

[24] 'Cinema only has a future if the camera ends up replacing the pen: this is why I say that its language is not the language of fiction, nor reporting, but of the essay. Or else if it wrests itself from the dictatorship of photography and representation faithful to reality. Or finally, if it becomes the port of call for the abstract' ['Le cinéma n'a d'avenir que si la caméra finit par remplacer le stylo: c'est pourquoi je dis que son langage n'est ni celui de la fiction, ni celui des reportages, mais celui de l'essai. Ou encore qu'il s'arrachera de la dictature de la photographie et de la représentation fidèle à la réalité. Et enfin qu'il deviendra lieu de passage de l'abstrait.'], Alexandre Astruc, 'L'avenir du cinéma', *Du stylo à la caméra... et de la caméra au stylo. Écrits (1942–1984)* (1992), 328–36, here 332 (my translation).

[25] Laura Rascaroli, *The Personal Camera: Subjective Cinema and the Essay Film* (2009), 21.

[26] Milan Kundera uses the expression 'romans qui pensent' to describe Robert Musil's *The Man without Qualities* and Hermann Broch's *The Sleepwalkers* (Milan Kundera, *Le Rideau* (2005), 87).

[27] Michael Richardson, *Surrealism and Cinema* (2006), 88. Carol Rosenthal suggests likewise that Marker 'detects the bizarre in the normal and explores surrealism in everyday urban life': see *New York and Toronto Novels after Postmodernism: Explorations of the Urban* (2011), 206.

differences; scenes that through their sheer otherness would astonish a European tourist. The exotic has always been of particular interest to essayists, most famously in Montaigne's 'On Cannibals', and again in works such as Barthes's *Empire of Signs* or Victor Segalen's 'Essay on Exoticism'. The defamiliarized customs of cultures that are not our own create an uncanny effect, since their structures are similar but nonetheless otherworldly.

Near the halfway point in the film, a representative scene provides hints at the crux of Marker's project. The narrator cites a message from Krasna:

> More and more, my dreams find their settings in the department stores of Tokyo, the subterranean tunnels that extend them and run parallel to the city. A face appears, disappears; a trace is found, is lost. All the folklore of dreams is so much in its place that the next day when I'm awake, I realize that I continue to seek in the basement labyrinth the presence concealed the night before. I begin to wonder if those dreams are really mine, or if they're part of a totality, of a gigantic collective dream of which the entire city may be the projection. [...] The train inhabited by sleeping people puts together all the fragments of dreams, makes a single film of them, the ultimate film. The tickets from the automatic dispenser grant admission to the show.[28]

The spectator wonders, in the film's meta-reference to film, whether *Sans soleil* is not an attempt to be the ultimate film, the stringing together of dream fragments into a collective vision. Marker's conjugation of essayism and the surreal in this segment shows with elegance and subtlety the compatibilities between the two.

Many of Krasna's reflections are dedicated to the problem of the image, in its mediated form, in its remembered form, and in its dream form. We might consider Marker's film an essay on the nature of the image. Krasna's Japanese friend Hayao Yamaneko, a computer artist, claims that 'electronic texture is the only one that can deal with sentiment, memory, and imagination' and thus spends his time creating synthesized images—what he calls non-images—of everyday places, things, people, and political events. In these brightly coloured digital renderings, figures are often barely recognizable; only when they move can the spectator be sure that the figures are human (Figure 17.7). This world of non-images, what Yamaneko calls 'the zone' in homage to Tarkovsky, is admired by Krasna: '[Hayao] plays with the signs of his memory. He pins them down and decorates them like insects that would have flown beyond time, and which he could contemplate from a point outside of time: the only eternity we have left.' These images do not pretend to be reality and are thus, he suggests, more honest; they reveal more clearly than unmanipulated pictures that they are

---

[28] Chris Marker, *Sans soleil*, Argos Films (1993), 100 minutes, VHS.

Figure 17.7 Still from *Sans soleil*.
Source: Chris Marker © 1983.

only representations. In this sense, the synthesized images play a similar function to the rotoscopic animation in Richard Linklater's film *Waking Life* (2001), which consists of meandering, reflective dialogues set in a dreamlike world, seemingly superimposed over actual actors. The animated or synthesized image allows us to grant the thoughts their own world, not simply blend them into our own. These altered states help the viewer to remember that what he or she perceives on screen is a mediated reality.

Marker could not have rendered the eeriness and atemporality of these synthesized images with words alone. Language insufficiently reproduces the alienating effect of the new media of his time, so the film essayist is reliant on the pictures to do the talking. To read the full transcript of *Sans soleil* without watching the film is to decrease its potency by one dimension—or two, if we keep sound in mind, which does its own kind of work. The same goes for the subtraction of words; viewing the images alone, we seem to be watching several ethnographic documentaries and some sci-fi and horror films whose footage has gotten mixed up. In words alone, Marker's avatar is an intellectual, a chronicler and analyst. As an image collector like Walker Evans, he is a voyeur and his dark sensibilities are made more palpable than in his words. The theme of this essay-film is the nature of the image, but Marker also uses the images themselves to test theories such as Yamaneko's claims that 'electronic texture is the only one that can deal with sentiment, memory, and imagination' and that the video game Pac-Man is 'the most perfect graphic metaphor of man's fate'. The images test or attest to what the words state. For this reason, the medium of essay-film becomes an ideal laboratory for an understanding of what is possible through pictures.

Through *Sans soleil*, one quickly understands the potential of the conflation of essay and moving image: tensions may be built by contrasting seemingly incompatible voiced thoughts and moving scenes; the reiterative poetics of repeated images creates a dream logic that may operate in consonance or dissonance with the spoken words; new media that allow for the manipulation of images allows the essay to be pushed into a different kind of reality, one that vaguely resembles our own but is by no means equivalent to it. Marker's essay-film is surreal in its themes, in its reiteration, manipulation, and choice of images, and in the digressive, displaced subjectivity of the essayist. This thinking film leaves the spectator with a breadth of meditative material and a set of images that work as visual analogues to the thought process. Marker provides the visual matter through which his ideas should be imagined. This ex-centric essay-film moves erratically like the Surrealist pinball, ricocheting from the digitized face of a cat to the opaque face of woman who knows she's being watched back to the smiling faces of three blonde Icelandic children playing together in 1965. Marker strings together his essayistic image theories in one long and tangled strand.

5. Bresland's Anxious Images

Marker, the self-veiling essayist, puts the narrator and several avatars between himself and his interlocutors. Other practitioners of hybrid essay forms such as the video essay are straightforward in their self-inclusion, much more in the spirit of Montaigne's autobiographical exhibitionism. Often, the medium itself determines how much of the self is visible. In contrast to film, which often requires a bulky camera and perhaps a crew, the video is more manageable and allows everyday life to be recorded in a less disruptive manner. For this reason, it is as portable as a journal, with which the essay shares many features, from its short prose form to its autobiographical imperative and its immediacy with its subject matter. This ability to record one's thoughts and impressions easily, to move through the world unhindered by a cumbersome apparatus, means that the film-maker can retrieve images that most closely resemble one's lived experience. The video essayist John Bresland writes:

> Film is analog. Film requires a shutter to convey motion. [...] Video, on the other hand, from the way it's acquired (on small, light digital cameras with startling image quality) to the way it's consumed (on mobile devices, on planes, as shared links across the ether) is now being carried everywhere, the way books and magazines once were. And there's a certain texture to video, a telltale

combination of compression artifacts, blown-out whites and noisy blacks, that isn't pretty. But it's not ugly, either. It's real.[29]

This realness would have perhaps attracted essayistic writers of the pre-cinematic age who wished to create a visible, audible analogue for their abstract musings. Perhaps Montaigne would have left behind a different kind of cultural artefact had a camera been available to him: 'Je suis moi-même la matière de mon film'.

Bresland's 2010 video essay *Mangoes*, a sustained, autobiographical reflection on paternal anxiety communicated through image, spoken word, and sound, illustrates the flexibility and the realness of the video format.[30] But it also shows the potential for a surreal treatment of everyday life while maintaining the essayist's posture (Figure 17.8). Bresland narrates the video essay, recorded on an iPhone and inspired by Lars Von Trier's *The Five Obstructions* (2003). Its ethereal, pulsing soundtrack, recorded using an app called Euphonics, and its handheld dynamism push everyday life into a dreamlike sequence. Bresland and

Figure 17.8 Still from *Mangoes*.
Source: John Bresland © 2010.

[29] John Bresland, 'On the Origin of the Video Essay', *Blackbird* 9.1 (Spring 2010), at http://www.blackbird.vcu.edu/v9n1/gallery/ve-bresland_j/ve-origin_page.shtml.
[30] *Mangoes* can be viewed online at http://www.blackbird.vcu.edu/v9n1/gallery/ve-bresland_j/mangoes-video.shtml.

his actual wife, child, and landlord are the key players. Over the first shot, which shows Bresland's wife walking outside with their child strapped to her chest, he narrates, 'We were on vacation when my wife asked, pretty much out of nowhere, why I hated the BabyBjörn.' The BabyBjörn, that baby carrier fastened to the mother, becomes the departure point for a reflection on the new emasculated father, the fragility of life, as well as a critique of capitalism and the enfeeblement of the male half of the human species. Bresland's stout landlord, a Vietnam vet with tattoos, a Harley Davidson, and a cigarette in his hand, considers the BabyBjörn 'gay', 'unnatural', and 'not manly' when worn by a male. The new man, softened by consumerism and the culture of fear, has become the unconvincing imitation of a woman. The video essay continues with amusing if not unsettling scenes, like the one in which Bresland's child giggles over and over each time he repeats the words 'Banana Republic' as his wife tries on clothes in the fitting room. In the most significant scene, the one that gives the video essay its title, Bresland feeds his son mangoes despite the fact that the child could have inherited an allergy from his mother. A mango in itself is not a threatening object. But Bresland delivers the mango slices to the baby on the flat side of a sharp knife, which he films moving across the room toward the child sitting in its high chair (Figure 17.9). Bresland cuts up the fruit next to a small toy human figurine

Figure 17.9 Still from *Mangoes.*
Source: John Bresland © 2010.

placed on the cutting board, and evokes in the viewer's mind the long cinematic history of prominently featured sharp edges. Recall that one of the most canonical Surrealist films, *Un Chien andalou* (1928), a collaboration between Buñuel and Dalí, shows in its first scene a man's hand appearing to slice a woman's eye with a razor.

Bresland reveals why he purposely fed his son the mangoes despite the risk: 'I didn't want him to become one of those effete little bubble boys, allergic to everything, allergic to the world.' The anxieties of fatherhood and the anticipation of his own failures and shortcomings permeate the full eight-and-a-half minute video. As a reader of Montaigne, Bresland was perhaps familiar with the essayist's writing on fatherhood and inheritance, such as the chapter 'Of the Resemblance of Children to their Fathers'. His video is a conduit for addressing his own mistakes and misunderstandings. There is no doubt who is the assaying subject; unlike the problematic doubled subjectivity of Agee and Evans's collaboration or Chris Marker's subjective deferral, the voice, thoughts, and images are identified squarely with Bresland. Using the video essay, he articulates the dilemma of the contemporary American man: have I become too feminine and, if so, how am I to reckon with this new femininity?

Of the new hybrid genre, Bresland writes, '[p]romiscuity of the image isn't a weakness of the essay-film. It's a feature. A volatile one, sure. And it's changing the way we write, changing our conception of what writing means.' An essayist who uses the image—moving or still—can deploy it as merely supplementary to her words, to ironize or complicate those words, or to convey something that words alone cannot. Bresland is cognizant of the image's power and makes full use of it to create a mood—along with the music—that is not part of daily life. Bresland employs the strong juxtaposition of gentle and dangerous images—for example, the mother and baby followed by a skull sitting on the landlord's table—which is a key feature of Surrealist film. Images recur and change meaning, toggling between life and death. Temporal linearity is uncertain. He frames shots in unexpected ways, placing the iPhone on the floor to show only the child's legs as he bounces in a suspended swing with bright natural light flooding the image; the landlord, a figure of darkness in his obscure dwelling, is filmed at an odd angle with the camera on the table among the man's pills and knickknacks, giving a biographical hint of how this person lives, even if he appears onscreen only momentarily. Again, the filmmaker pairs the mundane and the strange, offering yet another example of the congruity between essayism and Surrealism.

This video essay suggests that something in contemporary life is off kilter, a sensation reinforced by the haunting soundtrack. Bresland's essay is by no means as disorienting, sexually charged, or quick-cutting as many early Surrealist films, but he creates an atmosphere of precariousness and ephemerality through shots like a plastic shovel floating in the water, a *trouvaille* with an inexplicable symbolic charge, something like Dalí's and Montaigne's 'discovery' of our most useful

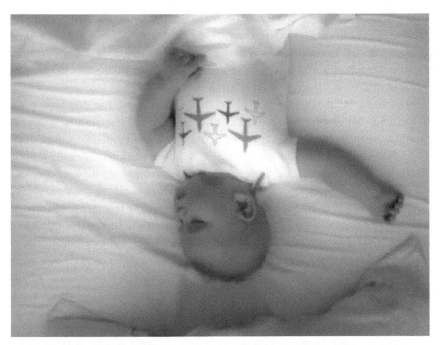

Figure 17.10 Still from *Mangoes*.
Source: John Bresland © 2010.

finger, the thumb, a neglected body part that remains invisible until it has been isolated and brought into the field of consciousness. His narration is minimal and suggestive, hinting that the autobiographically inflected meditations he offers are just the tip of a much larger existential iceberg. This attempt to reconcile the universal and the particular is a key feature of the essayist's practice; the images help in this task. He tries to render the subconscious conscious and to uncover the veiled aspects of his fear of fatherhood. Undermining the genre of parental home footage by transforming it into a series of self-interrogating pictures and adding a philosophical voice-over that demolishes any sentimentality the images might have had, Bresland shows that with a few adjustments, any art form can be made tentative (Figure 17.10). Like the Surrealists, who understood that any phenomenon can be transfigured through the lens of the surreal, Bresland realizes the potential of essayism to add a new contingency to life and art.

6. Conclusion

One might be tempted to think that the closest thing resembling an essay in the realm of the visual is the sketch—one of the definitions of 'essai'—that preliminary, rough, and impressionistic first attempt by an artist to prepare for the final image to come. Certain essayists undoubtedly think of their work as an opportunity for the kind of preparatory, free reflection unwelcome in other kinds of writing. But the essay's open-endedness and its willingness to subsume various genres to its ends have proven viable as a free-standing means of expression. It need not be followed by anything. It is not the preparation for something, but is that thing already. The essay nonetheless leaves room for mistakes, dreams, hypotheses, memories, anecdotes, and perhaps Freudian slips. It isn't interested in air-tight logic, cohesion, or foregone conclusions. By putting Surrealism into conversation with essayism, their many compatibilities become clear, particularly striking in the essay hybrids which combine image and text. For the essayist and the Surrealist, images may be strung together in digressive, associative chains that have aesthetic value in their own right and that don't lead to some grandiose and final work to come. Their images are externalizations of the internal, and what they present is inherently autobiographical since it seeks to show the most intimate conscious and subconscious mechanisms of the individual. The essayist, like the Surrealist, includes himself in his observations, if only implicitly.

Surrealism, which cultivated the dissolution of cohesion in general, offers a model for the hybrid essayist. Salvador Dalí, who provided readers of Montaigne's *Essays* with a set of illustrations to push their imaginations in unanticipated directions, showed the power of the picture to reshape the essay. Separated by centuries, these two very different minds made obvious a latent point about the literary essay: that it is image-friendly and, often, even image-dependent. The collaboration of James Agee and Walker Evans showed the flip-side of the Dalí-Montaigne fusion; instead of down-to-earth prose with fantastical imagery, they experimented with down-to-earth images accompanied by fantastical prose. The difference between the projects begins to show the potential of such hybrid combinations. As for the moving picture, Chris Marker perfected a tangled subjectivity by borrowing images from other directors and creating fictional avatars of himself to communicate his ideas. His essay-film challenged the conventions of essayistic authorship and sought to emphasize the mediated nature of all representation, particularly film. Finally, John Bresland takes up Montaigne's first-person subjectivity again only to 'surrealize' it through stark, unsettling juxtapositions and the logic and atmosphere of dreams. The vivid image, produced by and for the imagination, is essential to essayistic engagement, whether in written, photographed, animated, or filmed form.

From these examples, it is clear that Surrealism and essayism have many irons in a shared fire. Both have recognized the potential of the image to estrange daily life and to provide the occasion for reflective digression, underscoring the link between image and imagination. Given the increasing reliance on screens in everyday life across the globe, this image-centred ethos seems already endemic.

Essayism is no longer limited to the printed word nor even to the printed image. Its use of both has become lighter through virtualization and will undoubtedly continue to shed weight. The Surrealists would have delighted in the possibility of taking their digressive thought chains out of the actual world and putting them into a virtual one, the great collective and dreaming brain that Marker imagined the Tokyo underground to be.

Bibliography

Abrahamson, Robert-Louis, Richard Dury, Lesley Graham, and Alex Thomson, introduction to Robert Louis Stevenson, *Essays I: Virginibus Puerisque, and other papers* (2018).

Abrams, M. H., *The Mirror and the Lamp: Romantic Theory and the Critical Tradition* (1953).

Addison, Joseph and Richard Steele, *The Spectator*, 4 vols, ed. Gregory G. Smith (1950).

Addison, Joseph and Richard Steele, *The Spectator*, 5 vols, ed. Donald F. Bond (1965).

Addison, Joseph and Richard Steele, *The Tatler*, 3 vols, ed. Donald F. Bond (1987).

Adorno, Theodor, 'Cultural Criticism and Society (1949)', in *Prisms*, trans. Samuel Weber and Shierry Weber (1981).

Adorno, Theodor, 'The Essay as Form' [1958], trans. Bob Hullot-Kentor and Frederic Will, *New German Critique* 32 (1984), 151–71.

Adorno, Theodor, 'The Essay as Form' [1958], in *Notes to Literature, Volume One* [1958], ed. Rolf Tiedemann, trans. Shierry Weber Nicholsen (1991).

Adorno, Theodor and Max Horkheimer, *Dialectic of Enlightenment* [1944], trans. John Cumming (1997; reprinted 2008).

Agee, James and Walker Evans, *Let Us Now Praise Famous Men* [1941] (2001).

Ali, Kazim, 'Genre-Queer: Notes Against Generic Binaries', in *Bending Genre: Essays on Creative Nonfiction*, ed. Margot Singer and Nicole Walker (2013).

Allen, Judith, *Virginia Woolf and the Politics of Language* (2010).

Amis, Kingsley, *New Maps of Hell* (1961).

Ammons, A. R., *The Complete Poems of A. R. Ammons*, ed. Robert M. West, 2 vols (2017).

Anderson, Benedict, *Imagined Communities: Reflections on the Origin and Spread of Nationalism* (1991).

Arnold, Matthew, 'The Function of Criticism at the Present Time' [1865], in *The Complete Prose Works of Matthew Arnold*, vol. III, ed. R. H. Super, 11 vols (1962).

Arnold, Matthew, *The Poems of Matthew Arnold*, ed. Kenneth Allott, 4 vols (1965).

Arnold, Matthew, 'Emerson' [1883], in *The Complete Prose Works of Matthew Arnold*, vol. X, ed. R. H. Super (1974).

Ashton, Rosemary, *Thomas and Jane Carlyle: Portrait of a Marriage* (2002).

Astruc, Alexandre, 'L'avenir du cinéma', *Du stylo à la caméra... et de la caméra au stylo. Écrits (1942–1984)* (1992).

Atkins, G. Douglas, *On the Familiar Essay: Challenging Academic Orthodoxies* (2009).

Augst, Thomas, *The Clerk's Tale: Young Men and Moral Life in Nineteenth-Century America* (2003).

Bacon, Francis, *Of the advancement and proficience of learning*, trans. Gilbert Wats (1640).

Bacon, Francis, *The Works of Francis Bacon*, 14 vols, ed. James Spedding, Robert Leslie Ellis, and Douglas Denon Heath (1861–79).

Bacon, Francis, *Essays or Counsels, Civil and Moral* [1625], in *Francis Bacon: The Major Works*, ed. Brian Vickers (1996, 2008).

Bacon, Francis, *The Essayes or Counsels, Civill and Morall* [1625], ed. Michael Kiernan (2000).

Bahun, Sanja, 'Woolf and Psychoanalytic Theory', in *Virginia Woolf in Context*, ed. Bryony Randall and Jane Goldman (2012).

Baker, Nicholson, *Vox* (1992).

Baker, Nicholson, *The Size of Thoughts* (1996).

Baker, Nicholson, *The Way the World Works* (2012).

Bakhtin, Mikhail, 'The Problem of Speech Genres' [1979] in *Speech Genres and Other Late Essays*, ed. Michael Holquist, Vern McGee, and Caryl Emerson (1986).

Baldwin, James, *Notes of a Native Son* (1955).

Baldwin, James, *Nobody Knows My Name* (1961).

Baldwin, James, *The Fire Next Time* (1963).

Baldwin, James, 'If Black English Isn't a Language, Then Tell Me, What Is?', *New York Times* (29 July 1979).

Ballantyne, Thomas, *Passages Selected from the Writings of Thomas Carlyle* (1855).

Barbauld, Anna Laetitia, *Selected Poetry and Prose*, ed. William McCarthy and Elizabeth Kraft (2002).

Barnes, Julian, *A History of the World in 10½ Chapters* (1990).

Barnes, Julian, 'La Vida, una maldita cosa detras de la otra', *Clarín*, suplemento cultural (13 June 1996).

Barnes, Julian, *Levels of Life* (2013).

Bartels, E. B., 'Non-Fiction by Non-Men: Eula Biss', interview in *Fiction Advocate* (16 January 2017), at http://fictionadvocate.com/2017/01/16/non-fiction-by-non-men-eula-biss.

Bataille, Georges, 'The Big Toe' [1929], in *Visions of Excess: Selected Writings, 1927–1939*, ed. and trans. Allan Stoekl (1985).

Bayley, John, *An Essay on Hardy* (1978).

Beard, Jo Ann, *The Boys of My Youth* (1998).

Beer, Gillian, 'Introduction' in Sigmund Freud, *The Wolfman and Other Cases*, trans. Louise Adey Huish (2002).

Beetham, Margaret, 'Towards a Theory of the Periodical as a Publishing Genre', in *Investigating Victorian Journalism*, ed. Laurel Brake, Aled Jones, and Lionel Madden (1990).

Bell, Michael, *F. R. Leavis* (1988).

Bellah, Robert N., *Religion in Human Evolution: From the Paleolithic to the Axial Age* (2011).

Belloc, Hilaire, 'On the Pleasures of Taking up One's Pen', in *On Nothing & Kindred Subjects* (1908).

Belloc, Hilaire, 'On a Variety of Things', in *On* (1923).

Bense, Max, 'On the Essay and its Prose', in *Essayists on the Essay: Montaigne to Our Time*, ed. Carl H. Klaus and Ned Stuckey-French (2012).

Bensmaïa, Réda, *The Barthes Effect: The Essay as Reflexive Text* (1987).

Benson, Arthur, 'The Art of the Essayist', in *Modern English Essays*, ed. Ernest Rhys (1923).

Berlin, Isaiah, *The Hedgehog and the Fox: An Essay on Tolstoy's View of History* (1953).

'Bickerstaff, Isaac', *The Lucubrations of Isaac Bickerstaff, Revised and Collected by the Author*, 4 vols (1712).

Bishop, Wendy, 'Suddenly Sexy: Creative Nonfiction Rear-Ends Composition', *Creative Nonfiction*, a special issue of *College English* 65.3 (January 2003), 257–75.

Biss, Eula, *No Man's Land: American Essays* (2009).

Biss, Eula, 'It Is What It Is', in *Bending Genre: Essays on Creative Nonfiction*, ed. Margot Singer and Nicole Walker (2013).

Bizzotto, Elisa, 'The Imaginary Portrait: Pater's Contribution to a Literary Genre', in *Walter Pater: Transparencies of Desire*, ed. Laurel Brake, Lesley Higgins, and Carolyn Williams (2002).

Black, Scott, *Of Essays and Reading in Early Modern Britain* (2006).

Black, Scott, '*Tristram Shandy*'s Strange Loops of Reading', in *Without the Novel: Romance and the History of Prose Fiction* (2019).

Blair, Ann, *Too Much to Know: Managing Scholarly Information before the Modern Age* (2010).

Blanchfield, Brian, *Proxies* (2016).

Bloom, Harold, *The Anatomy of Influence* (2011).

Bloom, Lynn Z., 'The Essay Canon', *College English* 61.4 (March 1999), 401–30.

Booth, Wayne, *The Rhetoric of Fiction*, 2nd edn (1983).

Borges, Jorge Luis, *Ficciones*, trans. Anthony Kerrigan (1962).

Borsay, Peter, 'The Culture of Improvement', in *The Eighteenth Century*, ed. Paul Langford (2002).

Boswell, James, *Life of Johnson* [1791], ed. G. Birkbeck Hill and L. F. Powell, 5 vols (1934).

Boswell, James, *Life of Johnson* [1791], ed. R. W. Chapman (1998).

Boutcher, Warren, *The School of Montaigne in Early Modern Europe*, 2 vols (2017).

Box, M. A., *The Suasive Art of David Hume* (1990).

Boyle, Robert, *The Christian Virtuoso* (1690).

Brake, Laurel, '"A Juggler's Trick"? Swinburne's Journalism 1857–75', in *Algernon Charles Swinburne: Unofficial Laureate*, ed. Catherine Maxwell and Stefano Evangelista (2013).

Brake, Laurel, *Print in Transition, 1850–1910: Studies in Media and Book History* (2001).

Brant, Clare, *Eighteenth-Century Letters and British Culture* (2006).

Bresland, John, 'On the Origin of the Video Essay', *Blackbird* 9.1 (Spring 2010), at http://www.blackbird.vcu.edu/v9n1/gallery/ve-intro/intro_page.shtml.

Bresland, John, *Mangoes* film: http://www.blackbird.vcu.edu/v9n1/gallery/ve-bresland_j/mangoes-video.shtml.

Breton, André, *Manifestoes of Surrealism*, trans. Richard Seaver and Helen R. Lane (1972).

Brosnan, Leila, *Reading Virginia Woolf's Essays and Journalism* (1997).

Buell, Lawrence, *New England Literary Culture from Revolution Through Renaissance* (1989).

Burton, Robert. *The Anatomy of Melancholy what it is. With all the kindes, causes, symptomes, prognostickes, and severall cures of it* (1621).

Burton, Robert, *The Anatomy of Melancholy* [1621], ed. Holbrook Jackson (2001).

Butler, Samuel, 'Ramblings in Cheapside' [1890], in *Modern English Essays 1870–1920*, vol. II, ed. Ernest Rhys, 5 vols (1923).

Butrym, Alexander J. (ed.), *Essays on the Essay: Redefining the Genre* (1989).

Caines, Michael, 'Stick and Stickability', *TLS* blog (20 June 2016), at http://timescolumns.typepad.com/stothard/2016/06/stick-and-stickability.html.

Calvino, Italo, *Why Read the Classics*, trans. Martin McLaughlin (1999).

Camerarius, Philippus, *Les méditations historiques*, ed. Simon Goulart, 3 vols (1610).

Cameron, Sharon, *Impersonality: Seven Essays* (2007).

Cannadine, David, *Ornamentalism: How the British Saw Their Empire* (2001).

Carlyle, Thomas, *The Works of Thomas Carlyle*, 30 vols (1896–9, 2010).

Carter, Angela, *Shaking a Leg* (1997).

Cayton, Mary Kupiec, *Emerson's Emergence: Self and Society in the Transformation of New England 1800–1845* (1992).

Chandler, David, '"Elia, the Real": The Original of Lamb's *Nom De Plume*', *Review of English Studies* 58 (2007), 669–83.

Chatelain, Jean-Marc, 'Les recueils d'adversaria aux xvie et xviie siècles', in *Le livre et l'historien: études offertes en l'honneur du Professeur Henri-Jean Martin*, ed. Henri-Jean Martin and Frédéric Barbier (1997).

Chesterton, G. K., *A Shilling for my Thoughts* (1917).

Chesterton, G. K., 'The Essay' [1932], in *Essayists on the Essay: Montaigne to Our Time*, ed. Carl H. Klaus and Ned Stuckey-French (2012).

Chevalier, Tracy (ed.), *Encyclopedia of the Essay* (1997).

Cocozza, Paula, 'Poet Claudia Rankine: "The Invisibility of Black Women is Amazing"', *The Guardian* (29 June 2015), at https://www.theguardian.com/lifeandstyle/2015/jun/29/poet-claudia-rankine-invisibility-black-women-everyday-racism-citizen.

Cohen, Margaret, *Profane Illumination: Walter Benjamin and the Paris of Surrealist Revolution* (1993).

Coleman, Aaron, 'The History behind the Feeling: A Conversation with Claudia Rankine', *The Spectacle* (23 September 2015), at http://thespectacle.wustl.edu/?p=105.

Coleridge, Samuel Taylor, preface to 'Kubla Khan', in *Christabel; Kubla Khan, a vision; The Pains of Sleep* (1816).

Coleridge, Samuel Taylor, *Biographia Literaria* [1817], ed. James Engell and W. Jackson Bate, 2 vols (1983), in *Collected Works of Samuel Taylor Coleridge*, vol. VII, ed. Kathleen Coburn, 23 vols (1983–).

Colman, George, *The Connoisseur. By Mr Town, critic and censor-general*, 2 vols (1755–6).

Connolly, Cyril, *Enemies of Promise* (1938).

Connolly, Cyril, *Enemies of Promise*, revised edn. [1949], (2008).

Connor, Steven, *Dumbstruck! A Cultural History of Ventriloquism* (2000).

Cooke, George Willis (ed.), *Ralph Waldo Emerson: His Life, Writings and Philosophy* (1881).

Cornwallis, William, *Essayes* (2 vols, 1600–01).

Cornwallis, William, *Essayes* [2nd edn., 2 vols, 1606–10], ed. Don Cameron Allen (1946).

Cornwallis, William, *Essayes of Certaine Paradoxes* (1616).

Cowan, Brian William, *The Social Life of Coffee: The Emergence of the British Coffee House* (2005).

Cowley, Abraham, *Essays, Plays, and Sundry Verses* (1906).

Cowper, William, *Poetical Works*, ed. H. S. Milford, (1905).

Cox, R. G. (ed.), *Thomas Hardy: The Critical Heritage* (1970).

Culpeper, Thomas, *Essayes or Moral Discourses, on several Subjects* (1671).

Cummings, Robert, 'Versifying Philosophy: Thomas Blundeville's Plutarch', in *Renaissance Cultural Crossroads: Translation, Print, and Culture in Britain, 1473–1640* (2013).

Cutter, Weston, 'Doubling Down: An Interview with John D'Agata and Jim Fingal', in *Kenyon Review* (23 February 2012), at http://www.kenyonreview.org/2012/02/doubling-down-an-interview-with-john-dagata-and-jim-fingal.

D'Agata, John, *The Lifespan of a Fact* (2012).

D'Agata, John, *The Making of the American Essay* (2016).

D'Agata, John (ed.), *The Next American Essay* (2003).

D'Agata, John (ed.), *The Lost Origins of the Essay* (2009).

D'Agata, John and Deborah Tall, 'New Terrain: The Lyric Essay', *Seneca Review* 72.1 (Fall 1997), 7–8.

d'Argenson, Paulmy and Contant d'Orville, *Mélanges tirés d'une grande bibliothèque* (1779–88).

Davis, Hugh, 'The Making of James Agee' (unpublished PhD dissertation, University of Tennessee, 2005).

D'Israeli, Isaac, *Miscellanies; or, Literary Recreations* (1796).

D'Israeli, Isaac, *Literary Miscellanies: including a Dissertation on Anecdotes*, 2nd edn (1801).

Dalle, Réginald, 'Montaigne vu par Salvador Dalí', *Montaigne et les Essais, 1580–1980, Actes du Congrès de Bordeaux (Juin 1980)*, ed. Pierre Michel et al. (1983).

Dart, Gregory, *Metropolitan Art and Literature 1810–1840: Cockney Adventures* (2012).

David Ulin, 'Claudia Rankine, The Art of Poetry No. 102', *Paris Review* 219 (Winter 2016).

Davis, Hugh, '"Drinking at Wells Sunk beneath Privies": Agee and Surrealism', in *Agee Agonistes: Essays on the Life, Legend, and Works of James Agee*, ed. Michael A. Lofaro (2007).

De Bruyn, Frans, 'The English afterlife of the *silva* in the seventeenth and eighteenth centuries', in *La Silve: histoire d'une écriture libérée en Europe de l'antiquité au XVIIIe siècle* ed. Perrine Galand-Hallyn and Sylvie Laigneau-Fontaine (2013).

de Courcelles, Dominique (ed.), *Ouvrages miscellanées et théories de la connaissance à la Renaissance* (2003).

de Obaldia, Claire, *The Essayistic Spirit: Literature, Modern Criticism, and the Essay* (1995).

De Quincey, Thomas, *Confessions of an English Opium-Eater* [1821], ed. Barry Milligan (2003).

De Quincey, Thomas, *Confessions of an English Opium-Eater and Other Writings*, ed. Robert Morrison (2013).

De Quincey, Thomas, *The Works of Thomas De Quincey*, 16 vols (1878).

De Smet, Ingrid A. R., 'Isaac D'Israeli, Reader of Montaigne', in *Montaigne in Transit: Essays in Honour of Ian Maclean* , ed. Neil Kenny, Richard Scholar, and Wes Williams (2016).

DeMaria, Jr, Robert, 'The Eighteenth-Century Periodical Essay', in *The Cambridge History of Literature 1660–1780*, ed. John Richetti (2005).

Deresiewicz, William, 'In Defense of Facts', *The Atlantic Monthly* 319.1 (January/February 2017).

Dillane, Fionnuala, *Before George Eliot: Marian Evans and the Periodical Press* (2013).

Dillon, Brian, *Essayism* (2017).

Dix, Jonathan, *Lions: Living and Dead* (1854).

Douglas, Althea, 'The Indexes of 18th and early 19th-century magazines', *The Indexer* 14.3 (April 1985), 160–3.

Drake, Nathan, *Essays, biographical, critical and historical, illustrative of the Tatler, Spectator, and Guardian*, 3 vols (1805).

Drake, Nathan, *Essays, biographical, critical, and historical, illustrative of the Rambler, Adventurer, and Idler*, 2 vols (1809–10).

DuPlessis, Rachel Blau, 'f-Words: An Essay on the Essay', *American Literature* 68.1 (1996), 15–45.

Dzieza, Josh, 'John D'Agata's Fact-Checking Problem', *The Daily Beast* (21 February 2012), at http://www.thedailybeast.com/articles/2012/02/21/john-d-agata-s-fact-checking-bat tle.html.

Early, Gerald (ed.), *Speech and Power: The African-American Essay and Its Cultural Content from Polemics to Pulpit, Vols I and II* (1992, 1993).

Eckman, Fern Marja, *The Furious Passage of James Baldwin* (1966).

Eddo-Lodge, Reni, *Why I'm No Longer Talking to White People About Race* (2017).

Eden, Kathy, *The Renaissance Rediscovery of Intimacy* (2012).

Edwards, Owen Dudley, 'The Tone of the Preacher: Carlyle as Public Lecturer in *On Heroes*' in Carlyle, *On Heroes, Hero-Worship and the Heroic in History*, ed. David Sorensen and Brent E. Kinser (2013).

Eliot, George, *Adam Bede* [1859], ed. Valentine Cunningham (1996).

Eliot, George, *Silas Marner* [1861], ed. David Carroll (1996).

Eliot, George, *Middlemarch* [1871-2], ed. David Carroll (1986).

Eliot, George, *The George Eliot Letters*, ed. Gordon S. Haight, 9 vols (1954–78).

Eliot, T. S., 'The Function of Criticism', in *Selected Essays* [1932] (1991).

Eliot, T. S., 'The Pensées of Pascal', in *Selected Essays* [1932] (1991).

Eliot, T. S., 'The Perfect Critic', in *The Sacred Wood: Essays on Poetry and Criticism* (1921).

Ellul, Jacques, 'The Characteristics of Propaganda' [1962], in *Propaganda: The Formation of Men's Attitudes*, trans. Konrad Kellen and Jean Lerner (1969).

Emerson, Ralph Waldo, 'Nature' [1836], in *Nature, Addresses, and Lectures*, vol. I in *The Collected Works of Ralph Waldo Emerson*, ed. Robert E. Spiller and Alfred R. Ferguson (1971).

Emerson, Ralph Waldo, *Essays, First Series* [1841], vol. II in *The Collected Works of Ralph Waldo Emerson*, ed. Joseph Slater (1979).

Emerson, Ralph Waldo, 'Experience', in *Essays, Second Series* [1844], vol. III in *The Collected Works of Ralph Waldo Emerson*, ed. Joseph Slater (1984).

Emerson, Ralph Waldo, 'Montaigne; or, The Skeptic', in *Representative Men* [1850], vol. IV in *The Collected Works of Ralph Waldo Emerson*, ed. Wallace E. Williams (1987).

Emerson, Ralph Waldo, 'Eloquence', in *Society and Solitude* [1870], vol. VII in *The Collected Works of Ralph Waldo Emerson*, ed. Robert E. Spiller, Alfred R. Ferguson, Joseph Slater, and Jean F. Carr (1971).

Emerson, Ralph Waldo, *The Later Lectures of Ralph Waldo Emerson, Vol. 1: 1843–1854*, ed. Ronald A. Bosco and Joel Myerson (2001).

Emerson, Ralph Waldo, *The Later Lectures of Ralph Waldo Emerson, Vol. 2: 1855–1871*, ed. Ronald A. Bosco and Joel Myerson (2001).

Empson, William, *Seven Types of Ambiguity* (1966).

Epstein, Mikhail, 'Essayism: An Essay on the Essay' [1982], in *Russian Postmodernism: New Perspectives on Post-Soviet Literature*, ed. Mikhail Epstein, Alexander Genis, and Slobodanka Vladiv-Glover (2016).

Fadiman, Anne, *At Large and At Small: Confessions of a Literary Hedonist* (2007).

Fadiman, Anne, *Ex Libris: Confessions of a Common Reader* (1998).

Fadiman, Clifton, *A Party of One* (1955).

Federman, Raymond, 'Self-Reflexive Fiction or How to Get Rid of It', in *Critifiction: Postmodern Essays* (1993).

Felltham, Owen, 'Of Logick', in *Resolves*, 8th edn (1661).

Fielding, Henry, 'On Nothing', in *Miscellaneous Works: I*, vol. 14 in *The Complete Works of Henry Fielding*, 16 vols (1902).

Fielding, Henry, *Tom Jones* [1749], ed. Sheridan Baker (1995).

Fitzgerald, Percy, *Memoirs of an Author*, 2 vols (1894).

Florio, John, 'To the curteous Reader', in Montaigne, *Essayes*, trans. Florio (1603).

Forster, E. M., 'What I Believe' [1939], reprinted in *Two Cheers for Democracy* (1951, 1970).

Fraser, Nancy, *Rethinking the Public Sphere: A Contribution to the Critique of Actually Existing Democracy* (1990).

Freud, Sigmund, *The Future of an Illusion* [1927], in *Mass Psychology and Other Writings*, ed. Jacqueline Rose, trans. J. A. Underwood (2004).

Freud, Sigmund, *Civilization and its Discontents* [1930], *The Standard Edition of the Complete Psychological Works of Sigmund Freud, Volume XXI (1927-1931)*, 24 vols, ed. and trans. James Strachey (1961, 2001).

Freud, Sigmund, *The Standard Edition of the Complete Psychological Works of Sigmund Freud*, ed. James Strachey, 24 vols (1953–74, 2001).

Friedrich, Hugo, *Montaigne* [1949], ed. Philippe Desan, trans. Dawn Eng (1991).

Galand-Hallyn, Perrine and Sylvie Laigneau-Fontaine (eds), *La Silve: histoire d'une écriture libérée en Europe de l'antiquité au XVIIIe siècle* (2013).

Gasset, José Ortega y, 'To the Reader', in *Essayists on the Essay: Montaigne to Our Time*, ed. Carl H. Klaus and Ned Stuckey-French (2012).

Gay, John, *The present state of wit, in a letter to a friend in the country* (1711).

Gellius, Aulus, *The Attic Nights*, trans. Rev. W. Beloe, 3 vols (1795).

Gigante, Denise, *The Great Age of the English Essay: An Anthology* (2008).

Gigante, Denise, 'Sometimes a Stick is Just a Stick: The Essay as (Organic) Form', *European Romantic Review* 21.5 (2010), 553–65.

Gigante, Denise (ed.), *The Essay: An Attempt, A Protean Form, Republics of Letters* 4 (2014).

Gliddon, Anne, *The Gliddons in London 1760–1850*, ed. Wendy Norman (2000).

Goldberg, Shari, 'Emerson: Testimony without Representation', in *Quiet Testimony: A Theory of Witnessing from Nineteenth-Century American Literature* (2013).

Goldhill, Simon, *Victorian Culture and Classical Antiquity: Art, Opera, Fiction, and the Proclamation of Modernity* (2011).

Goldfield, Hannah, 'The Art of Fact-Checking', *The New Yorker* blog (9 February 2012), at http://www.newyorker.com/books/page-turner/the-art-of-fact-checking.

Goldsmith, Oliver, *Collected Works of Oliver Goldsmith*, ed. Arthur Friedman, 5 vols (1966).

Goldsmith, Oliver, *The Bee; Being Essays on the Most Interesting Subjects* (1759).

Good, Graham, *The Observing Self: Rediscovering the Essay* (1988).

Gopnik, Adam (ed.), *The Best American Essays: 2008* (2008).

Gordimer, Nadine, 'A Writer's Freedom' [1976], in *Telling Times: Writing and Living 1954–2008* (2010).

Gordimer, Nadine, 'English-Language Literature and Politics in South Africa' [1976], in *Telling Times: Writing and Living 1954–2008* (2010).

Greene, Thomas M., *The Light in Troy: Imitation and Discovery in Renaissance Poetics* (1982).

Greif, Mark, 'The Concept of Experience' [2005], in *Against Everything* (2016).

Grose, Francis, *The Olio* (1793).

Gross, John, 'Introduction' in *The Oxford Book of Essays*, ed. John Gross (1991).

Habermas, Jürgen, *The Structural Transformation of the Public Sphere* [1962], trans. Thomas Burger and Frederick Lawrence (1991).

Hardison, Jr, O. B., 'Binding Proteus: An Essay on the Essay', in *Essays on the Essay: Redfining the Genre*, ed. Alexander J. Butrym (1989).

Hardy, Thomas, *Far from the Madding Crowd* [1873–4], ed. Ronald Blythe (1978).

Hardy, Thomas, *Tess of the d'Urbervilles* [1891], ed. David Skilton (1978).

Hardy, Thomas & Florence Hardy, *The Early Life of Thomas Hardy, 1840–1891* (1928).

Hardy, Thomas, *Thomas Hardy's Personal Writings*, ed. Harold Orel (1967).

Harrison, Frederic, *Studies in Early Victorian Literature* (1895).

Harrison, Thomas, *Essayism* (1992).

Hartley, Lodwick, *Laurence Sterne in the Twentieth Century: An Essay and a Bibliography of Sterne Studies 1900–1965* (1966).

Hartman, Geoffrey, 'The Sacred Jungle', in *The Geoffrey Hartman Reader* (2004).

Hartman, Geoffrey, *The Third Pillar: Essays in Judaic Studies* (2011).

Hawkins, Angus, *Victorian Political Culture: Habits of Heart and Mind* (2015).

Hay, William, *Deformity: An Essay* [1754], ed. Kathleen James-Cavan (2004).

Haywood, Eliza, *The Female Spectator* (1744–6).

Hazlitt, William, 'On the Periodical Essayists [1819]', in *The Selected Writings of William Hazlitt*, vol. V, ed. Duncan Wu, 9 vols (1998).

Hazlitt, William, 'On Living to One's Self' [1821], in *The Selected Writings of William Hazlitt*, vol. VI, ed. Duncan Wu, 9 vols (1998).

Hazlitt, William, 'On Reason and Imagination' [1826], in *The Selected Writings of William Hazlitt*, vol. VIII, ed. Duncan Wu, 9 vols (1998).

Hazlitt, William, 'Jack Tars', extract from *Notes of a Journey through France and Italy* [1826], in *The Fight and Other Writings*, ed. Tom Paulin and David Chandler (2000).

Hazlitt, William, 'On a Sun-Dial' [1827], in *The Selected Writings of William Hazlitt*, vol. IX, ed. Duncan Wu, 9 vols (1998).

Hazlitt, William, 'Personal Politics' [1830], in *Literary Remains of the Late William Hazlitt*, ed. William Hazlitt [1836].

Hesse, Douglas, 'The Place of Creative Nonfiction', *Creative Nonfiction*, a special issue of *College English* 65.3 (January 2003), 237–41.

Hewitt, Martin, 'Aspects of Platform Culture in Nineteenth Century Britain', *Nineteenth-Century Prose* 29.1 (Spring 2002), 1–32.

Hill, Aaron, *Plain Dealer* (1730).

Hill, Geoffrey, 'Redeeming the Time', in *Collected Critical Writings*, ed. Kenneth Haynes (2008).

Himmelfarb, Gertrude, *The Spirit of the Age* (2009).

Hitchens, Christopher, 'Moderation or Death', *London Review of Books* 20.23 (26 November 1993), 3–11.

Hitchens, Christopher, 'Taking Sides', *The Nation*, (26 September 2002), at https://www.thenation.com/article/taking-sides.

Hitchens, Christopher, 'Preface' to *Arguably* (2011).

Hoagland, Edward, 'What I Think, What I Am', *The New York Times Book Review* (27 June 1976).

Holdheim, W. Wolfgang, *The Hermeneutic Mode: Essays on Time in Literature and Literary Theory* (1984).

Holloway, John, *The Victorian Sage: Studies in Argument* (1953).

Hone, William (ed.), *The Table Book*, vol. 2 (1828).

Horstmann, Rolf-Peter, *Beyond Good and Evil: Prelude to a Philosophy of the Future* (2001).

Houghton, Walter E., 'Periodical Literature and the Articulate Classes', in *The Victorian Periodical Press: Samplings and Soundings*, ed. Joanne Shattock and Michael Wolff (1982).

Houtchens, Lawrence Huston and Carolyn Washburn Houtchens (eds), *Leigh Hunt's Political and Occasional Essays* (1962).

Howells, William Dean, 'The Old-Fashioned Essay', *Harper's Magazine* (October 1902).

Howes, Alan B. (ed.), *Sterne: The Critical Heritage* (1974).

Hume, David, *A Treatise of Human Nature* [1739–40], ed. L. A. Selby-Bigge (1978).

Hume, David, *Philosophical Essays concerning Human Understanding* (1748).

Hume, David, *Essays Moral, Political, and Literary* [1758], ed. Eugene F. Miller (1987).

Hume, David, *Selected Essays*, ed. Stephen Copley and Andrew Edgar (1998).

Hunt, Leigh, *The Indicator* (1822).

Hunt, Leigh, 'Coffee Houses and Smoking', *The New Monthly Magazine and Literary Journal* 16.61 (January 1826), 50–4.

Hunt, Leigh, 'Men and Books', *The New Monthly Magazine and Literary Review* (January 1833), 31–7.

Hunt, Leigh, *Selected Writings of Leigh Hunt*, ed. Robert Morrison and Michael Eberle-Sinatra, 6 vols (2003).

Hurley, Michael and Marcus Waithe (eds), *Thinking Through Style: Non-Fiction Prose of the Long Nineteenth Century* (2018).

Hutton, Richard Holt, *A Victorian Spectator: Uncollected Writings of R. H. Hutton*, ed. Robert Tener and Malcolm Woodfield (1989).

Ifil, Gwen, 'Using Poetry to Uncover the Moments that Lead to Racism', interview on PBS NewsHour (4 December 2014), at https://www.pbs.org/newshour/show/using-poetry-uncover-moments-lead-racism.

James, Felicity, 'Charles Lamb, Samuel Taylor Coleridge, and the Forging of the Romantic Literary Coterie', in *Re-evaluating the Literary Coterie, 1580–1830*, ed. William Bowers and Hannah Leah Crummé (2016).

James, Henry, *The Art of the Novel: Critical Prefaces*, ed. R. P. Blackmur (2011).

James, William, 'Is Life Worth Living?' [1895], in *Writings 1878–1899*, ed. Gerald Myers (1992).

Jamison, Leslie, *The Empathy Exams* (2014).

Jefferson, D. W., 'Tristram Shandy and the Tradition of Learned Wit', *Essays in Criticism* 1.3 (1951), 225–48.

Johnson, Ralph, *The Scholars Guide from the Accidence to the University, or, Short, Plain, and Easie Rules for performing all manner of Exercise in the Grammar School* (1665).

Johnson, Samuel, *The Rambler* [1750–52], vols III–V of *The Yale Edition of the Works of Samuel Johnson*, ed. W. J. Bate and Albrecht B. Strauss (1969).

Johnson, Samuel, *A Dictionary of the English Language* (1755).

Johnson, Samuel, 'Addison', in *The Lives of the Poets* [1781], vols XXI–XXIII of *The Yale Edition of the Works of Samuel Johnson*, vol. XXII, ed. W. J. Bate and Albrecht B. Strauss (2010).

Johnson, Samuel, *The Letters of Samuel Johnson*, ed. Bruce Redford, 5 vols (1992–4).

Jonson, Ben, *Explorata, or Discoveries* [1640–41], ed. Lorna Hutson, in *The Cambridge Edition of the Works of Ben Jonson*, vol. 7, ed. David Bevington et al. (2012).

Kant, Immanuel, *The Critique of Judgment* [1790], trans. Werner S. Pluhar (1987).

Keats, John, *The Poems of John Keats*, ed. Jack Stillinger (1978).

Kenny, Neil, *The Palace of Secrets: Béroalde de Verville and Renaissance Conceptions of Knowledge* (1991).

Kermode, Frank, *The Sense of an Ending* (2000).

Keymer, Thomas, *Sterne, the Moderns, and the Novel* (2002).

Kiernan, Michael, 'General Introduction', in Francis Bacon, *The Essayes or Counsels, Civill and Morall* [1625], ed. Michael Kiernan (2000).

Klaus, Carl H., 'Toward a Collective Poetics of the Essay', in *Essayists on the Essay: Montaigne to Our Time*, ed. Carl H. Klaus and Ned Stuckey-French (2012).

Klaus, Carl H. and Ned Stuckey-French (eds), *Essayists on the Essay: Montaigne to Our Time* (2012).

Klein, Lawrence E., *Shaftesbury and the Culture of Politeness: Moral Discourse and Cultural Politics in Early Eighteenth-Century England* (1994).

Knox, Vicesimus, *Winter Evenings; or Lucubrations on Life and Letters*, 3 vols (1788).

Korhonen, Kuisma, *Textual Friendship: The Essay as Impossible Encounter from Plato to Montaigne to Levinas and Derrida* (2006).

Korshin, Paul, 'Johnson, the Essay, and The Rambler', in *The Cambridge Companion to Samuel Johnson*, ed. Greg Clingham (1997).

Krauss, Rosalind, 'Photography in the Service of Surrealism', in *L'Amour fou: Photography and Surrealism*, ed. Rosalind Krauss and Jane Livingston (1985).

Kreilkamp, Ivan, *Voice and the Victorian Storyteller* (2005).

Kundera, Milan, *Le Rideau* (2005).

Lamb, Charles, *Specimens of English Dramatic Poets, who Lived about the Time of Shakspeare* (1808).

Lamb, Charles, 'Imperfect Sympathies' [1823], in *The Works of Charles and Mary Lamb*, vol. I, ed. E. V. Lucas, 7 vols (1903).

Lamb, Charles, *Essays of Elia* [1823], ed. Phillip Lopate (2003).

Lamb, Charles, 'Detached Thoughts on Books and Reading' [1833], in *The Works of Charles and Mary Lamb*, vol. I, ed. E. V. Lucas, 7 vols (1903).

Lamb, Charles, *Everybody's Lamb, Being a Selection from the Essays of Elia, The Letters, and the Miscellaneous Prose*, ed. A. C. Ward (1933).

Lamb, Charles, *Letters of Charles and Mary Lamb*, ed. Edwin Marrs, 3 vols (1975).

Lamb, Jonathan, 'Sterne's Use of Montaigne', *Comparative Literature* 32 (1980), 1–41.

Landow, George P., *Elegant Jeremiahs: The Sage from Carlyle to Mailer* (1986).

Langer, Ullrich (ed.), *The Cambridge Companion to Montaigne* (2005).

Lanham, Richard, *Tristram Shandy: The Games of Pleasure* (1973).

Lawrence, D. H., *Studies in Classic American Literature* [1823], (2003).

Lazar, David, 'Queering the Essay', in *Bending Genre: Essays on Creative Nonfiction*, ed. Margot Singer and Nicole Walker (2013).

Leavis, F. R. (ed.), *Determinations* (1934).

Lee, Hermione, 'Virginia Woolf's Essays', in *The Cambridge Companion to Virginia Woolf*, ed. Sue Roe and Susan Sellers, 2nd edn (2010).

Le Faye, Deirdre (ed.), *Jane Austen's Letters* (1995).

Lennon, Brian, 'The Essay, in Theory', *diacritics* 38.3 (Fall 2008), 71–92.

Lewiton, Ariel, 'John D'Agata: What We Owe History [An Interview]', *Guernica* (15 February 2016), at https://www.guernicamag.com/what-we-owe-history/.

Lillywhite, Bryant, *London Coffee Houses: A Reference Book of Coffee Houses of the Seventeenth, Eighteenth and Nineteenth Centuries* (1963).

Lopate, Phillip, 'The Essay Lives—in Disguise', *The New York Times Book Review* (18 November 1984).

Lopate, Phillip (ed.), *The Art of the Personal Essay: An Anthology from the Classical Era to the Present* (1994).

Lopate, Phillip, *Notes on Sontag* (2009).

Lukács, György, 'On the Nature and Form of the Essay: A Letter to Leo Popper' [1911], in *Soul and Form*, trans. Anna Bostock, ed. John T. Sanders and Katie Terezakis (2010).

Lynch, Jack, 'The Relicks of Learning: Sterne among the Renaissance Encyclopedists', *Eighteenth Century Studies* 13.1 (2000), 1–17.

Lynd, Robert, 'On Doing Nothing', in *If the Germans Conquered England* (1917).

McFarland, Thomas, *Romantic Cruxes: The English Essayists and the Spirit of the Age* (1987).

McGann, Jerome J., *The Romantic Ideology: A Critical Investigation* (1983).

McGann, Jerome J., *Byron and Romanticism* (2002).

McGrath, F. C., *The Sensible Spirit: Walter Pater and the Modernist Paradigm* (1986).

McGrath, Patrick, 'Graham Swift', *BOMB Magazine* 15 (1 April 1986).

Mack, Peter, 'Rhetoric and the Essay', *Rhetoric Society Quarterly* 23.2 (1993), 41–9.

Mackie, Erin (ed.), *The Commerce of Everyday Life: Selections from* The Tatler *and* The Spectator (1998).

MacPhail, Eric, *Dancing Around the Well: The Circulation of Commonplaces in Renaissance Humanism* (2014).

Malcolm, James Peller, *Anecdotes of Manners and Customs of London* (1807).

Mandosio, Jean-Marc, 'La miscellanée: histoire d'un genre', in *Ouvrages miscellanées et théories de la connaissance à la Renaissance*, ed. Dominique de Courcelles (2003).

Markman Ellis, *The Coffee House: A Cultural History* (2004).

Marr, George S., *Periodical Essayists of the Eighteenth Century* (1923).

Marrs, Jr, Edwin W. (ed.), *The Letters of Charles and Mary Anne Lamb*, 3 vols (1975–8).

Marshall, Ashley, 'Henry Fielding and the "Scriblerians"', *Modern Language Quarterly* 72 (2011), 19–48.

Martineau, Harriet, *The Positive Philosophy of Auguste Comte, Freely Translated and Condensed by Harriet Martineau*, 3rd edn, 2 vols (1893).

Maxwell, Catherine, *Swinburne* (2006).

Mayhew, George, 'Swift's Bickerstaff Hoax as an April Fool's Joke', *Modern Philology* 61.4 (May 1964), 270-80.

Meisel, Perry, *The Absent Father: Virginia Woolf and Walter Pater* (1980).

Menand, Louis, *The Marketplace of Ideas: Reform and Resistance in the American University* (2010).

Michael, Ian, *The Teaching of English: From the Sixteenth Century to 1870* (1987).

Miller, Arthur, 'The Sin of Power', *Index on Censorship* 7 (May 1978), 3–6.

Milton, John, *Areopagitica* [1644], in *John Milton: The Major Works*, ed. Stephen Orgel and Jonathan Goldberg (1991).

Milton, John, *Complete Poems,* ed. Gordon Campbell (1980).

Montaigne, Michel de, *Essayes, or Morall, Politike and Millitarie Discourses,* trans. John Florio (1603).

Montaigne, Michel de, *Essays of Michael, seigneur de Montaigne in three books,* trans. Charles Cotton (1700).

Montaigne, Michel de, *Essays of Michael, seigneur de Montaigne in three books,* trans. Charles Cotton, 4th edn, 3 vols (1711).

Montaigne, Michel de, *Essays of Michael, seigneur de Montaigne in three books,* trans. Charles Cotton, 6th edn, 3 vols (1743).

Montaigne, Michel de, *Les Essais de Michel de Montaigne,* ed. Pierre Villey, 3 vols (1930–1).

Montaigne, Michel de, *Essays of Michel de Montaigne,* trans. Charles Cotton, illus. Salvador Dalí (1947).

Montaigne, Michel de, *The Complete Works,* trans. Donald Frame (2003).

Moore, Dinty W., 'D'Agata's Trickery and Manipulations: Dinty W. Moore Speaks Out', *Brevity's Nonfiction Blog* (27 February 2012), at https://brevity.wordpress.com/2012/02/27/dagatas-trickery

Moore, Marianne, *The Complete Poems of Marianne Moore* (1968).

Moss, Ann, *Printed Commonplace Books and the Structuring of Renaissance Thought* (1996).

Murphy, Kathryn, 'Anxiety of Variety: Knowledge and Experience in Montaigne, Burton, and Bacon', in *Fictions of Knowledge: Fact, Evidence, Doubt,* ed. Yota Batsaki, Subha Mukherji, and Jan-Melissa Schramm (2011).

Murphy, Kathryn, 'Montaigne, Robert Burton, and the Problem of Idiosyncrasy', in *Montaigne in Transit: Essays for Ian Maclean,* ed. Neil Kenny, Richard Scholar, and Wes Williams (2016).

Murphy, Kathryn, 'The Essay', in *The Oxford Handbook of English Prose, 1642-1714,* ed. Nicholas McDowell and Henry Power (forthcoming).

Murphy, Kathryn and Anita Traninger, 'Introduction', in *The Emergence of Impartiality,* ed. Murphy & Traninger (2014).

Murray, Albert, *The Omni-Americans: Black Experience and American Culture* (1970, 1990).

Musil, Robert, *The Man Without Qualities* [1930–43], trans. Sophie Wilkins (2011).

Nabokov, Vladimir, 'Breitenstäter—Paolino', in Vladimir Nabokov, *Think, Write, Speak,* ed. and trans. Brian Boyd and Anastasia Tolstoy (2019).

New, Melvyn, 'Introduction', *The Life and Opinions of Tristram Shandy, Gentleman*, vol. 3: *The Notes* (1984), in *The Florida Edition of the Works of Laurence Sterne*, ed. New, Richard A. Davies, and W. G. Day, 8 vols (1978–2000).

New, Melvyn, *Laurence Sterne as Satirist* (1969).

New, Melvyn, 'Sterne and the Narrative of Determinativeness', *Eighteenth-Century Fiction* 4 (1992), 315–30.

Nietzsche, Friedrich, *Human, All Too Human* [1878], trans. R. J. Hollingdale (1996).

Nkosi, Lewis, *Home and Exile* (1965).

Nkosi, Lewis, 'The Mountain', *Transition* 79 (1999), 102–125.

O'Neill, Bonnie Carr, '"The Best of Me Is There": Emerson as Lecturer and Celebrity', *American Literature* 80.4 (2008), 739-67.

Oates, Joyce Carol and Robert Atwan (eds), *The Best American Essays of the Century* (2000).

Ong, Walter J., *Orality and Literacy: The Technologizing of the Word* (1982).

Orwell, George, 'Looking Back on the Spanish War' [1942, published 1943], reprinted in *The Collected Essays, Journalism and Letters of George Orwell*, vol. 2, ed. Sonia Orwell and Ian Angus, 4 vols (1970).

Orwell, George, *The Road to Wigan Pier* (1958).

Osborne, Peter, Lynne Segal, and Judith Butler, 'Gender as Performance: An Interview with Judith Butler', *Radical Philosophy* 67 (Summer 1994), 32–9.

Ozick, Cynthia, 'She: Portrait of the Essay as a Warm Body', in *Quarrel & Quandary* (2000).

Paige, Nicholas D., *Before Fiction: The Ancien Régime of the Novel* (2011).

Parker, Samuel, *Sylva. Familiar letters upon occasional subjects* (1701).

Parnell, J. T., 'Swift, Sterne, and the Skeptical Tradition', *Studies in Eighteenth-Century Culture* 23 (1994), 221–42.

Pater, Walter, *Imaginary Portraits* [1887], ed. Lene Østermark-Johansen (2014).

Pater, Walter, *Plato and Platonism* (1893, 1910).

Pater, Walter, *The Renaissance: Studies in Art and Poetry: the 1893 Text*, ed. Donald L. Hill (1980).

Pater, Walter, *Gaston de Latour: The Revised Text*, ed. Gerald Monsman (1995).

Paulin, Tom, *The Day Star of Liberty: William Hazlitt's Radical Style* (1988).

Pebworth, Ted-Larry, 'Not Being, but Passing: Defining the Early English Essay', *Studies in the Literary Imagination* 10.2 (1977), 17–27.

Petrarch [Francesco Petrarca], *Rerum Familiarium Libri I–VIII*, trans. Aldo S. Bernardo (1975).

Petrarch [Francesco Petrarca], *Petrarch, the First Modern Scholar and Man of Letters: A Selection from His Correspondence with Boccaccio and Other Friends, Designed to Illustrate the Beginnings of the Renaissance*, trans. James Harvey Robinson (1909).

Phillips, Adam, *Side Effects* (2006).

Pierce, Edward L., *Memoir and Letters of Charles Sumner*, 4 vols (1839).

Pierre, José (ed.), *Tracts surréalistes et déclarations collectives* [1922–39], 2 vols (1980).

Plunkett, Erin, *A Philosophy of the Essay: Scepticism, Experience, and Style* (2018).

Plutarch, *Plutarch's Morals translated from the Greek by several hands*, 5 vols, ed. Matthew Morgan (1684).

Powell, Manushag N., *Performing Authorship in Eighteenth-Century Periodicals* (2012).

Praz, Mario, *The Hero in Eclipse in Victorian Fiction* (1956).

Priestley, J. B., 'On Doing Nothing', in *Essays of To-Day and Yesterday* (1926).

Rankine, Claudia, *Citizen: An American Lyric* (2014).

Rascaroli, Laura, *The Personal Camera: Subjective Cinema and the Essay Film* (2009).

Ray, Angela, *The Lyceum and Public Culture in the Nineteenth-Century United States* (2005).

Reynolds, Larry J. and Susan Belasco Smith (eds), *These Sad but Glorious Days: Dispatches from Europe, 1846–1850* (1991).

Richardson, Michael, *Surrealism and Cinema* (2006).

Richardson, Samuel, *Letters written to and for particular friends: on the most important occasions* (1741).

Riehl, Joseph E., *That Dangerous Figure: Charles Lamb and the Critics* (1998).

Root, Robert K. and Scott Russell Sanders, 'Interview with Scott Russell Sanders', *Fourth Genre* 1.1 (Spring 1999), 119–32.

Rose, Phyllis, *The Shelf: From LEQ to LES: Adventures in Extreme Reading* (2014).

Rosenberg, Beth Carole and Jeanne Dubino (eds), *Virginia Woolf and the Essay* (1997).

Rosenthal, Carol, *New York and Toronto Novels after Postmodernism: Explorations of the Urban* (2011).

Ross, Angus (ed.), *Selections from the Tatler and the Spectator of Steele and Addison* (1982).

Rothstein, Eric, *Systems of Order and Inquiry in Later Eighteenth-Century Fiction* (1975).

Rushdie, Salman, 'Introduction' to Günter Grass, *On Writing and Politics, 1967–1983*, trans. Ralph Manheim (1985).

Ruskin, John, 'The Political Economy of Art', in Lloyd J. Hubenka (ed.), *Unto This Last: Four Essays on the First Principles of Political Economy* (1967).

Russell, David, *Tact: Aesthetic Liberalism and the Essay Form in Nineteenth-Century Britain* (2017).

Rycroft, Charles, *Viewpoints* (1991).

Said, Edward, *Orientalism* (1978).

Said, Edward W., 'Introduction: Secular Criticism', in *World, The Text and The Critic* (1983).

Salomon, Randi, *Virginia Woolf's Essayism* (2012).

Sandbach-Dahlströhm, Catherine, '"Que scais-je?": Virginia Woolf and the Essay as Feminist Critique', in *Virginia Woolf and the Essay*, ed. Beth Carole Rosenberg and Jeanne Dubino (1997).

Sanders, Charles Richard et al. (eds), *The Collected Letters of Thomas and Jane Welsh Carlyle*, 44 vols (1970–).

Saunders, Max, *Self Impression: Life-Writing, Autobiografiction, and the Forms of Modern Literature* (2010).

Scarry, Elaine, *The Body in Pain* (1985).

Schlegel, Friedrich, *Friedrich Schlegel's* Lucinde *and the Fragments* [1799; 1798-1800], trans. and ed. Peter Firchow (1971).

Schneider, Gary, *The Culture of Epistolarity: Vernacular Letters and Letter Writing in Early Modern England, 1500–1700* (2005).

Scholar, Richard, *Montaigne and the Art of Free-Thinking* (2010).

Schultz, William, 'Off-Stage Voices in James Agee's *Let Us Now Praise Famous Men*: Reportage as Covert Autobiography', *American Imago* 56.1 (1999), 75–104.

Scott, B. K., *Refiguring Modernism*, vol. 1: *The Women of 1928* (1995).

Scott, Donald, 'The Popular Lecture and the Creation of a Public in Mid-Nineteenth-Century America', *Journal of American History* 66.4 (1980), 791–5.

Scott, Walter, 'Laurence Sterne', *Ballantyne's Novelist's Library*, ed. Walter Scott (1821–4).

Sebald, W. G., *The Emigrants* [1992], trans. Michael Hulse (1996).

Sebald, W. G., *The Rings of Saturn* [1995], trans. Michael Hulse (1998).

Sebald, W. G., *Austerlitz* [2001], trans. Anthea Bell (2001).

Sebald, W. G., *Campo Santo* [2003], trans. Anthea Bell (2006).

Seiler, R. M. (ed.), *Walter Pater: The Critical Heritage* (1980).

Seneca, Lucius Annaeus, *Epistulae morales/Moral Epistles* [c. 65 CE], trans. Richard M. Gummere (2014).

Shaftesbury, Anthony Ashley Cooper, 3rd Earl of, *Characteristicks of men, manners, opinions, times* [1711], ed. Philip Ayres, 2 vols (1999).

Shapin, Steven, 'Pump and Circumstance: Robert Boyle's Literary Technology', *Social Studies of Science* 14.4 (1984), 481–520.

Shelley, Percy Bysshe, *The Complete Poetical Works of Percy Bysshe Shelley*, ed. Thomas Hutchinson (1905, 1965).

Shields, David, *Reality Hunger* (2011).

Shklovsky, Viktor, 'The Novel as Parody: Sterne's Tristram Shandy', in *Theory of Prose* [1925], trans. Benjamin Sher (1990).

Sistare, Heidi and Jo Ann Beard, 'An Interview with Jo Ann Beard', *Slice* (4 November 2014), at https://slicemagazine.org/jo-ann-beard.

Sitter, John, *Literary Loneliness in Mid-Eighteenth-Century England* (1982).

Slater, Joseph (ed.), *The Correspondence of Emerson and Carlyle* (1964).

Smith, Alexander, 'On the Writing of Essays', in *Dreamthorp: A Book of Essays Written in the Country* (1863, 1913).

Solnit, Rebecca, *Wanderlust: A History of Walking* (2002).

Solnit, Rebecca, *A Field Guide to Getting Lost* (2005).

Solnit, Rebecca, 'Woolf's Darkness: Embracing the Inexplicable', *The New Yorker* (24 April 2014).

Sontag, Susan, *Against Interpretation and Other Essays* (1966).

Sontag, Susan, 'On Paul Goodman', *Under the Sign of Saturn* (1972, 2002).

Sontag, Susan, *Regarding the Pain of Others* (2003).

Sorel, Charles, *La bibliotheque françoise*, 2nd edn (1667).

Spenser, Edmund, *The Faerie Queene* [1590], ed. A. C. Hamilton (2001, 2007).

Squibbs, Richard, *Urban Enlightenment and the Eighteenth-Century Periodical Essay: Transatlantic Retrospects* (2014).

Stallybrass, Peter, 'Books and Scrolls: Navigating the Bible', in *Books and Readers in Early Modern England: Material Studies*, ed. Jennifer Andersen and Elizabeth Sauer (2002).

Stephen, Leslie, 'The Essayists' [1881], in *Men, Books, and Mountains: A Collection of Essays*, ed. S. O. A. Ullmann (1956).

Stephen, Leslie, *The Life of Sir James Fitzjames Stephen* (1895).

Sterne, Laurence, *The Life and Opinions of Tristram Shandy, Gentleman* [1759–1767], ed. Melvyn New and Joan New (2003).

Stevens, Wallace, *Selected Poems*, ed. John N. Serio (2010).

Stevenson, Lionel, *The English Novel: A Panorama* (1960).

Stevenson, Robert Louis, 'Walking Tours' [1876] and 'An Apology for Idlers' [1877], in *Virginibus Puerisque* [1881], *The Works of Robert Louis Stevenson*, vol. II, ed. Edmund Gosse, 20 vols (1906).

Stewart, Garrett, *Dear Reader: The Conscripted Audience in Nineteenth-Century British Fiction* (1996).

Stewart, Susan, *Nonsense: Aspects of Intertextuality in Folklore and Literature* (1978; 1979).

Sullivan, John Jeremiah (ed.), *The Best American Essays 2014* (2014).

Swift, Jonathan, *Journal to Stella* [1766], ed. George A. Aitken (1901).

Telle, E. V., 'À propos du mot "essai" chez Montaigne', *Bibliothèque d'Humanisme et Renaissance* 30.2 (1968).

Thompson, Denys, *Reading and Discrimination* (1934).

Thompson, Elbert N. S., *The Seventeenth-Century English Essay* (1927).

Thoreau, Henry David, 'Civil Disobedience' [1849], in *Collected Essays and Poems*, ed. Elizabeth Hall Witherell (2001).

Thoreau, Henry David, *The Portable Thoreau*, ed. Jeffrey S. Cramer (2012).

Toor, Rachel, 'How to Conquer the Admissions Essay', *New York Times* (2 August 2017).

Trevelyan, George Macaulay, *England Under Queen Anne*, 3 vols (1930–4).

Trublet, Nicolas Charles Joseph, *Essais sur divers sujets de littérature et de morale* (1735, 1749, 1754).

Tyndall, John, *Sound: A Course of Eight Lectures Delivered at the Royal Institution of Great Britain* (1867).

Vance, Norman, *The Victorians and Ancient Rome* (1997).

Vanden Bossche, Chris, *Carlyle and the Search for Authority* (1991).

Vardi, Amiel, 'Genre, Conventions, and Cultural Programme in Gellius' *Noctes Atticae*', in *The Worlds of Aulus Gellius*, ed. Leofranc Holford-Strevens and Amiel Vardi (2004).

Vidal, Gore, 'Montaigne', *Times Literary Supplement* 4656 (26 June 1992).

Walker, Alan, 'Indexing Commonplace Books: John Locke's Method', *The Indexer* 22.3 (April 2001), 114–18.

Walker, Hugh, 'Miscellaneous Prose', in *The Literature of the Victorian Era* (1910, 1921).

Walker, Hugh, *The English Essay and Essayists* (1915).

Wallace, David Foster, 'The Planet Trillaphon as It Stands in Relation to the Bad Thing' [1984], in *The David Foster Wallace Reader* (2014).

Wampole, Christy, 'The Essayification of Everything', *New York Times* (26 May 2013).

Ward, W. R., 'The Office for Taxes, 1666–1798', *Bulletin of the Institute for Historical Research*, 25 (1952).

Weber, Max, *The Theory of Social and Economic Organization*, trans. A. M. Henderson and Talcott Parsons (1924, 1947).

Wehrs, Donald, 'Sterne, Cervantes, Montaigne: Fideistic Skepticism and the Rhetoric of Desire', *Comparative Literature Studies* 25 (1988), 127–51.

Weinberger, Eliot, *An Elemental Thing* (2007).

Whitman, Walt, *Specimen Days: & Collect* (1882).

Whitman, Walt, 'Emerson's Books, the Shadow of Them' [1882], in *The Complete Writings of Walt Whitman*, ed. Richard M. Bucke, Thomas B. Harned, Horace Traubel, and Oscar L. Triggs (1902).

Whitmore, Charles, 'The Field of the Essay', *PMLA* 36.4 (1921), 551–64.

Wilde, Oscar, 'The Critic as Artist', in *Criticism: Historical Criticism, Intentions, The Soul of Man*, ed. Josephine M. Guy (2007), vol. IV of *The Complete Works of Oscar Wilde*, ed. Ian Small, ten vols (2000–).

Wilkinson, Emily Colette, 'The Miscellaneous: A Poetics of the Mode in British Literature, 1668–1759' (unpublished PhD dissertation, Stanford University, 2008).

Williams, Orlo, *The Essay* (1914).

Williams, W. E. (ed.), *A Book of English Essays* [1942], 2nd edn (1963).

Windell, Maria W., 'Citzenship in *Citizen*', from 'On Claudia Rankine's *Citizen: An American Lyric*, A Symposium, Part I,' *Los Angeles Review of Books* (6 January 2016), at https://lareviewofbooks.org/article/reconsidering-claudia-rankines-citizen-an-american-lyric-a-symposium-part-i.

Wittgenstein, Ludwig, *On Certainty*, trans. D. Paul and G. E. M. Anscombe (1969).

Womack, Peter, 'What are Essays For?', *English in Education* 27.2 (1993), 42–8.

Wood, Gaby, 'Do you feel these emotions too?', *Daily Telegraph* (28 February 2015).

Wood, James, 'V. S. Pritchett and English Comedy', in *The Irresponsible Self: On Laughter and the Novel* (2004).

Woolf, Virginia, *The Letters of Virginia Woolf*, 6 vols, ed. Nigel Nicolson and Joanne Trautmann (1975–1980).

Woolf, Virginia, *The Diary of Virginia Woolf*, 5 vols, ed. Anne Olivier Bell (1977–84).

Woolf, Virginia, *The Essays of Virginia Woolf*, 6 vols, ed. Andrew McNeillie and Stuart N. Clarke (1986–2011).

Woolf, Virginia, *A Passionate Apprentice: The Early Journals, 1897–1909*, ed. Mitchell A. Leaska (1992).

Woolf, Virginia, *A Room of One's Own and Three Guineas* [1929, 1938], ed. Morag Shiach (2008).

Woolf, Virginia, *Moments of Being: A Collection of Autobiographical Writing*, ed. Jeanne Schulkind (1985, 2002).

Wordsworth, William, 'Expostulation and Reply' in *Lyrical Ballads, and other Poems, 1797–1800*, ed. James Butler and Karen Green (1992).

Wordsworth, William, 'Preface to *Lyrical Ballads*', in *The Prose Works of William Wordsworth*, Vol. I, ed. W. J. B. Owen and Jane Worthington Smyser, 3 vols (1974).

Wright, Tom F., *Lecturing the Atlantic: Speech, Print and an Anglo-American Commons 1830–1870* (2017).

Wright, Tom F., 'Listening to Emerson's "England" at Clinton Hall, 22 January 1850', *Journal of American Studies* 46.3 (2012), 641–62.

Wright, Tom F. (ed.), *The Cosmopolitan Lyceum: Lecture Culture and the Globe* (2013).

Yelin, Amy, 'Jo Ann Beard Interview', *Yelinwords*, 5, at https://yelinwords.files.wordpress.com/2014/05/joannbeardfinal.pdf.

Yeo, Richard, 'Ephraim Chambers's *Cyclopædia* (1728) and the Tradition of Commonplaces', *Journal of the History of Ideas* 57.1 (1996), 157–75.

Zabriskie, Francis N., 'The Essay as a Literary Form and Quality', *The New Princeton Review* IV (July–November 1887).

Index

Note: Figures are indicated by an italic "*f*", respectively, following the page number.

For the benefit of digital users, indexed terms that span two pages (e.g., 52–53) may, on occasion, appear on only one of those pages.